Economic Forecasting
Volume I

The International Library of Critical Writings in Economics

Series Editor: Mark Blaug

Professor Emeritus, University of London
Professor Emeritus, University of Buckingham
Visiting Professor, University of Exeter

This series is an essential reference source for students, researchers and lecturers in economics. It presents by theme a selection of the most important articles across the entire spectrum of economics. Each volume has been prepared by a leading specialist who has written an authoritative introduction to the literature included.

A full list of published and future titles in this series is printed at the end of this volume.

For a list of all Edward Elgar published titles visit our site on the World Wide Web at
http://www.e-elgar.co.uk

Economic Forecasting
Volume I

Edited by

Terence C. Mills

Professor of Economics
Loughborough University, UK

THE INTERNATIONAL LIBRARY OF CRITICAL WRITINGS IN ECONOMICS

An Elgar Reference Collection
Cheltenham, UK • Northampton, MA, USA

Published by
Edward Elgar Publishing Limited
Glensanda House
Montpellier Parade
Cheltenham
Glos GL50 1UA
UK

Edward Elgar Publishing, Inc.
136 West Street
Suite 202
Northampton
Massachusetts 01060
USA

A catalogue record for this book is available from the British Library.

Library of Congress Cataloging in Publication Data
Economic forecasting / edited by Terence C. Mills.
    (The international library of critical writings in
  economics : 108)   (Elgar reference collection)
    Includes index.
    1. Economic forecasting.   I. Mills, Terence C.   II. Series.
  III. Series: Elgar reference collection.
  HB3730.E24   1999
  338.5′442—dc21
                                                                99–30947
                                                                CIP

3 2280 00677 9615

ISBN   1 85278 866 6 (2 volume set)

Printed and bound in Great Britain by MPG Books Ltd, Bodmin, Cornwall

Contents

Acknowledgements

The editor and publishers wish to thank the authors and the following publishers who have kindly given permission for the use of copyright material.

American Economic Association for article: Daniel B. Suits (1962), 'Forecasting and Analysis with an Econometric Model', *American Economic Review*, **LII** (1), March, 104–32.

American Statistical Association for articles: Warren M. Persons (1924), 'Some Fundamental Concepts of Statistics', *Journal of the American Statistical Association*, **XIX** (145), March, 1–8; A.C. Harvey and P.H.J. Todd (1983), 'Forecasting Economic Time Series With Structural and Box–Jenkins Methods: A Case Study', comments by Craig F. Ansley, David F. Findley and Paul Newbold and 'Response' by A.C. Harvey and P.H.J. Todd, *Journal of Business and Economic Statistics*, **1** (4), October, 299–315; Richard Meese and John Geweke (1984), 'A Comparison of Autoregressive Univariate Forecasting Procedures for Macroeconomic Time Series', *Journal of Business and Economic Statistics*, **2** (3), July, 191–200; Robert B. Litterman (1986), 'Forecasting With Bayesian Vector Autoregressions – Five Years of Experience', *Journal of Business and Economic Statistics*, **4** (1), January, 25–38.

Blackwell Publishers Ltd for articles and excerpt: R.L. Marris (1954), 'The Position of Economics and Economists in the Government Machine: A Comparative Critique of the United Kingdom and the Netherlands', *Economic Journal*, **LXIV** (256), December, 759–83; Alec Cairncross (1969), 'Economic Forecasting', *Economic Journal*, **LXXIX** (316), December, 797–812; P.J. Coen, E.D. Gomme and M.G. Kendall (1969), 'Lagged Relationships in Economic Forecasting' and discussion, *Journal of the Royal Statistical Society, Series A*, **132** (1), 133–63; Jeremy Bray (1971), 'Dynamic Equations for Economic Forecasting with the G.D.P.–Unemployment Relation and the Growth of G.D.P. in the United Kingdom as an Example' and discussion, *Journal of the Royal Statistical Society, Series A*, **134** (2), 167–227; George E.P. Box and Paul Newbold (1971), 'Some Comments on a Paper of Coen, Gomme and Kendall', *Journal of the Royal Statistical Society, Series A*, **134** (2), 229–40; P. Newbold and C.W.J. Granger (1974), 'Experience with Forecasting Univariate Time Series and the Combination of Forecasts' and discussion, *Journal of the Royal Statistical Society, Series A*, **137** (2), 131–64; Kenneth F. Wallis (1991), 'Macroeconomic Forecasting: A Survey,' in Andrew J. Oswald (ed.), *Surveys in Economics*, Volume I, Chapter 2, 48–81; David F. Hendry (1997), 'The Econometrics of Macroeconomic Forecasting', *Economic Journal*, **107** (444), September, 1330–57; Chris Chatfield (1997), 'Forecasting in the 1990s', *The Statistician*, **46** (4), 461–73.

Elsevier Science Ltd for article: Richard T. Baillie and Tim Bollerslev (1992), 'Prediction in Dynamic Models with Time-dependent Conditional Variances', *Journal of Econometrics*, **52**, 91–113.

Institutional Investor, Inc. for article: Paul A. Samuelson (1987), 'Paradise Lost and Refound: The Harvard ABC Barometers', *Journal of Portfolio Management*, **4**, Spring, 4–9.

John Wiley and Sons Ltd for articles: Stephen K. McNees (1982), 'The Role of Macroeconometric Models in Forecasting and Policy Analysis in the United States', *Journal of Forecasting*, **1** (1), 37–48; K. Rao Kadiyala and Sune Karlsson (1993), 'Forecasting with Generalized Bayesian Vector Autoregressions', *Journal of Forecasting*, **12**, 365–78; Michael P. Clements and David F. Hendry (1993), 'On the Limitations of Comparing Mean Square Forecast Errors', *Journal of Forecasting*, **12**, 617–37; Jin-Lung Lin and C.W.J. Granger (1994), 'Forecasting from Non-linear Models in Practice', *Journal of Forecasting*, **13** (1), January, 1–9; Michael P. Clements and David F. Hendry (1995), 'Forecasting in Cointegrated Systems', *Journal of Applied Econometrics*, **10**, 127–46.

Royal Society for article: Sir Terence Burns (1986), 'The Interpretation and Use of Economic Predictions' and discussion, *Proceedings of the Royal Society of London, Series A*, **407**, 103–25.

University of Chicago Press for article: Arthur W. Marget (1929), 'Morgenstern on the Methodology of Economic Forecasting', *Journal of Political Economy*, **XXXVII** (3), June, 312–39.

Every effort has been made to trace all the copyright holders but if any have been inadvertently overlooked the publishers will be pleased to make the necessary arrangement at the first opportunity.

In addition the publishers wish to thank the Library of the London School of Economics and Political Science and B & N Microfilm for their assistance in obtaining these articles.

Introduction

Terence C. Mills

Volume I

I Early Attempts

Economic forecasting has a long, and at times extremely chequered, history. While the forecasts from large-scale macroeconomic models have attracted most attention in recent times, attempts to find temporal patterns in economic data that might enable predictions to be made about future events stretch all the way back to a London cloth merchant, John Graunt, who in 1662 published several ingenious comparisons using bills of mortality. For example, in an attempt to make trade and government 'more certain and regular', Graunt searched for seasonal and other periodic patterns in mortality, conditioned the data on the plague, and determined the temporal pattern of 'sickliness' that would enable him to predict 'by what spaces, and intervals we may hereafter expect such times again', as quoted in Klein (1997, p. 55), who provides an authoritative account of these early attempts at statistical analysis using economic data.

As Klein recounts, attempts to detect periodic fluctuations in economic data continued throughout the eighteenth and nineteenth centuries, and links with meteorology became particularly fashionable, culminating in William Stanley Jevons's advocacy of the sunspot theory of the business cycle, in which he convinced himself that sunspot cycles and business cycles were of the same length, about ten and a half years, and that the causal relationship ran from sunspots to the economy, so that he could predict commercial cycle turning points from sunspot cycle peaks. Indeed, Jevons even used the evidence of a cyclical peak in corn prices to infer the presence of a preceding peak in the sunspot data. Jevons's sunspot theory is reviewed in Morgan (1990, chapter 1), which emphasizes the ridicule, rather than criticism, that the theory received from his peers, possibly the first in a long line of critiques of economic forecasting!

The presumed link between meteorology and the economy reached its apogee with Henry Moore's (1923) 'Venus theory', in which he outlined how recent discoveries in physics shed light on exactly how Venus, in conjunction with the earth and the sun, might cause rainfall cycles on earth, which then led on to cause economic cycles. As Morgan relates, Moore's theories had about as much support from other economists as had Jevons's, although the reaction was more of polite scepticism than the previous outrage and ridicule.

At around the same time as Moore was publishing his ideas about the causes of economic cycles, a different, more mainstream, view about measuring and using business cycles was coming to prominence through the statistical work of Wesley Mitchell (1913). Mitchell's analysis was primarily descriptive, and his belief that each cycle was different effectively excluded formal statistical analysis and, by extension, any role for forecasting. A parallel statistical approach to cycles did, however, purport to provide a methodology for forecasting. This was the business barometer approach of Warren Persons and the Harvard Economic

Society, a commercial venture set up by several of the economics staff at Harvard University and which specialized in providing a business forecasting service. This approach gained rapid popularity during the early 1920s, with institutes devoted to business cycle research being established in a number of countries. Chapter 1, Persons's Presidential Address to the American Statistical Association, outlines his methodological approach to statistical forecasting in business and economics, and a number of applications of this approach are collected in Persons (1924).

The Harvard A-B-C barometers, so termed because Persons combined groups of variables into three indices (A was the index, or barometer, of the group of leading series, B the index of current indicators, and C the index of lagging series), attempted to identify series, contained in A, that could be used to predict future movements in the stock market. For several years the barometers seemed to be a successful forecasting device, but, after they failed to predict the 1929 Crash, they swiftly fell out of favour and eventually into disuse. This episode is entertainingly recounted in Chapter 2, by Paul Samuelson, which also contains some trenchant comments on the supposed forecasting ability of academic economists!

Persons's view of statistics, that probability theory was unsuitable for business cycle analysis and forecasting, was shared by Oskar Morgenstern, who in 1928 published a thesis arguing that economic forecasting based on probability reasoning was impossible because economic data do not satisfy such conditions as homogeneity and independence. Morgenstern's thesis has never been published in English, but a reply to his criticisms was written by Arthur Marget, which is reproduced as Chapter 3. Although Marget accepts Morgenstern's claims that probability is not applicable to economic forecasting, he nevertheless disputes the conclusion that forecasting is therefore impossible in principle, arguing that most of the forecasting of the period used extrapolative methods rather than formal statistical techniques. Marget then argues that if any sort of causal explanation is available, then forecasting ought to be possible, and goes on to discuss Morgenstern's claim that forecasts can be invalidated by reactions to the forecasts – an early forerunner of the Lucas (1976) critique.

II Macroeconomic Forecasting and Policy Making

By the 1950s, there was a much greater emphasis in many countries on central economic planning, for which forecasts of future movements of macroeconomic variables became important inputs. How this forecasting was actually carried out is an interesting question, and Chapter 4, by Robin Marris, looks at the forecasting approaches of government economists in the United Kingdom and the Netherlands during this period. As well as providing an illuminating view on the workings of government economists in the two countries, it also highlights their contrasting approaches to forecasting. The British approach was to build up projections on a trial-and-error basis, deriving forecasts from broad general assumptions about the direction of the economy and its present, deflationary or expansionary, state. In the Netherlands, by contrast, under the Directorship of Jan Tinbergen and the research guidance of Henri Theil, the *Centraal Planbureau* were using econometric methods and a formal general equilibrium macroeconomic model to underpin their forecasting exercises.

During the 1950s, rapid advances in macroeconometric modelling were also being made in the United States, with the famous Klein–Goldberger model making its debut in 1955 (see Bodkin, Klein and Marwah, 1991, for a history of the American experience of macroeconometric modelling). While the focus of much of the analysis using these models was on policy simulations, multiplier implications and investigating their dynamic properties (namely, the famous Adelman and Adelman, 1959, study), forecasting performance was always closely monitored and published in a variety of outlets, both in academic publications and in the popular press. Chapter 5, by Daniel Suits, investigates the forecasting performance of a lineal descendant of the Klein–Goldberger model. Two features of this model are worth pointing out from a modern-day perspective: Suits uses data and presents forecasts in first differenced form, and estimates the parameters by ordinary least squares throughout. Both features were rather controversial at the time, which was an era of simultaneous equations estimation using levels data, but are much more in keeping with present-day econometric practices.

As the United States led, so other countries quickly followed, with both the Netherlands and the United Kingdom being in the forefront of macroeconomic modelling (see the chapters by Barten and by Ball and Holly in Bodkin, Klein and Marwah, 1991). The importance of macro-economic forecasting is amply demonstrated in Sir Alec Cairncross's 1969 Presidential Address to the Royal Economic Society, reproduced as Chapter 6, but so is the scepticism felt by many economists about formal macroeconometric models, particularly those in official circles. Notwithstanding these views, formal econometric models continued to gain influence in govern-ment macroeconomic policy making, and by the 1980s were the centrepiece of macroeconomic forecasting. Chapters 7 and 8, by Stephen McNees and Sir Terence Burns, discuss the roles of macroeconometric modelling in the United States and Britain, respectively. The final chapter, 9, in this part is Kenneth Wallis's authoritative survey of developments in macroeconomic forecasting in the twenty years after Cairncross's address.

III   Time Series Forecasting

The 1960s saw major advances in time series analysis, culminating with the publication of George Box and Gwilym Jenkins's (1970) pathbreaking book, which provided a detailed treatment of forecasting using ARIMA and transfer function models. This used as examples such 'economic' series as IBM stock prices, international airline passengers and company sales data, as well as a variety of chemical engineering series. Given this impetus, interest in economic forecasting using time series techniques greatly increased during this period and several important papers appeared. Some of the most influential were published in Series A of the *Journal of the Royal Statistical Society* and, as they were read before the Society, the papers also contain the subsequent discussions by the Society's members. We reproduce three of these papers, along with an extended comment on the first of them, as Chapters 10 to 13. The members' discussions are often as informative, and usually more entertaining, than the papers themselves, and offer a valuable insight into the way these ideas, which now form the basis of time series econometrics, began to influence the economic forecasting profession, although not without a great deal of initial opposition!

Time series approaches to economic forecasting continued to develop during the 1970s and, with the advent of more powerful computers and software, attention began to be focused on automated forecasted procedures, on models that were more complex than the ARIMA class, and on forecast comparisons across alternative procedures. A major example of the latter, employing as many as 1001 series from a variety of disciplines and 24 forecasting methods, was the 'M-Competition' of Makridakis et al. (1982). We content ourselves here with reproducing as Chapter 14 a somewhat smaller study, by Richard Meese and John Geweke, which is devoted to a comparison of automated autoregressive univariate forecasting procedures for macroeconomic time series. As examples of more complex time series models developed explicitly for economic forecasting, we present Andrew Harvey and Paul Todd's case study comparing their 'basic structural model' with standard Box–Jenkins models (Chapter 15), and two papers, by Robert Littermann and by Rao Kadiyala and Sune Karlsson, looking at the use of Bayesian vector autoregressions for forecasting (Chapters 16 and 17). Vector autoregressions (VARs) came into prominence with the publication of the influential paper by Sims (1980). This, however, was concerned with modelling aspects rather than forecasting. Bayesian VARs were subsequently developed to take advantage of the generality of VARs but to address the accompanying problem of their prolific parameterisation.

The final two chapters (18 and 19) in this part focus on recent developments in forecasting economic times series: nonlinear models are explicitly looked at by Clive Granger and Jin-Lung Lin, while Chris Chatfield provides a wide-ranging review touching on many aspects of modern time series forecasting.

IV   The Econometrics of Forecasting

The strength of time series approaches to economic forecasting is their requirement that a formal model be written down, from which point forecasts and measures of forecast error can be constructed using analytical methods. This is in marked contrast to the traditional macro-economic forecasting approach, where various adjustments and interventions (such as intercept corrections) are made by the modellers themselves. In recent years there has begun to develop a formal econometric theory of economic forecasting, building upon and linking the two approaches. Chapter 20, by Richard Baillie and Tim Bollerslev, provides a formal examination of prediction within a dynamic model with autoregressive conditionally heteroskedastic (ARCH) errors. The remaining three chapters in this part (21 to 23) are representative of the important research being undertaken by Michael Clements and David Hendry in developing a theory of economic forecasting that allows for misspecified models that need to be estimated using data taken from a non-stationary economy subject to unanticipated structural breaks. These papers take up a range of issues that have not previously been subject to formal econometric treatment.

Volume II

I   Forecast Evaluation

Assessing how accurate forecasts are should obviously be a major concern to any forecaster and an objective evaluation of forecast performance is thus of the utmost importance. Chapters 1 and 2, Geoffrey Moore's Presidential Address to the American Statistical Association and Victor Zarnowitz's survey, provide general reviews of forecasting performance from the 1920s. The first formal evaluation of the forecasts from several macroeconometric models are given in Chapters 3 and 4 by Herman Stekler and Charles Nelson. Forecast evaluation at this time usually took the form of comparing statistical measures such as the root mean squared error and computing Theil's (1958) U-statistic, which compares a model's mean squared forecast error with that obtained from a 'naive' no-change model. Chapters 5 and 6, by Clive Granger and co-authored with John Bates and Paul Newbold, respectively, critically assess model evaluation techniques and, in the former, consider for the first time the possibility of combining forecasts from alternative methods, an idea that has led to an enormous literature on forecast combining, which is reviewed by Robert Clemen in Chapter 7. An early exercise in combining forecasts was contained in Volume I, Chapter 13, by Paul Newbold and Clive Granger, which combined forecasts from various univariate techniques.

A related approach to forecast evaluation that became popular during the 1970s was to compare the forecasts from a macroeconometric model with those obtained from univariate models fitted to the individual series. A famous study of this type was that of Richard Cooper (1972), published in the influential volume edited by Bert Hickman, which compared the forecasts of seven quarterly models of the United States economy with those from autoregressive models fitted to individual endogenous variables. Since the forecasts from these univariate models had a pronounced tendency to outperform the macroeconometric model forecasts, not surprisingly this study generated a great deal of interest. Chapter 8, by Philip Howrey, Lawrence Klein and Michael McCarthy, reviews, criticizes and extends the Cooper study. It also introduces the notion of TLC (tender loving care), so beloved by macro-modellers, as a short-hand for the various adjustments made to forecasts by the modellers. Chapter 9, by Ray Fair, in contrast presents a structural model in which no adjustments are made to the forecasts at all. Fair argues that the application of TLC may lead to the conclusion that any improvements in forecast adequacy may be due solely to the 'informed' intervention of the modellers. In contrast, he finds, via a detailed model evaluation, that significant increases in forecast accuracy can be achieved through improved model specification and estimation techniques, rather than through interventions such as intercept adjustment. This type of analysis is continued by Fair in Chapter 10, in which he compares the forecasting performance of his own model, Tom Sargent's (1976) 'classical' model and Sims's (1980) VAR model, with that of a naive autoregressive model, breaking down forecast uncertainty into four components, due to random errors, parameter estimation error, model misspecification, and exogenous variable forecast errors. Chapter 11 provides an update on the forecast performance of alternative techniques by Stephen McNees.

The remaining chapters in this part are papers from the 1990s that look at various aspects of forecast evaluation. In Chapter 12, R.A. Kolb and Herman Stekler consider the question of whether macroeconomic forecasts improve significantly as the forecast horizon is reduced, while Chapters 13 and 14, by Roy Batchelor and Pami Dua and by Stephen McNees, consider questions of forecaster ideology, in the sense of the theory underlying the economic models used, and of the role of 'consensus' forecasts, which are essentially simple combinations of individual forecasts. Gordon Leitch and Ernest Tanner, in Chapter 15, argue that conventional statistical model evaluation criteria may be inappropriate in the context of explaining why firms purchase economic forecasts that often appear not to outperform those from naive models. They argue that a more plausible criterion in this context is the profit that can be made by acting on the forecasts and suggest that, if profits are not observable, then directional accuracy should be used. Leitch and Tanner also suggest that an implication of their analysis is that, if a squared error loss function is inappropriate, then least squares may not be the optimal estimation technique, a conclusion that harks back to earlier work of Clive Granger (1969). Chapters 16 and 17, by Francis Diebold and Roberto Mariano and by David Harvey,

Stephen Leybourne and Paul Newbold, provide new and formal econometric tests of relative forecast accuracy. Finally, Chapter 18 is a wide-ranging discussion by Clive Granger on the current state of economic forecasting, which touches upon many of the key issues involved in the reliability and quality of forecasts: for example, whether there is a limit to how far ahead forecasts can usefully be made, why different forecasters using different techniques have a tendency to be incorrect in the same direction, why forecasts tend to underestimate actual changes and, as an important consequence, why major business cycle turns may be poorly forecast.

II Forecasting with Leading Indicators

The use of leading indicators has a long history in forecasting, the earliest attempts being the Harvard A-B-C barometers, introduced in Volume I, Chapters 1 and 2. The use of business cycle indicators by the NBER was exemplified by the work of Burns and Mitchell (1946), but suffered a severe setback with the 'measurement without theory' critique of Koopmans. This famous debate is reprinted, with a commentary, in Hendry and Morgan (1995), who remark that, of all the great debates in econometrics, this was 'the best known but least understood' (p. 69). Chapter 19, by Sidney Alexander and Herman Stekler, is a subsequent example of a formal statistical examination of leading indicators in forecasting industrial production, comparing them with autoregressions, then still in their infancy as a technique for economic forecasting. Saul Hymans, in Chapter 20, returns to the use of leading indicators to predict cyclical turning points, while Alan Auerbach's Chapter 21 is a later critical evaluation of the technique. A detailed real-time evaluation of composite leading index forecasting is provided in Chapter 22 by Francis Diebold and Glenn Rudebusch, which shows marked deterioration in their post-sample forecasting ability. Nevertheless, the use of composite leading indicators for forecasting has undergone a considerable revival in recent years (see, for example, the book by Niemira and Klein, 1994) and Chapter 23, by Rebecca Emerson and David Hendry, offers a formal econometric evaluation of the approach, placing it within an integrated–cointegrated framework subject to regime shifts.

III Forecasting in Finance

The predictability of financial markets has engaged the attention of market professionals and academic economists and statisticians for many years, as well as numerous 'amateur' investors. Statistical work on stock market forecasting began in the 1930s, and Chapter 24, by Alfred Cowles, is one of the first that was published. Cowles investigated the ability of market analysts and financial services to predict future price changes, finding that there was little evidence that they could. The predictability of price changes has since become a major theme of financial research but, perhaps surprisingly, little more was published until Kendall's (1953) study, in which he found that the weekly changes in a wide variety of financial prices could not be predicted from either past changes in the series themselves or from past changes in other price series. This seems to have been the first explicit reporting of this oft-quoted property of financial prices, although further impetus to research on price predictability had to wait until the late 1950s. Chapter 25 presents Harry Roberts's famous demonstration of why successive price changes should be independent and why analysts can get 'fooled' into believing that the evolution of price levels contain patterns and regularities that can be exploited for forecasting: the random walk model of stock prices.

Most of the early papers on financial forecasting are contained in the collection by Cootner (1964), while the book by Granger and Morgenstern (1970) provides a detailed development and empirical examination of the random walk model and various of its refinements. Chapter 26 is Granger's concise survey of the field as it stood in the early 1970s, while Chapter 27 is his survey of twenty years later: the contrast between the two makes for fascinating reading. Probably the major development in the modelling of financial time series has been that of the ARCH process, which allows the variance of a series to be autocorrelated, and hence predictable, whereas the series itself may still be unpredictable: this enables the random walk assumption to be relaxed to that of a martingale. A detailed survey of financial applications of the ARCH model and its various extensions is Bollerslev, Chou and Kroner (1992). The ARCH process provides a method by which volatility, an important input into option and derivative pricing formulae, may be forecast. Chapters 28 to 31 provide four recent examples of volatility forecasting in the stock, option, commodity and foreign exchange markets. The ARCH process is but one example of a nonlinear time series model, and there has been great interest in trying to exploit various types of nonlinearities in financial markets. Chapter 32, by Steve Satchell and Allan Timmermann, assesses the economic value of alternative nonlinear exchange rate forecasts.

IV   Economic Forecasting Using Surveys

The use of survey data, and the ensuing analysis of the rationality of expectations, became a favourite forecasting technique in the decade between the mid-1970s and mid-1980s, no doubt in response to the great interest during this period in the rational expectations hypothesis (see, for example, the collection of readings in Lucas and Sargent, 1981). We provide three examples of the use of survey data as forecasts. Chapter 33, by Richard Rippe and Maurice Wilkinson, assesses the accuracy of the McGraw-Hill survey anticipatory data set, which contains up to four-year-ahead anticipations of investment, sales and capacity, comparing them favourably as predictors with both statistical and econometric models of investment. In Chapter 34 John Carlson analyses the famous Livingston inflation survey data set, while finally, in Chapter 35 Victor Zarnowitz analyses economic outlook survey data on six variables in terms of forecast bias and forecast error serial correlation.

References

Adelman, Irma and Frank L. Adelman (1959), 'The Dynamic Properties of the Klein–Goldberger Model', *Econometrica*, **27**, 596–625.

Bodkin, Ronald G., Lawrence R. Klein and Kanta Marwah (1991), *A History of Macroeconomic Model-building*, Aldershot: Edward Elgar.

Bollerslev, Tim, Ray Y. Chou and Kenneth F. Kroner (1992), 'ARCH Modelling in Finance: A Review of the Theory and Empirical Evidence', *Journal of Econometrics*, **52**, 5–59.

Box, George E.P. and Gwilym M. Jenkins (1970), *Time Series Analysis: Forecasting and Control*, San Francisco: Holden-Day.

Burns, Arthur F. and Wesley C. Mitchell (1946), *Measuring Business Cycles*, New York: National Bureau of Economic Research.

Cooper, Richard L. (1972), 'The Predictive Performance of Quarterly Econometric Models of the United States', in B.G. Hickman (ed.), *Econometric Models of Cyclical Behaviour*, No. 36 in National Bureau of Economic Research Studies in Income and Wealth, 813–947, New York: Columbia University Press.

Cootner, Paul A. (ed.) (1964), *The Random Character of Stock Market Prices*, Cambridge, MA: MIT Press.

Granger, Clive W.J. (1969), 'Prediction with a Generalized Cost of Error Function', *Operations Research Quarterly*, **20**, 199–207.

Granger, Clive W.J. and Oskar Morgenstern (1970), *Predictability of Stock Market Prices*, Heath: Lexington.

Hendry, David F. and Mary S. Morgan (eds) (1995), *The Foundations of Econometric Analysis*, Cambridge: Cambridge University Press.

Kendall, Maurice G. (1953), 'The Analysis of Economic Time Series – Part 1: Prices', *Journal of the Royal Statistical Society, Series A*, **96**, 11–25.

Klein, Judy L. (1997), *Statistical Visions in Time. A History of Time Series Analysis, 1662–1938*, Cambridge: Cambridge University Press.

Lucas, Robert E. (1976), 'Econometric Policy Evaluation: A Critique', in K. Brunner and A. Meltzer (eds), *The Phillips Curve and Labor Markets*, Vol. 1 of *Carnegie-Rochester Conferences on Public Policy*, 19–46, Amsterdam: North-Holland.

Lucas, Robert E. and Thomas J. Sargent (eds) (1981), *Rational Expectations and Econometric Practice*, London: Allen & Unwin.

Makridakis, S., A. Anderson, R. Carbone, M. Hibon, R. Lewandowski, J. Newton, E. Parzen and R. Winkler (1982), 'The Accuracy of Extrapolation (Time Series) Methods: Results of a Forecasting Competition', *Journal of Forecasting*, **1**, 111–53.

Mitchell, Wesley C. (1913), *Business Cycles and their Causes*, Berkeley: California University Memoirs, Volume 3.

Moore, Henry L. (1923), *Generating Economic Cycles*, New York: Macmillan.

Morgan, Mary S. (1990), *The History of Econometric Ideas*, Cambridge: Cambridge University Press.

Niemira, Michael P. and Philip A. Klein (1994), *Forecasting Financial and Economic Cycles*, New York: Wiley.

Persons, Warren M. (1924), *The Problem of Business Forecasting*, Pollak Foundation for Economic Research Publications, No. 6, London: Pitman.

Sargent, Thomas J. (1976), 'A Classical Macroeconometric Model for the United States', *Journal of Political Economy*, **84**, 207–37.

Sims, Christopher A. (1980), 'Macroeconomics and Reality', *Econometrica*, **48**, 1–48.

Theil, Henri (1958), *Economic Forecasts and Policy*, Amsterdam: North-Holland.

Part I
Early Attempts

[1]

NEW SERIES, NO. 145   (VOL. XIX)   MARCH, 1924

JOURNAL OF THE AMERICAN STATISTICAL ASSOCIATION

Formerly the Quarterly Publication of the American Statistical Association

SOME FUNDAMENTAL CONCEPTS OF STATISTICS [1]

By Warren M. Persons

The general topic for discussion at the present annual meeting of the American Statistical Association is, "the statistical basis for analyzing the current economic situation, with the object of making forecasts of business conditions in general and for the great groups of economic activities in the United States." This topic explicitly recognizes that statistics may be effectively utilized not merely to describe the past, but as a basis for estimating present and future tendencies. The point of view thus indicated is neither new nor revolutionary. When the Statistical Society of London was organized in 1834, five years before our own Association, the Prospectus announced that its functions were to "procure, arrange, and publish facts calculated to illustrate the conditions *and prospects* of society." The evaluation of "the prospects of society" was thus recognized in this early statement as a proper object of statistical research.

It was not by accident that the idea of utilizing statistics of the past condition of society for inferences concerning the future appeared in the Prospectus of 1834. That it was expressed deliberately and with comprehension of its significance is indicated by an interesting and pertinent incident in the organization of the London Society, related by its former president, Sir Athelstone Baines. A Statistical Section of the British Association for the Advancement of Science had been organized in 1833 in which the studies were limited to "Facts relating to communities of men which are capable of being expressed by numbers, and which promise, when sufficiently multiplied, to indicate general laws." "Several men of eminence on statistics," says Sir Athelstone, "chafed at being thus relegated to the position of 'hewers and

---

[1] The Presidential address read at the Eighty-fifth Annual Meeting of the American Statistical Association, Washington, D. C., December, 1923.

drawers for political economy and philosophy,' so they joined in promoting the Statistical Society of London, now the Royal Statistical Society, with the view of providing therein a wider scope for their inquiries." [1] They considered it to be the function of *the statistician* to interpret and draw inferences from his statistics, and organized the Statistical Society for the purpose of furthering the development of that function.

It is my object tonight to discuss some fundamental concepts of statistics. I will consider, particularly, the logical significance of a statistical exhibit, the nature of statistical inference, and some of the important concepts involved in making forecasts of economic conditions on the basis of statistical analyses of limited periods in the past.

The necessity of the accumulation of statistics of the complex world of affairs in which we are immersed and the equal necessity of the development of special methods, different from those of the exact sciences, for summarizing these data have been admirably expressed by John T. Merz in his *History of European Thought in the Nineteenth Century*. "That which everywhere oppresses the practical man," he says, "is the great number of things and events which pass ceaselessly before him, and the flow of which he cannot arrest. What he requires is the grasp of large numbers. The successful scientific explorer has always been the man who could single out some special thing for minute and detailed investigation, who could retire with one definite object, with one fixed problem into his study or laboratory and there fathom and unravel its intricacies, rising by induction or divination to some rapid generalization which allowed him to establish what is termed a law or general aspect from which he could view the whole or a large part of nature. The scientific genius can 'stay the moment fleeting. . . .' The practical man cannot do this; he is always and everywhere met by the crowd of facts; by the relentlessly hurrying stream of events. What he requires is grasp of numbers, leaving to the professional man the knowledge of detail. Thus has arisen the science of large numbers or statistics, and the many methods of which it is possessed." [2]

The contrast, indicated by Merz, between the experimental method of the natural sciences and the statistical method of the social sciences may be expressed in greater detail. The natural scientist sets up and tries his experiment; repeats it as often as he pleases under the same or varying conditions; isolates the factor in which he is interested; and arrives at a demonstrable conclusion concerning the operation and effects of that factor. The social scientist, on the other hand, must ac-

[1] *The History of Statistics*, edited by John Koren, p. 385.
[2] Vol. II, pp. 554–5.

cept and analyze the mixed situation as it comes to him; gather pertinent statistics, not such as he would like, but such as are available;
study figures which embody the combined effects of many factors; and
express his conclusions in terms of probabilities.

It is obvious that the scope and nature of statistical inquiries are
determined, in the first instance, by the extent and kind of records
yielded by the "relentlessly hurrying stream of events". Many of
these records, which constitute the material for statistical research,
have resulted by accident rather than by design. For instance, in the
seventeenth century the French government sold to a group of pur-
chasers, bonds containing the provision that upon the death of any
holder the income from his bond was to be distributed to the surviving
holders; the record of this bond issue constituted the material for one
of the first tables of mortality. But we need not go back to the seventeenth century for illustrations of the accidental origin of useful statistics. Our figures for the personal distribution of incomes are a by-
product of tax administration; bank clearings are a consequence of the
process of check collection; and figures for building permits have resulted from the regulation of urban construction. It is only in comparatively recent times that such statistical by-products have been
supplemented by special collections of data definitely planned, and
designed to answer specific social or economic questions. And it is a
still more recent development for various organizations, such as journals, trade associations, and governmental agencies, to collect and
publish current data expressly for the purpose of estimating tendencies
with the object of moulding private and public policies. The body of
new statistics which has been added to our store during the five years
since the war shows that we are making rapid progress toward securing
a more adequate statistical record of "the relentlessly hurrying stream
of events."

The boundaries of statistical research set by the material available,
are obviously being widened, particularly in the field of economics.
But it is not now my purpose to consider either these widening boundaries or their limitations upon research. My purpose, as I have said, is
to consider the nature of the argument which proceeds from an examination of series of economic statistics, such as prices, interest rates, and
the output of goods for consecutive time-units in a given period.

The primary function of an investigation of the economic statistics
of a selected period of time is purely descriptive of that period.[1] Statistical devices, such as tables, charts, averages, measures of dispersion,
lines or curves of trend, periodic functions, and coefficients of correla-

[1] See Keynes, *A Treatise on Probability*, p. 327.

tion, are not arguments. All of this machinery enables one merely to describe more or less completely and, at the same time, more or less simply, the economic fluctuations and inter-relations of the given period. The inclusion of such a function as the coefficient of correlation among the descriptive devices of statistics indicates and emphasizes our point of view. Keynes accurately characterizes the last named statistical device in these words, "the mere existence of a particular correlation coefficient as descriptive of a group of observations, even of a large group, is not in itself a more conclusive or significant argument than the mere existence of a particular frequency coefficient would be." [1] And a frequency coefficient, such as average wholesale prices or the ratio between bank loans and deposits, is of itself no argument at all. So that the immediate result of any research in social statistics is merely the description of a limited field.

But the statistician whom we are considering has not as his object the securing of an isolated description in a world of isolated descriptions. His aim is to draw an inference. In the specific case which we are considering at the present annual meeting of the American Statistical Association his object is the definite one of getting a notion of the economic "prospects of society". To attain his end he has selected a suitable body of statistics and a period for study. Back of this selection, back of the study itself, is a fundamental belief. The statistician, in common with every other scientific investigator, has a deep-seated belief in the continuity and orderliness of affairs.

"The grasp of large numbers," says Merz, "the methodical array of figures and the registration of events, would in itself be of little use were it not for a fundamental assumption which appeals to common sense and has been confirmed by science, though it is hardly anywhere expressly stated—namely, the belief in a general order, in a recurrent regularity or a slow but continuous change and orderly development of the things and events of the world. . . . It may also be well to note that this belief in a general order is common to all schools of thought." [2]

The recognition of this belief in a general orderliness of affairs is necessary if we are to understand the manner in which the statistician moulds his investigation and arrives at a statistical inference. In the first place, he follows, as well as his material allows, the method of the experimental scientist when he selects, as a basis for forecasting, a past period for study as nearly as possible like that of the present. He attempts to find a specific analogy existing in an orderly universe. But

[1] *A Treatise on Probability*, p. 426.
[2] *History of European Thought in the Nineteenth Century*, Vol. II, p. 556.

he realizes that analogies differ greatly in their persuasive quality. The importance for an inference of a given statistical result pertaining to a given period is greatly increased, first, if similar or consistent statistical results obtain for sub-periods; second, if similar or consistent statistical results obtain for other periods and under different circumstances; and third, if all of the statistical results agree with, are supported by, or can be set in the framework of, related knowledge of a statistical or non-statistical nature. To illustrate the first point, if we have found, for instance, that a periodic function with a period of 40 months fits a time series of money rates for a span of 50 years the conclusion that there is a real period of 40 months for the entire span is strengthened if we obtain the same periodic function for each of two or more segments of the given 50 years. Also, to illustrate the second point, the conclusion is further strengthened if the same function is found for other than the given 50-year span and its segments. Likewise, the conclusion of a 40-month period would be further supported by the securing of evidence, statistical or otherwise, of corresponding fluctuations in business affairs. In other words, stability of statistical results and agreement with non-statistical results are potent arguments for continued stability in an orderly universe.

The method of argument just described is essentially empirical. Oftentimes when arguments from statistics are so characterized the word "empirical" is used to classify statistical inference as a lower, and hardly respectable, order of human thought. It is not in this way that I use the term. For I conceive that the term empirical "means simply what belongs to or is the product of experience or observation," and that a stable empirical statistical result persisting over the entire range of our experience is precisely the same thing as a "law of nature."

You will say to me, "There is nothing novel in the type of argument which you ascribe to the statistician; it is induction, neither more nor less." To this, I assent. "But the statistician," you may continue, "unlike other investigators deals with large numbers relating to classes of phenomena, in which, though it is impossible to predict what will happen in an individual case, there is nevertheless a significant regularity of occurrence if the phenomena be considered in successive sets. From this regularity," you say, "and from the likeness of the stream of human events to games of chance, the mathematician has built up a technique of statistical probability. In this technique a given statistical series becomes a random sample and the various statistical devices used, such as averages and coefficients of correlation, consequently have determinable probable errors. From these probable errors we can state precisely the future result which we may reasonably expect. For instance," you continue, "the maximum coefficient of correlation between the monthly items of pig-iron production and money rates for the period January 1903–July 1914 (133 pairs of items), after having made due allowance for secular trend and seasonal influences, is for a lag of 5 or 6 months in money rates and amounts to +0.75. The probable error of this coefficient is 0.03. The coefficient of correlation and the probable error together mean, according to the theory of inverse probability, that if we should take another sample of equal size the chances are equal that the resulting coefficient would be between +0.72 and +0.78. That is to say, one can state the mathematical probability that given economic relations will obtain in the future. This," you conclude, "is the special contribution of mathematical statistics to forecasting."

The view that the mathematical theory of probability provides a method of statistical induction or aids in the specific problem of forecasting economic conditions, I believe, is wholly untenable. Let us take a simple case. Suppose we are considering the probability that 1924 will be a year of business depression and that we have the record of business conditions for the past 100 years in which there were 40 years of depression and 60 years of non-depression. Then, according to the statistical record, the probability that a year taken at random would be depressed is 4/10. But this probability cannot refer to 1924 unless that year is a random year, that is, unless we have no specific information that differentiates it from other years. In fact, we do have specific information about the economic conditions in 1923 and about the relation of economic conditions in consecutive years, which we cannot reasonably ignore, so that we cannot view 1924 as "any" year taken at random. Every item of knowledge which we obtain bearing upon the situation in 1923 removes not only that year, but also 1924 one step further from its classification as "random." Such items of knowledge do not lead merely to continued revisions of the numerical probability that next year will be a year of depression; rather, they render inapplicable the method of mathematical probability, to the problem of making a rational forecast. Moreover, the actual statistical data utilized as a basis for forecasting economic conditions, such as a given time series of statistics for a selected period in the past, cannot be considered a random sample except in an unreal, hypothetical sense; that is to say, unless assumptions be made concerning our material which cannot be retained in actual practice. Any past period that we select for study is, in fact, a special period with characteristics distinguishing it from other periods, and is not "random" with respect to the present. We must, therefore, discard statistical probability and arrive at a forecast for 1924 on another basis.

There is a special objection to the application of the theory of probability to the particular economic data which constitute our material. If the theory of probability is to apply to our data, not merely the series but the individual items of the series must be a random selection. In fact, a group of successive items with a characteristic conformation constitutes our material. Since the individual items are not independent, the probable errors of the constants of a time series, computed according to the usual formulas, do not have their usual mathematical meaning. Thus, the "probable error" of 0.03 in a coefficient of correlation of +0.75 between the monthly items of pig-iron production and money rates six months later does not indicate, as one would conclude from the theory of probability, that the chances are billions to one against the independence of the two variables; or, to state the idea more specifically, that if we compute a coefficient from data of "any" other actual period the chances are more than ten millions to one that its value would be over +0.50. In fact, the significance of the "probable error" of a constant computed from time series is not known, and, in practice, we do not view the world from the standpoint of mathematical probability. So that we are not surprised when we actually find that the coefficient of correlation between the adjusted figures for pig-iron production and money rates six months later for the period 1915–18 is only +0.38. We find sufficient explanation of this result, which is almost impossible and really astounding when viewed from the standpoint of random sampling, in the war demands for pig-iron, the tremendous imports of gold, government financing, and the inauguration of the federal reserve system during the period in question. Neither are we surprised when we find that for the period 1919–23 the maximum correlation between the two series is for a lag in money rates, not of six months, but of nine to twelve months. For this period includes the severe crisis and great financial stringency of 1920–21, which dominated most of the items and hence the results. Thus in actual practice the statistician cannot reasonably assume ignorance of the peculiar circumstances pertaining to the special cases which constitute his material, and therefore he does not think in terms of random sampling and numerical probabilities. Granting as one must that consecutive items of a statistical time series are, in fact, related makes inapplicable the mathematical theory of probability.

The thesis that statistical probabilities give us no aid in arriving at a statistical inference has been developed with great skill and, I think, success by John Maynard Keynes in his *Treatise on Probability*, which I have already quoted. Summarizing his position, he says, "In order to get a good scientific argument we still have to pursue precisely the same methods of experiment, analysis, comparison, and differentiation as are recognized to be necessary to establish any scientific generalization. These methods are not reducible to a precise mathematical form. . . . But that is no reason for ignoring them, or for pretending that the calculation of a probability which takes into account nothing whatever except the numbers of instances, is a rational proceeding. . . . Generally speaking, therefore, I think that the business of statistical technique ought to be regarded as strictly limited to preparing the numerical aspects of our material in an intelligible form, so as to be ready for the application of the usual inductive methods. Statistical technique tells us how to 'count the cases' when we are presented with complex material. It must not proceed also, except in the exceptional case where our evidence furnishes us from the outset with data of a particular kind, to turn its results into probabilities; not, at any rate, if we mean by probability a measure of rational belief." (pp. 391–392.)

For the purposes of drawing inferences from economic statistics, in which the data are not of the "particular kind" indicated by Keynes, the theory of numerical probability gives no assistance. In particular, reasonable forecasts of economic developments can only be made by application of the usual methods of argument. To be sure, the conclusions of such arguments are expressed. not as certainties, but as probabilities. They are not, however, numerical probabilities. It is obviously impossible to state in terms of numerical probability a forecast or an inference based upon both qualitative and quantitative evidence; and even if all the evidence were quantitative, we have seen that it does not express a numerical measure of rational belief for the future. So when we say that "the conclusions of the social scientist are expressed in terms of probabilities" we merely mean that his conclusions do not have the certainty of those of the natural scientist. The probabilities of the economic statistician are not the numerical probabilities which arise from the application of the theorems of Bernoulli and Bayes; they are, rather, non-numerical statements of the conclusions of inductive arguments.

[2]

Paradise Lost & Refound: The Harvard ABC Barometers

Plus some insights into Town–and–Gown in the world of finance.

Paul A. Samuelson

These unauthenticated memoirs were evoked by Peter Bernstein's editorial queryings. Rather than check carefully the historic facts described here, I leave to some future researcher the identification of any myths that have crept into the oral traditions of my generation. I only tell it, as it was told to me! I owe thanks to the MIT Center for Real Estate Development for de Medici support of macroeconomic research.

By unhappy chance, Harvard University got into the forecasting business during the 1920s. Many of the great names in its economics department were connected with the Harvard Economic Society, a commercial venture that used some of its revenue to start and continue the *Review of Economic Statistics*, renamed the *Review of Economics and Statistics* in the 1930s when Seymour Harris was its editor.

Warren M. Persons (1878-1937) was a Harvard statistician who, around World War I, was an expert on the theory of index numbers. Apparently, Persons had the notion of starting a forecasting service. It must have prospered early, as the handsome outsize volumes of the *Review of Economic Statistics* were subsidized by the Harvard Economic Society. Besides Persons, other Harvard luminaries must have received some income from this commercial venture:

C. W. Bullock, John H. Williams, Edwin Frickey, and perhaps Allyn Young were a few such. The statistician W. L. Crum was presumably brought to Harvard in part because the Harvard Economic Society needed his mathematical skills.

The story is an interesting one, but in the end an unhappy case study of the risks a university runs when it lends its name to for-profit activities.

THE BAROMETERS

The most memorable activity of the Harvard Economic Society, and certainly its most interesting scientific contribution, was its famous A, B, and C barometers of business activity. These were the forerunners of the leading, current, and lagging indicators later developed at the National Bureau of Economic Research by Arthur F. Burns and Wesley Mitchell, by Geoffrey Moore, and later, in connection with the federal government's statistical services, by Julius Shiskin.

Persons, as I recall it, collected numerous time series. Some had downturns and upturns that occurred on the average a bit *earlier* than most of the series: He classified these as A or *leading* series, and the A barometer was a mean of them. Some of the series tended to move down and move up a bit *later* than the mob: These were the *lagging* series classified under C. The rest were B series, which more or less constituted *current indicators*. Although the act of clas-

PAUL A. SAMUELSON is Institute Professor Emeritus at MIT in Cambridge (MA 02139). A former student recently described him as "a human main frame, linked with a spreadsheet on a PC."

sification was mechanically empirical, the A series tended to represent Speculation; the B series were to represent Business; the C series, called Money, tended to be such finance items as interest rates and the stock of money.

The hope was to find in the A series a philosopher's stone that would tell customers when to get into the wild and woolly stock market of the 1920s and when to get out. (Even in my time at Harvard, just outside the walls of the Yard was the office of Curtis & Jackson — later merged with Paine Webber. Students and bold assistant professors could chance their arm against Lady Luck at little personal inconvenience.)

Persons used graphical methods, such as transparent charts that could be shifted until the series in question got into phase with the mean of the business cycle. Also, I seem to remember, he used cross-correlations of the form $r[x_t, y_{t+k}]$. If this Personian r reached its maximum for k equal to the positive integer 3, that was interpreted to mean that x tended to move three months earlier than y did. For k negative, y led x.

Students of monetarism will be surprised only momentarily that M tended to be in the C, or lagging, barometer rather than in the A, or leading, barometer. Any early positivistic Friedman could handily resolve this violation of what today might be called "Granger causality" by noting that M's growth rate (or first difference) tended in smooth oscillations to precede in its turning points M's own turning points: If M_t was in C, dM_t/d_t or $M_t - M_{t-1}$ tended to be in A.

SUCCESS!

The mail and the money rolled in — rolled into Holyoke and Little Halls, the holy temples of the old Harvard economics department in pre-Littauer days. President Emeritus A. Laurence Lowell once told me that one of his smarter moves was to divorce Harvard from the Harvard Economic Society: He just felt that this was not the kind of activity a university should be engaged in. (President Eliot apparently had no such compunction when he lent his name to the Five Foot Shelf of *Harvard Classics*, with which our parents used to line their bookshelves, and which we used as trots to help translate the *Aeneid*. There were no biologically instructive items in Eliot's selection: Much of what my generation knew about sex had to come from the famous eleventh edition of the *Encyclopedia Britannica*.)

Lowell's is a good story, which speaks well for his acumen and caution. But perhaps it wells out from imperfect memory, as some of my elders who have heard me tell the tale claim that it was well after Oc-

tober 1929 that the would-be money fructifiers were driven out of the temples of Holyoke and Little Halls. In any case, they moved only a few paces down Massachusetts Avenue, and their advertisements and letterheads still carried Harvard Square as their address.

UNTIL THE CRASH

Legend has it that the Harvard Economic Society let its customers down badly in the 1929 crash. Twice I heard Leonard Crum agree to recount for graduate students the failure of the barometers to predict or even recognize the 1929 financial panic. Really he had little to glean from the experience, coming up only with remarks like the following:

> "There was one statistical clerk [maybe Dorothy Wescott?] who said she didn't like the looks of the ABC barometers. But we failed to heed her warning."
>
> "Perhaps if Allyn Young had not died in 1928, the Harvard Economic Service would have done less badly."

Needless to say, empiricists who live by the sword die by the sword. The customers melted away, and the professors had to go back to teaching Radcliffe sections for their pin money. A number of economist stars, young and old, dropped a bundle in the 1929 crash. Some dowagers in Cambridge were still saying in my time: "I shouldn't have listened to Lauchlin Currie's guesses." A Back Bay society dentist, in the late 1930s, when he held me captive in the chair, used to complain endlessly: "John Williams may be vice president of the New York Federal Reserve Bank now, but in 1929 he sure was optimistic."

I have no reason to single out the Persons barometer methodology as particularly misleading in a time when a tulip-mania craze was sweeping both Wall Street and Main Street. Actually, though, it is of scientific interest that the National Bureau upper turning point of the late-1920s business cycle is marked in mid-1929, months prior to Black Friday of October 1929. Only rarely in history does the stock market *follow* the coincidental indicators instead of *leading* them. (When I am dead, I will not so much be remembered for my countless wisdoms as for my flippant remark: "Yes, Wall Street does call the turns of business. The Dow Jones index has predicted *nine* of the last five recessions.")

The fact that stock prices, for whatever reason, are so early an indicator of cyclical downturns suggests that speculators ought not to have hoped for much from subscribing to the ABC barometers. What the speculator wants is the time series that comes *before* the A series: They want Irving Berlin's pup, the "pup who gets the bugler up!" Such pups are hard to locate, and expensive to rent. Thus, it was a legend of the 1930s that Roger Babson, the sage of Wellesley Hills, had predicted the Wall Street collapse of 1929. Indeed he had. But Babson did it first in 1925 — a call that did not do a lot for the net worth of his clients.

In the middle of the 1930s, the *Review of Economic Statistics* was still carrying in an unenthusiastic way the ABC barometers in each quarterly issue. One day these disappeared from the new mailing. Few noticed. The universe and economic science carried on.

THE PHOENIX FLIES AGAIN

The museums of science are replete with fossils of species that could not last the course. The leading-coinciding-lagging indicators might be buried forever in old footnotes. But occasionally Sleeping Beauty is brought back to life by the kiss of a new Prince Charming. It must have been Arthur F. Burns who played the Prince. As the historian of science Robert K. Merton would expect, Darwins and Wallaces come in pairs like Newtons and Leibnizes. So it was with Burns and Persons. Impressed as he was by the regularities of the business cycle that the Mitchell group at the National Bureau had discerned and classified, it was only natural for Burns to look for regularities of phase shifts. And, working with Moore (and, later, with Shiskin), Burns found regularities that we economists still use today.

The ABC barometers live on in the Leading Indicators methodology of government agencies and private forecasters. What I still continue to find astonishing, but which I gratefully accept, is the finding that the mechanical leading indicators — imperfect as they are — still convey useful information. Even more surprising, they still stand up well in comparison with a myriad of close cousins. Like the late Tjalling Koopmans, I prefer paradigms that combine plausible Newtonian theories with observed Baconian facts. But never would I refuse houseroom to a sturdy fact just because it is a bastard without a name and a parental model.

CHARLES RIVER LEGENDS

We can appraise the influence of the Harvard Economic Society better if we know something about how the depression hit a community like Cambridge and a university like Harvard. Stories become taller in their retelling.

More than once I heard the following doubtful tale. One March morning in 1933, a Radcliffe student was supposed to have put to her money and banking professor the following question: "Professor Wil-

liams, could all the banks be shut down?" "No, that is quite impossible," he is reported to have replied. "What then does this headline in the *Boston Herald* mean, sir?"

The story is too pat to have a plausible ring. Perhaps it was accorded a false credence because reliable legend tells that the janitor in Holyoke Hall had to lend the department members funds to carry them through the Bank Holiday, because he was the only one in the building to have withdrawn his funds from the Cambridge Trust Company.

Wait, though, before we infer that the amateur is a better forecaster than the expert. It would perhaps not have been considered quite good form for professors to initiate a run on the banks. All my teachers knew well the opprobrium that descended on Professor Arthur Dewing, finance expert at the Harvard Business School, when, against the pleas of distraught bankers, he withdrew a large amount of gold from the Harvard Trust and put it in a bank deposit vault for safekeeping. Rightly or wrongly, this was considered the unsocial act of a survivor at sea who, in bolting out of the lifeboat, rocks it into hazardous instability.

For a score of years, Dewing would justify his behavior even to casual strangers, averring that, as a fiduciary for his public utility companies, it had been his duty to conserve their assets. (We graduate students believed the story that Dean Donham of the Harvard Business School asked for Dewing's formal resignation in order to alleviate public criticism but that, immediately on receiving that document, Donham proceeded to accept it. Do things happen like this outside C. P. Snow novels?)

Although the Harvard Economic Society happened to put some of its reliance on the ABC barometers, the service was essentially one of those many desert blooms called into existence by the sunshine of a long bull market. The cartoon books were full of similar debacles. "Where are the Customers' Yachts?" and "Oh Yeah?" were only two of the many titles of works in this genre.

AN EARLY KEYNESIAN CONTROVERSY

The magnificent collected works of John Maynard Keynes remind me of an old dispute about the 1920s bull market. Keynes and Ralph Hawtrey were on one side of the debate. Among those on the other side were Carl Snyder of the Federal Reserve Bank of New York and that same Bullock whom I have already mentioned in connection with the Harvard Economic Society. The issue deserves some paragraphs.

Bullock was a leading Harvard elder throughout the first third of the century, along with Frank

Taussig (truly a great scholar, and dean of American economists), Thomas Nixon Carver, and the wordless great man in economic history, Edwin F. Gay. These well-paid luminaries did not get along well with one another, as the failure of Taussig's prize pupil in Jacob Viner's oral examination attests.

Bullock's fiefdom was public finance, and he brought to it a knowledge of Greek and Latin and perhaps some smattering of Hebrew and Aramaic. In case you are too dull to guess how that confers deep insight into taxation and fiscal policy, Bullock's writings would have driven home to you that throughout all history unbalanced budgets contrived the downfall of Greece and the decline of Rome. Bullock's disciples, Harold Hitchings Burbank at Harvard and Harley Lutz at Princeton, perpetuated his theses.

Although Ralph Hawtrey and John Maynard Keynes were scholars of deeper analysis and wider reputation, one cannot in retrospect be sure that theirs was a more correct position than Bullock's in the late 1920s. Hawtrey and Keynes discerned no deep danger to the United States and the world macroeconomy from the Wall Street Bubble. Although Bullock could not articulate the precise basis for his apprehension, he had forebodings that the speculative "excesses" in Wall Street would lead to future disasters: As it had been in Sodom and Gomorrah, so might it come to be in New York and Chicago.

Some features of the securities markets in 1986 would no doubt be regarded by a Rip van Bullock as equally ominous. Rather than dismiss as ridiculous any such fears, I would have to take more comfort from the consideration that what was crucial for the Great Depression was not so much the October 29 Crash as the cumulative falling dominoes of bank failures, mortgage foreclosures, and bankruptcies that were subsequently allowed to take place in that era of relative laissez-faire.

UNIVERSITY FINANCES

Harvard and Cambridge were if anything less hard hit by the depression than most places. I remember few Greater Boston banks failing after 1935. When I once told the story that no local bank would take a Harvard student's deposit in those days, it was not to document the rigors of the academic life but, rather, to report on the possible relevance of a contemporary liquidity trap.

President Lowell's successful wooing of Mr. Harkness for the House system meant that Dunster and Lowell Houses were built in the teeth of the Great Depression, costing the economy in the end possibly a negative amount. Professors who kept their jobs in some cases never had it so good as in the slump.

Instructors in the Harvard economics department earned as much as $2500 a year, more perhaps than full professors at some land grant institutions and certainly several times what Harvard assistants in philosophy and the humanities were doled out. The best and the brightest in mathematics, physics, and biology — as certified by the National Research Council — were unable to a man to find jobs, much less permanent chairs, in the years just after 1933–1934.

The total returns earned on the Harvard portfolio in the years 1930 to 1939 can hardly explain its having been an oasis of serenity. Like others' organs, the Harvard nose was being ground down by the deflation, but it was a very long nose to begin with. The assets of universities were not to be unitized for another thirty years at least, so no one knew which universities did well as investors and which did badly. One had to settle for impressions. Hopkins, McGill, and Stanford were among those considered not to have been lucky in the depression years. Harvard was supposed to have done better than Yale. Once reputation is formed, however unwarrantedly, it tends to have a life of its own. One suspects that Yale did less badly than the casual world believes — and that Harvard did less well.

TRUE "THAT THOSE WHO TEACH, CAN'T"?

A treasurer of Harvard, William Claflin, once told me at a Society of Fellows dinner: "I have only two rules for investing the Harvard portfolio. Never consult the Economics Department, and never consult the Business School." Would that it were so simple!

Later in the postwar period, there were times when the University of Chicago, Rochester, (Connecticut) Wesleyan, the Alumni Foundation of the University of Wisconsin, and one or another educational institution were rumored to be particularly astute and innovative as investors. Often their short-term reputations were based on no more than the happenstance that the institution in question happened to allocate a high fraction of wealth to common stocks or unconventional equity instruments when markets were strong. By the time their college treasurers levitated up to important positions with a large Wall Street firm, their green thumbs too often reverted to the gray mean.

One needs sophisticated academic theory to understand the Mandelbrot–Pareto–Levy and less leptokurtic probability distributions that conduce to spurious appearances of superlative performing ability. Those who decry broad diversification or "settling for mediocrity" often have no conception of how to discern and test *long-run risk-corrected* investment prowess. Thus, in its fifteen years of existence, the

Common Fund (set up to permit smaller schools and colleges to pool their assets under professional management) has earned a higher "alpha" of total return than has the S&P 500 Index or CREF. Insiders understand that most of this superiority came from one of many money managers — one terminated at this time. Hiring several money managers and firing those with least recent luck has yet to be authenticated as the best strategy or even as a good strategy.

Irving Fisher, now recognized to have been a great scholar, became a laughingstock for his bullish pronouncements. Keynes's scholarly prowess did not inhibit his investment judgment. The typical college at Oxford and Cambridge tended to have on its endowment board one or more economist dons. I doubt that a Richard Kahn, a James Meade, or a Brian Reddaway lowered the batting averages of their ancient colleges. Certainly it was not long after Claflin jested that modern finance theory, from the pens of Harry Markowitz, John Lintner, Irwin Friend, and William Sharpe, demonstrated its usefulness to money managers. CREF, the largest common stock fund in the world, has benefited much from its trustees drawn from the world of professional finance. From my own observations over a long period of years, I would have to conclude that, at the same time, CREF's academic trustees have brought to the common effort much that the Claflins of the world neglect at their peril.

Paul Cabot was certainly one of Harvard's more effective treasurers. In retrospect, was it wise that his antipathy to government and to debt was permitted to delay Harvard's taking advantage of tax-exempt borrowing for the building of dormitories? Did Harvard's descending to the public trough kill off private philanthropy, as State Street pundits had warned would be the case?

When Seymour Harris led a 1951 revolt of the Harvard faculty against investing all of professors' pensions in fixed-principal securities, that move coincided with Vannevar Bush's threat to pull the Carnegie Institution out of TIAA. William C. Greenough's proposal for variable annuities based on the changing market values of a representative portfolio of common stocks therefore got its chance when TIAA established CREF in 1952. Meanwhile, back at the Harvard Yard, Cabot grudgingly awarded the rebelling activists a pension contract yielding as much more than 3-odd percent as the declared yield on the market value of the Harvard portfolio exceeded that percent.

The result was an incipient disaster. Neither Cabot nor the rebel professors realized that the latter were selling out their birthright for a mess of pottage that left all the capital gains of the Harvard portfolio

with the university and not with the professors. Had a competent assistant professor of finance been commissioned to study the setup at an early stage, the disaster might have been averted, and a later Harvard administration could have been spared the need to devise Robin Hood compensations for a generation of professors who had opted against CREF–TIAA and for the unfavorable local option.

A modern reader may be tempted to say, "Surely, when observers examined the *total returns* of CREF-TIAA, the Harvard portfolio, and the contractual provisions of the Harvard-controlled defined-benefit pensions, they would have recognized early on the inadequacy of the local alternative to CREF-TIAA."

Such a remark would betray naivete. No university provided data for observers to calculate total returns and other data that would enable an auditor to know whether its endowment was being poorly or cannily invested. I have no way of judging whether Henry Shattuck, or Claflin, or Cabot were astute investors. In the absence of unitization, neither can anyone else. To its credit, Harvard was one of the first finally to unitize its holdings so that a) *total returns* could be estimated, and b) a donor could discover when the university's central headquarters was standing to usurp the future capital gains from his/her gift. (Threat of suits by donors, I seem to remember, helped speed overdue action on this unitization front.) *After* Harvard moved, so did MIT and Yale and — as so often is the case. Let us be grateful.

GOING FOR IT

Judging performance of college and foundation trustees inevitably recalls McGeorge Bundy's pressure, from the Ford Foundation and onto non-profit organizations, to pursue a more aggressive strategy for improved expected return. Just when James Tobin's q factor — the ratio of what the economy's assets sell for in Wall Street, relative to what it would cost (net) in goods markets to construct such assets — was warning against possible overvaluation of equities, the Robert Barker report commissioned by Bundy urged colleges to invest more rationally. What Barker *et al.* meant to communicate was, "Be more rational." I fear this was interpreted by readers as, "Be more bold — especially if you hope for Ford Foundation grants."

I do not fault Bundy or Barker. I do reproach the economist members of the Barker committee, good friends of mine (Howard Bowen and James Lorie), for not incurring personal unpopularity by insisting in a minority dissent to the effect that long-run riskiness received inadequate attention in the Barker report. Academic scholars in economics departments and business schools — Eugene Fama, Fischer Black, Robert C. Merton, Myron Scholes, and a myriad of others — do have inputs that college treasurers, pension managers, and mutual fund directors will neglect only at their peril.

THE HOLY SANCTUM

All this, I agree, is a fair distance away from the comedy-tragedy of the Harvard Economic Society. Still, this digression to efficient market theory does bring up a basic question.

Even if the A barometer contains some useful knowledge for predicting share price declines, who is to say that this knowledge is not *already* registered in Wall Street pricings?

What is truly discouraging — or reassuring? — is the considerable evidence that the universe of those who seek to be "timers," and vary the fractional shares of their portfolios committed to common stocks in the hope of enlarging average long-term total return, in fact fail to achieve on the average any plus gain in comparison with simply buying and holding a fixed fraction of common stocks.

First it was my physicist and electrical engineer colleagues who became instant millionaires. Now it is the turn of the molecular biologists. That is their business. But as the comic-sad history of the Harvard Economic Society reminds us, it is the university's main business to mind its soul.

[3]

MORGENSTERN ON THE METHODOLOGY
OF ECONOMIC FORECASTING

THIS[1] is one of those rare books which, if only they are received with the serious attention that they deserve, sometimes succeed in forcing an entirely new orientation in the field of scientific endeavor with which they deal. The book would deserve the closest attention, even if its specific arguments were found to be either unsound or of little permanent value for further research along positive lines, by virtue of the vision of its conception, the saneness with which it sets limits to the discussion, and the boldness with which it states its conclusions. It required an imaginative vision to pull one's self consciously away from the details both of present methods of "business forecasting" and of the "cycle theories" which, consciously or unconsciously, lie at the base of those methods, in order to examine the methodological assumptions common to all methods and theories. It required a saving sense of balance to prevent the inevitably abstract and formal nature of the treatment from leading to fruitless juggling with metaphysical subtleties of doubtful relevance. It required courage of a high order to issue a challenge, couched in the most uncompromising terms, to the vested interests represented by those "institutes," commercial and "scientific," which are at this moment devoting a huge expenditure, in time and effort, to the study of business forecasting.

What will claim the primary interest of most readers of Dr. Morgenstern's book—though they will be superficial readers indeed who will find nothing of permanent positive value in the details of his analysis—is its essentially iconoclastic conclusion, and the arguments by which it is reached. His attack, against which a defense must be devised, may be summarized[2] as attempting to prove the following three propositions:

[1] Oskar Morgenstern, *Wirtschaftsprognose: Eine Untersuchung ihrer Voraussetzungen und Möglichkeiten* (Vienna, 1928).

[2] The nearest our author comes to presenting a summary under the three heads here indicated is on p. 108 of the volume under review. There is a more

MORGENSTERN ON ECONOMIC FORECASTING   313

I. Forecast in economics by the methods of economic theory and statistics is "in principle" impossible.[3]

II. Even if it were possible to develop a technique of economic forecasting, such a technique would be incomplete, by virtue of its necessary limitation to methods based on a knowledge of economics alone; it would therefore be incapable of application in actual situations.[4]

III. Moreover, such forecasts can serve no useful purpose.[5] All attempts to develop a formal technique for forecast are therefore to be discouraged.[6]

Each of these main propositions is supported, in turn, by a series of subsidiary propositions. At the risk of an awkward schematization, it will help to clarify the issues if, against each of these subpropositions, we set up a series of counterpropositions, which may be held to represent the position of those who would still break a lance in defense of business forecasting and its ultimate possibilities.

I

The subpropositions which are held to provide unequivocal support for the first major proposition, viz., that "forecasting in economics, by the methods of economic theory and statistics, is in principle impossible," may be stated somewhat as follows:

A. The data with which the economic forecaster must deal are of such a nature as to make it certain that the prerequisites for adequate induction must always be lacking.

B. Economic processes, and therefore the data in which their action is registered, are not characterized by a degree of regularity sufficient to make their future course amenable to

---

formal summary, consisting of six propositions, on pp. 109 ff., on lines somewhat different from those followed by me in the text. The propositions adduced throughout this review as representing the author's position are therefore not to be regarded as direct quotations, unless they are explicitly represented as such. In every case, however, I have given sufficient page references to enable the reader to judge whether my summary is a fair one.

[3] For instances of the formal statement of this conclusion see, e.g., pp. 108, 112, 113, 119.

[4] See esp. pp. 112 ff.   [5] Pp. 117 ff.   [6] Pp. 117, 121 ff.

forecast, such "laws" as are discoverable being by nature "in-exact" and loose, and therefore unreliable.

C. Forecasting in economics differs from forecasting in all other sciences in the characteristic that, in economics, the very fact of forecast leads to "anticipations" which are bound to make the original forecast false.

We may begin by laying down, as against subproposition A, the following counterproposition (A'):

A'. Most—though, in strictness, not all—of what Dr. Morgenstern says concerning the peculiar unfitness of economic data for treatment by certain formal methods of induction is true, especially if the differences in these respects between the data of economics and those of the other sciences be regarded as differences of degree and not of kind. Nevertheless, this conclusion does not have as crucial a significance for the problem of business forecasting as Dr. Morgenstern implies, for the reason that the conclusion challenges merely either (1) a basis of forecast that is not now, and has hardly ever been used, in any formal way, by those actually engaged in economic forecasting, though its theoretic possibilities have been canvassed by some workers interested in the more formal aspects of the problem of forecasting; or (2) a basis which, unfortunately, has been and is being used by certain forecasting agencies, but is by no means the only possible basis for forecasting. The most that Dr. Morgenstern proves, in other words, is that some business-forecasting enthusiasts have looked for light in the wrong direction; he does not prove that attempts at forecasting which start from premises quite different from those he attacks must necessarily fail.

It is primarily in connection with the question as to the possibility of applying to the problem of economic forecasting the formal technique of probability analysis,[7] regarded as a method of "scentific induction," that Dr. Morgenstern develops his arguments as to the unfitness of the data of economics as a basis for such "induction." As to the essential accuracy of Dr. Morgenstern's distinction between the data of economics and those of other sciences, in this connection, little need be said beyond

[7] See esp. pp. 66 ff.

the simple statement that there are grounds for questioning the formal rigidity with which our author draws the distinction as to kind between the types of data in question. The criteria, for example, of homogeneity[8] and of independence[9] in the data treated, which are postulated by the theory of probability, after all are, strictly speaking, relative, and not absolute criteria; what is desiderated is more or less homogeneity or independence, not absolute homogeneity or independence. Indeed, a general insistence upon the possession of these qualities in the degree of unadulterated purity which Dr. Morgenstern would seem to demand of economic data would forbid the practical application of the technique of probability analysis in fields where, as a matter of fact, it has shown its greatest usefulness. It is idle to labor this point, however, for the reason that, if one can quarrel with the rigidity with which Dr. Morgenstern contrasts economic and other data as to kind, it is hardly possible to quarrel with his implication that the differences in degree are so important as to be equivalent in effect to a difference in kind. The differences following from the relative smallness of the number of cases available in economics,[10] as compared with the other sciences, for example—especially in the light of the difficulty, familiar to every economic statistician, of honoring the criterion of homogeneity along with the criterion of the largest possible number of cases—are so familiar that we should be prepared to grant at once that the distinction between the two types of data, if it cannot be drawn with the formal exclusiveness with which Dr. Morgenstern seems to draw it, is at least sufficiently sharp to justify his conclusion that whatever may be the case in the other sciences, the formal technique of probability analysis can only rarely, if ever, be applied to economic data with any hope of obtaining reasonably significant results.

The real question, however, is how far this conclusion, granting its essential accuracy, takes us in the direction of establishing our author's central proposition that forecasting in economics is "in principle" impossible. That Dr. Morgenstern him-

[8] See pp. 66, 72, 97.

[9] Pp. 67 f., 70.   [10] See pp. 70 f.

316 ARTHUR W. MARGET

self regards it as taking us very far indeed is abundantly clear.[11] Nevertheless, it is possible to ask whether the significance of the conclusion is not greatly attenuated by the fact that our author would seem here—there is no other part of his book of which the like may be said—to be engaged in flogging a horse which is not only now dead, but which at no time, especially if one has regard to the actual practice of economic forecasting, was very much alive. One has only to try to recall concrete instances of formal attempts to employ the technique of probability analysis to the problem of business forecasting to be convinced that our author is, after all, fighting with a shadow.[12]

[11] Cf., e.g., p. 66, where the thesis as to the unsoundness of a "so-called statistical induction" based upon probability theory is declared to be "one of the most important of the whole treatment."

[12] The origin of the shadow, I suspect, lies in the looseness of expression to be found in certain continental writers upon the significance of the application of modern statistical methods to economics. See especially the suggestive but extremely dangerous article by E. Altschul, "Konjunkturtheorie und Konjunkturstatistik," *Archiv für Sozialwissenschaft*, Vol. LV (1926), from which one would gain the impression that the so-called "Harvard methods" are actually based upon the formal technique of probability analysis—an achievement apparently greeted with hearty approval by Altschul himself. If there are others who cherish illusions as to the extent to which the Harvard methods make use of that technique, they should consult again W. M. Persons, in Persons, Foster, and Hettinger, *The Problem of Business Forecasting* (Boston and New York, 1924), esp. pp. 8 ff. Altschul speaks repeatedly (e.g., pp. 63, 80 n.) of the theory of correlation as being "built upon" the formal technique of probability analysis. The explanation would seem to be that Altschul has taken too seriously—or, perhaps, too literally—the discussions by such writers as A. A. Tschuprow (see, e.g., his *Grundbegriffe und Grundprobleme der Korrelationstheorie* [Berlin, 1925]) of the "stochastic basis" of the theory of correlation—"stochastics" being defined as "applied probability theory" (so Altschul, *op. cit.*, p. 64 n.). Professor Persons, it is true, can be quoted as saying that "the problem of correlation . . . . is one aspect of the general problem of probability" (*Review of Economic Statistics*, July, 1925, p. 186). Nevertheless, in the absence of any suggestion by Professor Persons, in this later article, that he has abandoned the perfectly clear position indicated in his earlier paper, we may be permitted to assume that he is here speaking with the looseness with which, according to his earlier paper, we always speak when we say that "the conclusions of the social scientist are expressed in terms of probabilities" (*The Problem of Business Forecasting*, p. 12); and that he would hold fast to the proposition that "the view that the mathematical theory of probability provides a method of statistical induction or aids in the specific problem of forecasting economic conditions . . . . is wholly untenable" (*ibid.*, p. 8).

MORGENSTERN ON ECONOMIC FORECASTING   317

The fault would not be serious—indeed, it would hardly be describable as a fault—if it were not for the fact that Dr. Morgenstern proceeds to draw from his admittedly demonstrated proposition as to the inapplicability of the technique of probability analysis to the problem of economic forecasting, conclusions, both specific and general, which are not warranted simply upon the basis of that proposition itself. No one will quarrel, for example, with Dr. Morgenstern's specific corollary,[13] from the criterion of necessary independence of the observed cases, to the effect that probability analysis, per se, cannot foretell the individual event, but can only establish the probability that the chances of the individual event's occurring are, say, one in four. It is certainly possible, on the other hand, to quarrel with his clear implication[14] that, because it is wrong to attempt to forecast the individual event by means of the technique of probability analysis, it is wrong, in principle, for economic forecasting in general to set itself the task of forecasting the individual event. It can hardly be granted that Dr. Morgenstern has proved more than that, if these attempts were based upon the use of the formal technique of probability analysis, they would rest upon an unsound foundation.

In the same way, it may be said of Dr. Morgenstern's implications with regard to the general significance of his conclusion[15] that the whole of the formal technique of probability analysis should be allowed to pass once and for all beyond the pale of permissible bases for forecast in economics, that they make the calamity seem greater than it really is not only by greatly exaggerating, consciously or unconsciously, the part which the use of these methods has played in economics itself, but by conveying the impression that the whole technique has a much higher standing, among the tools available to the general scientist, than is actually the case. For some forms of scientific forecast, it is true, it is virtually the only tool available; but it is wrong to give the impression that it is the only one which general science knows, or even the one it most commonly uses. In the attempt to forecast the number of suicides or accidents which are likely

---

[13] See pp. 67 f.   [14] E.g., pp. 110, 116.   [15] P. 73.

ARTHUR W. MARGET

to occur over a given period, the technique of probability analysis is probably the best tool available; but neither suicides nor
accidents represent the typical material with which science
works. Dr. Morgenstern lists[16] weather forecast as an instance
of scientific forecast co-ordinate with the two instances just cited; but surely the actual work of the weather forecaster from
day to day—it is to be observed, in passing, that here, as in economics, we are certainly dealing with forecast of the individual
case—is not based primarily, if at all, upon the use of the formal
technique of probability analysis. Weather forecasting from day
to day is very definitely based primarily upon a theory of causation and upon a system of "symptomatics"—both of which are
not only not a necessary complement to analysis by means of
the technique provided by probability theory, but, as Dr. Morgenstern himself points out,[17] are, in a very real sense, actually
inconsistent with it!

If it has been found necessary to protest against what may
be regarded as an overrating by Dr. Morgenstern of the practical importance, for the future of business forecasting, of any putative claims which the formal technique of probability analysis
might put forward as a basis for forecasting in economics, it
would be bitterly unfair to our author to imply that he has
failed to deal with those broader and much less formal bases for
"induction" which are actually in use by business-forecasting
agencies at the present time. Here, indeed, the horse which Dr.
Morgenstern flogs is anything but a dead horse; and it is his argument on this head—the argument is woven into the very tex-
ture of the book itself, rather than developed at length at any
one point—which gives the book its chief value on the purely
critical side. Here is where it is possible for everyone anxious
for the establishment of a basis for forecasting in economics
with some claim to the designation "scientific" to utter a hearty
"Amen" to Dr. Morgenstern's strictures; the disagreement with
him will come, once more, only upon the question whether our
author, having shown the inadequacy of the way actually being
followed, has shown also that we have reached a final *impasse*

[16] P. 110.   [17] Pp. 69, 70.

MORGENSTERN ON ECONOMIC FORECASTING   319

which gives us no alternative but retreat and an ultimate abject surrender.

The whole drift of a great part of Dr. Morgenstern's detailed argument—an attempt to summarize the details themselves here would involve rehearsing a great deal of argument, extraneous to our present interest, through which the central conviction runs like a scarlet thread—centers around the proposition that economic statistics, from their very nature, provide an incomplete understanding of economic processes; that "purely statistical" considerations can never satisfy as a means of explanation and so ultimately of forecast.[18] This has been argued by others, by intelligent statisticians[19] no less than by theorists; the novelty of Dr. Morgenstern's contribution lies in the persistent, remorseless way in which this central point of view is applied to the successive problems in hand. The fresh and extremely illuminating discussion of the real meaning of time-series, from the point of view of what Dr. Morgenstern chooses to call the "time-quality" of prices;[20] the consistent attempt to provide an economic meaning to the results obtained by the use of modern statistical devices;[21] the insistence upon a study of the mechanism[22] of economic processes which find merely their reflection and symbol in prices; the categorical refusal to regard as self-sufficient the method of historical analogy[23]—all this cannot fail to gladden the hearts of those who still believe that economic theory will remain a chief tool for an understanding of economic events. The practical bearing of all that Dr. Morgenstern has to say on these points of detail—even if it is not always possible to agree in all particulars with some of his more positive contributions[24]—will be obvious to anyone who is frank enough

[18] So, e.g., pp. 64, 71. Cf. also pp. 10, 109 (on the "incompleteness" of the data recorded in time-series).

[19] Cf., e.g., Persons, *op. cit.*, p. 5.   [20] See esp. pp. 57 ff; also p. 78.

[21] See, e.g., pp. 10 f., 47, 51 f., 56 f., 58 ff., 74 ff., 85 ff.

[22] Cf. e.g., pp. 12, 25 ff., 28, 58.

[23] See, e.g., p. 90 and also, in this connection, the extremely stimulating discussion of the proper treatment of lags (pp. 74 ff.).

[24] Such as, for example, the suggestive differentiation (pp. 10 f., 47, 58, 75 f.) of trend, seasonal, and "cyclical" factors, on the basis of their relative dependence

　　　　　ARTHUR W. MARGET

to recognize that much, if not all, of business forecasting, at least in so far as it lays claim to the possession of a formal technique, has not yet passed beyond the infantile outlook which cherishes hopes that by some dark processes it may be possible to discover devices that will dispense with everything except the collection of statistics and the application of statistical formulas.

We have still to consider, however, the precise significance of these strictures for Dr. Morgenstern's central thesis. It is to be remembered that our author holds, not that some forms of forecasting are inadequate, but that all forms are, in principle, doomed to failure. Yet it is hard to see how all these considerations can be made to constitute anything more than an argument as to the inadequacy of the "statistical approach," taken by itself alone. If the nature of economic statistics is such that they cannot, taken alone, provide a basis for "statistical induction" which shall serve as a basis for forecast, we have still to ask whether it may not be possible to devise methods, of a type entirely different from those in common use today, which will provide an adequate basis. One might indicate again the precise limitations of the whole of Dr. Morgenstern's argument on this head by repeating the proposition that an attack designed to prove the inadequacy of "statistical induction" as a basis of forecast—an attack the details of which are directed, in the one case, against a method never seriously applied by business forecasters, and, in the other, against current methods the precise nature of whose present inadequacies have been recognized by the more thoughtful defenders of the possibilities of business forecasting[25]

---

upon non-economic causes, and their relative tendencies to persist *(Beharrlich-keit)*. One might agree with the broad differentiations which Dr. Morgenstern makes, and yet not be inclined to go all the way with him in his treatment of some of the details of this differentiation. One would hesitate to agree, for example, with the statement that changes in the record of seasonal variation are unlikely to result from causes other than such things as amplification of the statistical material (p. 11 n.). One thinks of such things as the modification of the seasonal movement in money rates as a result of the establishment of the Federal Reserve System. But such differences of opinion concern matters of minor detail, representing, in most cases, differences in emphasis rather than in principle.

[25] Cf., e.g., Edmund E. Day, "The Rôle of Statistics in Business Forecasting," *Journal of the American Statistical Association*, Vol. XXIII (March, 1928).

—does not prove that the road to further progress in economic forecasting is forever barred to those who will seek other paths. If there is a permanent bar to such progress, it must be held to lie in the nature of economic processes themselves. Such, indeed, seems to be Dr. Morgenstern's position, to an examination of which, from this new angle, we now turn.

Again it will help to clarify the issues involved if, against subproposition B, as stated above, we set up the following counterproposition (B′):

B′. No greater assumption of regularity in economic processes is necessary for forecast than is necessary for scientific explanation of economic events. Moreover, there is no inherent reason why, if the concept of "law" be employed in the sense of a "rule of adequate causation," rather than in some sense implying conformity to a formal external pattern, the "laws" which are to serve as a basis for forecast need forever be so "inexact" and loose as to be useless for that purpose.

It is characteristic of this excellent book that its author gives his opponents few chances to charge him with having failed altogether to include, in his more or less schematic presentation of possibilities, the particular concept or device which will present itself to those opponents as the way of ultimate salvation. The differences, therefore, between him and his critics will turn upon differences in the weighting to be assigned to one or the other of these possibilities. In the present instance, our author, though he wisely avoids any far-flung excursion into the field of discussions as to the precise nature of "economic laws," is careful to distinguish[26] between at least two types of "law": the term "law," in the one instance, being equivalent to the notion of a "rule of adequate causation," and, in the other, to a tendency to "continuous[27] repetition." Closely allied to the latter, again, is our author's use of the term "law" in the sense of a tendency of observed data to conform to a pattern measurable, and ultimately predictable, by a mathematical formula.[28] It is Dr. Morgen-

[26] Pp. 42 ff.

[27] On the meaning to be assigned to the adjective "continuous" see esp. pp. 48 ff.

[28] For instances of this usage see pp. 14, 52, 55, 84, 107. In the general argument the word "law" is often used without further definition, only the context

stern's opinion—and surely most economists, if we except the small group of patient searchers after "hidden periodicities" and other evidence of a "normal" cycle, will agree with him— that the evidence has not yet disclosed, and, from the very nature of economic processes, cannot be expected to disclose regularities of the kind suggested by the latter two notions of law; that, moreover, economic processes being what they are, the discovery of such regularities by purely empirical[29] means would carry with it no assurance of the indefinite continuance of these regularities, and so would represent no reliable basis for forecast.[30]

To all of this, it may be repeated, most economists would again utter a hearty "Amen"; and yet there are still some who would insist that to confine one's attention to regularities and laws only of this formal sort is not to do justice to that concept of law which is really at the basis of most attempts at scientific explanation: the concept of law, that is to say, which is represented, in Dr. Morgenstern's phrase, by the notion of a "rule of adequate causation." There is no indication that our author would deny[31] the possibility of explaining, from a reasonably modern and sophisticated view as to the nature of causation, the movements in recorded statistical data; indeed, to do so would

---

showing which of the three senses is meant. Contrast, e.g., the usage on p. 55 (in the third sense), or p. 114 (in the second sense), with the usage (in the first sense) in sec. 36 (esp. p. 50).

[29] It may be pointed out that Dr. Morgenstern does not bother to protect himself against the familiar charges of those who might attack his pessimism as to the strength of "merely empirical" laws, or, as he sometimes calls them (e.g., pp. 82, 111), "laws of experience," on the alleged ground that all scientific laws are empirical laws, in the sense that they all appeal to the facts of the world of experience. Such a criticism would, in the present case, involve merely a question of terminology. Granting that all laws are "empirical laws" in the sense indicated, the question becomes one of subdividing such laws into two or three categories similar to those indicated by Dr. Morgenstern, and of determining the degree of permanent validity attaching to each type. The question whether the specific type of "law" which Dr. Morgenstern distinguishes as a "rule of adequate causation" should be called an "empirical law" is essentially a terminological one.

[30] Cf., e.g., pp. 47, 50 f., 54, 57, 77 f., 79, 82, 111.

[31] Quite the contrary; cf., e.g., p. 112 n.

amount virtually to denying the possibility of scientific explanation in economics at all. For explanation of past events, of the kind indicated, the assumption of some kind of order—of a "rational filiation in the succession of events," as Comte[32] put it—is of course necessary; but the order which is assumed is one represented by the thesis that a given group of factors in a given combination will tend to produce a given result. Support of the proposition that further progress in economic forecasting is not forever barred demands no greater assumption as to the existence of "order," or "tendencies," or "laws," than this.

Indeed—it is a paradox which runs through the whole of Dr. Morgenstern's book—the ways to such further progress have, in fact, been suggested by our author himself, though in some instances with a reserve which may be attributed in part to the modesty of his whole performance, and in part to the pessimistic devil within him who will not down, and who finally registers a formal triumph at the end of his book. Consider, for example, the plea, already referred to,[33] for a closer study of the mechanism by which the results that are registered in economic statistics are brought about. An objective description of a sequence in events—which is what a description of mechanism essentially reduces to—is of course not in itself a theory of causation; but it provides at once a check on other theories of causation, in the sense that it challenges the very possibility of occurrence of some of them, and, at the same time, by the fact that it brings into juxtaposition two or more events which had heretofore seemed unrelated, provides a clue to other possible theories of causation. Consider, also, the recognition[34] by Dr. Morgenstern—although his treatment of this particular approach will strike some of his readers as neither as complete[35] nor

[32] See Cairnes, "M. Comte and Political Economy," *Essays in Political Economy*, p. 302.

[33] See the references given above in n. 22.

[34] Cf. pp. 18 ff. The idea recurs elsewhere, without formal use of the expression "potential factors"; see, e.g., p. 60 and esp. p. 61.

[35] The direct use of the concept by Dr. Morgenstern really represents, as he himself suggests (p. 19), merely a kind of application of the law of definite proportions, in the special sense that these factors "must" be present, in given pro-

quite as sympathetic[36] as its importance in their eyes would warrant—of the possibility of listing a set of "potential factors," the combination of which will give different results according to the differing quantitative importance of the several factors in a given combination. Consider, finally, his recognition of the need for the development of "cycle theory"—a need which, as he never tires of emphasizing, implies a prior need for the develop-

---

portions, in order to produce a cycle. But of course the idea should be extended far beyond so simple a notion—far enough, in fact, to include the explanation of the effects following from the action of those factors which have been dubbed, with increasingly less justification after the work of Professor Wesley Mitchell in destroying the idea of a "normal" cycle, "erratic" or "irregular" factors, in contrast to "cyclical" (so Dr. Morgenstern, persistently; cf., e.g., pp. 13, 15, 23, 76, 96 n.). Our author even goes so far as to define "erratic" fluctuations as those "for which a cause cannot be given" (p. 58; cf. also p. 102, for a similar contrast between the "erratic" and that which is "comprehensible" [*verständlich*]). There are other indications of an apparent failure, on the part of Dr. Morgenstern, to recognize the bearings of the concept of "potential factors" upon the problem of explaining the so-called "erratic" in economic phenomena. Cf., for example, the proposition (p. 41) to the effect that whereas forecast is possible only upon the assumption of "a certain order and conformity to law [*Gesetzmässigkeit*]," erratic fluctuations are "the negation of order," so that (p. 13), upon the assumption that there are in economic life only "irregular" fluctuations and "erratic movements," "every theory of forecast collapses hopelessly" and leaves the field to the view that "complete anarchy" prevails in industrial fluctuations. For the special difficulties which our author sees for the explanation of the "erratic," when the latter is identified with the effects of non-economic factors (e.g., p. 90), see the argument on p. 334 of this review and n. 57.

[36] Cf., e.g., the arguments on p. 116: "The combination of factors which are recognized as being involved in the situation is always a new one, and never repeats itself"; and, again: "The number of the factors is too great for all possible combinations to be exhausted," as is evidenced by "the theory of permutations." To these suggestions the answer is twofold: (1) The attempt at explanation and forecast in the physical sciences is based upon the assumption that, while every situation does represent a new combination of factors, the action of the factors in their new combination may be forecasted with a considerable degree of success from their action in a previous combination, providing that the previous action has made it possible to build up a workable "rule of adequate causation." (2) Research in the physical sciences does not prepare itself to solve future problems by imagining in detail all the possible situations which may arise. It attempts, by the construction of a system of "rules of adequate causation," to provide an analytical technique which will be able to solve these problems as they arise. Fortunately for the world, science has not yet degenerated into a memory exercise, by means of which the practical worker may recall the particular formula which might be expected to fit a particular case.

MORGENSTERN ON ECONOMIC FORECASTING   325

ment of general economic theory[37]—in the entirely new directions which are called for by the revolutionary work which has
been done in the field beginning, say, with the publication of
Professor Wesley Mitchell's first *Business Cycles*.

All this is of course simply to reiterate the conviction of
those who, so far from admitting that "economic theory" is
either merely a scholastic relic from an era of misguided effort
or a finished volume of authoritative doctrine, would insist that
the field of economic theory still offers new worlds for conquest
by another and fresher generation of workers. The point for the
present argument, however, lies in the suggestion that the progress of scientific explanation in economics, which will be represented by the further development of economic theory, will
necessarily be identical with progress in economic forecasting,
progress in the latter field involving no greater assumption of
law or regularity than it does in the former. Whether the task
of explanation would not be better accomplished if there were
no thought of the use of its results in forecasting is a question of
private judgment, which will concern us when we have finally
disposed of the central question as to the possibility of economic
forecasting. For the present, it should suffice to repeat the proposition that to insist, even by implication, that forecasting in
economics is "in principle impossible," upon the ground that economic processes do not evidence that minimum of regularity
which will provide a sufficient basis for economic forecasting, is
simultaneously to deny the possibility of explanation in economics, and to bar the road to the further development of economic theory which the attempt at such explanation must involve.

It is to what we have distinguished as the third of our author's chief subpropositions that Dr. Morgenstern obviously[38]
attaches the greatest importance of all, and rightly so; for if his

[37] Cf. the quotation from Böhm-Bawerk in this connection, on p. 1, and see
also pp. 4, 12, 75. On the particular desirability of a further development of the
theory of pricing in terms which might be described as "dynamic" see pp. 12,
32, 43 n., 61.

[38] See p. 92 : "We are here concerned with one of the . . . . most central
problems that the theory of forecast can present."

argument on this head be sound, everything that we may have shown thus far with regard to the possibilities of forecast in economics becomes irrelevant. Our criticisms of Dr. Morgenstern up to this point have simply attempted to show that the statement that forecasting in economics is "in principle" impossible should be restated to read that some bases of forecasting are unsatisfactory, and therefore doomed to failure. If, however, what we have designated as proposition C be true, then all these gradations of merit are of no practical significance whatever; all forms and all bases of economic forecasting are to be rejected as equally devoid of scientific or practical utility.

To this third proposition, which alleges[39] that the attempt to forecast in economics carries within itself the seed of its own destruction, because of the fact that the forecast itself inevitably sets up reactions which necessarily make the original forecast false, we may set up the following counterproposition (C'):

C'. The distinction between the social sciences, on the one hand, and all other sciences, on the other, upon the basis of the alleged fact that only in the social sciences can the forecast itself affect the subsequent event, is too sharply drawn, unless the term "social sciences" be extended to include all studies of those factors in human environment capable of modification at the hands of man. In any event, it is not clear that forecasting in these sciences is bound to prove a failure, for the reasons that (1) forecasting has in fact been made possible in these sciences, by the device of including the possible reactions of man to the forecast itself as one of the "potential factors" affecting the final result; and that (2) it is by no means certain that the nature and extent of the reaction set up by the forecast itself will necessarily be such as to falsify the original forecast.

Our central problem is, of course, that of the possibility of forecast in economics, not in science generally. In the present instance, however, since Dr. Morgenstern may be said to be forced, in the last analysis, to rest his whole argument as to the

[39] See esp. sec. 42 (pp. 92–106). There are indirect references to the proposition at many other points in the argument (see, e.g., pp. 8, 28, 112 f.), and it is itself applied to other specific problems, such as, e.g., the homogeneity of economic data (p. 71 f.), and the constancy of lags (p. 83).

MORGENSTERN ON ECONOMIC FORECASTING   327

impossibility "in principle" of forecast in economics upon the consequences of one of these alleged differences, it might be well, without going into detail or multiplying instances, to question the rigidity with which our author draws a distinction[40] in this particular matter between the social sciences and "all others." Fortunately for our purposes, Dr. Morgenstern himself provides a test case when he adduces[41] the science of medicine as one in which forecast is practiced, apparently with profitable results. Physicians forecast the decomposition of tissues, let us say, under the influence of certain degenerative diseases; but, fortunately for humanity, the forecast may be made "false"— in Dr. Morgenstern's sense of the term—by the fact that, aware of this tendency to decomposition, man may choose to submit to treatment which may set up a certain corrective reaction. The possible "modification" of the original forecast as a result of the forecast itself—we are accepting, for the moment, Dr. Morgenstern's implication as to the rigidity of the form which the original forecast must take—is a contingency which, it may be repeated, is to be faced not only in economics, but in any science dealing with man or his material environment, where that environment is capable of modification by man.

Recognition of the vastness of the area over which one may witness the operation of this peculiar—and, to Dr. Morgenstern, crucial—difficulty, resulting from the causal influence of the forecast itself, will naturally breed curiosity as to the way in which the difficulty has been met in these other sciences. Obviously, we have in this factor of possible "anticipations," as Dr. Morgenstern calls them, simply one more "potential factor" operating upon the situation immediately following upon the forecast. If it were indeed true, as our author implies[42] at this stage of his argument, that the forecasting agency finds itself

[40] Cf., e.g., pp. 5 ff., 30. An exception is of course made as to the effect of economic forecasts the terms of which are "kept secret" (pp. 103, 105).

[41] E.g., p. 5. It may well be that Dr. Morgenstern thinks of forecasting in medicine as being concerned primarily with vital statistics, and their possible treatment by the tools of probability analysis. Yet that fact would not weaken the force of our illustration.

[42] E.g., p. 95. But see *infra*, pp. 331 f., of this review.

ARTHUR W. MARGET

confronted by the necessity for making a forecast which should exclude the listing of the possible alternatives which may be expected to follow according to the way in which men may prove to react, Dr. Morgenstern's expectation that the forecast would be proved false might be confirmed, though, as I shall attempt to show presently, still not with the unfailing certainty that he implies. There is in fact, however, no reason to confine the forecasting agency within any such strait-jacket. To the ready objection that a forecast which envisages many alternative possibilities forecasts nothing, the answer to be made is that the course of subsequent events will itself limit the number of these possibilities and still leave room for forecast; and that it will be the task of the forecasting agency to issue a second forecast—not, as Dr. Morgenstern persistently assumes,[43] by way of correction of the first forecast, but by way of supplement to it—in the sense that the forecasting agency, upon the basis of as many symptoms[44] as it can survey, becomes increasingly able to establish the fact that men have begun to commit themselves definitely to a course of action which may be expected to continue for some time to come.

The possibility just outlined—that the conceivable effects of the forecast upon economic activity may be included among the potential factors affecting the final result, and so may be incorporated into the details of a correctly phrased initial forecast—represents the most inclusive answer to Dr. Morgenstern's categorical proposition that the forecast itself, by introducing a "new datum" into the ensuing situation, necessarily makes the initial forecast false. For it would take care even of those cases in which it is to be expected that the anticipations of enterprisers would result in action directly contrary to that which might

[43] Cf., e.g., pp. 96 f.; and see the ironical remarks on pp. 98, 110, concerning "prophecy with privilege of recantation" *(Prophetie auf Wiederruf)*.

[44] It must be obvious that this use of a set of "symptomatics," in the sense of a possible use of a group of sensitive variables as indicators of the inauguration of certain processes the action of which is to be interpreted only in the light of a carefully developed theory of causation which would allow for all reasonable contingencies, has nothing in common with the type of blind reliance upon a "constancy" of the "symptoms," which Dr. Morgenstern repeatedly, and rightly, rejects (cf., e.g., pp. 25, 71, 87 ff.).

MORGENSTERN ON ECONOMIC FORECASTING 329

have been undertaken in the absence of such anticipations. Yet it would be well to point out also that this whole difficulty of the effect of anticipations which looms so large in Dr. Morgenstern's vision becomes, when the realities of the situation are viewed at closer range, still less acute; for it is possible to ask whether the anticipatory actions of enterprisers need necessarily be of this disruptive sort.

It is to be noted, for example—and the illustration given by Dr. Morgenstern himself[45] of a forecast of rising prices illustrates the point admirably—that, in many cases, all that results from these anticipations by enterprisers possessing the new datum—assuming that such anticipations are really inevitable—is an intensification, instead of a contradiction, of the action that would have been inaugurated in any case. Dr. Morgenstern, after having himself indicated this possibility, attempts to show that the very admission of the likelihood of such intensification is *ipso facto* admission of the inevitable falsity of the original forecast, because it amounts to saying that "the real change is under all circumstances much greater than the forecasted change."[46] Yet the forecasting agency is not necessarily obligated to say by precisely how much prices may be expected to rise; and so long as it refrained from doing so, it would be making a forecast which, despite the anticipations (in a sense, indeed, because of them), would be both true and useful.[47]

Moreover, even if we grant, as under the strictest assumptions presented by our author we must, that the forecast is unquestionably a new datum for the enterpriser, there is no reason to assume that the new datum must so outweigh all the other data at the disposal of the enterpriser as necessarily to cause him to abandon the course which he had decided upon on the

[45] Pp. 94 f.

[46] P. 95; cf. also p. 118.

[47] At only one point (p. 96) does our author seem to deny that forecasts couched in general terms are useful. He does say elsewhere (p. 37) that of course "the goal of forecast is in the direction of the greatest possible specification" of the details of future events; but he is careful to point out immediately (p. 38) that a "general" forecast may be more valuable—may be more nearly "optimal," as he would put it—than a narrowly specified one.

      ARTHUR W. MARGET

basis of such "points of orientation"[48] as he could command before he was in possession of the new datum. The "total forecast"[49] might simply confirm the enterpriser in the decision he had made on the basis of an "individual forecast," just as an experienced, though non-technical, observer of weather conditions may find his conviction that the weather is likely to be fair confirmed by the official weather forecast. In such cases, it is difficult to see why we are forced to believe that the very fact of forecast must, through its putative effect upon the subsequent actions of enterprisers, make that forecast false.

It must be pointed out, finally, that it is, after all, only upon the "strictest assumptions" that we are compelled to accept even the thesis that economic forecasting necessarily introduces a new datum for the business world—"datum" being used in the sense of something which individual enterprisers may be expected to take into account in determining their "points of orientation." In the light of the actual facts with regard to the probability of acceptance, by the business world, of a single "authoritative" forecast, or indeed, of any published forecast, Dr. Morgenstern could hardly fail to be perfectly well aware of this; and he is in fact extremely careful to present[50] a schematic list of the possibilities with regard to the generality with which a given forecast may be accepted. He argues,[51] however, that if the forecast is accepted only by a section of the business world, or if, as at present, we have a situation in which there are several competing forecasts, each with its group of supporters, forecasts have still less likelihood of becoming true than if there were a single, authoritative forecast. For to the previous diffi-

[48] For the meaning of the concept, and instances of its application, cf. pp. 26 ff., 92 ff. The proposition in the text above would be true, even if we recognized, with Dr. Morgenstern (see, e.g., pp. 27, 102), that our "points of orientation" may be "unstabilized" from the simple fact that others change their plans. For it is still possible to assume that others will not necessarily change their plans— which is all that is necessary for the present argument.

[49] This notion, together with that indicated by the expression "individual forecast," is introduced early in the book (e.g., p. 7), but the terms are not formally defined until pp. 30 ff.; see esp. pp. 33, 35.

[50] Pp. 93 ff.

[51] Cf. pp. 97, 99, and esp. pp. 100 ff.

MORGENSTERN ON ECONOMIC FORECASTING 331

culties, which resulted from the fact that the forecast itself may have provided a new datum which changed the plans of enterprisers, we now have the difficulty of determining not only how many new data—in other words, how many forecasts—there are current, but also what proportion of enterprisers are likely to follow what forecasts, and what proportion will follow none of the forecasts at all.

It will be observed that the very fact that Dr. Morgenstern raises this type of difficulty indicates a subtle shift of front on his part with respect to the inevitably disruptive effects of "anticipations"; for it must be clear, on reflection, that the difficulty he now raises has significance only for the problem of including the possible effects of the forecast in the terms of the forecast itself, a saving possibility which he had heretofore virtually ignored. There is no reason, however, why we should not meet him on his new ground, especially since it happens to be the one we have ourselves chosen. From this standpoint it may be said that the specific difficulty which our author now raises is a factitious one, in that it arises only upon the assumption of a procedure by the forecasting agency which will not, in actual practice, be found necessary. There is no reason why, even assuming diversity in forecasts and in the number of adherents to each, such an agency should give its attempt to gauge the future course of economic events the form of a literal enumeration of the number of forecasts and an effort at precise measurement of the quantitative importance of the following of each among business men. The fundamental fact—fortunately both for science and for the struggle of everyday life—is that over a wide range of human activity the alternatives for human action are in fact, whatever they may be in theory, comparatively few in number. The actual possibilities of a given business situation are limited; the number of possible reactions is likewise limited.[52] All these possibilities of human action may be assumed

[52] This is of course the answer to Dr. Morgenstern's very amusing analogy of a guessing contest between Sherlock Holmes and Moriarty (p. 98 f.). Holmes, in pursuit of Moriarty, bases his own action upon a forecast of the way in which Moriarty will forecast his (Holmes's) action: and Dr. Morgenstern asks us to imagine the complications in the event that Moriarty had gone one step farther,

ARTHUR W. MARGET

to have been latent before the advent of the economic forecast; there is no reason to believe that the advent of the forecast itself made the situation worse. The forecast, if properly conceived, should have envisaged all of these possibilities, and, if properly stated, should have taken account of them, with the intention of following up the first clues presenting themselves as to which of the possibilities are in fact being realized. The threat of a necessity for counting forecasts, and then seriously attempting to count the noses of the supporters of each, supposes a *naïveté* of procedure which is hardly likely to be found anywhere in practice. One feels that Dr. Morgenstern has here given us what, despite his declared intention,[53] can be described only as a satire.

II

All the considerations thus far adduced combine to show that it is not possible to provide unequivocal proof for Dr. Morgenstern's proposition that forecasting in economics is, as a matter of principle, impossible. It is at this point, however, that we encounter the second of our main propositions, viz., that even if such a thing as a "positive theory of forecasting in economics" were attainable, it would not be adequate for the task which economic forecasters have in practice set themselves, for the reason that the data with which they have to deal are the resultant of other forces than merely economic ones.

It is difficult to gauge the real importance of this second objection in Dr. Morgenstern's own mind; in any case, it is hard to believe that he would be prepared to follow to their extremity

---

and forecasted the way in which Holmes had reasoned, and so on *ad infinitum*. Aside from the fact that the actions of business men are predictable with considerably greater ease than those of a detective and his quarry engaged in a battle of wits, it may be pointed out that, even in the case cited, the possibilities of Moriarty's actions were extremely limited. He might have left from Victoria Station, or from the halfway station. What was there to prevent Holmes from dispatching one agent to meet Moriarty at the halfway station, and to leave another at Victoria Station, to take care of all contingencies? And what is to prevent a business man from weighing the possible contingencies, and being prepared for action along more than one line? Or the forecasting agency from surveying these possible lines of action and being prepared to note the definitive adoption of one of them by these same business men?

[53] P. 101.

the consequences, for further research in economics, that a literal acceptance of this dictum must entail. For it may be pointed out once more, that the objection is just as valid against all attempts at explanation in economics as it is against all attempts at forecasting. As to the objection itself: Of course all the social sciences are one; so is all human knowledge. Yet when it is a question of drawing up actual programs for scientific research, surely Dr. Morgenstern is not seriously proposing that we revert to the view of the Greeks, who took the proposition as to the unity of all knowledge so seriously as to combine it under one name, "philosophy," and to treat it as a single unified discipline. The reason for the change, as everyone[54] recognizes (it is difficult to avoid repeating here the most obvious of platitudes), has been that our practical choice lies between accurate knowledge of a few detailed, specialized fields, or even of a single specialized field, and superficial knowledge of many. He is the wise scholar who will not condemn himself to insulation from influences in fields other than his own, but at the same time will refuse to renounce his privilege of attempting to master his own field as well as a short lifetime will permit.

For practical purposes, Dr. Morgenstern's inhibitions arising from his contemplation of the ramifications of the various branches of human knowledge, considered as a bar to further progress in economic forecasting, seem to derive from two leading considerations. The first[55] is that sociology—it would have to be defined in a sense very close to the "philosophy" of the Greeks if it were to do justice to all the difficulties involved—is not yet sufficiently advanced, as a discipline, to be of practical utility to the business forecaster. To this, again, the answer is twofold. In the first place, the unsatisfactory condition of what must remain, under any definition, essentially a synthesizing discipline is no necessary criterion for the state of our knowledge within the several fields whose contents are being synthesized. In the second place, the incompleteness of knowledge is no argument for the denial of the possibility of the attainment of further

[54] Including, apparently, Dr. Morgenstern himself. See, at any rate, p. 113 n.
[55] See p. 115.

knowledge. At most, it would be an argument for humility in the stating of our present conclusions, and a willingness to modify them upon the appearance of new evidence.

Dr. Morgenstern's other proposition as to the futility of attempting to forecast economic events because of the complications introduced by forces whose detailed study belongs outside the province of economics proper would seem to be, in one sense at least, in direct contradiction to his first proposition. Having argued that economics itself is not sufficient for the solution of the problem, he would seem actually to forbid economists the use of the results obtained in other fields, on the grounds that "for an economic forecast, only economic theory and the data as refined by the methods of economic statistics may be used."[56] This is scientific parochialism, with a vengeance! Of course nobody seriously suggests that economists should themselves undertake the forecast of, let us say, movements in natural phenomena, such as rainfall and climatic conditions generally; but why should not an economist, interested, for example, in the forecast of cotton prices, combine with his own first-hand knowledge of how a man is likely to economize on the basis of a given material situation, the knowledge he is likely to obtain from the first-hand work of meteorologists and agronomists, as to what that material situation is likely to be in fact?[57] Again, therefore, it may be held that Dr. Morgenstern's argument, properly interpreted, is an argument for the careful use of our tools in the practice of forecasting, not for the abandonment of the task itself, as being "in principle" impossible.

III

We come now to a consideration of the practical questions of immediate policy which Dr. Morgenstern raises at the very end of his book: Can the attempt to forecast economic events serve any useful purpose? Is Dr. Morgenstern right in urging, with-

---

[56] P. 113.

[57] This is of course the answer to the problem as to how the economist is to deal with "erratic" fluctuations, when these are defined as involving "meta-economic processes" (p. 90). Contrast Dr. Morgenstern's treatment of the problem (p. 41 and esp. p. 114).

out qualification, that all scientific approval be withdrawn from the present attempts to develop a technique of forecast?

That the attempt to forecast economic events is "without purpose" would follow naturally, and does follow, in our author's treatment, from an alleged proof that such attempts are bound to lead to failure. It is a tribute to Dr. Morgenstern's fairness, however, that he does more to support his counsel as to abandonment of all attempts at forecast than to draw this simple conclusion. He approaches[58] the problem rather from the concrete standpoint of the possible use of forecasting as an instrument for the social control of industry—especially from the standpoint of the possibilities of "stabilization"—and comes to the conclusion[59] that forecast, in the sense of a formally published forecast enjoying fairly wide acceptance, so far from assisting efforts toward stabilization may well endanger those efforts, by threatening the "rationality"[60] of the economic process through its shifting of the enterprisers' "points of orientation." Obviously, this conclusion will command acceptance or not, according as our author's analysis as to the necessarily disruptive nature of the relationships between forecasts and "anticipations" is regarded as sound or not. It is hardly necessary to go over this ground again. It is most certainly necessary, on the other hand, to challenge the fundamental proposition which obviously suggested the problem of stabilization as a test case for the usefulness of attempts at forecast, and which underlies the

[58] Pp. 118 ff.

[59] This conclusion is hinted at various points in the argument (e.g., p. 30), and is explicitly stated elsewhere (pp. 92, 106, and esp. p. 119). It may be pointed out, in passing, that if the mere publication of a new datum thus threatens the stability of the economic structure, it is difficult to see why the publication of more information of the kind approved by Dr. Morgenstern partly in the interests of stabilization (p. 123) would not be just as likely to cause a "shift in the points of orientation" and so (by Dr. Morgenstern's own argument) a tendency toward instability!

[60] A state of "rationality," as the term is used by Dr. Morgenstern, is obviously to be understood in the sense of one in which the means used are found to be perfectly adapted to the accomplishment of the end. So, e.g., pp. 8 ff., 26 ff., 30. There are scattered instances of other usages (e.g., p. 42) but this is obviously the chief one.

336   ARTHUR W. MARGET

whole of Dr. Morgenstern's position as to the purposelessness
of such attempts; the proposition that forecast itself can have
significance only for economic policy,[61] and not for the development of economic science as such.

What Dr. Morgenstern would seem to fail to recognize is
the value which the persistent attempt to forecast has for the future development of economic theory. One would imagine, from
reading certain of his pages,[62] that a failure in forecasting is to
be regarded as an unmitigated calamity. As a matter of fact,
such failures, like failure in attempts at "verification" of economic theories, should be greeted with the greatest enthusiasm,
since the chances are that the failure was due to inadequate attention to some "potential factor" which may turn out, in some
instances, to be the point about which everything revolves.[63]
The danger that confronts every discipline, such as economics,
which is, for practical purposes, deprived of the opportunity of
experiment, is the danger of complacency with the results obtained by theoretical analysis. Attempts at "verification" of
theories on the basis of concrete historical episodes, if they are
pursued constructively—that is to say, in the frank hope of finding that the theory does not "work," with the intention, at the
same time, of amplifying it and restating it subsequently in such
wise that it will work—have their value, as thorns in the side of
this complacency. In verification on the basis of recorded data
of the past, however, the danger is always that, even with the
firmest intention on the part of the investigator to avoid bias,
the investigation may suffer from a tendency toward the selection of facts, such as will give support to a concealed bias. Nothing is easier than to give lip service to certain theoretic possibilities, and then, in actual controversy, to forget that these
possibilities exist. The test of successful forecast, as applied to
economic theory, is a bitter one—if not carefully handled, in
some respects an unfair one—but it does have the inestimable ad-

---

[61] See p. 118.   [62] Cf., e.g., pp. 95, 107.

[63] As Dr. Morgenstern himself seems on occasion to recognize (cf., e.g., pp.
82, 108); and yet this recognition does not change his conviction that no possible
good can come from the attempt to forecast!

vantage of putting theory on its mettle; of pointing out new variables, and new possibilities of mechanism which, except for the
spur which a failure in forecast provided, might never have been
discovered or properly estimated. From the standpoint of this
testing function of attempts at forecast, Dr. Morgenstern's strictures as to the usefulness of unpublished forecasts[64] and his discussion of the possible effect of published forecasts upon the
task of stabilization are seen to be, if not unfounded, at least irrelevant. So far as the special problem of stabilization is concerned, it may be said that forecast will aid stabilization by aid-
ing in the acquisition of that knowledge of economic processes
which should be at the basis of all attempts at stabilization; the
real gain, however, which it is to be hoped will come from the
attempt at forecast, will be the additions accruing to that body
of analytical technique which constitutes the heart of our science.

   This is not to say, by any means, that the present organization of research into the possibilities of business forecasting
merits the unqualified approval and good wishes of those whose
major interest lies in the further progress of economic science.
Opinions on this head, as Dr. Morgenstern suggests,[65] are bound
to differ. With all hesitancy, I should make these two suggestions:

   1. It is time seriously to consider the possibility of a permanent dissolution of that marriage of convenience between scientific investigation into the possibility of forecasting in economics,
and the sale of a "service" to the public, which may have been
necessary when the first attempts were being inaugurated, but
which does not find a similar justification under present conditions. Like most marriages of convenience, this one has turned
out far better than anyone had a right to expect; but it is hardly
to be doubted that the present arrangement possesses certain
features which are bound to prove troublesome in the future.
The desire to please one's paying customers may lead to one of
two opposite results, neither of which is desirable. The fear of
error, which would cause the loss of some of the paying custom-

   [64] So, e.g., pp. 72, 105, 112.   [65] P. 121.

338   ARTHUR W. MARGET

ers, may lead to inhibitions in the matter of clear and unequivocal statement of the forecast,[66] with the result that it is impossible, after the event, to say whether the forecast has succeeded or
failed. Or the inevitable demand of the "customers" for specific
and detailed forecasts may force the making of a definite forecast at a time when, either because of the present unsatisfactory
state of our scientific knowledge or from the peculiar nature of
an individual[67] situation, no definite forecast is possible. There
is also the inevitable danger of lack of candor in admitting mistakes in the past, and this only because of the fear of losing these
same paying customers. No agency of research should ever be
forced to choose between its scientific honesty and its continued
existence as a going concern.

2. In all forecasting, a much sharper distinction[68] should be
drawn than has heretofore been the case between the theoretical
basis of the forecast, which should attempt to lay out the factors
which may possibly[69] operate in a given situation, and that part

[66] In this connection see the remarks of Dr. Morgenstern on p. 78, though
they seem a bit strange coming from one who would reduce the function of "institutes" at present engaged in the study of business forecasting to the publication of statistics "with as little interpretation as possible" (p. 122), and the production of merely a new-fashioned type of "economic history" *(ibid.)*.

[67] The difficulties, in such a situation, might arise either from the fact that
not enough statistical information was available or that the situation had not yet
crystallized sufficiently to make clear which of several potentialities was likely to
be realized. The admission of either possibility in the individual case has of
course nothing whatever in common with the categorical denial, "in principle,"
of the possibility of forecasting in economics.

[68] On the necessity for a clear distinction between the "theory" and the forecast based thereon, see Morgenstern, pp. 73 f.

[69] It should hardly be necessary for me to defend myself here at length
against the accusation that I oversimplify the whole problem by assuming that
the variables operating in a given situation are very few in number. I make no
such assumption; I assume only that the number of possible significant variables
is not so great that they cannot be distinguished and their action studied. The scientific correctness of the proceeding would be protected by the use of the impounding device, "other things being assumed constant"—in the special sense of
being assumed to remain, as they have been found to be in the past, insignificant in their influence. The validity of this device, in actual experiment, would
depend upon whether the variables excluded from direct consideration did, in
fact, exercise any appreciable effect upon the final result. If they did, it would
be necessary, in order to keep our theory in a state of relevance to the problems
of life, to add a new variable to the "active" part of our scientific equipment;
to that extent one must agree with Dr. Morgenstern when he says (p. 112 n.)

of the forecast which consists of the attempt to assign relative importance to each of these factors, upon the basis of quantitative measurement, in the existing situation. It is of the greatest importance for the progress of economics, as a science, that it should be possible to determine whether the failure in forecast was due to inadequate or mistaken measurement, or to faulty theoretic analysis in the first place. Mistakes with regard to the former affect only the truth or falsity of the original forecast; mistakes with regard to the latter affect the validity of a part of that "body of analytical technique" which has already been referred to as the heart of our science. To know that we have failed in forecasting is no disgrace; the disgrace would come from being forever doomed to fail simply because we are unable to tell why we have failed in each case.

What is called for, in other words, is much more self-consciousness as to the presuppositions and the methods underlying the attempt to forecast. That there has been much blind "tapping about in the dark," with so little to show in the way of definitive achievement,[70] is to be attributed, above all else, to this lack of methodological self-consciousness. It is this fact which gives this courageous and challenging attempt of Dr. Morgenstern its chief significance. No difference of opinion on minor detail, no difference of opinion even with regard to his central conclusion, can for a moment lessen the magnitude and the importance of his contribution.

ARTHUR W. MARGET

UNIVERSITY OF MINNESOTA

that, in forecasting, the *ceteris paribus* which forms part of the theorem must be "resolved" *(aufgelöst)* (cf. also p. 115). Yet it will always be true that, for practical purposes, we can confine our attention to a comparatively small proportion of the forces which have a remote chance of acting significantly in a given situation. Here, as always, the problem would be one of steering a middle course between a scientifically correct but fairly useless statement to the effect that certain broad movements will result, if all other things are held constant, when, in fact, they are not at all likely to be constant, and the statement, equally correct scientifically, but still more useless practically, to the effect that there are many millions of forces operating upon a given situation, and that a complete list of them, to say nothing of a complete description of their operation in particular cases, would be an undertaking of tremendous dimensions.

[70] On the meagerness of the achievement in proportion to the outlay, cf. the mournful remarks of Morgenstern, p. 93 n.

Part II
Macroeconomic Forecasting
and Policy Making

[4]

THE POSITION OF ECONOMICS AND ECONOMISTS IN THE GOVERNMENT MACHINE

A COMPARATIVE CRITIQUE OF THE UNITED KINGDOM AND THE NETHERLANDS

THAT professional economists in government service should confine themselves to technique, leaving it to political leaders to set the objectives and take the decisions, is easier said than done. The border-line between the two rôles is blurred : most social scientists are possessed of sufficiently strong political views to find it almost impossible to keep their impartial analyses genuinely impartial. And most economists are so unconfident of the accuracy of their techniques that they are tempted to abdicate not only responsibility for value-judgments, but also for final decisions as to the technical advice Ministers should receive. Hence the relations between government economists and other government officials are almost as important a matter for study as the relations between officials and economic ministers. Nowadays, in most of the world's capitals, nearly every official fancies himself as an economist, and, particularly in this country, nearly every economist fancies himself as something of an administrator.

In a large group of Western European countries, and to some extent in the United States, there has been a remarkable similarity in the post-war development of relations between government economists, other government officials, Ministers and Parliament. In Western Europe the similarity is so marked that deterministic explanations are strongly indicated. But similarity of temperament, educational systems, political institutions and economic situation seem not the only factors ; much is evidently attributable to the nature and significance of economic science. The development does not necessarily imply a process of evolution towards an ideal ; one finds repetition (but little conscious copying) of bad things as well as good.

The distinguishing features of this similar development are :

(1) In all the countries a conscious general economic policy from the government, combined with a varying degree of direct intervention, in predominantly capitalist economies. The nature and scope of these policies have been such that the governments have inevitably required much more day-to-day advice from professional economists than before the war.

(2) The advent of (1) did not, in any of the countries, result in a general accession to power by professional economists. There was an increasing specialisation in economic affairs by officials, some with formal training as economists and academic standing, some as " amateurs." In addition, each government recognised the need for some central group, manned by trained economists recruited largely from the universities. Several such organisations were named economic planning bureaux, several were given less ambitious titles, but the functions of nearly all were essentially advisory rather than operational. A feature common to several of the countries was the emergence of one man, who as director of the central bureau, or as the government's chief economic adviser, exerted a strong personal influence on affairs, somewhat independently of his staff.

(3) In all of the countries there is a strong constitutional and administrative tradition of Departmental independence. Formal responsibility for the new economic policy was therefore morcellated among the various Departments of State; in a pattern basically much the same everywhere. In nearly all the countries, for example, a strong Ministry of Finance continued to be responsible for fiscal policy, budget making, internal financial policy and often the balance of payments, while the Central Bank, now nationalised to serve the broader ends of economic policy, acquired power to ensure that the bankers' point of view prevailed more than ever in the counsels of government, particularly in the new field of exchange control. The heterogeneous group of responsibilities which devolved upon the United Kingdom Board of Trade is also recognisable in similar ministries in other capitals, often under the name of a Ministry of Economic Affairs.

This morcellation was bound to present serious problems. Much delegation of responsibility was necessary. But all economic policy questions, even minor ones, are essentially interdependent. Further, the new concepts of macroeconomic policy—concerning employment, the balance of payments, the general level of prices and so forth—had, self-evidently to be operated centrally. There was thus a definite conflict between traditional administrative *desiderata* and the needs of the newly shouldered economic responsibilities of the governments.

(4) The conflict described in (3) usually resulted in a compromise. If a question was " inter-departmental " in the

administrative sense, then central intervention (by the central economic advisers, or some body such as the United Kingdom Central Economic Planning Staff, or both) might occur as a matter of right. If, however, a question, though involving the entire economy, fell administratively into the sphere of one Department only, then central intervention could occur only through persuasion, and always with the danger of provoking bad feeling. Central economic groups were given a clear field in the macro-economic work, but, because of the nature of the administrative set-up, much of this was left rather in the air : it was unusual, for example, for taxation departments to agree to frame their estimates of next year's revenue on the basis of the central economists' assumptions about income.

(5) Despite these constitutional and administrative difficulties, and despite the fallibility of their science, the trained economists in central bureaux, in all these countries, succeeded nevertheless in exerting some definite influence on policy at all levels. Sometimes it appears to the outside observer that the major part of their work lay in the preparation and publication of annual economic surveys or national budgets, but this impression mainly arises from the fact that much of their other work was confidential.

This development has now had some eight years to mature.[1] It does not seem too early, therefore, to begin to ask certain questions about the work of these central bureaux :

(1) What professional methods have been used ?

(2) How has the work been organised, and what has been its scope ?

(3) What has been its influence ?

The similarities do not extend to the subjects of these questions. In working methods, organisation and results, as well as in important secondary details, there are major variations from country to country and major similarities. Thus comparative study should be fruitful.

The present article compares the *Centraal Planbureau* of the Netherlands' Government [2] with the organisation of professional economists in Her Majesty's Treasury, most of whom are con-

---

[1] In the United Kingdom there was also, of course. an important war-time development.

[2] One of the reasons for selecting this organisation for study was that it is directed by the author of a work on the theory of economic policy (see note 1, p. 767 below), and therefore has a *prima facie* case for investigation as a meeting ground of theory and practice.

centrated in the Treasury's " Economic Section." The article is based on information gained during an extended visit to the *Planbureau* [1] and on the author's personal experience and knowledge of the Treasury. The reader is warned, however, that whereas the Dutch officials willingly discuss their methods and problems with outside research workers, the Treasury pursues a policy of deliberate secretiveness—which its members are bound to follow—often extending even to the finer points of social accounting.[2] Hence with respect to the descriptive passages below which relate to the British side of the comparison, in contrast to those which relate to the Dutch, it was not possible to obtain confirmation, or denial, on any points of fact; some of these therefore take the form of deduction or surmise, though to the best of the author's knowledge and belief the account given here is reasonably accurate for comparative purposes. *Opinions* expressed are, of course, entirely personal, and none should be taken as representing the views of the *Centraal Planbureau*, the Netherlands Government, the Treasury, the Economic Section, its members or Her (Britannic) Majesty's Government.

THE METHODS OF WORK

In many matters the methods of Dutch and British government economists are much the same—the methods used by economists the world over. One studies the available qualitative information; one turns a sharp eye upon the available statistics of present situation and past trends; one searches for supplementary data; one performs a few simple computations; then, making liberal use of one's pre-conceived ideas, one writes one's opinion in a few well-chosen words, illustrated by one or two simple, well-chosen tables. More elaborate computations will be

---

[1] The author is extremely grateful to the Director and many individual members of the staff of the *Bureau* for giving him a great deal of their time, for providing material facilities and for general encouragement. He is also grateful to the Governing Body of King's College, Cambridge, for financial assistance in meeting research expenses.

[2] The only available published source is the article, " The Recent Uses of Social Accounting in the United Kingdom," by E. F. Jackson, printed in *Income and Wealth, Series I* (Cambridge, 1951), to which extensive reference is made below. The article is, however, an unhappy source for the investigator to rely upon because : (i) it was apparently written during the summer of 1949, and is therefore almost certainly considerably out of date; and (ii) it is prefaced by a footnote reading ". . . although I am an official, nothing in this paper must be taken as expressing the views of the Central Statistical Office or any other part of H.M. Government," a statement whose poignancy is enhanced when it is appreciated that the Central Statistical Office is entirely independent of the Economic Section.

relegated to an appendix, because, however important, they are unsuitable *pabulum* for one's seniors. In more technical language, these methods may be described as a mixture of qualitative and quantitative analysis, such as involves only the more elementary theoretical concepts and the most elementary statistical methods —inspection, simple derived statistics, index numbers and other weighted averages, national income arithmetic. These methods are used in the *Centraal Planbureau* of the Netherlands Government in any appropriate work, in particular work concerning monetary policy, the problems of particular industries and work concerning economic developments in foreign countries. The difference between the Hague and Whitehall is that whereas in Whitehall these are, as far as is known, the only methods allowed, in the Hague there is a consistent attempt to exploit in addition the " econometric " or statistically " advanced " methods of modern applied economics.

Simple econometric methods are widely employed by Professor Tinbergen's staff, not only in basic research but also as aids to the analysis of current problems of policy. The latter are subjected to the discipline of a general-equilibrium macro-economic decision model, expressed in algebra, and based on the assumption of a reasonable stability in the behaviouristic and structural relationships between the variables identified in it, albeit with liberal allowances for specific disturbances. Time-series analysis, family budget analysis, input–output analysis and the like are employed both in basic research into the values of parameters in the model and also to help with guesses of the future movement of its exogenous variables.

This major difference in the methods used in Holland and Britain not only appears to exist at the time of writing but also was certainly present throughout the period when a considerable amount of detailed economic planning or " programming " was still occurring in the United Kingdom, particularly in the field of balance-of-payments control. Somewhat surprisingly, in Holland, the classic methods of the *Planbureau* were not applied to the operation of import controls, and quantitative controls generally seem to have played a rather less dominant rôle in balance-of-payments policy than they have in this country. The *Planbureau* is mainly concerned with the total amount of the overall balance of payments; something they consider as (partly) endogenous to their general model of the economic system, something to be attacked with general, rather than specific, weapons of policy. In the United Kingdom, short-term control of the balance of payments seems to be an operation conducted rather independently of other economic policy operations, although it is evident from public statements that the connection in principle between internal and external equilibrium is very well appreciated. Holland's very large foreign trade multiplier, small share in world trade and heavy concentration on trade with Europe—as against the structural, geographical, bilateral and " monetary " [1] character of the external difficulties of this country—must provide much (but not all) of the explanation.

Nevertheless, it is extremely interesting to compare in more detail the *Planbureau's* methods for constructing balance-of-payments projections with the type of procedure which appears to correspond to typical British practice. Periodically, the governments of both countries, whether they liked it or not, have been forced to take a fairly definite quantitative view as to what would happen to the balance of payments if existing policies and economic trends remained unchanged, and have had to call for estimates of the quantitative effects of possible corrective policies. And for both governments there were major elements in the situation—foreign demand and supply conditions—which were entirely beyond their control, and thus self-evidently exogenous variables in any form of decision model; but, as will be seen, the methods used for estimating even these variables were very different in the two countries.

In Holland, next year's export demand is assumed to depend on Dutch export prices, a specially constructed and weighted index of competing prices (short-term elasticity assumed is usually the Tinbergen Two), incomes in Dutch overseas markets (income-elasticity just over unity) [2] and special factors. Dutch export prices are assumed partly to follow world prices for similar products and partly costs in the export industries (which come from

[1] " Monetary " is intended as a short-hand reference to the United Kingdom's difficulties in controlling its external capital account.

[2] This is a weighted average of individual commodity and market elasticities, as follows :

$$\bar{y} = \sum_j w_j \sum_i e_{ij} y_{ij}$$

where $\bar{y}$ is the aggregate export income-elasticity; y_{ij} is the income-elasticity of the ith commodity in the jth market; e_{ij} is the proportion of Dutch exports of the ith commodity to the jth market in total Dutch exports to that market, in some base year; w_j is the proportion, in some base year, of total Dutch exports to the jth market, in total Dutch exports to all markets.

The y_{ij}'s are estimated from family budget data, or any other information available, relating to country j.

$\bar{y}$ is fed into the model as a constant : errors due to changes in the distribution of the w's and e's are, rightly or wrongly, assumed unimportant, because $\bar{y}$ is applied only to changes.

the model as the cumulative consequence of changes in labour costs, import prices, etc.). The competitive price index has been found to show a good lagged correlation with world prices. Foreign incomes are forecast piecemeal from whatever qualitative and quantitative information is available about each country, and depend imprecisely on the *Bureau's* view of cyclical tendencies in the United States. The volume of next year's imports is entirely given by the model, but import prices, of course, must be forecast independently : the Dutch are fortunate compared with their British colleagues in that they can reasonably regard their importers as facing conditions of infinitely elastic supply. The Netherlands raw materials import price index has been found to possess a mysteriously reliable lagged correlation with the Reuters' Economic Service index of London prices of internationally traded raw materials, and this can be heavily exploited because raw materials form a very high proportion of total Dutch imports. Thus apart from invisibles, which are largely forecast by the same methods as in the United Kingdom—projection of trends, use of special knowledge, etc., item by item—the forecast change in the overall balance of payments is completely determined by the various assumptions determining internal developments, together with two major judgments about the external world—the change in real incomes abroad and the change in world prices. Any change in either group of assumptions changes quite explicitly the balance-of-payments forecast.

In the United Kingdom the volume of exports next year is projected as a single quantitative guess, taking some rough general account of all the factors, both on the demand side and the supply side, considered relevant. One of these, probably not the most important in the minds of those responsible, presumably is price, but the concept of the elasticity of demand is not certainly and consciously brought into play. At one time United Kingdom export forecasts were based on more detailed market research, country by country or commodity by commodity ; here again the individual studies were largely concerned with qualitative factors, though each led up to a single quantitative estimate.[1]

The value and volume of imports into the United Kingdom is the assumed result partly of an administrative programme governing the issue of import licences and partly of internal demand for " liberalised " goods. The administrative programme is made to conform with whatever it is government policy to

[1] The Board of Trade, not the Treasury, has primary responsibility for export forecasts.

" afford " in the light of the total estimate of foreign earnings.[1]
Bids for commodities are submitted to an interdepartmental committee (on which the central economists are usually represented),
scrutinised for general economic reasonableness, added up and
then if necessary " cut " after reference to Ministers to decide the
cases thought to involve thorny politico-economic consequences.
It is not known how the estimate for the liberalised sector is made,
but given the types of commodities involved and the prevailing
methodological tone, it seems unlikely that any use is made of a
specific income-elasticity or set of elasticities.

The above description does not provide any evidence, either
way, as to whether the Dutch methods are more likely to be
successful in forecasting what actually happens to the balance of
payments : in the present state of knowledge there exists no
conclusive demonstration of the general superiority of econometrics over intuition and extrapolative guesswork.[2] But the

[1] See Jackson, *op. cit.*, p. 155.

[2] Professor H. Theil, of the *Bureau*, contributed an article on this subject to
De Economist entitled " Whose forecasts are best ? ", February 1954. He compared the published, Economic Survey type of official forecast with actual results
in the United Kingdom, the Netherlands, Denmark, Norway and Sweden by
means of an index which reaches infinity for a set of perfect forecasts, and tends
to zero for extremly bad forecasts. The precise definition is

$$\text{Index of quality of forecast} = 1/V$$

where $V = \sqrt{\dfrac{\overline{\sigma_v^2}}{\sigma_r^2}}$

$$\sigma_v^2 = \frac{1}{n} \sum_{t=1}^{n} (v_t - r_t)^2. \quad (v_t = \text{forecast of variable for year } t)$$

and $\quad \sigma_r^2 = \frac{1}{u} \sum_{t=1}^{n} (r_t - r_{t-1})^2 \quad (r_t = \text{result})$

The *rationale* of this is that it compares the second moment of errors in forecast
changes with the second moment of actual changes. If one were forecasting an
index number which consistently changed, in one direction or the other, by 5
points each year and one was always correct as to direction but always underestimated (or over-estimated) the degree of fluctuation by 3 points, 2 points or 1
point, the corresponding values of $1/V$ would be 1·7, 2·5 and 5·0. Thus anything
under 2 is pretty hopeless, anything over 3 not at all bad.

The British and Dutch forecasts come out generally substantially better than
the Scandinavian. Professor Theil has kindly provided me with some adjusted
results which permit a direct comparison between the United Kingdom and Holland for the whole period 1948–52. Here is the tally :

$1/V$, 1948–53

	United Kingdom.*	Netherlands.†
Value of Exports . . .	3·3	3·8
Value of Imports . . .	3·8	1·3
Invisibles	1·1	1·0
Export Prices	no forecast	2·7
Import Prices	no forecast	5·2

* Economic Surveys. † Annual Plans.

Dutch system is probably more effective in exposing, insistently and systematically, the essential interdependence of internal and external factors. Also, in the author's view, it derives from a superior methodological philosophy; that it is better to frame estimates on the basis of general factors in the first place and then take account of special factors secondarily, rather than to compute the final result as the sum-total of a set of imprecisely stated special factors behind which the general assumptions, if any, lie obscured.

That philosophy runs right through the *Planbureau's* model, the whole of which need not be described in detail here. Reference may be made to publications of the director and staff of the *Bureau.*[1] Readers should be warned : (1) that the system in use is substantially simpler and generally less *recherché* than the kind of thing described in the published descriptions, and (2) that those descriptions are made unnecessarily difficult by frequent failure to explain sufficiently explicitly the basic economic theory (especially of price formation) which lies behind the equation.

The model is, of course, frequently changed, both in structure and in detail, in the light of circumstances and according to the current predilictions of those responsible. But it always consists of a set of linear equations relating one-year changes in a substantial number of selected macro-economic variables. It is always " Keynesian "; always, so far, static. Disturbances, including disturbances to parameters, thought to be caused by factors special to the year in question are dealt with by the insertion of separate autonomous terms in the equations : parameters are adjusted only when they are believed to be undergoing some permanent change. These autonomous corrections are the vehicle for the injection of common sense and qualitative judgment : they are subjected to frequent adjustment, both deduced and induced, so that the system is not slavishly followed when it offers silly results.

An example of a typical equation in the model is :

$$\Delta \text{ Imports} = \mu_1 \Delta \text{ Consumption} + \mu_2 \Delta \text{ Investment} + \mu_3 \Delta \text{ Exports} + M \text{ (all at year O prices).}$$

where the Δs are increases from this year (year O) to next year, the μs the " normal " marginal import contents of consumption,

[1] Tinbergen, *Econometrics* (Blakiston Co., Philadelphia, 1951), Chapter 7.

Tinbergen, *On the Theory of Economic Policy* (North-Holland Publishing Co., Amsterdam, 1952).

Sandee and Schouten, " A Combination of a Macro-Economic Model and a Detailed Input–Output System," *Input–Output Relations* (Netherlands Economic Institute), p. 196.

investment and exports, respectively, estimated from time-series. M is the sum of corrections for special factors.

The most complicated model tried so far was that used in the initial stages of constructing the 1954 Plan (it was subsequently simplified for publication). This contained about 20 basic equations and involved 65 symbols. Of the latter (in round figures) 20 were parameters (marginal coefficients or constant trends); 5 represented variables which are exogenous both to the model and to the economy, being quite beyond the reach of Dutch economic policy, and hence requiring to be forecast independently; 20 represented variables exogenous to the model but endogenous to the Dutch economy and capable (in principle) of being influenced to some extent by government policy. That left room for 20 variables fully endogenous to the model, *i.e.*, 20 determinable " unknowns," such as employment, production, personal consumption and the balance of payments. These variables are of the type which can only be influenced by government policy *via* operations on the previous group : given specific policy *desiderata* —quantitative " targets "—for any number, x, of them, only $20-x$ of the exogenous variables in the previous group are still free to vary; the remainder must be manipulated by policy if the targets are to be hit. In other words, x of the unknowns have become " knowns " (targets), hence, for the number of unknowns to remain equal to the number of knowns, some of the items initially assumed known must change their spots.

Of the initial division between exogenous and endogenous variables it is worth picking out the following, some of which have been indicated already : *endogenous*—tax receipts, labour productivity,[1] entrepreneurial saving on both personal and business account (the two together taken as a single function of total entrepreneurial income), employment and (partly) the general levels of the prices of consumption, investment, exports and government expenditure; *exogenous*—wage-rates, wage-earners' savings and the volume of investment, the last two mainly because no reliable functional relations with the wage bill and corporate income respectively have so far been found.

A large proportion of the 20 equations merely represent

[1] Productivity is assumed to vary directly with output, and output to depend on effective demand. Each 1% rise in output yields 0·525 of a 1% rise in productivity, an empirical relationship which has worked in the period 1948–52. The *Bureau* recognises, however, that this simple relationship may represent the compounding of an underlying trend with a much lower (or negative) short-period elasticity (of productivity on output). In which case it would break down in a period of stagnant effective demand.

national accounting identities, or conversions of quanta into current prices. Several could be eliminated by substitution, but are more convenient given separately. Basically the system is much simpler than superficially it appears.

Given any set of assumed values for the knowns, with their consequent values for the unknowns, the Dutch model can easily be, and is, translated for presentational purposes into a set of numerical projections of the national accounts, in a form quite familiar in this country. Indeed, the tabular details and refinements involved are in some features probably less complicated than in the projections provided to the government as a basis for the Economic Survey and for the consideration of short-run macro-economic problems generally. The difference between the systems of Whitehall and the Hague is less of form than of method.

The British, inserting appropriate determining assumptions at each stage, build up, step by step, numerical projections of next year's income and expenditure accounts (both current and capital) of enterprises, the government and households;[1] in recent years there has evidently been some further subdivision of the sectors in order to help analyse the balance of supply and demand in certain individual branches of industry very broadly defined (such as " all metal-using industries "). From these tables, and from the determining assumptions about wages, prices, productivity, tax rates, government expenditure, investment, etc., the important dependent volumes—total production, personal consumption, etc. —can be derived by simple arithmetic. The tables are brought into internal consistency by constant adjustment and re-adjustment of the assumptions: the method is that of Trial and Error.

At the outset, it appears, there is set up a broad general assumption about the directional tendency of effective demand and prices; this choice determines the *path* of the subsequent operations. Thus, if the *conjuncture* were thought to be expansionary, involving certainly full employment and probably rising prices, a sequence of trial assumptions thereafter would be chosen which is appropriate to the characteristic conditions and problems of an economy in full employment whose government is trying to prevent inflation. Production rises according to trend, employment according to the natural increase in working population, hence the volume of production is determined. Wage-rates rise from trade-union pressure, prices probably a little more than wage-rates.

The balance of payments must, by rule, be assumed to accord

[1] See Jackson, *op. cit.*, p. 156.

with its programme (see above).[1] Then the magnitudes determined to this point are sufficient to determine national income
and resources available for consumption or investment at home.
Profits, also, are determined. Hence, with a guess about the
proportion which will be distributed, the major items in the
account of enterprises can be written down. With an eye to
these accounts and to existing administrative and technical plans,
investment (government and private) can now be forecast.
Government consumption is taken as given. Personal consumption emerges as a residual. Given the transfers (estimated by
trend projection, etc.), the wage-bill and the accounts of enterprises, the accounts of households could be constructed, their tax
liabilities (as also those of enterprises) being taken as a specific
function of income, and the gap between liabilities and payments
estimated administratively. There is now only one figure for
private savings by households (" personal savings ") which will
allow the tables to balance. If this figure seems improbably high,
the Government is advised to try to reduce government consumption, tighten the screw on government-controlled investment or
cause a reduction in disposable income by means of an increase in
taxes. There is no second round; no explicit recognition, for
example, of the likelihood, expressed in the Dutch model by a
definite functional relationship, that a reduction in income will in
turn reduce the " plausible " level of *ex-ante* savings (one good
reason for this being the near-impossibility of deriving any
plausible consumption function from post-war British time series).

If, at the outset, deflationary tendencies are suspected,
employment must be taken as dependent on effective demand
rather than demographic factors; it is therefore necessary to
choose an initial arbitrary value for effective demand (and hence
production) to be adjusted later as necessary. Appropriately
non-inflationary assumptions would then be made about wages and
prices; output per man-year would be assumed to rise less than
trend, or even fall, because of the sag in production. The procedure followed thereafter is then similar to the first, except at the
final stage of interpretation for policy.

In principle there appears little difficulty in bringing the Dutch
and British systems together. The British operating procedure
could undoubtedly be expressed as a system of equations.
Although, at present, most of these would be no more than
identities—the only explicit functional relationship is that of
tax liabilities with income—some of what appear to be working

[1] See also Jackson, *op. cit.*, p. 156.

rules concerning the relations between changes in prices, wages, productivity and production imply belief in certain linearities which could easily be expressed in mathematical language; the discontinuities would be handled by the technique of applying boundary conditions.[1] Similarly, the Dutch model, which in the form described above is not applicable to a potentially inflationary situation, can easily be made so by the application of a boundary condition to employment.

Despite this similarity of principle, the existing differences of practice are most important. True, the British model would need very little formal alteration to make it symmetrical to the problems of inflation and deflation, and could be used, as is the Dutch, to help decide *whether* there is danger of (*e.g.*) too much deflation. But in practice—because of the enormous scope for the exercise of subjective judgment during the process of adjusting the assumptions—there is all the difference in the world between that procedure and the present British one of deciding in advance, on the basis of broad intuitive judgment, what is the direction the *conjuncture* is taking, and then using the " model " mainly as a vehicle for expressing that judgment in detailed quantitative terms. The British, with some justification, do not believe that econometric models of present-day vintage are much good at foretelling the *direction* of cyclical tendencies, although they may help, once the direction is established, to assess their extent. This philosophy, in my view, would make the British technique methodologically superior to the Dutch, if the latter were used over-mechanically : on the whole, however, it is not.

In a general comparison of the advantages and disadvantages of the Dutch " algebraical," *versus* the British " arithmetical," methods, one may list the following clear advantages for the Dutch :

(i) It is more systematic, intellectually tidier.

(ii) There is less danger of ignoring important but round-about or otherwise unobvious, consequences of policy decisions or sets of decisions.

(iii) It is less cumbersome, more " streamlined," and hence much quicker to manipulate. With the British methods it must take anything from five minutes to five days of work by quite senior officials to follow out the effects of changed assumptions. The Dutch system needs to be inverted only from time to time, *i.e.*, when a fundamental coefficient is

---

[1] See Tinbergen, *On the Theory of Economic Policy* (already cited), Chapter IV.

adjusted or the structure of the model modified. This inversion requires several days work from the staff of a computing pool, but thereafter there is available a standard tabular matrix from which the effect on all the other variables of any set of changes in determining variables can be read off at a glance. The importance of speed can hardly be exaggerated. In modern administrative politics, it is the quickest answer to a question which is most likely to be accepted. Also, if one is faced with onerous labour every time an assumption is changed, one is likely to put up a dangerous irrational defence of the *status quo*.

(iv) Partly because of (iii) and partly from its general structure the Dutch model is peculiarly well adapted to the presenting of policy problems in the form of a series of alternative possibilities. There is nothing in principle to prevent this form of presentation under the British system, but it would be relatively more cumbersome and, as far as one can tell from Economic Surveys and other indications, is not often done.

Against the above, the following are the advantages of the British methods :

(i) In some senses greater flexibility : greater adaptability (no more labour is involved in changing the structure of the model than in changing major assumptions) and greater scope for the insertion of non-linearities and discontinuities.[1]

(ii) Less danger of its operators becoming wedded to belief in the stability of relationships (parameters) which are not in fact stable.

Any overall judgment as to which methods are " best " is bound to be heavily influenced by subjective predilections : the present writer must declare a personal bias in favour of the Dutch. It may be argued that the Dutch system is particularly vulnerable to the danger that some members of its operating team may fail to apply adequate common sense : they may become so fascinated by the mathematical manipulations that they forget reality. But the British system also has its dangers; for example, the failure, already mentioned, to underline sufficiently explicitly the relation

---

[1] Clearly, most of such cases can be linearised, or dealt with by boundary conditions (see, for example, the supply price equation, number 3 in the table on p. 19 in *The Theory of Policy*), but the process becomes cumbersome. On the other hand, in many of these cases the higher terms of the Taylor's expansion turn out to be of much less quantitative importance than is sometimes supposed.

between savings and taxation. Alternatively, it may be said that, since the Dutch method cannot be proved to have been overwhelmingly more successful at economic forecasting,[1] the extra intellectual discipline involved is hardly worth while. But the question of forecasting has become something of a red-herring in public discussion of this subject. The basic function of this branch of the work of government economists—in the Hague, Whitehall, Oslo or anywhere—is the systematic presentation of policy alternatives; the analysis of the consequences of particular decisions, sets of decisions or, equally important, failures to decide; the imposition of the inescapable logic of national income identities. Governments, so long as they pursue any general economic policy whatsoever, face their advisers with two, almost separate, technical tasks : first, the forecasting of variables beyond government influence, and second, quantitative analysis of the multiple, interdependent, consequences of the policies under consideration. Forecasting may be given up as hopeless—we may decide mostly to wait and see, then act [2]—but the second task still remains. For that purpose the Dutch methods do seem clearly better.

The most powerful attack is one which falls on the British and Dutch methods together : the attack which comes from those who believe that all attempts to develop a successful general theory of economic policy are doomed to failure; that economic advisers should confine themselves to limited, relatively simple, micro-economic questions where there is some chance of providing answers of true scientific accuracy; that they may suggest small structural improvements in the economy, perhaps occasionally venturing so far as to make proposals for the improvement of a single industry, or interference with one particular price-relationship, but never further. This view is perfectly tenable, and in some quarters increasingly popular. But it implies that governments should abandon all attempts at general economic policy, or alternatively that if they do not, they will manage better without professional advisers than with them. It also involves a proposition which is itself both general and in essence unprovable; that a largely *laissez-faire* general equilibrium is in some way " better " than any calculable equilibrium resulting from policy.

[1] But see note 2 on p. 766 above.

[2] All economic policy involves *some* assumption about the future. What this plan really means is always assuming that things will stay exactly as they are. This form of assumption has very little rational basis, since it rarely corresponds to anybody's best guess. For example, few people, if compelled on pain of death to bet half their income on next year's change in production, would put their money on " no change," except in very particular circumstances.

THE SCOPE AND ORGANISATION OF THE WORK

The *Centraal Planbureau* is formally part of the Dutch Ministry of Economic Affairs; its British opposite number, having been lodged in the Cabinet Offices for the first eight years of its post-war life, has recently been taken into the Treasury. But the *Bureau* has always been housed in a separate building, some distance from the administrative centre of the Hague, and has always possessed complete policy independence from the Ministry of Economic Affairs, whose Minister is quite content to regard Professor Tinbergen as economic adviser to the government as a whole. While the *Bureau's* attachment to a senior Ministry thus represents little more than an administrative formality, the Economic Section both geographically and metaphorically, has worked very close to, if not always closely with, the Treasury and the Chancellor for some time past. This difference is of substantive significance : in the United Kingdom central responsibility for economic policy at the official level now lies fairly and squarely with the Treasury as a whole, and the Economic Section is only one of several bodies serving the Treasury for that purpose. In Holland, responsibility is more divided : the United Kingdom has in fact probably progressed further in overcoming the constitutional difficulties of centralisation[1] than almost any other country in Western Europe. Hence in Holland greater reliance has to be placed on " co-ordination," and the *Centraal Planbureau* is the official co-ordinating body at the advisory level (although of course there exists other co-ordinating machinery at the decision-taking level).

Professor Tinbergen's position as head of the *Bureau* is designated " Director," and the same appellation is given to Sir Robert Hall at the head of the Section. Both of these are special appointments in which the holders' position in the official hierarchy is not precisely defined, although it appears from the *Imperial Calendar* and other indications that Sir Robert Hall is formally significantly better placed in the official hierarchy than is Professor Tinbergen in the Dutch. However, Professor Tinbergen's personal standing in Dutch political and official life is such that this fact is probably of no great importance, although clearly it might become so if for any reason he were to leave. As is always the case, the difference between the character of the two organisations must be more than a little due to differences in the personal views and

---

[1] See p. 760, sub-paragraph 3 above.

interests of the two Directors,[1] a matter which cannot easily be discussed in print. Suffice it to say that it is not a coincidence that Professor Tinbergen is one of the world's leading econometricians and the *Bureau* he directs has a distinct econometric twist.

The Director of the *Bureau* is served by two deputy directors, a senior adviser on social problems and an adviser on statistical problems. The latter two are both employed full time, but they operate in free-lance fashion without direct organisational responsibility for any large group of staff. The main body of the *Bureau's* staff consists of twenty-five trained economists or economic statisticians about equivalent in rank to a Whitehall Principal, another eight to ten people about equivalent to Assistant Principals or Executive Officers and fifteen to twenty statistical officers and statistical assistants of various ranks : in the total of this professional staff, including Professor Tinbergen, five are part-time university teachers. In addition, there is a fully fledged computing pool, of five persons, trained to be able to undertake (*e.g.*) the inversion of the economic policy matrix [2] inside about three days. The whole body is divided into three divisions, each headed by a division chief carrying a civil service rank equivalent in British parlance to something between an Assistant Secretary and an Under-Secretary.

By contrast, the Economic Section has an establishment for one Deputy-Director (at present Mr I. M. D. Little), two Senior Economic Advisers (Assistant Secretaries), about six to eight Economic Advisers (Principals) and two or three juniors : there are no professional statisticians and there is no computing pool, but the Section may be assumed to have access to the computing staff of the Central Statistical Office which is in the same building. Thus the Economic Section is constructed on a much smaller scale than the *Bureau*—a difference more significant when it is remembered that not only is the real national income of the United

[1] The following selection of publications illustrates this point :

Sir Robert Hall : *Earning and Spending*, 1934; *The Economic System in a Socialist State*, 1936; and a number of articles, of which the best known is " Price Theory and Business Behaviour " (with C. J. Hitch), *Oxford Economic Papers No. 2*, the famous article which among other things established the kinked demand curve.

Professor Tinbergen : *Statistical Testing of Business Cycle Theories*, League of Nations, Geneva, 1939; *International Economic Co-operation*, Elsevier, 1945; *The Dynamics of Business Cycles* (with J. J. Polak), London, 1950; *Business Cycles in the United Kingdom, 1870–1914*, Amsterdam, 1951; *Econometrics* (text-book), Philadelphia, 1951; *On the Theory of Economic Policy*, Amsterdam, 1952; plus numerous articles on econometrics and other topics in applied economics.

[2] See p. 771, sub-paragraph (iii) above.

Kingdom of the order of ten times the Dutch but also that the scale of government operations in relation to national income is considerably higher in the United Kingdom. Holland probably has as high a proportion of economists to other officials as any country in the world; on the other hand, among " advanced " countries, where a good supply of trained economists exists, the United Kingdom must have one of the lowest. In Holland, quite apart from the *Bureau*, there are important economic staffs in several other economic ministries, whereas in the United Kingdom the number of official economists outside the Treasury could probably be counted on the fingers of one hand.

A description of the three internal divisions of the *Centraal Planbureau* will serve also to describe the substantive differences in the scope and nature of its work compared with that of the Section. One division is built round, although by no means exclusively concerned with, the operation of the econometric model already described. In it there are subsections devoted, as it were, to each basic group of equations. One such, for example, contains specialists in the field of wages and prices. These officials have operational responsibility for the measurement of parameters and the observation of variates, as well as for persistent attempts to improve the equation structure in this field. At the same time they will help in more general matters, such as the preparation of briefs for Ministers about wages policy or price control. Another subsection is concerned with the supply equations, and thus with the factors determining productivity. Another is concerned with final demand : consumption and investment totals and patterns. Another with the balance-of-payments and to some extent short-term export forecasts. Finally, there is a large and important section concerned with the equations relating to government operations, both on the side of revenue and of expenditure. This section contains, *inter alios*, two research assistants specialising in forecasts of revenue and transfer payments. It also takes responsibility for the *Bureau's* views on fiscal policy and monetary policy generally. In addition to these subsections, the Division employs one fairly senior officer and a small staff to take general care of the model : central co-ordination of its actual operation and improvement in its overall structure. The relations between this unit and the rest of the division are not rigidly defined and, as in all bureaucratic organisations, the lines of demarcation are constantly being blurred in response to the requirements of particular problems and the abilities and personalities of particular individuals. On the whole, however, there is in the *Planbureau*

more conscious organisational structure based directly on theoretical economic considerations than in most other similar offices,
and certainly more than in the Economic Section.

The second division of the *Bureau* is built up of specialists in
the economic and technical problems of individual branches of
industry, and in various general " industrial " or technical-
economic questions (for example, emigration, flood control policy,
transport co-ordination). This division is also possessed of a
small but important general section which, *inter alia*, runs an
input–output model in collaboration with the Central Bureau
of Statistics. The principle of industrial specialisation is self-
evidently a good one. But there are a number of psychological
and organisational difficulties which seem bound to arise in any
attempt to apply this principle; these the *Bureau* has certainly
encountered and does not pretend to have resolved. One suspects
the failure may have occurred partly because the difficulties were
at first thought to be accidental, whereas in fact they are inherent :
inevitably there must be difficulties in achieving the proper
intimacy of interaction with the other divisions and inevitably a
psychological tendency for the industrial specialists to feel that
their work is regarded as inferior and less " glamorous " than that
of those engaged on the " horizontal " economic questions. It
may well be that the time is ripe for an experiment in dual
organisation : a single division in which all of the staff were
fully qualified to take, and did take, responsibility for particular
horizontal questions—in the Dutch case particular macroeconomic equations—while at the same time each would also be
required to carry out the work of specialist in some one or other
branch of industry.

The third and final division of the *Bureau* is concerned, *inter
alia*, with research into long-term economic problems of the
Dutch economy and also with research into the long- and medium-
term development prospects of foreign countries which are important Dutch trading partners. This division is working on a long-
term development model of a fairly refined type, and because it is
therefore equipped more in the manner of an economic research
organisation, it also takes on a certain amount of the research
involved in revising the basic parameters of the short-term model,
such as, for example, the calculation of income-elasticities
described in footnote 2 on p. 764. The main feature of the work
is that it is essentially not concerned with day-to-day questions :
the division's job is to undertake the sort of research which may
take months or even years to complete.

The existence of a division specialising in long-term research provides one of the most important contrasts with the arrangements current in the United Kingdom. Here, there is no administrative provision for such work, and little or no economic research in fact occurs within the government machine. Further, there has up to now been little deliberate farming out of this kind of economic research by the Government to Universities and other outside research organisations. In the United Kingdom, if an aspect of economic policy requires for its rational implementation that some substantial piece of economic research be carried out, the normal procedure, by and large, is to drop the policy or to implement it irrationally. This state of affairs almost certainly arises from the traditional British administrative impatience with anything which is not of obvious urgent practical usefulness; in the social sciences, particularly, good men and good money cannot be spared for back-room work. At the other extreme the Netherlands *Planbureau* and also the Netherlands Central Statistical Bureau are accustomed to undertaking much research on their own initiative, and often, it appears, solely for the sake of the intrinsic interest of the research itself. Many of the results are published, and the *Bureau* seems at times to be carrying out national functions similar to those of a semi-academic research institution : it is often consulted by outside bodies, for example. British officials, at the other extreme, are strongly discouraged and frequently prohibited from publishing anything which could be identified by readers as directly connected with official work, except in the purely statistical field.

We now come to describe the internal organisation of the Economic Section, and a question which immediately arises is to what extent the other elements in the Treasury—Central Economic Planning Staff and Overseas Finance—should be brought within the purview. The Central Economic Planning Staff is, in effect, a central secretariat mainly concerned with the administrative co-ordination of departmental economic policies. In the United Kingdom, despite the now fundamental central responsibility of the Treasury for economic policy as a whole (see pp. 760 and 774 above), the greater part of the responsibility for specific aspects of policy, especially for initiation, remains, of course, basically decentralised. At the present stage of constitutional development, this is inevitable : the Minister of Food, for example, has to answer to Parliament for food supplies, although the Treasury wields great influence over the amount of foreign exchange he has with which to buy them. In order to achieve co-ordination and, as far as possible, consistency in the policies initiated by the departments, there exists an elaborate network of interdepartmental committees, and it is these which form the main vehicle of British economic planning. In order to strengthen that system most of the chairmen and secretaries of the committees are now drawn from this specialised branch of the Treasury, the C.E.P.S., which mainly exists for that purpose—an ingenious administrative device which has no counterpart in Holland, although the staff of the *Planbureau* play an important rôle in the work of a number of economic committees. Attendance at committees to present the view of the Section may be taken also to be a major function of the staff of the Economic Section. The C.E.P.S., however, does not apparently, at the time of writing, any longer contain any economists, and therefore need not be further considered.

The Overseas Finance Division of the Treasury is another matter. In the field of balance-of-payments control, British post-war economic planning has been carried on at an entirely different level of intensity from that in any other field. Ever since the end of the war, the complicated machinery of exchange control and import licensing has been constantly in use as part of a continuous attempt to implement a conscious operational programme for controlling the balance of external payments in general, and the dollar balance in particular, while at the same time inhibiting as little as possible the development of the internal economy. The direct controls, though largely of the negative type, have been powerful, far-reaching and detailed.[1] Policy direction of the whole of this apparatus of planning and control was centred in the Overseas Finance Division of the Treasury, with the Bank of England and the Import Licensing branch of the Board of Trade as executive arms. The Division contained a substantial statistical section, responsible for the collation of all statistics relating to the balance of payments, both those published in the Balance of Payments White Papers and those kept for internal circulation only, and it had a large group of administrative officers organised into geographical sections, each of which was responsible for all policy relating to the United Kingdom balance of payments with particular overseas countries or groups of countries—exchange control, international lending, payments agreements and so on. In addition to these specific responsibilities, Overseas Finance was thought of as the Cabinet's primary

---

[1] That some would say that the controls do not appear to have been powerful enough, nor the planning show a conspicuous record of success, is not a comment which is directly relevant to our present enquiry.

adviser on all general policy in this field, for example on convert-
ibility, on relations to the I.M.F. or the E.P.U. and so on. (The
Board of Trade was responsible for external *commercial* policy, the
general encouragement of exports and so on.) The division at its
peak contained some thirty to forty officials of the rank of Assistant
Principal and above, including two or three economists.

The existence of so large and powerful a body, responsible for
both general and detailed policy in the most important economic
policy field, must inevitably have exerted a profound influence on
the rôle and organisation of the Economic Section, and for that
matter of the Planning Staff. There was something of a similar
division of responsibilities in Holland, but because exchange-
control and import programming have always been more rudi-
mentary in that country and the balance of payments there
regarded more exclusively as an aspect of the problem of general
equilibrium, the effect on the rôle of the *Bureau* in overall policy-
making was almost certainly smaller. The general question
raised here is important. It is widely believed that if some aspect
of economic policy requires a substantial degree of detailed
administration for its implementation, from the very nature of
the case professional administrators must play the major " entrepreneurial " rôle in the determination of policy over the whole of
the relevant field : the professional economic advisers may suggest
and criticise, and thereby exert considerable influence, but always
as it were from the sidelines. The advantages of this arrangement
are obvious; the disadvantages unfortunately less so. For
whereas an administrative break-down, due to an attempt to
apply an over-academic prescription, is there for all to see, the
aggregate loss caused by a multitude of administrative decisions
based on amateur economic reasoning is never measurable and
rarely noticed. It might be suggested that " administration "
should be regarded as a technique which the professional economist in government service must undertake to learn as an essential
" secondary ability " in the same way in which he must learn, say,
statistical method. On that showing there could be little apparent
case for not putting economic policy, at the official level, entirely
in the hands of the economists. But that is not a way of looking
at things which is likely to gain early acceptance in this country.

By contrast with the *Planbureau* the internal organisation of
the Economic Section appears to be relatively loose, an arrangement which might be expected in the light of what has already
been said about the Section's size, rôle and methods. Specialisation has almost certainly occurred, but probably in consequence of

individuals' personal interests and aptitudes, rather than of any abstract concept of organisational structure. Given the general nature of its work and responsibilities, such a form of organisation seems best designed to extract the maximum from the total potential of the Section's small and extremely able staff. Clearly, however, it would no longer do so well if at any time the work were to become more " operational " in character, or if methods such as those of the *Bureau* were to be adopted.

THE INFLUENCE OF THE WORK

We have seen that, from the point of view of the economist, the scope of the work of the *Bureau* is considerably wider than that of the Section. We have not seen, so far, any evidence that from the point of view of the political scientist, the *Bureau* has wielded any greater influence at the keystone points in the formation of economic policy. Indeed, organisationally the Section is much more closely integrated into the rest of the government machine than is the *Bureau* : the Section is " in " the Treasury. That difference is partly inevitable : legislation enacted by the Dutch Parliament in 1947 defined the *Bureau's* independent function and at the same time charged the *Bureau* with the preparation of an annual economic " Plan " (we British would call it a Survey).[1] The plan is submitted to the Government and, eventually, to the Parliament, but the Plan does not commit the Government; it is more in the nature of a statement of policy by the *Bureau* than by the Government, an arrangement unthinkable in the United Kingdom.

A major point in any final assessment is the delicate question of the relative personal influence of the two Directors. Sir Robert Hall has clearly great influence in Whitehall, just how much no ordinary member of the public can ever know. It is, however, known that he believes strongly in trying to see problems from the administrator's point of view, in contrast with the extremer faults of outlook which many administrators complain are often associated with academic economists. The position of Professor Tinbergen is different, and in a way unique. He

---

[1] Although it is dangerous in this context to draw any parallels between Western Europe and the United States—because of the radical differences in the underlying constitutional rôles of Legislature and Executive in the two cases—the legal position of the *Bureau* does seem to have considerable affinity with that of the Federal Government's *Council of Economic Advisers* under the terms of the Federal Employment Act, 1946. See *Congress Makes a Law*, by S. K. Bailey, New York, 1950, and *Economics in the Public Service*, by Edwin G. Nourse, New York, 1953.

attends the weekly meetings of the Dutch Cabinet's economic committee, he is Vice-Chairman of the Council of the Netherlands Bank and he is, in general, a well-known public figure. To a considerable extent the *Centraal Planbureau* wields its influence through Tinbergen : while he relies heavily on the work done by his staff in making up his mind about economic affairs, and takes a close personal interest in all stages of the research, the staff rely on him to sell the results of their combined cogitations to the Cabinet. In the Economic Section the staff are probably more independent of their Director ; in the nature of normal Whitehall arrangements they would be expected to operate at all levels in the hierarchy, engaging in direct argument with their official opposite numbers in the Treasury or in other departments. That is not to say that members of the *Bureau* are completely cut off from direct contacts with other officials. They do in fact, in committee and elsewhere, intervene at various levels, and there is evidence that when they intervene they are influential. But one suspects that the interventions of the Section are considerably more numerous, even making no allowance for the different sizes of the two bodies. Thus the influence of the Section on economic policy as a whole must be regarded as the sum total of the influence of its individual members in their capacity as members of the Treasury (although they no doubt display a strong group outlook on particular issues), whereas in the case of the *Bureau*, which is itself the official co-ordinating authority, the proposition must be reversed ; there the influence of its members depends on the influence of the *Bureau* as a corporate entity with independent direct access to the Cabinet. Although both bodies remain essentially advisory, and neither is at present possessed of operational functions, the *Bureau* gives its advice to politicians directly, while the Section must, presumably, work to a much greater extent through or in collaboration with other (non-economist) officials.[1]

It is quite impossible to say whether the British or the Dutch solution has to date been more " successful." [2] One suspects that on balance there is little in it. Certainly there is no evidence that Professor Tinbergen's body has had to pay a price—in terms of

[1] One could say this with more certainty were it not for the Section's previous history of an independent existence in the Cabinet Offices, for at one time its services were regarded as being available to any Department which asked for them and, also, presumably, to the Prime Minister directly. As a result, therefore, of its history, its professional status and the official title of " Economic Adviser to H.M.G." which is now given to the Director, the Section may well be possessed of rather more independence than is normal.

[2] It would be possible to be less indefinite were it not for the security blanket at the British end.

lost potential influence—for its independence. Nor is there evidence that the Economic Section's situation has compromised the overall quality of its professional work, although the difference in status must have been a major factor accounting for the difference in methodology. Both bodies could probably gain by moving in the direction of the other. In the author's personal view—and let it be frankly admitted that this stems partly from an intellectual bias in favour of the Dutch which has run right through his judgments—the Dutch approach carries greater prospects of professional development, *if* such development is wanted. At the present point in Whitehall it seems difficult to see where things can go from there, except in the sense of a continuing process of infiltration. Whether that is a criticism depends on whether one believes that economic policy on the modern scale requires from its official votaries a genuine professionalism : a university training in economics and economic statistics, followed by full-time engagement in teaching, or in research, or as a government economist, ever since. The contrary view is at present dominant in this country : it is believed that adequate results can be obtained by the selection of suitable officials from the administrative class for training " on the job," coupled with the safeguard of constant advice from the sidelines from the small group of full-time professional economists. Great hopes are also placed in the increasing number of entrants to the Administrative Class who originally read economics at the university.[1] Thus a reasonable familiarity with economic problems is now regarded as a useful accomplishment for an administrator, and economic policy as an important new branch of the traditionally amateur British system of civil government. Indisputably that system has worked brilliantly in the past. Can it accommodate the new situation—where some half of the work of government has become an aspect of applied social science—by modest adaptions, or are the implications of the situation more revolutionary than has yet been generally realised ? The fundamental question posed here may be just as relevant in Holland. For we have seen that the combination of a high degree of professional independence with a substantial degree of political influence achieved by the staff of the *Centraal Plan-bureau* is based partly on special circumstances.

R. L. MARRIS

King's College,
    Cambridge.

[1] See, for example, a distressingly complacent *Times* leading article, "The British Civil Service II—Choosing and Training the Policy Makers," *The Times*, November 24, 1953.

[5]

FORECASTING AND ANALYSIS WITH AN ECONOMETRIC MODEL

By Daniel B. Suits*

Although an econometric model is the statistical embodiment of theoretical relationships that are every economist's stock in trade, its discussion has largely been kept on a specialized level and confined to the more mathematical journals. Models are rarely explored from the point of view of their usefulness to the profession at large, yet there is nothing about their nature or their application—aside, again, from a solid grasp of economic theory—that requires anything more than an elementary knowledge of school algebra. The compilation of an econometric model requires a certain degree of technical specialization, but once constructed, any competent economist can apply it to policy analysis and economic forecasting.

The purpose of this article is to present an actual econometric model of the U.S. economy, to demonstrate its use as a forecasting instrument, and to explore its implications for policy analysis. To minimize the technical background required, the presentation is divided into two main parts. Part I deals with the general nature of econometric models, and, using a highly simplified schematic example, illustrates how forecasts are made with a model, how a model can be modified to permit the introduction of additional information and judgment, and how short-run and long-run policy multipliers are derived from the inverse of the model. Part II presents the 32-equation econometric model of the U.S. economy compiled by the Research Seminar in Quantitative Economics. This model is the most recent product of a research project whose initial output was the well-known Klein-Goldberger model [1] [3]. In Part III the outlook for 1962, as calculated and published in November 1961, is studied as an example of an actual forecast; and earlier forecasts of this kind that have been prepared by the Research Seminar annually since 1953 are compared with actual events as a demonstration of the potential of the method.

In Part III the inverse of the model is also presented and its application to policy evaluation is reviewed. Short-run and long-run multipliers are calculated for selected policy variables. Part III also includes

* This is the report of a continuing project of the Research Seminar in Quantitative Economics, sponsored by National Science Foundation grant G-13423. The author is professor of economics at the University of Michigan.

a digression on deficit financing, covering an interesting and important theoretical implication of the model.

I. *Econometric Models and Their Applications*

The science of economics can be variously defined, but for the present purpose it is useful to think of it as the study of the relationships among a system of observable and essentially measureable variables: prices, costs, outputs, incomes, savings, employment, etc. These relationships derive from the complex behavior and interaction of millions of households, millions of firms, and thousands of governmental units, producing and exchanging millions of products. The relationships can be represented by a system of mathematical equations, but unfortunately a theoretically complete representation (e.g. a Walrasian system) would involve trillions of equations—surely millions for each household and firm. Moreover these equations would be individually as complex as human behavior, and involve the elaborate interaction of numberless variables.

We have neither the time nor the resources to deal with such a vast system of equations; to proceed at all we must simplify and condense. Millions of individual households become a single "household sector," millions of products become a single item of expenditure, e.g., "durable goods." Moreover, complex mathematical relationships among thousands of variables become simple linear approximations involving two or three aggregates. An econometric model of the economy is obtained by confronting these highly simplified equations with data arising from the historical operation of the economic system and, by appropriate statistical techniques, obtaining numerical estimates for their parameters.

The minimum number of equations necessary for an adequate representation of the economic system depends on a number of considerations, but clearly the fewer the equations the greater must be the level of aggregation and the less accurate and useful the result. On the other hand, the larger the number of equations and the greater the detail shown in the variables, the more complicated it is to derive the individual equations, to manipulate the resulting system, and to see the implications of the model. Where modern computing facilities can be used the mere size of the model is no longer a serious barrier to its effective application, but for purposes of exposition the smaller and simpler the model the better.

A. *A Simple Illustrative Example*

To illustrate the principles of application, let us suppose that the statistical procedure gave rise to the following, purely schematic, model of four equations.

$$(1) \qquad C = 20 + .7(Y - T)$$

$$(2) \qquad I = 2 + .1Y_{-1}$$

$$(3) \qquad T = .2Y$$

$$(4) \qquad Y = C + I + G$$

According to equation (1), consumption (C) depends on current disposable income ($Y-T$). In equation (2), investment (I) depends on income lagged one period. The third equation relates taxes (T) to income, while the last defines income as the sum of consumption, investment and government expenditure G.

While this model is small, it illustrates most of the properties of the larger model. The single consumption function in equation (1) corresponds to the set of four equations (01), (02), (03), and (04) that describe the behavior of the consumer sector in Part II. The investment behavior represented in (2) corresponds to equations (05), through (10) The single tax equation (3) corresponds to a combination of the eleven tax and transfer equations, while the relationship of production to income embodied in equation (4) is indicated in much greater detail by equations (11) through (20).

This econometric model approximates the economy by a system of equations in which the unknowns are those variables—income, consumption, investment, and tax yield—whose behavior is to be analyzed. The "knowns" are government expenditure and lagged income. When projected values for the "knowns" are inserted in the equations, the system can be solved to forecast the values of the unknowns.

Quotation marks are used advisedly on the word "knowns." For, while some economic variables move so slowly along secular trends that their future values can be projected with considerable accuracy, others —for example new government expenditures—are unknown in advance of their occurrence, even in principle. Moreover, even the values of lagged variables are unknown at the time of the forecast, since a useful forecast must be made some months before the end of the preceding year. For example, each of the forecasts shown in Table 3 (p. 123) was made during the first week of November of the preceding year. To make such forecasts, lagged variables are estimated from data for the first three quarters of the year, with the third quarter given double weight.

At any rate, suppose we expect next year's government expenditure to be 20, and the preliminary estimate of this year's income is, say, 100. Substituting $G=20$ and $Y_{-1}=100$ into the equations above and solving gives $C=86.2$, $I=12$, $T=23.7$, $Y=118.2$.

B. *Introducing Outside Information*

It may appear from the foregoing that this kind of forecasting is a blind, automatic procedure; but while an econometric model looks like a rigid analytical tool, it is actually a highly flexible device, readily modifiable to bring to bear additional information and judgment. For example, the investment equation in our little model is surely an unreliable predictor of capital formation. If no other information were available the equation would have to serve the purpose. But suppose we have available a survey of investment intentions reported by business. An estimate derived from such a survey is clearly superior to any that equation (2) could produce. To introduce the information into the forecast we simply remove equation (2) from the model and, in the remaining equations, set I equal to the survey value. Forecasts made from the Research Seminar model have frequently involved use of a figure for gross investment in plant and equipment derived from the McGraw-Hill Survey of Investment Intentions rather than from equation (05) of the model.[1]

Information can also be used to modify individual relationships short of replacing them entirely. For example a prospective improvement in consumer credit terms—a variable that does not appear in our schematic model—would be expected to stimulate consumption expenditure. It is often possible to set an upper limit to this stimulating effect, and by increasing the constant term in the consumption function by this amount, to set an upper limit to the forecast economic outlook. An adjustment of this kind was applied to equation (01) to allow for the probable influence of the compact car on the outlook for automobile sales during 1960. For the same forecast, a similar modification of the housing starts equation (06) was made in anticipation of activity of the Federal National Mortgage Association.

Using the flexibility to full advantage permits the forecaster to explore any desired number of alternative sets of projections and modifications, and to bring to bear all information and judgment he possesses. The econometric model is not, therefore, a substitute for judgment, but rather serves to focus attention on the factors about which judgment must be exercised, and to impose an objective discipline whereby judgment about these factors is translated into an economic outlook that is consistent both internally, and with the past observed behavior of the economic system.

C. *The Inverse Matrix*

In principle, the exploration of a range of alternative projections and other modifications of the model consists of inserting each set of alternatives in turn as "knowns" in the equations and solving for the resulting

---

[1] The McGraw-Hill Survey of Investment Intentions is conducted annually in the fall. It becomes available just in time to be incorporated in the forecast presented before the Conference on the Economic Outlook, held annually during the first week of November at the University of Michigan. For several years the Conference has been the occasion for the release of the data by *Business Week*.

forecast. The process is greatly expedited by further simplifying the model and by the use of the inverse matrix. Simplification of the model is made possible by the fact that one of the unknowns, I, depends only on knowns. I helps to determine the current values of C, T, and Y, but the latter do not, in turn, feed back into the determination of the current value of I. As a result, once the knowns are given, I can be directly calculated from (2) without reference to any other part of the model, and hence, as far as the remaining equations are concerned, I can be treated as a known in the sense used above. (Indeed it is this fact that enables us to replace equation (2) with survey values for I.)

The process of solving the system of equations can then be divided into two parts. First: using the values of the knowns, calculate the value of I. Second: substitute the knowns (now including I) into the remaining equations, and solve for the other unknowns.

The inverse matrix facilitates the second step. For those unfamiliar with matrix manipulations the following will help clarify the nature and use of this table. Since I is now considered as known, the model is reduced to the system of three equations (1), (3) and (4) above. By transferring all unknowns to the left side, and representing the right sides by P_1, P_3, and P_4, these equations can be expressed as:

$$(1) \qquad C - 0.7Y + 0.7T = 20 = P_1$$

$$(3) \qquad -.2Y + 1.0T = 0 = P_3$$

$$(4) \qquad -C + Y = I + G = P_4$$

Now using any convenient method to solve this system for C, Y, and T in terms of P_1, P_3, and P_4 will yield:

$$C = 2.273P_1 - 1.591P_3 + 1.273P_4$$

$$T = .445P_1 + .682P_3 + .455P_4$$

$$Y = 2.273P_1 - 1.591P_3 + 2.273P_4$$

That is, the value of each unknown is obtained as a specified weighted total of P_1, P_3, and P_4. Where a large number of equations is used, and a lot of calculating is to be done, it is convenient to display the weights used for each unknown as a column of numbers in a table, with the detail of the P's shown in a separate column at the right:

Equation No.	C	T	Y	P
(1)	2.273	.455	2.273	20
(3)	−1.591	.682	−1.591	0
(4)	1.273	.455	2.273	$I + G$

To make a forecast we first substitute Y_{-1} into equation (2) and solve for I. Then I and G are substituted in the P column of the table and the

SUITS: ECONOMETRIC MODEL   109

values of P_1, P_3 and P_4 calculated. These values, weighted by the numbers shown in the C column of the inverse and summed, give the forecast value of consumption; use of the weights in column Y gives the forecast for income, etc.[2] For example if we set $Y_{-1} = 100$ and $G = 20$, we first find from (2) $I = 12$. Substituting these values in column P of the table gives the forecast values: $C = 86.2$, $T = 23.7$, $Y = 118.2$.

D. *Short-Run Policy Multipliers*

It is an obvious step from economic forecasting to short-run policy analysis. To investigate any specified set of prospective government actions, we insert them in the proper place in column P and solve for the forecast implied by these assumptions. The analysis is expedited if we first calculate short-run multipliers for the individual components of government action. These can then be applied in any desired policy mixture.

Short-run multipliers for any policy variable are readily calculated by inserting $+1$ for the variable everywhere it appears in column P, and then (ignoring all terms that do not contain the variable in question) extending a forecast using the columns of the inverse. For example, to calculate the government expenditure multiplier, set $G = 1$ in row (4) of column P. This makes $P_4 = 1$. To find the effect of this value of G on, say, income, multiply this value of P_4 by the weight in row (4) of the Y column to get $Y = 1 \times 2.273 = 2.273$. That is, the income multiplier on government expenditure is 2.273. Likewise, $T = 1 \times .455 = .455$. That is, the tax-yield multiplier on government expenditure is .455. In other words, for every dollar of additional government expenditure, tax receipts rise by nearly 46 cents. A corollary is that—according to our schematic model—an increase in government expenditure of 1 with no change in tax legislation will generate an increase in deficit of only:

$$G - T = 1 - .46 = .54$$

In addition to changing the value of exogenous variables like government expenditure, government policy can produce changes in the equations themselves. An extensive change—e.g. a substantial alteration in tax rates—can only be studied by replacing the old tax equation by a new one, but less extensive changes can be studied as shifts in the levels of existing equations, the coefficients being unaltered.

Multipliers for such shifts are easily determined by placing $+1$ in the row of column P that corresponds to the equation being shifted. The extensions are then made as before. For example, to calculate the multipliers on a $+1$ shift in the level of the tax equation, we put $+1$ in the row marked (3) of column P, since the tax equation is (3). The multi-

[2] As those familiar with matrix algebra will recognize, the inverse matrix is tabulated here in its transposed form, and goes into the P vector at the right column by column.

plier effect of this shift is then calculated by multiplying this 1 by the weight in the corresponding row of the appropriate column, as shown above. For example for income:

$$Y = 1 \times (-1.591) = -1.591$$

For consumption:

$$C = 1 \times (-1.591) = -1.591$$

In other words, the multipliers associated with the shift of any equation are merely the weights in the row of the inverse corresponding to that equation.

Note that according to our simplified model, the tax-yield multiplier is .682. That is, an upward shift of $1 billion in the tax *schedule* actually increases *yield* by only $682 million. The difference is due to the decline in income arising from the shift in the tax schedule.

The small size of our illustrative model limits the policy variables to government expenditure and the level of taxes. In the more extensive model below, policy is given considerably more scope; a number of individual tax and transfer equations can be shifted, and a number of different kinds of expenditure altered. The number of possible combinations of action is correspondingly very large; but one important advantage to a linear system lies in the fact that once multipliers for the individual components have been calculated, the economic implications of a complete policy "package" can be estimated by summing the effects of the individual components.

For example, an increase of $1 in government expenditure coupled with an upward shift of $1 in the tax schedule would generate a change in income given by the sum of the two individual multipliers:

$$Y = 2.273 - 1.591 = .682$$

This is what might be called an *"ex-ante-*balanced" government expenditure multiplier. That is, the change in the law is such as to increase tax yield at the *existing* level of income by enough to balance the planned expenditure, but the budget will not necessarily be balanced *ex post*. The tax and expenditure program will alter income, and hence will change tax yields. Analysis of the complete fiscal impact of the operation requires the examination of all revenue and outlay items combined. Adding together the two tax-yield multipliers we find that the additional expenditure of $1 is offset by a tax yield of:

$$.682 + .455 = 1.137$$

That is, the *ex-ante-*balanced expenditure of $1 billion would, in our example, be accompanied by an increase of $1.137 billion in tax yield and give rise to an *ex-post* surplus of $137 million.

E. *Dynamics and Long-Run Multipliers*

An increase in government expenditure of 1.0 will increase income by 2.273 the same year. But the long-run effect of expenditure sustained at this level will differ from this. According to equation (2), an increase in income this year will generate an increase in investment next year. This will again raise income and add further stimulus the following year, etc. Once the inverse has been tabulated, however, the sequence can easily be calculated by inserting the forecast values of one year as the "knowns" of the next. Thus an initial increase in G of 1 will raise Y by 2.273. This will raise I by $.2 \times 2.773 = .455$ the following year. The value of P_4 is then $G + I = 1.455$ and the second year income rises to 3.307 above its initial value, etc. The five-year sequence of values would be:

Year	1	2	3	4	5
Income	2.273	3.307	3.775	3.989	4.087

This means, for example, that if government expenditure is increased by 1 in 1961, and sustained at that new level, the level of income in 1965 will—other things equal—be 4.087 higher than it was in 1960.

Similar sequences can be worked out for other policy variables. For example a shift of 1 in the tax schedule in year 1 would imply the following sequence of annual income values:

Year	1	2	3	4	5
Income	-1.591	-2.314	-2.643	-2.793	-2.862

Like short-run multipliers, these long-run multipliers can be combined by simple addition. For example, a permanent rise of 1 in government expenditure coupled with an *ex-ante* shift of 1 in the tax schedule would raise income by $2.273 - 1.591 = .682$ the first year. After 5 years, however, income would be $4.087 - 2.862 = 1.225$ higher than its initial level.

Although the discussion has been focused on a highly simplified example, the principles developed apply equally to any linear econometric model. The presentation of the actual Research Seminar model in Part II will follow the same pattern as the illustration of Part I.

II. *The Model of the U.S. Economy*

The model developed by the Research Seminar in Quantitative Economics consists of 32 equations, most of them least-squares linear regressions fitted to annual first differences in the variables.[3]

---

[3] The exceptions are definitional equations, and those approximating tax laws. Use of least squares is unnecessary for the former, and inappropriate to the latter. The frequency of change in tax laws makes past data irrelevant to their current analysis. Tax equations were fitted by eye through a few relevant points.

Five advantages are gained by the use of first differences. In the first place, the autocorrelation of residuals from time series regressions causes a downward bias in calculated standard errors, giving an exaggerated appearance of precision to the result. The use of first differences serves to reduce this bias. Secondly, many of the equations—e.g. the demand for consumer durables—involve stocks for which data are not currently available. The increase in a stock is composed of current acquisitions less retirements. Since the latter tends to be a smooth series, exhibiting little year-to-year variation, the first difference in stock is well represented by acquisitions, a figure readily available on a current basis. Thirdly, in short-run analysis and forecasting, the present position is known, and *ceteris paribus* will continue. The important question is what change from that position will result from projected changes in other factors. The use of first differences serves to focus the power of the analysis on these changes. Fourthly, the use of first differences minimizes the effect of slowly moving variables such as population, tastes, technical change, etc., without explicitly introducing them into the analysis. The net effect of changes in these factors is represented in the constant term of the equation. Finally, use of first differences minimizes the complications produced by data revision when the model is applied. Revisions usually alter the level at which variables are measured, rather than their year-to-year variation.

In calculating the equations, the prewar and postwar periods were explored separately to determine whether there was any indication of a change in the coefficients. Except for institutional relationships—tax laws, transfers, etc.—no important shifts were discovered. Nevertheless the final equations are fitted only to data drawn from the period 1947–1960 to maximize their applicability to current problems.

The equations of the model are presented and discussed below by sectors, and the symbol for each variable is explained the first time it appears. In general the variables correspond to the magnitudes as given in the national accounts, measured in billions of 1954 dollars. In calculating the equations, however, all imputations were removed from the Department of Commerce figures for consumer expenditure and disposable income. These imputations, mainly associated with services rendered by financial institutions and by owner-occupied dwellings, are added back in after a forecast is made to maintain comparability with the national accounts. First differences are indicated throughout by prefixing Δ to the symbol of the variable. Note, however, that lagged undifferenced values of certain variables appear at some points (e.g. in the automobile demand equation (01) below). These undifferenced values serve as proxy variables for first differences in stocks as explained above. Figures in parentheses are the standard errors of the regression coefficients.

SUITS: ECONOMETRIC MODEL 113

A. *Aggregate Demand*

1. Consumption

(01) Automobiles and Parts:

$$\Delta A = .177\ \Delta(Y - X_u - X_f - X_s) - .495\ A_{-1}$$
$$(.086) (.168)$$
$$+ .260\ \Delta L_{-1} + 4.710$$
$$ (.082)$$

Consumer expenditure for new and net used automobiles and parts (ΔA) depends on disposable income (Y), net of transfers for unemployment compensation (X_a), and other federal (X_f) and state (X_s) transfers. These transfers are deducted on the ground that they are unlikely to find their way into the automobile market. Servicemen's insurance dividends (X_{GI}) are not deducted from disposable income. In addition, automobile demand depends on the stock of cars on the road (A_{-1}) and on the real value of consumer liquid assets at the end of the preceding year (ΔL_{-1}). For this purpose liquid assets are defined as household holdings of currency and demand deposits plus fixed-value redeemable claims as estimated by the Federal Reserve Board. The sizeable constant term in the equation probably reflects replacement demand.[4]

(02) Demand for Other Durables:

$$\Delta D = .176\ \Delta Y - .0694\ D_{-1} + .0784\ \Delta L_{-1} + .262$$
$$ (.015) (.029) \phantom{D_{-1} + } (.016)$$

This equation relates ΔD, consumer expenditure for durables (other than automobiles and parts) to disposable income (ΔY), the accumulating stock of durables (D_{-1}) and liquid assets.

(03) Demand for Nondurable Goods:

$$\Delta ND = .224\ \Delta Y + .205\ \Delta ND_{-1} + .143\ \Delta L_{-1} - .149$$
$$ (.060) (.135) \phantom{\Delta ND_{-1} + } (.059)$$

Nondurable expenditure depends on disposable income, liquid assets, and last year's nondurable expenditure (ΔND_{-1}). Notice the difference between this and the foregoing equations. In (01) and (02) the lagged values were undifferenced representing accumulation of stock. In this equation the difference itself is lagged, representing a dynamic adjustment in nondurable expenditure: an initial rise in level is followed by a subsequent secondary rise.

(04) Demand for Services:

$$\Delta S = .0906\ \Delta Y + .530\ \Delta S_{-1} + .0381\ \Delta L_{-1} + .363$$
$$ (.029) (.170) \phantom{\Delta S_{-1} + } (.029)$$

This equation is similar to (03) and relates expenditure for services

[4] This equation is a simplified version of that given in [5].

(ΔS) to disposable income, liquid assets, and lagged service expenditure. It should be remembered that service expenditure is here defined to exclude imputed items.

These four equations constitute the demand sector. Note that the aggregate marginal propensity to consume can be estimated by summing the income coefficients in the four equations. The sum, .67, is an estimate of the marginal propensity to consume, at least as an initial impact. The lagged terms in the individual equations, however, generate a dynamic response of consumption to income. As the equations show, the long-run response of nondurables and services tends to be greater, and that of automobile and durables less, than the initial impact. The implications of this fact for the calculation of multipliers will appear below.

2. Gross Capital Expenditure

(05) Plant and Equipment Expenditure:

$$\Delta PE = .605\ \Delta(P^*_{-1} - T_{fc-1} - T_{sc-1}) - .124\ PE_{-1} + 4.509$$
$$(.238)\phantom{\Delta(P^*_{-1} - T_{fc-1} - T_{sc-1})\ }(.216)$$

ΔPE, expenditure for new plant and equipment, includes producers' durables, nonfarm nonresidential construction, and all farm construction. It is related to the preceding year's corporate profits (P^*_{-1}) after federal (T_{fc}) and state (T_{sc}) corporate income taxes and to its own lagged, undifferenced value (PE_{-1}). The latter represents growth in the stock of plant and equipment. As in (01) above, the large constant term probably represents replacement.

(06) Housing Starts:

$$\Delta HS = 19.636\,\Delta\left(\frac{FHA + VA}{2} - Aaa\right) - .702\ HS_{-1} + 66.147$$
$$(17.0)\phantom{\Delta\left(\frac{FHA + VA}{2} - Aaa\right) - }(.312)$$

This equation, which applies only to the postwar period, relates the number of nonfarm residential housing starts (ΔHS), measured in thousand of units per month, to the gap between the simple average of the FHA and VA ceiling interest rates on the one hand, and the *Aaa* bond yield on the other (both expressed in percentage points). This interest rate differential reflects the substantial influence of credit availability on the volume of FHA and VA financed residential construction.[5] It can function, however, only in the presence of a strong underlying housing demand. With the accumulation of a large stock as a consequence of construction in recent years, this interest rate differential

---

[5] This aspect of credit availability has been recently discussed by J. M. Guttentag [2]. Guttentag is skeptical of the influence of the ceiling rates. Our equation was, of course, developed independently of his work, and was first introduced into the model in the fall of 1959 in making the forecast for 1960.

may lose its role in the model.[6] The term HS_{-1}, the lagged undifferenced value of housing starts, only partially represents the effect of this accumulation, and equation (06) is probably due for revision.

(07) Housing Expenditure:

$$\Delta H = \underset{(.013)}{.125}\ \Delta HS + \underset{(.012)}{.024}\ \Delta HS_{-1} + \underset{(5.42)}{6.580}\ \Delta C + .083$$

Expenditure on housing, (ΔH), depends on the rate at which residential construction is carried forward, and thus on current and lagged starts. In addition it depends on construction costs. The term ΔC is the ratio of the index of construction costs to the GNP deflator.

(08) Durable Goods Inventory:

$$\Delta ID = \underset{(.100)}{.291}\ \Delta(A + D) + \underset{(.157)}{.591}\ \Delta PD + \underset{(.085)}{.305}\ \Delta M_{+1} - \underset{(.109)}{.669}\ ID_{-1}$$

Accumulation of durable inventories, ΔID, depends on sales of consumer durables, producers durables ΔPD, and the stock of inventory already accumulated ID_{-1}. In addition an important component of inventory is associated with government military orders. Production on such orders appears in the national accounts as goods in process, and exerts a strong impact on the economy long before delivery of the finished product materializes as government expenditure. A wide variety of arrangements and lead times are involved in this process.[7] As a proxy for such orders in any given year, we use ΔM_{+1}, federal military purchases from private industry the following year.

The equilibrium sales-inventory ratio implied by this equation compares favorably with that observed from other data.

(09) Nondurable Goods Inventory:

$$\Delta IND = \underset{(.111)}{.427}\ \Delta ND - \underset{(.248)}{1.121}\ IND_{-1}$$

Accumulation of nondurable inventory, ΔIND, depends on consumer sales of nondurables and the stock already on hand, IND_{-1}.

(10) Imports:

$$\Delta R = \underset{(.03)}{.0602}\ \Delta G^* + .369$$

This relates the aggregate level of imports to the private GNP (G^*).

3. Private Gross National Product

$$(11)\ \Delta G^* = \Delta(A + D + ND + S) + (\Delta F - \Delta R) + \Delta ID + \Delta IND$$
$$+ \Delta PE + \Delta H + \Delta g$$

---

[6] Guttentag argues that this is not necessarily the case [2, p. 297].

[7] For an excellent study of these see [6].

Private GNP is defined as the sum of its parts including net exports $(\Delta F - \Delta R)$ and government purchases from private firms (Δg).

B. *Income and Employment*

(12) Wage and Salary Workers, Private Sector:

$$\Delta E = .068 \Delta G^*$$

This production function, relating ΔE, the number of full-time equivalent employees in the private sector (measured in millions of persons) to the private GNP, applies specifically to the forecast of 1962 and is based on the first three quarters recovery experience during 1961.

(13) Unemployment:

$$\Delta U = \Delta LF - \Delta E_0 - \Delta E_G - \Delta E$$

Unemployment is the difference between labor force (ΔLF) on the one hand, and the number of self-employed and unpaid family workers, (ΔE_0), government workers, including armed services (ΔE_G) and employees of private industry (ΔE).

(14) Average Annual Earnings:

$$\Delta w = -\ .0216\ \Delta U + .00436\ P^*_{-1} - .0743$$
$$ (.0076) (.0025)$$

Δw, average annual earnings (including wages and salaries plus "other labor income," and measured in thousands of dollars) is related to unemployment and last year's profits. This relationship reflects two facts. First and probably more important, annual earnings are heavily influenced by overtime pay which varies inversely with the level of unemployment. Secondly, pressure of union demands varies directly with profits and inversely with the level of unemployment. The undifferenced level of profits is used since the *existence* of profits acts as a target for wage demands.

(15) Private Wage Bill:

$$\Delta W = \Delta(wE) = w_{-1}\Delta E + E_{-1}\Delta w$$

By definition the wage bill is the product of average earnings and employment. To keep the model linear, this nonlinear relationship is replaced by the linear approximation shown.

(16) Depreciation:

$$\Delta Dep = .0456\ \Delta G^* + .763$$

(17) Property Income:

$$\Delta P = \Delta G^* - \Delta W - \Delta Dep - \Delta T_{fe} - \Delta T_{cd} - \Delta T_{bp}$$
$$ - \Delta T_{ss} - \Delta T_{os} - \Delta SI_r$$

Property income (ΔP) is a residual from the GNP after deducting wage costs, depreciation (ΔDep), employer contributions for social insurance (ΔSI_r), and indirect business taxes: federal excises (ΔT_{fe}), customs duties (ΔT_{cd}), business property (ΔT_{bp}), state sales (ΔT_{ss}), and other state taxes on business (ΔT_{os}).

(18) Corporate Profits:

$$\Delta P^* = .902\ (\Delta P - \Delta P_f) - 1.027$$

This relates profits (ΔP^*) to total property income net of farm income (ΔP_f). There is, of course, no strong theoretical basis for the particular distribution of corporate business found in the U.S. economy. This equation is an empirical representation of the distribution of property income under existing institutional arrangements.

(19) Dividends:

$$\Delta Div = \underset{(.064)}{.229}\Delta(P^* - T_{fc} - T_{sc})$$

$$+ \underset{(.052)}{.0198}\ (P^* - T_{fc} - T_{sc} - Div)_{-1} - .0191$$

Current dividends (ΔDiv) depend on current profits after federal (T_{fc}) and state (T_{sc}) corporate profits taxes, and on last year's level of undistributed profits.

(20) Disposable Income:

$$\Delta Y = \Delta W + \Delta W_G + (\Delta P - \Delta P^*) + \Delta Div + \Delta i_G + \Delta X_u + \Delta X_f + \Delta X_s$$

$$+ \Delta X_{GI} - \Delta T_{fy} - \Delta T_{sy} - \Delta T_{eg} - \Delta T_{op} - \Delta SI_e + \Delta T_{ref}$$

Disposable income is the sum of wages, including government wages (W_G), noncorporate property income $(\Delta P - \Delta P^*)$, dividends, government interest payments (i_G), plus transfers, less personal taxes: federal (ΔT_{fy}), and state (ΔT_{sy}) income, estate and gift (ΔT_{eg}), other personal taxes (ΔT_{op}) and personal contributions for social insurance ΔSI_e, all net of tax refunds ΔT_{ref}.

C. *Taxes and Government Transfers*

1. Federal Taxes

(21) Federal Corporate Profits Tax:

$$\Delta T_{fc} = .500\Delta P^*$$

(22) Federal Personal Income Tax Receipts:

$$\Delta T_{fy} = .111(\Delta W + \Delta W_G) + .150(\Delta P - \Delta P^* + \Delta i_G) + .195\Delta Div$$

This equation relates income tax receipts in the form of withholding, quarterly payments on estimated tax, and final tax payment to the several income components. The coefficients reflect both variation in income shares by tax bracket and the effect of the dividend tax credit.

(23) Federal Personal Income Tax Liability:

$$\Delta T^*_{fy} = .100(\Delta W + \Delta W_G) + .114(\Delta P - \Delta P^* + \Delta i_G) + .154\Delta Div$$

Tax receipts commonly exceed liability. The difference (ΔT_{ref}) appears as a tax refund the following year.

(24) Federal Excise Taxes:

$$\Delta T_{fe} = .099\Delta A + .011\Delta D + .003\Delta ND + .010\Delta G^* + .015\Delta Y$$

(25) Customs Duties:

$$\Delta T_{cd} = .083\Delta R + .012$$

2. State and Local Taxes

(26) State Corporate Income Taxes:

$$\Delta T_{sc} = .019\Delta P^*$$

(27) State and Local Sales Taxes:

$$\Delta T_{ss} = .033(\Delta A + \Delta D + \Delta ND + \Delta S)$$

(28) State and Local Personal Income Taxes:

$$\Delta T_{sy} = .010(\Delta W + \Delta W_G + \Delta P - \Delta P^* + \Delta Div + \Delta i_G)$$

3. Social Insurance Programs

(29) Private Employer Contributions for Social Insurance:

$$\Delta SI_r = .149\Delta E$$

(30) Personal Contributions for Social Insurance:

$$\Delta SI_e = .129(\Delta E + \Delta E_G) + .050(\Delta P - \Delta P^*)$$

(31) Covered Unemployment:

$$\Delta U_c = .675\Delta U - .140(\Delta LF - \Delta LF_{-1})$$

The relationship of unemployment covered by compensation programs (ΔU_c) to total unemployment varies with the rate of increase in the labor force. When the labor force is growing rapidly, new entrants, not yet covered, make up a larger proportion of total unemployment.

(32) Unemployment Compensation:

$$\Delta X_u = 1.77 \Delta U_c + .101$$

III. *The Model as a Forecasting Instrument*

A. *The Forecast of 1962*

The unknowns of the model are the 32 variables like automobile demand, disposable income, private GNP, etc. that stand on the left side of the equations. The knowns are variables like government pur-

SUITS: ECONOMETRIC MODEL   119

TABLE 1—PROJECTIONS UNDERLYING FORECAST OF 1962

Equation

(01) $A_{-1}=14.3$ $\Delta L_{-1}=16.9$ $X_f=\Delta X_s=0$
(02) $D_{-1}=27.3$ $\Delta L_{-1}=16.9$
(03) $\Delta ND_{-1}=1.2$ $\Delta L_{-1}=16.9$
(04) $\Delta S_{-1}=3.4$ $\Delta L_{-1}=16.9$
(05) $\Delta PE=1.3^a$
(06) $\Delta Aaa=+.02$ $\Delta\left(\dfrac{FHA+VA}{2}\right)=-.06^b$ $HS_{-1}=93.1$
(07) $\Delta HS_{-1}=3.2$ $\Delta C=0$
(08) $\Delta PD=.7^a$ $\Delta M_{+1}=1.0$ $ID_{-1}=0.0$
(09) $IND_{-1}=1.7$
(10) —
(11) $\Delta F=0$ $\Delta PE=1.3^a$ $\Delta g=6.9$
(12) —
(13) $\Delta LF=1.2$ $\Delta E_0=.2$ $\Delta E_G=.6$
(14) $P^*_{-1}=39.6$
(15) $w_{-1}=4.38$ $E_{-1}=46.9$
(16) —
(17) $\Delta T_{bp}=.730$ $\Delta T_{os}=.087$
(18) $\Delta P_f=0$
(19) —
(20) $\Delta X_f=\Delta X_s=\Delta X_{GI}=0$ $\Delta W_G=1.5$ $\Delta i_G=.1$ $\Delta T_{op}=.35$ $\Delta T_{ev}=.08$ $\Delta T_{ref}=0$
(21) —
(22) $\Delta W_G=1.5$ $\Delta i_G=.1$
(23) $\Delta W_G=1.5$ $\Delta i_G=.1$
(24) —
(25) —
(26) —
(27) —
(28) $\Delta W_G=1.5$ $\Delta i_G=.1$
(29) —
(30) $\Delta E_G=.6$
(31) $\Delta LF=1.2$ $\Delta LF_{-1}=1.0$
(32) —
(Addendum) Δ Imputed Services $=1.5$

ᵃ Based on McGraw-Hill survey showing 4 per cent increase in plant and equipment expenditure.

ᵇ FHA ceiling rates are projected at their present level throughout 1962. The projected decline reflects the fact that they were above this level in early 1961.

chases from private firms, labor force, household liquid assets, etc. that appear only on the right side of the equations, and whose values must be projected or assigned before the unknowns can be forecast.

The forecast of 1962, calculated and presented in November 1961, employed the projected values shown in Table 1. The most important single item was the $16.9 billion increase in consumer holdings of liquid assets. A few of the other key items were: a $6.9 billion projected increase in government purchases from private firms; an increase of .6 million in government employment; increase in government wage payments of $1.5 billion; and a $1 billion rise in military orders. Note that investment in plant and equipment is projected directly on the basis of the McGraw-Hill survey rather than from equation (05). All monetary values are in 1954 dollars.

When the projections of Table 1 were inserted in the equations, the solution gave the outlook for 1962 shown in Table 2. The first two columns contain a detailed comparison of the forecast of 1961 with the preliminary actual values. The middle column contains the solutions obtained from the equations. These are in first differences and are expressed as increases over 1961. When the forecast increase is added to the preliminary actual level for 1961 the result is the forecast level of 1962 shown in the fourth column. In the last column this forecast has been translated into approximate 1962 prices.[8]

The forecast entails substantial increases in consumption expenditure, especially for automobiles. The forecast level of $18.8 billion for this sector constitutes a record level of automobile sales, exceeding the $17.9 billion reached in 1955. This large increase derives primarily from the high level of consumer liquidity and the small addition to stocks of cars during 1961.

Aside from the consumer sector the main stimulus to the economy derives from projected increases in government outlays, associated with the trend of state and local expenditures and federal defense expenditure. In preparing the forecast no allowance was made for the possible effect of a steel strike during 1962. Inventory accumulation in anticipation of interruption of steel supplies will probably accelerate inventory accumulation in the first half of the year and depress it in the second half. There is no indication that this will alter the over-all level for the year.

The forecast increase in production is adequate to absorb more than the growth of the labor force, and the outlook concludes by showing a reduction of 1.3 million in unemployment, reducing the average for the year to 3.6 million or 5 per cent of the civilian labor force.

B. *Review of Past Forecasts*

The Research Seminar in Quantitative Economics has been making annual forecasts since 1953, each a matter of record published in advance of the year forecast. The econometric model has been revised and improved several times over this period (the version presented here was first used for the 1962 forecast), but the review of past forecasting performance in Table 3 will illustrate the general reliability of the method.[9]

---

[8] To convert the values from 1954 to 1962 prices they were multiplied by deflators obtained by raising 1961 deflators 1½ per cent across the board. The result serves to put the forecast in proper perspective, but should not be thought of as part of the forecast itself.

[9] The review of the 1961 forecast, compared with the actual outcome, is provided in Table 2.

SUITS: ECONOMETRIC MODEL   121

TABLE 2—REVIEW OF 1961 AND OUTLOOK FOR 1962

(Monetary figures, except column 5, are billions of 1954 dollars)

	1961		Forecast Increase	Forecast 1962	
	Forecast	Actual[p]		(1954 prices)	(1962 prices)
Gross National Product	450.1	446.8	27.5[a]	474.3	559.9
Consumption Expenditures					
Automobiles and Parts	14.6	14.3	4.5	18.8	21.2
Other Durables	25.1	24.8	1.9	26.7	28.7
Nondurables	144.7	142.7	5.3	148.0	163.6
Services	119.9	119.6	5.5[a]	125.1	147.9
Private Gross Capital Expenditure					
Plant and Equipment	39.0	37.3	1.3	38.6	48.1
Residential Construction	19.9	17.7	0.1	17.8	21.4
Inventory Investment					
Durables	} 2.4	0.0	2.6	2.6	2.8
Nondurables		1.7	0.4	2.1	2.3
Imports	24.8	22.2	1.9	24.1	24.8
Exports	24.6	26.4	—	26.4	28.7
Government Expenditure on Goods and Services	84.7	84.5	7.8	92.3	120.0
Corporate Profits	40.3	39.6	5.1	44.7	52.5
Dividends	12.4	12.3	0.7	13.0	15.3
Civilian Labor Force[b] (millions of persons)	71.3	71.6	0.9	72.5	
Private Wage and Salary Workers		46.9	1.7	48.6	
Govt. Employees (Civilian)	}67.0	8.8	0.3	9.1	
Self-employed		11.0	0.2	11.2	
Unemployed[b]					
Number (millions)	4.3	4.9	−1.3	3.6	
Per cent of Civilian Labor Force	6.0	6.8	—	5.0	

[p] Preliminary.

[a] Includes imputed services.

[b] Annual average.

Each forecast is shown as it was presented, and compared with the actual outcome.[10] Note that from 1953 to 1956 the figures are given in 1939 dollars; thereafter the price level employed was changed almost every year. The increasing elaboration of the model is evident in the table.

As plotted in Figure 1, the general accuracy of these forecasts speaks for itself. The direction of movement was correctly forecast each year,

[10] Since data revisions occur frequently, there is some question as to what figures should be taken as "actual." Since we want the "actual" figures as close as possible in definition and economic context to the data on which the forecast was based, they are taken from the issue of the *Survey of Current Business* appearing in the February following the forecast year. E.G. the "actual" GNP for 1954 is the value for 1954 published February 1955.

and the levels were generally well predicted. The recession of 1954 was forecast with considerable precision. The recovery of 1955 was likewise forecast, but the magnitude of the boom that developed was grossly underestimated. The fact that the error of the 1955 forecast is concentrated in the consumer sector lends support to the idea that this was a consumer-generated movement. The recession of 1958 was well predicted. The recovery of 1959 was somewhat underestimated.

In many respects the forecast of 1960 was the most interesting of all. Made in November 1959 at the height of business optimism, and amidst

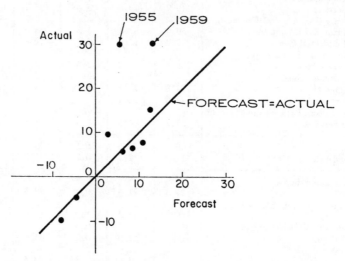

FIGURE 1. COMPARISON OF FORECAST WITH ACTUAL CHANGES IN GNP (1953–61)
(billions of 1954 dollars)

general anticipation of the "soaring 'sixties," its pessimistic outlook for 1960 was greeted with almost complete skepticism, but it proved to be more exact than any other forecast placed on record in advance.

C. *Short-Run Policy Multipliers*

Simplification of the model is carried out as illustrated in Part I. Inspection shows that in equation (05), plant and equipment expenditure (ΔPE) depends only on "known" values: last year's profits after taxes, and the stock of plant and equipment available at the beginning of the year. Similarly in equations (06) and (07), housing starts (ΔHS) and expenditure for nonfarm residential construction (ΔH) depend only on credit availability, construction costs, last year's starts, and the stock of houses at the beginning of the year. To make a forecast, therefore, we

TABLE 3—REVIEW OF PAST FORECASTS

	1953[a]		1954[a]		1955[a]		1956[a]		1957[b]	
	Forecast	Actual	Forecast	Actual	Forecast	Actual	Forecast	Actual	Forecast	Actual
Gross National Product	177.4	178.6	174.8	173.9	176.4	188.5	191.6	191.2	337.0	335.2
Consumption Expenditure	114.4	115.9	117.3	116.7	118.6	125.1	127.4	128.5	226.2	226.1
Private Gross Capital Formation	24.2	24.9	22.7	23.6	25.2	25.9	28.7	26.3	47.2	44.4
Employee Compensation	80.4[f]	79.8[f]	82.3[f]	83.0[f]	81.2[f]	89.5[f]	107.1	104.3	196.5	196.3

	1958[c]		1959[d]		1960[e]	
	Forecast	Actual	Forecast	Actual	Forecast	Actual
Gross National Product	432.7	432.5	456.7	475.7	432.0	439.2
Consumption Expenditure	282.1	287.3	295.4	310.7	287.1	296.8
Automobiles	—	—	—	—	16.7	15.6
Other Durables	—	—	—	—	25.2	25.2
Non Durables	—	—	—	—	138.9	141.9
Services	—	—	—	—	106.3	113.7
Private Gross Capital Expenditure	61.9	53.7	61.2	70.4	62.4	60.5
Plant and Equipment	—	—	44.0	43.0	40.5	39.3
Residential Construction	—	—	17.8	21.6	19.7	18.0
Inventory	—	—	-.6	5.8	2.2	3.2
Government Purchase of Goods and Services	88.8	90.5	100.1	94.6	83.7	80.3
Net Exports					-1.3	1.6
Employee Compensation	254.3	251.8	261.0	273.4	236.3	257.1
Corporate Profits	39.5	36.5	47.7	45.8	42.7	38.7
Dividends	—	—	—	—	12.2	12.2
Civilian Employment	66.4	66.5	66.0	65.6	65.5[g]	66.7[h]
Unemployment	4.8	4.7	3.4	3.8	4.4[g]	3.9[h]

[a] 1939 prices
[b] 1947 prices
[c] 1954 prices
[d] 1958 prices
[e] 1957 prices
[f] private sector only
[g] excludes Alaska and Hawaii
[h] includes Alaska and Hawaii

TABLE 4—INVERSE MATRIX

Equation No.	ΔA	ΔD	ΔND	ΔS	ΔID	ΔIND	ΔR	ΔG^*	ΔE
01	1.113	.089	.113	.046	.350	.048	.100	1.660	.113
02	.117	1.092	.118	.048	.351	.050	.101	1.676	.114
03	.130	.103	1.130	.053	.068	.483	.112	1.854	.126
04	.091	.072	.091	1.037	.047	.039	.078	1.298	.088
08	.092	.073	.093	.037	1.048	.040	.078	1.304	.089
09	.092	.073	.093	.037	.048	1.040	.078	1.304	.089
10	−.095	−.076	−.097	−.040	−.050	−.041	.921	−1.318	−.089
11	.092	.073	.093	.037	.048	.042	.078	1.304	.089
12	.884	.623	.793	.321	.439	.339	.192	3.205	1.218
13	−.118	.091	.116	.047	−.008	.049	.010	.167	.011
14	8.621	8.030	10.220	4.133	4.845	4.364	2.283	37.929	2.579
15	.184	.171	.218	.088	.103	.093	.049	.809	.055
16	−.040	−.037	−.047	−.019	−.022	−.020	−.012	−.175	−.012
17	.040	.037	.047	.019	.022	.020	.012	.175	.012
18	−.179	−.166	−.212	−.086	−.100	−.090	−.047	−.786	−.053
19	.202	.188	.240	.097	.114	.102	.054	.890	.061
20	.254	.237	.302	.122	.143	.129	.067	1.119	.076
21	−.046	−.043	−.055	−.022	−.026	−.024	−.012	−.204	−.014
22	−.254	−.237	−.302	−.122	−.143	−.129	−.067	−1.119	−.076
24	−.040	−.037	−.047	−.019	−.022	−.020	−.012	−.175	−.012
25	−.040	−.037	−.047	−.019	−.022	−.020	−.012	−.175	−.012
26	−.046	−.043	−.055	−.022	−.026	−.024	−.012	−.204	−.014
27	−.040	−.037	−.047	−.019	−.022	−.020	−.012	−.175	−.012
28	−.254	−.237	−.302	−.122	−.143	−.129	−.067	−1.119	−.076
29	−.040	−.037	−.047	−.019	−.022	−.020	−.012	−.175	−.012
30	−.254	−.237	−.302	−.122	−.143	−.129	−.067	−1.119	−.076
31	.101	.391	.498	.201	.143	.213	.088	1.461	.099
32	.058	.221	.281	.114	.081	.120	.050	.825	.056

Projections

01	$4.710 - .495A_{-1} + .260\Delta L_{-1} - .177\Delta X_f - .177\Delta X_s$
02	$.262 - .0694D_{-1} + .0784\Delta L_{-1}$
03	$-.149 + .205\Delta ND_{-1} + .143\Delta L_{-1}$
04	$.363 + .530\Delta S_{-1} + .0381\Delta L_{-1}$
08	$0 + .591\Delta PD + .305\Delta M_{+1} - .669ID_{-1}$
09	$0 - 1.121IND_{-1}$
10	$.369$
11	$0 + \Delta F + \Delta PE + \Delta H + \Delta g$
12	0
13	$0 + \Delta LF - \Delta E_0 - \Delta E_G$
14	$-.0743 + .00436P^*_{-1}$
15	0
16	$.763$
17	$0 - \Delta T_{bp} - \Delta T_{os}$

SUITS: ECONOMETRIC MODEL 125

TABLE 4—(*Continued*)

Equa- tion No.	ΔW	ΔP^*	ΔDiv	$\Delta(P-P^*)$	Federal Tax Receipts	State and Local Tax Receipts	Social Ins. Contr.	ΔX_u	ΔY
01	.609	.694	.076	.076	.585	.066	.035	−.135	.506
02	.615	.780	.085	.084	.545	.068	.036	−.136	.525
03	.680	.875	.096	.096	.600	.072	.040	−.151	.583
04	.476	.606	.066	.066	.414	.060	.028	−.105	.407
08	.478	.638	.070	.069	.432	.028	.028	−.106	.414
09	.478	.638	.070	.069	.432	.028	.028	−.106	.414
10	−.483	−.719	−.079	−.078	−.546	−.030	−.029	.107	−.431
11	.478	.638	.074	.069	.458	.030	.030	−.106	.438
12	6.568	−3.586	−.395	−.390	−1.002	.076	.319	−1.455	3.539
13	−.952	.997	.109	.109	.430	.016	.009	1.181	.516
14	60.808	−25.478	−2.806	−2.767	−4.726	1.091	.579	−3.082	45.619
15	1.297	−.543	−.059	−.060	−.101	.023	.012	−.066	.973
16	−.064	−.980	−.107	−.107	−.544	−.026	−.009	.014	−.211
17	−.064	.980	.107	.107	.544	.026	.009	−.014	.211
18	−.288	.651	.075	−1.038	.106	−.021	−.067	.064	−.946
19	.326	.395	1.040	.043	.497	.045	.019	−.072	1.070
20	.410	.496	.040	.054	.378	.045	.024	−.091	1.346
21	−.075	−.090	−.238	−.010	.886	−.010	−.004	.017	−.245
22	−.410	−.496	−.040	−.054	.622	−.045	−.024	.091	−1.346
24	−.064	−.980	−.107	−.107	.456	−.026	−.009	.014	−.211
25	−.064	−.980	−.107	−.107	.456	−.026	−.009	.014	−.211
26	−.075	−.090	−.238	−.010	−.114	.990	−.004	.017	−.245
27	−.064	−.980	−.107	−.107	−.544	.974	−.009	.014	−.211
28	−.410	−.497	−.040	−.054	−.378	.955	−.024	.091	−1.346
29	−.064	−.980	−.107	−.107	−.544	−.026	.991	.014	−.211
30	−.410	−.497	−.040	−.054	−.378	−.045	.976	.091	−1.346
31	.535	.661	.072	.072	.486	.059	.031	1.651	2.224
32	.303	.374	.041	.041	.274	.033	.018	.932	1.256

Projections—*Continued*

18	$-1.027-.902\Delta P_f$
19	$-.0191+.0198(P^*-T_{fc}-T_{sc}-Div)_{-1}$
20	$0+\Delta W_G+\Delta i_G+\Delta X_f+\Delta X_s+\Delta X_{GI}-\Delta T_{op}-\Delta T_{eg}+\Delta T_{ref}$
21	0
22	$0+.111\Delta W'_G+.150\Delta i_G$
24	0
25	$.012$
26	0
27	0
28	$0+.010(\Delta W_G+\Delta i_G)$
29	0
30	$0+.129\Delta E_G$
31	$0-.140(\Delta LF-\Delta LF_{-1})$
32	$.101$

use the knowns to estimate ΔPE, ΔHS, and ΔH via equations (05), (06), and (07), and then use these values, together with the other knowns, to solve the remaining equations. The inverse of the model is shown in Table 4. This is merely an enlarged version of the little table shown earlier for the illustrative model of Part I, and is used in the same way. For example, if the projected values of Table 1 are inserted in column P of Table 4, multiplied by the weights in the Automobile column and summed, the result is 4.5, the forecast increase in automobile demand shown in Table 2.[11] Short-run multipliers for any policy variable are readily calculated as before by inserting 1 for the variable everywhere it appears in column P and then (ignoring all terms that do not contain the variable in question) extending a forecast using the columns of Table 4.

For example, to find the multiplier on government purchases from private firms, set $\Delta g = +1$ everywhere it appears in column P. The term Δg is found in only one place: in row (11) it is multiplied by 1. To find the effect of $\Delta g = \$1$ on, say, private GNP, we multiply the weight in row (11) of the GNP column by 1:

$$\Delta G^* = 1 \times 1.304 = 1.304$$

That is to say, the short-run multiplier on government purchases is about 1.3. Similarly, the effect on, say, automobile demand is given by

$$\Delta A = 1 \times .092 = .092$$

i.e. the short-run "automobile demand multiplier" on government purchases from the private sector is .092.

In working out a policy multiplier, care must be taken to include changes in *all* exogenous variables affected by the policy action. For example, an increase in government employment involves hiring additional people [ΔE_G in rows (13) and (30)] and paying them wages [ΔW_G in rows (20), (22), and (28)]. At an average annual wage of $5000, an addition of $1 billion to the government wage bill will hire .2 million additional employees. To find the multipliers on government wages, therefore, we set $\Delta E_G = .2$. This gives $-.2$ in row (13) and .0258 in row (30) of column P. We also set $\Delta W_G = \$1$ to get 1 in row (20), .111 in (22) and .010 in (28) of column P. The impact of additional government employment on private GNP is then found by extending

[11] To save space some of the less interesting columns of the matrix have been omitted from Table 4. Moreover the tax and transfer equations have been consolidated to show only totals for federal taxes, state and local taxes, and social insurance contributions. If values of any omitted variable are required, they can be calculated from the others. For example, to calculate the federal corporate profits tax yield, use the inverse to calculate ΔP^* and substitute this value in equation (21).

these figures by the weights in the corresponding rows of the GNP column:

$$\Delta G^* = -.2 \times .167 + 1 \times 1.119 - .111 \times 1.119 - .010 \times 1.119$$
$$- .0258 \times 1.119$$
$$= .692$$

To find the effect of the action on total GNP, we must add in the additional value added by government (i.e. government wages and salaries). Thus:

$$\text{Total GNP} = .692 + 1 = 1.692$$

We also recall that government tax policy can be expressed by shifts in the equations themselves. As shown in Part I, these shift multipliers are equal to the weights found in the row of the inverse matrix that corresponds to the equation being shifted. Thus we see from the -1.119 in row (22) of the GNP column that a \$1 billion shift in the federal personal tax function will reduce private GNP by \$1.1 billion, etc. Note again [row (22) of the federal tax column] that an upward shift of \$1 billion in the federal income tax *schedule* increases federal tax *yield* by only \$622 million due to the decline in personal income and expenditure associated with the rise in taxes.

Some multiplier effects of a selection of government actions are given in Table 5. As before, once the multipliers are worked out they can be combined in any desired proportions. Thus an increase in government purchases of \$2 billion coupled with additional government wages of \$.5 billion and an upward shift of the personal tax schedule of \$1.3 billion would produce a total change in GNP of $(2 \times 1.304) + (.5 \times 1.692) + (1.3 \times -1.119) = \$2$ billion. The same program would raise total employment by .211 million, and add \$.67 billion to the federal deficit.

D. *A Digression on Deficit Financing*

An interesting and important conclusion to be drawn from Table 5 is that the impact of a government action cannot be measured by merely the existence, or even the size of a surplus or deficit. In the first place it makes a great deal of difference whose deficit is under discussion, and it is not always clear whether deficit "multipliers" are supposed to be applied to the federal deficit or to the consolidated government sector. In what follows we confine ourselves to the latter. In the second place, surpluses and deficits result from courses of action; they are the difference between certain expenditures and receipts. While it is elementary that expenditures promote and taxes retard economic activity, the net

TABLE 5—SELECTED MULTIPLIERS

Multiplicand	Multiplier for Impact on:												
	GNP		Employment		Tax Receipts		Social Insurance		Government Surplus or Deficit (−)			
	Private	Total	Private	Total	Federal	State and Local	Contributions	Transfers	Federal	State and Local	Social Insurance	Total
Plant & Equipment[a]	1.690	1.690	.115	.115	.586	.058	.038	−.137	.586	.058	.175	.819
Federal Purchases from Firms	1.304	1.304	.089	.089	.458	.030	.030	−.106	−.542	.030	.136	−.376
Federal Employment[b]	.692	1.692	.063	.263	.209	.016	.044	−.314	−.791	.016	.358	−.417
Federal Personal Income Tax Shift	−1.119	−1.119	−.076	−.076	.622	−.045	−.024	.091	.622	−.045	−.115	.462

a Additional expenditure of $1 billion of which half is spent for producers' durable equipment.
b Additional expenditure of $1 billion in government wages to hire .2 million new workers.

result depends not only on the amounts of expenditures and tax yields, but also on the kinds, and we cannot speak unqualifiedly of a deficit multiplier.

Although this point can be made from purely theoretical considerations [4, pp. 133–55], the econometric model shows the substantial order of magnitudes involved. We see from Table 5, for example, that a $1 billion consolidated deficit will result from either $1 ÷ .376 = $2.66 billion of federal government purchases or, say a cut of $1 ÷ .462 = $2.16 billion in the federal income tax schedule. Yet the former action raises total GNP by 1.304×2.66 = $3.47 billion, while the latter generates an increase of only 1.119×$2.16 = $2.42 billion.

This result can be generalized. According to the multipliers in the last column of Table 5, the consolidated balance (surplus or deficit) is given by

$$\Delta b = -.376\Delta g + .462\Delta a$$

where Δb is the change in the balance and Δa is the shift in the federal income tax schedule. A wide range of combinations of expenditures and taxes will produce the same budgetary balance. In fact, if we set Δb at some fixed value, say $\Delta b = 2$, then

$$2 = -.376\Delta g + .462\Delta a$$

is the equation of an "isobalance" locus. That is, every combination of expenditures and taxation that satisfies this equation produces a $2 billion increase in consolidated surplus. Three isobalance lines—corresponding to a $1 billion surplus, a balanced budget and a $1 billion deficit—are plotted as solid lines in Figure 2.

By the same token, the increase in total GNP is given by:

$$\Delta GNP = 1.304\Delta g - 1.119\Delta a,$$

and if we assign, say $\Delta GNP = 5$, then

$$5 = 1.304\Delta g - 1.119\Delta a$$

is the equation of an "iso-GNP" locus. Three of these are plotted as broken lines in Figure 2.

Inspection of the figure immediately shows that any specified increase in GNP can be attained in association with a wide range of balances and that any deficit or surplus may be associated with a wide range of impacts on GNP. In fact, a government program can simultaneously generate a substantial deficit and a sharp deflation, or a substantial surplus and general expansion. Since transfers, corporate profits taxes, defense orders, and government employment will have still other isobalance and iso-GNP lines, this merely scratches the surface of the possibilities.

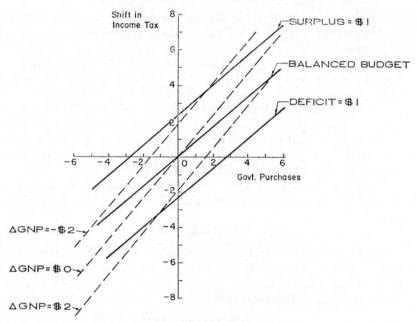

FIGURE 2. RELATIONSHIP OF GNP AND DEFICIT TO GOVERNMENT PURCHASES AND
LEVEL OF PERSONAL TAXES

E. *Dynamic Responses and Long-Run Multipliers*

As shown in Part I, dynamic responses are studied by iteration.
Among the initial impacts of any program, we must find the effects on
automobile demand, inventory accumulation, plant and equipment,
and other variables whose values re-enter the system with a lag. These
form a set of additional knowns for the next year. Using these values,
in turn, gives rise to another set, etc. Repeating this operation enables
us to follow the implications of a given program over as long a period
as desired. It appears, however, that the dynamic elements stabilize by
the end of the fifth year, and the system can be treated as in equilibrium
after five iterations.

A complete study of the dynamic behavior of each variable in response to each possible policy action cannot be presented here, but
Table 6 shows the response of the GNP and its components to a permanent increase of $1 billion in government expenditure. The tabulated
figures are the values of the variables measured as deviations from their
levels as of year 0 before the shift in expenditure policy.

In response to increased government expenditure, the GNP rises by
$1.3 billion the first year and under the stimulation of the dynamic fac-
tors climbs to a maximum of $1.6 billion over its initial level. It declines

TABLE 6—DYNAMIC RESPONSES TO A PERMANENT INCREASE OF $1 BILLION IN
GOVERNMENT EXPENDITURE

(Tabulated figures are deviations from initial levels)

	Year				
	1	2	3	4	5
Gross National Product[a]	1.304	1.619	1.582	1.545	1.335
Automobiles and parts	.092	.088	.050	.042	.014
Other Durables	.073	.104	.113	.117	.104
Nondurables	.093	.159	.193	.215	.213
Services	.037	.075	.104	.126	.134
Plant and Equipment	0.	.186	.173	.133	.082
Inventory					
Durable Goods	.048	.079	.017	−.010	−.031
Nondurable Goods	.040	.023	.012	.008	−.002
Net Foreign Investment	−.078	−.101	−.103	−.103	−.098
Government Purchases	1.	1.	1.	1.	1.

[a] Detail may not add to total because of rounding.

thereafter under the back-pressure of accumulating stocks. The behavior of the individual components is in keeping with their respective
natures. Automobile demand rises immediately to its maximum and
declines slowly as the stock of cars on the road accumulates. Consumer
expenditure for durables rises sharply and levels off, while outlays on
nondurable goods and services continue to rise throughout the period,
although at declining rates.

Investment in plant and equipment spurts in response to the immediate improvement in corporate profits and tapers off as the new plant
becomes available. Inventory accumulation occurs at a high rate, but
durable inventory overshoots and the rate of accumulation is forced
somewhat below the year 0 level.

IV. *Conclusion*

To approximate the behavior of a complex economy by a set of 32
linear approximations is a heroic simplification. Yet experience has
shown the statistical model to be a useful and flexible device for economic forecasting. Moreover, while the system of equations is small in
relation to the vast structure of pure theory, it is considerably more
elaborate than other devices that can be brought to bear on a practical
level. Indeed, if an econometric model is nothing else, it is a highly
sophisticated method of observing the past operation of the economy
and systematizing the information obtained.

Yet, once the technical work of constructing the model is completed,
a competent economist needs little more than a knowledge of elementary
algebra to understand its nature, or to apply it to a wide range of ana-

lytical problems. Properly used, the model provides quantitative estimates of economic responses to specified changes in conditions. It goes
without saying that the accuracy of these estimates is below the level
that might be inferred from the precision of their statement in the text.
But they show the proper order of magnitude involved and fall well
within the practical tolerances required for effective policy evaluation.

REFERENCES

1. A. S. GOLDBERGER, *Impact Multipliers and Dynamic Properties of the
   Klein-Goldberger Model*. Amsterdam 1959.
2. J. M. GUTTENTAG, "The Short Cycle in Residential Construction,"
   Am. Econ. Rev., June 1961, *31*, 275–98.
3. L. R. KLEIN AND A. S. GOLDBERGER, *An Econometric Model of the United
   States, 1929–1952*. Amsterdam 1955.
4. P. A. SAMUELSON, "The Simple Mathematics of Income Determination," in *Income, Employment and Public Policy: Essays in Honor of
   Alvin Hansen*, New York 1948.
5. D. B. SUITS, "The Demand for New Automobiles in the United States
   1929–1956," *Rev. Econ. Stat.*, Aug. 1958, *40*, 273–80.
6. M. L. WEIDENBAUM, *Government Spending: Process and Measurement*.
   Seattle, The Boeing Co., 1958.

[6]

ECONOMIC FORECASTING[1]

" If we could first know where we are and whither we are tending,
we could better judge what to do and how to do it."

Abraham Lincoln

A trend is a trend is a trend
But the question is, will it bend?
Will it alter its course
Through some unforeseen force
And come to a premature end?

Stein Age Forecaster

FORECASTING occupies us all for much of our lives. It begins with the speculative wagging of heads over our cradles and continues until the prayers with which we are hopefully laid to rest. Sometimes it is an idle amusement, sometimes a matter of life and death, sometimes—and this is where the economist takes a hand—it carries rewards and punishments in the form of profit or loss.

There is nothing new, therefore, either about forecasting or about economic forecasting as such. Both are as old as human activity, of which economic activity has always been a prominent part. What is new is the kind of economic forecasting that is now carried on and the way in which it is organised. It is accepted as an integral and necessary part of policy-making at all levels of economic management, and tends to be undertaken systematically by a specialised group of experts recruited for this specific purpose. Whether it takes the form of market research, investment analysis or national-income forecasting, it has become a full-time occupation requiring preliminary training and is the subject of an expanding literature designed to assist such training.

I cannot discover any occasion on which the Royal Economic Society has ever discussed this new activity, in which an increasing number of economists are now engaged. I have thought it appropriate, therefore, to select this topic for a Presidential Address, all the more because I have myself been preoccupied with forecasting over the past few years to the almost complete exclusion of other aspects of economics. My preoccupation has been that of a consumer rather than a producer; but perhaps economists should be invited for once to swallow one of their own favourite prescriptions and have a look at the market before putting too much effort into production. In any event, I am not qualified to enter in detail into the technical issues involved in the preparation of forecasts. I shall also limit what I have to

---

[1] Presidential address to the Royal Economic Society, July 3, 1969.

say to national-income forecasting, although I believe that a good deal of my argument has a wider application.

National-income forecasts are essentially forecasts of the behaviour of aggregate demand over a period which is usually between one and two years. Sometimes the forecast is expressed in the form of a year-on-year comparison, but in Britain it is almost always prepared so as to show the changes quarter by quarter, and the focus of interest is the situation predicted at the end of the period and the path by which it is reached rather than the average change in demand and output between one year and the next. National-income forecasts are usually coupled with balance-of-payments forecasts, and in these the absolute size of the expected surplus or deficit over the period is of interest equally with the changes that are predicted in the balance of payments from quarter to quarter.

Forecasts of this kind serve in principle important administrative purposes. First of all, they provide a frame of reference for policy decisions. So far as they express the best available judgment of future prospects, they allow the Government to act incrementally on the economy: that is, to take for granted the changes already in progress and concentrate policy on reinforcing or modifying these changes. Instead of reacting to events as they occur, the Government can frame its policies ahead of the events predicted in the forecasts.

Secondly, the forecasts form a channel of communication between those concerned with day-to-day administration and those who are involved in policy formulation. The preparation of a set of forecasts involves the first group, because their knowledge of what is going on currently ought to be consistent with the figures for the near future and the recent past; and it also involves the second group, because if the outcome of existing policies as revealed in the forecast is unsatisfactory fresh policies will have to be introduced. The dissemination of official forecasts throughout Whitehall provides Departments simultaneously with a common view of the current situation and a common view of what will happen unless something is done. Each can then react knowing what view of the future is held elsewhere and can either challenge that view or propose action based upon it.

Thirdly, the forecasts can serve a monitoring function and provide a basis against which to judge how policies are working out. Any serious divergence from forecasts rings an alarm bell and makes it easier to concentrate attention and effort on corrective action.

Although economic forecasts serve these purposes in principle, there are a number of practical difficulties that should not be overlooked. There are no doubt great advantages in using a single set of forecasts known to a large number of officials and Ministers and accepted by them as a consistent basis for the management of the economy. But no Ministers in any well-conducted government are likely to devolve completely on a small group of experts responsibility for formulating an authoritative view of future economic prospects; the risks of error are only too obvious whatever the auspices under which forecasts are prepared. Ministers (and officials) may well hesitate to commit themselves to a single set of forecasts to be appealed to in all contexts and for all purposes. It may also be far from self-evident to them that what emerges at the end of the day from a large-scale forecasting exercise by specialists drawn from each of the leading economic departments is necessarily a better basis for policy-making than the judgment of a single careful observer of current trends; statistical haggling has not always been the path to economic wisdom.

There are also great advantages in making official forecasts as widely available as possible. If it is helpful to involve the whole government machine in economic forecasting it would also seem helpful to involve the community at large. Since the forecasts underlie some at least of the decisions that Ministers take, an explanation and defence of these decisions is incomplete without reference to the forecasts that form the background to them. But this is only half the story. The very size of the government machine creates problems in communication within it which are not overcome and may easily be aggravated by giving forecasts precise quantitative shape. As for the general public, any government has to give careful thought to the way in which it presents its policies and may scruple to blurt out its worst fears because they happen to be dignified as economic forecasts. What one Minister hesitates to reveal to another he is not likely to reveal to the Press—although his colleague may.

To some of these issues I shall return later. First, however, I propose to discuss some of the problems involved in forecasting.

A short-term economic forecast has to be based on two things: an informational system and an economic model. Some people lay the emphasis on one, and some on the other. For example, many economists who construct forecasting models take the availability of suitable data for granted or assume, usually mistakenly, that it does not matter in what form the data are fed into the model. Sometimes models are constructed from annual data, and so implicitly reject the contribution that can be obtained through access to the latest available information.

Just as some people feel in no need of recent data, others feel in no need of elaborate models. They find it sufficient to establish a trend and extrapolate. Or they conduct surveys of business expectations and build a forecast round the results. The origins of the trend may remain unexamined and shifts in expectations be treated as inherently unpredictable.

My own sympathies lie more with the unsophisticated second group, who at least have an ear to the ground, than with the often over-sophisticated first group, who take a bird's eye view of the situation. It is in practice quite possible to make forecasts of short-term prospects without a model; but it is impossible to make quantitative forecasts without quantitative data. Moreover, any model that is worth using has itself to be based on an analysis of such data. The system of relationships in the model may be derived partly from theoretical considerations, but it must also embody the results of empirical investigation of past experience in the values assigned to all the parameters. In a forecasting model, as distinct from an explanatory model, this dependence on statistical data is enhanced by the use of a large number of exogenous variables as forward indicators of investment, exports and so on.[1]

Forecasts based on economic models convey an illusion of continuity that can be highly dangerous. We may try to smooth the past or crush it into a Procrustean bed of econometric relationships, but we know that it is made up like the future of a series of discontinuous and unique events. The economic outlook may be dominated by the likelihood of some specific event, such as a major war, an exchange crisis, an international agreement and so on, so that the only forecast that matters is whether and, if so, when that event will take place. In a state of crisis improvisation takes over from planning, uncertainties multiply and forecasting becomes a waste of time. The only thing to do is to react to a succession of emergencies, recognising that it is impossible to be ahead of events that are inherently unpredictable. In the summer of 1940, for example, it would have been of little help in deciding what to do over the next few months to have a forecast of G.N.P. extending into 1941.

The models may also mislead by implying a constancy in the pattern of economic events which experience belies. The same key variables may be present in successive cycles, and may operate on one another in much the same way: so far as this is so, ordinary economic theory can tell us what to expect. But the interactions are never *quite* the same, because the circumstances are different, the strength of the economic forces at work varies from one cycle to the next and the time taken for a given effect to show itself—a matter hardly touched upon in economic theory—is far from constant. In addition, the parameters are changing through time, so that in trying to establish them from the statistical record of the past we are analysing an economic system that has already ceased to exist. I would stress particularly our ignorance of the speed of response of economic variables, because any forecasting system that assumes this to be constant takes for granted what may well be one of the principal uncertainties that a forecast is intended to resolve.

I do not propose to deal with the technical problems of model-building, on which there is a considerable literature. I shall concentrate instead on the constraints imposed by the available data. These constraints may in due course be relaxed by improvements in the collection and processing of statistical information, but in my view they are largely inherent in the economic system itself, and should not be dismissed or ignored as a minor or

---

[1] For a fuller discussion of the issues involved see " Short-term Economic Forecasting at the Treasury" (in *Models for Decision*, British Computer Society, 1964).

transient affair. It is precisely because the variables are so numerous and complex and our information about them inevitably so imperfect that economics (and economic forecasting) is so much more difficult than it looks.

The ideal situation would be one in which all the data were bang up to date, completely reliable and mutually consistent. We should then be able to say with confidence what had been happening and where we were. Unfortunately this is hardly ever possible. The first thing we have to forecast is the past. So far from being easy, this is usually very difficult. In fact, it often makes more sense to project a forecast backwards as a guide to what the statistics should look like than to construct a forecast of the future on an uncritical acceptance of current figures. I have frequently had to confess that the best available guide to what was happening was the latest forecast of what was expected to happen.

First of all, the forecaster has to contend with the inevitable lag of statistics behind events. Sometimes this lag may be negligible: for example, we can keep track of the gold reserves from day to day. Sometimes it is extremely long: census data were collected until recently at intervals of ten years and published up to five years later, so that in 1966 the latest information might relate to 1951. Most of the data necessary for the construction of national-income estimates relate to a period at least one month ago, and often as much as three months ago. The quarterly figures, which give the most comprehensive picture of the economic situation, appear three months or more after the event. This means that when the February forecasts are being prepared in advance of the Budget the latest available national accounts relate to the third quarter, *i.e.*, to the quarter centred on August. Obviously a lot can happen in the seven months between August and April.

Next comes the issue of reliability. One index of this is the frequency with which the figures are subsequently amended, usually in the light of later information. An obvious example is the series for personal saving. The published statistics represent a residual, arrived at from figures of income on one side and figures of expenditure on the other. But until a few years ago there appeared to be a systematic tendency for new items of expenditure to be omitted, so that, in course of time as more and more of the omissions were identified, the figures of consumer spending crept up, and the residual was correspondingly narrowed.[1] In recent years the revisions have been comparatively small, but it would be rash to assume that the figures have greatly improved in reliability.

A second illustration is provided by the index of industrial production. In the first nine months of 1964 the index stayed obstinately level at a time when other signs pointed to increasing pressure of demand. To-day the figures for the first three quarters read 126, 128, 129—a very different picture. Similarly, the revised figures for 1962 indicate a much slower climb up to the third quarter of the year than the unrevised figures at the

[1] National Institute of Economic and Social Research, *Economic Review*, May 1963, p. 11.

time of publication. I cite these examples not in order to point an accusing finger at British statistics (other countries, including the United States, amend their figures at least as often and as much) but because they relate to periods at which misinterpretation of the figures could have had serious consequences. Indeed, in 1964 press comment on the figures did contribute to the inertia of the Government.

A more recent illustration has been provided by the discovery that exports have been consistently understated for nearly six years. Quite apart from the uncertainties introduced by this discovery, it has always seemed to me dangerous to treat the change in exports recorded in the Trade Returns from year to year (not just from month to month) as an entirely reliable guide to the actual change either in the value of work done on exports or in export proceeds or even in the flow of goods to foreign destinations.

One consequence of this unreliability is that one can never be sure whether a new trend for which there is no obvious explanation really exists. It is possible to build all kinds of interesting hypotheses around a series of figures until the bubble is pricked by an unpublicised amendment, and the theories lose their iridescence with a bang. Time and again in my experience, a disturbing but inexplicable change in the situation turns out to need no explanation, because it eventually proves that there has in fact been no such change. You can be just as wrong about the past as about the future.

One particular source of unreliability that needs emphasis is the difficulty of making seasonal adjustments. It is easy to overlook this problem when the figures in regular use have been purged, nominally at least, of seasonal influences. But seasonal influences are neither invariable from year to year nor over longer periods. Walter Heller's remark that " seasonally corrected, the weather in January was lousy " epitomises part of the problem; and the shifting habits of car buyers points to another.

It is not possible in my judgment to dodge this problem by working out all the necessary econometric relations in terms of raw data and concealing the implicit seasonal adjustments from the sceptical eye. One might with equal justice exclude price changes and make all the calculations at current prices. On the other hand, there is no uniquely right way of making seasonal corrections, any more than there is a uniquely right way of constructing an index number.

The importance of making the right adjustments can best be illustrated by reference to the unemployment statistics. Broadly speaking, it is possible to apply a correction to these in one of two ways: either by making absolute adjustments to the figures, up or down, to remove the seasonal understatement or overstatement, or by using proportionate adjustments, on the assumption that the size of the seasonal correction is itself dependent on the current level of unemployment and not fixed independently of it. There are good reasons for thinking that part of the adjustment should be additive and part proportionate. But the two sets of adjustments can lead to very different results. In the early months of 1959, for example, the picture would have looked entirely different if the proportionate method had been used; and the difference would have been particularly striking at the very moment when the Chancellor of the Exchequer was looking for advice on how to frame his Budget. In the six months between August 1958 and February 1959 the rise in unemployment on one basis was 70,000, while on the other it was no more than 20,000, and the peak had already been passed.

The unemployment statistics raise a further problem in reliability: the problem of comparing figures over time. Unemployment in 1969 is not the same phenomenon as in 1959, and other indices of pressure on the labour market may move in a quite different way. It is dangerous, therefore, to treat the recorded change in unemployment from one year to another as a reliable guide to the actual change in pressure. In Britain the various labour-market indices—unemployment, vacancies, hours of work, participation rates, migration flows, recruitment through the Labour Exchanges— did in fact agree remarkably well until a year or two ago, but in 1968 the unemployment figures diverged rather strikingly from the others. This posed a major problem, since the unemployment figures are usually the most up to date, reliable, unambiguous and significant of all the leading British indicators. It takes time to become alive to such an unaccustomed divergence, to make sure that it is not an aberration, to investigate its origins and decide how far to abandon changes in unemployment as a guide to policy decisions.[1] Indeed, one of the greatest hazards in forecasting is that a statistical series which is generally highly reliable may suddenly and without warning prove quite unreliable.

As the unemployment figures show, the data may tell different stories. The fact that the statistical picture is inevitably full of inconsistencies is the most awkward problem of all. Even measures that in principle are equal to one another are often in flat contradiction. To take what may be an extreme example, between the first quarter of 1966 and the first quarter of 1967 the expenditure measure of G.N.P. increased by 2%, the income measure fell by $\frac{1}{2}$% and the output measure was unchanged. Yet all these measure the same thing. Even when they all show the same direction of change, they often differ very perceptibly as to amount. By the second quarter of 1968, for example, one measure was 2% above the level of 1966, another $5\frac{1}{2}$% and the third 4%.

How is one to reconcile evidence of this kind? Not surely by accepting implicitly the expenditure estimate because it happens to be the aggregate

---

[1] In case anyone interprets this (like some readers of the Brookings Report on *Britain's Economic Prospects*) as implying that the British Government habitually overlooks the lag of unemployment behind output, let me hasten to point out that the Hopkin Loop illustrating this lag was part of Treasury lore by 1961 or earlier, and that the idea that the lag is a fixed one was abandoned long ago. (See J. R. Shepherd, " Productive Potential and the Demand for Labour," *Economic Trends*, August 1968, p. xxvi.)

of the demand components of which forecasts are made up. Nor, in my view, by striking a simple average and treating the result as a firm estimate. One has to look at all the other evidence and judge what is most plausible.

Forecasts suffer from a number of occupational diseases of which I shall mention three. First there is what I should call the Jonah syndrome or Variant I. By this I mean the tendency to dwell on possible disasters ahead and to call for immediate action to avoid them. It is, of course, a powerful position to be in, since if disaster does occur the forecaster's reputation is made, while if it does not occur people will either be too relieved to call for the forecaster's head or will attribute the outcome to some action set on foot after his predictions. When Nineveh was saved Jonah had no real need to go off and sulk; he could have taken credit by attributing Nineveh's good luck to his intercession with the Lord.

A more common disorder is the Overgrown Hedge or Variant II. The forecaster, instead of predicting a specific outcome, wisely takes refuge in quoting a range of figures, but sets the upper and lower limits so far apart that the policy-maker to whom the forecast is presented is no wiser than he was before. The forecaster suffering from Variant II may be led to claim that he has not suggested any outcome within the limits set as more probable than any other outcome within those limits. But if he is honest with himself he knows only too well that his forecast will be treated as implying that the most probable outcome lies mid-way between the upper and lower limits.

A third variant is what I would designate " the phony average." There was a time in the early fifties when the Royal Statistical Society used to invite its members in May to predict the average increase in G.N.P. in the current year over the preceding year. It does not require much elementary arithmetic to show how valueless such a forecast would be to the policy-maker. By May two-thirds of the two-year period is already over; and if the available statistics showed a steady expansion up till March it would require a very large and sudden change of trend to move the expected outcome up or down by one percentage point. If, for example, production is rising every month from 100 by half a percentage point the increase in Year Two over Year One should work out at $8\frac{3}{4}\%$. To bring this down to $7\frac{3}{4}\%$ would mean either that production had to stop increasing in April and remain flat until December or that a turning-point should be reached later, with production falling towards the end of the year—a change of trend far more violent than the layman would deduce from a wobble in the forecast by one percentage point.

None of these variants lacks for professional support. I have heard Variant III stoutly defended by the head of the forecasting staff of a continental country whose practices are held up to our admiration by British journalists. It is true that year-on-year forecasts are usually made about November rather than in the following May. But this still means that the forecast is made nearly half-way through the period to which it relates and is subject to a very wide margin of error as an indication of the situation at the end of the period. For purposes of economic management in Britain such a forecast would be largely valueless if not highly misleading.

Variant II has also many respectable and eminent defenders who argue that the uncertainties behind any forecast can be adequately conveyed only if the forecast is expressed in terms of a range of possible outcomes. The difficulty is that in practice it is at least as hard to state precise limits to the range as it is to plump for some central outcome. The unsophisticated user is inclined either to pooh-pooh the forecast or simply strike an average, while the sophisticated user is usually well aware that any figure is subject to a wide margin of error and wants not a measure of the timidity of the forecaster but detailed information about the vulnerability of the forecast to specific alternative assumptions.

As to the Jonah syndrome, which you may think a rather attractive form of disorder, it may be true that those afflicted with it could usefully have bitten British policy-makers more severely during the sixties. But if so this is not because it would be right to erect into a principle that one should always forecast the worst possible outcome, but because in the circumstances of the last decade or two it would probably have been appropriate to err more strongly on the side of caution.

This brings us to the interesting question of errors in forecasting. These are of various kinds.

First of all, the forecast may rest on bad theory. The model used may be wrong in the sense that it either selects the wrong variables or specifies wrong relationships between them. As to what I mean by " bad " theory or " wrong " relationships, let it suffice that one characteristic of what is " bad " or " wrong " is that it could be superseded with advantage by something which would give a more satisfactory and consistent account of the inner logic of the observed phenomena. For example, the forecast may rest on a model which excludes from the parameters monetary influences such as the rate of interest or the money supply when it is clear that economic activity does respond to changes in monetary conditions. Or it may introduce monetary influences as if they operated mainly on business investment rather than on, say, housing, when better results can be obtained from a model connecting monetary factors and house-building more closely.

On the whole, I doubt whether bad theory has played a major part in forecasting errors in this country over the past decade or two. It is conceivable, to take the example I have given, that the model has allowed too little influence on the economy to monetary factors. For what it is worth, this is not my own impression. There have been a number of occasions— notably the introduction of S.E.T. in 1966, with the consequent forced loan to the Government, and the import deposits scheme of 1968/69—when it might have been reasonable to allow a good deal for the reflection of financial restriction on business outlays. But on these occasions it has proved difficult if not impossible to trace such effects—in marked contrast to the clear reflection of hire-purchase restrictions on consumer spending.

The next source of error is a change in some variable outside the model. This covers everything that the model assumes to remain constant, and hence everything assumed to have no systematic relationship with the rest of the model. But this obviously covers a great deal of what does in practice determine the movement of economic activity: strikes, assassinations, elections, chance events like the closing of the Suez Canal, and so on. Some of these things are capable of being included in the model, and others can to some extent be allowed for. But the economy is never

> " A creature that moves
> In determinate grooves "

so that even in principle there is no reason to expect economic forecasting to become an exact science. The difficulty is to decide whether, when an error occurs, the forecaster's alibi is sound because the error springs from the unfathomable complexity of the real world and the inherent randomness of events.

These sources of error apart, mistakes can arise out of misinterpretation of the statistical data. First of all, it is very easy to get the starting-point wrong, especially as the data for the past three months or even the past year are necessarily highly uncertain. Anyone conducting a post mortem on a forecast has to face an almost invariable discrepancy between the current level (*e.g.*, of G.N.P.) assumed at the time when the forecast was made and as seen retrospectively when the post mortem is undertaken. He has then to ask himself whether the forecast was related to the level x months away or to the increase in the level over x months. But at this point it almost always emerges that the two things are part and parcel of the same forecast: had a different starting-point been taken for the forecast, both the eventual level and the rate of increase to that level would have been altered. Sometimes this reflects technical factors: for example, if G.N.P. is put at a higher initial level this alters the stock–output ratio, and so the amount of stock-building required in order to restore equilibrium. Sometimes what is involved is the changed view of future prospects that is occasioned by a changed view of the recent past. If it became clear that an upswing in business investment was in progress instead of the level trend previously assumed this would automatically change the forecast, perhaps quite radically. The forecaster might claim that the only satisfactory way of testing his accuracy would be to allow him to repeat the forecast in the light of the newly available information about the past. But here as over other errors the recipient of the original forecast might view the matter less sympathetically and ask in all innocence whether there were no other ways of checking on the starting-point.

The data may give rise to other kinds of misinterpretation. Any forecasting model has to use a large number of equational relationships, complete with coefficients and lags which are bound to be of uncertain magnitude, if only because the relationships have to be based on a limited number of observations, and these extend over a period in which the whole system of relationships is itself likely to have been changing. No one can be very confident, however successful his curve-fitting, that he has found the unique explanation of past experience. Anyone who has watched econometrics applied to short-term forecasting knows that a wide selection of equations can be generated with highly impressive R^2's from the same set of past observations, and that there tends to be a distressing scatter in the predictions yielded by these same equations when they are projected into the future. I believe that the Board of Trade have used over twenty equations, all with impeccable credentials, to forecast imports, but without any means of deciding which is right.

There is, of course, no reason why an equation which is intended to represent some underlying relationship should hold in the special circumstances of any single year. But it is a more serious matter if one cannot be sure that the underlying relationship will reassert itself or re-emerge after a wobble as a quite different relationship. Take, for example, the familiar story of consumer spending in 1968. The public, observing the spending spree at the beginning of this year, was inclined to conclude that personal saving would remain negligible for the rest of the year and that the imposition of higher taxation would have a very limited effect in checking consumption. It became an article of faith in some quarters that there had been a fundamental change in saving habits and that fiscal methods of regulating demand were ineffective. All this was idle talk and showed little appreciation of what goes to make up personal savings. But there *might* have been a continuing shift in propensities; we don't know for sure that there wasn't.

It is often assumed that forecasting errors would be reduced if use were made of a computable model rather than the less elaborate forecasting models usually employed. I see nothing inevitable about this.[1] Indeed, there is a serious danger that computable models will yield less reliable results, particularly if they are fed with statistics in a very raw state. At least half the problem lies in the need to refine the data and ensure self-consistency. This requires detailed inspection of the kind which the methods hitherto used in Britain are calculated to provide. What is undoubtedly true is that computers are indispensable to forecasting for the analysis of specific equational relationships, for exploring alternative hypotheses and for providing rather quicker results by dispensing with iterative processes. They do not necessarily reduce the risk of error.

Anyone engaged in forecasting has always to be jogging back to see what went wrong. But this is not as easy as it sounds. If the Government took

---

[1] See " Short Term forecasting at the Treasury," in *Models for Decision*. This essay, although attributed to me, is almost entirely the work of Mr. A. D. Roy.

action in the light of the forecast that in itself would give rise to a change in the forecast. But how big a change it is impossible to say without resort to the very model and system of equations on which the original forecast rested. So in assessing forecasting errors it may be necessary to take for granted the very apparatus that is being tested.

Much the same applies in allowing for random events outside the model. Both in the forecast and in the post mortem it is necessary to assign to such events a precise value for their impact on the economy—something which the average administrator would rarely make bold to do and which he may never imagine going on all the time in a different area of government. There may be no way of testing whether the allowance made is correct except by methods that are themselves of the nature of a forecast. Once again a post mortem may involve forecasting backwards.

When we come to errors that clearly originate within the equational system and cannot be explained away in terms of a wrong starting-point, external events or a change of policy, the trouble usually lies in the speed or violence of reaction, on the one hand, or in a shift in the underlying relationships, on the other. Either of these may be associated with a change in mood or attitude which can originate outside economic events altogether or have as much to do with the way in which policy is presented as with policy itself. Whatever the source, it is not easy to predict accurately how quickly smoke will give way to flame so that all the normal interactions are speeded up. Even when one is on one's guard for the evidence of acceleration after an obvious turning-point, it may first be extraordinarily slow to appear and then exceed expectations in the most disconcerting way. Both in 1959–60 and in 1964–65 these cumulative effects seem to have been inadequately foreseen in the forecasts of G.N.P. and still more of the balance of payments. It is always a little sinister when the forecasts begin to be revised uniformly in one direction.

Given the obvious need to revise forecasts, how often should this be done? The answer inevitably depends on the frequency with which policy adjustments can be contemplated: in this sense a fresh forecast should be available at any time. Yet something must also be allowed for the logistics of forecasting. Where this involves extensive consultation with other Departments, the preparation of a new set of forecasts may stretch over weeks and can rarely be undertaken at short notice. The normal practice in the Treasury is to engage in three major forecasting exercises every year: in January/February before the Budget; in June/July after the Budget; and in October/November to allow a preliminary view of the Budget to be taken. But of course other less elaborate forecasts are made more or less monthly, and the forecasting staff is also called upon to predict the effect of particular acts of policy. My personal impression is that the less elaborate forecasts are subject to a wider margin of error than the others. The reason for this in my view is that it is usually only when the major exercises are undertaken that the situation is radically re-examined and a fresh view taken of current trends. It is much easier in a month-by-month approach to persist in discounting evidence of a change in the underlying situation and preserving the basis of earlier forecasts unchanged.

I come finally to the way in which forecasts are used. How should one look at a forecast, and how ought one to frame advice on it?

It is important to make clear at the start that policy is not governed exclusively by economic forecasts. A government, being a government, cannot isolate economic policy and decide what to do or when to do it on economic grounds alone. It may wish quite properly to defer action or draw up plans undeterred by the latest forecast in order to strengthen its political position at home or for reasons of defence or foreign policy. It has also to weigh up different objectives of economic policy, and when these are in conflict no forecast can by itself resolve the conflict. Short-term considerations may point one way, long-term considerations the other; domestic and external pressures may be opposed to one another; the particular interests that would benefit from one kind of policy may have to be balanced against other interests that would suffer. No Chancellor ever feels, therefore, that the forecasts as such tell him what to do.

Secondly, it is important not to treat forecasts as gospel truth. It may seem odd to insist on this in view of the fallibility of economic forecasters. But the world is full of people who are only too willing to treat a forecast with excessive reverence (or in revulsion dismiss all forecasts as mumbo-jumbo). There are no more dangerous men in government than those who take figures literally, and this applies both to statistics of the past and to forecasts of the future. Such readers appal the righteous forecaster, who regards the figures he sets down as no more than the beginning, not the end of the story. For he knows that the essential function of a forecast is to help Ministers in deciding what risks they are running and how they should run them; and although the figures summarise the most probable outcome as the forecaster sees it, they are far from conveying all that is in his mind. They do not reveal the conviction with which he regards his own forecast; the margin that separates it from other quite plausible outcomes; its vulnerability to a change of assumptions at critical points; the direction in which departures from forecast seem most likely. All this may be elaborated in the text accompanying the forecast, but cannot be incorporated in the forecast itself.

Thirdly, the forecaster has to ask himself, not: " Is the forecast likely to be right? "—it is better to assume that all forecasts are *ipso facto* wrong— but: " How wrong might the forecast be? How seriously would it matter if it were that much out? What action would I then recommend which I would not recommend on the basis of the forecast? " In other words, the forecast has to be judged in terms of the policy advice to which it leads, not in terms of the accuracy of the forecast itself.

This may seem strange doctrine to those who want to be shown the basis of policy and imagine that it would be revealed in its nakedness if only all official forecasts were made public. But as I have argued above, policy rests on an assessment of risks taken in a state of ignorance and uncertainty; and advice consists fundamentally in emphasising particular risks and indicating how those that are least acceptable could be reduced or avoided. Forecasting is one stage in this process of assessing and coping with risks; but it is one stage only, and not always the most important.

If forecasts are published this introduces a further element into the calculations of the forecasters. For they may find it necessary to forecast public reactions to the forecast itself. These reactions will form part of the economic system, and may affect the balance of payments, domestic investment, labour attitudes and so on. In ordinary circumstances one might disregard such repercussions as of secondary importance. But if business confidence is low, the external situation is precarious and official forecasts are believed, the release of a gloomy balance-of-payments forecast could have major consequences.

The forecaster may have to concern himself with other consumer reactions. If he is trying to take a view of the future honestly he may have to ask himself whether it is reasonable to start from the assumption that official policy will remain unchanged. Later, in framing policy advice, he cannot escape raising from time to time the question whether Ministers will persist resolutely in their policies and whether therefore it is wise to encourage them to set out on a course from which they may yet have to beat a retreat. Forecasting what Ministers will yet do may be a necessary preliminary to analysing the choices open to them now, and assessing the risks to which the various alternatives expose them.

I have raised rather obliquely the issue of publication of official forecasts, and perhaps I might conclude by commenting on this at more length.

It seems to me that the reasons why Ministers have been reluctant to publish forecasts have little or nothing to do with the accuracy of the forecasts. Of course, it is always embarrassing to be wrong; but the average man knows enough about forecasts from his study of form or his weekly flutter on the pools to recognise that error is human (even if he does not couple this with forgiveness). Error is not the main hostage that a Chancellor thinks he is giving to his political opponents. It is rather that an official forecast becomes in the act of publication a plan. As soon as the figures are released they imply that the Government is content that events should be in accord with forecast. This exposes the Government to immediate criticism not for what it has done but for what it has not done. Some people are bound to be dissatisfied with the prospects summarised in the forecast; they will agitate for a change of plan where previously they found no fault in the actual policies of the Government. On the other hand, if things fall out differently from forecasts the Government will be asked what it proposes to do where there might otherwise be no presumption at all that policies were in need of change.

On top of this must be put the reluctance of any government to give publicity to a situation plainly calling for action when it has still to decide what to do. This means that while a government may publish a forecast after the Budget (*i.e.*, after it has taken all the action it thinks necessary), it will be reluctant to publish forecasts at set times throughout the year. Governments hate issuing bad news at any time; but they like it still less if they have not had time to couple it with mitigating announcements outlining how they propose to improve matters.

There is also a real risk that the Government will insist on cooking the forecasts rather than reveal how awful the situation is. If things are worse than is commonly believed the Government may well hesitate to give a jolt to opinion, especially if it has reason to expect an early improvement. Forecasts are in fact no different from other pieces of information which governments would like to withhold: a government which jibs at revealing the state of its reserves of foreign exchange or its short-term foreign debts is hardly likely to want to parade the size of the external deficit that it expects. Similarly, where government thinking on other matters is shrouded in secrecy it would be surprising if there were full and regular disclosure of official economic forecasts. But there are, I admit, some paradoxes. In the United States, where in other respects government is more open than in the United Kingdom, there is no appreciable difference in public access to official forecasts. And in the United Kingdom governments that were unwilling to issue forecasts covering the next twelve months have been known to issue plans covering the next four or five years.

I am not, of course, seeking to argue against publication of forecasts. I am merely emphasising some of the inconveniences from the Ministerial point of view in putting official forecasts in front of an unsophisticated public. Publication exposes them to pressure, and the pressure may be misguided. They may be less free to decide what to do or forced into acting at the wrong time and in the wrong way. But it is axiomatic that Ministers are always under pressure and that they may be no less misguided than their critics. It is arguable that they should not have the freedom of manoeuvre that they derive from non-disclosure and that if publication were on a regular footing Ministers would be at more pains to avoid situations in which publication would be a serious embarrassment.

My own view is that the issue is not nearly as important as it appears. There is no particular reason to publish official forecasts if outside forecasts are as reliable. The Government has no monopoly of forecasting, and the more competition there is the better. Non-official forecasters may lack the resources at the disposal of the Government,[1] and there is always some secret

[1] Particularly in Britain. I know of no more appalling fact about British industry than that it subscribes less than £30,000 annually to the National Institute for Economic and Social Research.

information to which they do not have access. But there is no reason why they need stand at any great disadvantage. It should be an aim of government to put them on as equal a footing as possible in respect of access to information: not just current economic information but the analysis and research that goes on in government into how the economy is actually working. The official forecasters on their side have much to learn from the weight of research that is carried on outside the government machine, particularly if it can be focussed more clearly on the specific problems encountered in forecasting. Econometric analysis of specific relationships should be the subject of a joint programme of research, and these relationships should be kept under continuous review.

What is needed most is a deeper appreciation of the purposes of economic forecasting and of its limitations. At best, forecasting amounts to no more than a full and systematic review of the evidence in the light of the best available understanding of the way in which the economic system works. This calls for a considerable staff of high quality, which up till now has been hard to recruit: too few first-class economists have been willing to dedicate themselves to this kind of work. Moreover, although techniques have greatly improved and methods have grown enormously in sophistication in the last twenty years, the margins of error in the forecasts themselves, even when small in relation to the magnitudes involved, remain large in relation to policy objectives and to the reserves held against contingencies. This seems to me to imply not that forecasting is a waste of time but that the policy objectives have been in the circumstances too ambitious. It is not possible to run an economy without some fluctuations in economic activity and unwise to try to run it without considerable fluctuations in the balance of payments. If fluctuations are avoided we ought not to give all the credit to the forecasters and policy-makers: luck plays its part too. But if fluctuations do occur—as they will—let us not blame the forecaster too hastily for failing to predict them in time.

ALEC CAIRNCROSS

St. Peter's College,
Oxford.

[7]

Journal of Forecasting, Vol. 1, 37–48 (1982)

The Role of Macroeconometric Models in Forecasting and Policy Analysis in the United States

STEPHEN K. McNEES
Vice-President and Economist, Federal Reserve Bank of Boston, Boston, Massachusetts, U.S.A.

ABSTRACT

This article stresses how little is known about the quality, particularly the relative quality, of macroeconometric models. Most economists make a strict distinction between the quality of a model *per se* and the accuracy of solutions based on that model. While this distinction is valid, it leaves unanswered how to compare the 'validity' of conditional models. The standard test, the accuracy of *ex post* simulations, is not definitive when models with differing degrees of exogeneity are compared. In addition, it is extremely difficult to estimate the relative quantitative importance of conceptual problems of models, such as parameter instability across 'policy regimes'.

In light of the difficulty in comparisons of conditional macroeconometric models, many model-builders and users assume that the best models are those that have been used to make the most accurate forecasts are those made with the best models. Forecasting experience indicates that forecasters using macroeconometric models have produced more accurate macroeconomic forecasts than either naïve or sophisticated unconditional statistical models. It also suggests that judgementally adjusted forecasts have been more accurate than model-based forecasts generated mechanically. The influence of econometrically-based forecasts is now so pervasive that it is difficult to find examples of 'purely judgemental' forecasts.

KEY WORDS   Econometric models   Unconditioned models   Exogeneity
(degree of)   Ex-post simulations   Invariance across
'policy regimes'

The quality of the major macroeconometric models is hotly disputed. Use of these models is widespread and growing (Naylor, 1981). In business, government, and research, macro-econometric models are widely employed as a tool for forecasting and policy analysis. While reliance on macroeconometric models is clearly increasing, criticism of these models has been escalating. The professional literature contains numerous severe objections to the economic theories on which the models are based, the ways the models are estimated, and their ability to cope with the problems of forecasting and policy analysis. A significant portion of the academic community seems to feel these models are so fundamentally flawed that they are worthless, at best, and more probably pernicious. Lurid descriptions of forecasting failures appear regularly in the press. Senior decision-makers express scepticism about the value of the information generated with the models.

0277–6693/82/010037–12$01.20
Received August 1981

This paper considers three common claims made against macroeconometric models:

(1)   Forecasts from these models are generally poor and specifically inferior to judgemental forecasts.

(2)   Econometrically generated forecasts are inferior to those generated with statistical time series models.

(3)   Existing models are worthless for policy analysis.

This paper finds no strong support for any of these claims, even though, when properly rephrased, each of the claims contains a kernel of truth—the major models must be managed intelligently (and extensively) to produce good forecasts, these models often exhibit substantial residual autocorrelation and other signs of 'misspecification', and the models seem unlikely to be strictly invariant to dramatic changes in the behaviour of exogenous variables such as policy instruments.

The issue is not, however, whether the major macroeconomic models are ideal. They clearly are not. Model-builders themselves freely acknowledge that their models are misspecified and continually seek to improve them. The question raised here is whether any *other* existing model is immune from these and other criticisms. Specifically, is there evidence that any *alternative* models (or non-model techniques) are available which are more useful for economic forecasting and policy analysis?

A definitive answer to this question would require a methodology for model evaluation. Unfortunately, no definitive methodology exists for weeding out deficient models and guiding users to the model (or models) best suited to their purposes. In addition, existing model evaluation procedures have seldom been implemented so that remarkably little useful evidence is available for choosing among alternative models.

THE ROLE OF ECONOMETRIC MODELS IN FORECASTING

Models versus judgement: the two-way interaction of 'art' and 'science'
Much of the confusion about models stems from the debate about the relative contributions of 'models' and 'judgement' in forecasting. This debate typically overlooks a simple fact: The models used in forecasting and policy analysis are *conditional* models.[1] A conditional model is a system of equations (or a solution procedure) which cannot be solved without additional information, typically the values of the variables the model takes as exogenous. Conditional models cannot forecast; their forecasting accuracy is undefined.

All forecasting requires some degree of judgement. Forecasting with an econometric model requires, at a bare minimum, that the forecaster choose the future values of the exogenous variables of the model. This degree of judgement is an integral, inevitable part of forecasting with an econometric model.

Model-based forecasts reflect the *interaction* of a model and a forecaster. The accuracy of the forecast depends on *both* the quality of the model *and* the skill of the forecaster. Forecast evaluation involves the search for the best forecaster/model combination, not the best forecasting model. Only in the unlikely event that *all* forecasters could forecast more accurately with the *same* model might that model accurately be described as 'the best forecasting model'.

Although a model can be combined with estimates of the future values of its exogenous variables to produce a forecast, few forecasts are generated so mechanistically. Forecasters are aware of the formidable conceptual problems in constructing a system of equations to represent an entire

---

[1] Forecasts of unconditional models are discussed in the next section of the paper.

economy, and are aware of some of the specific weaknesses of the models they use. In addition, forecasters recognize that models are only models, approximations of what are regarded to be the essential characteristics of the economy. They are aware that numerous political, social, cultural, psychological, and even economic factors generally believed to be important in influencing economic behaviour are not incorporated in formal models. Consequently, virtually all forecasters who try to present the most accurate forecasts possible, adjust the mechanical or 'first pass' forecast generated with their models in an attempt to account for these limitations.

Although these adjustments could either add to or detract from the accuracy of forecasts, the widely held presumption is that these adjustments contribute significantly to greater accuracy. The primary reason for this presumption, however, is probably the simple fact that the practice of adjusting is so commonplace. This, of course, is not really evidence that adjustments do help. In fact, there is remarkably little empirical evidence on whether and how much these types of adjustment add to the accuracy of forecasts. The best available evidence on this subject comes from an experiment conducted at the Bureau of Economic Analysis (BEA) of the U.S. Commerce Department.[2] In the early 1970s the BEA generated both 'mechanical' and judgementally adjusted forecasts. The accuracy of the two sets of forecasts has been described in some detail elsewhere (McNees, 1975, pp. 28–29). The *adjusted* forecasts of the GNP implicit price deflator and of personal consumption expenditures for non-durable goods and services were substantially more accurate than the mechanically generated forecasts. However, the *mechanical* forecasts of business fixed investment and nominal GNP were noticeably more accurate than the adjusted forecasts. The accuracy of the two sets of forecasts was about the same for the other seven variables examined.

The role of judgemental adjustments in forecasting accuracy is an important but neglected subject. The conventional wisdom on the matter seems to be that these modifications contribute to much greater accuracy, and the inference is often drawn that the underlying models are unsatisfactorily unstable. This conventional view may well be correct, but the question is of sufficient importance that it would be desirable to try to gather additional evidence. Once some ground rules were established, this evidence would be fairly easy and inexpensive to generate; econometric forecasters would need only to store their 'first pass' or 'mechanically generated' forecasts for comparison with their final, adjusted or 'control' forecasts.

This kind of information could provide an estimate of the effects of judgemental adjustments other than the inevitable judgements involved in selecting future values of exogenous variables. This information might help to distinguish the different roles that judgement can play in econometric forecasting but it would *not* enable us to disentangle the roles of models and judgement because the interaction runs both ways. Many of these adjustments should be regarded as insights gained from preliminary experimentation with the model.

Some scholars have attempted to estimate the role of econometric models versus judgement in forecasting by comparing the accuracy of adjusted, model-based forecasts with 'purely' judgemental forecasts. Such comparisons ignore important interactions between model-based results and judgemental forecasters. Judgemental forecasters (myself included) continually experiment with various individual econometric relationships very much like, and probably

---

[2] The only other evidence is from a series of forecasts Ray Fair generated mechanically with his forecasting model. The mechanically generated forecasts were generally inferior to other ex ante forecasts, though the margin of inferiority varied widely (from substantial for real GNP, the implicit GNP price deflator, and personal consumption expenditures for durable goods to negligible for net exports, business fixed investment, and personal consumption expenditures for non-durable goods and services). (McNees, 1975, pp. 25–26.) These results are not a clean test of the role of judgemental adjustments, however, because they also reflect differences in the quality of the different models and in the skill of the forecasters in selecting future values of exogenous variables.

inspired by, those that appear in formal, simultaneous models. Paul Samuelson, a judgemental forecaster with a sound background in economic theory, has put the point clearly: 'It is idle to pose the debate in the form of judgement versus quantitative science. For in plain truth every judgement of the modern age rides piggyback on the output of hundreds of operating computers. When, abacus in hand, I confront the blank back of an envelope, my views are already contaminated by knowledge of what is being said by Klein's Wharton model, Otto Eckstein's model at Data Resources, Inc., the UCLA and Ann Arbor models and a dozen other econometric systems'. (Samuelson, 1980).

Whereas there is precious little relevant information to use to disentangle the roles of models and judgement, there is a large amount of published data on the accuracy of the judgementally adjusted, econometrically based economic forecasts. To summarize briefly the record of several prominent forecasters over the past decade (McNees, 1979a):

(1) None of the major forecasters dominates the others for all or even most variables and forecast horizons. Even for a specific variable and horizon the differences in accuracy among the major forecasters are typically, though not invariably, rather small. In addition, there is no test to determine whether the differences are significant in the statistical sense.

(2) Although there is a natural tendency for the accuracy of predicted quarter-to-quarter changes to deteriorate over longer forecast horizons, this tendency is *not* universal. For some variables the two-quarter-ahead change is predicted no more accurately than the six-quarter-ahead change. More important, although errors of cumulative changes tend to increase in absolute magnitude over longer horizons, for some variables the increase is less than proportionate to the increase in the horizon due to offsetting errors. Thus, when cumulative changes are all expressed as annual rates of growth, the forecasts of some variables are more accurate over longer horizons. For example, the mean absolute error of forecasts of next quarter's real GNP growth expressed at an annual rate is about 2.0 to 2.5 percentage points whereas the mean absolute error of the four- or six-quarter-ahead annual rate of growth of real GNP is about 1.5 percentage points. (This result obviously stems from expressing cumulative changes at a standard, e.g. annual, rate. Comparisons of cumulative changes over varying time spans require some form of standardization to make much sense.)

(3) The most important source of variability in forecast accuracy is the period of time being predicted, not the forecaster or the forecast horizon. Some periods are clearly harder for everyone to forecast than others. The size of forecasting errors has varied widely during the last decade. (This feature highlights the importance of using *identical* forecast periods when comparisons of different forecasters are made.)

Perhaps because forecast errors have varied so widely over the past decade, forecasting performance has been both praised and ridiculed. An intelligent assessment of the quality of this performance should be *relative* because there is no absolute standard for judging a forecast. A large absolute error may correspond to a brilliant forecast if all other forecasters were even further off the mark. Similarly, a small error is not a sign of forecasting skill if all other forecasters were even more accurate. The only sensible answer to the question of 'How good were these forecasts?' is to answer the question 'Were other forecasts better or worse?' If a systematically superior record can be documented, these performances are not impressive. If no one can document a systematically superior performance, condemnation of these forecasts is equivalent to a wish that the future were less uncertain or dismay that we were not smarter than we in fact were.

Comparisons with forecasts of unconditional models

The standard of comparison for judging economic forecasts traditionally has been very 'naïve' unconditional models, such as no-change, same-change, or average-change rules-of-thumb. More recently, the most popular standard of comparison has become the statistically more sophisticated 'time series' models, typically univariate stochastic processes of integrated autoregressive moving average (ARIMA) form in the Box–Jenkins format. An extensive literature has developed comparing time series forecasts with others. Here, I will focus solely on that part of the literature that deals with time series forecasts of macroeconomic variables in the United States.

In the early 1970s, several studies (Cooper, 1972; Nelson, 1972; Cooper and Nelson, 1975; Ibrahim and Otsuki, 1976) compared time series forecasts with ex post simulations of econometric models.[3] All of these studies found time series equations were more accurate for most variables, often by rather large margins. However, all of these studies focused *exclusively* on one-quarter-ahead predictions. This limitation is a critical one that severely restricts the usefulness of the results.

Zellner and Palm (1974) have shown that, under the assumption that all exogenous variables are generated by covariance stationary processes, *any linear* econometric model can be transformed into 'final equations' in the time series form. In other words, some set of time series equations implicitly incorporates the *complete* structure of any linear model. If the two are the same, it would hardly be surprising to find their error characteristics are similar. If time series equations were less accurate than any model that met these assumptions, it would only indicate that the appropriate set of time series equations had not been used.

Virtually all models used in macroeconomic forecasting contain many elements of nonlinearity and thus have no stable time series counterparts. However, over a very short, one-quarter period a nonlinear model can be closely approximated by a linear version which in turn would also have its exact time series counterpart. One of the most important differences between macroeconometric forecasting models and time series equations will emerge only over longer, multi-period horizons. To repeat, all of these early studies ignored multi-period forecast horizons.

Moreover, all of these studies were based on ex post simulations of econometric models. Ex post simulations obviously reflect the information in the actual, future values of the exogenous variables in the model. Extrapolations of time series equations, on the other hand, contain only information available at the start of the projection period. Comparisons of ex post model simulations and time series forecasts reflect, therefore, both the quality of the models, including their different assumptions about linearity, and differing amounts of external information. This type of comparison, in other words, must be interpreted with extreme caution because of the major inherent differences in the two approaches. Whatever can be learned from such comparisons—and in my view it is usually very little—these early comparisons of ex post simulations tell us very little about our present subject, comparative ex ante forecasting ability.

Three more recent studies (Hirsch, Grimm and Narasimham, 1976; McNees, 1979b; and Eckstein, 1981) compared time series forecasts with ex ante forecasts (see Table 1). These more recent multi-period studies reach conclusions directly opposite to those of the earlier one-period studies. They all suggest that time series forecasts of the major macroeconomic variables are usually, though not always, less accurate than ex ante forecasts. All of these recent studies also indicate that the margin of superiority usually, though not always, increases with increases in the forecast horizon, as would be expected if nonlinearities are important.

How solid is this evidence? Two of the studies cover several variables—Hirsch *et al.* eight and Eckstein 20—but are based on fairly small samples—Hirsch *et al.* seven to 12 observations, Eckstein four and seven. My study deals with only four macroeconomic aggregates but covers a seven and one-half year period. In my study, univariate time series equations were refitted each

---

[3] Cooper and Nelson also examined what they refer to as 'ex ante model forecasts'. This part of their paper is discussed in the following section of the paper.

Table 1.   Forecast accuracy relative to time series equations ratio, root mean squared errors

Variable	Forecast horizon (quarters)					
	1	2	3	4	5	6
A. (Hirsch, Grimm and Narasimham, 1976) 1970:3–1973:2						
Mechanically generated BEA forecast						
GNP	0.51	0.53	0.52	0.48	0.44	0.49
Real GNP	0.49	0.39	0.39	0.42	0.44	0.45
Real personal consumption expenditures	0.72	0.75	0.67	0.73	0.68	0.58
Real non-residential fixed investment	0.78	0.65	0.46	0.29	0.45	0.30
Real changes in business inventories	2.15	2.09	2.87	1.70	1.57	0.94
Corporate profits	1.01	1.07	0.84	0.59	0.46	0.43
GNP Deflator	0.60	0.53	0.57	0.61	0.58	0.36
Unemployment Rate	0.83	0.45	0.32	0.32	0.33	0.31
Judgementally adjusted BEA forecast						
GNP	0.30	0.37	0.31	0.35	0.36	0.26
Real GNP	0.29	0.37	0.30	0.35	0.32	0.20
Real personal consumption expenditures	0.71	0.70	0.75	0.71	0.70	0.49
Real non-residential fixed investment	0.60	0.61	0.58	0.40	0.64	0.48
Real changes in business inventories	1.22	1.44	1.87	1.20	1.06	0.78
Corporate profits	0.93	0.92	0.70	0.53	0.44	0.39
GNP deflator	0.64	0.64	0.65	0.67	0.57	0.28
Unemployment rate	0.39	0.29	0.22	0.30	0.31	0.29
B. (McNees, 1979) 1970:3–1977:4						
ASA/NBER survey						
Real GNP	0.55	0.59	0.65	0.67	0.69	—
GNP deflator	0.88	0.95	0.95	0.88	0.87	—
Unemployment rate	0.50	0.57	0.64	0.64	0.63	—
GNP	0.57	0.55	0.51	0.45	0.39	—
Chase econometrics						
Real GNP	0.47	0.54	0.62	0.64	0.69	0.73
GNP deflator	0.89	0.95	0.91	0.88	0.87	0.82
Unemployment rate	0.75	0.86	0.73	0.71	0.75	0.78
GNP	0.47	0.55	0.51	0.43	0.39	0.38
DRI						
Real GNP	0.60	0.66	0.73	0.75	0.77	0.79
GNP deflator	1.11	1.11	1.05	0.92	0.90	0.85
Unemployment rate	0.75	0.71	0.64	0.64	0.69	0.67
GNP	0.53	0.52	0.51	0.48	0.44	0.36
Wharton EFA						
Real GNP	0.60	0.61	0.59	0.58	0.63	0.67
GNP deflator	0.72	0.84	0.86	0.81	0.77	0.76
Unemployment rate	0.75	0.86	0.73	0.71	0.63	0.61
GNP	0.66	0.62	0.56	0.45	0.41	0.38
C. (Eckstein, 1979) DRI, 1977:4–1979:2						
Real GNP	0.94	—	—	0.87	—	—
GNP	0.66	—	—	0.63	—	—
Personal consumption expenditures	0.80	—	—	0.96	—	—
Non-residential fixed investment	0.71	—	—	1.01	—	—
Government purchases	0.85	—	—	0.78	—	—
State and local government purchases	0.83	—	—	0.74	—	—
Changes in business inventories	0.99	—	—	1.06	—	—
Consumer price index	0.84	—	—	0.89	—	—
Federal funds rate	0.46	—	—	0.41	—	—
Treasury bill rate (3 month)	0.47	—	—	0.42	—	—

Table 1.—*contd.*

Variable	Forecast horizon (quarters)					
	1	2	3	4	5	6
C. (Eckstein, 1979) DRI, 1977:4–1979:2						
Corporate bond rate	0.84	—	—	1.16	—	—
Industrial production	0.56	—	—	0.39	—	—
Capacity utilization	0.46	—	—	0.35	—	—
Unemployment rate	1.09	—	—	1.32	—	—
Housing starts	0.27	—	—	1.01	—	—
Auto sales	0.96	—	—	0.99	—	—
Corporate profits	0.81	—	—	0.79	—	—
Consumer sentiment index	0.83	—	—	0.87	—	—
Standard & Poors 500 Index	0.41	—	—	0.36	—	—
M-1	0.62	—	—	0.60	—	—
D. (McNees, 1981b) (Nelson BMARK) 1976:1–1980:3						
ASA/NBER survey						
GNP	0.83	0.87	0.75	0.67	—	—
GNP deflator	1.00	0.80	0.80	0.73	—	—
Real GNP	0.74	0.79	0.79	0.48 ·	—	—
Chase						
GNP	0.96	1.10	1.07	0.99	—	—
GNP deflator	0.80	0.70	0.87	0.91	—	—
Real GNP	0.93	0.90	0.88	0.86	—	—
DRI						
GNP	0.89	0.90	0.77	0.76	—	—
GNP deflator	1.00	0.90	0.87	0.82	—	—
Real GNP	0.82	0.73	0.58	0.50	—	—
Wharton						
GNP	0.88	0.83	0.68	0.57	—	—
GNP deflator	1.00	0.90	0.87	0.77	—	—
Real GNP	0.89	0.71	0.57	0.46	—	—
(McNees, unpublished) (Litterman time series) 1980:2–1981:1						
DRI						
Real GNP	0.93	1.22	1.17	0.95	—	—
GNP deflator	0.75	0.92	0.57	0.57	—	—
Unemployment rate	1.00	0.75	0.56	0.70	—	—

quarter up to the start of the forecast period with the most recently revised data. Since these were also the data used as 'actuals' to calculate errors, this may have given some advantage to the time series equations. On the other hand, construction of time series equations is itself a matter of judgement. For this reason, I recently examined the ex ante forecasts of two acknowledged experts, Charles Nelson of the University of Washington and Robert Litterman of MIT, who uses a vector-autoregressive model. The samples are very small but the results are sufficiently similar to the published results to provide some confidence that the published results are not due simply to inept time series modelling.

Time series modelling is still in its infancy and is rapidly developing beyond the univariate ARIMA stage upon which most forecast comparisons have been based. Either alone or in combination with more traditional techniques, time series modelling may be extremely valuable for forecasting, especially for those variables where the relevant theory or data are lacking. As Zellner has shown, time series approaches can be a valuable *complement* to econometric modelling, for purposes of model design and diagnostic checking.

44   *Journal of Forecasting*   *Vol. 1, Iss. No. 1*

Time series modelling, however, is certainly not a satisfactory *substitute* for econometric modelling. In particular, I know of *no* convincing evidence that suggests unconditional time series macroeconomic forecasts have been more accurate than those issued by prominent forecasters.

THE ROLE OF ECONOMETRIC MODELS IN POLICY ANALYSIS

Conceptual problems of macroeconometric models

The strongest criticisms of econometric models stem not from their role in forecasting but from their use in policy analysis. The strongest critic, Robert E. Lucas, Jr., has argued that policy 'simulations using these [major macroeconometric] models can, in principle, provide *no* useful information as to the actual consequences of alternative policies'. (Lucas, 1976, p. 20)

Lucas' criticism of the use of the major econometric models for policy evaluation is that the estimated structure of these models may be unstable under arbitrary changes in the behaviour of exogenous variables. He provides several theoretical examples that suggest that major policy can induce shifts in the estimated parameters. While the conceptual point seems valid—that dramatic changes in determinants of the behaviour of exogenous variables, changes in 'policy regimes', may alter the structure of a model from that which can be estimated before the shift occurred—the empirical importance of the point is not at all clear. How are we to distinguish 'major' shifts or changes in 'policy regimes' from the normal changes in exogenous variables? How many past changes of regimes have occurred and how large an impact did they have on the structure? When a major shift is under consideration, can we estimate how large an impact it may have or even the direction of the impact? Will a given change of regime alter the stability of some sectors of the model or the performance of the entire model? Will its short-run performance change little while its 'long-run' performance changes a lot? Or, will the instability be only temporary and the 'long-run' relationships unchanged? Are any models immune to the criticism? Do models which are more invariant to policy interventions have significantly different short-run or long-run policy implications? Questions like these would have to be answered in order to assess the empirical significance of the Lucas critique. To my knowledge, the answers are not available.[4]

Lucas disassociates his criticism 'from any denial of the very important advances in forecasting ability recorded by the econometric models, and of the promise they offer for advancement of comparable importance in the future'. He states that 'the major econometric models are (well) designed to perform the... task' of short-term forecasting but stresses that '... the unquestioned success of the forecasters should *not* be construed as evidence for the soundness or reliability of the structure proposed in that theory [of economic policy]'. (Lucas, 1976, pp. 20 and 23). Lucas is clearly insisting on a strict distinction between the quality of a model and the reliability of a forecast generated with the aid of the model.

The fundamental difficulty in policy evaluation

The problem of policy evaluation is extremely complex, and can perhaps best be introduced by a simple example to illustrate one of the primary reasons why the problem is so difficult to resolve. The fundamental problem can be illustrated in a decision-making context with one decision-maker and one policy adviser. The adviser must recommend either policy A or policy B. Suppose the

---

[4] The only evidence bearing on these questions appears in (Fair, 1979). Fair analyses the expected predictive accuracy of four macroeconometric models and concludes that the expected accuracy of his model is greater than that of the 'equilibrium' models developed by Sargent and Sims and a naïve statistical model. Fair's method of model evaluation (Fair, 1980) attempts to measure all sources of model error and does not provide an estimate of the importance of the point Lucas has stressed. For an assessment of Fair's procedure for comparing models, see (McNees, 1981a).

adviser recommends policy A and suppose, by stretching the imagination a little, that policy A is adopted by the decision-maker. If the outcome is a 'success', the policy adviser receives accolades. His advice is regarded as having been correct; he believes his analysis (model) was correct. He believes, in other words, he was right for the right reason, that the success was not due to 'luck' or other factors. If the outcome is a 'failure', the policy adviser is dismissed. His advice is deemed wrong; his analysis is believed to be in error.

The policy adviser may still claim that his advice was good and his analysis was correct. He may argue that policy A had the expected effect but that some *other* factor caused the failure. He may argue that if policy B had been adopted things would have turned out even worse than they did.

As we know, the adviser's defence may have been correct despite the 'failure' outcome, just as the acclaim he received in the 'success' case may have been undeserved.

The point of this simple example is that, in contrast to a forecasting situation where subsequent experience is sufficient to answer the question 'What will be?', *in policy analysis historical experience is not sufficient to resolve the hypothetical, counter-factual question* 'What would have been?' Policy analysis asks hypothetical questions, 'How would conditions have differed under (actual) policy A rather than under (alternative) policy B?'.

Answers to such hypothetical questions are inevitably contingent on some explicit or implicit model. If there were general agreement about how best to model the structure of the economy—if there were an explicit statement of all the relevant factors that may influence the success or failure of a policy—policy disputes could be resolved; or, with a stochastic model, the range of uncertainty could be described.

In practice, as we know, the problem cannot be resolved so simply. There are not one but many policy advisers, and their advice is based on many different models, all with different policy implications. Suppose there are several different models with drastically different policy implications. How can we determine which model is likely to be more reliable?

The dilemma of model comparison

Traditionally, economists have measured the quality of an econometric model by the accuracy of its (ideally, outside-sample) ex post simulations—i.e. model solutions based on the actual values of the exogenous variables. Actual values of exogenous variables *must* be used to *isolate* the quality of a conditional model. If *any* other than the actual values are used to simulate the model, any errors in the solution may not be due to misspecification of the model but may instead reflect the fact that the model was solved with inaccurate information. Strictly speaking, *an ex post simulation is the only pure test of the quality or 'validity' of a conditional model.*

On the other hand, ex post simulations inevitably combine both the quality of the model *and* the informational content of the actual values of the exogenous variables used to solve the model. Differences in the size and composition of the appropriate set of exogenous variables are a primary reason why different models have different 'policy multipliers' and differing policy implications. Comparisons of ex post simulations of different models with different degrees of exogeneity—different sets of exogenous variables—reflect not only the quality of the models but also the differing amounts of information in the exogenous variables. *Comparisons of ex post simulations do not, therefore, isolate the quality of different models,* their ability to convert the information contained in the values of their exogenous variables into information about the values of their endogenous variables.

This dilemma—that *only* ex post simulations isolate the quality of a conditional model but that ex post simulations of models with different degrees of exogeneity do *not* isolate the quality of the models—can be called 'the dilemma of model comparisons'.

One response to the dilemma of comparing models with different degrees of exogeneity has been

46   *Journal of Forecasting*   *Vol. 1, Iss. No. 1*

to construct models to explain the exogenous variables. Cooper and Nelson (1975), for example, compared model simulations with exogenous variable values taken from univariate time series models. This approach is subject to two problems:

First, it is particularly difficult, if not impossible, to construct a model that would accurately represent model-users' ability to choose exogenous variable values.[5] The future values of some exogenous variables, particularly policy instruments, could be known exactly. Any description based on the historical behaviour of these variables would be likely to overstate the difficulty of determining their values. In practice model-users can rely not only on their own past histories, but also on the paths of other exogenous variables. (For example, the corporate income tax rate is likely to depend on personal income tax rates as well as the investment tax credit and depreciation rules.) The model-user may also attempt to relate the behaviour of exogenous variables to the expected behaviour of endogenous variables—e.g. the monetary policy instrument will vary with the predicted rates of inflation and real growth. The exact relationship between any exogenous variable and the other variables in the model would depend on the type of policy experiment under investigation. It is hard to see how interdependencies such as these could be modelled in a way that would adequately depict the usefulness of the model in different applications.

However, even if this problem could be ignored or overcome, this approach could not succeed in isolating the quality of alternative models. At best, this approach would provide a test of expanded, hybrid models in which the exogenous variables of the original models had been made endogenous. This would be a *joint* test of the original models *and* a procedure for generating exogenous variables. This whole approach, in other words, seems to violate a critical feature of conditional models—the separation of variables into endogenous and exogenous categories, of which the latter is defined as outside the scope of the model. The dilemma of comparing conditional models with different degrees of exogeneity seems to be a real one with no escape.

Model 'validity' and performance

Many model practitioners would argue that the dilemma of model comparisons reflects the impossibility of evaluating conditional models apart from the quality of their performance in a particular application. Solution procedures can only be assessed by examining the accuracy of the solutions they yield. From this perspective, a model can be regarded as a tool which cannot itself perform a task but which may assist its user in accomplishing a task. The role of an econometric model is to capture the essential features of the economy enabling the model user to devote his attention to the novel or controversial features including those beyond the scope of the formal model. One feature of a useful model is to enhance the judgement of the model user. In this sense, the quality of a model cannot be separated from the quality of the performance that can be achieved using the model. With this perspective, many practitioners assume 'that best predictions will be made from best structural models' (Klein, 1971, p. 99) and take forecasting performance as the single best way to compare models that differ significantly in exogeneity (Klein, 1979, p. 312).

CONCLUSION

This article has stressed how little is known about the quality, particularly the relative quality, of macroeconometric models. Most economists make a strict distinction between the quality of a model *per se* and the accuracy of solutions based on that model. While this distinction is valid, it leaves unanswered how to compare the 'validity' of conditional models. The standard test, the

---

[5] This reservation also applies to Fair's method for estimating the expected predictive accuracy of econometric models.

accuracy of ex post simulations, is not definitive when models with differing degrees of exogeneity are compared. In addition, it is extremely difficult to estimate the relative quantitative importance of conceptual problems of models, such as parameter instability across 'policy regimes'.

In light of our inability to make definitive comparisons of conditional macroeconometric models, many prefer to focus instead on comparisons of model performance. Most model-builders and users assume that the most accurate forecasts are those made with the best models. Macroeconometric models have been used as a forecasting tool for more than a decade. This experience indicates that forecasters using macroeconometric models have produced more accurate macroeconomic forecasts than either naïve or sophisticated unconditional statistical models. It also suggests that judgementally adjusted forecasts have been more accurate than model-based forecasts generated mechanically. The influence of econometrically-based forecasts is now so pervasive that it is difficult to find examples of 'purely judgemental' forecasts.

There may have been a time when it was thought that macroeconometric models could foretell the future and decide questions of public policy. If there ever were such a time, the rain of criticisms that has fallen on macroeconometric models during the 1970s has brought welcome return to a more balanced perspective. No one now is willing to bestow blind faith upon any system of equations as a complete representation of the past and future structure of the economy.

In my view, however, the pendulum has now swung too far. The major models have been characterized as 'meaningless', 'without content', and providing '*no* useful information' about the economy. For these allegations to have content, there would have to be some superior, alternative models (or non-model techniques). Despite the acknowledged limitations of existing macroeconometric models, the superiority of available, alternative techniques is yet to be demonstrated.

ACKNOWLEDGEMENTS

I am indebted to my colleague Richard Kopcke for many helpful discussions. The opinions expressed in this paper are my own and do not necessarily reflect the views of the Federal Reserve Bank of Boston or the Federal Reserve System.

REFERENCES

Cooper, J. Phillip, and Nelson, Charles R., 'The ex ante prediction performance of the St. Louis and FRB-MIT-PENN econometric models and some results on composite predictors', *Journal of Money, Credit, and Banking*, 7 (1975), 1–32.

Cooper, Ronald L., 'The predictive performance of quarterly econometric models of the United States' in Hickman, B. G. (ed.), *Econometric Models of Cyclical Behavior*, Studies in Income and Wealth, no. 36, vol. II, New York: Columbia University Press, 1972, pp. 813–925.

Eckstein, Otto, 'Econometric models for forecasting and policy analysis: the present state of the art' in Sanderson, A. R. (ed.), *DRI Readings in Macroeconomics*, New York: McGraw-Hill, 1981, 2–18.

Fair, Ray C., 'An analysis of the accuracy of four macroeconometric models', *Journal of Political Economy*, 87(4) (1979), 701–718.

Fair, Ray C., 'Estimating the expected predictive accuracy of econometric models', *International Economic Review*, 21(2) (1980), 355–378.

Hirsch, Albert A., Grimm, Bruce T., and Narasimham, Gorti V. L., 'Some multiplier and error characteristics of the BEA quarterly model', in Klein, L. R., and Burmeister, E. (eds.), *Econometric Model Performance*, Philadelphia: University of Pennsylvania Press, 1976, pp. 108–125.

Ibrahim, I. B., and Otsuki, T., 'Forecasting GNP components using the method of Box and Jenkins', *Southern Economic Journal*, 42 (1976), 461–470.

Klein, Lawrence R., *An Essay on the Theory of Economic Prediction*, Chicago: Markhan Publishing Co., 1971.

Klein, Lawrence R., 'Use of econometric models in the policy processes' in Ormerod, P. (ed.), *Economic Modelling*, London: Heinemann, 1979, pp. 309–329.

Lucas, Robert E., Jr., 'Econometric policy evaluation: a critique in Brunner, K., and Meltzer, Allan H. (eds.), *The Phillips Curve and Labor Markets* (Carnegie-Rochester Conferences on Public Policy, 1), Amsterdam: North Holland; New York: American Elsevier, 1976, pp. 19–46.

McNees, Stephen K., 'An evaluation of economic forecasts', *New England Economic Review*, November/December (1975), 3–39.

McNees, Stephen K., 'The forecasting record for the 1970s', *New England Economic Review*, September/October (1979a), 1–21 of reprint.

McNees, Stephen K., 'The accuracy of macroeconometric models and forecasts of the U.S. economy' in Ormerod, Paul (ed.), *Economic Modelling*, London: Heinemann Educational Books (1979b), 245–264.

McNees, Stephen K., 'The methodology of macroeconometric model comparison' in Kmenta, J. and Ramsey, J. (eds.), *Methodology of Macroeconometric Models*, Amsterdam: North Holland, 1981a.

McNees, Stephen K., 'The recent record of thirteen forecasters', *New England Economic Review*, September/October (1981b), 5–21.

Naylor, Thomas H., 'Experience with corporate econometric models: a survey', *Business Economics*, **16**(1) (1981), 79–83.

Nelson, Charles R., 'The prediction performance of the FRB-MIT-PENN model of the U.S. economy', *American Economic Review*, **62**(5) (1972), 902–17.

Samuelson, Paul A., 'A Nobel for forecasting', *Newsweek*, November 3 (1980), 72.

Zellner, Arnold and Palm, Franz, 'Time series analysis and simultaneous equation econometric models', *Journal of Econometrics*, **2** (1974), 17–54.

Author's biography:
Stephen McNees is a vice-president and economist at the Federal Reserve Bank of Boston where his duties include the preparation and assessment of economic forecasts. Mr. McNees has published research on forecast evaluation, econometric model comparison, consumer spending and wage determination. He has served as chief economist at the Bureau of Economic Analysis of the U.S. Department of Commerce and taught at Harvard and Northeastern Universities and Williams College.

Author's address:
Stephen K. McNees, Vice-President and Economist, Federal Reserve Bank of Boston, Boston, Massachusetts, U.S.A.

[8]

Proc. R. Soc. Lond. A **407**, 103–125 (1986)
Printed in Great Britain

The interpretation and use of economic predictions

By Sir Terence Burns

H.M. Treasury, Parliament Street, London SW1P 3AG, U.K.

Treasury forecasts, both published and unpublished, of GDP and retail prices are analysed with reference to average absolute forecast errors and a benchmark index of variation. Forecasts of both GDP and the RPI looking two years ahead have become more accurate since the early 1970s, but there has been no marked improvement in one year ahead forecasts. The accuracy of annualized forecasts of GDP improves, and that of the RPI forecasts deteriorates, as the forecast time horizon is progressively extended from one to eight quarters ahead. Some evidence of forecast bias is presented; in the period up to 1979, GDP tended to be over-predicted, and inflation under-predicted. Since 1980 this pattern has been reversed. Analysis of Treasury forecasts and an average of U.S. forecasts shows them to be about equally accurate.

The role of forecasts in the implementation of economic policy is discussed. Systematic model-based forecasts provide a consistent framework of analysis, which can improve the operation of economic policy. But prediction errors, and the inertia of the economy, imply that there is only limited scope for discretionary, forecast-based, stabilization policy. Under the medium term financial strategy, MTFS, the policy emphasis has shifted to the medium term. The forecasts have been used to articulate assumptions for output, inflation and money GDP, and to provide the tax and expenditure framework behind the illustrative path of the PSBR. Without the forecasts, the conduct of monetary and fiscal policy would have been considerably more difficult. The paper concludes that, while reductions in the forecast errors of short-term forecasts may be difficult to achieve, there is hope that the accuracy of longer-term forecasts may continue to improve.

Introduction

It is difficult to imagine the conduct of economic policy without predictions. Either explicitly or implicitly the conduct of any policy implies a view about the future.

Marshall (1919, p. 7) was able to argue:

> 'A chief purpose of every study of human action should be to suggest the probable outcome of present tendencies; and thus to indicate, tacitly if not expressly, such modifications of those tendencies as might further the well-being of mankind.'

I have chosen to limit my attention to macro-economic predictions; that is, predictions about the behaviour of the economy as a whole. I will concentrate on their use in helping Government to conduct stabilization policy; that is, the

[103]

104   Sir Terence Burns

operation of policy (primarily fiscal and monetary) directed towards achieving
stable economic growth and the control of inflation. For convenience I will be using
the Treasury model and forecasts to illustrate my argument. But many of my
comments would apply to other models and forecasts.

Macro-economists routinely produce two types of prediction; a forecast for the
appropriate period ahead of the consequences of existing policies; and simulations
of the effects of changes in policy instruments or states of the world. In this lecture
I will be concentrating on the former. I will begin with some introductory
observations about the methodology of macro-based economic predictions before
examining some aspects of the Treasury forecasting record over recent years. After
a discussion of the implications of those results, I will conclude by examining the
role they can play in the implementation of policy.

THE METHODOLOGY OF ECONOMIC PREDICTIONS

Treasury forecasts and simulations are both produced by some combination of
man and machine. The machine is the Treasury model, a set of 1000 statistical
and accounting relationships. Man, in the first instance, is the collective group of
economists who operate the model. The machine is, of course, man-made. It
combines hardware in the shape of a computer and software in the shape of the
economic model. The group of economists who operate the model will include those
who helped to develop it.

The model plays a key role. It gives the analysts a consistent and comprehensive
structure that captures the economic relationships that can be identified from
historical data. A formal model ensures that the various interrelationships are
taken consistently into account, both in forecasting and in policy advice. It makes
possible many of the calculations that we do.

Although progress is being made, we are still some way from a position where
the model answers can be accepted without further human intervention. This is
standard international practice. McNees surveyed the large U.S. forecasting
organizations in 1981; they attributed between 20 and 50 % of the final forecast
to judgmental adjustments (McNees 1981). Adjustments are made in the light of
other information, commonsense judgements, past model error, and a knowledge
of its deficiencies. The useful exercise of this judgement is not limited to the
specialists. Non-specialists may also make a valuable contribution providing that
the issues are put to them clearly.

There are a number of characteristics of economic models that need to be taken
into account when applying judgement to results. First, models are necessarily
simplifications of an extremely complex structure and the model builder's task is
to devise a framework which captures the key inter-relations. The process of
simplification inherent in model building removes aspects of the real world. Faced
with new circumstances, a number of adjustments may be required to allow for
factors that are not fully captured already. For example, following the 1984
Corporation Tax changes, special allowance had to be made for their impact on
the timing of expenditure, the cost of capital and methods of finance.

Second, the range of experience available is often insufficient to discriminate

Economic predictions   105

clearly between alternative views of the world. In particular it is often difficult, statistically, to distinguish between models which are internally coherent in terms of different theories. No experimental data are available for estimating economic relationships; instead, we are forced to rely upon often fragile historical data. Third, a related point; economic models are inevitably dominated by the range of historical experience. This means they are more suitable for analysing relatively small changes from the current situation and can give misleading answers if confronted with extreme situations. If we are faced with a large shock (for example, the recent halving of oil prices) it is necessary to examine the results in much greater detail and question whether some of the effects may need exaggerating or attenuating. Fourth, there are difficulties in measuring the scale of responses and the time lags involved. Estimated coefficients can be imposed while doing relatively little damage to the 'fit' of the relationship. This is particularly important in relation to the longer-term properties of a model. Changes which have only a small impact on the short-term accuracy of predictions may greatly affect the longer-term properties of a relationship. Some progress has been made in recent years. More rigorous econometric tests and procedures are followed, some of which help in the incorporation of desirable theoretical properties. However, data limitations are a serious constraint.

Finally, it is very difficult to cope with significant changes to the way expectations are formed. Decisions of economic agents can be dominated by expectations about the future. Often, these expectations will be dependent upon experiences of the past, but not in any mechanistic way. We have seen some advances in considering and modelling expectations formation, but they only scratch the surface. It remains necessary to question whether the process of expectations formation built into the model is likely to change. This is particularly important with predictions that involve a sharp change of government policy or the environment. This may sound a formidable list of difficulties but I regard them as factors to be taken into account, rather than insuperable obstacles.

FORECASTING PERFORMANCE

A sensible interpretation of predictions must begin with an analysis of the forecasting record. The Treasury has a long tradition of making, and more recently publishing, evaluations of economic forecast against out-turn. Ever since the Industry Act Forecasts were first published in December 1976 they have included assessments of errors from past forecasts. There is, of course, an inherent interest in the extent to which past forecasts were in error. Even more important, however, errors in past forecasts provide the best, although still fallible, guide to the likely extent of errors in current forecasts. In this paper I use mainly unpublished, internal, forecasts, although some use is made of forecasts published at budget time.

Assessing the accuracy of past forecasts is not, however, easy, although this claim risks being interpreted as evasion. The problems have been well documented by those who have attempted to compare and contrast forecasting records; data revisions, changes to economic policy and unanticipated changes to the economic

106   Sir Terence Burns

environment being the most prominent. In this lecture I will try to give an outline
of the accuracy of Treasury forecasting over the past 15 years in relation to GDP
and inflation. I will examine the size of errors; the extent to which they deteriorate
as the forecast horizon is extended; any tendency towards bias; and whether there
are any signs of improvement as methods have become more sophisticated.

I am conscious that, by concentrating on a few variables, I may appear to
understate the progress that has been made in producing comprehensive and
detailed forecasts that help us to monitor a wide variety of information. Even so,
the ability to predict output and inflation remains a crucial test. By limiting the
analysis in this way I am able to look at the predictions in greater detail.
Comparing one forecaster with another, for the same period of history, and using
the same data, is fraught with problems. It is even more difficult to evaluate the
relative accuracy of forecasts made in, say, the 1960s with those in the 1970s or
1980s. This is because the variability of the data changes, sometimes drastically.
The relatively placid years of the 1960s, although not always perceived as such
at the time, look in retrospect to be fairly easy to forecast by comparison with
the 1970s, which were subject to a number of major surprises from both the world
economy and from policy.

To measure the accuracy of forecasts, I have chosen to compute the average
absolute error. I have also attempted to give an estimate of forecasting difficulty
to help put some of the errors into perspective. For this purpose, I have computed
an index of variation. In a technical sense, it measures the average absolute value
of the next higher order of difference compared with the difference we are
attempting to forecast. To give an example, we wish to evaluate our record in
forecasting the one-year ahead growth of GDP. The index of variation measures
the average absolute value of the difference between last year's growth and next
year's growth. This, if GDP always grew by 2%, the index of variation would have
a value of zero. If growth alternated between $+2\%$ and -2%, the index of
variation would have a value of 4. We can extend the definition to cover n-year
or n-quarter variation.

The index of variation provides a benchmark in the following way. If we always
forecast that the change in the next period will be the same as the change in the
previous period, the average absolute error will be the same as the index of
variation. We should be able to produce average absolute forecasting errors that
are smaller than the index of variation. It is not suggested that this is an absolute
standard but the index does provide a useful measure of changes in the difficulty
of forecasting for different variables or for different periods. I have not adjusted
the results for subsequent policy changes. Such adjustments are difficult. The
overall message is changed little if allowance is made using the forecasters'
judgements at the time about the effect of the policy changes. Next I shall present
some analysis of forecast errors; then I shall suggest some implications.

GDP forecasts

For GDP forecasts, I will examine two sets of information. The first is a set of
annual growth forecasts made early in each year. Each forecast measures the
change in (real) GDP between the previous calendar year and the current calendar

Economic predictions   107

year. I should emphasize that this is not a strong test, even if data are only available to the end of the previous year. The movement of output during the previous year, an early estimate of which is already known, will have a significant weight in the out-turn. However, annual growth forecasts are the most readily accessible information for the 1960s. These have been available since 1960 for the year in question, and since 1965 for two years ahead. The second data set includes 46 quarterly forecasts made between 1970 and 1985. Most of them cover a forecasting horizon of eight quarters; some made around the time of the first oil shock are for less than eight quarters; and for the most recent forecasts we do not have out-turn data for all quarters.

Figures 1 and 2 show uncentred five-year moving averages of the absolute error from one-year and two-year predictions. The two-year errors have not been

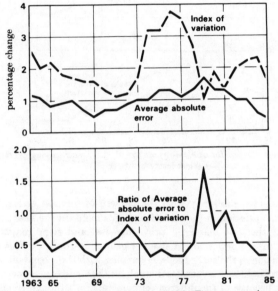

FIGURE 1. Forecast errors for GDP, one year ahead. (Five-year moving averages shown against last year of period.)

annualized and are therefore larger than the one-year errors. The diagrams also show the five-year moving average of the index of variation for one-year and two-year moving average of the index of variation for one-year and two-year growth rates. The lower part of the frame plots the ratio of the absolute error to the index of variation (both measured as five-year moving averages).

For both one-year and two-year forecasts the errors are bigger in the 1970s than in the 1960s or 1980s. By the end of the period shown the errors are similar to, if anything a little lower than, those experienced in the 1960s. The index of data

108   Sir Terence Burns

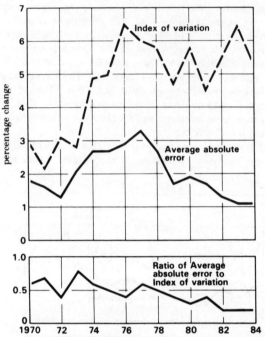

FIGURE 2. Forecast errors for GDP, two years ahead. (Five-year moving averages shown against last year of period.)

variation shows some similarity with the pattern of forecast errors. There is a sharp increase in variation in the mid-1970s. This included the final stages of the 'Barber boom', the first major oil price increase, and some major industrial disputes. Then, after a few years of steadier growth in the late 1970s there is an increase in variation in the early 1980s, coinciding with the second oil price shock.

It is difficult to make any generalizations about the trend of accuracy of one-year ahead forecasts because of the different circumstances, although recent forecasts compare well. The ratio of the absolute error to the index of variation shows no trend for the one-year forecasts. This suggests there has been little, if any, progress in forecasting GDP one year ahead. There are clearer signs of improvement in the accuracy of the two-year forecasts after allowing for the changing degree of difficulty. The ratio of the absolute error to the index of variation has been declining. The errors are less than those from the late 1960s even though the degree of data variation has been much bigger.

The quarterly GDP calculations are complicated by substantial revisions to the historical data. We have tried to allow for this by focusing on the predicted changes relative to the last quarter for which information was available at the time. In computing the out-turn, we have followed a similar procedure using the latest estimate of the change.

Economic predictions 109

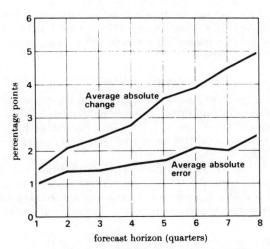

FIGURE 3. Forecast errors for GDP: 1970–1985.

Figure 3 shows the average errors by time horizon for the level of GDP for 46, mainly internal, quarterly forecasts made since 1970. The results show the extent to which forecast errors increase as we extend the time horizon of the forecasts. The pattern for GDP is that the errors increase relatively slowly, so that forecast errors from annualized data decline as the time horizon is extended.

I have also presented estimates of the index of variation over the eight quarter time horizon. In this context, they are equivalent to the average absolute errors from a predictor based on the rule that growth over the next n quarters will be the same as over the past n quarters, where n is the time horizon of the forecast. The pattern of forecast errors is broadly the same as the estimate of data variability. The ratio of the two series shown is relatively stable. If anything, the ratio of the absolute error to the index of variation is higher in the early quarters. A comparison of sub-periods is shown in table 1.

As with the annual data, the comparison is complicated by the changing degree of difficulty. They support the tentative conclusion I reached earlier. There has been some reduction in average errors but the index of variation is also lower after the first half of the 1970s. After allowing for that, the signs of improvement are most noticeable for the longer forecast horizon.

TABLE 1. FORECAST ERRORS FOR GDP BY SUB-PERIOD: 1970–1985

(Index of variation in parentheses.)

| | forecast horizon (quarters) | | | |
	2	4	6	8
1970–74	2.1 (3.2)	2.7 (4.0)	3.3 (4.8)	4.5 (5.6)
1975–79	1.4 (2.0)	1.3 (1.9)	1.7 (3.3)	1.9 (4.3)
1980–85	0.9 (1.4)	0.9 (2.7)	1.3 (3.6)	1.9 (5.1)

110   Sir Terence Burns

Table 2 shows the average errors which are an estimate of bias. There is a
tendency towards over-prediction between 1970 and 1979, although it is weaker
after 1975. Since 1980 the tendency is reversed, with evidence of under-prediction
for the longer forecast horizon.

Inflation forecasts

I have followed the same procedures in examining the inflation forecasts. The
comparison is more straightforward, however, as the Retail Prices Index is not
revised. Figures 4 and 5 show, for the RPI, the same information I presented earlier
for GDP. Forecasts are available since 1966 and hence the five-year moving
averages since 1970.

There are some similarities with the pattern of GDP errors, but there are also
some differences. In particular the four quarter errors behave in an unexpected
way. There is little change in the size of the error over the period shown; and errors
are small in the second half of the seventies. The index of variation follows a

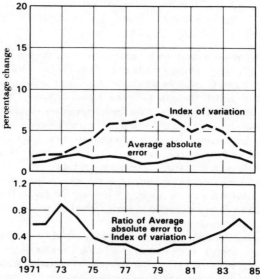

FIGURE 4. Forecast errors for RPI, one year ahead. (Five-year moving averages shown
against last year of period.)

TABLE 2. AVERAGE FORECAST ERROR (BIAS) FOR GDP FOR SUB-PERIODS: 1970–1985

	forecast horizon (quarters)		
	4	6	8
1970–74	2.4	2.6	3.0
1975–79	0.2	0.7	1.7
1980–85	−0.4	−0.9	−1.7

Economic predictions 111

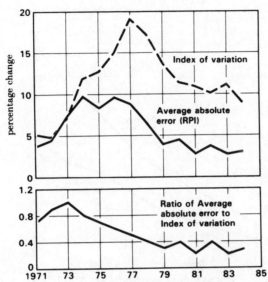

FIGURE 5. Forecast errors for RPI, two years ahead. (Five-year moving averages shown against last year of period.)

broadly similar pattern to the GDP variation. This suggests that inflation was rather more difficult to predict in the mid to late 1970s. However, the profile of four quarter errors does not reflect the variations in the data. As a result there is no convincing sign of steady improvement for the four quarter forecasts. There are large differences in the variation of inflation itself and no trend in the ratio of the absolute error to the index of variation.

The pattern of eight quarter errors is more like the GDP error pattern and the index of variation. The eight quarter inflation errors were rather bigger in the 1970s than in the late 1960s, or so far in the 1980s. There is more evidence of improvement with the eight quarter ahead predictions. The pattern of steady improvement is similar to the results for GDP. The detailed figures by time horizon for the quarterly forecasts are shown in figure 6, and the data are also tabulated by sub-periods in table 3. The annualized errors rise as we extend the forecast horizon. If anything the tendency is for the errors to rise relative to the estimate of variation.

Within the sub-periods the reduction of error in later years is concentrated in quarters 6 and 8; in the final period there is also a lower measure of variation of inflation.

The estimates of bias, shown in table 4, tend to be of opposite sign to those for output. Until 1974, there is a tendency for under-prediction; it is also evident in a weaker form until 1979. Since 1980 the pattern has been reversed with some over-prediction on average.

112   Sir Terence Burns

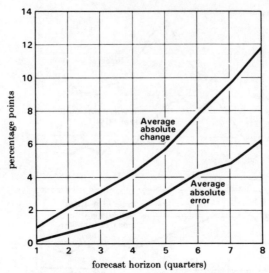

FIGURE 6. Forecast errors for RPI; 1970–1985.

TABLE 3. FORECAST ERRORS FOR RPI BY SUB-PERIODS: 1970–1985

(Index of variation in parentheses.)

	forecast horizon (quarters)			
	2	4	6	8
1970–74	0.7 (1.6)	2.2 (4.1)	5.9 (8.4)	10.5 (12.1)
1975–79	0.7 (3.3)	1.5 (6.1)	3.4 (8.8)	5.2 (12.7)
1980–85	0.7 (1.6)	1.9 (2.6)	3.4 (5.8)	4.4 (10.2)

TABLE 4. AVERAGE FORECAST ERRORS (BIAS) FOR RPI FOR SUB-PERIODS: 1970–1985

	forecast horizon (quarters)		
	4	6	8
1970–74	−2.1	−5.9	−10.5
1975–79	−0.9	−1.7	−3.5
1980–85	1.4	2.5	3.7

INTERPRETATION OF FORECASTING ERRORS

I interpret these results as suggesting that the forecasts of GDP and inflation do contain information. Forecast appraisal must be subjective. It is difficult to make firm statements and most of my remarks refer to tendencies. But for my own part I find the results encouraging.

Economic predictions   **113**

Changing forecasting methods

In considering the progress of errors over the years it is important to remember that Treasury forecasting methods have changed. (For a history of macro-economic model building in the U.K. see Ball 1984). Through most of the 1960s, Treasury forecasting was very much a matter of hand crafting with different parts being done in separate compartments, often in different Government Departments and not all at the same time. There were considerable doubts expressed in the 1950s and 1960s about the potential for using models for these purposes. A common conclusion was that this was impractical. It was feared that models inevitably would be rigid, over-precise and inflexible. It was argued that they would not be a substitute for the careful examination and adjustment of recent data; reading the tea-leaves of recent indicators; and adding a twist of judgement that can only be acquired by many years of experience.

From 1966 onwards, forecasts were produced at the London Business School by using a quarterly econometric model (Ball & Burns 1968). Initially the forecast errors were probably larger than those generated using conventional techniques, but with experience performance improved. One of the achievements of the past 15 years has been the successful integration of the two cultures. Writing in 1969, Sir Alec Cairncross (Cairncross 1969) feared that the use of models would mean trying to crush the past into a Procrustean bed of econometric relationships, when in reality the future is a series of discontinuous and unique events. In practice, within the framework of a model, it has still been possible to adjust recent data, assess trends and highlight special factors. Indeed, the model serves a valuable role in that process, and is part of the continuing exercise in monitoring the economy and its statistics as they appear. The comparison of the model's predictions and the out-turn for recent quarters provides valuable information about the extent to which special factors seem to have been at work. It has become possible to monitor a huge amount of information and build it into a consistent picture of developments. Without the use of models, only a limited amount of data can be monitored and interpreted.

The appearance of the Treasury model, beginning in about 1969, had implications for the organization of official forecasting, and led to forecasting becoming much more centralized in the Treasury. In the late sixties and early 1970s, there was growing confidence in forecasting. Extra resources were put in, and there were hopes that the accumulation of data and more sophisticated techniques would lead to major improvements in accuracy of forecasts and understanding of the economy. These hopes for forecasts were not realized. As we have seen, the forecasting record in the 1970s was in many way worse than in the 1960s. This largely reflected the much greater turbulence of the post-1971 world.

Is forecast performance improving?

The results I have presented suggest it is not possible to reach any decisive view about the development of forecast accuracy for one-year ahead forecasts, although there is some sign of improvement in recent years. If anything, we must conclude that, as far as the short-term horizon is concerned, there has not been much improvement in accuracy.

For two-year ahead forecasts the picture is clearer, with rather greater evidence of improvement. This probably reflects, in part, the extra resources devoted to modelling. The attention to longer-term properties of the model, better estimation techniques, and theoretical developments seem to have yielded returns. I also suggest that it reflects an increase in value of the human capital. Many members of the forecasting teams were engaged in forecasting for many years.

Learning from oil price shocks

The problems in the mid-1970s are themselves instructive. The model at the time had been estimated using data from a relatively quiet and trend-like period. As a result the coefficients were probably poorly determined. The forecasters then had to cope with the unexpected oil price shock. Following the oil price rise forecasters correctly predicted that it would damage economic performance, but the scale of the effect was underestimated. However, as a result of that experience, the models improved. We learned more about the response of the economy to inflation shocks, for example via the saving ratio, and the potential impact of the exchange rate. As a result, the forecasters handled the implications of the second oil price increase, and the disinflationary policy of the 1980s, much better.

Tendency to bias

Another interesting feature of the errors has been some tendency for persistent bias to occur. During the late 1960s and first half of the 1970s, the growth of money GDP was underestimated and the forecasts tended to be optimistic about the implications for output and inflation. In other words, the division of money GDP between output and inflation was worse than expected. Since 1980, money GDP has been over-predicted a little, and the forecasts have tended to be pessimistic about the prospects for inflation and output. The output–inflation split has been rather better than expected.

These biases broadly coincide with changes in the overall stance of policy. In the earlier period, fiscal policy was generally expansionary; monetary policy tended to be accommodating and the exchange rate fell considerably. In the second period, the budget deficit has been brought down, monetary policy has been actively directed towards disinflationary monetary conditions and the exchange rate has not shown any pronounced trend over the period even though it has been volatile. These forecast errors are consistent with the view that there is too much inertia in the modelling of inflation and output, and maybe too small an impact of inflation changes on output. They are also consistent with the view that forecasters may have paid too much attention to demand factors and not enough to supply factors.

Errors and the forecast horizon

I would also draw attention to the differences in error profiles as we extend the forecast horizon. Figure 7 shows the errors for GDP and the RPI on an annualized basis as we extend the time horizon of the forecast. The actual and predicted values

Economic predictions   115

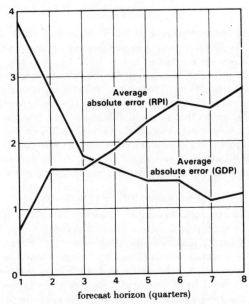

forecast horizon (quarters)

FIGURE 7. GDP and RPI annualized forecast errors: 1970–1985.

were annualized before computing the absolute error. For real GDP, annualized errors decline as we extend the forecast horizon; for the RPI they increase.

This result emphasises the inherent difficulty in predicting short-run movements of activity. They can be dominated by shocks like strikes or rapid changes in inventory levels. They can also be influenced by sudden changes in policy. However, there appear to be built-in stabilizers, which keep the average rate of growth of the economy fairly constant. The longer the period we cover, the more this tendency of the economy to converge on a fairly constant growth path becomes apparent. By contrast, there is no tendency for longer-term inflation to be more predictable than short-term changes. We have a fairly good knowledge of short-term price movements, but there is no inherent tendency for inflation to converge on any particular rate.

Comparison with univariate estimates

It is difficult to know how to judge forecast errors. We have tried to estimate univariate time series estimators for real GDP and inflation to serve as a benchmark. In each case, we only used the information that was available at the time. These time series estimators have been clearly outperformed by the actual forecasts since 1975. Between 1970 and 1975 there is less difference. However, I am very conscious that we have not put many resources into this exercise. Even so, it is worth noting that in the U.S., where *ex-ante* time series predictions have been issued to serve as a benchmark, the model based forecasts do better (see McNees 1979, 1983).

116   Sir Terence Burns

Data revisions

One interesting comparison is with the revisions to the GDP data. One of the complications to be faced in making short-term GDP forecasts is that the national accounts data, which the forecasters use, is itself subject to considerable revision over a period of years. For example, my earlier results suggested that forecasts of real GDP growth over the next four quarters have, on average, been subject to an absolute error of about 1.6 % since the 1970s. The estimate of growth over the most recent four quarters that was available at the time that these forecasts were being made was itself subject to an absolute error of 1.3 % on average. It is almost inevitable that errors in the data will have materially affected the accuracy of the GDP forecasts. Forecasters' views about the near future are, in many respects, conditional on their perception of what has been happening in the recent past.

Comparison with other forecasts

In principle it is interesting to compare these error statistics with those of other forecasters but I do not have time to address that today. Other U.K. forecasters have published forecast post-mortems (Robinson 1983; Savage 1983; NIESR 1984). Some of the characteristics of Treasury forecasts that I have described are present in other forecasts, but there are also some differences. It is also interesting to compare the errors I have presented today with the typical U.S. results. I appreciate that this runs into even more trouble than the comparison across time periods. Even so, it is of some interest. The U.S. figures are from McNees (1983, pp, 14 and 15) and cover the period of 1976–1983. They are an average of the early quarter forecasts produced by the major U.S. forecasters. We have calculated average Treasury forecast errors for the same period. I also show our computed index of variation for both U.S. and U.K. data.

TABLE 5. COMPARISON OF U.K. RPI AND U.S. CPI FORECAST ERRORS
PERCENTAGE POINTS; ANNUALIZED RATES OF GROWTH: 1976–1983

(Index of variation in parentheses.)

	time horizon (quarters)			
	2	4	6	8
H.M. Treasury	1.7 (4.8)	2.1 (4.4)	2.3 (5.0)	2.2 (5.4)
United States†	2.0 (2.4)	2.1 (2.6)	2.5 (3.3)	2.9 (4.0)

† Average of five U.S. forecasts.

TABLE 6. COMPARISON OF U.K. REAL GDP AND U.S. REAL GNP FORECAST ERRORS
PERCENTAGE POINTS; ANNUALIZED RATES OF GROWTH: 1976–1983

(Index of variation in parentheses.)

	time horizon (quarters)			
	2	4	6	8
H.M. Treasury	2.4 (3.6)	1.3 (2.4)	1.0 (2.5)	0.9 (2.4)
United States†	2.4 (4.1)	1.8 (3.3)	1.4 (2.7)	1.3 (2.9)

† Average of six U.S. forecasts.

Economic predictions   117

In table 5, I show the comparative figures for inflation. The annualized U.K. errors seem to be less than the equivalent U.S. errors, but the pattern is very similar. The estimate of variation is rather less for the U.S. than the U.K., particularly in the short-run, according to the measure I have been using.

The average GDP errors are shown in table 6 on the same basis. Again, the pattern seems to be that the U.K. average errors are less than the U.S. errors. However, our measure of variation also suggests that the U.K. GDP series varied a little less. Allowing for that, there seems to be very little difference in forecast performance.

My general, and provisional, conclusion from the comparison is that there is not a great deal of difference between the two forecasting records. There is no evidence in these figures that the U.K. performance is any worse.

The use of economic predictions

So far I have concentrated on the interpretation of economic predictions. I would now like to turn to the second part of my title; the use that can be made of predictions in the implementation of policy. I will discuss, in turn, the extent to which predictions are necessary to the conduct of policy; some limitations in their use; and their role in the implementation of the MTFS.

Are predictions necessary for the conduct of policy?

Some commentators have argued that we can do without these predictions altogether. Some of that scepticism derives from the feeling that anyone who involves themselves in predictions must be, at heart, an interventionist. However, the essence of prediction is an attempt to use the considerable array of information available systematically in the assessment of economic developments. Decisions have to be made against the background of an uncertain current position; they cannot be easily reversed, and many policy changes have consequences stretching years ahead. Some kind of forward look is therefore essential and it is best to do this in a consistent way. Once they are produced, forecasts have an important monitoring function as they provide a basis against which to judge subsequent developments.

Forecasting does not depend upon the objectives of short run demand management. Monetary policy, taxation and public expenditure decisions require forecasts of the whole economy because of the influence of the movement of output and inflation upon, for example, interest rates, tax collection and expenditure.

It is sometimes suggested that the alternative to prediction is the operation of policy rules. The idea of policy without predictions is an attractive prospect but, I suggest, impractical. In practice, the operation of policy rules themselves will involve the use of predictions. Even apparently straightforward policy rules, such as balanced budgets or monetary targets, require a considerable amount of technical expertise for their successful implementation. If the necessary predictions are not made in a systematic manner, they will simply be done in an *ad hoc* manner. The strength of model-based predictions is that they bring consistency and attention to detail. It is likely that the operation of economic policy of any kind can be improved by the use of systematic model-based forecasts. The discipline of recording predictions along with the logic involved in their preparation is an essential part of the learning process, along with regular post-mortems of the results. The model itself provides a description of how the economy works, and a benchmark against which to set our judgements.

The forecasting process in the Treasury serves a crucial coordinating role. In part, it is an attempt to bring together much of the forecasting work of the rest of the Treasury, the Inland Revenue, Customs & Excise and other Departments to provide a coherent, integrated picture of economic prospects and developments. It is important to stress that the extent to which the forecasting and policy analysis work, based in part upon model simulations, is an integral part of the Treasury administrative process.

Some limitations in their use

In summary, I am persuaded of the contribution of model-based predictions to the technical competence with which a government implements its policy. But there are limitations to their use; I will mention two.

First, it is my view that predictions from one type of model, on their own, are an unreliable basis to determine the operation of fiscal and monetary policy. The size of forecast errors means that it is dangerous to place excessive reliance on one approach. This suggests the need to monitor a range of forecasts and policy simulations based upon different views of the way economies function and respond. We also need to consider the implication of the tendency for inflation forecast errors to increase rapidly as we extend the forecast horizon without any pressure for inflation to converge on a particular rate, and for inflation forecasts to show a downward bias when the underlying inflation rate has been increasing. My own interpretation is that it suggests the need for a clear financial framework to maintain control of inflation. Whether that policy should be a fixed exchange rate, monetary targets or a money GDP objective is a secondary issue for the purpose of this exposition. Forecasts have a role to play within such a framework, and I will return to this later.

Second, there are important limitations in the extent to which predictions can be used in fine tuning demand, whether in real or money terms. The short-term forecast errors are large in relation to the scale of the measures Government can contemplate, particularly in the shorter term. Short-term fluctuations of demand due to inventory changes or world demand movements can be both surprising and, to a degree, self-correcting. Even if we could correctly forecast short-term fluctuations, it is very difficult to devise control techniques whose effect is exhausted in a short period. Thus, policies have to be reversed sharply to offset their longer-term effect. Such changes in policy are both disturbing and costly to administer. This does not mean that discretionary stabilization policy is impossible; but its scope is limited (see Committee on Policy Optimisation, H.M. Treasury 1978).

Many of the problems became evident during the years of demand management. During this period, short-term forecasts played an increasing role. Despite this growing influence, a view also emerged that neither domestic nor balance of

Economic predictions   119

payments forecasts were good enough guides for the policy decisions which were based upon them. The ambitions to fine tune demand within a narrow path meant forecasting fluctuations with greater accuracy than forecasters could reasonably be expected to deliver. In hindsight, it is striking how little tolerance could be permitted either with the unemployment or balance of payments objective.

It was inevitable that forecasts would be uncertain and liable to be wrong. It is clear from the various articles written by Chief Economic Advisers to the Treasury (see Hall 1959; Cairncross 1969; MacDougall 1974) that no-one realized the uncertainty more than the Treasury forecasters themselves. The conclusion I draw from this is that the design of policy must pay full regard to the limitations of the predictions. If excessive demands are made for forecast accuracy this can only lead to growing frustration with the forecasters. In turn, the forecasters can become unnecessarily defensive about the status of their predictions.

The problem of fine tuning the level of real demand is also one of not having the appropriate policy instruments to stabilize the economy in response to major disturbances such as unexpected wage and price shocks. The Korean war price shock in 1951 and both oil price hikes fall into this category. The breakdowns of wages policies have had effects similar in nature, if more subdued. The forces at work can be so powerful that it is difficult to imagine any policy response that would stabilize them. There may be no time to take any action that will stabilize the initial situation.

It can be difficult to accept that situations can arise unexpectedly or with a force that makes stabilization policy ineffective to deal with them; and yet the temptation to override this reality can lead to even greater instability in the future. The important role of predictions may be to anticipate the way in which the economy will unwind from the shocks and to help in making a judgement about the action that will help that adjustment. It is not to attempt to foresee what policy changes would stabilise the situation in the short term.

The role of prediction in the MTFS

I would like to close with some brief comments about the economic predictions that have been used during the years of the MTFS. They have played a different role to that of the 1960s and 1970s. During the years of Demand Management, the purpose of the short-term forecast and policy analysis was to help the Government to decide whether to run risks of unemployment on the one side, or of overheating and balance-of-payments deficits on the other; and to advise on the scale and type of measures that would bring the economy into line with the Government's objectives. Until the early 1970s, the striking feature was the extent to which the aim set out in the 1944 White Paper of maintaining 'high and stable' employment was, by all past and subsequent standards, successfully achieved. Even so, many commentators argue that frequently policy was destabilizing; emphasizing recovery when it was already under way, and restraining demand when activity was already slowing down.

I have already mentioned some of the growing doubts about economic predictions. From 1972 onwards, the major difficulties with demand management emerged. By 1976, there was not only disillusion with demand management; there

120   Sir Terence Burns

was also growing frustration with the forecasts. A number of changes in balance
have emerged. Within the framework of the MTFS, introduced in 1980, judgements
about fiscal and monetary policy have not relied solely upon short-term forecasts
of activity and inflation. Instead, the forecasts have taken on a slightly different
role; one that I suspect is more comfortable. The focus of the forecasts and policy
simulations has shifted to a more medium-term horizon. There has been less
emphasis on the short-term outlook and the evaluation of measures that would
be involved in bringing output quickly back to its desired path. The essence of
the MTFS has been a series of monetary ranges with an illustrative path for the
budget deficit, that was judged to be consistent with the profile for monetary
growth and the implied growth of money GDP; but which recognized the inevitable
uncertainty surrounding the forecasts.

The forecasts and assumptions that have been presented were not detailed
planning assumptions for the MTFS; they were primarily illustrative. They have
not been the only basis for setting the monetary targets and the illustrative PSBR
path, but they played a part in attempting to ensure that the financial framework
was consistent with the overall objectives. In operational terms, they were used
to compute the appropriate tax and expenditure framework that was consistent
with the illustrative PSBR.

There has been less emphasis on the detailed components of demand and more
on the government's finances and monetary developments. Treasury resources
have been increased in areas (such as the public sector and the financial system)
of direct concern to, and the responsibility of, Government. Other areas of
modelling and forecasting, such as the balance of payments and the industrial
forecasts, have been allocated fewer resources. Within the medium term horizon,
increased attention has been given to trying to identify balance-sheet pressures
upon the various sectors. As we have seen, the forecast errors have declined again;
maybe partly because of improved techniques but also because the profile of
inflation and output has become smoother and more predictable. Space prohibits
a detailed examination of their profiles, but I have presented the data for two
variables, money GDP and real GDP.

Table 7 shows the growth of nominal GDP over this period shown in successive
versions of the MTFS. For the first two years, the assumptions were not published
but were prepared for internal purposes. This is one indicator of the extent to

TABLE 7. MTFS ASSUMPTIONS FOR NOMINAL GDP (PERCENTAGE CHANGE)

date of publication

	1980†	1981†	1982	1983	1984	1986 Out-turn
1979–80	17¼	—	—	—	—	19.9
1980–81	17	13	—	—	—	13.8
1981–82	12	10¼	10½	—	—	10.1
1982–83	9¼	9¼	10	8¼	—	9.3
1983–84	10¼	10	9¼	8	8.0	7.8
1984–85	—	—	9¼	8½	7.9	6.9
1985–86	—	—	—	—	6.8	9.6

† Assumptions for nominal GDP were not published in the 1980 and 1981 MTFS.

Economic predictions   121

which the pressures from monetary and fiscal policy have been operating as anticipated. The table shows that in the early years we did not foresee fully the extent of the deceleration of nominal GDP that would be brought about by the MTFS framework. However, in general terms the outcome has been very much as expected.

A similar conclusion applies to the record on real output, which is shown in table 8. The output profile as presented in the 1980 MTFS involved a sharp reduction of output in 1980, a further small reduction in 1981 followed by some recovery in 1982 and 1983. The profile has been very much as expected, although the fall in 1981 was a little greater than anticipated in the 1980 MTFS. By the time of the 1981 MTFS however we had revised the outlook and this revised profile has been almost spot on.

TABLE 8. GDP 1980 PRICES†; ASSUMPTIONS FOR MTFS (PERCENTAGE CHANGE)

date of publication

	1980‡	1981‡	1982	1983	1984	1986 Out-turn
1980	−2.5	−2.5	—	—	—	−2.4
1981	−0.5	−2.0	−2.0	—	—	−1.4
1982	1	1	1¼	0.7	—	1.9
1983	2¼	2¼	2¼	2	2.8	3.3
1984	—	—	—	2¼	3	2.6
1985	—	—	—	—	2¼	3.3

† MTFS assumptions published between 1980 and 1983 were based on 1975 prices.
‡ Average growth from 1980 to 1983 as published was 1 % a year in the 1981 MTFS.

Although our experience of this type of medium-term framework is relatively short, so far the predictions are encouraging; and they have been useful. The operation of fiscal and monetary policy has been conducted against the background of the assumptions for output, inflation and money GDP. At times of unexpected velocity changes, the profile of money GDP has provided *ex-post* reassurance of the appropriateness of monetary conditions. The monitoring of the wage, price, productivity developments against expectations has helped in understanding some of the unexpected developments. The conduct of monetary and fiscal policy would have been considerably more difficult if we had not set out for our own use an articulate, coherent set of projections for the main variables.

CONCLUSIONS

I shall not attempt to summarize the material I have presented. Instead I shall conclude with some general observations.

Economic forecasting has been a growth industry over the past 25 years. In the early 1960s only the Treasury and National Institute undertook detailed forecasts. In 1966, at the London Business School, James Ball and I began preparing the first regular model based forecasts of the U.K. economy. Since then, there has been an explosion of forecasting activity. At the Treasury we monitor about 30 forecasts on a regular basis. The evidence I have presented suggests that over this

122   Sir Terence Burns

period, there has not been any marked improvement in Treasury forecasts of
output and inflation up to a forecasting horizon of about a year. But the results
for longer horizons are more encouraging, with some evidence of improvement.
Although some modest gain is possible, I do not expect to see any major
breakthrough in the accuracy of short-term forecasts in the years ahead.
There is only limited scope for improved estimation techniques and theoretical
developments to add to the accuracy of short-term forecasts.

Short-term forecasts of GDP are hampered because of difficulties with the quality
and timeliness of data. I emphasise this is not a U.K. problem alone, but applies
to macro-economic data everywhere. Forecasts of the inflation rate are less
troubled by measurement problems, although there is a separate problem with the
volatility of the housing costs element of the RPI, which is heavily dependent upon
interest rate changes. I am more hopeful of further reducing errors in longer-term
forecasts. Many of the developments in our understanding of the way economies
work are likely to have their pay-off in a better appreciation of some of the
medium-term pressures facing the economy; that is, over a forecast horizon of
between one and four years.

The two most likely developments that will bring that reduction of forecast
error are in our understanding of the supply behaviour of the economy and the
modelling of government behaviour. For many years supply behaviour was
neglected. This was understandable when the main focus of the forecasters'
attention was the short-term horizon, as demand factors are probably the most
important influences on output over that period apart from unpredictable supply
side disturbances (such as the oil price fall). The more we attempt to extend the
forecast horizon the more we need to give attention to supply factors; for example,
the determination of productive capacity, the extent to which demand is met from
home and abroad and the split of nominal demand growth between output or
inflation. For many years it was forecasting practice to assume unchanged
government policies in a very narrow sense; that is, planned expenditure levels,
unchanged tax and benefit rates, and unchanged interest rates and exchange rates.
Missing from this formalization was any constraint on the sustainability of policy
and the impact of that upon interest rates, the exchange rate and tax rates. In
part, this was because forecasts were being used to estimate the scope for
discretionary government action rather than to make unconditional predictions
of how events might unfold.

However, if we wish to provide a picture of the likely evolution of the economy
on the basis of the Government's broad policy objectives, it is necessary to define
'unchanged policies' in a more general sense, taking account of the likely policy
response in the event of pressures of one kind or another. This modelling of policy
responses is a relatively new activity, but a necessary aspect of any medium-term
prediction. In recent years we have been able to make some progress in this
direction by forecasting within a framework of money supply targets and an
illustrative path for the PSBR. Interest rate and tax changes have been built into
the forecasts as necessary. There are clearly other formulations depending upon
the particular way that Government choose to conduct policy.

Finally we must remind ourselves that in this lecture I have been discussing a

Economic predictions   123

type of prediction that has been formalized for 15–20 years. Over that period progress has been made; and it has been an exciting adventure for those who have participated. We set out with considerable hope but also considerable ignorance of what might be achieved.

I have attempted to give a personal interpretation of the achievements and failures. I will be surprised and dissappointed if further progress is not made in the years ahead.

I thank James Ball, Alan Budd, Huw Evans, Lawrence Klein, Chris Melliss and Bill Robinson for helpful discussions during the preparation of this paper; and Chris Allen, Gideon Bierer, John McLaren and Rod Whittaker for help with data and calculations.

REFERENCES

Ball, R. J. 1984 Macro-econometric model building in the United Kingdom, Discussion Paper no 121, London Business School Centre for Economic forecasting.
Ball, R. J. & Burns, T. 1968 An econometric approach to short run analysis of the U.K. economy 1955–66. *Opl Res. Q.* 19, 225–256.
Cairncross, A. 1969 Economic forecasting. *Econ. J.* 79, 797–812.
Hall, R. L. 1959 Reflections on the practical application of economics. *Econ. J.* 69, 639–652.
H.M. Treasury 1978 Committee on Policy Optimisation: Report. (Chairman: R. J. Ball). Cmnd 7148.
Klein, L. 1981 *Economic models as guides for decision making.* New York: Free Press.
MacDougall, D. 1974 In praise of economics. *Econ. J.* 84, 773–786.
McNees, S. 1979 Accuracy of macroeconometric models and forecasts of the U.S. Economy. In *Economic modelling* (ed. P. Ormerod), pp. 245–264. Heinemann.
McNees, S. & Ries, J. 1983 The track record of macroeconomic forecasts. *N. Engl. econ. Rev.,* November/December, pp. 5–18.
Marshall, A. 1919 *Industry and trade.* Macmillan.
National Institute 1984 The National Institute's forecasts of inflation 1964–82. *Natn. Inst. Econ. Rev.,* no. 107 (February), pp. 47–50.
Roberthall, Lord 1969 Introduction to NIER 50th issue. *Natn. Inst. econ. Rev.,* no. 50 (November), pp. 3–7.
Robinson, B. 1983 Forecasting errors: the LBS track record. *Econ. Outlook,* July. London Business School.
Savage, D. 1983 The assessment of the National Institute's forecasts of GDP 1959–82. *Natn. Inst. Econ. Rev.,* no. 105 (August), pp. 29–36.

Discussion

A. BRITTON (NIESR, 2 *Dean Trench Street, Smith Square, London SW1P 3HE, U.K.*). Measuring the accuracy of forecasts is one way of assessing the reliability of macroeconomic models. It is also possible to use the same forecasting record to assess more directly the reliability of these models in estimating the effects of economic policy. When policy is changed after a forecast has been made it is customary to make a correction for this change before examining the accuracy of that forecast. These policy corrections are calculated by the macroeconomic models. Then, when a regression equation is calculated relating out-turn to forecast, the policy correction can be included as an additional variable. If the regression coefficients are both close to unity, the policy correction as well as the

124   Sir Terence Burns

forecast is free from serious bias. Exercises done by using short-term forecasts
made by the NIESR and by the Treasury suggest that this is broadly the picture
in both cases.

SIR RANDOLPH QUIRK, P.B.A. (*The British Academy*, 20–21 *Cornwall Terrace*,
*London NW*1 4*QP, U.K.*). The similarities between the economic predictions (both
individually and in improvement over time) for Britain and the United States are
very striking. In view of the especially close relations between British and
American thinkers that one notes in many fields of inquiry, to what extent do
these similarities derive from shared features in the models producing them?

SIR TERENCE BURNS. The Treasury model, other large models of the U.K.
economy, and most of the models included in the data on U.S. forecasts, are large
quarterly models in the mainstream of work in this field. Because of the historical
development of economic model building they share common intellectual and
empirical foundations.

In addition, the economies of Britain and the United States share many features.
In the short term they tend to be dominated by random shocks; in the longer term
underlying cyclical movements, influenced by policy, tend to be more important.

P. MATHIAS, F.B.A. (*All Souls College Oxford OX*1 4*AL, U.K.*). The British
economy seems to have been growing since about 1780 at between 1.5 and 2.5%
per annum (at least for most of the time) with low deviations round this bracket.
Perhaps it is not so surprising that the longer term forecasts have tended to be
more accurate than the short-term forecasts, approximating more to this very
long-term long-established trend.

SIR JOHN MASON, TREAS.R.S. (*Centre for Environmental Technology, Imperial
College, London SW*7 1*LU, U.K.*). From what Sir Terence has said, it does not seem
reasonable to expect econometric models to provide accurate predictions either of
short-term changes or of very long-term developments far removed from recent
experience on which the models are based. It does seem sensible to use them to
indicate underlying trends in the medium term, to investigate the sensitivity and
response time of the economy to various fiscal and monetary controls and to help
decide between alternative ways of achieving a particular set of policy options
involving inflation, unemployment, economic growth, balance of payments, etc.

But although the ultimate objective of modelling is to make predictions I think
that, in their present state of development, it would be wrong to judge their value
solely in terms of the accuracy of their forecasts. Would Sir Terence agree that,
at present, they probably have even greater value in the synthesis, diagnosis and
simulation of the major components of the economy and for experimentation
designed to improve understanding of how the economy works and its sensitivity
to various uncertainties introduced by deficiencies in the input data or in the
model itself?

Since tne Treasury two-year forecasts of GDP are rather more successful than

Economic predictions   125

the one-year forecasts, and this may be due partlyto better input data, I wonder if this has been confirmed by making hindcasts with data sets of comparable quality?

SIR TERENCE BURNS. In the Treasury, at least as much time is devoted to the type of model-based policy and analytical studies that you describe as to forecasting. It is only for reasons of space that I have not covered policy simulations in my paper. These use a similar methodology to the forecasts, and in fact one can regard policy simulations as a forecast in which one component of the exogenous or input data has been altered. However, there are difficult problems in evaluating the accuracy of such exercises since there is no outturn data with which they can be compared.

Sir John also asked whether the comparative success of two-year ahead forecasts could be attributed in part to better input data. Although no formal tests have been done I think it unlikely that world economic conditions, and the setting of exogenous policy instruments, which comprise the main input data for forecasts, are relatively more accurate two years ahead. In the case of tax rates, for example, these are known with almost complete certainty for the year ahead.

[9]

MACROECONOMIC FORECASTING: A SURVEY*

Kenneth F. Wallis

Developments in macroeconomic forecasting over the last twenty years are surveyed in this paper, which takes the 1969 Presidential Address to the Royal Economic Society (Cairncross, 1969) as its starting point. Sir Alec Cairncross had found no previous occasion on which the Royal Economic Society had discussed 'this new activity', and so selected economic forecasting as the topic for his address. As retiring Chief Economic Adviser to the Treasury he had been preoccupied with forecasting for the preceding few years, and was well placed to reflect on the new kind of economic forecasting that was emerging and the new ways in which it was being organised. At the time these were changing fast, with forecasting becoming in particular more heavily based on computable models. A conference in April 1969 heard that in the Treasury 'a more elaborate fully formalised model is being programmed for a computer' (Roy, 1970); in August 1969, at the National Institute of Economic and Social Research (NIESR), an econometric model of the whole economy became an integral part of the quarterly forecasting exercises that had begun, with the publication of the *National Institute Economic Review*, in 1959. These developments followed the inauguration by the London Business School (LBS) in 1966 of the first series of published forecasts based on the direct application of a complete statistical model of the economy.

In the late 1960s and early 1970s confidence in forecasting was growing. 'Extra resources were put in, and there were hopes that the accumulation of data and more sophisticated techniques would lead to major improvements in accuracy of forecasts and understanding of the economy' (Burns, 1986). This confidence rested in part on the wide acceptance of the neoclassical synthesis as a framework for macroeconomic analysis. The phrase originated with Samuelson, who was largely instrumental in constructing and promulgating the 'grand neoclassical synthesis', which was given considerable prominence in the third edition of his textbook. Here it was noted that economists, instead of being Keynesian or anti-Keynesian, 'have worked toward a synthesis of whatever is valuable in older economics and in modern theories of income determination. The result might be called neo-classical economics and is accepted in its broad outlines by all but about 5 per cent of extreme left wing and right wing writers' (Samuelson, 1955, p. 212). In his *New Palgrave* entry on the neoclassical synthesis, Blanchard (1987) observes that it 'did not expect full employment to occur under *laissez-faire*; it believed however that, by proper use of monetary and fiscal policy, the old classical truths would come back into

* This chapter was first published in the ECONOMIC JOURNAL, vol. 99, March 1989. The support of the Economic and Social Research Council is gratefully acknowledged, as are the helpful comments and/or research assistance of M. J. Artis, A. J. C. Britton, P. G. Fisher, C. W. J. Granger, C. L. Melliss, A. J. Oswald, S. K. Tanna, D. S. Turner, J. D. Whitley and two anonymous referees.

relevance. This synthesis was to remain the dominant paradigm for another twenty years, in which most of the important contributions, by Hicks, Modigliani, Solow, Tobin and others, were to fit quite naturally.' The neoclassical synthesis enjoyed considerable empirical success in the 1960s: as a result Heller *et al.* (1968, p. 16) could conclude that 'governments have, to a large extent, succeeded in subduing or overcoming the rhythmic fluctuations which used to be called the trade cycle' and Cairncross (1969, p. 805) could 'doubt whether bad theory has played a major part in forecasting errors in this country over the past decade or two'.

Growing confidence in the use of more sophisticated techniques rested on developments in econometric modelling and forecasting that had taken place largely outside the United Kingdom. The construction of economy-wide models had been pioneered by Tinbergen, who had subsequently served as the first director of the Central Planning Bureau of the Netherlands; this had become the official forecasting agency whose activities were the most heavily model-based. An account of the methods of short-term forecasting used by the governments of six member countries was published by the OECD in 1965, and in his introductory survey McMahon reported that 'All the participating countries except the United Kingdom use an econometric model; but except for the Netherlands it is used primarily as a consistency check, rather than as the primary method of making the forecast itself.' Theil's classic *Economic Forecasts and Policy* (1958) and *Applied Economic Forecasting* (1966) represented in part a contribution to the research programme of the Central Planning Bureau. In the United States Klein had led the way, and his brief stay in the United Kingdom had resulted in the first serious attempt to develop a large-scale quarterly model of any national economy, the model being estimated for the most part on seasonally unadjusted data (Klein *et al.*, 1961). The annual Klein–Goldberger model had been built at the University of Michigan in the early 1950s, and its descendants were subsequently used for forecasting by the Research Seminar in Quantitative Economics (Suits, 1962); forecasts based on a quarterly model of the US economy were distributed by the Wharton School at the University of Pennsylvania from 1963 onwards (see Klein, 1968 and references therein). Important work on the evaluation of forecasts came from an NBER project on short-term economic forecasting (Zarnowitz, 1967; Mincer and Zarnowitz, 1969). This literature provided a foundation for the initial developments indicated in the opening paragraph, and for subsequent developments that occurred in the period under consideration.

A feature of the last twenty years that is immediately apparent on attempting a survey is that the literature on forecasting has grown apace with forecasting activity. From the three groups in existence in the late 1960s, macroeconomic forecasting activity has grown to the point where the Treasury's monthly compilation *Forecasts for the UK Economy* now covers nineteen forecasts. As for the literature, it remains the case that forecasting has scarcely featured in this JOURNAL, no major article having dealt with the subject in the intervening period, but in this time two journals devoted entirely to forecasting have been established. Notable books on the production and use of macroeconomic forecasts have been published by leading practitioners, for example, Keating (1985), Klein and Young (1980), and Llewellyn *et al.* (1985), respectively from UK, US and international perspectives. More general textbooks have appeared, for example, Fair (1984), Granger and Newbold (1977), and Pindyck and Rubinfeld (1976). A substantial section of the literature deals with the assessment of forecasts, both in theory and in practice, and in turn with the use of forecasts in model evaluation. An early study of UK forecasts is that by Ash and Smyth (1973); subsequently numerous authors, including the forecasters themselves, have contributed assessments. Various aspects of macroeconomic forecasting are touched on in the international conference volumes edited by Chow and Corsi (1982), Kmenta and Ramsey (1981), and Malgrange and Muet (1984); the UK scene is represented by Hilton and Heathfield (1970), Renton (1975), Ormerod (1979a), and the sequence of reviews by the ESRC Macroeconomic Modelling Bureau (Wallis *et al.*, 1984–7).

The paper proceeds as follows. In the next section the essential ingredients of a forecast are described, by way of background, and some basic data on forecasts and outcomes are presented as a point of reference. The events and consequences of some important episodes are then considered: first 1974–5, when in many countries unprecedented forecast errors were made, which provided a focus for important challenges, both empirical and theoretical, to the prevailing consensus; next 1979–81, which saw a recession, a change of regime and notable forecasting errors, heralding further developments. Forecast evaluation is touched on as much as is necessary throughout this account, but is then treated more thoroughly in a separate section, which includes consideration of a final episode, namely 1986, when the dramatic fall in the world price of oil, fortunately for the forecasters, was not anticipated. Concluding comments follow, the paper closing, like Cairncross (1969), on the issue of the publication of forecasts. The principal orientation of the paper is towards the UK economy, with occasional glances elsewhere, although developments in economic analysis and econometric methods know no frontiers.

I. CONSTRUCTION OF FORECASTS

The need for forecasting in economic policy-making, and the essential ingredients of a forecast, have scarcely changed over twenty years. Thus Cairncross (1969, p. 798) notes that forecasts 'provide a frame of reference for policy decisions' and 'a base against which to judge how policies are working out', and the current Chief Economic Adviser to the Treasury similarly states 'Decisions·have to be made against the background of an uncertain current position; they cannot easily be reversed, and many policy changes have consequences stretching years ahead. Some kind of forward look is therefore essential and it is best to do this in a consistent way. Once they are produced, forecasts have an important monitoring function as they provide a basis against which to judge subsequent developments' (Burns, 1986, p. 117). Outside the policy-making context, two further quite different motives for forecasting exist.

MACROECONOMIC FORECASTING: A SURVEY   5I

One is to anticipate events, whether for private gain or for public good, and it is largely in respect of the former that the growth in forecasting activity has occurred; the other is to put hypotheses about the behaviour of the world to test, which helps explain why independent research groups engage in forecasting.

Although the key ingredients of a forecast have remained quantitative data and a framework for their interpretation and analysis, substantial developments have occurred in respect of the methods of analysis. Early forecasts were based on a limited number of variables, which were analysed in the context of an implicit, perhaps informal model, not necessarily written down. The process relied on the assessment of data and the evaluation of new information by the experienced forecaster. 'A few people possess the extraordinary gift of being able to do this in their heads...The process involved is not well understood, but it seems to involve the checking of data against the predictions and workings of a mental model of how the economy works. The disadvantage of such a method is that the number of people truly gifted in this way is small, and the technique is difficult to explain and transmit to others' (Llewellyn *et al.*, 1985, p. 83) – and to replicate. In the 1960s the use of explicit, more formal models increased, with these models becoming increasingly based on estimated equations. The models distinguish between endogenous and exogenous variables, that is, those determined by the system of equations and those treated as being determined outside the system. In a forecasting context, these latter variables have to be set by projection or assumption, which leads to the further distinction between an unconditional and a conditional forecast. The former represents the conventional understanding of a forecast, namely a prediction of a future event, whereas the latter represents an if–then statement, resting on the occurrence of certain specified conditions. The pure prediction problem is the main concern of this paper, although the distinction is less clear-cut than might appear, since exogenous variables that are policy instruments may be treated in different ways. One possibility is to assume no change in policy instruments, irrespective of the forecast; another is to project a policy response to the forecasted developments.

With greater computerisation the size of the models could be increased, allowing attention to be paid to a greater number of variables, including the components of aggregates previously treated as one. The intervening years have seen such developments in computing that computer capability is no longer a constraint, either on the size and complexity of the model to be managed, or on the frequency with which forecasts and policy exercises can be constructed and revised, or on the econometric estimation and testing procedures applied to the models, these procedures themselves having been substantially developed over the last twenty years.

The removal of the computing constraint and the use of more fully elaborated accounting frameworks should not obscure the fact that some practical limitations, in particular concerning data, remain much as in Cairncross' (1969) description. 'First of all, the forecaster has to contend with the inevitable lag of statistics behind events...when the February forecasts are being prepared in advance of the Budget the latest available national accounts relate to the third quarter' of the preceding year. This remains the case today. Moreover, the inevitable lags differ from one variable to another, so there is not a clean break between periods for which data are available and those for which they are not; rather, the dataset has a 'ragged edge', presenting additional complications (Wallis, 1986). 'Next comes the issue of reliability', one indication of which is the frequency with which preliminary data are subsequently amended, and another is the frequency of changes in definition of a given series. Some errors are systematic and survive the revision process, the most notable current example being in international trade, where on a balance of payments basis imports considerably exceed exports, globally, by an amount which, as a proportion of total imports, is of the same order of magnitude as the UK current balance. Less frequently, reconstruction of the real national accounts data using revised relative price weights can lead to very substantial revision of data, going back perhaps to the origin of the data series, and affecting both the level of the series and its growth rate over given periods. Last, but not least, is the discrepancy between the statistician's measurement and the economist's concept. The problem of the valuation of stocks, and the decomposition of a given change into price and volume changes, arises in a number of areas, and is part of the well-known problem of the measurement of capital stock; a related problem is that of the measurement of capacity utilisation. In the absence of adequate direct measurements, indirect measurements or 'proxy' variables have to be used. Moreover 'even measures that in principle are equal to one another are often in flat contradiction. To take what may be an extreme example, between the first quarter of 1966 and the first quarter of 1967 the expenditure measure of GNP increased by 2 per cent, the income measure fell by $\frac{1}{2}$ per cent and the output measure was unchanged. Yet all these measure the same thing' (Cairncross, 1969, p. 803). Such contradictions remain in the 1980s. For example, in October 1983 it was estimated that the expenditure measure had risen by $1\frac{1}{4}\%$ between 1980 and 1982, while the output measure had fallen by $\frac{1}{2}\%$ and the income measure had not changed. Just one year later, in October 1984, the expenditure increase was revised to $\frac{1}{2}\%$, that of output to $\frac{1}{4}\%$ and income was estimated to have increased by $1\frac{3}{4}\%$!

The continuing presence of data discrepancies and delays is one reason why there remains a role for informed judgement in forecasting, often expressed through a process of adjustments to model-based forecasts. The use of such adjustments, variously termed constant adjustments, residual adjustments, add factors, etc. is widespread, despite the models having come to represent a more complete framework for analysis. Indeed, the more complete is the model, the greater is the internal consistency with which a given adjustment to a variable or an equation is carried through the forecast calculations. The use of 'conjunctural analysis' to supplement the official macroeconomic data and so to suggest adjustments is well described by Keating (1985); other reasons for making adjustments, based on knowledge of further developments not incorporated in the model or of other model deficiencies, feature in

MACROECONOMIC FORECASTING: A SURVEY   53

general terms in all practitioners' accounts of their art. An attempt to appraise the impact of these adjustments, *ex post*, is presented in Section IV.5 below.

As a point of reference for subsequent discussion, data on one-year-ahead forecasts of GDP and inflation published by independent UK forecasting groups, LBS, NIESR and LPL (the Liverpool University Research Group in Macroeconomics) are presented in Figs. 1 and 2. The upper panel of each figure shows the actual outcome, and the lower panel the forecast errors, defined as actual minus forecast. Public discussion usually focuses on the annual (real) GDP growth rate and the annual rate of inflation, so the data are presented in these terms, which also has the merit of reducing the basic GDP and price level variables to (near) stationarity. That is, the proportionate rates of change are trend-free, and their variances and autocovariances can be treated as time-invariant. The forecasts described as one-year-ahead are

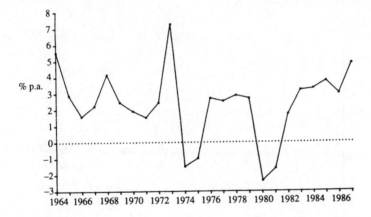

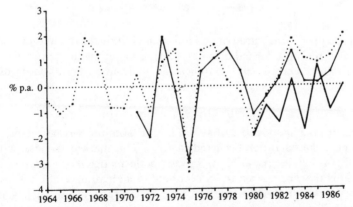

Fig. 1. GDP growth. Upper panel, actual; lower panel, one-year-ahead forecast errors.
Key: LBS (—■—), NIESR (··■··) and LPL (——).

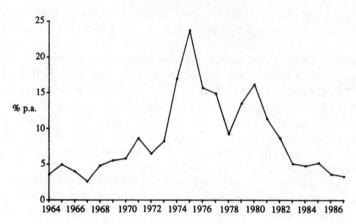

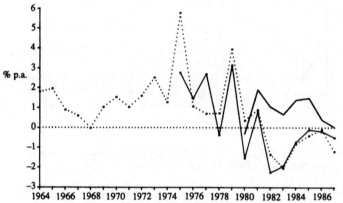

Fig. 2. Inflation. Upper panel, actual; lower panel, one-year-ahead forecast errors.
Key: —■—, LBS; ··■··, NIESR; ----, LPL.

forecasts of a given year's growth and inflation published early in that year, and
hence which rest on a formal database ending sometime in the previous year,
although other, more timely, conjunctural information may also be used, as
noted above.

II. THE 1974-5 RECESSION·

It is clear from Figs. 1 and 2 that the largest absolute forecast errors in the
period under consideration occurred in 1975. This marked the low point of a
period of gradual deterioration in forecast performance. For example Osborn
(1979) finds that, compared to its accuracy in forecasting real GDP over the
1965-70 period, the NIESR performance deteriorates in the 1970-5 period,
most markedly so in 1974-5. In the United States, McNees (1979a) finds that,
for a sequence of quarterly one-year-ahead forecasts of real GNP growth

MACROECONOMIC FORECASTING: A SURVEY 55

through the 1970s, all of the 'failures', with one minor exception, occurred in forecasts of the periods ending between 1974:1 and 1976:1, all but one of these nine forecasts being a 'failure': a 'failure' is defined as the median absolute error across five leading US forecasters substantially exceeding its average value over the entire period. For the OECD area, Llewellyn *et al.* (1985, ch. 6) find that, of the seventeen year-ahead forecasts of real OECD GNP growth over the period 1966–82, those for 1974 and 1975 exhibit the two largest errors. In the analytical framework of the time, an overestimate of real growth would be expected to be associated with an underestimate of unemployment, which indeed occurred: McNees (1979a) notes the 'extraordinarily large under-estimates of unemployment in early 1975'. Emphasis on the absolute forecast errors may underestimate the ability of the forecasters, since, as indicated by Figs. 1 and 2, for example, the situation they were attempting to predict showed a sharp increase in variation. In these circumstances their relative performance, assessed more fully below, might even be considered laudable. It is clear from contemporary writings, however, that this provided little solace, and the absolute errors prompted a vigorous search for forecasting improvements.

The economic scenario in which these forecasting errors occurred was the coexistence, not previously experienced, of rapid inflation and high unemployment, leading into recession. Writing from a US perspective, Lucas and Sargent (1978) in their well-known polemic laid the blame for these reversals very clearly at the door of the neoclassical synthesis. That macroeconomic policies predicated on models in this tradition had not produced the predicted results represented 'econometric failure on a grand scale'. Moreover, not only were the predictions 'wildly incorrect' but 'the doctrine on which they were based is fundamentally flawed'; it was argued 'that the difficulties are *fatal*: that modern macroeconomic models are of *no* value in guiding policy and that this condition will not be remedied by modifications along any line which is currently being pursued'. The models should be replaced by equilibrium models (Lucas, 1975, 1977), which assume that prices and quantities continuously clear markets and that agents continuously optimise, which in turn leads to the imposition of the hypothesis of rational expectations. In such equilibrium or 'new classical' models, fluctuations are caused by agents' reactions to unanticipated shocks.

This recommendation was not followed by the forecasters, whose attention focused on other perceived inadequacies of their models. First among these was the models' oversimplified treatment of supply factors, since the 'first oil price shock', that is, the quadrupling of the price of imported oil in late 1973, was in particular blamed for the 1974–5 recession. 'This unique external supply-side shock provided a severe challenge to the conventional, demand-oriented forecasting techniques' (McNees, 1979b) not because it was unanticipated but because its repercussions were not understood and in consequence were underestimated. Thus, in revising their forecasts for 1974 after observing the oil price increase, US forecasters made adjustments to show more inflation and lower growth, but these, while in the right direction, were not nearly large

56   KENNETH F. WALLIS

enough, as McNees (1979 *b*) notes: 'the upward pressure on prices and downward pressure on output were far stronger than...anticipated'. Writing at the time, Klein (1974) noted that 'The US models, which have been not only demand oriented, but also overly domestic in character have few provisions for indicating how high import prices (fuel in this case) contribute to domestic inflation. This is not a problem for European and UK model builders, however, because they have generally been alert to problems of imported inflation and allow for that factor in their domestic price formation equations'. Subsequently elaborate energy sectors were introduced into the Wharton model, to allow routine analysis of oil-price changes in particular. Likewise the DRI model moved into its third generation after 1975, to remedy the shortcomings in the existing ('second generation') models that became apparent during 1973–5. Specifically, the design of these models did not 'offer sufficient points of contact with external matters such as raw material prices, oil prices, worldwide booms and recessions, shortages and the financial instability which only became more evident during that period' (Eckstein, 1983, p. 8). They had been fitted over the sample period 1953–73, which enjoyed relatively smooth growth and 'did not reveal the full cyclical vulnerability of the economy'. Appropriate extensions to the model were accordingly made.

For the OECD area as a whole, forecast errors also reflected underestimates of the scale of the response to the oil-price shock. Again, once the oil price increase was known, growth forecasts for 1974 were revised downwards, but insufficiently so. 'Anyone who was involved in managing a macroeconometric model at the time of the 1973 oil-price rise will never forget the strain this supply shock placed on an apparatus largely attuned to coping with demand disturbances' (Higgins, 1988). Since the continuation of the recession into 1975 was not foreseen in forecasts prepared in late 1974, Llewellyn *et al.* (1985) emphasise the lack of understanding not only of the magnitude of the economic responses to the shock but also of their timing. An international analytic framework and an appropriate set of quantified relationships was not available at the time, and the oil shock provided a strong impetus for the development of globally consistent projections, as Higgins notes. Whereas it was immediately apparent that there would be large transfers of financial resources from oil-importing to oil-exporting countries through the current account of the balance of payments, their continuing consequences were unclear. As the OPEC countries began to react to their new wealth, work began on an international linkage model to focus on the effects of the various transmission mechanisms.

In the United Kingdom the inflationary explosion of 1974–5 was attributed not only to the oil-price shock but also, by monetarists in particular, to the surge in monetary growth in 1972–3. A rapid rise in public borrowing was associated with the expansionary fiscal policy of 1971–2, which produced unprecedented output growth in 1973, and rapid growth in bank lending followed the move towards a more liberal regulatory regime in 1971 (the 'competition and credit control' measures). The broad money measure in use at the time (M3) grew by 27·8% in 1972 and 27·6% in 1973, the inflationary

MACROECONOMIC FORECASTING : A SURVEY   57

explosion following with a two-year lag and an intervening temporary output rise, exactly as in the basic Friedmanite analysis, although the oil-price rise exaggerated the magnitude of the inflationary response. Foreign prices had a role in the models, as indicated by Klein (1974), quoted above, but no distinction was drawn between oil and other imports, nor between oil and other commodities, whose prices were also rising exceptionally quickly in 1973. The inclusion of foreign prices was by no means enough to prevent the 1975 forecasting errors shown in Figs. 1 and 2; similarly large errors were observed in other variables such as consumption and employment. As elsewhere, the depth of the recession was not correctly anticipated. Again as elsewhere, the response was a pragmatic one, with forecasters attempting to learn from the new information and new experience in order to improve future performance, rather than jettisoning their whole approach.

In the light of the events described above, and of the 1973 move to a system of floating exchange rates, attention concentrated on the modelling of the financial sector, exchange rate equations, and the influence of monetary policy. A new financial sector for the Treasury model became operational in 1978 (Spencer and Mowl, 1978; Spencer, 1986), and a simple financial system was introduced into the NIESR model (Ormerod, 1979 b). The fullest account of their learning and respecification process or, in Flemming's (1978) phrase, their 'intellectual odyssey', is provided by the LBS group in papers presented at conferences in late 1977 and mid-1978 (Ball and Burns, 1978; Ball *et al.*, 1979). The LBS approach followed the 'international monetarist' tradition (Dornbusch, 1976), that changes in relative money supplies affect prices via changes in the exchange rate, given long-run purchasing power parity. More generally, the LBS group undertook a 'fundamental reappraisal of the properties of the system as a whole'. In the personal sector, for example, failure to anticipate the sharp fall in consumers' expenditure in 1975 led to a reconsideration of the impact of inflation on real spending, in which consumers were assumed to save more as inflation increased in order to preserve the real value of their financial assets.

Given the central place of the consumption function in neoclassical synthesis econometrics, the rise in the savings ratio that occurred in the early to mid-1970s in association with a rising rate of inflation prompted much empirical research by forecasters and others, which continues to this day. Notable examples in this JOURNAL are the papers by Davidson *et al.* (1978) and Pesaran and Evans (1984), and the current forecasting models incorporate the effect of inflation on consumers' expenditure, occurring either directly, or indirectly via an adjustment to real income for the inflation loss on liquid assets and/or wealth. The detection of this effect provides a good example of the model development opportunities offered by turbulent periods of history, alluded to in the quotation by Eckstein, above.

The technical point is that forecasts based on a mis-specified model, for example, one that omits a relevant explanatory variable, will continue to perform as well as expected from past experience and hence arouse no suspicions as long as the omitted variable continues to behave in the same

58   KENNETH F. WALLIS

manner as before. Once its behaviour changes, however, then so does that of variables related to it, and forecasts of these variables based on the mis-specified model exhibit unexpected errors, so drawing attention to the model's inadequacy. Over the time span of this paper the changes have been from relatively smooth to relatively turbulent behaviour, and it may be that only after the perturbation of the data, and a period in which events appear inexplicable, is it possible to identify and estimate an appropriately extended model. On the other hand, there may have been enough information in the 'smooth' data to permit the satisfactory estimation of a revised model, once the inadequacies of the original model are revealed. In the case of the consumption function, Davidson *et al.* (1978) find that there is enough variation in the 1960s data to allow the estimation of a new equation, incorporating inflation effects, that does not suffer from the mid-1970s predictive failure of the old equation. The forecast errors in consumers' expenditure could have been avoided if the inflation effects had been looked for and, in an *ex ante* forecast context, if inflation itself had been well predicted.

In the case of the exchange rate, other UK forecasters, like the LBS group, introduced exchange rate equations and made other related changes post-1975. None of the exchange rate systems performed well when used for forecasting, however, and the exchange rate equations often had to be overridden or subject to heavy residual adjustments. In the first instance the modelling difficulties were not surprising, given the short series of data available for the 'floating' regime and the completely uninformative nature of the 'fixed' regime. These have persisted, however, Isard (1988) concluding in his international survey that 'empirical modeling of exchange rates over the past decade has been largely a failure', which is evident 'from documentation of the poor post sample forecasting accuracy of the models, from data that appear to reject important building blocks for the monetary models (in particular, the assumption of uncovered interest rate parity), and from the lack of statistically significant in-sample support for existing portfolio-balance models of the exchange risk premium'. Forecasting the exchange rate remains arguably the greatest single problem facing UK forecasters.

The experience of the 1974–5 recession was a major blow to the growing confidence in forecasting of the 1960s and early 1970s. It represented a valuable learning experience, however, and caused a sharp spurt in the continuing evolution of forecasting models, as existing systems were amended, not abandoned. In any event the advice that they should be abandoned was by the end of the decade itself amended, Lucas (1980) observing 'To what extent this forecast error should be interpreted as a "fatal" error in models based on the neoclassical synthesis or simply as one suggesting some modifications is not so easy to determine.'

III. THE 1979–81 RECESSION

The second oil-price shock occurred in several stages in 1979 and initiated a second recession in the OECD economies. 'Inflation re-accelerated, current account deficits increased, public sector deficits swelled, and unemployment

MACROECONOMIC FORECASTING: A SURVEY   59

rose yet further. Taken together, these presented a greater problem for policy in nearly all economies than in any previous post-war cycle' (Llewellyn *et al.*, 1985, p. 39), although unlike the first oil price shock, there was now no substantial disagreement among the OECD economies about the appropriate policy response. The UK experience differed from that of the rest of the OECD, however. Despite its near self-sufficiency in oil by 1979, the United Kingdom suffered a recession which started earlier than elsewhere and was of much greater severity. Many authors have compared this recession with the Great Depression of the 1930s, output falling by 5% in both 1929–31 and 1979–81. Unemployment rose from 1·2 million in mid-1979 to reach 2 million in late 1980 and 3 million by autumn 1982.

May 1979 had seen the election of a new Conservative government in the United Kingdom, committed to the reduction of inflation and the creation of conditions favourable to sustained economic growth, but no longer accepting responsibility for high employment. Inflation was to be controlled by restrictive monetary policy, not incomes policy, and the supply side was to be strengthened through fiscal measures such as a shift from direct to indirect taxation and a reduction in public expenditure, and through the liberalising of financial markets and the labour market. Thus in the June 1979 Budget monetary policy was tightened, public expenditure cuts were announced, income tax was reduced and the rate of indirect taxation (value added tax) was increased. In October 1979 exchange controls were abolished. The March 1980 Budget introduced the medium-term financial strategy (MTFS) comprising a four-year declining target path for the growth of a broad monetary aggregate (sterling M3) and an accompanying path for the public sector borrowing requirement (PSBR), which implied a declining PSBR/GDP ratio. The immediate result of these policies, in conjunction with external developments, was a major loss of competitiveness accompanied by a large fall in production and the rise in unemployment noted above. Company finances were adversely affected, real profitability falling to its lowest recorded level in the second half of 1980, and the reaction was a massive reduction in inventories. Arithmetically, the reduction in real GDP between 1979 and 1980 was more than accounted for by the reversal in stockbuilding; substantial destocking continued in 1981. Inflation increased to 18% in 1980, but then began to fall, reaching 5·4% by the end of 1982.

This brief description serves to set the scene for the discussion of forecast performance over this period, of which a good account is given by Barker (1985), and of subsequent developments. The 'Thatcher experiment', or what is now the 'Thatcher experience', has a considerable literature of its own, two notable early contributions being the Brookings papers of Buiter and Miller (1981, 1983), and that literature falls outside the scope of the present survey.

The recession was not well forecast, being unanticipated until mid-1979, although the errors were smaller than in 1974–5. As Barker (1985) points out, the difficulties are demonstrated by an exercise presented to the Bank of England Academic Panel (Worswick and Budd, 1981), in which the LBS and

NIESR models were used to explain the shortfall of output over 1978–80 relative to its trend. (Budd's contribution also includes a post-mortem analysis of LBS forecasts over this period; Surrey (1982) likewise examines the NIESR track record.) The shortfall in output was estimated at 4%, the main contributions being

    (i) policy changes in the June 1979 Budget, in particular the VAT increase and the planned cuts in public expenditure (1·6–1·7%);

   (ii) the deterioration in competitiveness (1·1–1·3%);

  (iii) the oil price rise (0·8–1·3%).

As all these factors appeared in the models as relevant exogenous variables, three possible explanations of the forecast errors remain. First, the movements in these variables may not have been correctly anticipated. Secondly, their effects on the economy may not have been accurately modelled. Thirdly, the model forecasts may have been adjusted to show less dramatic changes, although no evidence on this is available (an analysis of the impact of adjustments on later forecasts is presented in Section IV.5 below). After the onset of the oil price increases and the June 1979 Budget growth forecasts were revised downwards, with the LBS correctly forecasting that output would fall in 1980, although the extent of the fall, and in particular the collapse of GDP in the fourth quarter of 1980, was not anticipated. The NIESR forecast of growth in 1980 was revised to a negative number only in February 1980, and again the fall in output was considerably underestimated. By this time the full extent of the oil-price rise was appreciated, but the extent of the financial squeeze on the company sector was not. Cuts in public expenditure continued to be forecast into 1980, but these never materialised, and these errors served to offset the failure to capture the large volume of destocking. As Budd notes, to predict the speed of adjustment to major shocks, particularly financial shocks, is especially difficult, and the previous recession offered little guidance. Whereas companies allowed exceptionally high deficits to accrue in 1974 and did not adjust inventories and employment until 1975, in 1980 the adjustment occurred almost instantaneously. Thus the rise in unemployment was also underpredicted. Finally the exchange rate was underpredicted, and this would have remained the case even had the oil price increase been fully anticipated.

Once again the experience of forecasting through a relatively turbulent period led to a reappraisal of the forecasting models. While this resulted in further small steps in the continuing process of model evolution, such as the introduction of financial considerations into the determination of investment and stockbuilding, two major items appeared on the agenda, namely expectations and the supply side.

Expectations of future developments have long been recognised as important determinants of current behaviour and, as Klein (1987, p. 420) notes, forecasters have long endeavoured to use survey data on expectations and anticipations wherever possible. Reliable quantitative data on expectations are relatively rare, however, and auxiliary hypotheses about the way in which expectations are formed are commonly used in their place. In the forecasting

MACROECONOMIC FORECASTING: A SURVEY   61

models of the 1960s and 1970s expectations were assumed to be formed by extrapolating from past experience, usually in respect of the variable of interest alone. The simplest example of this approach is the adaptive expectations hypothesis, which was widely used, and in this and more general cases the resulting model can be described as backward-looking. The need to accommodate explicit forward-looking behaviour was increasingly recognised, at the theoretical level through the attention given to the rational expectations hypothesis and at the practical level through the experience of 1979–81. The role of expectations in the face of a change of policy regime and the associated questions of credibility began to feature in the discussion. Credibility featured without agreement, however. On the one hand Buiter and Miller (1981, p. 362) assert

> The government established the credibility of its restrictive policy stance at the start of its term of office. The perception that current and future monetary policy would be restrictive was reflected promptly in the exchange rate, interest rates, and financial markets generally, but only gradually in domestic costs, especially wages. This led to a major appreciation of the real exchange rate along the lines of the overshooting model, a rise in real interest rates, and a decline in Tobin's q.

On the other hand, Matthews and Minford (1987, p. 62) argue that 'in fact, most people had written off the early actions of the government as unlikely to be followed through,...so if anything people expected a "U-turn" towards much looser policies. It was for this reason, the lack of credibility, that prices and wages in 1979–80 were accelerating towards 20% p.a. growth.'

In March 1980 the first forecasts based on the Liverpool model (Minford *et al.*, 1984) were published. This model represented a break with the existing models of the UK economy, being a new classical equilibrium model, incorporating the hypothesis of rational expectations; it is a monetarist model in the sense that higher monetary growth directly increases inflation, with no role for cost factors. The rational expectations literature is usually assumed to start with Muth (1961), although following much older discussions of the influence of forecasts on outcomes, Grunberg and Modigliani (1954) had already shown that where agents react to forecasts and thereby alter the course of events, this reaction can be taken into account to yield a correct, self-fulfilling forecast. This same kind of internal consistency is imposed by the rational expectations algorithms used to calculate a sequence of forecasts based on a model containing explicit forward-looking expectations variables, in that each period's future expectations coincide with the model's forecasts for the future period. The approach is more appropriately and perhaps less controversially termed 'model-consistent' expectations. In policy evaluation exercises, the use of consistent expectations allows policies to be tested under conditions in which their effects are understood. As Currie (1985) argues, good performance in these conditions is a necessary condition for a satisfactory policy: 'a policy that performs badly when its effects are understood must be unsatisfactory'. In both

62   KENNETH F. WALLIS

forecasting and policy analysis, the explicit treatment of forward expectations allows such issues as the announcement effects of future policy changes, their credibility and, indeed, the consequences of false expectations to be dealt with.

Fischer (1988)[1] recalls that his 1976 survey with Barro drew 'a clear distinction between the rational expectations hypothesis as a theory of expectations, and the type of equilibrium model in which the hypothesis was typically embodied at the time'. This distinction was blurred by leading US forecasters, however; thus in discussing the 'rational expectations school', both Eckstein (1983) and Klein (1986) associate the rational expectations hypothesis with the policy ineffectiveness proposition, and Klein *et al.* (1983) describe the 'many ways in which the thinking of monetarists and proponents of rational expectations are congruent'. Given the opposition of the 'mainstream models' to the positions of the 'rational expectations school' and the extreme monetarists indicated in these writings, it is perhaps not surprising that consistent expectations were not widely embraced in the US models. In the United Kingdom, however, despite the first appearance of rational expectations being in the new classical Liverpool model, the distinction appears to have been more clearly appreciated, and the incorporation of explicit forward-looking expectations handled in a model-consistent manner was part of the post-1981 revision process of other, more mainstream 'sticky price' and quantity adjustment models.

In the case of the LBS model, the introduction of consistent expectations was associated with the introduction of a detailed financial sector, in which asset demands are determined in a general portfolio choice model featuring expected future prices of gilts, equities and overseas assets, and in which the exchange rate is determined as a market-clearing price. Various questions, now of increased importance, such as the conduct of monetary and exchange rate policy, the use of open-market operations and debt management, and the finance of fiscal deficits could then be addressed.

The introduction of forward-looking behaviour into the NIESR model (Hall and Henry, 1985) was motivated by its forecasting performance: backward-looking equations for employment, investment and stockbuilding, depending mainly on lagged output, missed the turning point in 1979, as noted above, and did not capture the speed and depth of the recession. Accordingly, forward-looking behaviour was introduced into these equations, together with wage equations, money demand and exchange rate equations. Not only do expectations of various prices appear, as in the LBS and Liverpool models, but also expectations of future output and personal income, so retaining the model's neo-Keynesian quantity adjustment approach.

The influence of the supply side on macroeconomic phenomena received increasing attention as a result of the major supply shocks of the 1970s and the criticisms of the new classical macroeconomists. Among US modellers and forecasters, for example, Klein (1978) in his AEA Presidential Address and Eckstein (1983), cited above, advocate a consensus approach in which mainstream models, now recognised to be over-emphasising effective demand, are extended by incorporating a full supply-side analysis into an appropriately

---

[1] See previous chapter.

MACROECONOMIC FORECASTING : A SURVEY   63

elaborated IS–LM system. The over-emphasis on the demand side does not imply that supply theory had been neglected in the academic literature in preceding decades, as Eckstein (1983, p. 56) notes, but that body of work had had little impact on the macroeconomics used for policy. In the United Kingdom the Conservative government elected in May 1979 paid increasing attention to supply-side policies, and the Liverpool model contained powerful supply effects in its representation of the labour market. As Matthews and Minford (1987) note, the size of the effects attributed to variations in unemployment benefits, direct taxes and trade union membership (proxying the power of unions) remain controversial, and their claim that these are well-determined empirically has been rejected by other researchers (for example, Nickell, 1987; Wallis *et al.*, 1986, ch. 5). A further model, specifically designed as a supply-side model, namely that of the City University Business School (Beenstock *et al.*, 1986) was first used for forecasting at the time of the June 1983 general election. The CUBS model abandoned the usual income-expenditure framework and determined the supply of output through a KLEM production function (capital, labour, energy, materials); it also included a formal labour supply schedule, unlike other models. Like the Liverpool model, it is an annual, not quarterly model, and emphasises the medium-term development of the economy. In the quarterly models the consensus has been slower to arrive than in the United States, but the current version of the LBS model (Dinenis *et al.*, 1989) incorporates explicit supply influences into the income–expenditure framework. Output is determined not as the sum of the expenditure components but by both supply and demand factors at the sectoral level, with prices in the long run ensuring that the goods market clears.

IV. EVALUATION OF FORECASTS

The evaluation of past forecasting performance is an important input into the forecasting process and, since it provides a forecast of future performance, it is of interest to the users of forecasts. The forecasters themselves regularly publish accounts of their own performance, and occasionally contrast this with that of other groups. Several authors have undertaken independent studies of the performance of different forecasters with respect to a range of variables and forecast horizons, for example, in the United Kingdom Ash and Smyth (1973), Holden and Peel (1983, 1986) and Wallis *et al.* (1986, 1987), and in the United States McNees (1982, 1986) and Zarnowitz (1979, 1985) and references therein, including papers cited above; Artis (1988) examines the forecasting record of the IMF World Economic Outlook, and compares it with that of the separate national forecasting agencies. Evaluations range from descriptive accounts of forecasting ability in particular periods, especially turning points, as in the preceding sections, to the statistical analysis of forecast errors over a period of years, considered in this section. Evaluations are typically addressed to one variable at a time, whereas a multivariate assessment may be more relevant, particularly if trade-offs between different variables have a bearing on the specific decision problem.

   Given time series of forecasts and outcomes, the first step is usually to

64   KENNETH F. WALLIS

calculate summary statistics such as the mean absolute error (MAE) and root mean square error (RMSE), or comparable statistics for the forecasts and outcomes separately, or even their correlation coefficient. An immediate difficulty is that there is no absolute measure of the forecastability of a series, and so there is no absolute standard against which to compare these summary statistics. For a given definition of optimality, usually linear least squares, statistical prediction theory provides the optimal forecast with respect to a given information set, but economic forecasters may not agree about the relevant information set, which in the widest sense is in any event unknown, *ex ante* and *ex post*, and unmanageably large. In the absence of an absolute standard, various comparative procedures have been developed, discussed in the following sections. The first approach is to test whether the forecast satisfies certain properties of an optimal forecast, other than that of minimum mean square error. The second approach is to limit attention to a particularly restricted information set, namely that comprising past values of the variable of interest alone, and to compare a given forecast with the 'pure time series' forecast based on this 'own-variable' information set. The proper interpretation of such comparisons is considered, together with some recent evidence on the variation over time of the performance of economic forecasts relative to a particularly simple time series forecast. A third possibility is to conduct comparisons across a number of models or forecasts, and the issues that these raise, together with the possibility of combining forecasts, are discussed next. Whereas all these approaches limit attention to the published *ex ante* forecast, some recent systematic appraisals of the major sources of forecast error, *ex post*, are then described. Finally, the assessment of forecast uncertainty is considered.

IV.1 *Properties of Optimal Forecasts*

An optimal forecast, which is the same thing as a rational expectation in the macroeconomic context, is unbiased and efficient. That is, the forecast error has an expected value of zero and cannot be predicted by any variable in the information set: full use of the given information has already been made in constructing the forecast.

A simple test of unbiasedness is to calculate the sample mean forecast error and compare it to its standard error. Many studies, instead or in addition, estimate the realisation-forecast regression

$$A_t = \alpha + \beta F_t + u_t,$$

where A and F denote actual value and forecast respectively, and test the (joint) hypothesis $\alpha = 0$, $\beta = 1$. While this is often interpreted as a test of unbiasedness, since if $\alpha = 0$ and $\beta = 1$ the forecasts are unbiased, it is in fact a stricter test, and was originally presented as a test of efficiency by Mincer and Zarnowitz (1969, p. 9). Since

$$A_t \equiv F_t + e_t,$$

where e_t is the forecast error, the estimate of β in the above regression only deviates from 1 if F_t and e_t are correlated. Such a correlation indicates an

MACROECONOMIC FORECASTING: A SURVEY 65

inefficient forecast, since the correlation could be exploited to help predict the forecast error and so improve the forecast. But a significant deviation of the estimates of α and β from 0 and 1, respectively, does not necessarily imply significant bias, for it is possible that the sample mean forecast error, $\bar{e}$, is nevertheless close to zero in such circumstances. Since the regression estimates of α and β are in general correlated, their individual t ratios provide inappropriate tests of the efficiency hypothesis, and a *joint* test is required: Artis (1988) presents examples in which the individual and joint tests are in conflict.

Granger and Newbold (1977, p. 284) raise a practical objection to the realisation-forecast regression, namely that the validity of the usual test procedures rests on the non-autocorrelation of u_t, which need not necessarily hold for sub-optimal one-step-ahead forecasts, and does not generally hold for optimal forecasts more than one step ahead: Hansen and Hodrick (1980) provide corrected estimates of the asymptotic covariance matrix to accommodate this possibility. These are used by Holden and Peel (1985), for example, who study NIESR forecasts of six variables one to four quarters ahead over the period 1975–80: the hypothesis $\alpha = 0$, $\beta = 1$ is rejected in only one of the twenty-four cases, namely for forecasts of inflation four quarters ahead. Zarnowitz (1985) studies ASA–NBER business outlook survey respondents and likewise finds that inflation is the difficult variable: across six variables, five horizons and 79 respondents, the hypothesis $\alpha = 0$, $\beta = 1$ is rejected at the 5 % level in 15·4% of the tests, but nearly half of these rejections refer to the inflation forecasts. In both of these papers the hypothesis $\alpha = 0$, $\beta = 1$ is referred to as the unbiasedness hypothesis.

The NIESR inflation forecasts presented in Fig. 2 are similar to the four-quarter-ahead forecasts considered by Holden and Peel, but cover a longer period. It is clear from inspection that the forecast errors are positive during the period 1964–81 (except 1968, which has a zero error), indicating persistent underprediction of inflation, followed by persistently negative errors during 1982–87. Given this pattern it is not surprising that the realisation-forecast regression has a significant Durbin-Watson statistic, and in a joint test based on the corrected coefficient covariances the hypothesis $\alpha = 0$, $\beta = 1$ is rejected. The mean forecast error overall is 1·0% p.a. The GDP forecasts, however, are unbiased according to these tests.

It is now recognised that the concept of efficiency underlying the realisation-forecast regression is a relatively weak one. Granger and Newbold (1977, p. 284) argue that $\alpha = 0$, $\beta = 1$ 'constitutes a necessary condition for forecast efficiency, but according to any acceptable interpretation of that word it cannot be regarded as a *sufficient* condition'; in particular, it neglects possible autocorrelation of the forecast error, as their counter-example implicitly suggests. Autocorrelation of one-step-ahead forecast errors indicates that the forecast is not making efficient use at least of the own-variable information set, since knowledge of past forecast errors for the variable in question can then improve current forecasts. Errors in forecasts more than one step ahead cumulate step-by-step and so are autocorrelated, as noted above, but the errors in an optimal n-step-ahead forecast exhibit autocorrelation of order n-1, not n,

66   KENNETH F. WALLIS

so this cannot be exploited to improve the forecast: it is efficient with respect
to the own-variable information set. This efficiency property can be tested in
a variety of ways. Holden and Peel (1985) regress the forecast error on the four
most recent values of the variable known when the forecast was made. Of the
twenty-four cases considered, only the inflation forecasts over three and four
quarters fail this test, and the remaining NIESR forecasts could not be
improved by using own-variable information more efficiently.

Increased use of the rational expectations hypothesis has been associated
with a further strengthening of the concept of efficiency, which in its most
extreme form, 'full rationality', requires that all available information be used
in an optimal manner in constructing a forecast. Efficiency with respect to an
information set containing other variables can be tested as in the preceding
paragraph, by regressing the forecast error on lagged values of these variables
known at the time the forecast was prepared. But the notion of 'all available'
information presents practical difficulties, and whereas a rejection of full
rationality in such a test is convincing, a failure to reject does not dispel the
thought that there might be a relevant variable, untested, lurking around the
corner. Brown and Maital (1981) assess one of the best-known surveys of
experts' anticipations, namely the Livingston data, over the period 1962–77. Of
the nine variables considered, only the wholesale price inflation expectations
were found to be inefficient with respect to own-variable information, and the
forecast errors in this variable and consumer price inflation could each be
partly explained by past values of the other variable, indicating that their
interrelationship was not properly appreciated by the forecasters. The more
interesting finding, however, was that monetary growth helped to explain the
forecast errors in both inflation variables, indicating that had monetary growth
been correctly understood and fully incorporated into expectations over this
period, the forecasts would have been considerably improved. Neglect of
monetary influences does not appear to be the explanation of the problems in
the NIESR annual inflation forecasts described above, however.

IV.2 *Comparisons with Time-series Forecasts*

Forecasts based exclusively on the statistical time-series properties of the
variable in question have often been used to provide a yardstick against which
economic forecasts, whether model-based or not, can be assessed. At a
conference in 1972, Granger and Newbold (1975) commented that 'so far the
sparring partner [the time series forecast] is consistently out-pointing the
potential champion [the econometric model]', but the potential champion
quickly reached match-fitness. A typical result is that of McNees (1982), who
finds that published model forecasts generally outperform their time series
competitors, the margin being greater four quarters ahead than one quarter
ahead.

Comparison of a given forecast with a particularly naive alternative is
implicit in a widely used 'inequality coefficient', attributed to Theil, defined as
the ratio of the RMSE of the forecast to the RMSE of a 'no-change' forecasting
rule. This rule projects forward the last available observed value, and so the

MACROECONOMIC FORECASTING: A SURVEY   67

error in such a one-step-ahead forecast is simply the first difference of the variable in question. This inequality coefficient appears in Theil's *Applied Economic Forecasting* (1966), also in Ferber and Verdoorn (1962), Zarnowitz (1967), and elsewhere; in *Economic Forecasts and Policy* (1958) Theil had proposed a coefficient with a different denominator, designed to ensure that the coefficient lies between 0 and 1, but this has other disadvantages, as noted by Ferber and Verdoorn (1962, ch. 10.4), Sims (1967), Granger and Newbold (1977, pp. 281–2), and by Theil (1966, p. 28) himself. Sims (1967) and Zarnowitz (1967) also use inequality coefficients in which the denominator is the RMSE of less naive time series forecasts, initiating a trend in forecast comparisons that has continued since that time. After the initial use of no-change or 'same-change' forecasting rules, autoregressive models and the ARIMA models of Box and Jenkins (1970) were employed as benchmarks. The increased complexity of these time series methods itself indicates the progress that has occurred in forecasting models since their early development. Finally, moving to a multivariate context, vector autoregressive (VAR) models as used for forecasting by Litterman (1986) have entered the competition. In this last respect the US picture is somewhat mixed: VAR forecasts are part of the comparison carried out by McNees (1982), summarised above; with Litterman's Bayesian modification they also feature in the comparison of McNees (1986), where they are generally the most accurate or among the most accurate for real GNP, unemployment and investment. Curiously, for four of the seven variables considered by McNees, the RMSE of the VAR forecast declines as the forecast horizon increases from one to eight quarters. In the United Kingdom, however, VAR forecasts have not been found to dominate published model-based forecasts (Wallis *et al.*, 1986, 1987).

Formal comparisons between model-based forecasts and time series forecasts face two difficulties. First, since the data used in empirical specification and estimation of the two forms are the same, their forecasts, forecast errors and resulting summary measures are not statistically independent, hence a formal test based on a direct comparison of the two forecast error variances, such as an F test, cannot be employed. Secondly, at the theoretical level, a univariate ARIMA model can be regarded as an approximation to a solution form of an econometric model (its 'final equation'), and hence again cannot provide an independent check on the econometric model, in terms of forecast or any other comparison. Since the time series models emphasise dynamic and stochastic features of the data, early comparisons in which they outperformed econometric models simply suggest that the latter were deficient in these respects (Prothero and Wallis, 1976). Indeed, the equations of such models often exhibited substantial residual autocorrelation. Subsequently, the dynamic and stochastic specification of the large-scale econometric models has improved, through the application of developments in time-series econometrics. In the UK context, these stem from the classic Colston paper by Sargan (1964); see, for example, Wallis (1972), Hendry (1974) and Hendry and Richard (1983). In particular, comparisons with time series models now can be seen to represent a useful diagnostic device during the model specification process. The advice offered at

68   KENNETH F. WALLIS

that same 1972 conference, 'that a suggested specification should be tested in all possible ways, and only those specifications which survive and correspond to a reasonable economic model should be used' (Sargan, 1975) has been heeded, and a range of diagnostic tests is readily available in user-friendly micro-computer software (for example, Hendry, 1986).

Finally, an inequality coefficient based on a naive time-series forecast is reconsidered, for a different purpose. In his analysis of Treasury forecasts, Burns (1986) calculates five-year moving averages of absolute forecast errors and compares these to an index of variation which gives some impression of the difficulty of forecasting at different points in time. The index is defined as the five-year moving average of the absolute error of a no-change forecast of the growth rate or the inflation rate, that is, the average of the absolute difference between successive years' growth or inflation rates; appropriate extensions are needed for comparison with two-year-ahead forecasts. The resulting ratio modifies the Theil inequality coefficient for forecasts of growth and inflation in two ways: it replaces RMSEs by MAEs, and it replaces the overall sample means by five-year moving averages. Burns' results for Treasury forecasts over one-year and two-year horizons are shown, slightly updated, in Fig. 3, together with equivalent information for LBS and NIESR forecasts. His broad conclusion about Treasury forecasts over this period is that while there has not been any marked improvement in accuracy of the short-term forecasts, the results for the two-year-ahead forecasts are more encouraging, with some evidence of improvement over time. Over the shorter period for which data are available, the LBS and NIESR two-year forecasts show no substantial change in performance in respect of these two variables, and the Treasury forecasts appear to dominate, which may reflect their more effective incorporation of policy measures. For the one-year-ahead forecasts, however, the ranking of the three groups varies over time, and at any point in time is not consistent across the two variables considered. This is illustrative of a general finding in cross-model comparisons, discussed next.

IV. 3 *Cross-model Comparisons and Combinations*

Comparisons of the *ex ante* forecasts published by different forecasting groups place all competitors on an equal footing with respect to information about the future. If one forecaster uses a model which treats as exogenous a variable which another treats as endogenous, then the former needs to provide an off-model projected value for that variable. The difference in classification of variables is immaterial, provided that it is recognised that a forecaster-model combination is under scrutiny. Remembering also the process of adjustments described in Section I, it is clear that *ex ante* forecasts do not provide useful evaluations of models alone. Furthermore, since models evolve, as discussed above, comparisons based on summary statistics such as MAE or RMSE over a period of years are in effect evaluating forecasting groups together with whatever model specification was in use at the time. Their personnel changes over time, too, although Burns (1986) attributes some of the improvement in Treasury medium-term forecasts to an increase in human capital: 'many

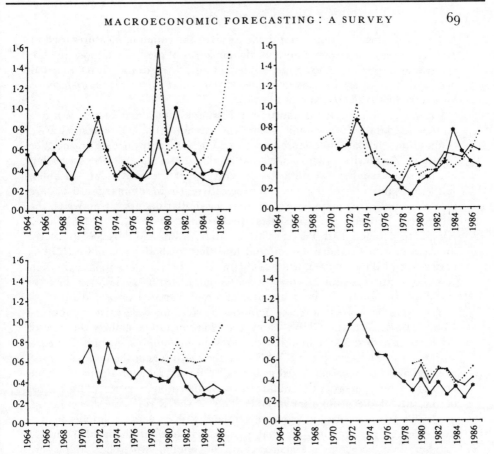

Fig. 3. Ratio of mean absolute error to index of variation (five-year moving averages shown against last year of period). Upper left, GDP growth, one-year-ahead forecast; lower left, GDP growth, two-year-ahead forecast; upper right, Inflation, one-year-ahead forecast; lower right, Inflation, two-year-ahead forecast. Key: —■—, LBS; ··■··, NIESR; —*—, HMT.

members of the forecasting teams were engaged in forecasting for many years'.

One practical use of forecasts is in informing decision-making, and in principle the evaluation of forecasts can be associated with any specified loss function, relevant to the particular objective. Given the dynamic multivariate nature of the forecasts, this would then help to specify the time horizon and the set of variables to be considered. In practice this does not feature in the literature, since decision makers and the users of forecasts seldom discuss such matters, at least not in public. As a result comparative studies usually focus on the small number of key macroeconomic indicators that feature in public discussion, and the possibility that one forecaster may offer information about a further group of variables about which another forecaster is completely silent is usually ignored. Clearly, however, if a user's interest is in that further group of variables, then there is no difficulty in deciding which forecaster is 'best'.

70 KENNETH F. WALLIS

Although the loss function is not made explicit, the common measures used to evaluate forecast accuracy imply particular forms of the loss function, the use of mean square error, for example, implying that it is quadratic. Also the period over which these are calculated implies a particular interest in short-term or long-term forecasts, for example.

Given the rather general nature of the criteria, and the existence of a free market in data and economic ideas, the common finding of comparative studies that there are no unambiguous rankings is perhaps not surprising. For example, Zarnowitz (1979) finds that rankings among six US forecasting groups show appreciable differences with respect to particular variables, subperiods and forecast horizons, but the differences in summary statistics are typically small: 'the main lesson...is that the similarities greatly outweigh the differences between the forecasters' performance records'. In the United Kingdom, Holden and Peel (1986) compare LBS and NIESR quarterly forecasts of growth and inflation, and find that for both variables NIESR is preferred to LBS in 1975–9, whereas the ranking is reversed in 1980–4 (in each case both are superior to the forecasts published by a London firm of stockbrokers, however). As an example of a multivariate exercise, Wallis *et al.* (1987) consider a single forecast published in autumn 1984 by four groups – LBS, NIESR, LPL and CUBS – and study four variables, namely the level of GDP, its growth rate, the inflation rate and the unemployment rate. For each variable and each group the RMSE over the two years of the forecast period is calculated and then expressed as a ratio of the average for a given variable across all groups, in order to standardise the comparison in respect of the degree of difficulty of forecasting that variable. The relative RMSEs are shown in Fig. 4: a value less than one for a given group and a given variable implies better-than-average performance for that variable. If one tetrahedron lies inside another, then there is an unambiguous ranking not only when the variables are deemed to have equal importance, as in the illustration, but for all values of their relative weights. While this occurs in this particular short-term forecast for one pair, LBS and LPL, in all other pairwise comparisons the tetrahedra intersect and so no rankings that are invariant to the choice of weights on the different variables can be derived.

The statistical significance of differences in summary statistics such as the RMSE cannot be directly tested, as noted above, since the competing forecasts are not independent. The idea of combining forecasts (Bates and Granger, 1969) offers an alternative approach to testing the *ex post* performance of competing forecasts, and also a method of improving *ex ante* forecasting performance. Consider a combination of one forecast with its competitor: if the combined forecast has an error variance that is not significantly smaller than that of the first forecast then the competing forecast appears to offer no useful additional information. On the other hand, different forecasts based on different informations sets, different models, or even different approaches to data analysis, as in econometric vs. time series comparisons, in general may each be expected to contribute usefully to the forecasting problem, and so the combined forecast may be more accurate than any of the individual

MACROECONOMIC FORECASTING : A SURVEY 71

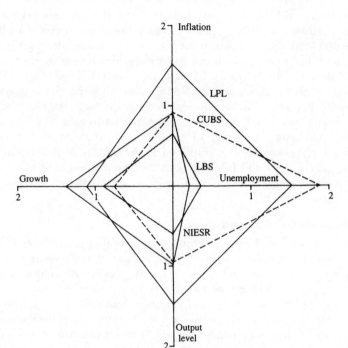

Fig. 4. Relative root mean square errors. The average root mean square errors are: GDP level, 2 % of actual; GDP growth rate, 1·0 % per annum; inflation rate 1·8 % per annum; unemployment rate, 0·7 %.

components. Thus an *ex post* comparison of two forecasts, F_{1t} and F_{2t}, may be based on the regression equation

$$A_t = \beta F_{1t} + (1 - \beta) F_{2t} + u_t$$

and a test of the null hypothesis $\beta = 1$, while a combination of *ex ante* forecasts for subsequent use may be based on the estimated coefficient.

Recent discussion (Granger and Ramanathan, 1984; Clemen, 1986; Holden and Peel, 1986) has focused on the general combination of k forecasts through the equation

$$A_t = \alpha + \beta_1 F_{1t} + \beta_2 F_{2t} + \ldots + \beta_k F_{kt} + u_t$$

and the question of whether or not the coefficient restrictions

$$\alpha = 0, \quad \beta_1 + \beta_2 + \ldots + \beta_k = 1$$

should be imposed. The unconstrained regression clearly achieves a smaller residual sum of squares *ex post*, as Granger and Ramanathan indicate, but the practical objective is to improve *ex ante* forecast performance, and Clemen shows that the imposition of the restrictions can improve forecast efficiency. Whereas some forecasts may be found to be biased, *ex post*, over certain periods, each individual *ex ante* forecast is offered as a best estimate of the future

72   KENNETH F. WALLIS

outcome, corrected for any past bias through the best endeavours of the forecaster. Holden and Peel (1986) estimate the above regression using only data available at a given point in the past, and with the estimated coefficients form a combined forecast of a future outcome, which is then compared with the actual outcomes: for quarterly forecasts of growth and inflation, a restricted combination always has a smaller RMSE than an unrestricted combination. The three 'economic' forecasts noted above are considered, along with three time series forecasts, and the winning combination is that based on the three economic forecasts. However, given the need to estimate the regression coefficients, the comparison is restricted to the later period of available data, namely 1980–4: here the LBS provides the best economic forecast, as noted above, and this single forecast also dominates the combined forecast over this period.

IV.4 *Decomposition of Forecast Error*

Ex ante forecasts are of little assistance in the evaluation of models, as noted above, since the forecast is a joint product of model and forecaster. Statistical summaries of errors in published forecasts provide no information about possible causes of forecast error. Errors may arise because the model is inadequate and because exogenous variables behave in a different manner to that on which the forecast is conditioned. Recomputation of the forecast, *ex post*, using realised values of exogenous variables, allows this latter source of error to be assessed. Forecasters make adjustments to the pure model forecasts in an attempt to overcome perceived model inadequacies and to improve the forecast in other ways, and the extent to which this succeeds may be assessed by recomputing the forecast with such adjustments removed. There is little consideration in the literature of these various sources of forecast error, an exception being Osborn and Teal (1979), who analyse two NIESR forecasts. In general, independent researchers have not been able to recompute forecasts under alternative assumptions, using the precise models on which the forecasts were based. An exception, however, is the ESRC Macroeconomic Modelling Bureau, which has taken successive deposits of models and forecasts since autumn 1983, and archived this information. With the passage of time comparative *ex post* forecast error decompositions become feasible, as described in this section, based on Wallis *et al.* (1986, ch. 4; 1987, ch. 4).

Ex post forecast comparisons give an advantage to a model that treats as exogenous a variable that is difficult to forecast, when other models are trying to explain its behaviour. Accordingly such comparisons are often criticised, because different models may have different degrees of exogeneity. Practical experience with the UK models, however, is that the broad classification of variables as endogenous or exogenous does not differ across models. In general, the variables treated as exogenous in models of small open economies fall into three main groups, describing respectively the economic environment in the rest of the world, domestic economic policy, and various natural resource and demographic trends, such as the growth of North Sea oil production and changes in the population of working age. Within these generally agreed

MACROECONOMIC FORECASTING: A SURVEY 73

exogenous areas differences of detail may arise, for the same reasons that apply in other areas of the models. For example, different models may measure an identical concept (the world price of oil, the real wage) in different ways; some concepts (world money supply) may appear in some models but not in others; the level of aggregation (distinguishing the price of oil from the general price level) may differ. Also, where the line is drawn between exogenous assumption and endogenous consequence may differ, particularly in respect of domestic economic policy: the more medium-term models tend to take as given a broad policy stance and allow the response of public expenditure and taxation to emerging pressures to be determined by the model, whereas the more short-term models take the detailed policy settings as given. Nevertheless these differences are not sufficient to inhibit cross-model comparisons.

Wallis *et al.* (1986, 1987) compute two variant forecasts after the event. First, the projected values of variables treated as exogenous are replaced by the actual outcomes: a comparison with the published forecast indicates the effect of incorrect anticipations about external developments. Secondly, by setting all residual adjustments to zero an *ex post* forecast, variously described as pure model-based, mechanical, or hands-off, is obtained. The error in this forecast includes the effect of model misspecification and the contribution of random disturbances in the forecast period, together with any effect of data revisions not explicitly accommodated elsewhere. The forecaster's residual adjustments represent an attempt to reduce this error and a comparison with the first variant indicates how successful this was. The error in the published forecast can then be decomposed as illustrated in Fig. 5, which describes the 1983 and 1984 forecasts of the price level, one and two years ahead, from four groups. In each segment of the figure the first block gives the error in the *ex post* hands-off forecast ('model error'), and the second block is the contribution of the forecaster's adjustments. These should be of opposite sign if the adjustments indeed act in an offsetting manner: in the majority of cases this has occurred, although the adjustment is seldom of the correct magnitude and sometimes rather large offsets were called for. The third block gives the contribution of errors in projecting exogenous variables, and these three contributions sum to the fourth block, namely, the error in the published forecast. In all cases these last errors increase as the forecast horizon increases, as expected. Overall the LPL group persistently underestimated inflation, that is, took an overoptimistic view in this respect, whereas the other three groups tended to be unduly pessimistic. It is often argued that a good track record in forecasting is a prerequisite for the use of a model in policy analysis, but it is important to disentangle the role of the model and the role of the forecaster, as in this illustration.

Perhaps the most striking feature of Fig. 5 is the contribution of exogenous uncertainty to the forecasts for 1986. In the first three cases the fortuitous choice of wrong exogenous assumptions has resulted in a relatively small final error, while in the LPL forecast the exogenous outcome transposes a pessimistic *ex post* adjusted forecast into an optimistic one. The principal cause is the unanticipated and unprecedented fall in the world oil price in 1986. This

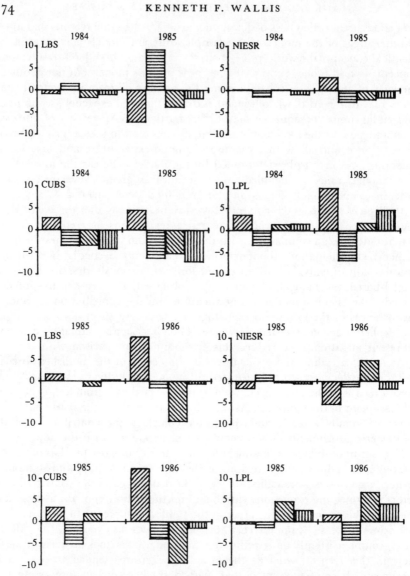

Fig. 5. Contributions to errors in price level forecasts, one and two years ahead (% of actual). Upper panel, autumn 1983 forecasts; lower panel, autumn 1984 forecasts. Key: ▨, model error; ▤, contribution of residuals; ◩, contribution of exogenous uncertainty; ▥, error in published forecast.

variable appears directly in the LBS, NIESR and CUBS models, which would have produced substantial forecast errors had its movements been anticipated, as the first block of the decomposition indicates. The fall in the world oil price was associated with a level of world demand lower than anticipated, the depressing impact of lower oil prices on the oil-producing countries being more immediate than the expansionary impact in the oil-importing countries, and this is the principal source of exogenous error in the LPL model, where oil prices do not appear. In the other three cases there is no agreement: LBS and CUBS show a large positive model error and knowledge of the forthcoming oil price fall would have led them to underestimate the domestic price level by a considerable amount, whereas in the NIESR forecast lower oil prices would have increased domestic prices via the lower exchange rate. This is the principal transmission mechanism in this case, and the actual impact on exchange rates of the oil price fall was much smaller than suggested by the then-current models. These were projecting forward from a different kind of sample experience and did not reflect whatever asymmetric effects were in operation. Once again, a change in data characteristics has been informative, and including this episode in the sample period has resulted in newly estimated equations that are much less sensitive to world oil prices.

A principal use of *ex post* forecast assessment is in studying the performance of models, as noted above. As far as the forecasts themselves are concerned, whereas calculations such as those that lie behind Fig. 5 permit discussion of what might have been, they cannot tell what would have been. The production of a forecast is an interactive process, and had the oil price fall been anticipated forecasters might have realised that its effects would not simply be the negative of the effects of the preceding oil price rise. Adjustments to the pure model-based forecast might then have been made, anticipating the model modifications that occurred subsequently. However forecasters seldom reveal the rationale for specific adjustments that they make (revelation of the adjustments themselves is a relatively new phenomenon, as discussed below), and it is not possible to reconstruct the forecasting team and its state of mind at the time in order to answer 'what-if' questions. Nevertheless a model that produces accurate *ex post* forecasts only after substantial adjustment must represent an unreliable vehicle for policy analysis.

IV.5 *Assessing Uncertainty*

Forecasts are subject to errors, and the user of forecasts needs to know the likely margin of error. Theoretical discussion of model-based forecasts usually takes the model as given and then analyses the forecast error in terms of its three sources: the model's random disturbance terms, its coefficient estimation errors, and forecast errors in exogenous variables. In the textbook linear model formal expressions for the variance attributable to each source are available, and in the practical nonlinear model stochastic simulation can be employed to estimate these quantities. This approach is of little help to the practitioner. It neglects the contribution of the forecaster's subjective adjustments, and its last element simply pushes the problem of assessing the margin of forecast error one stage further back, from endogenous to exogenous variables. More fundamentally, the model's specification is uncertain. At any point in time competing models coexist, over time model specifications evolve, and there is no way of assessing this uncertainty. Thus the only practical indication of the likely margin of future error is provided by the past forecast errors. Published evaluations of

76　　　　　　　　　　　　KENNETH F. WALLIS

forecasts, such as those cited above, are a source of this information, and the forecasters themselves commonly provide an estimate of their past performance. For example, Treasury forecasts published in the annual *Financial Statement and Budget Report* (the 'Red Book') are accompanied by the MAE of the preceding ten years' forecasts.

Estimating the future margin of error is itself a forecasting problem, in that not only the first moment but also the second moment of the conditional probability distribution of future outcomes is now under consideration. As with the first moment, errors in forecasting the second moment are likely to occur at times of rapid change in the underlying situation, when the economy becomes harder or easier to forecast for some reason. Standardising measures of forecast performance with reference to the underlying variation, as in the examples in Fig. 3, accommodates such changes in the past, but in projecting forward the underlying variation is assumed to remain constant, unless this forecast is in turn subjectively adjusted. For example, in discussing the margin of error of Treasury forecasts, the *Financial Statement and Budget Report* that accompanied the June 1979 Budget noted the 'possibility that large changes in policy will affect the economy in ways which are not foreseen'.

The uncertainty of a single forecast, indicated by the spread of the probability distribution of possible outcomes, should be distinguished from disagreement among several (point) forecasts, as Zarnowitz and Lambros (1987) note. Consensus among forecasters need not imply a high degree of confidence about the commonly predicted outcome. To study this question, Zarnowitz and Lambros analyse the ASA-NBER survey responses on GNP growth and inflation, in which individual respondents provide their subjective (joint) probability distribution of outcomes. It is found that the variance of point forecasts tends to understate uncertainty as measured by the variance of the predictive probability distributions. The former varies much more over time than the latter, although these measures of consensus and uncertainty are positively correlated.

V. CONCLUDING COMMENTS

This paper surveys developments in macroeconomic forecasting over the last twenty years, during which forecasting methods have become more formalised and considerable progress has been made. 'Success in forecasting may be occasional and fortuitous or intuitive, but progress in forecasting, to the extent it is possible, can only come from advances of science, not art or chance' (Zarnowitz, 1979). Such advances have occurred gradually, with small improvements building on one another, 'but nothing really has been a complete breakthrough for solving the problems that confront us' (Klein, 1987). Forecasting disappointments led not to complete changes of direction but to constructive reappraisals and eventual improvements, also changes of emphasis. McNees (1988) concludes that 'annual forecasts of real GNP and the inflation rate have improved over time. Summary error measures have

MACROECONOMIC FORECASTING: A SURVEY 77

declined slightly in absolute terms but even more relative to either naive standards of comparison or the variability of the actual outcomes.'

The role of forecasts in macroeconomic policy-making, and the policy-making itself, have seen considerable changes during this period. Although the uncertainty in forecasting was clearly appreciated, Cairncross (1969) noting that 'the margins of error...even when small in relation to the magnitudes involved, remain large in relation to policy objectives and to the reserves held against contingencies', during the years of demand management short-term forecasts played an increasing role in fine tuning the level of demand. But by 1976, as Burns (1986) notes, 'there was not only disillusion with demand management; there was also growing frustration with the forecasts' as the increased level of noise in the economic system led to increased margins of error. In the 1980s the focus of the forecasts and policy analysis has shifted to a more medium-term horizon, and it is here that 'many of the developments in our understanding of the way economies work are likely to have their pay-off', again quoting Burns.

Cairncross (1969) concluded his Presidential Address by commenting on the issue of the publication of official forecasts. While acknowledging that there were 'great advantages in making official forecasts as widely available as possible', he also emphasised 'some of the inconveniences from the Ministerial point of view in putting official forecasts in front of an unsophisticated public' and expressed his own view 'that the issue is not nearly as important as it appears'. In any event, the Bray amendment to the 1975 Industry Act required the Treasury to publish forecasts produced with the aid of the model at least twice a year, and the first 'Industry Act forecast' was published in December 1976. As noted above, these are accompanied by indications of forecasting error, also as required by the Act. Five years after the Act, the Treasury could conclude that 'the impact of the Government's publishing forecasts has been, perhaps, more limited than was suggested by some of the strongly-held beliefs – pre-1976 – for and against publication' (HM Treasury, 1981).

Considerable improvements in publication and dissemination of forecasts have occurred in the period under review. Models and forecasts have become better documented and more widely accessible, most recently being disseminated for implementation on micro-computers. In the United Kingdom, forecast analysis such as that described in Section IV.4 is possible because the models, forecasts, and associated databases are made available to an independent research group (the ESRC Macroeconomic Modelling Bureau) charged with improving accessibility and undertaking comparative research. Before the establishment of the Bureau in 1983, the LBS forecasters had begun to publish the residual adjustments used in each forecast in their *Economic Outlook*. (Treasury forecasts do not enter such comparative analysis, however, since although the model is publicly available, again thanks to the Industry Act, the forecast assumptions and adjustments are not.) This degree of openness is unique, and perhaps could not be achieved in countries where the leading forecasting groups are commercial. Nevertheless in such countries public bodies

78   KENNETH F. WALLIS

are often among the main customers of commercial forecasters, and when such forecasts enter the public debate the same arguments about understanding the assumptions and replicating the results apply. Models and forecasts benefit from public discussion and assessment, and in most countries much more could be done.

REFERENCES

Artis, M. J. (1988). 'How accurate is the World Economic Outlook? A post mortem on short-term forecasting at the International Monetary Fund.' In *Staff Studies for the World Economic Outlook*, July 1988, pp. 1–49. Washington, DC: International Monetary Fund.

Ash, J. C. K. and Smyth, D. J. (1973). *Forecasting the United Kingdom Economy*. Farnborough: Saxon House.

Ball, R. J. and Burns, T. (1978). 'Stabilisation policy in Britain 1964–81.' In *Demand Management* (ed. M. V. Posner), pp. 66–100. London: Heinemann.

——, —— and Warburton, P. J. (1979). 'The London Business School model of the UK economy: an exercise in international monetarism.' In *Economic Modelling* (ed. P. A. Ormerod), pp. 86–114. London: Heinemann.

Barker, T. S. (1985). 'Forecasting the economic recession in the U.K. 1979–1982: a comparison of model-based *ex ante* forecasts.' *Journal of Forecasting*, vol. 4, pp. 133–51.

Barro, R. J. and Fischer, S. (1976). 'Recent developments in monetary theory.' *Journal of Monetary Economics*, vol. 2, pp. 133–67.

Bates, J. M. and Granger, C. W. J. (1969). 'The combination of forecasts.' *Operational Research Quarterly*, vol. 20, pp. 451–68.

Beenstock, M., Warburton, P., Lewington, P. and Dalziel, A. (1986). 'A macroeconomic model of aggregate supply and demand for the UK.' *Economic Modelling*, vol. 3, pp. 242–68.

Blanchard, O. J. (1987). 'Neoclassical synthesis.' In *The New Palgrave: A Dictionary of Economics*, vol. 3 (ed. J. Eatwell, M. Milgate and P. Newman), pp. 634–6. London: Macmillan.

Box, G. E. P. and Jenkins, G. M. (1970). *Time Series Analysis, Forecasting and Control*. San Francisco: Holden–Day.

Brown, B. W. and Maital, S. (1981). 'What do economists know? An empirical study of experts' expectations.' *Econometrica*, vol. 49, pp. 491–504.

Buiter, W. H. and Miller, M. H. (1981). 'The Thatcher experiment: the first two years.' *Brookings Papers on Economic Activity*, no. 2, pp. 315–67.

—— and —— (1983). 'Changing the rules: economic consequences of the Thatcher regime.' *Brookings Papers on Economic Activity*, no. 2, pp. 305–65.

Burns, T. (1986). 'The interpretation and use of economic predictions.' *Proceedings of the Royal Society of London*, A, no. 407, pp. 103–25. Reprinted in *Predictability in Science and Society* (ed. J. Mason, P. Mathias and J. H. Westcott). London: Royal Society and British Academy.

Cairncross, A. (1969). 'Economic forecasting.' ECONOMIC JOURNAL, vol. 79, pp. 797–812.

Chow, G. C. and Corsi, P. (eds.) (1982). *Evaluating the Reliability of Macroeconomic Models*. New York: Wiley.

Clemen, R. T. (1986). 'Linear constraints and the efficiency of combined forecasts.' *Journal of Forecasting*, vol. 5, pp. 31–8.

Currie, D. A. (1985). 'Macroeconomic policy design and control theory – a failed partnership?' ECONOMIC JOURNAL, vol. 95, pp. 285–306.

Davidson, J. E. H., Hendry, D. F., Srba, F. and Yeo, S. (1978). 'Econometric modelling of the aggregate time-series relationship between consumers' expenditure and income in the United Kingdom.' ECONOMIC JOURNAL, vol. 88, pp. 661–92.

Dinenis, E., Holly, S., Levine, P. and Smith, P. (1989). 'The London Business School econometric model: some recent developments.' *Economic Modelling*, vol. 6, pp. 243–351.

Dornbusch, R. (1976). 'Expectations and exchange rate dynamics.' *Journal of Political Economy*, vol. 84, pp. 1161–76.

Eckstein, O. (1983), *The DRI Model of the U.S. Economy*. New York: McGraw-Hill.

Fair, R. C. (1984). *Specification, Estimation and Analysis of Macroeconometric Models*. Cambridge, Mass: Harvard University Press.

Ferber, R. and Verdoorn, P. J. (1962). *Research Methods in Economics and Business*. New York: Macmillan.

Fischer, S. (1988). 'Recent developments in macroeconomics.' ECONOMIC JOURNAL, vol. 98, pp. 294–339.

Flemming, J. S. (1978). Review of *Demand Management* (ed. M. V. Posner), Heinemann, 1978. *Times Higher Educational Supplement*, 15 September.

Granger, C. W. J. and Newbold, P. (1975). 'Economic forecasting: the atheist's viewpoint.' In *Modelling the Economy* (ed. G. A. Renton), pp. 131–47. London: Heinemann.

MACROECONOMIC FORECASTING : A SURVEY   79

—— and —— (1977). *Forecasting Economic Time Series*. New York: Academic Press. (Second edition, 1986.)

—— and Ramanathan, R. (1984). 'Improved methods of combining forecasts.' *Journal of Forecasting*, vol. 3, pp. 197–204.

Grunberg, E. and Modigliani, F. (1954). 'The predictability of social events.' *Journal of Political Economy*, vol. 62, pp. 465–78.

Hall, S. G. and Henry, S. G. B. (1985). 'Rational expectations in an econometric model: NIESR model 8.' *National Institute Economic Review*, No. 114, pp. 58–68.

Hansen, L. P. and Hodrick, R. J. (1980). 'Forward exchange rates as optimal predictors of future spot rates: an econometric analysis.' *Journal of Political Economy*, vol. 88, pp. 829–53.

Heller, W. W. *et al.* (1968). *Fiscal Policy for a Balanced Economy*. Paris: OECD.

Hendry, D. F. (1974). 'Stochastic specification in an aggregate demand model of the United Kingdom.' *Econometrica*, vol. 42, pp. 559–78.

—— (1986). 'Using PC-GIVE in econometrics teaching.' *Oxford Bulletin of Economics and Statistics*, vol. 48, pp. 87–98.

—— and Richard, J. F. (1983). 'The econometric analysis of economic time series.' *International Statistical Review*, vol. 51, pp. 111–63.

HM Treasury (1981). 'Forecasting in the Treasury.' *Economic Progress Report*, No. 134 (June), pp. 2–6.

Higgins, C. I. (1988). 'Empirical analysis and intergovernmental policy consultation.' In *Empirical Macroeconomics for Interdependent Economies* (ed. R. C. Bryant *et al.*), pp. 285–302. Washington, DC: Brookings Institution.

Hilton, K. and Heathfield, D. F. (eds.) (1970). *The Econometric Study of the United Kingdom*. London: Macmillan.

Holden, K. and Peel, D. A. (1983). 'Forecasts and expectations: some evidence for the UK.' *Journal of Forecasting*, vol. 2, pp. 51–8.

—— and —— (1985). 'An evaluation of quarterly National Institute forecasts.' *Journal of Forecasting*, vol. 4, pp. 227–34.

—— and —— (1986). 'An empirical investigation of combinations of economic forecasts.' *Journal of Forecasting*, vol. 5, pp. 229–42.

Isard, P. (1988). 'Exchange rate modeling: an assessment of alternative approaches.' In *Empirical Macroeconomics for Interdependent Economies* (ed. R. C. Bryant *et al.*), pp. 183–201. Washington, DC: Brookings Institution.

Keating, G. (1985). *The Production and Use of Economic Forecasts*. London: Methuen.

Klein, L. R. (1968). *An Essay on the Theory of Economic Prediction*. Helsinki: Yrjo Jahnsson Foundation.

—— (1974). 'Supply constraints in demand-oriented systems: an interpretation of the oil crisis.' *Zeitschrift fur Nationalokonomie*, vol. 34, pp. 45–56.

—— (1978). 'The supply side.' *American Economic Review*, vol. 68, pp. 1–7.

—— (1986). 'Economic policy formation: theory and implementation (applied econometrics in the public sector).' In *Handbook of Econometrics*, vol. 3 (ed. Z. Griliches and M. D. Intriligator), pp. 2057–93. Amsterdam: North-Holland.

—— (1987). 'The ET interview: Professor L. R. Klein interviewed by Roberto S. Mariano.' *Econometric Theory*, vol. 3, pp. 409–60.

—— Ball, R. J., Hazlewood, A. and Vandome, P. (1961). *An Econometric Model of the United Kingdom*. Oxford: Basil Blackwell.

—— Friedman, E. and Able, S. (1983). 'Money in the Wharton quarterly model.' *Journal of Money, Credit and Banking*, vol. 15, pp. 237–59.

—— and Young, R. M. (1980). *An Introduction to Econometric Forecasting and Forecasting Models*. Lexington, Mass: D. C. Heath.

Kmenta, J. and Ramsey, J. B. (eds.) (1981). *Large-Scale Macroeconometric Models: Theory and Practice*. Amsterdam: North-Holland.

Litterman, R. B. (1986). 'Forecasting with Bayesian vector autoregressions – five years of experience.' *Journal of Business and Economic Statistics*, vol. 4, pp. 25–38.

Llewellyn, J., Potter, S. and Samuelson, L. (1985). *Economic Forecasting and Policy – the International Dimension*. London: Routledge and Kegan Paul.

Lucas, R. E. (1975). 'An equilibrium model of the business cycle.' *Journal of Political Economy*, vol. 83, pp. 1113–44.

—— (1977). 'Understanding business cycles.' In *Stabilization of the Domestic and International Economy* (Carnegie-Rochester Series on Public Policy, vol. 5, ed. K. Brunner and A. H. Meltzer), pp. 7–29. Amsterdam: North-Holland.

—— (1980). 'Methods and problems in business cycle theory.' *Journal of Money, Credit and Banking*, vol. 12, pp. 696–715.

—— and Sargent, T. J. 'After Keynesian macroeconomics.' In *After the Phillips Curve: Persistence of High Inflation and High Unemployment*, pp. 44–72. Federal Reserve Bank of Boston, Conference Series No. 19.

80   KENNETH F. WALLIS

McNees, S. K. (1979a). 'The forecasting record for the 1970s.' *New England Economic Review* (September/
    October), pp. 33–53.
—— (1979b). 'Lessons from the track record of macroeconomic forecasts in the 1970s.' In *Forecasting* (TIMS
    Studies in the Management Sciences, vol. 12, ed. S. Makridakis and S. C. Wheelwright), pp. 227–46.
    Amsterdam: North-Holland.
—— (1982). 'The role of macroeconometric models in forecasting and policy analysis in the United States.'
    Journal of Forecasting, vol. 1, pp. 37–48.
—— (1986). 'Forecasting accuracy of alternative techniques: a comparison of U.S. macroeconomic forecasts
    (with discussion).' *Journal of Business and Economic Statistics*, vol. 4, pp. 5–23.
—— (1988). 'How accurate are macroeconomic forecasts?' *New England Economic Review* (July/August),
    pp. 15–36.
Malgrange, P. and Muet, P. A. (eds.) (1984). *Contemporary Macroeconomic Modelling*. Oxford: Blackwell.
Matthews, K. G. P. and Minford, A. P. L. (1987). 'Mrs Thatcher's economic policies 1979–87 (with
    discussion).' *Economic Policy*, vol. 5, pp. 59–101.
Mincer, J. and Zarnowitz, V. (1969). 'The evaluation of economic forecasts.' In *Economic Forecasts and
    Expectations*, National Bureau of Economic Research Studies in Business Cycles No. 19 (ed. J. Mincer),
    pp. 3–46. New York: Columbia University Press.
Minford, A. P. L., Marwaha, S., Matthews, K. and Sprague, A. (1984). 'The Liverpool macroeconomic
    model of the United Kingdom.' *Economic Modelling*, vol. 1, pp. 24–62.
Muth, J. F. (1961). 'Rational expectations and the theory of price movements.' *Econometrica*, vol. 29, pp.
    315–35.
Nickell, S. J. (1987). Discussion (of Matthews and Minford, 1987). *Economic Policy*, vol. 5, pp. 93–5.
Organisation for Economic Co-operation and Development (1965). *Techniques of Economic Forecasting*. Paris:
    OECD.
Ormerod, P. A. (ed.) (1979a). *Economic Modelling*. London: Heinemann.
—— (1979b). 'The National Institute model of the UK economy: some current problems.' In Ormerod
    (1979a), pp. 115–40.
Osborn, D. R. (1979). 'National Institute gross output forecasts: a comparison with US performance.'
    National Institute Economic Review, No. 88, pp. 40–9.
—— and Teal, F. (1979). 'An assessment and comparison of two NIESR econometric model forecasts.'
    National Institute Economic Review, No. 88, pp. 50–62.
Pesaran, M. H. and Evans, R, A. (1984). 'Inflation, capital gains and U.K. personal savings: 1953–1981.'
    ECONOMIC JOURNAL, vol. 94, pp. 237–57.
Pindyck, R. S. and Rubinfeld, D. L. (1976). *Econometric Models and Economic Forecasts*. New York: McGraw-
    Hill. (Second edition, 1981.)
Prothero, D. L. and Wallis, K. F. (1976). 'Modelling macroeconomic time series (with discussion).' *Journal
    of the Royal Statistical Society*, Series A, vol. 139, pp. 468–500.
Renton, G. A. (ed.) (1975). *Modelling the Economy*. London: Heinemann.
Roy, A. D. (1970). 'Short-term forecasting for central economic management of the U.K. economy.' In *The
    Econometric Study of the United Kingdom* (ed. K. Hilton and D. F. Heathfield), pp. 463–73. London:
    Macmillan.
Samuelson, P. A. (1955). *Economics* (3rd edn.). New York: McGraw-Hill.
Sargan, J. D. (1964). 'Wages and prices in the United Kingdom: a study in econometric methodology.' In
    Econometric Analysis for National Economic Planning (ed. P. E. Hart, G. Mills and J. K. Whitaker), pp.
    22–54. London: Butterworth. Reprinted in *Econometrics and Quantitative Economics* (ed. D. F. Hendry and
    K. F. Wallis), pp. 275–314. Oxford: Basil Blackwell.
—— (1975). 'Discussion on misspecification.' In *Modelling the Economy* (ed. G. A. Renton), pp. 321–22.
    London: Heinemann.
Sims, C. A. (1967). 'Evaluating short-term macro-economic forecasts: the Dutch performance.' *Review of
    Economics and Statistics*, vol. 49, pp. 225–36.
Spencer, P. D. (1986). *Financial Innovation, Efficiency and Disequilibrium: Problems of Monetary Management in the
    United Kingdom 1971–1981*. Oxford: Clarendon Press.
—— and Mowl, C. J. (1978). 'A financial sector for the Treasury model.' Government Economic Service
    Working Paper No. 17.
Suits, D. B. (1962). 'Forecasting and analysis with an econometric model.' *American Economic Review*, vol. 52,
    pp. 104–32.
Surrey, M. J. C. (1982). 'Was the recession forecast?' *National Institute Economic Review*, No. 100, pp.
    24–8.
Theil, H. (1958). *Economic Forecasts and Policy*. Amsterdam: North-Holland. (Second edition, 1961.)
—— (1966). *Applied Economic Forecasting*. Amsterdam: North-Holland.
Wallis, K. F. (1972). 'Testing for fourth order autocorrelation in quarterly regression equations.' *Econometrica*,
    vol. 40, pp. 617–36.
—— (1986). 'Forecasting with an econometric model: the "ragged edge" problem.' *Journal of Forecasting*,
    vol. 5, pp. 1–13.

—— (ed.), Andrews, M. J., Bell, D. N. F., Fisher, P. G. and Whitley, J. D. (1984). *Models of the UK Economy: A Review by the ESRC Macroeconomic Modelling Bureau.* Oxford: Oxford University Press.

—— (ed.), ——, ——, —— and —— (1985). *Models of the UK Economy: A Second Review by the ESRC Macroeconomic Modelling Bureau.* Oxford: Oxford University Press.

—— (ed.), —— Fisher, P. G., Longbottom, J. A. and Whitley, J. D. (1986). *Models of the UK Economy: A Third Review by the ESRC Macroeconomic Modelling Bureau.* Oxford: Oxford University Press.

—— (ed.), Fisher, P. G., Longbottom, J. A., Turner, D. S. and Whitley, J. D. (1987). *Models of the UK Economy: A Fourth Review by the ESRC Macroeconomic Modelling Bureau.* Oxford: Oxford University Press.

Worswick, G. D. N. and Budd, A. P. (1981). 'Factors underlying the recent recession.' Paper presented to the Panel of Academic Consultants, No. 15, Bank of England.

Zarnowitz, V. (1967). *An Appraisal of Short-Term Economic Forecasts.* National Bureau of Economic Research Occasional Paper, No. 104. New York: Columbia University Press.

—— (1979). 'An analysis of annual and multiperiod quarterly forecasts of aggregate income, output and the price level.' *Journal of Business,* vol. 52, pp. 1–33.

—— (1985). 'Rational expectations and macroeconomic forecasts.' *Journal of Business and Economic Statistics,* vol. 3, pp. 293–311.

—— and Lambros, L. A. (1987). 'Consensus and uncertainty in economic prediction.' *Journal of Political Economy,* vol. 95, pp. 591–621.

Part III
Time Series Forecasting

[10]

Lagged Relationships in Economic Forecasting

By P. J. COEN, E. D. GOMME and M. G. KENDALL

Scientific Control Systems Ltd, London

[Read before the ROYAL STATISTICAL SOCIETY on Wednesday, January 15th, 1969,
the President, Mr F. A. COCKFIELD, in the Chair]

INTRODUCTION

1. FOR some years econometricians have been aware of the critical dependence of economic systems on the lag between cause and effect. It has been shown that the very stability of a system may depend on the length of time taken for a stimulus to pass through the transient to full response. However, not much is known about the actual lengths of these lags, at least in the U.K. economy, and surprisingly little effort has been devoted to determining them. Such writers as are concerned with dynamic systems usually write in lags of one or two time units (and occasionally up to four in quarterly data to describe seasonal effects) and hope that autoregression will take care of any important lag effects. We felt that work in this area being done, for example, in the U.S.A. (e.g. by the National Bureau of Economic Research in *Business Cycle Indicators*) might not be applicable in the U.K. and decided to approach the British problem *ab initio*.

2. In December 1966 Mr Gomme approached Scicon to undertake, in the first place, a critical appraisal of the lag concept for predicting economic events, because he had already, after two years' study, had some success in developing a basic equation which predicted the July 1966 crisis in real time. He was faced with pronounced scepticism in the City and in the academic world, but held to the conviction that the whole concept should be critically examined. It was decided to proceed with a joint project which would systematically explore the existence of relationships among a wide range of economic variables. We were in a favourable position to do this because of our access to powerful computers and our program for determining optimum regression equations. Before very long some rather remarkable relationships emerged and our work, though not yet terminated, has reached a stage at which we feel that the results are worth reporting. At this stage we offer the results as empirical phenomena requiring explanation. We are not, for the present, concerned with what that explanation might be.

INITIAL EXPLORATION

3. We began by considering whether a Stock Exchange index of securities, namely the *Financial Times*† ordinary share index, could be related to one or more of the following variables: the *F.T.* commodity index, Reuter's commodity index, bank advances, sterling liability, Standard and Poor‡ share index (425 industrials on Wall Street), U.K. car production, value of U.K. cars produced, expenditure on consumer durables, bank rate, 2½ per cent consols yield, government expenditure, Stock Exchange activity, weekly wage rates, unemployment, vacancies outstanding, U.S. car production, production of bricks and electricity consumed. The data for the last 20 years for variables used in the equations here are exhibited in Table 1. All the data displayed here and used in this work are quarterly.

† *Financial Times* = F.T.   ‡ Standard and Poor = S. and P.

TABLE 1

Year and quarter	F.T. index	F.T. commodity index	Reuter's commodity index	Total bank advances (£ million)†	2½ per cent Consols yields (%)	Sterling liability (£ million)	S. and P. index	U.K. production of cars seasonally adjusted	Government securities index	U.K. bank rate (%)
1948/1	118·2		368·7				14·18	82,361	113·0	
1948/2	118·4		380·5				15·92	82,499	112·1	
1948/3	113·4		358·2				15·83	84,896	112·4	
1948/4	119·8		404·1				15·33	84,820	113·4	
1949/1	118·9		404·3				14·84	97,131	113·8	
1949/2	110·8		401·4				14·29	93,840	113·1	
1949/3	104·2		408·8				14·93	108,522	107·3	
1949/4	103·4		465·4				15·92	116,137	105·4	
1950/1	105·0		470·2				16·83	131,092	104·9	2·0
1950/2	109·8		487·6				18·18	123,583	105·8	2·0
1950/3	113·4		532·9				18·32	135,620	106·5	2·0
1950/4	116·3		561·6				20·01	135,889	108·1	2·0
1951/1	120·5		609·1		3·64	2,932	21·81	122,481	105·6	2·0
1951/2	133·7		622·3		3·78	3,119	22·14	115,384	102·9	2·0
1951/3	133·5		601·0		3·74	3,255	23·21	120,588	101·9	2·0
1951/4	129·1		592·9		3·98	3,281	23·57	121,576	99·3	2·33
1952/1	113·0		576·0	2,031	4·14	3,299	24·33	111,172	95·0	3·0
1952/2	108·7		545·4	1,966	4·32	3,164	24·19	109,355	93·0	4·0
1952/3	112·7	96·21	544·1	1,849	4·29	3,128	25·36	105,761	93·0	4·0
1952/4	115·0	93·74	517·9	1,871	4·24	3,099	25·34	121,874	94·7	4·0
1953/1	121·4	91·37	508·0	1,850	4·21	3,063	26·23	126,260	95·3	4·0
1953/2	118·4	86·31	498·2	1,830	4·10	3,121	24·66	145,248	97·4	4·0
1953/3	122·7	84·98	491·1	1,786	4·03	3,118	24·04	160,370	98·1	3·9
1953/4	128·8	86·46	480·6	1,792	3·92	3,073	24·44	163,648	100·4	3·5
1954/1	135·7	90·04	485·6	1,831	3·88	3,060	26·13	178,195	100·6	3·5
1954/2	148·5	94·74	490·0	1,855	3·76	3,067	28·87	187,197	102·6	3·25
1954/3	165·4	92·43	484·2	1,922	3·63	3,091	30·33	195,916	105·2	3·0
1954/4	178·5	92·41	492·7	2,013	3·74	3,153	34·62	199,253	105·4	3·0
1955/1	187·3	91·65	503·3	2,090	3·92	3,244	37·50	227,616	100·6	3·67
1955/2	195·9	89·38	490·9	2,149	4·13	3,232	39·79	215,363	96·6	4·5
1955/3	205·2	91·05	495·3	2,200	4·39	3,250	45·46	231,728	91·1	4·5
1955/4	191·5	89·89	485·0	2,034	4·40	3,237	46·83	231,767	90·9	4·5
1956/1	183·0	90·16	483·7	1,964	4·54	3,216	48·20	211,211	87·3	5·0
1956/2	184·5	86·78	484·7	1,948	4·67	3,191	50·13	185,200	86·4	5·5
1956/3	181·1	88·45	474·9	1,985	4·79	3,082	51·45	152,404	84·2	5·5
1956/4	173·7	90·69	493·3	1,979	4·85	3,265	49·41	156,163	83·7	5·5
1957/1	185·4	86·03	489·0	2,007	4·56	3,366	47·13	151,567	88·0	5·17
1957/2	201·8	84·85	472·8	2,040	4·84	3,329	49·82	213,683	85·2	5·00
1957/3	198·0	84·07	449·8	2,038	5·21	3,403	49·86	244,543	81·2	5·33
1957/4	168·0	81·96	426·9	1,976	5·46	3,038	43·71	253,111	78·6	7·00

† The "Total bank advances" are the figures given in Table 151 of the *Monthly Digest of Statistics*. There was an alteration in the basis in the first quarter of 1967. An adjustment of £2,000 million has been made to take account of this change.

TABLE 1—*continued*

Year and quarter	F.T. index	F.T. commodity index	Reuter's commodity index	Total bank advances (£ million)†	2½ per cent Consols yields (%)	Sterling liability (£ million)	S. and P. index	U.K. production of cars seasonally adjusted	Government securities index	U.K. bank rate (%)
1958/1	161·6	80·03	413·5	1,948	5·13	2.924	44·32	266,580	80·7	6·87
1958/2	170·2	79·80	412·4	1,995	4·96	2,825	46·41	253,543	83·2	5·50
1958/3	184·5	80·19	416·6	2,078	4·87	2,812	50·82	261,675	84·1	4·67
1958/4	211·0	80·13	415·9	2,270	4·86	2,811	55·92	249,407	84·6	4·25
1959/1	218·3	80·42	407·5	2,473	4·74	2,788	59·13	246,248	86·4	4·00
1959/2	231·7	82·67	413·9	2,633	4·63	2,972	61·59	293,062	85·7	4·00
1959/3	247·4	82·78	418·9	2,846	4·79	2,990	63·06	285,809	85·6	4·00
1959/4	301·9	82·61	425·8	3,064	4·93	3,156	62·02	366,265	86·3	4·00
1960/1	323·8	82·47	430·2	3,246	5·23	3,238	60·19	374,241	83·5	4·67
1960/2	314·1	81·86	423·7	3,401	5·42	3,255	59·79	375,764	81·6	5·90
1960/3	321·0	79·70	422·3	3,503	5·48	3,243	59·06	354,411	79·6	6·00
1960/4	312·9	77·89	408·7	3,642	5·56	3,199	58·67	249,527	80·0	5·50
1961/1	323·7	77·61	408·7	3,713	5·83	3,248	65·58	206,165	78·6	5·00
1961/2	349·3	78·90	419·6	3,832	6·08	3,272	69·82	258,410	77·7	5·00
1961/3	310·4	79·72	419·6	3,903	6·52	3,316	70·58	279,342	74·1	6·33
1961/4	295·8	78·08	411·6	3,762	6·51	3,241	73·98	264,824	75·5	6·17
1962/1	301·2	77·54	408·5	3,841	6·28	3,128	77·14	312,983	77·9	5·75
1962/2	285·8	76·99	409·3	3,866	6·09	3,089	65·43	300,932	78·1	4·67
1962/3	271·7	76·25	413·5	3,987	5·72	3,039	60·32	323,424	82·2	4·50
1962/4	283·6	78·13	421·8	4,113	5·73	3,038	62·05	312,780	85·4	4·50
1963/1	295·7	80·38	446·6	4,312	5·81	3,040	68·54	363,336	84·0	4·00
1963/2	309·3	81·78	464·6	4,457	5·48	3,104	73·31	378,275	85·7	4·00
1963/3	295·7	82·81	460·4	4,563	5·43	3,175	74·30	414,457	87·8	4·00
1963/4	342·0	84·99	484·3	4,650	5·72	3,268	77·39	459,158	86·3	4·00
1964/1	335·1	86·31	479·9	4,801	5·90	3,650	82·15	460,397	83·8	4·33
1964/2	344·4	85·95	468·9	4,867	6·01	3,503	85·28	462,279	82·7	5·00
1964/3	360·9	90·73	470·5	5,091	6·05	3,622	87·72	434,255	82·1	5·00
1964/4	346·5	92·42	476·0	5,345	6·22	3,813	89·61	475,890	81·1	5·67
1965/1	340·6	87·18	453·1	5,307	6·27	3,895	91·38	439,365	79·0	7·00
1965/2	340·3	85·20	454·9	5,427	6·53	4,077	92·65	431,666	77·5	6·67
1965/3	323·3	85·44	451·3	5,474	6·43	4,235	92·18	399,160	78·0	6·00
1965/4	345·6	87·85	451·7	5,458	6·40	4,139	97·63	449,564	79·7	6·00
1966/1	349·3	89·95	466·1	5,590	6·53	4,351	97·90	437,555	78·4	6·00
1966/2	359·7	90·20	462·4	5,749	6·72	4,502	94·39	426,616	77·0	6·00
1966/3	320·0	88·89	450·1	5,658	7·08	4,580	87·15	399,254	74·0	6·90
1966/4	299·9	83·25	426·7	5,391	6·85		84·87	334,587	76·8	7·00
1967/1	318·5	81·21	424·2	5,315	6·40		93·03	367,997	80·0	6·50
1967/2	343·1	79·70	435·5	5,421	6·51		98·53	393,808	80·5	5·67
1967/3	360·8	78·70	430·0	5,697	6·82		102·15	375,968	78·4	5·50
1967/4	397·8	81·50	465·0	5,921	7·01		103·09	381,692	76·9	7·00

† The "Total bank advances" are the figures given in Table 151 of the *Monthly Digest of Statistics*. There was an alteration in the basis in the first quarter of 1967. An adjustment of £2,000 million has been made to take account of this change.

4. We tried many relations among these variables with different lags; there is no space to report them all and we shall concentrate most of our attention on the forecasting of the Stock Exchange index, which until recently could be regarded as a fair barometer of the country's economy. One feature which became apparent at an early stage was that good regressions were obtainable with only two or three explanatory variables—bringing in more, rarely if ever improved the representation as measured by R^2. This is not because the economy or the stock market is a simple process which is nearly completely determined by one or two factors, but because there are groups of highly correlated factors of which these are representatives. This raises a practical difficulty when using these equations for forecasting. If variable A, which has not been included in an equation because of its high correlation with variable B which has been included, has a real effect on the dependent variable and ceases to be correlated with B, then the forecasts produced can be misleading. However, some of the regressions on one or two variables were astonishingly good. The best set of equations for the *F.T.* ordinary share index which we had established early in 1967 is shown in Table 2.

TABLE 2

*Coefficients in regressions of F.T. ordinary share index
on the three variables shown*

Equation No.	Period of fit (year and quarter)	Constant	Coefficients			R^2
			(U.K. car production)$_{t-6}$	F.T. (commodity index)$_{t-7}$	(Reuter's commodity index)$_{t-7}$	
(1)	1948/1–1958/1	82·06	0·00063 (10·34)		−0·05 (−1·54)	0·75
(2)	1954/2–1960/4	750·96	0·00039 (2·99)	−7·07 (−5·65)		0·81
(3)	1954/2–1962/1	757·64	0·00041 (4·89)	−7·16 (−5·96)		0·85
(4)	1954/2–1964/1	716·87	0·00042 (5·83)	−6·74 (−7·66)		0·88
(5)	1954/2–1965/1	717·88	0·00044 (7·30)	−6·78 (−8·42)		0·90
(6)	1958/1–1965/4	897·51	0·00035 (7·879)	−8·675 (−8·49)		0·87
(7)	1954/2–1966/4	653·16	0·00047 (14·114)	−6·127 (−9·89)		0·90

Values of t are in brackets under the coefficients.

5. Much of this early work was done by graphing the series on transparencies to a roughly comparable scale and then superposing them, sliding them along the time-axis to see whether there was any fairly obvious coincident variation. This method has dangers, and we refer later to the steps we took to avoid false conclusions. But as a preliminary screening device it has many advantages, especially where a number of series are involved and one wishes to compare them in many different ways,

sometimes superposing several. The method brought to light some very unexpected effects. Fig. 1 shows (to comparable vertical scale) (1) the S. and P. index from 1951 to 1967 and (2) the production of motor cars in the U.K. (seasonally adjusted) displaced 6 quarters to the right (that is, cars lead the stock market index by 6 quarters).

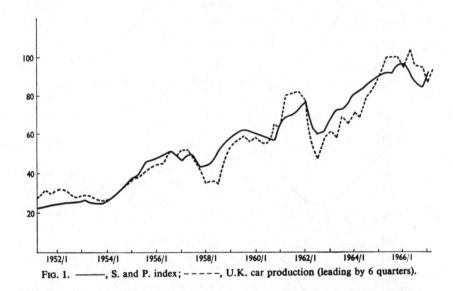

FIG. 1. ———, S. and P. index; - - - - -, U.K. car production (leading by 6 quarters).

It is, we think, difficult to believe that the fidelity with which one series follows the fluctuations in the other is a chance phenomenon. The actual figures are given in Table 1.

6. We also calculated cross-correlation coefficients between the dependent variables (principally *F.T.* share index for London and the S. and P. index for Wall Street) and a number of possible indicator variables at a range of positive lags.

The results for the *F.T.* index and other variables in detrended terms are displayed graphically in Fig. 2. Most of the lagged correlations observed by using transparencies were confirmed and attention was directed to some possible new relationships. The statistical meaningfulness of these relationships is discussed in the Appendix and paragraphs 20–22 below.

The lags at which the maximum values of the cross-correlation coefficient, r_k, occur may be considered to mark the stages of a business fluctuation. Commodity prices tend to be at a peak 7 to 9 quarters before a trough in the *F.T.* index. Sterling liability, which depends, in part, on commodity prices, tends to reach a peak about 7 quarters before the *F.T.* index low point and for bank rate the best correlation is 2 to 4 quarters ahead of the *F.T.* index.

7. We also calculated the cross-correlations of some of the series, notably the *F.T.* index and the S. and P. index, differenced at periods of one year (for instance, the values were 1961/1–1960/1, 1961/2–1960/2, 1961/3–1960/3, 1961/4–1960/4, 1962/1–1961/1, etc.). These are shown in Figs. 3 and 4.

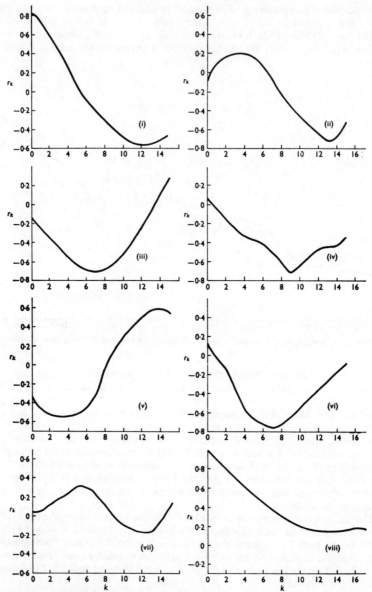

FIG. 2. Values of the cross-correlation coefficients r_k between the *F.T.* share index (detrended) and the following variables (detrended):

    (i) Bank advances,   (v) Bank rate,
   (ii) Government securities index,   (vi) Sterling liability,
  (iii) Reuter's commodity index,   (vii) U.K. car production,
  (iv) *F.T.* commodity index,   (viii) *F.T.* share index,

plotted against k, the lag of the *F.T.* index.

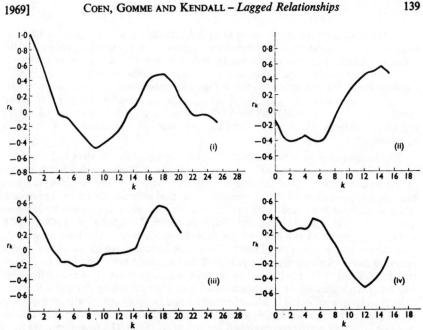

FIG. 3. Values of the cross-correlation coefficients r_k between the *F.T.* share index and
    (i) *F.T.* share index,   (iii) S. and P. index,
    (ii) Bank rate,   (iv) U.K. car production,
plotted against k, the lag of the *F.T.* share index. (All variables are in four-quarter
difference terms.)

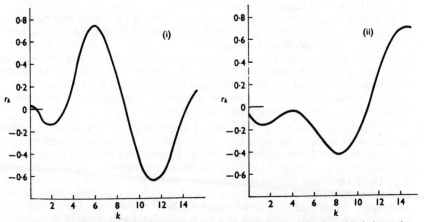

FIG. 4. Values of the cross-correlation coefficients, r_k, between the S. and P. index and
    (i) U.K. car production,   (ii) U.K. bank rate,
plotted against k, the lags of the S. and P. index. (All variables are in four-quarter
difference terms.)

8. The graphs of the cross-correlations indicate the length of lags most likely to yield good correspondence in regression analysis. We then proceeded to the regression stage. This was conducted by including among the regressors a variable at several lags around the value where the cross-correlation was a maximum in absolute value, for example, if y_t had a high correlation with x_{t+u} we might include among the regressors $x_{t+u-4}, x_{t+u-3}, ..., x_{t+u+4}$. The program for rejecting redundant variables (Beale *et al.*, 1967) will then tell us which are the best to retain. Thus the regression analysis effectively determines the lags to be included in the final equations.

9. The equations shown in Table 2 have only two regressor variables and "explain" between 75 and 90 per cent of the variation in the *F.T.* index, depending on the period used in fitting. Fig. 5 shows the predictions which these equations could have been used to produce beyond their periods of fit; that is to say, they give the forecasts which could have been made with the information then available. These results were quite good for the period 1961 and 1967. Equation (1), fitted from 1948 to 1958, would have predicted the start of the 1958/59 boom but would have missed the second part of the boom in 1959/60. Even that equation, which was fitted over a period of lower variation than the post-1958 period, could have been used to forecast the shape of the *F.T.* index curve up to 1964, although it underestimated the level. The other equations which have used data up to 1960 for fitting give good forecasts of level and shape up to 1967. These forecasts could be produced for almost 6 quarters ahead (that is, the shortest lag, 6, minus the time taken for data to become available). A crude equation had been developed by one of us (E. D. G.) in autumn 1965 and successfully forecast in advance the fall in the index which followed "the July 1966 measures".

10. We arrived at equation (7) early in 1967 and decided to use it to forecast the *F.T.* index over the next year, by quarters. The resulting prediction was quite unambiguous: before the end of the year a downward swing would start on the stock market and would be equivalent to a serious recession.

As things turned out the market went on rising until the most optimistic bulls had doubts about its stability. It looked as if our first attempts at forecasting were a spectacular failure. We had, however, correctly forecast a major sterling crisis of such gravity that we were forced to devalue and the ensuing budget, to quote the Chancellor, Mr Jenkins, called for "greater tax increases than had ever before been imposed in peace or war and the incomes policy had been backed by legal powers to an extent which is unparalleled in western countries". The anomaly of this equation is discussed more fully in paragraphs 13 and 14 below.

11. The equations shown in Table 2, even when fitted over 1959–61, underestimate the level of the index at the top of that boom. This led us to consider other variables which might give a better fit over this period. In particular we tested the hypothesis that when the index is rising it gains a certain momentum which will keep it rising (this is probably becoming increasingly important with the development of unit trusts) until some major event such as a budget or bank rate adjustment destroys the market's confidence. We defined an artificial variable called "the euphoria index" which had a value zero in the decreasing part of a fluctuation and had a value in the increasing part equal to the rise since the last trough multiplied by the number of quarters since the last trough. Troughs were considered to have occurred in 1958, 1962 and 1966. The inclusion of the euphoria index in an equation of the Table 2 type improved the

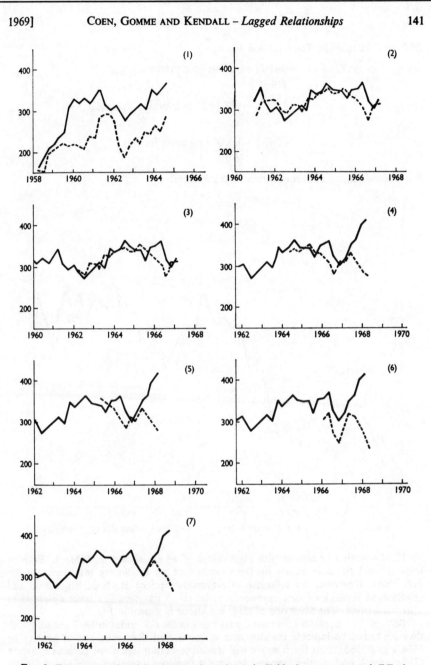

FIG. 5. Forecasts produced by the equations shown in Table 2. ——, actual *F.T.* share index; ‒‒‒‒‒, forecast. Equations are identified by the number shown in brackets.

R^2 from 0·91 to 0·95. The equation was

$$(F.T. \text{ index})_t = 541·17 + 0·00046 \text{ (car production)}_{t-6}$$
$$(19·1)$$
$$-4·88 \text{ } (F.T. \text{ commodity index})_{t-8}$$
$$(9·5)$$
$$+0·0080 \text{ (euphoria index)}_t.$$
$$(6·0) \tag{8}$$

Fig. 6 shows the fit of this equation to the *F.T.* index.

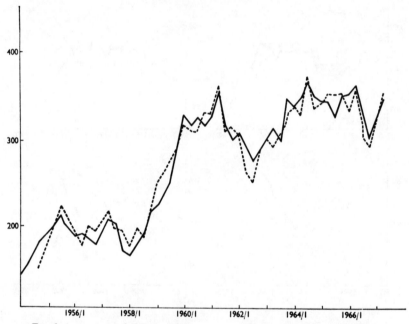

FIG. 6. ———, actual *F.T.* share index; – – – –, fitted values (for equation (8)).

12. Two other equations with high values of R^2 are shown in Table 3. Both of these depend to some extent on the existence of an oscillatory movement in the *F.T.* index. However, the influence of commodity prices at about 8 quarters and government securities index or interest rates at 13 quarters has been observed in other equations. The fit of one of these equations is shown in Fig. 7.

Both of these equations forecast the recovery in the *F.T.* index in 1967 and although they continued to indicate the direction of movement they were out of control by 1968/1 and 1968/2. At the time we had tended to favour equations such as equation (7) because it had shorter lags and because it required no assumption about a cycle of constant length in stock market prices.

TABLE 3

Fitting equations for (F.T. share index)$_t$

Equation No.	R^2	Constant	Coefficients			
			(F.T. index)$_{t-17}$	(S. and P. index)$_{t-17}$	(Reuter's commodity index)$_{t-8}$	(Government securities index)$_{t-13}$
9	0·957	681·66	0·334 (6·89)		−0·09 (4·48)	−5·00 (18·93)
10	0·975	501·39		2·241 (12·21)	−0·06 (4·4)	−3·44 (12·5)

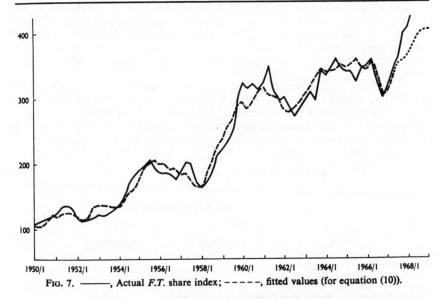

FIG. 7. ————, Actual *F.T.* share index; – – – – –, fitted values (for equation (10)).

13. As mentioned in paragraph 10, the equation type shown in Table 2 produced forecasts for the *F.T.* index for 1967/4 and early 1968 which were badly wrong. In the previous twenty or so years two variables had been sufficient to "explain" and predict the movement of the *F.T.* index. These were car production and a commodity price index. (The commodity indices are in fact highly correlated with sterling liability.) There is little doubt that if an attempt had been made to bring the U.K. trade account into balance without resort to devaluation, drastic deflation would have been necessary and this would bring a serious setback in equity share prices. But this did not happen and the market has continued to rise through the first half of 1968. The economy was now being managed in a different way. After devaluation there was no immediate deflationary action, there was a consumer-spending spree, and a stock market boom and imports rose to a level which caused acute concern. We continued our study and concentrated on looking for further explanatory variables.

We had been aware all along of the danger that a variable, which had not seemed important during the period used for fitting the equation, could suddenly become a key factor. This is a problem for all model builders and there is no easy solution. One can monitor the levels of variables which are suspected of being potentially important but there is still the problem of identifying the potentially important.

14. We re-examined several variables and particularly their recent levels. The 1967/68 boom on the London market was not accompanied by any corresponding movement on Wall Street and the two markets often move together. There were no very definite signs of improvement in the economy. Interest rates were at a very high level which usually means a bad time for equity prices. High interest rates are usually the signs of a restriction on consumer demand and we were being told by the government that we would have to consume less and that the next two years would be very difficult.

The deflationary package used by Chancellors since 1950 has usually involved an increase in bank rate and a brake on consumer spending through reductions in money supply and total bank advances. This can be seen in Fig. 11. However, the high interest rates following November 1967 were not accompanied by any reduction in total bank advances. In fact, as can be seen from Fig. 9, bank advances rose quite sharply.

This led us to reconsider total bank advances at a short or zero lag as a possible explanatory variable. Fig. 10 shows the fit of bank advances to the *F.T.* share index; both are in four-quarter first differences. The value of R^2 for the equation is 0·53, but the patterns of movement are closer than is suggested by this value. The fit can be improved by including other explanatory variables. See, for example, Fig. 11; the fit is given by:

$$(F.T.\ \text{index})_t = 11{\cdot}218 + 0{\cdot}0565\ (\text{bank advances})_t$$
$$(4{\cdot}57)$$
$$- 0{\cdot}396\ (F.T.\ \text{commodity index})_{t-9}$$
$$(3{\cdot}92)$$
$$- 0{\cdot}00016\ (\text{U.K. car production})_{t-12}, \qquad (11)$$
$$(2{\cdot}92)$$
$$R^2 = 0{\cdot}61.$$

All variables are expressed as four-quarter differences.

Bank advances and money supply are the only series which we have investigated so far which "explain" even statistically the strong upward movement in share prices in 1968. We do not pretend to know the mechanism by which bank advances or money supply might influence share prices, whether it is through increased purchasing power of investors or whether it is through a stimulation of consumer spending which is, in the short term at least, good for trade and is seen as being good for share prices. It may even be that there is some other factor to which share prices and bank advances both respond.

THEORETICAL CONSIDERATIONS

15. The series which we used were all taken from official sources or published data like the *F.T.* index. We had no control over their accuracy or the interval of observation. There were four points in particular we had to consider in some detail:

(a) Monthly and quarterly data are often subject to seasonal variations. This affects short-term autocorrelations and hence autoregressions. It may also affect lags in cross-correlations.

(b) It may be better to use logarithmic transforms of some series, for the usual reasons, e.g. that price changes are relative, or that the combined efforts of different variables are multiplicative.

(c) A great many of our series contained trend. We have to be careful that our lagged relations are not just the kind of covariation which one would expect from two qualities trending in the same direction. On the other hand, if we eliminate trend we have to be equally careful that relations between residuals are not contaminated by the trend-removal process (see, for example, Kendall and Stuart, 1967, Vol. 3, 46.14).

(d) In particular, we tried taking four-quarter differences of some of the series to eliminate linear trend. This is equivalent to taking a moving average with weights $(1, 0, 0, 0, -1)$.

16. As regards seasonal effects, we removed them in every case where we thought, on general grounds, that they might exist. The program used was the one developed in the U.S.A. by Julius Shiskin (1960). In effect, it fits a moving average to the series, works out the ratio of actual to the average and constructs a factor for each month or quarter which is divided into the actual to give the deseasonalized figure. The program allows for slow changes in seasonal pattern by a moving average of seasonal indices which, in effect, discounts remotely past history. This method, in one form or another, is commonly used for the elimination of seasonal variation and appears to work quite well in practice. The last word on deseasonalization has not been said (there are no last words in time-series analysis), but we think it very unlikely that the method we used has seriously distorted the data.

17. In some cases we did not attempt any further manipulation of the data. Table 2 is a case in which one variable is regressed on the others with no corrections except for seasonality. Most of our series, however, contained trend and we felt it necessary to extract the trend element before embarking on the detection of comparatively short-term relationships.

18. In economic relationships there is a good deal to be said, on theoretical grounds, in favour of using logarithms of the variable rather than the variables themselves. When we construct linear regressions of the usual type, it may look rather remote from reality to express a price, say, as the sum of a physical quantity of production, an interest-rate and a monetary measure of bank advances. To a physicist such an equation would be suspect as being dimensionally heterogeneous. Economic equations with this kind of complexity are often more realistically expressed as products—for example the Cobb–Douglas equation. Equivalently, they are better expressed as linear in the logarithms of the variables involved. This reinforces what has already been mentioned, that it is relative changes which are often of greater interest. The same thought lies at the basis of a good deal of current projective forecasting which assumes an exponential rate of growth or a fixed percentage rise in gross national product.

19. In many cases, then, we worked with the logarithms of quantities, at least in the first instance. But in practice there is an easy escape from the danger of over-sophisticating the data: when in doubt do it both ways. On a number of occasions we reworked equations expressed one way in the other, and relied on the reality of the effects only when both methods gave the same kind of result.

The following, for example, is the equivalent of equation (7) in terms of logarithms:

$$(\log F.T. \text{ index})_t = 7\cdot355 + 0\cdot512 \ (\log \text{ U.K. cars production})_{t-6}$$
$$(12\cdot76)$$
$$- 1\cdot847 \ (\log F.T. \text{ commodity index})_{t-8}, \qquad (12)$$
$$(-8\cdot04)$$

$$R^2 = 0\cdot89.$$

20. Trend-elimination is a more serious problem for the theoretician. The cases we considered were either trend-free—so far as the eye could see—or were over a period in which the trend was approximately linear. As a general rule, therefore, we simply fitted a linear regression on time. This is not the usual method, which prefers a moving average to a polynomial fitted over the whole course of the data, but for our purposes it had two important advantages concerning the possible distribution of residuals:

    (a) If there are short-term fluctuations of a pseudocyclical kind the method will not seriously affect the residuals, provided that over the course of experience there has been time for several swings to take place. Failure of the fitted line to correspond exactly to the real line may somewhat affect the amplitudes of the fluctuations in the observed residuals, but will not affect their turning points; and it is the point of reversal of movements which is often of major interest.

    (b) Likewise, if random (unautocorrelated) residuals are imposed on a linear trend, the fitting of a linear regression will not seriously affect the general behaviour of the observed residuals.

21. The subject is considered in more detail from the theoretical and experimental viewpoint in the Appendix.

22. The taking of first differences eliminates linear trend. In a series of random residuals it will generate a serial correlation of about 0·5 but no serial correlations of higher order. Its effect on oscillatory movements depends on the pseudo-period, but for those of more than two time-intervals it will reduce the amplitude, and may do so seriously. For most purposes we have preferred the fitting of a linear trend by regression but, as noted above, have tried the variate-difference method on occasion, particularly in equations using bank advances. Once again, when there was doubt about the reality of the results, several methods were tried.

23. The apparent relationship between the S. and P. index and U.K. car production shown in Fig. 1 was tested by regression; the equation with $R^2 = 0\cdot94$ is

$$(\text{S. and P. index})_t = 3\cdot34 + 0\cdot00021 \ (\text{U.K. car production})_{t-6}. \qquad (13)$$
$$(34\cdot9)$$

This was also tested in four-quarter first-difference terms and the fit is shown in Fig. 8 (i). The fit is particularly good up to 1966. The deviation led us to look for other and perhaps more meaningful leading variables. We had never suggested that the level of car production in the U.K. directly influenced the level of the Wall Street stock market but believed that both variables depended on some other monetary or trade factor to which U.K. car production reacted sooner. We tried several American series including car production but without success. Finally, we observed the relationship, displayed in Fig. 8 (ii), between the S. and P. index and the U.K. bank

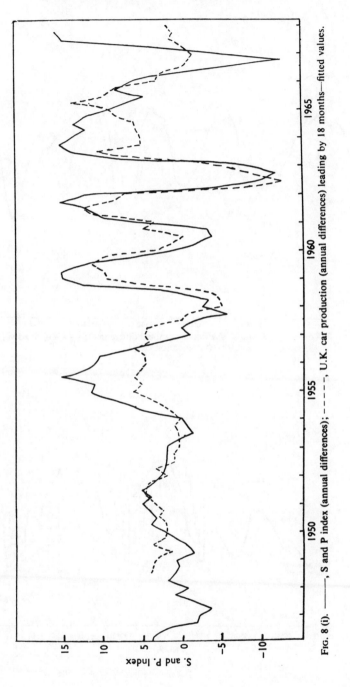

FIG. 8 (i). ———, S and P index (annual differences); – – – –, U.K. car production (annual differences) leading by 18 months—fitted values.

Economic Forecasting I

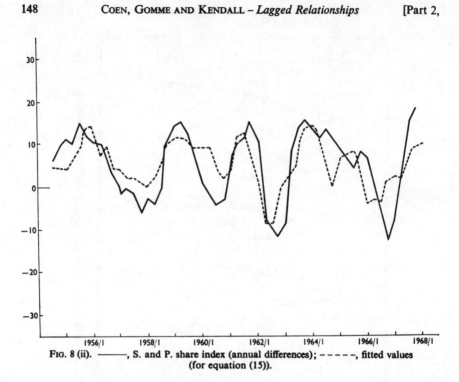

FIG. 8 (ii). ———, S. and P. share index (annual differences); – – – –, fitted values
(for equation (15)).

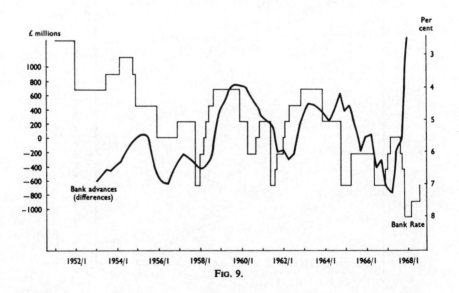

FIG. 9.

rate which still seems to hold good up to the present time. The equations for the fits shown in Figs 8 (i) and (ii) are:

$$(\text{S. and P. index})_t = 3{\cdot}30 + 0{\cdot}000092 \ (\text{U.K. car production})_{t-6}, \qquad (14)$$

$$(7{\cdot}6)$$

$$R^2 = 0{\cdot}52,$$

and

$$(\text{S. and P. index})_t = 4{\cdot}7 + 4{\cdot}71 \ (\text{U.K. bank rate})_{t-14}, \qquad (15)$$

$$(6{\cdot}5)$$

$$R^2 = 0{\cdot}44.$$

All variables are in four-quarter difference terms.

24. We have reported here a selection of the results obtained and of the regression runs attempted. Space and the wish to avoid confusion prevent us from exhibiting them all, but in presenting a selected set we have to guard against two further possible theoretically based criticisms. The first is that if one calculates a mass of relations on a large number of variables, some of them are likely to turn out "significantly" by sheer chance. This is a difficult point to meet with the precision which a statistician likes to bring to bear on his significance tests. There are no such tests available to condition our judgment whether the various relations to which we call attention are significant in any ordinary sense of the word. It seems to us, however, that they are significant in the statistical sense, namely that they are not effects which one would get in unrelated series of a stochastic kind.

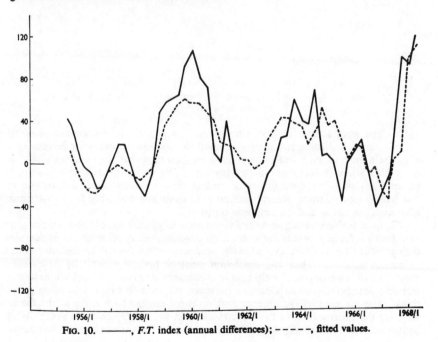

Fig. 10. ———, *F.T.* index (annual differences); – – – –, fitted values.

25. The second criticism is that, over the time-period examined, there are short-term fluctuations which, not having had time to get out of step in the usual way, may generate autocorrelations and hence lag-effects which are not permanent. From the purely empirical viewpoint of short-term forecasting this may not be important, but from the explanatory point of view it is.

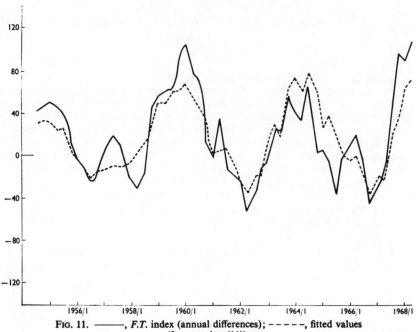

Fig. 11. ———, *F.T.* index (annual differences); – – – – –, fitted values
(for equation (11)).

26. The results reported here were essentially empirically determined although we, of course, had some hypotheses in mind in selecting variables for inclusion. It is of the nature of empirically determined relationships that the statistics alone tell us nothing about the causality underlying them. We do not propose at this stage to advance any well-developed theory to explain these statistical relationships. To do this would require more general economic analysis and probably the construction of a model in causal and deterministic terms.

27. Even for forecasting some caution is necessary in the use of these relationships as indeed it is for any forecasting method. Socio-economic systems may be undergoing change either by ordinary evolutionary processes or by the deliberate intervention of human agencies. Thus any prediction must be hedged around by government regulation of the economy, by changes in consumers' or producers' behaviour and by technological development. Changes, however, may not be so quick as some people think. The evidence so far suggests that no rapid change took place in the factors affecting the general level of the stock markets in the last fifteen or so years. While equations such as these may sometimes be wrong for the various reasons mentioned,

some of these reported here have been shown to produce good forecasts and did forecast the major turns in the *F.T.* index in 1966 and the 1966 and 1967 economic crises in real time. It seems to us that the method of lagged relationships deserves serious consideration for short-term (one or two years ahead) economic forecasting.

ACKNOWLEDGEMENTS

We should like to acknowledge the very useful help we have had in the analysis and preparation of diagrams from Mr John Rees, Mr Philip Hurst and Mrs Elizabeth Rawlings of Scientific Control Systems Ltd.

REFERENCES

BEALE, E. M. L., KENDALL, M. G. and MANN, D. W. (1967). The discarding of variables in multivariate analysis. *Biometrika*, **54**, 357–366.

KENDALL, M. G. and STUART, A. (1967). *The Advanced Theory of Statistics*, Vol. 3. London: Griffin.

MOORE, G. H. (ed.) (1961). *Business Cycle Indicators*, I. Published for National Bureau of Economic Research by Princeton University Press.

SHISKIN, J. (1960). Electronic computer seasonal adjustments—tests and revisions of U.S. census methods. *Technical Paper No. 5, U.S. Bureau of the Census.*

APPENDIX

The Effect on Random Residuals of Eliminating Trend by Regression Methods

1. We owe the following general investigation to Professor E. M. L. Beale. Assume that we have a model

$$y_i = \sum_r x_{ir}\beta_r + \epsilon_i,$$

where the ϵ's are independently distributed with variance σ^2 and zero means.

Assume further that we fit the model

$$y_i = \sum_r b_r x_{ir} + e_i$$

by conventional least squares, e_i being the actual residual.

To calculate the b_r we set up the normal equations

$$\sum_s a_{rs} b_s = \sum_i y_i x_{ir},$$

where the matrix $\mathbf{A} = (a_{rs})$ has elements

$$a_{rs} = \sum_j x_{jr} x_{js}.$$

We then find that

$$b_s = \sum_r \sum_j a_{rs}^* y_j x_{jr},$$

where $(a_{rs}^*) = A^{-1}$.

This is equivalent to

$$b_s - \beta_s = \sum_r \sum_j a_{rs}^* x_{rj} \epsilon_j.$$

Further, since

$$e_i = \epsilon_i - \sum_s (b_s - \beta_s) x_i s$$

we see that

$$e_i = \epsilon_i - \sum_r \sum_s \sum_j a_{rs}^* x_{jr} x_{is} \epsilon_j$$

$$= \sum_k c_{ik} \epsilon_k,$$

where

$$c_{ik} = \delta_{ik} - \sum_r \sum_j a_{rs}^* x_{kr} x_{is}$$

and δ is the Kronecker delta.

It follows that

$$\mathrm{corr}\,(e_i\, e_j) = \frac{\sum_k c_{ik} c_{jk}}{\{\sum_k c_{ik}^2 \sum_k c_{jk}^2\}^{\frac12}}.$$

In the particular case when there are $N = 2n+1$ values of the time variable $-n$ to n, and we fit (about means)

$$y = \beta_0 + \beta_1 t,$$

we find

$$e_t - \epsilon_t = - \left[\bar\epsilon + \frac{\sum t\epsilon}{S_2} \right] t,$$

where $S_2 = \sum t^2 = \frac13 n(n+1)(2n+1)$.

Now t and ϵ are independent. The expectation of $\sum t\epsilon$ is zero and its variance is σ^2/S_2. Its range of variation is then of the order of $\sigma/\sqrt{S_2}$. t never exceeds n in absolute value, so the difference between e and ϵ is of the order of $\sigma/\sqrt{N}$. Hence the serial correlations of ϵ will not differ much from those of e unless N is small. For our particular purposes we wished to observe the behaviour of the serial correlations of residuals in a time series with linear trend. We therefore constructed four series of the type

$$u_t = t + \epsilon_t \quad (t = 1, 2, ..., 40).$$

In all series ϵ was a discrete integer variable chosen from a table of random numbers. For series 1 the range of ϵ was 0 to 9; for series 2, 0 (2) 18; for series 3, 0 (3) 27; and for series 4, 0 (4) 36. For each of the four series there was calculated a regression on t, the residuals, and the first 30 serial correlations of these residuals. We also calculated the 10 cross-correlograms from -30 to $+30$ lags but omit them to save space. They have the same irregular appearance as the serials. The diagrams are sufficiently unlike the smooth curves of Fig. 6 to indicate that the latter are not artefacts created by the trend-removal process, at least so far as concerns random residuals.

DISCUSSION ON THE PAPER BY MR COEN, MR GOMME AND DR KENDALL

Professor J. DURBIN (London School of Economics): I do not know which gives one greater pleasure on this sort of occasion, to welcome an old friend or to welcome new authors. Dr Kendall is, of course, an old friend, and Mr Gomme and Mr Coen are, I believe, new authors as far as the Society is concerned, so I am in the happy position of being able to enjoy both pleasures simultaneously.

There are, it seems to me, essentially two basic views on the role of statistics in scientific investigation. In the first of these, one regards statistics as a substantial subject in its own right. According to this view, one would in any particular situation assemble as much as possible of the relevant information and then examine it dispassionately and rigorously for evidence of statistical regularities and relationships, trying to keep one's mind free from preconceived ideas and expectations. This approach is therefore essentially pragmatic and empirical.

An alternative view of statistics is that it is essentially a humble subject, playing a rather subsidiary role in any particular investigation. According to this view, one would first go to a specialist in the field under review usually a non-statistician, and one would ask him to provide the theoretical model or class of models for the phenomena under investigation. The statistician's job is then to fit the models, carry out tests of significance and so on, the object being either to evaluate the extent to which the evidence supports or refutes the specialist's hypotheses, or alternatively to emerge with the best-fitting model.

As stated, these two views are extreme and many of us hold somewhat intermediate positions. My own approach is that, although on the whole I am generally sympathetic to the latter view, I am quite happy to see both approaches tried and to let the results decide which approach is better on any particular occasion.

As far as short-term economic forecasting is concerned, my feeling is that it is not clear at present whether one does better to fit economic models based on postulated relationships between the variables, or to use statistical forecasting of a frankly *ad hoc* character. This is not to say that an econometric approach to the subject does not have considerable value in other directions—for example, in understanding the nature of the causal forces at work or in predicting the effects of a change of the structure of the system. The difficulty in using the econometric approach in practice is often that there is not sufficient independent variation in the data during the period for which observations are available to enable one to estimate all the desired relationships with sufficient accuracy, and it may well be that one can actually gain greater forecasting accuracy by throwing away some of the theoretical structure and using a more empirical approach.

The basic approach of the authors is to take as their forecasting relation the multiple regression or best fit. This approach has its dangers as they themselves admit since if the relationship is not based on a well-founded causal connection, there is no guarantee at all that it will continue to hold outside the period of fit. Many have pointed out that where there are trends in two variables which are unconnected causally, one can obtain a high degree of apparent correlation between the variables concerned. It is not quite so obvious that if one adopts the frequency approach to time series analysis the same phenomenon holds. Whenever there is oscillation in the data which has a period longer than the period of observation, then by moving two series along the time axis relative to each other until the observed correlation is highest it is possible to obtain a high degree of spurious correlation between variables. In other words, low frequency oscillation as well as trends can induce nonsense correlation between time series.

Having said this, I must confess that the degree of fit achieved by the authors in predicting the share index such a long period of time ahead was a surprise to me. I would be interested to know whether one could do any better by fitting a well-formulated econometric model using the same data, and hope that some econometrician will rise to the challenge.

I notice that the regression relations in the paper contain lagged values only of the explanatory variables and I would like to ask the authors why no lagged values of the dependent variables are included. If all that is required is a forecasting relation, I would expect the fit to be improved by including variables of this type as predetermined variables.

Another feature of this exercise is that the analysis is done entirely in the time domain. When lagged relations are under study there are some advantages in using frequency-domain concepts and I wondered whether the authors had considered this approach at all. For example, using spectral concepts it is a fairly easy matter to allow for linear filtering operations such as a trend-elimination or the elimination of seasonal effects where this is done by linear or approximately linear methods. Essentially, all one has to do is make a Fourier transformation of the data, divide through by the transfer function of the filter and then either stay in the frequency domain or transform back to the time domain.

Finally, there is the question of the serial-correlation of the disturbances in the regression model. In time series regression problems there is often a certain amount of serial-correlation present, and if this is so, it is advisable to allow for this in the fitting procedure. I wonder if the authors have considered this. I would be interested to see what the effect of allowing for it would be on the results.

I have much pleasure in moving the vote of thanks to the authors for their most interesting paper.

Mr J. P. BURMAN (Bank of England): The way in which economists nowadays tackle the analysis of our economic system is painstaking construction of models of different parts of it; discussion of the formulation of these with the statistician; great care to indicate the direction of causation; testing; rejecting; testing again; and finally assembling the parts into a coherent set of equations. Often non-linearities appear in the relationships. This is the humbler of the two roles for the statistician described by Professor Durbin.

As I understand them, Dr Kendall, Mr Coen and Mr Gomme want us to treat the economic system as a "black box". We read various inputs into the box and see whether the output resembles one of the inputs at some earlier time, or a linear combination of inputs at different times. We are to take no notice of the nature of the series or the probable direction of causation; and most of the equations estimated in this paper are based on only 40 or 50 quarterly observations of series whose cycles are 16–20 quarters in length. I suggest we would not be at all surprised to find some apparently significant R^2 in a random collection of such series. But even if we found an R^2 as high as 0·9, in the absence of any causal explanation we would do well to be very sceptical of its future performance.

To give an example, several years ago I published a regression with 20 observations on one variable that gave a correlation of 0·995 and had a good causal connection. Yet in later years the prediction errors in the equation became much larger and it had to be abandoned.

In Sections 1 and 2, the paper refers to long lags as if econometricians had ignored them: there has been a great deal of work in the United States on accelerator models for fixed investment in manufacturing industry, that is, depending on a distributed lag of growth of output; and there is evidence that a distributed lag averaging two years gives a good fit for U.K. data.

As one would expect from Dr Kendall, this paper displays a mastery of statistical techniques and a thorough analysis of a large range of figures, but one needs to examine them from the viewpoint of an economist.

The authors "predict" the *Financial Times* share price index from past values of other economic and financial series, but nowhere is there any mention of the fact that a share price index reflects people's expectations about the *future*. Stock Exchange lore suggests about 18 months forward, but this is perhaps exaggerated. Investors may have tended to be guided in the past by the publication of annual profits, somewhat out of date. But the modern institutional investor looks at the latest national income estimates and is much more closely in touch with current trends. This will tend to upset any lag correlations based on the past. Dr Kendall mentioned that they had tested some of the series for lag correlations in the reverse direction. Equation 15 is an obvious candidate for this treatment, replacing a lag of 14 quarters by a lead of 4 quarters. Professor Durbin referred to the use of cross-spectral analysis for estimating lags and I would strongly support this. I have recently made a first essay into this field with money supply and the index of production multiplied by a price index. The result is a uniformly high coherence and no evidence of phase shift. But the fact that the series is synchronous does not mean—as Dr Kendall suggested—that control of money will affect production. It depends on the direction of causation and it may well be that money is the dependent variable. That is what the current monetary argument is about.

The authors' selection of explanatory variables seems curious: why not look at Gross Domestic Product or the index of industrial production? A glance at a chart of industrial production suggests that the troughs of 1956, 1963 and 1966, lagged the *F.T.* index by between 1 and 3 quarters (bearing in mind the delay in publication of production). One also wonders what cross-correlations exist between the "independent" variables. And would it be unreasonable to ask why the commodity price index always has a negative coefficient in Table 2? Apart from its effect on the shares of commodity producers, none of which are in the 30-share index, high prices generally indicate expanding world trade, which is probably good for the U.K.

In Section 10 the authors say that early in 1967 they forecast a marked downward swing in the share index before the end of the year. "We have, however, correctly forecast a major sterling crisis. . . ." This seems to imply several unstated assumptions: that car production is being used to predict the balance of payments cycle; that when the latter is in deficit, restrictive monetary or fiscal actions have in the past been taken; and that the latter produce a fall in the share index. Why not then regress the balance of payments against lagged car production, etc. and the share index against, say, bank rate and the Central Government's net balance of surplus or deficit?

In Section 12, the authors have lapsed into the use of causative language by saying that "the influence of commodity prices on the *F.T.* index has been observed".

In Section 13 they seem to class themselves among the model builders, but their concept of a model is completely different from that of economists. The latter would insist that each equation be supported by rational argument.

In Section 14, after the two-variable equation has broken down, they try to restore the situation by bringing in a series called "bank advances"; and even then R^2 becomes only 0·61 and the coefficient of car production has now changed sign. Moreover, I am afraid that Dr Kendall's conclusion, that a change in monetary policy has occurred since devaluation, is based on a misunderstanding of the bank advances series. This contains large loans to foreigners—mainly in foreign currency—the so-called Euro-dollars (see last column of the table in the *Monthly Digest* to which the authors refer). These loans to foreigners account for £500 million of the total increase of nearly £1,000 million between November 1967 and May 1968 (not seasonally adjusted) and they largely represent foreign deposits in London being on-lent abroad and revaluation adjustments due to the devaluation of sterling. Also, because of the change of coverage of the series at the end of 1966, which raised its level by some 40 per cent (see footnote to Table 1), the official statisticians have not yet attempted to seasonally adjust it. The seasonal movement is certainly upward between November and May, so the underlying increase in advances to U.K. residents was probably quite modest and would not go far in explaining the rise in share prices. A more appropriate series for this paper would be London clearing banks' "advances to customers and other accounts" as published in Table 35 of *Financial Statistics*.

I am strongly tempted to ask Dr Kendall a question, which is always appropriate for those who make forecasts about the stock market. Has he risked any money on them yet?

To sum up, Mr President, in view of Dr Kendall's distinguished reputation, both in this Society and outside, and his great textbook from which many of us have learnt so much of statistical method, I think it is a great pity that he should have presented his paper in a form which cannot but provoke a hostile reaction from all those who believe that in economics rational explanation should always accompany high correlations. As Dr Kendall said on a previous occasion, "We clearly cannot be satisfied with the mere eliciting of pattern, even if we go about the process systematically and discover a good deal more regularity than has been observed in the past. For a number of very obvious reasons we must go behind the manifest phenomena to see whether some model of the generating process can be set up. Not until we have a satisfactory model can we be said to understand the process fully or to retain control over it in changing circumstances."

I have pleasure in seconding the vote of thanks to Dr Kendall.

The vote of thanks was put to the meeting and carried unanimously.

Dr K. F. WALLIS (London School of Economics): The opening sentence of this paper tells us one thing of which econometricians are aware. It is probably worth while to mention some other relevant concepts from econometrics, first for practical reasons in the interpretation of this study, second to exemplify the earlier discussion (Professor Durbin's first view of the role of statistics) of measurement without theory, and, in general, to persuade students of econometrics that the route so thoroughly pursued by Mr Coen, Mr Gomme and Dr Kendall is not the only road to take.

A useful idea in econometrics is that of the *distributed* lag. It is often the case that the reaction of a dependent variable to a change in an explanatory variable is not concentrated at some particular point in time, but is spread over an interval. In general

$$y_t = \sum_{j=0}^{\infty} \beta_j x_{t-j} + u_t.$$

Irving Fisher realized that restrictions on the lag coefficients, β_j, would be necessary for successful estimation, and problems of multicollinearity would still remain if the infinite upper limit were replaced by some $n < \infty$. Koyck used the assumption that, after some point, the coefficients β_j decline geometrically; if this decline begins with β_0 we have

$$y_t = \beta_0 \sum_{j=0}^{\infty} \lambda^j x_{t-j} + u_t,$$

which gives the estimating equation

$$y_t = \lambda y_{t-1} + \beta_0 x_t + v_t.$$

This simple equation can be generalized by incorporating additional lagged values of either variable. Jorgenson (1966) shows that such "rational distributed lag functions" can approximate any lag distribution; an application in a slightly different context is contained in the work of Box and Jenkins. (It is not clear whether this is what the authors mean when they speak of autoregression taking care of any important lag effects. Little use of these techniques is made in *Business Cycle Indicators*, in any case.) For the general case, the calculation of such summary statistics as the mean lag is straightforward. A useful discussion of this whole area is given by Griliches (1967); note especially his remarks on "theoretical ad-hoccery".

Also useful in econometrics is the distinction between endogenous variables (whose variations are explained by the system) and exogenous variables (which are determined outside the system). Most economists would regard the explanatory variables used by the authors to be endogenous; in which case their forecasting equations could not be regarded as reduced forms of some underlying structure. Within a single market, for example, where price is regarded as endogenous, specification of an underlying structure would require demand and supply functions to be spelled out, for price is determined by the interaction of demand and supply.

Taking an example from the paper, if we were to set up an economic model relating, *inter alia*, U.K. car production, U.K. bank rate and a Wall Street index, and we were able to reduce it to some simple form as equations (13)–(15) by not worrying about the endogenous/exogenous distinction, then the dependence, as Mr Burman indicates, could just as well be the other way round. (And, of course, cyclical variations in the two series make quite possible a relation between U.K. bank rate and the lagged S. and P. index.)

Share prices seldom appear in macro-econometric models (of the 10 U.S. models described by Nerlove (1966), only the Tinbergen (1939) model contains share prices). Concern is generally centred on the "real" economy, and interest is concentrated on forecasting income, consumption, investment, and so forth. A well-known *ex-ante* forecasting model is that of the Research Seminar in Quantitative Economics at the University of Michigan, and one might expect the authors to rise to the challenge implied in the statement by Suits (1967) that "The proper evaluation of the accuracy of a forecast is to compare it, not with the outcome of events, but with the *other forecasts* that were actually made at the same time. In this comparison econometric forecasts have compiled a remarkable record", in that forecasting errors are smaller than those produced by other methods.

Macro-econometric models are also used for *policy analysis*, whereas the methods in this paper do not permit an evaluation of, for example, the probable effects of change in tax rates, government expenditures or institutional arrangements. See, for example, the discussion of paragraphs 13–14; also note the absence of any explicit consideration of institutional changes in and around the stock market, regularly discussed in such journals as *The Economist*. "This is [indeed] a problem for all model builders"—a group from which the authors presumably exclude themselves at the present time. Progress towards a solution is surely to be made by explicitly considering all elements of the causal chain, and closely examining all the interlocking relationships. The possibility of incorporating structural changes, such as those referred to in the closing paragraph, is then always available.

Two technical points. First, with regard to seasonality, the Shiskin methods have been shown to remove from a series more variation than could reasonably be called seasonal. Not much is known about the effect of separate seasonal adjustment of a number of series on the relationships between them—except that these procedures preserve neither sums nor ratios. In these circumstances, the usual practice in econometrics is to work with unadjusted data, adding seasonal variables to the equations if necessary. This also admits the possibility that seasonal variation in the dependent variable is explained, along with other kinds of variations, by the variations in the regressors.

Second, with regard to trend. The same regression coefficients are obtained either when variables are expressed as deviations from a linear regression on time or when a trend variable is added to a regression in the original observations. The regression residuals will also be the same, but R^2 in the former case will be decreased, and appearances are worsened. It would be more consistent with the general spirit of the authors simply to add a trend variable to all equations, and let the data determine whether or not it is needed.

Since stock market operators work in a non-detrended, non-deseasonalized world, predictions which would be useful to them would have trend and seasonality added back in. Is it the case that the summary statistics reported here can be interpreted as describing the accuracy of such forecasts of the actual variables, or are these R^2 for regressions in transformed variables?

Perhaps a compact summary to these remarks can be achieved by referring to a paper given to the Society by Dr Kendall some 16 years ago, entitled "The analysis of economic time series". Among the discussants was H. S. Houthakker now, if not then, an econometrician of repute. All the remarks which he made on that occasion, about the absence in the reported work of an acceptable theoretical framework which can be utilized in interpreting the results, are relevant today.

Dr S. ROSENBAUM (Central Statistical Office): I am glad of the opportunity to comment on the paper by Beale *et al.* (1967) on which this analysis of lag relationships has been based. It appeared in *Biometrika* and has not been discussed at a meeting of the Society. Beale *et al.* gave an economical method for selecting a best set of regression variables but, like its predecessor—the article by Efroymson (1960)—it did not consider the effect this would have on significance levels.

In the special case of analysis of variance with orthogonal components, an appropriate test entails the distribution of the largest *F*-ratio, namely the ratio of the largest mean square to an independent mean square. An approximation due to Hartley (1938) permits one simply to alter the significance level in the ordinary *F*-tables by a factor equal to the number of treatment mean squares. An exact test, tabled by Nair (1948), is available for the case where each mean square has 1 degree of freedom. This would therefore be suitable for a multiple regression if the regressor variables were independent, but the presence of correlation affects the significance level. Recently Chien-Pai Han (1968) showed that the effect of correlation on the distribution of $F_{\max}$, defined differently as the ratio of the largest to the smallest sample variance, was to introduce the factor $\sqrt{(1-\rho^2)}$ into the test criterion.

When there are lag relationships they may perhaps be considered as falling into K groups, in each of which there is a choice of different lags. The size of K, and the correlation if any between groups, determines the level of significance in selecting them, while within a group one would use an independent criterion to find the best lag.

Professor D. E. BARTON (Institute of Computer Science): Two or three years ago Mr E. D. Gomme and Mr M. R. W. Burrows introduced me to an earlier version of the present data and the analysis we made then is of interest in that it provides to some degree an independent study of the problem. In particular we looked at one or two of the questions which Professor Durbin and Dr Wallis have raised and it would be interesting to know whether our answers to these coincide with Dr Kendall's. It should be made clear, however, that not only were we using a set of regressor variables which differed by several items from the present set but, more critically, we did not have the advantage of the Beale–Kendall–Mann programme (or equivalent) to pick out the best regressors. Thus our conclusions may differ in detail from those here because of these limitations. Broadly, they were very similar.

We found that autoregression of the linear-trend-corrected log *F.T.* index on previous values, even so few as the two immediately preceding, gave as good prediction as multiple regression on the linear-trend-and-seasonal-corrected regressions. This was a point Professor Durbin raised.

Generally, all those variables expressed in cash terms had logarithms showing marked linear trend but no significant higher-order terms. This is, presumably, mostly inflation but also increased affluence, productivity and working population, since items like employment and electricity consumption show similar but less marked behaviour. This relates to Dr Wallis's remarks.

Dr Kendall says he has taken the data as given. This has unfortunate consequences though it is probably unavoidable. The regressors, like the *F.T.* index itself, are highly complex indices whose components have different trends and seasonalities. This introduces more variability than "purer" figures would, since one cannot remove seasonalities as effectively from composite series. Mr Burman's differentiation between foreign-currency and sterling bank advances is a case in point.

The remarkable phenomenon described in this paper [of the marked (lagged) correlations on particular regressors] may well be as much political as economic. That is, it may be largely generated by the artificially stimulated pre-election boom with its painful post-election disinflationary hangover. Mr Burrows has argued this more fully elsewhere; in his Chairman's address to the Industrial Section of the Market Research Society in July 1966 (which received some newspaper publicity at the time) and in *The Investment Analyst*, November 1966 ("Computer forecasting and the politico-economic trade cycle"). It could well be that the decision to hold the last election so soon after its predecessor has interrupted the rhythm of the cycle and that it is this as much as anything which has made recent predictions go astray.

Professor M. S. BARTLETT (Oxford University): No doubt this problem is of particular interest in relation to the economy but, as previous speakers have indicated, this is a general problem of methodology and statistics of interest in many fields. It may be illuminating to consider what the situation is, say, in the field of forecasting in meteorology. I am not an expert in meteorology, but remember some years ago, when in the United States, discussion with a meteorologist examining the problem of forecasting by using statistical methods. I got from him the information that at that time the success of the empirical statistical method of forecasting on the basis of statistical patterns in previous data was running parallel with forecasting based on a detailed mathematical model which you have then to estimate as best you can and run through a computer to elicit what will happen to the weather in future. You had these two methods, one empirical and one theoretical, which at that time—I do not know the present position—were rather neck and neck. This is rather intriguing because surely if you have two quite different methods like that which are producing rather similar results, somehow you ought to be able to strike a mean and use both methods more efficiently to give even better results, but I do not know how to suggest that it should be done.

I do think it worth bearing in mind, although I am in favour of model building myself to a certain extent, that even if you do have the perfect model, if you know what the model is but it involves rather complicated equations with lots of coefficients, you have to estimate these, and it by no means follows that you will do better than with the more empirical methods. This means you must distinguish between the problem of interpreting what is going on and the problem of predicting what is going to happen. Prediction is one thing, and the problem of interpreting is another, and it does not always mean that procedures should synchronize for the two purposes.

Professor G. B. WETHERILL (Bath University of Technology): I am grateful to the authors for tackling this problem, because it seems to me that there is a great deal to be learned about the methodology of this kind of an analysis.

My first point concerns the use by the authors of the Beale *et al.* (1967) multiple regression programme. Now in any multiple regression analysis there will usually be a whole set of regression equations which attain nearly as high a sum of squares as the optimum set. It seems to me that the choice within this group has to be made with great care, and in particular an equation which made sense physically may be preferred, even if it were not the best.

Suppose one has several different sets of data. Then if an equation were fitted to each, there will be (in general) a different optimum equation for each. If there is an equation which does reasonably well for all the different sets of data, this equation would be preferred to other equations which did very well in some, but badly in others.

Now suppose our different sets of data are combined in some way, then it is always possible that because of some fluke variation, a single optimum equation is produced which in fact is spurious.

Finally, it always seems to me that situations of this kind are really more suitable for analysis as a functional relationship, and I wonder if the authors have considered it. I would also like to know if the authors used multiple regression because they think it really is appropriate or because there is no other technique which can be conveniently used.

The AUTHORS thanked the participants in the discussion for their remarks, and later replied in writing, as follows:

1. We are well aware, as several speakers from Professor Durbin onwards pointed out, that the empirical detection of relationships is only part of the scientific process. But several speakers, especially Mr Burman and Dr Wallis, seem to think that no empirical results should be published except when accompanied by rational argument (Mr Burman) or presented in an acceptable theoretical framework (Dr Wallis).

In short, Kepler should not have published the laws of planetary motion because he could not explain them; he should have presented them in the acceptable framework of Ptolemaic epicycles. Newton should not have published the *Principia* because he could not explain gravity; Jenner, Prout, Michelson and Morley, Doll and Bradford Hill should have kept quiet until they could explain what they observed.

2. The crux of the argument is whether our results are reproducible. We have followed them through long enough to suggest that they may be, but we acknowledge quite freely

160   *Discussion on the Paper by Mr Coen, Mr Gomme and Dr Kendall*   [Part 2,

that the only valid test is the experimental one. We strongly rebut any criticism based on the rejection of evidence simply because it cannot be explained. Mr Burman says that we want to treat the economic system as a "black box". We are as anxious as anyone to look inside the "black box" to find out how it works. All we would say is that, until such a thing is possible, it is worth while examining the stimulus–response relationships exhibited by the economy; or the lead–lag relationship where even "stimulus–response" may be thought tendentious.

3. Mr Burman is slightly less than fair in his reference to the length of experience. He has compared the shortest length of experience from one equation with the longest length from another: see Fig. 12 for the comparison of bank advances and share price over 18 years. The apparent relationship between U.K. car production and the S. and P. index, about which we do not wish to make any issue, is shown in Fig. 8(i) for 1948–68.

4. Both Professor Durbin and Mr Burman advise the use of spectral methods in time-series analysis. We think that in econometrics such methods are largely a waste of time. But we are willing to be convinced and will repeat a challenge which one of us made many years ago: can somebody tell us, by the use of spectral methods, something about economic time-series which was not already known or derivable more simply from correlation analysis?

5. Mr Burman questions our choice of explanatory variables. We have in fact tested the variables Mr Burman mentions and found that they are not as good as those in our equations at "explaining" the variation in the *F.T.* index.

6. We have been unable to find any convincing evidence that the stock market is able to anticipate. The market probably is based on people's expectations of the future but examination of any London share price index will suggest that these expectations are often not realized.

7. We were aware of the significant proportion of the increase in bank advances which was accounted for by lending to overseas residents. We would like to point to the similarity in movements in money supply and equity prices: see Fig. 13. We do not think that London clearing banks' advances, as suggested by Mr Burman, are an appropriate series for the more recent years because lending by these banks is becoming a less important part of total bank lending.

8. Dr Wallis's discussion on econometrics is not really our concern in this paper. What we have to say about distributed lags, the estimation of parameters in mixed systems, identifiability problems and so forth will be said on some later occasion. We do not, as Mr Burman and Dr Wallis both suggest, exclude ourselves from the group of model builders, only from the group of bad model builders.

9. Dr Wallis's quotation from Suits is one we wish we had found ourselves, for nothing reveals the invincible resistance to fact so much as this. One is, apparently, to judge of the *accuracy* of a forecast, not by whether it was anywhere near the eventuality, but by whether it agrees with other forecasts made at the same time. Now it is possible to be right for a bad reason just as it is possible, and even creditable, to be wrong for a good reason. But one must not forget that whole classes of forecasters may be wrong because their reasons are bad.

10. We agree with most of Professor Barton's comments. It is true that an autoregressive scheme may produce high values of R^2, but since one of the primary purposes of the type of forecasting equation which we have been trying to develop is to indicate major turning points we have not pursued autoregressive schemes with one or two terms. There are some interesting theoretical points here which we intend to develop in later studies.

11. Certain pressures probably do exist to increase economic activity before elections and to hold elections when conditions are favourable. However, the coincident movements in bank advances, money supply and equity share prices have not been upset around any recent election. We have also developed equations, which we do not propose to publish here, to predict interest rates. These have not been significantly off course in

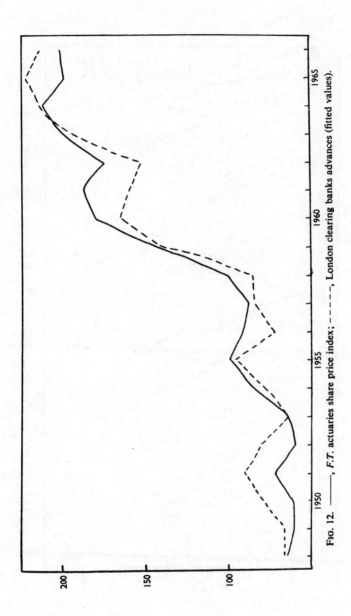

Fig. 12. ———, *F.T.* actuaries share price index; - - - -, London clearing banks advances (fitted values).

162   *Discussion on the Paper by Mr Coen, Mr Gomme and Dr Kendall*   [Part 2,

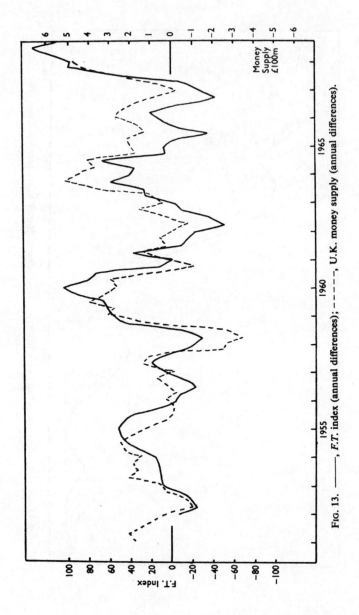

Fig. 13. ⸻, *F.T.* index (annual differences); – – – –, U.K. money supply (annual differences).

the past ten years and, incidentally, produced forecasts nine months ago for 1969/1 which are very close to the actual levels.

12. We should like to thank Professor Bartlett for his very helpful analogy with meteorological forecasting. We entirely agree with his comments.

13. Professor Wetherill is quite right about the solution of variables in regression analysis. Optima being by nature flat, there is often a fairly wide degree of variation for the regression variables in the neighbourhood of the optimal set. A good program should print out the values in the neighbourhood to enable similarity to be gauged.

14. We would agree with Professor Wetherill about functional relationship, but used the regression because of its greater computational simplicity. Even with linear systems the estimation of functional relationship depends on assumptions about scale or sampling variance; and with lagged variation of the autoregression type there are further problems. It would be interesting to see some theoretical work on this subject.

Note: At the time of reading our paper attention was already being focused on bank advances although no reduction had yet been achieved. We would have expected, on the basis of the fits shown in Figs. 10 and 11, that a reduction in bank advances would be accompanied by a fall in equity prices and we were aware that special efforts were being made to reduce bank advances and money supply. In fact the *F.T.* index had fallen by 100 points to 423 on May 13th.

REFERENCES IN DISCUSSION

CHIEN-PAI HAN (1968). Testing the homogeneity of a set of correlated variances. *Biometrika*, **55**, 317–326.
EFROYMSON, H. A. (1960). Multiple regression analysis. In *Mathematical Methods for Digital Computers* (edited by Ralston, A. and Wilf, H.S.), pp. 141–203. London and New York: John Wiley.
GRILICHES, Z. (1967). Distributed lags: a survey. *Econometrica*, **35**, 16–49.
HARTLEY, H. O. (1938). Studentization and large-sample theory. *J. R. Statist. Soc. Suppl.*, **5**, 80–88.
JORGENSON, D. W. (1966). Rational distributed lag functions. *Econometrica*, **34**, 135–149.
KENDALL, M. G. (1953). The analysis of economic time series. *J. R. Statist. Soc.* A, **116**, 11–34.
NAIR, K. R. (1948). The studentized form of the extreme mean square test in the analysis of variance. *Biometrika*, **35**, 16–31.
NERLOVE, M. (1966). A tabular survey of macro-econometric models. *Int. Econ. Rev.*, **7**, 127–175.
SUITS, D. B. (1967). Applied econometric forecasting and policy analysis. In *Forecasting on a Scientific Basis*, Proceedings of an International Summer Institute held in Curia, Portugal, September 1966. Also *Arquivo do Instituto Gulbenkian de Ciencia* (B) **2**, 91–147.
TINBERGEN, J. (1939). *Business Cycles in the United States of America*, 1919–32. Geneva: League of Nations.

As a result of the ballot taken during the meeting, the following were elected Fellows of the Society:

BOLDY, Duncan Peter, M.Sc.
EVANS, Edward Andrew, Ph.D.
FREEMAN, Stanley Roger, M.Sc.
GROVE, Daniel Michael, B.Sc.
IMBER, Valerie, B.A.
JOYCE, Peter John, B.Sc.
KANITKAR, Yechwant Gajanan, M.Sc.
KU, Hsien Hsiang, Ph.D.
MARTIN, Keith Baillie, M.Sc.
ORTON, Clive Robert, B.A.

PEACOCK, Robert Avenel, B.A.
PEARE, Charles William Derek, B.A.
PEPPER, Jon Vivian, M.Sc.
PEPPER, Michael Peter Gregory, B.Sc.
ROBINSON, Peter Michael, B.Sc.
ROE, Peter Alan, B.Sc.
SHANAHAN, Michael Francis, M.Sc.
SMITH, Bernard John Alan, B.A.
SOLOMON, Vethamani, M.Sc.

[11]

Dynamic Equations for Economic Forecasting with the G.D.P.–Unemployment Relation and the Growth of G.D.P. in the United Kingdom as an Example

By Jeremy Bray

Mullard Ltd, London†

[Read before the Royal Statistical Society on Wednesday, January 20th, 1971, the President, Dr B. Benjamin, in the Chair]

1. Introduction

This paper describes a method for estimating dynamic equations for systems undergoing structural change, and applying them in economic forecasts made as an aid to current policy decisions. Though suitable for any type of computer operation, the method is designed particularly for conversational mode operation on line through a teletype terminal. A description of the procedure is followed by a theoretical justification and an example showing its application to a study of the relationship between gross domestic product and unemployment in the United Kingdom between 1955 and 1970, from which conclusions emerge regarding possible rates of growth of the United Kingdom economy.

Methods used in econometrics for estimating dynamic relationships have not lent themselves to a tidy theoretical system, and the considerable efforts devoted to their development have produced a mass of ingenious arguments and many unsolved problems. A good impression is given in the textbooks by Malinvaud (1966) and Christ (1967), and a recent review paper by Leser (1968).

On the basis of experience of time-series analysis in other fields, particularly in process control, Box and Jenkins (1970) have developed practical methods and the necessary underlying statistical and mathematical ideas which econometricians are likely to find powerful and illuminating. The method set out in this paper may be considered a stepping stone to the use of Box and Jenkins' methods by economists used to previous methods of analysis.

Less developed versions of the methods used in this paper have been used by the author and others for modelling and optimizing chemical plant operation (Bray *et al.*, 1959, 1961, 1966).

The method of mathematical statistics is to postulate a model giving relationships between variables x_i and random variables e_j, and then estimate these relationships using observations of the x_i. Because in econometric practice the underlying structure is not known for sure, there is a circular process, hypothesizing the structure, estimating parameters and making predictions from observations, seeing where these depart from the behaviour to be expected from the hypothesized structure and revising it accordingly, using fresh estimation methods, and so on.

This paper gives estimation and prediction methods without first discussing the statistical structure of the relations being estimated. This is no indication of any wish to revert to a more primitive concept of statistical method. The paper sets out to describe practical methods, which are easy to use, for tackling a number of problems in lagged relationships which are well recognized by economists.

† Formerly Member of Parliament for Middlesbrough West.

2. METHOD

The procedure is carried out in the following stages:

Stage 1

Plot both the endogenous and exogenous time series that might be used against time and against each other.

Stage 2

Examine the graphs in the light of the economic hypotheses to be tested and quantified, to see the broad behaviour of the system—the existence of time trends, changes in the period of variations, apparent correlations and other characteristics. Select the endogenous and the principal and subsidiary exogenous variables in the light of economic theory.

Stage 3

Edit and transform the data into time series suitable for linear relations found by multiple regressions: for example, correct for changes of base, definition or classification; consider the elimination or adjustment of non-typical behaviour like strikes and extremes of weather conditions. Seasonally correct the data where appropriate. *Do not* smoothe data or take differences, since these operations introduce lags into the system which should be handled in the ensuing forecasting process.

Stage 4

Consider the endogenous variable $y(t)$, and the exogenous variable $x(t)$. Further exogenous variables may be treated simultaneously in the same way as $x(t)$. Compute recursively $y1(t)$, $y2(t)$, $y3(t)$, $y4(t)$, $y5(t)$ and $x1(t)$, $x2(t)$, $x3(t)$, $x4(t)$ and $x5(t)$ as lagged exponentially weighted moving averages of $y(t)$ and $x(t)$ as follows:

$$y1(0) = y2(0) = y3(0) = y4(0) = y5(0) = y(0).$$

For $t>0$,

$$y1(t) = 0{\cdot}5y(t-1)+0{\cdot}5y1(t-1),$$

$$y2(t) = 0{\cdot}4y1(t-1)+0{\cdot}6y2(t-1),$$

$$y3(t) = 0{\cdot}3y2(t-1)+0{\cdot}7y3(t-1), \quad \text{etc.,}$$

$$\tag{1}$$

and $x1(t)$, $x2(t)$, $x3(t)$, $x4(t)$, $x5(t)$ are defined similarly in terms of $x(t)$.

If D is the backward displacement operator, so that we can write $Dy(t) = y(t-1)$, equations (1) may be written, for $t>0$,

$$y1(t) = 0{\cdot}5Dy(t)+0{\cdot}5Dy1(t-1),$$

or

$$(1-0{\cdot}5D)y1(t) = 0{\cdot}5Dy(t),$$

or

$$y1(t) = \frac{0{\cdot}5D}{(1-0{\cdot}5D)}y(t).$$

Similarly,

$$y2(t) = \frac{0 \cdot 4D}{(1 - 0 \cdot 6D)} y1(t),$$

$$y3(t) = \frac{0 \cdot 3D}{(1 - 0 \cdot 7D)} y2(t), \quad \text{etc.}$$

These functions are the exponentially weighted moving averages (supposing $y(t) = y(0)$ for $t < 0$),

$$yJ(t) = \sum_{i=0}^{\infty} AJ_i y(t - i). \tag{2}$$

The weighting coefficients AJ_i, plotted in Fig. 1, give a set of moving averages $yJ(t)$ of increasing order, lag and dispersion.

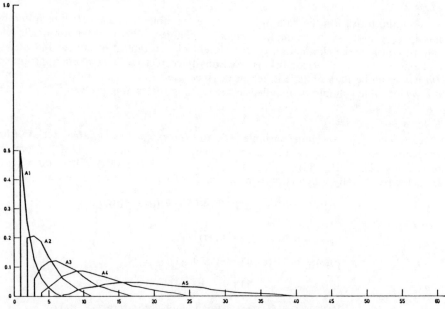

FIG. 1. Weighting coefficients for lagged averages.

Stage 5

Compute the single-stage least-squares multiple regression

$$y(t) = Q_1 y1(t) + Q_2 y2(t) + Q_3 y3(t) + P_0 x(t) + P_1 x1(t) + P_2 x2(t)$$
$$+ P_3 x3(t) + c + e(t) \tag{3}$$

to give estimates of the coefficients c, Q_i and P_i and the usual parameters of the estimation with $e(t)$ a random variable with zero mean and standard deviation giving the standard error of the regression. More or fewer different order averages may be included. The constant c may be omitted if there is a good reason to do so.

Further terms may be added representing exogenous variables other than x and their similarly lagged averages. But the above equation is sufficient to deal with quite complex lagged systems with lags up to 2 years on quarterly data, provided data are available for at least 10 years and for two cycles at the principal periodicity (5 years). If singularity and significance problems are suspected in any regression computation, results can be checked by including the same regression terms in a different order.

Compute the regression first using only an initial segment of data for, say, $t = 4, 5, ..., T$. The reason for not starting with $t = 0$ is to allow the lagged averages time to adjust. For examples, if $N = 59$ (15 years of quarterly data), take $T = 43$ (11 years), say.

Stage 6

Substituting from equations (1), equation (3) can be written in the form

$$\frac{(1 - B_1 D)(1 - B_2 D)(1 - B_3 D)}{(1 - 0.5D)(1 - 0.6D)(1 - 0.7D)} y = P_0 \frac{(1 - A_1 D)(1 - A_2 D)(1 - A_3 D)}{(1 - 0.5D)(1 - 0.6D)(1 - 0.7D)} x + c, \quad (4)$$

where A_i, B_i are calculated from P_j, Q_j, B_i being the poles and A_i the zeros of the transfer function relating y and x. If there is a pole B_i near 1 and particularly if it is greater than 1, taking successive differences

$$\Delta y(t) = (1 - D) y(t) = y(t) - y(t - 1)$$

in place of y in equations (1) and in the regression equation (3) may reduce the standard error, and may also be needed to keep the system stable. If there are two poles near 1, take second differences $\Delta^2 y(t)$, and so on. If there is a zero A_i near 1, $(1 - D)x$ may be taken similarly in place of x in equations (1) and (3).

Stage 7

A more general form of equation (3) is

$$y(t) = Q_0 y(t - n) + Q_1 y1(t - n) + ... + Q_5 y5(t - n)$$
$$+ P_0 x(t - m) + P_1 x1(t - m) + ... + P_5 x5(t - m) + c + e(t). \quad (5)$$

By substituting from equations (1) in equation (5), the autoregressive coefficients b_i and the moving average coefficients a_i may be obtained for the equation

$$y(t) = \sum_{i=0}^{\infty} \{b_i y(t - i) + a_i x(t - i)\} + c + e(t). \quad (6)$$

For $n = 1$ in equation (5), $b_0 = 0$ in equation (6). This equation may therefore be used to predict $y(T + 1)$, given $y(t)$ for $t \leqslant T$ and $x(t)$ for $t \leqslant T + 1$.

Successive applications of equation (6) for $t = T + 1$, $T + 2, ..., T + L$, give the L-step prediction of $y(T + L)$, that is the prediction at time T of $y(T + L)$ given the values of $y(t)$ for $t \leqslant T$, and of $x(t)$ for $t \leqslant T + L$. This is equivalent to the equation,

$$y(t) = \sum_{i=L}^{\infty} b_{Li} y(t - i) + \sum_{i=0}^{\infty} a_{Li} x(t - i) + c_L + e_L(t), \quad (7)$$

where the coefficients b_{Li}, a_{Li}, c_L and the standard error e_L of the random variable $e_L(t)$ are derived from equation (6).

For all $L > i$, $a_{Li} = a'_i$, where a'_i are the moving average coefficients in the purely moving average form

$$y(t) = \sum_{i=0}^{\infty} a'_i x(t-i) + c' + e'(t). \tag{8}$$

The coefficients a'_i are also called the "impulse response" since they give the response of $y(t)$ to a unit impulse in $x(t)$. The "step response", $A'_j = \sum_{i=0}^{j} a'_i$, may also be calculated.

The 1-step coefficients, the L-step coefficients for any L, the pure moving average coefficients or "impulse response", the "step response" and the L-step prediction errors may be computed to show different aspects of the behaviour of the predicting equation (5).

Compute the L-step predictions $y'(T+L)$, for $L = 1, 2, ..., 8$, say, using equation (6) repeatedly, with the actual values of $y(t)$ for $t \leqslant T$, the predicted values for $t > T$, and the actual values of $x(t)$ for all t, comparing the errors of prediction $y'(T+L) - y(T+L)$ with e_L.

Stage 8

Carry out Stages 5, 6 and 7 for at least two values of T less than N, and for $T = N$, using the latest data available. Postulate different values of the exogenous variable $x(t)$ and, using equation (6), compute the prediction $y'(t)$ of $y(t)$ for $t > N$, giving predictions and standard errors of the predictions $y'(t)$ $(t > N)$ conditional on alternative values of $x(u)$ $(N < u \leqslant t)$. These predictions should be interpreted and qualified in the light of how accurate the predictions turned out to be for values of $t > T$ in the earlier regressions.

Stage 9

It is desirable to experiment with different selections of terms in equations (3) or (5). A danger to avoid is the introduction of too many terms which, while improving the fit over the data used in the regression, introduce instabilities into the predictions for times not used in the regression. This can arise when there is insufficient information in the data to justify the use of the functional form assumed. Such instabilities are shown by irregular behaviour of the coefficients in Stage 7. If because of such instabilities or because of changes in the system, predictions go very much astray, the standard errors of the prediction, taking into account error in the estimates of the coefficients, will generally show the predictions have little meaning.

A particular type of equation (5) which may be tried are equations which give direct estimates of L-step predicters, by making $u > 1$, omitting the Q_0, Q_1 terms and so on. This is an alternative to repeated application of the 1-step predicter. Its interest lies in that it offers different ranges of possible coefficients, and that it facilitates calculation of the errors of predictions due to errors in estimating coefficients. But there are complications in that because of the serial correlation of errors inherent in L-step predictions, generalized rather than ordinary least-squares regression should be used.

Stage 5(a)

Since the behaviour of most systems changes over time it may be desirable to give less weight to less recent data. Accordingly, the sum of squares

$$\sum_t \{y(t) - y'(t)\}^2$$

minimized by the regression equations (3) to (6) may be replaced by

$$\sum_{t=0}^{P}\{y(t)-y'(t)\}^2 b^{P-t},$$

where $0<b<1$. To reduce the weighting to $0\cdot 5$, 20 steps (5 years) before, $b = 0\cdot 9659$. The value of b can be adjusted so as to give the best fit when the predicter is applied for $t > P$, though this must be a matter of trial and error, since it depends on how fast the structure of the system is changing.

3. THEORY

3.1. *Comparison with Other Methods*

Various forms of autoregressive and moving average relations have been considered or used by Malinvaud (1966, p. 479), Fisher (1925, 1937), Koyck (1954), Solow (1960), Theil and Stern (1960), Almon (1965), Jorgenson (1966) and Griliches (1967). The latest methods of Box and Jenkins (1970) are more general and so more powerful than all of these, though Almon's method differs somewhat from the rest. Box and Jenkins estimate, by non-linear least squares, relations of the form

$$y = \frac{P(D)}{Q(D)}x + \frac{R(D)}{S(D)}e, \qquad (9)$$

where P, Q, R, S are polynomials in D of low order and e is white noise. Before estimation they identify the order of model to be considered and afterwards check the model.

The methods of this paper estimate relations of the form

$$\frac{Q(D)}{K(D)}y = \frac{P(D)}{K(D)}x + e, \qquad (10)$$

where $K(D)$ is of the class K of polynomials with factors $(1-0\cdot 5D)$, $(1-0\cdot 6D)$, $(1-0\cdot 7D)$, $(1-0\cdot 8D)$, $(1-0\cdot 9D)$. This can be written

$$y = \frac{P(D)}{Q(D)}x + \frac{K(D)}{Q(D)}e.$$

This has an unrestricted operator on x, and the noise operator is less general than the form considered by Box and Jenkins in two respects only. First $K(D)$ is any function having factors only of the set $(1-k_i D)$ where $k_i = 0\cdot 5$, $0\cdot 6$, $0\cdot 7$, etc., instead of a general polynomial. Second, after allowing for cancellation of factors, any factor in the denominator of the operator on x other than a factor $(1-k_i D)$ has to appear in the denominator of the operator on the noise e, but not vice versa. In many cases these are not severe restrictions, since the distribution of k_i covers those parts of the unit circle most likely to contain important roots of the operator. Important periodicities, causing complex roots, will often have been removed by seasonal corrections of y and x. The effect of roots k on the real axis between 0 and $0\cdot 5$ damp out very rapidly, and any near 1 become indistinguishable from 1. While models estimated and forecasts made by these methods will therefore sometimes be nearly as good as Box and Jenkins results, since their model is more general, the results obtained by their methods must be in every respect superior to those obtained by the methods of this paper. So it does not seem necessary to develop further the methods of this paper to deal with difficulties in estimation and prediction that will occur in some cases, to provide for iterative estimations to improve predictions by choosing different sets of numbers k_i, and so on.

While Box and Jenkins' methods in their present form are more difficult to understand, and perhaps to use, than the methods of this paper, they are well worth the effort. The methods of this paper are likely to be superior to previous methods used by economists in many cases, but they should only be considered a stepping-stone to the use of full Box and Jenkins' methods.

3.2 Prediction

Suppose the predicting equation (5) above, obtained by regression, is expressed in the form (6), and the residual error e_{1t} is not serially correlated, and has zero mean and standard deviation e_1. The L-step predicting equation (7) above is obtained by multiplying equation (6) for $t = t - i$ by M_i for $i = 0, 1, ..., L-1$, and adding them together, where

$$M_0 = 1 \quad \text{and} \quad M_i = \sum_{j=0}^{i-1} M_j b_{i-j}.$$

The standard error e_L of the L-step predicting equation is then given by

$$e_L = e_1 \sqrt{(M_0^2 + M_1^2 + ... + M_{L-1}^2)} \tag{11}$$

since the errors e_{1t} are uncorrelated.

If there is a pole B_i, found in Stage 6 above, near to the unit circle, the factor $(1 - B_i D)$ in the denominator of the transfer function will cause any error in the estimate of B_i to give corresponding difficulties with the errors $e_L(t)$ of L-step predictions. If $|B_i| > 1$, an error $e_1(t)$ will cause an associated error $e_L(t)$ growing with L. If $|B_i| = 1$, the effects of an error $e_1(t)$ will persist indefinitely in e_L, and if $|B_i| < 1$, but near 1, the effect will only die away slowly. This may be a feature of the system itself, but since an error in estimating B_i will cause $e_L(t)$ to depart from its expected distribution in the same way, the effect must be watched. Pathological error behaviour could be, but would not usually be, a feature of the system and is likely to arise from a mis-specification of the form of the predicting equation.

One way of avoiding error instabilities with a pole near 1 is to take successive differences of the dependent variable. If n poles are near 1, nth-order differences can be taken. The result is to introduce a bias into the structural form of the predicting equation, but by removing the cause of instability, the result may well be to give smaller standard errors of predictions over data not used in the regression. The effect of taking differences is to improve the prediction of short-term effects at the cost of poorer prediction of long-term effects, for any particular functional form or set of data. This may well be desirable where there is not the data available to make significant longer-term predictions.

Another way of avoiding these predicting instabilities due to the accumulation of errors is to obtain an L-step predicting equation not by repeated application of a 1-step predicting equation as above, but directly by regression, as indicated in Stage 9. Since from repeated applications of the 1-step predicting equation,

$$e_{(L+1)t} = e_{Lt} + M_L e_{1(t-L)}$$

the *L*-step predicting errors are serially correlated, so, strictly speaking, generalized rather than ordinary least squares should be used for estimating the equations. Poles outside the unit circle can equally arise in *L*-step predicting equations, particularly due to mis-specification and redundancy in the number of auto-regressive terms, but any difficulties likely to arise can be seen by the growth or violent oscillation of the *L*-step predicting coefficients or of the impulse response. The standard error of predictions given by equation (11) is the error due to the random variable residual $e(t)$ and takes no account of errors in the estimation of the coefficients of the equation. For non-serially correlated residuals the standard error allowing for error in the estimation of coefficients may be obtained in the usual way from the covariance matrix of the coefficients. Where the equation has been reasonably well specified, the error in predictions due to error in the estimation of coefficients is usually small by comparison with that due to the random variable residual.

3.3. *New Systems and Series*

The extreme problem of structural change is when a totally new system is created and no data are available for past times. In economics this may arise with new taxes or other factors, or more commonly with new time series resulting from new systems of measurements. It is possible in these circumstances to use predicters, complete with covariance matrices, estimated from theoretical considerations, however crudely, and then use the updating method described in Stage 5(a) above to embody practical experience as it is accumulated. In such extreme conditions, it is useful to arrange to update some aspects of the predicters faster than others, by combining the selective weighting for different "observations", described above, with selective weighting of different terms in the regression (cf. Malinvaud, 1966, p. 355).

This way of incorporating an initial theoretical construct is particularly important in going beyond forecasting to consider optimal control. I have obtained results on these lines on a chemical plant (Bray *et al.*, 1966), where the problem frequently arose in optimizing dynamic behaviour, since, when the control computer was switched on, the model it started with, left over from the previous run, did not fit at all well and had to be rapidly updated. It proved possible, in starting from scratch, that is with the most crudely estimated coefficients and covariance matrix, to converge quite rapidly on a model describing the current behaviour of the plant, which could be used effectively for optimization.

Brown and Durbin (1969) have examined the behaviour of recursive residuals, that is the residuals of recursively updated regressions. It seems possible to develop their use of the recursive residual as a measure of whether or not a regression relationship is changing into a measure of how fast it is changing, and use this to adjust the value of *b*.

3.4. *Objectives and Tests in Regression Methods*

Christ (1966, p. 546) discusses whether in testing a model it is better to use all the available data to derive the model and then examine the prediction errors over the sample data used in the regression, or whether it is better to derive the model from part of the data—usually the earlier part—and see how it predicts over the latter part. He concludes reasonably enough that if in 1966 the purpose is to predict for 1966–70 then the best that can be done is to use the model that fits best up to 1966. But because statistical tests based on the distribution of random variables are not applicable when maintained hypotheses have been chosen so as to conform to the data on which hypotheses will be tested, he advocates testing a model over fresh data which was not available when the model was constructed, either by updating it, or by examining its prediction errors. He argues that in time-series work, because of the limited amount of data available, it is better to update the model.

It is suggested that the best course is to do both the alternatives considered by Christ. This is the only way by which it is possible to demonstrate the possible impact of structural change on predictions and their estimated standard errors. For example, when 12 years of quarterly data are available, the model might be derived on data for 8, 10 and 12 years, and used to predict over the data used and on to the fourteenth year in each case.

If the structural form of the predicter is a reasonable representation of the system and if the system is reasonably stable, then the actual errors of prediction, from the end of data used in the regressions, will have a distribution with a standard error equal to the standard error of the regression itself. If this is not so either the form of the predicter is not right or the system is changing.

Where models are built or forecasts made from which policy conclusions are to be drawn, the statistical analysis should be continued into the arguments about policy, evaluating proposed policies or deducing that policy which will best achieve the desired objectives. If the analysis stops short at the forecast, however good the forecasts, policies based on them may well prove unstable or otherwise unsatisfactory. This further analysis requires the application of control theory.

3.5. *Types of Dynamic Situations in Economics*

The estimation methods considered in this paper, and still more those of Box and Jenkins, cover a very wide range of linear relationships which occur in economics, including relations between lagged derivatives of any order on either side. The one estimating method will thus deal with, for example, pipeline models (e.g. orders—deliveries), deviation from steady-growth models (e.g. G.D.P.—unemployment), cumulative backlash models and pressure equalization models, without having to choose in advance the form of the model. In particular these estimation methods do not simply identify the lag in an effect that is otherwise known: they identify the dynamics, which may include important derivative and integral effects of various orders which can be very different from simple unimodal, one-sign distributed lags. While any insight available from economic theory should be used, the estimation methods will be able to test and choose between a wider range of hypotheses than those usually considered in studying an economic relationship. The relationship finally used must of course be plausible on theoretical grounds as well as being indicated as the most likely on empirical grounds.

4. EXAMPLE: THE G.D.P. – UNEMPLOYMENT RELATION 1955–70

4.1. *Previous Work*

A method used in the Treasury for forecasting unemployment from gross domestic product and hence deriving the "productive potential" of the economy and its rate of growth has been described by Godley and Shepherd (1964), and amendments to it by Shepherd (1968). The equivalent work for the United States is by Okun (1962) and Black and Russell (1969).

Although the hypothesis on which economic policy decisions are based are seldom defined clearly enough to test them on the record, it has been widely assumed that

176   BRAY – *Dynamic Equations for Economic Forecasting*   [Part 2,

there is a "rate of growth of productive potential", which sets a limit to achievable growth rates. If a faster rate of growth is attempted, the economy will run up against ineluctable structural constraints in the domestic economy. If the rate of growth falls below the potential this will be shown by mounting unemployment. Paish (1962) and others have drawn conclusions for economic policy, laying the basis of, and drawing on, the work of Godley and Shepherd (1964).

The concept of "productive potential" is distinct from the constraints imposed by the balance of payments and by acceptable rates of inflation. Thus, an argument against removing the balance of payments constraint by devaluation or by floating exchange rates has been that it would still not make possible a faster rate of growth, since this is limited by "the rate of growth of productive potential". An argument in support of incomes policy norms has been that any increase in earnings above the "rate of growth of productive potential" is bound to be inflationary, and "the rate of growth of productive potential" was set by other factors.

These arguments have been contested by economists who believe faster growth is possible. They have argued that the level of investment, and hence the rate of growth, is affected by the pressure of demand. Trade unionists have argued that wage increases can secure faster growth through greater incentives to efficiency and higher demand.

Since 1966 the unemployment—G.D.P. relationship seems to have changed, with a higher level of unemployment than would have been expected from the behaviour of G.D.P. This is supported by indirect evidence, in that the level of vacancies has been higher for the level of unemployment than in previous years. The Godley–Shepherd relationships between output, unemployment and employment are used not only in the Treasury's short-term forecast for forecasting unemployment (Roy, 1970, p. 468), but also in the principal loop connecting output, unemployment, employment, wages and salaries, imports and exports in the Treasury's medium-term assessment (Sowerbutts, 1970, p. 490). Miss Sowerbutts says:

> "It is well known that these (Godley–Shepherd) relationships are unsatisfactory over the most recent past, partly because of an apparent increase in productivity and partly because unemployment is less efficient as a measure of the pressure of demand. Currently the equation (taking the growth of capacity as exogenous) is used with an arbitrary adjustment term which takes different values according as one assumes that the present situation regarding the increase in productivity is a temporary aberration, a once-and-for-all increase or indicates movements to a higher rate of growth. This procedure does not resolve the difficulty and work is in hand to try to find a more satisfactory solution."

There is thus a case for re-examining the G.D.P.–unemployment relation.

The Godley–Shepherd method uses a two-equation relationship between employment, population changes, unemployment, G.D.P. and the average hours worked per week. The method will be described and analysed below, and the results from this method compared with those from the use of the methods of this paper.

The earlier work of Okun (1962) assumes that the magnitude of all other effects (employment, productivity, etc.) is related to unemployment and proceeds from there. Black and Russell (1969) estimated the labour force. Their relation between employment demand and output incorporated a lagged value of employment demand, thus eliminating iterative estimations used by Godley and Shepherd. Corrections were made for hours worked per man, and for dual-job holding, to give final estimates of potential G.N.P. Their work was aimed at providing historic estimates of potential G.N.P. rather than at giving the best possible current forecasts of unemployment in relation to output.

In the treatment of lags none of this work goes beyond what economists call a Koyck lag, what control engineers call a single pole, and what mathematicians call a first-order differential or difference equation. Godley and Shepherd estimate lags graphically (permitting non-linearity) or *a priori*. Black and Russell estimate lags by autoregression. Both make liberal use of logarithms, and Black and Russell of first differences of logarithms in the usual treatment of Cobb–Douglas production functions.

This much-studied problem therefore presents a good test of a forecasting method. This paper does not attempt to consider all the factors taken into consideration by Okun, Godley and Shepherd, and Black and Russell. It assumes that other factors are related to unemployment and shows what emerges directly from a more sensitive treatment of dynamics and structural change by a standard forecasting method.

4.2. *Forecasting Unemployment from G.D.P.*

The data used in the Godley–Shepherd method are graphed and defined in Fig. 2 (p. 178) and tabulated in Table 1 (Stage 1 above). Fig. 2 shows G.D.P. (P) is cyclical about a rising trend. Unemployment (UN) is cyclical with a cycle broadly corresponding to the cycle in the rate of growth of P. UN is asymmetric with sharper peaks than valleys, and in economic behaviour the zero of UN is a singularity with behaviour likely to become more singular as UN approaches zero. It is therefore reasonable to try $U = \log UN$ in linear relationships with P, though as may be seen from Fig. 2, the effect of taking log UN is not very great. It does facilitate comparisons with Godley and Shepherd's method which uses log UN. The population change (D) relative to 1956 shows a single period of increase between 1960 and 1965, with very little short-term variation. Employment (E) shows the kind of behaviour which could result from the combination of changes in population and unemployment after allowing for lags. Also reliable employment data have only been available 6-monthly and with considerable delay, by contrast to the monthly unemployment figures. For a first examination, it is therefore reasonable to omit employment on the grounds that it introduces no evidence not implicit in other variables. It can be introduced later to see if it helps represent this evidence more accurately than do the other variables alone. Hours worked (H) shows two periods of reduction in 1960–61 and 1965–66, with very little short-term variation. The main effect is the relationship between G.D.P. (P) and U. From economic considerations unemployment is the natural endogenous variable. G.D.P. is treated as a control variable which can be adjusted by policy decisions, and not as a leading indicator.

The data for 1955 I to 1970 II were supplied by the Treasury as those estimates most suitable for the Godley–Shepherd work. It is seasonally corrected as described by Shepherd (1968) (Stage 3).

4.3. *Lagged Averages*

The lagged averages of U are shown in Fig. 3 (p. 181). The data are unlikely to be sufficient to identify lags greater than 3 or 4 years, so only the first three lagged averages are used. The effect of longer lags can be eliminated or reduced by suitable weighting in

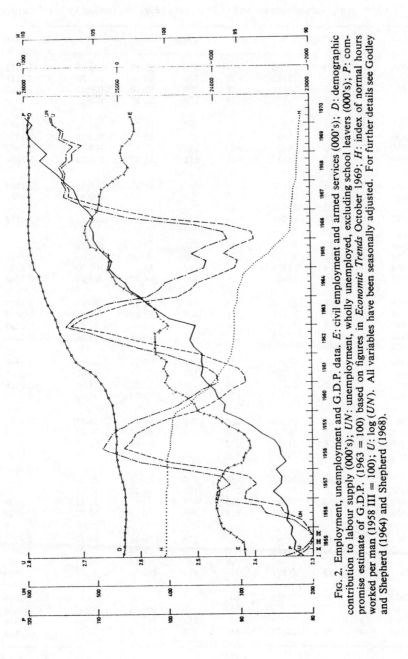

FIG. 2. Employment, unemployment and G.D.P. data. *E*: civil employment and armed services (000's); *D*: demographic contribution to labour supply (000's); *UN*: unemployment, wholly unemployed, excluding school leavers (000's); *P*: compromise estimate of G.D.P. (1963 = 100) based on figures in *Economic Trends* October 1969; *H*: index of normal hours worked per man (1958 III = 100); *U*: log (*UN*). All variables have been seasonally adjusted. For further details see Godley and Shepherd (1964) and Shepherd (1968).

TABLE 1

Employment, unemployment and G.D.P. data (Fig. 2) supplied by the Treasury

Year	Q	T	E	D	UN	P	H	log (UN/1000)
1955	1	0	23715	−11	225	81·37	100·35	2·3522
1955	2	1	23732	−14	208	82·60	100·32	2·3181
1955	3	2	23845	−18	201	82·30	100·32	2·3032
1955	4	3	23920	−26	199	83·00	100·32	2·2989
1956	1	4	23927	−34	207	82·87	100·32	2·3160
1956	2	5	23947	−40	215	83·60	100·32	2·3324
1956	3	6	24004	−42	240	83·33	100·32	2·3802
1956	4	7	23970	−41	245	83·53	100·32	2·3892
1957	1	8	23921	−37	295	84·27	100·32	2·4698
1957	2	9	23978	−32	293	85·50	100·32	2·4669
1957	3	10	23914	−20	279	84·33	100·23	2·4456
1957	4	11	23891	−5	287	84·30	100·07	2·4579
1958	1	12	23734	13	331	85·07	100·05	2·5198
1958	2	13	23729	27	396	83·60	100·05	2·5977
1958	3	14	23654	31	432	84·37	100·00	2·6355
1958	4	15	23664	29	462	84·50	99·95	2·6646
1959	1	16	23738	24	454	85·20	99·95	2·6571
1959	2	17	23791	26	446	87·07	99·94	2·6493
1959	3	18	23924	34	426	88·40	99·88	2·6294
1959	4	19	23994	48	402	90·03	99·84	2·6042
1960	1	20	24174	67	363	92·30	99·49	2·5599
1960	2	21	24209	91	342	92·13	98·45	2·5340
1960	3	22	24277	126	325	93·17	98·09	2·5119
1960	4	23	24452	174	312	93·50	97·59	2·4942
1961	1	24	24564	220	291	94·77	96·83	2·4639
1961	2	25	24500	263	293	95·37	96·43	2·4669
1961	3	26	24581	332	304	95·03	96·12	2·4829
1961	4	27	24507	401	330	95·23	95·76	2·5185
1962	1	28	24643	468	357	95·07	95·54	2·5527
1962	2	29	24654	537	401	96·40	95·45	2·6031
1962	3	30	24648	575	447	96·97	95·41	2·6503
1962	4	31	24581	615	483	96·50	95·37	2·6839
1963	1	32	24495	653	535	96·16	95·37	2·7284
1963	2	33	24665	693	520	99·79	95·37	2·7160
1963	3	34	24682	728	489	101·14	95·37	2·6893
1963	4	35	24821	764	456	102·95	95·23	2·6590
1964	1	36	24869	801	386	103·96	95·17	2·5866
1964	2	37	24936	836	368	105·28	95·04	2·5658
1964	3	38	25039	861	358	105·81	94·89	2·5539
1964	4	39	25118	886	330	107·14	94·71	2·5185

[*Continued overleaf*

TABLE 1 (*cont.*)

Year	Q	T	E	D	UN	P	H	log (UN/1000)
1965	1	40	25187	909	306	108·07	94·12	2·4857
1965	2	41	25174	933	304	107·64	93·61	2·4829
1965	3	42	25167	943	321	108·87	92·82	2·5065
1965	4	43	25299	954	305	109·75	92·45	2·4843
1966	1	44	25342	965	279	110·20	91·81	2·4456
1966	2	45	25321	967	282	110·20	91·39	2·4502
1966	3	46	25279	968	318	110·90	91·29	2·5024
1966	4	47	25066	965	414	110·40	91·27	2·6170
1967	1	48	24928	956	463	111·00	91·27	2·6656
1967	2	49	24923	948	506	112·10	91·23	2·7042
1967	3	50	24897	948	538	112·50	91·13	2·7308
1967	4	51	24814	948	536	113·00	91·09	2·7292
1968	1	52	24769	946	544	114·30	90·99	2·7356
1968	2	53	24722	946	541	115·10	90·97	2·7332
1968	3	54	24687	944	547	116·40	90·97	2·7380
1968	4	55	24738	942	532	117·80	90·94	2·7259
1969	1	56	24749	940	532	116·80	90·87	2·7259
1969	2	57	24721	932	519	117·80	90·85	2·7152
1969	3	58	24645	923	547	119·00	90·77	2·7380
1969	4	59	24634	910	544	119·60	90·77	2·7356
1970	1	60	24653	902	561	118·70	90·69	2·7490
1970	2	61	24650	893	563	119·90	90·59	2·7505

Stage 5(a). Fig. 3 shows that these three lagged averages, taken with their negatives, effectively span the full range of phase shifts, with peaks spaced evenly between the peaks of unemployment.

4.4. *Exploratory Direct Regressions of U on P*

The first regressions $B1$ took for the 1-step predicter the equation

$$U(t) = c + Q_1 DU(t) + Q_2 DU1(t) + Q_3 DU2(t) + Q_4 DU3(t)$$
$$+ P_0 P(t) + P_1 P1(t) + P_2 P2(t) + P_3 P3(t), \tag{12}$$

where D is the backward displacement operator such that $DU(t) = U(t-1)$, and $U1$, $U2$, $U3$, $P1$, $P2$ and $P3$ are the lagged averages of U and P respectively. Seven regressions were carried out on data starting in 1956 II (to allow the lagged averages time to settle down) and ending respectively in the fourth quarter in each year from 1963 to 1969. The results are given in Table 2(a), for 1-step predicters.

The standard errors of the regressions (around 0·02) rise sharply in 1966 and then fall again, suggesting a considerable disturbance in 1966. R_1^2 and R_2^2 are both near 1, as would be expected from a 1-step predicter, drawing information from the immediately preceding value. The Durbin–Watson statistic, while starting off reasonably, does show a tendency to fall, particularly at the 1966 disturbance, but it does not fall to the point where errors are clearly correlated.

The 1-step predictions using data for regressions, since they are only 1-step-ahead predictions look good, and there is little drift of predictions away from the actual values after the end of the regression data. But these results tell us little.

In looking further ahead, it is natural to consider repeated application of the 1-step predicter to give predictions L steps ahead, for $L = 2, 3, 4...$. However inspection of the poles and zeros of these $B1$ regressions in Table 5 show that there is a pole near to 1, and it is usually greater than 1. The repeated application of such a predicter is liable to produce instabilities of prediction as was found with the very similar weighted regressions $B3$ which will be described later.

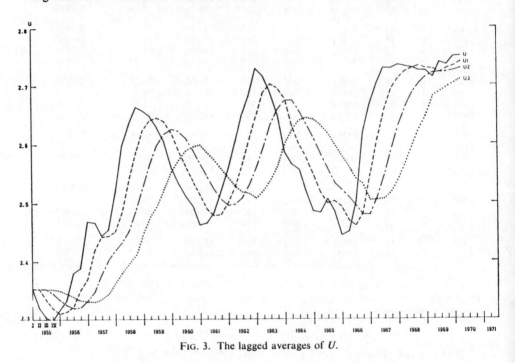

FIG. 3. The lagged averages of U.

For 2-, 4- and 8-step predictions we therefore carry out separate regressions using the equations for 2 steps

$$U(t) = c + Q_1 D^2 U(t) + Q_2 D^2 U1(t) + Q_3 D^2 U2(t) + Q_4 D^2 U3(t)$$
$$+ P_0 P(t) + P_1 P1(t) + P_2 P2(t) + P_3 P3(t), \tag{13}$$

for 4 steps

$$U(t) = c + Q_1 D^3 U1(t) + Q_2 D^3 U2(t) + Q_3 D^3 U3(t)$$
$$+ P_0 P(t) + P_1 P1(t) + P_2 P2(t) + P_3 P3(t) \tag{14}$$

and for 8 steps

$$U(t) = c + Q_1 D^7 U1(t) + Q_2 D^7 U2(t) + Q_3 D^7 U3(t)$$
$$+ P_0 P(t) + P_1 P1(t) + P_2 P2(t) + P_3 P3(t). \tag{15}$$

The regression results are given in Table 2(b), (c) and (d), and 8-step predictions with regressions using data up to 1965 IV and 1969 IV, in Figs. 4 and 5 respectively.

TABLE 2

Regression results for B1 regressions of U on P†

(a) *For 1-step predicters with data starting in 1956 II*

Finish of data used	Degrees of freedom left	Standard errors of predictions	R_1^2	R_2^2	DW
1963 IV	22	0·02139	0·99995	0·96988	2·079
1964 IV	26	0·02226	0·99994	0·96176	1·957
1965 IV	30	0·02271	0·99994	0·95612	1·862
1966 IV	34	0·02600	0·99992	0·93935	1·635
1967 IV	38	0·02495	0·99992	0·95059	1·795
1968 IV	42	0·02386	0·99993	0·95959	1·812
1969 IV	46	0·02372	0·99993	0·96209	1·804

(b) *For 2-step predicters with data starting in 1956 III*

Finish of data used	Degrees of freedom left	Standard errors of predictions	R_1^2	R_2^2	DW
1963 IV	21	0·02688	0·99992	0·94637	1·120
1964 IV	25	0·02784	0·99991	0·93214	1·143
1965 IV	29	0·02987	0·99990	0·91503	1·073
1966 IV	33	0·03724	0·99983	0·86252	0·951
1967 IV	37	0·03765	0·99983	0·87707	0·893
1968 IV	41	0·03606	0·99984	0·89998	0·900
1969 IV	45	0·03573	0·99984	0·90712	0·921

(c) *For 4-step predicters with data starting in 1956 III*

Finish of data used	Degrees of freedom left	Standard errors of predictions	R_1^2	R_2^2	DW
1963 IV	22	0·02829	0·99991	0·93779	0·920
1964 IV	26	0·02960	0·99990	0·92022	0·964
1965 IV	30	0·03113	0·99988	0·90456	0·943
1966 IV	34	0·03626	0·99984	0·86569	0·911
1967 IV	38	0·04309	0·99977	0·83463	0·625
1968 IV	42	0·04187	0·99978	0·86184	0·603
1969 IV	46	0·04141	0·99978	0·87249	0·638

(d) *For 8-step predicters with data starting in 1957 III*

Finish of data used	Degrees of freedom left	Standard errors of predictions	R_1^2	R_2^2	DW
1963 IV	18	0·03173	0·99990	0·90476	1·048
1964 IV	22	0·02953	0·99990	0·90183	1·050
1965 IV	26	0·02879	0·99990	0·90397	1·228
1966 IV	30	0·03078	0·99989	0·89020	1·326
1967 IV	34	0·03368	0·99986	0·88580	1·029
1968 IV	38	0·04029	0·99980	0·85573	0·753
1969 IV	42	0·03903	0·99981	0·87172	0·766

† In Tables 2, 3 and 6, R_1^2 denotes the multiple correlation coefficient with constant suppressed, and R_2^2 the corresponding coefficient with constant included. DW is the Durbin–Watson statistic.

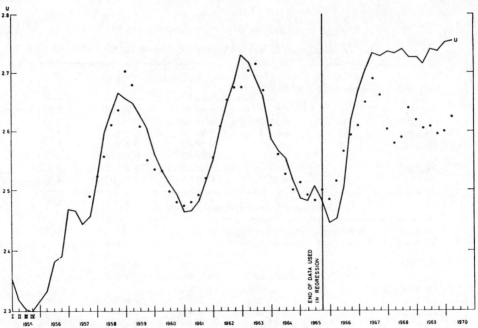

FIG. 4. Eight-step predictions using data to 1965 IV with regressions B1.

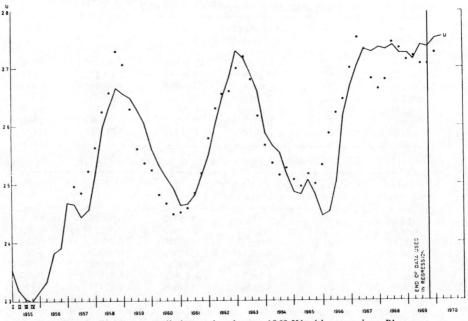

FIG. 5. Eight-step predictions using data to 1969 IV with regressions B1.

184   BRAY – *Dynamic Equations for Economic Forecasting*   [Part 2,

The standard errors in the 2-step regressions are greater than in the 1-step, and in the 4-step than in the 2-step. The 8-step errors might be expected to be greater than the 4-step errors, and they would be if the structure of the 8-step and 4-step equations were equally suitable, but evidently the form of the 8-step equation is "better" since its standard errors are generally smaller. Also the coefficients in the 8-step predicter are highly significant. The Durbin–Watson statistic shows that errors of the 2-, 4- and 8-step predictions are serially correlated, as would be expected from the theoretical discussion above.

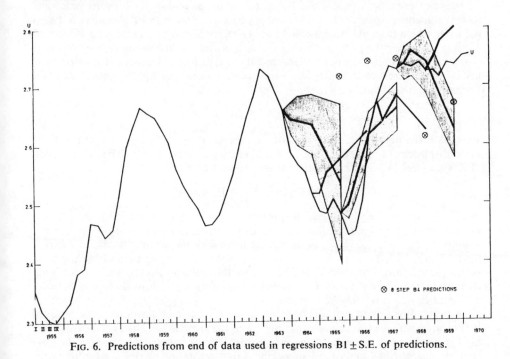

FIG. 6. Predictions from end of data used in regressions B1 ± S.E. of predictions.

Operationally we are concerned with the prediction of U running ahead from the present, given predicted or alternative future values of P. We know U and P in the past. It is therefore appropriate to derive L-step predicters for different L, using all data available up to the present, and use these for making 1-, 2-, 3-, ... step-ahead predictions from the present. Each L-step predicter may be obtained directly by regression or by repeated application of a 1-step predicter.

The results of doing this with the regressions $B1$, using data up to the fourth quarter of each successive year from 1963 to 1968, is shown in Fig. 6, together with the errors of the forecasts (taking into account the error in the estimation of the L-step coefficients as described above, and not merely the standard error of the random variable after L steps). The predictions are shown ± standard errors from 1963 IV, 1965 IV and 1967 IV only, to avoid confusion in the figure.

The full set of standard and actual errors is tabulated in Table 7 together with their root-mean squares. The root-mean square of the $B1$ actual errors is substantially greater than that of the standard errors of the regressions and the ratio

(2·03) is significant at the 95 per cent level for the ratio of two standard deviations with 6 degrees of freedom in the numerator and 30 to 50 in the denominator. If the system is sufficiently stationary and its behaviour adequately represented by the form of the predicting equations, this should not differ significantly from 1. We conclude that either the system is changing or the structure of the equations is not adequate.

4.5. *Directions for Further Exploration*

It is not possible to apply the 1-step $B1$ predicter repeatedly since its pole near to and sometimes greater than 1 makes it unstable. One way of obtaining a 1-step predicter which it would be possible to apply repeatedly is to take first differences of U, thus absorbing the pole and giving a stable system. While doing so, since there is also a zero near unity, it would be reasonable to take first differences of P. However, taking first differences of U prejudices the question of the asymptotic behaviour of U. For suppose we obtain the equation

$$Q(D)\Delta U = P(D)\Delta P + c,$$

where Δ is the first differencing operator $1-D$, and $Q(D)$, $P(D)$ are rational functions in the displacement operator D. This would mean that there is only one rate of growth of P which would keep U constant. If the true system is

$$Q(D)(1-bD)U = P(D)\Delta P + c,$$

there are different levels of equilibrium unemployment corresponding to different rates of growth. It would require very sensitive estimation to identify b, since it lies so near 1. There is, however, some sign of instability on the actual data in the predictions using $B1$, 2-, 4- and 8-step predicters too in Fig. 6, particularly in the most recent period from 1967 and 1968. So despite the prejudice to the question of long-term asymptotic behaviour of U, it is worth exploring regressions on first differences of U and P, which we call $B2$ regressions.

Another direction to explore is whether better system identification can be achieved if allowance is made for any possible change in the structure of the system with time. So it is worth trying using the $B1$ equations but with the squared deviation in the total sum of squares to be minimized so weighted that greater emphasis is given to recent than to long-past data (by Step 5(a) above). It may be that this would not only give more accurate 1-, 2-, 4- and 8-step predictions in the recent past, but would also give a 1-step predicter that could be applied repeatedly while allowing b above to be different from 1. We call these weighted regressions $B3$.

4.6. *Regressions $B2$ of ΔU on ΔP*

Equation (12) in first differences was fitted seven times over to data starting in 1956 III and ending in the fourth quarter in each year from 1963 to 1969. In Tables 3 and 7 the standard errors for the $B2$ regressions is that due to the random variable alone, with no allowance for errors of the regression coefficients. They are reasonably uniform showing an increase from 1966. The R_1^2 and R_2^2 are naturally much lower than for the $B1$ regressions, due to differencing. The Durbin–Watson statistics uniformly show no signs of serial correlation of the residuals. The pattern of the coefficients, particularly the larger coefficients, and of the standard errors is regular.

TABLE 3

Regression results for B2 regressions of ΔU on ΔP with data starting in 1956 III

| Finish of data used | Degrees of freedom left | Standard errors for L-step predictions | | | | R_1^2 | R_2^2 | DW |
		$L = 1$	$L = 2$	$L = 4$	$L = 8$			
1963 IV	21	0·02264	0·03270	0·03891	0·04784	0·72761	0·70070	2·159
1964 IV	25	0·02220	0·03072	0·03594	0·04420	0·73550	0·72959	2·130
1965 IV	29	0·02210	0·03072	0·03632	0·04561	0·70923	0·70556	2·052
1966 IV	33	0·02496	0·03912	0·04571	0·05781	0·68902	0·67968	2·091
1967 IV	37	0·02471	0·03921	0·04991	0·06280	0·68011	0·66383	2·136
1968 IV	41	0·02380	0·03791	0·04865	0·06323	0·67236	0·65739	2·155
1969 IV	45	0·02316	0·03642	0·04646	0·06061	0·66255	0·64773	2·125

| Finish of data used | Const. | ΔDU | $\Delta DU1$ | $\Delta DU2$ | $\Delta DU3$ | ΔP | $\Delta P1$ | $\Delta P2$ | $\Delta P3$ |
			Regression coefficients/standard errors of coefficients of above regression						
1963 IV	0·05725	0·04217	−0·65477	0·34934	−0·71201	−0·01142	−0·02350	−0·05153	0·01954
S.E.	0·01846	0·20447	0·38573	0·53271	0·59921	0·00458	0·00975	0·02556	0·02695
1964 IV	0·06106	−0·04378	−0·66011	0·33078	−0·69879	−0·01151	−0·02668	−0·05493	0·02142
S.E.	0·01713	0·18909	0·36154	0·48132	0·55989	0·00439	0·00934	0·02391	0·02567
1965 IV	0·06136	−0·03466	−0·64168	0·42728	−0·72844	−0·01198	−0·02989	−0·04500	0·00958
S.E.	0·01694	0·18207	0·34818	0·46259	0·54101	0·00421	0·00904	0·02310	0·02421
1966 IV	0·05844	0·20693	−0·91458	0·68041	−0·74867	−0·01372	−0·02655	−0·04420	0·01045
S.E.	0·01801	0·18125	0·34440	0·47624	0·53191	0·00469	0·00999	0·02550	0·02728
1967 IV	0·05156	0·23192	−0·61833	0·43938	−0·68976	−0·01239	−0·02423	−0·03578	0·00918
S.E.	0·01583	0·15410	0·28852	0·41723	0·51135	0·00452	0·00969	0·02288	0·02663
1968 IV	0·04857	0·23993	−0·60686	0·49069	−0·57803	−0·01242	−0·02497	−0·03644	0·01544
S.E.	0·01471	0·14638	0·27539	0·37252	0·47121	0·00432	0·00921	0·02184	0·02376
1969 IV	0·04902	0·21389	−0·59284	0·45962	−0·50667	−0·01251	−0·02508	−0·04081	0·01958
S.E.	0·01410	0·14022	0·26313	0·36048	0·40352	0·00393	0·00840	0·02002	0·02132

This is brought out particularly clearly in Table 5 giving the poles and zeros, which shows little movement in their values. The poles near 1 have of course disappeared, having been absorbed by the differencing. The covariance matrix in Table 4 shows the expected high covariance between different lagged averages of the same variable, explaining the accuracy of forecasts despite the standard errors of individual coefficients.

TABLE 4 *Covariance matrix for B2 regression on data to* 1969 IV

$C[1, 1] =$	0·370771014				
$C[1, 2] =$	−1·5871798	$C[2, 2] =$	36·6665046		
$C[1, 3] =$	−2·67410166	$C[2, 3] =$	−9·17993012	$C[3, 3] =$	129·116081
$C[1, 4] =$	−1·40715788	$C[2, 4] =$	12·3505124	$C[3, 4] =$	−112·97259
$C[1, 5] =$	−1·95749324	$C[2, 5] =$	−0·89208649	$C[3, 5] =$	83·8888034
$C[1, 6] =$	−0·00262843052	$C[2, 6] =$	0·0369426438	$C[3, 6] =$	0·0534970385
$C[1, 7] =$	−0·0500802463	$C[2, 7] =$	0·856471042	$C[3, 7] =$	0·0160543561
$C[1, 8] =$	−0·189403521	$C[2, 8] =$	1·64711072	$C[3, 8] =$	3·83733496
$C[1, 9] =$	−0·238021267	$C[2, 9] =$	−0·569562467	$C[3, 9] =$	−0·701988989
$C[4, 4] =$	242·328303				
$C[4, 5] =$	−155·241708	$C[5, 5] =$	303·659808		
$C[4, 6] =$	−0·544706493	$C[5, 6] =$	−0·314778289	$C[6, 6] =$	0·0287407257
$C[4, 7] =$	−0·641673101	$C[5, 7] =$	−0·833276809	$C[6, 7] =$	0·0079597292
$C[4, 8] =$	0·158019249	$C[5, 8] =$	−4·17166995	$C[6, 8] =$	−0·00236837051
$C[4, 9] =$	3·45608994	$C[5, 9] =$	6·60665852	$C[6, 9] =$	−0·0251505162
$C[7, 7] =$	0·13163909				
$C[7, 8] =$	−0·0357062334	$C[8, 8] =$	0·747358093		
$C[7, 9] =$	−0·026620535	$C[8, 9] =$	−0·46076546	$C[9, 9] =$	0·847312683

The $B2$ predictions in Figs 7(a), (b), (c) and (d) for the regression on data to 1965 IV and in Fig. 8 for that to 1969 IV for the 8-step predictions show similar characteristics to the $B1$ predictions in Figs 4 and 5, but the drift after the end of the regression data is less for the 8-step predictions. In Table 7 it will be seen that not only are root-mean squares of the actual prediction errors substantially smaller with the $B2$ than the $B1$ regressions, but also the ratio to the root-mean square of the regression standard errors of the $B2$ regressions is very near 1. This shows that the system is reasonably stationary, and that the structural form of the $B2$ equations is reasonable. Stationarity in the stronger sense of the same coefficients derived from data up to 1963 IV applying over the whole period 1964–70 has not been tested except in so far as Fig. 7 shows that the $B2$ predicter derived on data up to 1965 IV remains a reasonable predicter up to 1969 IV. The 1966 disturbance appears as in fact an unexpectedly low level of unemployment in 1966 II relative to that predicted from 1965 IV, followed by an unexpected rise by 1966 IV relative to that predicted from 1965 IV. But the disturbance passes through the system with little effect on the system equation, which picks up the new level of unemployment relatively quickly. Furthermore, the $B2$ form could have been identified on data up to 1965 IV available in 1966.

In every respect therefore the $B2$ regressions appear as a stable characterization of the short-term behaviour of the G.D.P.–unemployment relation. The only drawback is that it has been necessary to sacrifice the unbiased characterization of the longer-term relation between G.D.P. and unemployment.

4.7. *Attempts at Characterization of the Longer Term*

To sharpen up the $B1$ regressions to try to locate the pole without fixing it at 1 by taking differences, it can be argued that if the pole is moving, the data should be

TABLE 5

Poles and zeros from 1-step predicters for B regressions

	Year	Poles	Zeros
B1 {*U* on *P*}	1963	0·907 ± *i*0·040, 0·450 ± *i*0·518	1·040, 0·234 ± *i*0·094
	1964	1·023, 0·432, 0·603 ± *i*0·313	1·016, 0·368, 0·033
	1965	1·034, 0·315, 0·677 ± *i*0·277	1·004, 0·573, −0·124
	1966	1·037, 0·733, 0·563 ± *i*0·456	1·012, 0·323 ± *i*0·220
	1967	1·039, 0·692, 0·570 ± *i*0·435	1·010, 0·308 ± *i*0·210
	1968	1·038, 0·655, 0·589 ± *i*0·409	1·008, 0·310 ± *i*0·178
	1969	0·995, 0·650, 0·614 ± *i*0·321	1·009, 0·576, −0·037
B2 {Δ*U* on Δ*P*}	1963	0·775 ± *i*0·246, 0·146 ± *i*0·582	0·789, −0·009 ± *i*0·806
	1964	0·768 ± *i*0·240, 0·110 ± *i*0·569	0·791, −0·075 ± *i*0·794
	1965	0·782 ± *i*0·237, 0·101 ± *i*0·579	0·749, −0·098 ± *i*0·581
	1966	0·793 ± *i*0·227, 0·210 ± *i*0·713	0·755, 0·039 ± *i*0·630
	1967	0·798 ± *i*0·246, 0·218 ± *i*0·597	0·758, 0·032 ± *i*0·571
	1968	0·798 ± *i*0·222, 0·222 ± *i*0·601	0·790, −0·003 ± *i*0·588
	1969	0·789 ± *i*0·211, 0·218 ± *i*0·591	0·802, −0·003 ± *i*0·651
B3 {*U* on *P* with weighting factor *b* = 0·9659}	1963	0·949, 0·842, 0·516 ± *i*0·462	1·037, 0·325 ± *i*0·182
	1964	1·029, 0·694 ± *i*0·308, 0·264	1·013, 0·409, 0·131
	1965	1·041, 0·735 ± *i*0·257, 0·183	0·997, 0·684, −0·143
	1966	1·061, 0·789, 0·594 ± *i*0·535	1·013, 0·404 ± *i*0·358
	1967	1·063, 0·703, 0·587 ± *i*0·497	1·009, 0·371 ± *i*0·372
	1968	1·050, 0·657, 0·614 ± *i*0·441	1·007, 0·385 ± *i*0·325
	1969	0·930, 0·788, 0·603 ± *i*0·337	1·012, 0·574, 0·043

The poles are the *B(I)* and the zeros the *A(I)* when the regression results are written in the form:

$$\frac{\{1-B(1)D\}\,\{1-B(2)D\}\,\{1-B(3)D\}\,\{1-B(4)D\}}{(1-0\cdot5D)\,(1-0\cdot6D)\,(1-0\cdot7D)}\,y = \frac{\{1-A(1)D\}\,\{1-A(2)D\}\,\{1-A(3)D\}}{(1-0\cdot5D)\,(1-0\cdot6D)\,(1-0\cdot7D)}\,x.$$

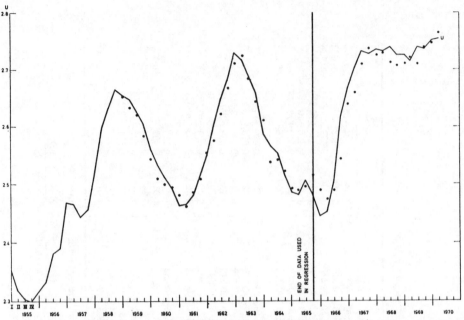

FIG. 7(a). One-step predictions using data to 1965 IV with regression *B*2.

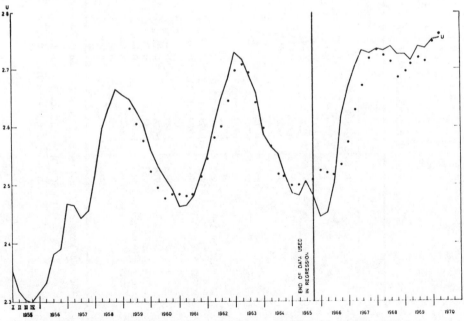

FIG. 7(b). Two-step predictions using data to 1965 IV with regression *B*2.

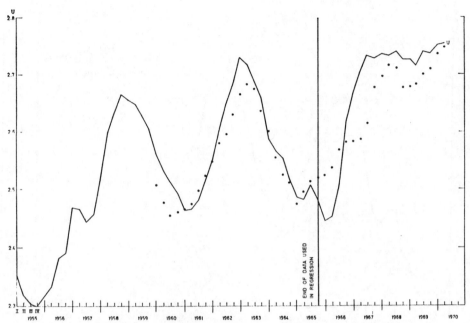

FIG. 7(c). Four-step predictions using data to 1965 IV with regression *B*2.

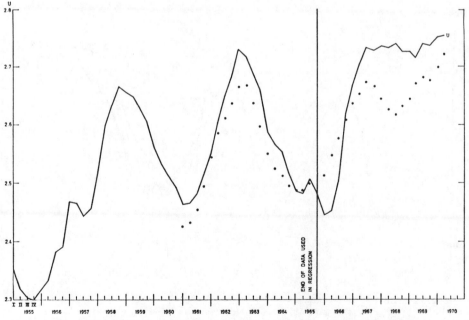

FIG. 7(d). Eight-step predictions using data to 1965 IV with regression *B*2.

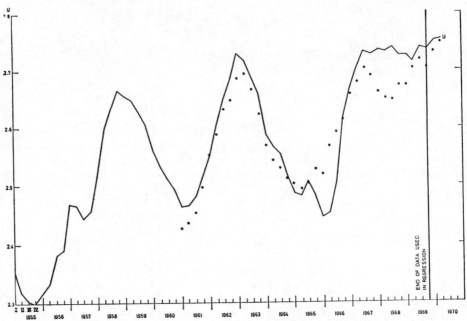

FIG. 8. Eight-step predictions using data to 1969 IV with regression *B*2.

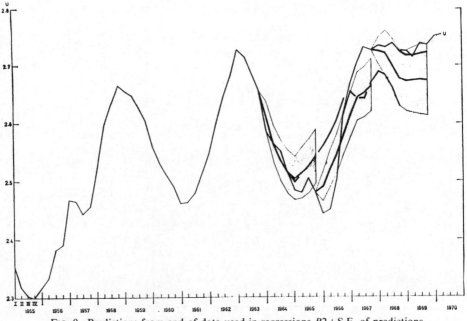

FIG. 9. Predictions from end of data used in regressions *B*2 ± S.E. of predictions.

weighted in the regressions to make the fit closest on the more recent data. This is a dubious argument, since long-term behaviour only manifests itself over the longer term, and this effect is reduced by weighting. But it is a matter of seeing if there is a medium-term effect which can be identified.

Equations (12), (13), (14) and (15) were fitted by the method of Stage 5(a) above with a weighting factor $b = 0.9659$ (such that $b^{20} = 0.5$), with data to the fourth quarter in each year from 1963 to 1969 as for $B1$ and $B2$. The standard errors of the regressions and the actual errors of predictions are compared in Table 7. $B3$ comes out marginally better than $B1$ on actual errors mainly due to its better performance in 8-step predictions, so we shall examine this predicter more closely. The ratio of the root-mean square of actual to that of standard errors at 2·06 is still poor, showing that $B3$ is no more structurally satisfactory than $B1$ as would be expected since it has the same structure. The poles and zeros of the 1-step $B3$ predicters given in Table 5 suggest there would be difficulty in repeated application of these predicters, and this is indeed the case: predictions from the end of the data run away because of the amplification of errors by the pole greater than 1.

Like the 8-step $B1$ predicter, the 8-step $B3$ has large auto-regressive coefficients. Fig. 10 gives, using data up to 1969 IV, the autoregressive and moving average coefficients of the 1-step $B2$ predicter as in equation (6) above, the derived 8-step predicter as in equation (7), the derived impulse response or pure moving average coefficients as in equation (8) and the step response. The comparable coefficients are given for the 8-step $B3$ predicter. It will be seen that the large coefficients of $D^7 U1$, $D^7 U2$ and $D^7 U3$ combine to give a very sharp peak at b_8 (the first autoregressive coefficient in the 8-step predicter) with a subsequent swing, both very much larger than in the 8-step predicter derived from the $B2$ regression. This peak in b_8 comes through in the impulse and step responses as a strong and continuing cycle of period 8, which is plainly spurious and would lead to bad predictions in repeated application. The 8-step $B1$ predicters would show similar behaviour.

So we still have no stable predicter the repeated application of which can give an unbiased indication of the long-term characteristics of the G.D.P.–unemployment relation.

Fig. 10 also gives the corresponding data for an 8-step predicter obtained by dropping the $U3$ term in $B1$, and lagging $U1$ and $U2$ as $D^7 U1(t)$ and $D^7 U2(t)$. This regression equation we call $B4$. It has the reasonably small autoregressive coefficients obtained in the 8-step predicter from repeated application of the stable 1-step $B2$ predicter, without the constraint the latter has on its long-term behaviour, and it is stable. The predicter $B5$ using $D^6 U2(t)$ and $D^6 U3(t)$ is also stable. But if $D^6 U4(t)$ is added as a regression term to the latter, the predicter becomes unstable again.

$B4$ and $B5$ are thus the only stable equations we have found which are unconstrained in their long-term characteristics. The $B4$ equation (20) gives the smaller prediction errors of the two (Table 7). The $B4$ predictions are shown in Fig. 6 for comparison with the $B1$ 8-step predictions. The predictions obtained from the repeated application of the $B4$ equation derived from data up to 1965 IV and 1970 II, for 2, 3, 4 and 5 per cent per annum growth of P from these times are shown in Fig. 11. These contrast with the asymptotic behaviour of the $B2$ predictions in Fig. 15, showing unemployment levelling out at different levels, depending on the growth rate. Note that the $B4$ predictions for a 2 per cent growth rate from 1965 IV (the average growth from 1965 IV to 1969 IV was 2·2 per cent) is much the most accurate long-term prediction of unemployment made from 1965 IV for the years 1967–69. Although its performance as an 8-step predicter is worse than that of any other predicter, that does not mean that, if it is structurally more correct than the other equations, its longer-term predictions need be worse. All that can be said is that the long-term behaviour of the G.D.P.–unemployment relation is unresolved. It is doubtful whether the data available permit any conclusion about it. Certainly any such conclusion would need more finely tuned estimation methods than those of this paper. It is possible that

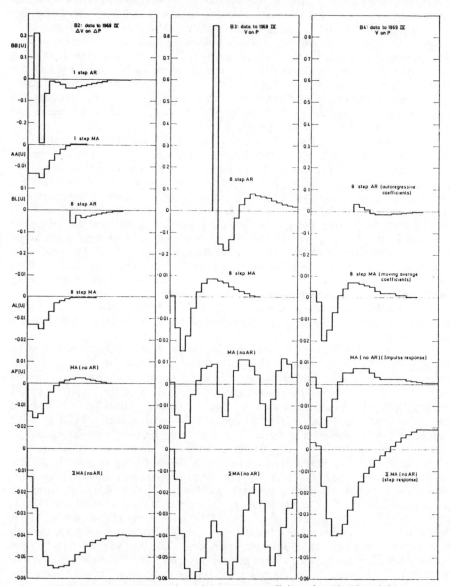

Fig. 10. Autogressive and moving average coefficients for *B*2, *B*3 and *B*4.

Box–Jenkins methods might be able to identify long-term behaviour, but it is also possible that the data needed are not there.

It was a family of regressions of the type *B5* which led the author to suggest (Bray, 1970) in the *Economist* that in fact there may be no such thing as "the underlying rate of growth of productive potential" and indeed that any of a range of rates of growth are possible leading to different levels of unemployment. The further work reported in this paper has not been able to prove or disprove this suggestion.

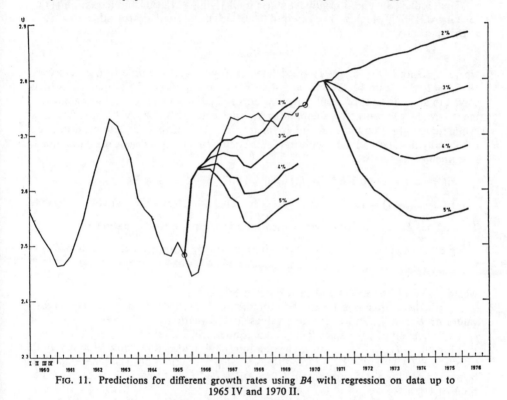

FIG. 11. Predictions for different growth rates using *B4* with regression on data up to 1965 IV and 1970 II.

For any interest it may have, the rates of growth (per cent per annum) estimated in successive years which would keep unemployment stable if *B2* were an unbiased and accurate long-term predicter (which it is not) are given below.

1963 IV	3·3
1964 IV	3·2
1965 IV	2·9
1966 IV	2·9
1967 IV	2·9
1968 IV	2·8
1969 IV	2·8

These rates of growth are of course related to the average rate of growth over the period of the regression (but biased through having worked with ΔP rather than $\Delta P/P$). The interest of these figures lies only in that they end up close to more directly calculated rates of growth.

4.8. *The Godley–Shepherd Method*

The Godley–Shepherd argument starts by deriving a relationship (equation (1) in (Shepherd, 1968), which will be referred to as (GS1), and similarly for other equations in that paper)

$$E - D = c_1 - gU + P_1 t + P_2 t' \qquad \text{(GS1)}$$

where E, D and $U = \log(UN)$ are defined in Fig. 2, and $t =$ time in quarters with 1955 I $= 1$, $t' = 0$ up to 1960 IV and then rises 1 per quarter. This equation is then solved to give the level of employment L, corresponding to a fixed level of unemployment UN ($1\frac{1}{4}$ per cent). Two equations are then estimated iteratively, introducing a synthetic variable "equilibrium employment" E^*. One of these equations, estimated graphically in 1964 and kept with the same coefficients in all subsequent estimations, is segmented as follows:

$$E(t) - E(t-1) = 0 \cdot 7\{E^*(t) - E(t-1)\} \quad \text{if} \quad E^*(t) - E(t-1) < 30,$$

$$E(t) - E(t-1) = 13 \cdot 5 + 0 \cdot 25\{E^*(t) - E(t-1)\} \quad \text{if} \quad E^*(t) - E(t-1) \geqslant 30. \qquad \text{(GS4)}$$

This defines E^*, given E, and E^* is then used in the regression equation

$$\log E^*(t) - \log L(t) = c_2 + k\{\log P(t) - 0 \cdot 5 \log L(t) - 0 \cdot 25 \log L(t-4) - 0 \cdot 25 \log H(t)$$
$$+ P_3 t + P_4 t'' \ldots\}, \quad \text{(GS3)}$$

where $t'' = 0$ up to 1960 II and then rises 1 per quarter.

To use these equations at time T for predicting $U(t)$ for $t > T$, for postulated future values of D and H, and alternative values of P, equation (GS1) gives all values of $L(t)$ independent of any values P may take. Equation (GS3) then gives $\log E^*(t)$ given $P(t)$ for all $t > T$. $E(T)$ is known, so equation (GS4) makes it possible successively to calculate $E(T+1)$, $E(T+2)$, ..., being 1-, 2-, ... step predictions of $E(t)$. These can then be used in equation (GS1) to obtain $U(T+1)$, $U(T+2)$, ..., being 1-, 2-, ... step predictions of $U(t)$.

A difficulty is that if this procedure is carried out for $t = T$, the prediction of $U(T)$ may be substantially different from its actual value, causing a stepwise difference of the prediction $U(T+1)$ from $U(T)$, instead of a smooth transition. This can be countered in a number of ways. The coefficients C_1 and/or C_2 may be adjusted (a process known as "estimating the residuals"). The published work contains no description of what is done, but this seems to be the practice in the Treasury. However, since in the comparisons in this paper predictions are only made from the end of the data used in the regressions, it is not clear on what principle the constant should be adjusted immediately. If the constant is adjusted it affects all future values of U. A better solution seemed to be to set the value of $E(T)$ to satisfy equation (GS1) exactly. The equation (GS4) then ensures that $E(t)$ and hence $U(t)$ $(t > T)$ moves off smoothly, without prejudicing the longer-term future by adjusting the constants. This also has the practical merit that employment figures come much later than unemployment figures. The systematic adjustment of the constants according to the stochastic structure of the residuals would of course amount to a full Box–Jenkins estimation, but that would rather be standing the estimation process on its head.

The equations (GS4) and (GS3) were estimated on data up to the fourth quarter in each year from 1963 IV to 1969 IV. The regression results are given in Table 6. The 1-, 2-, 4- and 8-step predictions from the regressions on data to 1965 IV are given in Fig. 12(a), (b), (c), (d) and the 8-step predictions from data to 1969 IV in Fig. 13. Predictions ahead from the end of the regression data using the equations estimated from them, are given in Fig. 14. The Godley–Shepherd papers and indeed the equations do not produce a standard error of the predictions of U, so this has been estimated indirectly as the root-mean-square error in the predictions of U over the data used in the regressions, for each lead time $L = 1, 2, 4, 8$, allowing 8 degrees of freedom for the regression coefficients. These "standard errors" and the actual errors of prediction are listed in Table 7, for comparison.

It will be seen that while the root-mean square of the errors over the regression data is less than the root-mean square of the $B2$ *standard* error for the 1-, 4- and 8-step predicters, the root-mean square of the *actual* errors of all the Godley–Shepherd predictions are greater. In fact the ratios of the root-mean squares of the actual errors of prediction to the standard errors indicate that the structure of the system is not correctly determined by the Godley–Shepherd equations. (1 step: 1·36; 2-step: 1·71; 4-step: 1·61; 8-step: 2·33; all lead times: 1·83.)

The ratio of the root-mean square of all the actual prediction errors for $L = 1, 2, 4$ and 8 predicting from the ends of the regression data for the $B2$ regression to that for the Godley–Shepherd method is 0·75. As a ratio of standard errors from a sample of 23, this is significant at the 90 per cent level. The slight correlation between successive 8-step errors might reduce the number of degrees of freedom by 1, but this hardly affects the significance.

Since the Godley–Shepherd equations are highly non-analytic, their dynamic characteristics and the structural contraints they impose are not immediately obvious. The short-term dynamic characteristics in fact depend very largely on the process of "estimating the residuals" and this is not defined at all by Godley and Shepherd (1964) or Shepherd (1968). The long-term characteristics can be derived as follows.

With the Godley–Shepherd equations (GS1) and (GS3), derived from data up to time $t = T$, the "productive potential" $C(t)$ is defined as that level of G.D.P., $P(t)$, which would make the "equilibrium employment" $E^*(t)$ equal to the labour supply $L(t)$. k (in equation (GS3)) is the one and only coefficient relating G.D.P. to employment, and g (in equation (GS1)) the one and only coefficient relating unemployment to employment. It can be shown that once these are determined, so is the asymptotic behaviour of unemployment for rates of growth differing from the "rate of growth of productive potential". Furthermore, for any rate of growth above "the rate of growth of productive potential", unemployment tends to zero, and for any rate below, unemployment tends to infinity. This is inherent in the form assumed for the equations and is quite independent of the data.

The "rate of growth of productive potential" is itself in effect an average of the rate of growth achieved in recent years. The Godley–Shepherd method thus assumes that if G.D.P. grows faster than the average of recent years unemployment will tend to zero, and if slower, unemployment will tend to infinity. This should certainly be recognized as an assumption and an assumption that should be tested. As the earlier discussion in this paper has shown, given the data, it is not at all easy to test it. (Mr. Godley has said that he himself does not make this assumption.)

TABLE 6

Godley–Shepherd regression results

Equation (GS1)

| Data used | | Degrees of freedom left | Standard error | R_1^2 | R_2^2 | DW | Regression coefficients/S.E. | | | |
Start	Finish						C_1	$-g$	P_1	P_2
1955 I	1963 IV	32	71·86	0·99999	0·86151	0·916	27,942 / 354	−1,786 / 151	31·39 / 2·43	−24·03 / 5·35
	1964 IV	36	70·66	0·99999	0·86410	0·926	27,766 / 324	−1,713 / 138	31·28 / 2·38	−28·59 / 4·33
	1965 IV	40	68·43	0·99999	0·88513	0·932	27,707 / 297	−1,688 / 127	31·19 / 2·30	−29·41 / 3·87
	1966 IV	44	65·51	0·99999	0·90341	0·944	27,702 / 273	−1,685 / 117	31·02 / 2·15	−28·80 / 3·38
	1967 IV	48	63·72	0·99999	0·90231	0·991	27,700 / 233	−1,684 / 99	31·03 / 1·84	−28·86 / 2·63
	1968 IV	52	66·72	0·99999	0·89556	0·873	27,918 / 230	−1,780 / 98	32·91 / 1·80	−32·53 / 2·42
	1969 IV	56	68·17	0·99999	0·89392	0·793	28,014 / 232	−1,824 / 98	34·05 / 1·78	−34·88 / 2·27

Equation (GS3)

| Data used | | Degrees of freedom left | Standard error | R_1^2 | R_2^2 | DW | Regression coefficients/S.E. | | | |
Start	Finish						C_2	k	P_3	P_4
1955 II	1963 IV	31	0·003169	0·65636	0·65119	2·670	0·8493 / 0·1312	0·4502 / 0·0699	−0·001155 / 0·000172	−0·000412 / 0·000235
	1964 IV	35	0·003056	0·63434	0·62585	2·656	0·8340 / 0·1232	0·4421 / 0·0657	−0·001135 / 0·000156	−0·000394 / 0·000203
	1965 IV	39	0·003057	0·61556	0·60132	2·557	0·8406 / 0·1226	0·4456 / 0·0654	−0·001156 / 0·000153	−0·000334 / 0·000187
	1966 IV	43	0·002947	0·61860	0·60694	2·553	0·8526 / 0·1158	0·4520 / 0·0618	−0·001169 / 0·000147	−0·000340 / 0·000160
	1967 IV	47	0·002906	0·65665	0·65597	2·427	0·9083 / 0·1091	0·4818 / 0·0582	−0·001200 / 0·000144	−0·000465 / 0·000138
	1968 IV	51	0·002956	0·68798	0·68602	2·188	0·9432 / 0·1098	0·5005 / 0·0586	−0·001223 / 0·000145	−0·000548 / 0·000132
	1969 IV	55	0·002870	0·73426	0·72593	2·179	0·9538 / 0·1043	0·5061 / 0·0556	−0·001238 / 0·000139	−0·000552 / 0·000119

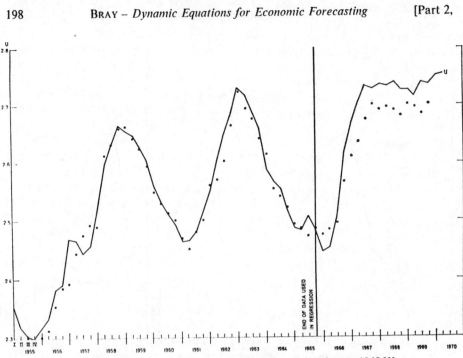

FIG. 12(a). Godley–Shepherd 1-step predictions using data to 1965 IV.

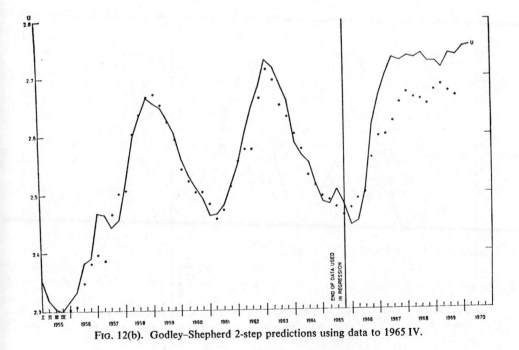

FIG. 12(b). Godley–Shepherd 2-step predictions using data to 1965 IV.

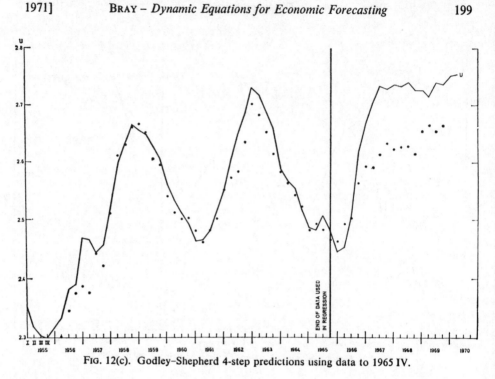

Fig. 12(c). Godley–Shepherd 4-step predictions using data to 1965 IV.

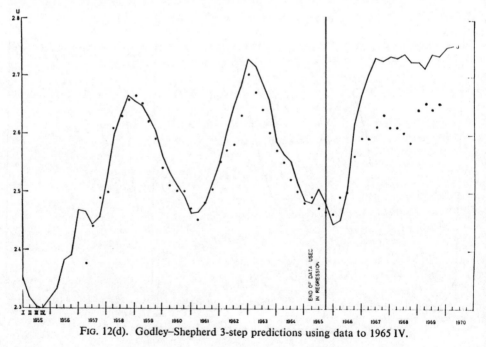

Fig. 12(d). Godley–Shepherd 3-step predictions using data to 1965 IV.

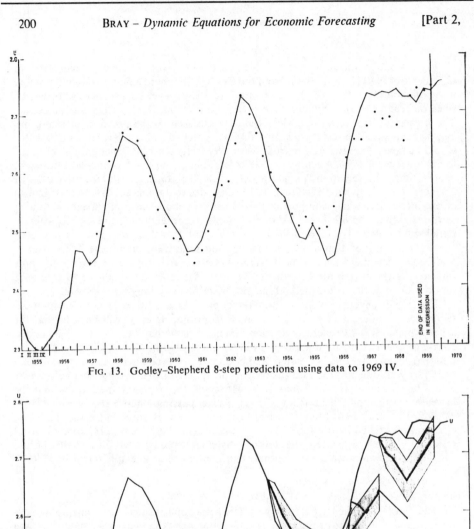

Fig. 13. Godley–Shepherd 8-step predictions using data to 1969 IV.

Fig. 14. Godley–Shepherd predictions from end of data used in regressions ± R.M.S. error over regression data.

4.9. *Future Prospects*

Fig. 15 shows the prospects for unemployment, given different growth rates of G.D.P. from 1970 II. Both the *B*2 and the Godley–Shepherd equations were estimated using all data up to 1970 II. The standard errors shown are those of the *B*2 forecasts, since no reliable error estimates have been found for the Godley–Shepherd forecasts. The biggest difference is that while both forecasts show the prospect of rising unemployment for 2 per cent growth of *P*, the Godley–Shepherd forecasts suggest this would be faster than the *B*2 forecasts, with seasonally corrected unemployment in the fourth quarter of 1971, reaching 850,000 according to the Godley–Shepherd forecast, while falling probably in the range 600,000–750,000 according to the *B*2 forecast. For 3 per cent growth the Godley–Shepherd forecast, tied to the concept of a "rate of growth of productive potential" still greater than 3 per cent shows unemployment continuing to rise slightly. The *B*2 forecast shows unemployment tending to fall slightly after an initial rise in 1970. The forecasts for higher rates of growth do not differ very greatly.

It can be argued that a further independent time trend should be introduced in the Godley–Shepherd method in (GS1) and (GS3) starting in 1964 or 1965, to allow for any change in the rate of growth. This is reasonable. It would be to recognize that the Godley–Shepherd method has not identified any long-term growth rate.

Fig. 15, however, also shows the predictions on data up to 1965 IV of the consequences of different rates of growth of *P* from that date. It will be seen that the 2 per cent Godley–Shepherd prediction reaches and perhaps crosses over the actual course of unemployment at about 1970 IV. That is why the Godley–Shepherd prediction (particularly the 1967 IV 8-step prediction in Table 7) comes back in line for the end of 1969. Were this not the case the root-mean square of the Godley–Shepherd errors would be considerably worse than it is. However, the implication of this is that the increase in unemployment from 1967 II was a passing phase, and the extra unemployed have by 1970 been absorbed back into the work force in the same relation to output as existed before 1967. This does not seem likely. A simple "adjustment of residuals" which increased the Godley–Shepherd predictions during the period 1967–69 would show an earlier and more dramatic rise of unemployment in 1970.

4.10. *Long-term Behaviour*

The question of the long-term asymptotic behaviour of the G.D.P.–unemployment relation and of whether or not there is such a thing as "the underlying rate of growth of productive potential" remains unresolved. The Godley–Shepherd method on its own does not answer these questions. It assumes answers and clothes them with figures. The previous analysis in this paper has not answered them either. The doubt remains as to whether there is such a thing as "the underlying rate of growth of productive potential" or whether in fact different rates of growth are possible leading to an equilibrium level of unemployment dependent on the rate of growth. Indeed it seems probable that the answer cannot be found without reference to other aspects of the economy, such as investment. Since investment is needed to increase capacity, if there were a clear long-term relation between unemployment and G.D.P. alone, the implication would be that the level of investment is uniquely (and with low error) determined by past values of G.D.P. and unemployment alone. It seems unlikely that this is the case. One reason why the Godley–Shepherd method has been accepted by some economists may be that it has appeared to them to give mathematical form to the underlying economic principle that all output stems from resources of labour,

TABLE 7. *Standard errors and actual prediction errors for B regressions and Godley–Shepherd regressions*

Data ending qtr IV	1-step				2-step			
	B1	B2	B3	GS	B1	B2	B3	GS
S.E. / Deg. of freedom	*Standard errors over regression data*							
1963	0·02139 (22)	0·02264 (21)	0·01937 (23)	0·02424 (26)	0·02688 (21)	0·03270	0·02484 (21)	0·03088 (25)
1964	0·02226 (26)	0·02220 (25)	0·02052 (27)	0·02437 (30)	0·02784 (25)	0·03072	0·02476 (25)	0·03089 (29)
1965	0·02271 (30)	0·02210 (29)	0·02095 (31)	0·02426 (34)	0·02987 (29)	0·03072	0·02709 (29)	0·03111 (33)
1966	0·02600 (34)	0·02496 (33)	0·02651 (35)	0·02566 (38)	0·03724 (33)	0·03912	0·03960 (33)	0·03207 (37)
1967	0·02495 (38)	0·02471 (37)	0·02519 (39)	0·02786 (42)	0·03765 (37)	0·03921	0·03949 (37)	0·03520 (41)
1968	0·02386 (42)	0·02380 (41)	0·02329 (43)	0·02760 (46)	0·03606 (41)	0·03791	0·03685 (41)	0·03479 (45)
1969	0·02372 (46)	0·02316 (45)	0·02294 (47)	0·02707 (50)	0·03573 (45)	0·03642	0·03561 (45)	0·03399 (49)
R.M.S.	0·0236	0·0234	0·0228	0·0259	0·0333	0·0354	0·0332	0·0328
Actual error S* R* (See note on p. 203)	*Actual errors of predictions from end of regression data*							
1963	0·05729 (4)	0·0273 (1)	0·05108 (3)	0·0414 (2)	0·07463 (4)	0·0005 (4)	0·05999 (3)	0·0324 (2)
1964	0·03230 (4)	0·0168 (2)	0·02754 (3)	0·0160 (1)	0·07198 (4)	0·0331 (2)	0·06950 (3)	0·0314 (1)
1965	0·05433 (4)	0·0468 (2)	0·04970 (3)	0·0298 (1)	0·09714 (4)	0·0725 (2)	0·09044 (3)	0·0459 (1)
1966	0·01389 (2)	−0·0077 (1)	0·03174 (3)	−0·0551 (2)	−0·06271 (2)	−0·0601 (2)	−0·07087 (3)	−0·1066 (4)
1967	0·00106 (2)	−0·0103 (1)	0·00113 (3)	−0·0299 (2)	0·02519 (2)	−0·0111 (1)	0·04084 (3)	−0·0426 (4)
1968	0·02359 (2)	−0·0061 (1)	0·02792 (3)	0·0258 (2)	0·06325 (3)	0·0038 (1)	0·06809 (4)	0·0403 (2)
R.M.S.	0·0366	0·0239	0·0357	0·0352	0·0692	0·0410	0·0682	0·0562
R.M.S. actual/R.M.S. S.E.	1·55	1·02	1·57	1·36	2·08	1·16	2·05	1·71
R.M.S. actual/R.M.S. actual for GS	1·04	0·68	1·01	1	1·23	0·73	1·22	1
R.M.S. actual all L					0·0653	0·0453	0·0649	0·0585
R.M.S. S.E. all L					0·0321	0·0410	0·0315	0·0319
R.M.S. actual all L/R.M.S. S.E. all L					2·03	1·10	2·06	1·83

TABLE 7 (cont.)

	4-step				8-step					
Data ending qtr IV	B1	B2	B3	GS	B1	B2	B3	GS	B4	B5
S.E. (Deg. of freedom) — *Standard errors over regression data*										
1963	0·02829 (22)	0·03891	0·02119 (20)	0·03303 (23)	0·03173 (18)	0·04784	0·02963 (18)	0·03035 (19)	0·02659	0·02837
1964	0·02960 (26)	0·03594	0·02314 (24)	0·03298 (27)	0·02953 (22)	0·04420	0·02701 (22)	0·03026 (23)	0·02826	0·02818
1965	0·03113 (30)	0·03632	0·02815 (28)	0·03318 (31)	0·02879 (26)	0·04561	0·02652 (26)	0·03159 (27)	0·03939	0·03311
1966	0·03626 (34)	0·04571	0·03657 (32)	0·03319 (35)	0·03078 (30)	0·05781	0·03027 (30)	0·03180 (31)	0·05516	0·04730
1967	0·04309 (38)	0·04991	0·04641 (36)	0·03679 (39)	0·03368 (34)	0·06280	0·03343 (34)	0·03585 (35)	0·05421	0·04903
1968	0·04187 (42)	0·04865	0·04402 (40)	0·03749 (43)	0·04029 (38)	0·06323	0·04134 (38)	0·03740 (39)	0·05213	0·04921
1969	0·04141 (46)	0·04646	0·04184 (44)	0·03654 (47)	0·03903 (42)	0·06061	0·03867 (42)	0·03639 (43)	0·05030	0·05124
R.M.S.	0·0364	0·0435	0·0358	0·0348	0·0337	0·0551	0·0328	0·0335	0·04518	0·04206
Actual error (S*, R*) — *Actual errors of predictions from end of regression data*										
1963	0·11544 (4)	−0·0002 (1,1)	0·10630 (3)	0·0377 (2,2)	0·04855 (3)	0·0607 (4,2)	−0·00827 (1)	0·0412 (2,1)	0·23297	−0·24473
1964	0·09387 (3)	0·0620 (2,2)	0·11373 (4)	0·0108 (1,1)	−0·01269 (2)	0·0275 (4,2)	0·02003 (3)	−0·0105 (1,1)	+0·14579	−0·12972
1965	0·00133 (2)	−0·0350 (3,1)	−0·00015 (1)	−0·0490 (4,2)	−0·06686 (2)	−0·0624 (1,1)	−0·06716 (3)	−0·0974 (4,2)	+0·01813	−0·01380
1966	−0·04553 (1)	−0·0565 (3,1)	−0·04733 (2)	−0·0958 (4,2)	−0·09909 (3)	−0·0943 (1,1)	−0·09594 (2)	−0·1386 (4,2)	−0·11048	−0·17185
1967	0·02808 (1)	−0·0470 (2,1)	0·05851 (3)	−0·0741 (4,2)	−0·11205 (4)	−0·0607 (2,2)	−0·10117 (3)	−0·0093 (1,1)	−0·06547	−0·17478
1968	−0·07292 (3)	−0·0134 (1,1)	0·07914 (4)	0·0188 (2,2)						
R.M.S.	0·0711	0·0421	0·0776	0·0562	0·0766	0·0647	0·0699	0·0782	0·1357	0·1655
R.M.S. actual/R.M.S.S.E.	1·95	0·97	2·17	1·61	2·27	1·17	2·13	2·33	3·00	3·94
R.M.S. actual/R.M.S. actual for GS	1·27	0·75	1·38	1	0·98	0·83	0·89	1		

*S: accuracy ranking between B2 and GS.   R: accuracy ranking between the four regressions.

204   BRAY – *Dynamic Equations for Economic Forecasting*   [Part 2,

capital and land, and that increases in output cannot come without increases in
resources. In the Godley–Shepherd method the increase in output, which is a fact of
economic life, is wrapped up in time trends representing the spontaneous creation of
resources, irrespective of what we do with the resources of manpower we already have.
There is no fundamental economic principle here. In fact, of course, a more sensitive
treatment of the stochastics and dynamics of economic systems does not offend against
economic principles at all.

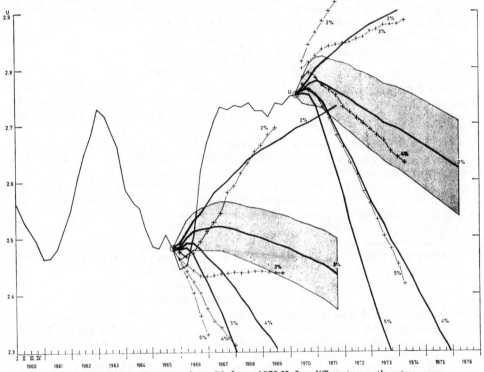

FIG. 15. Predictions by regressions $B2$ from 1970 II for different growth rates: ▬▬.
Godley–Shepherd predictions from 1970 II for different growth rates: + +.

4.11. *Conclusions on the G.D.P.–unemployment Relations*

The $B2$ equation is the best that has been found for predicting the level of unemployment, given alternative courses for G.D.P. in the short term, that is, up to 2
years. The error distribution of forecasts made predicting ahead from the end of
data used in regressions has shown the same error distribution as was estimated over
the regression data, indicating a stable relationship over the whole period 1963–70.
The $B2$ equation predicts more accurately than the Godley–Shepherd method, and
without using employment or other variables used in the Godley–Shepherd method.
The $B2$ equation should be capable of improvement by the use of fully general
rational function operators found by Box and Jenkins' methods, and possibly by the
introduction of other variables, particularly employment, used by Godley and

Shepherd. The Godley and Shepherd method could also be improved by *ad hoc* adjustments to cope with the period 1967–70, but this would not fundamentally improve the method which imposes, *a priori*, a particular dynamic structure that is not fitted to the data.

Longer-term behaviour has not been identified satisfactorily either by the method of this paper or by Godley and Shepherd's methods, and it probably requires the consideration of other economic factors such as investment. The suggestion remains that different rates of growth of G.D.P. over a considerable range covering 2–5 per cent per annum lead to different "equilibrium levels of unemployment" after 3 or 4 years, but it has not been possible to prove it or to disprove it.

5. MODEL-BUILDING METHODS AND OBJECTIVES

5.1. *The Possibility of a New Approach*

Box and Jenkins' methods will only prove themselves by being shown to predict ahead of data used in estimating relations, with actual error distribution as estimated at the time of the forecast. This must first be done for the past for a number of different economic relations.

If they are then shown to work effectively over the next 2–3 years that will be needed to digest them in the policy-making machinery, it is likely they could then be used for policy-making purposes because present methods are known to be unsatisfactory or would fail the test on past data. Also, if systems are of the character indicated by Box and Jenkins' methods, it is unlikely that the trial-and-error use of individual autoregressive and independent variable terms would identify them satisfactorily, and such estimates would show the kind of unsatisfactory behaviour that has often been found.

In order to test Box and Jenkins' methods thoroughly, a new approach is needed to model building which is set out in the following principles.

5.2. *Principles of Model Building*

1. The record of the main variables in an economic system contains a very limited amount of information. Fifteen years of quarterly data with a principal periodicity of 5 years is scant. It is therefore only possible to identify main effects on any one variable.

2. For any dependent variable start with one or at most two independent variables and derive the most economical (or in Box and Jenkins' terminology "parsimonious") representation. This will include an autoregressive noise model. Test actual error distribution over subsets of the data, predicting ahead of the data used in estimating operators.

3. Try the addition of another variable which, as well as reducing the residual, may make it possible to reduce the order of the previous operator on one/or more existing variables, and reduce the "tail" of past information required in such an operator by taking out of it a pole near the unit circle.

4. When another independent variable is introduced, unless it is directly and wholly controllable, it becomes a possible dependent variable in another equation. If there are no variables on which it depends, and it is not directly and wholly controllable, predict it autoregressively.

5. For each estimation the Box–Jenkins method reduces the residual for the 1-step predicter to an uncorrelated random variable, or white noise, and tests that this is so.

If the model is structurally correct the residual for other lead times will also be a minimum. There is therefore a unique scalar measure of fit in the standard error of the 1-step predicter. Also the problems of serial correlation of residuals and multi-collinearity do not arise. If the residuals are significantly correlated, the estimation is not complete. If a variable is completely collinear with existing variables in the circumstances in which the model is to be used, it has no information to offer and will be rejected.

6. Since as time passes more information becomes available, economic models can grow in complexity, but they will not produce significant results if they try to outgrow the available information.

7. For any particular dependent variable and a particular set of independent variables there is a combination of complexity of transfer function for each independent variable, and the selection of independent variables, which will give the smallest residual. It is not possible therefore to separate the estimation of the dynamics from the estimation of the statics of a system for which no static data are available. Furthermore, the use of appropriate transfer functions with rather fewer dependent variables makes the system simpler to handle in practice because fewer measurements are required.

8. Relations may be estimated simultaneously for more than one dependent variable if this produces smaller residuals for the respective dependent variables than single-equation estimation.

9. For any specific degree of complexity of model there is no uniquely correct model for a system.

10. It is unlikely that a complex model can be specified *ab initio* without application: the complexity has to grow by an iterative process with its application.

11. In particular where even only a two- or three-equation model has been built, and it is to be used for policy guidance, the policy objectives, which should be discussed from every point of view, should be made the basis for the design of a control algorithm, matching the setting of controllable variables to the objectives. Purely verbal arguments using a single or several forecasts are likely to be seriously defective, especially when formulated without insight into the nature of dynamic stochastic systems. Once formulated, the control algorithm, its assumptions and prescriptions can and should be criticized again from every available point of view, both in general and, where time is available as with economic systems, on each occasion when action is possible.

12. The seasonal correction, smoothing, and displacement of data in time should be treated as part of the time series analysis and not handled by preliminary treatment which can throw away or contaminate useful information.

5.2. *Current Model-building Practice*

None of the short-term models of the United Kingdom economy seem to have been built on these principles. Too often simple relations have been estimated and then found to predict poorly, both in that the errors of prediction prove to be large and in that they are larger than the standard error of the regressions, indicating an inadequate structure. Instead of having their structure put right, the equations, which are often not constructed as predicting equations at all, are then adjusted by a factor which is an average of recent prediction errors, thus introducing the beginnings of a serious time series analysis at the end, but in an inefficient manner.

Two causes of difficulty often quoted are the lateness of data and the extent of data revision. The status of unrevised data should be recognized: it can be treated as a separate variable or longer lead time predicters can be used.

It is sometimes argued that economic systems have unique characteristics, related to objectives, structural change, data revision, the unavailability of necessary data, random events, unexpected feedback effects like "confidence", and so on, which make it impossible to apply higher standards of dynamic stochastic analysis. Such arguments are sometimes attempts to verbalize concepts already well recognized in control applications. But undoubtedly the circumstances of the application of control theory in economics are unique as they are in every other field of application. The importance of economics only makes it the more important to get the stochastics and dynamics right and understood.

5.3. *Present Models*

It is uncertain whether the reconstruction of the very large London Business School and Southampton University models (Hilton and Heathfield, 1970) with Box and Jenkins' methods or the equivalent will give as interesting or as useful results as the construction of models guided in the first place by these methods and the principles based on them which are outlined above. The simpler National Institute and Treasury models may offer a more suitable base for a central model. Indeed even these latter models are far more complex than any model control engineers have thought it sensible to analyse as a single system, and any further model-building effort would be well advised to seek the co-operation of control theorists with experience of handling large systems. Livesey (1970) has applied control theory concepts to a simpler model, but using estimation methods which do not identify economic behaviour as well, or in as convenient form, as Box and Jenkins' methods.

To handle the complexity of economic systems, hierarchies of models and sectoral models are certainly needed. But the same thorough estimation and testing of the stochastics and dynamics of a sectoral model is needed before it is linked with other sectoral models, as is needed of a particular equation before it is put into a sectoral model. The fitting together of sectoral models and of levels in a hierarchy also need careful handling.

5.4. *Economic Management*

The estimation and forecasting methods at present used in the Treasury, of which the Godley–Shepherd method is by no means a bad example, are not satisfactory. Arguments that the defects do not matter because they are overcome, or at least overlaid, by methods of economic management of which these forecasts are only a part (and a part which may sometimes be ignored), would be more convincing if the performance of the United Kingdom economy had been better in the past 25 years. But the arguments are right in setting forecasts in the context of economic management. The methods of economic management themselves are not satisfactory.

Though the forecasting models used in the Treasury are relatively complex, the control models inherent in practical decisions in economic management are very much simpler. That such models are at present mainly verbal and sometimes unwitting attempts to represent the stochastics and dynamics of the economy, does not protect them from all the hazard of mis-estimation and misunderstanding that can arise in handling such systems.

The author has argued elsewhere (Bray, 1970a) that the management of aggregate demand has limitations due to inherent noise and structural change, which may make it inadequate as an economic management system. But it is necessary first to establish the limits of performance of aggregate demand management, limits which present practice has neither attained not explored, nor even identified as a concept.

The greatest practical merit of Box and Jenkins' forecasting methods, and related principles and methods, is that even at the level of the simplest of aggregate models (or sectoral models), the estimation stage is matched directly to the policy guidance stage that must follow. With better tools available, the development of better estimation and policy guidance methods should be a high priority, with Treasury officials encouraged to co-operate fully with outside workers.

ACKNOWLEDGEMENTS

I am grateful to Mr Martin Joyce, Mr Anthony Paris and Mr Del Wright who wrote library programmes for the Time Sharing Limited system, and to Mr Richard Evans, Managing Director of Time Sharing, for the loan of a terminal to carry out this work.

Mr David Jeffery of the Economic and Statistical Analysis Division of the former Ministry of Technology, Mr Solomon Khela and Mr Jeremy Hall of General Electric Information Services Limited assisted with computations in the earlier stages of this work, and Mr Robert Matthews of Mullard Limited in the latter stages.

I am particularly grateful to the Royal Statistical Society reviewer and to Professor G. M. Jenkins for comments on an earlier version of this paper, which was written before I was aware of the extent of Box and Jenkins' recent work on rational function operators. The iteration of 1-step predicters and the associated treatment of errors were subsequently borrowed directly from Box and Jenkins' methods. Comparisons with results obtained by Professor Jenkins by the application of his own methods to the same data helped to illuminate the nature and limitations of the estimation methods described here.

I am also grateful to Professor J. Durbin, Professor J. H. Westcott, Mr W. A. H. Godley, Mr J. R. Shepherd, Sir Donald MacDougall, Mr M. V. Posner, Mr. H. P. Evans and Mr S. G. B. Henry for useful correspondence and discussion about this work.

I alone am responsible for the results and views expressed.

REFERENCES

ALMON, SHIRLEY (1965). The distributed lag between capital appropriations and expenditures. *Econometrica*, **33**, 178–196.

BLACK, S. W. and RUSSELL, R. R. (1969). An alternative estimate of potential G.N.P. *Rev. Econ. Statist.*, **51**, 70–76.

BOX, G. E. P. and JENKINS, G. M. (1968). Some recent advances in forecasting and control. *Appl. Statist.*, **17**, 91–109.

—— (1970). *Time Series Analysis, Forecasting and Control.* San Francisco: Holden-Day.

BRAY, J. W. (1970a). *Decision in Government.* London: Gollancz.

—— (1970b). The road to faster growth. *Economist*, 30 May 1970.

BRAY, J. W., HIGH, R. J., JEMMERSON, H. and ROBSON, V. (1966). A continuously updated dynamic optimization system. *Proc. 3rd Congr. Int. Feder. Automat. Control*, Paper 48b.

BRAY, J. W., JOHNSON, C. A., NEEDHAM, R. W. and STONEHEWER, S. E. (1961). An investigation of computer control of a polythene reactor. Report, I.C.I. Ltd.

BRAY, J. W., MITCHELL, P. R., PAYNE, F., STONEHEWER, S. E. and WATSON, K. J. (1959). Operating conditions of an oil cracker: a dynamic regression analysis. Report, I.C.I. Ltd.

BROWN, R. G. (1962). *Smoothing, Forecasting and Prediction of Discrete Time Series*. Englewood Cliffs, N.J.: Prentice-Hall.
BROWN, R. L. and DURBIN, J. (1969). Methods of investigating whether a regression relationship is constant over time. Paper delivered to European Statistical Meeting, Amsterdam.
CHOW, G. C. (1970). Optimal stochastic control and linear economic systems. *Money, Credit and Banking*, 291–302.
CHRIST, C. F. (1966). *Econometric Models and Methods*. New York: Wiley.
FISHER, I. (1925). Our unstable dollar and the so-called business cycle. *J. Amer. Statist. Ass.*, **20**, 179–202.
—— (1937). Note on a short cut method for calculating distributed lags. *Bull. Inst. Int. Statist.*, **29**, 323–328.
GODLEY, W. A. H. and SHEPHERD, J. R. (1964). Long term growth and short term policy. *Nat. Inst. Econ. Rev.*, **29**, 26–58.
GRILICHES, Z. (1967). Distributed lags: a survey. *Econometrica*, **35**, 16–49.
HILTON, K. and HEATHFIELD, D. F. (1970). *The Econometric Study of the U.K.* London: Macmillan.
JORGENSON, D. W. (1966). Rational distributed lag functions. *Econometrica*, **34**, 135–149.
KOYCK, L. M. (1954). *Distributed Lags and Investment Analysis*. Amsterdam: North-Holland.
LESER, C. E. V. (1968). A survey of econometrics. *J. R. Statist. Soc.* A, **131**, 530–566.
LIVESEY, D. A. (1970). The modelling and control of the U.K. economy. *Second World Cong. Econometric Soc.*
MALINVAUD, E. (1966). *Statistical Methods of Econometrics*. Amsterdam: North-Holland.
OKUN, A. M. (1962). Potential G.N.P.: its measurement and significance. *Proc. Amer. Statist. Ass.*, 98–104.
PAISH, F. W. (1962). *Studies in an Inflationary Economy. The United Kingdom 1948–1961*. London: Macmillan.
ROY, A. D. (1970). Short term forecasting for central economic management of the U.K. economy. In Hilton and Heathfield (1970), see above, pp. 463–473.
SHEPHERD, J. R. (1968). Productive potential and the demand for labour. *Econ. Trends*, No. 178, xxv–xxvii.
SLATER, LUCY JOAN (1967). *Fortran Programs for Economists*. University of Cambridge, Department of Applied Economics, Occasional Paper 13. Cambridge University Press.
SOLOW, R. (1960). On a family of lag distributions. *Econometrica*, **28**, 393–406.
SOWERBUTTS, ANNE (1970). The D.E.A. medium term macro-economic model. In Hilton and Heathfield (1970), see above, pp. 489–494.
THEIL, H. and STERN, R. M. (1960). A simple unimodal lag distribution. *Metroeconomica*, **12**, 111–119.

DISCUSSION ON DR BRAY'S PAPER

Professor J. D. SARGAN (London School of Economics): It is a great pleasure to propose the vote of thanks to Dr Bray for his stimulating paper. I am sure it is stimulating to us in several directions.

May I first of all talk about the method of estimation of equations similar to equation (15) of the paper? As he pointed out we can represent this in the form of $Q(D)y_t = P(D)x_t + K(D)e_t$. The point is that $K(D)$ is an arbitrarily specified polynomial and we are not estimating these parameters of the model. I would like to compare this specification with the Jorgenson general rational distributed lag model which essentially was the same equation except for the specification of the stochastic error. The equation can be written $Q(D)y_t = P(D)x_t + W_t$. If one ignores the difference in the error terms of these equations it can be seen that they have essentially the same implications. The difference in the error term can be expressed by saying that $w_t = K(D)e_t$. The difference in the two forms is simply in the assumptions we are making about the stochastic behaviour of the error on the equation and that essentially, if we estimate in this form, we are implicitly saying we believe the e_t are independent. On the other hand if we estimate this equation by ordinary squares we are assuming that the w_t are serially independent. We shall produce inconsistent estimates if we mis-specify the stochastic nature of the error. The relative advantages of the Jorgenson rational distribution lag estimated by ordinary least squares compared with Dr Bray's procedure depends upon whether we believe that the hypothesis that the e_t are serially independent is more reasonable than the hypothesis that the w_t are serially independent. This should be settled by testing to see which is correct in terms of the serial covariance matrixes, and without this kind of test, I should be reluctant to believe that it is necessary to go through the extra stages required for Dr Bray's procedure compared to the straightforward regression for the rational distributed lag estimates. However, if Dr Bray had the purely autoregressive model it might be that in some cases that would be a more reasonable approximation than alternative treatments.

Turning to the author's more general discussion of econometric technique in the last section of his paper, I do not wish to appear too unenthusiastic about the use of control methods in econometrics. Econometricians have been aware of the possibility of this kind of technique being available since the 1950s when Phillips wrote, and Theil and the Netherlands Econometric Institute were building models of the Dutch economy in which control theory methods of producing optimal public policies were computed. But if we look at the Netherlands work, it is clear that there are many problems unsolved. Let me start first of all at the estimation end of things. It is convenient that if one wants to make optimal predictions, one can assume that they will be obtained by specifying appropriately a suitable model, and then estimating it, using the usual criteria for optimal estimation. Of course, this is a large sample property, but it is not too clear to me that one gains a great deal by considering the prediction problem at the time of estimation. Of course, if you have estimated a model and then used it to predict, especially if you use it to predict outside the sample period, that is a convenient and crucial test of the appropriate specification of the model. If one predicts for longer lags, that probably is a pretty good test of the dynamic specification of the model and the stochastic properties of the errors. But it seems to me a relatively crude test, and it would be better to set up tests which are specific in the sense of indicating which constraints on the parameters in the model that has been estimated are incorrect, and this kind of test does not very satisfactorily produce specific information of this sort. Econometricians on the whole prefer to look at tests which refer to particular *a priori* descriptions of their models. One combines this sort of testing with an attempt to build into the model as much economic theory as possible. If one is only interested in short-period forecasting, then it is probably appropriate to look at simple autoregressive models involving only a few variables, but if we are interested in understanding how the economy works to predict over longer periods, or in order to see what will happen if the Government changes one of the equations in the model, then essentially we need to know something about the structural form of the model. We are also faced with the problem of what criterion to use. In the public policy sphere, we have many objectives that we wish to pursue; to name a few, we should take account of the advantages of reducing the variance occurring in the balance of payments, so reducing the necessary stock of foreign exchange. Other objectives are higher G.D.P., lower unemployment and a lower rate of inflation. But if we use a criterion function which depends on all these things, we need a model which explains them all, and that certainly requires a fairly large size of model. The model of Livesey which was described in his paper at the Cambridge meeting of the Econometric Society covers some of these variables and it is probably about the minimum size that would be useful. But even with all this, we still need to specify a criterion which balances out the advantages, say, of a higher level of G.N.P. per head against a higher level of unemployment. This is clearly an interesting field to work in and I would be happy to see more work carried out in this field. But in the initial stages, if we started to compute optimal control policies we should probably learn more about problems in econometrics than we would increase our understanding of the problems of Government.

Dr Bray has not really had time to discuss the Godley–Shepherd model, but perhaps since one of the things he must have done is to cause econometricians to look again at that model, I can be allowed to say a little about this. I find it difficult in the model to understand how one could expect two equation models which contain only one current endogenous variable to work particularly well. I do feel probably that the answer is that the supply equation should be looked upon as determining the current level of unemployment, and if this were the case, it would be then possible to produce a reduced form for the model which had unemployment as one of its endogenous variables, and with such a model one might produce better predictions of unemployment.

Since I obviously have found rather too much to say about Dr Bray's paper, I repeat my congratulations to the author on the stimulating and interesting work he is doing.

Professor G. M. JENKINS (University of Lancaster): Dr Bray is to be congratulated for drawing the Society's attention to the very important statistical problem of dynamic regression analysis. This has applications not only in economics but also to problems in business, engineering and the natural sciences. The models used by Dr Bray are similar, but less general, than those used by other people, such as Aström, and also by Professor Box and myself.

The first slide shows that these more general models are such that an appropriately differenced output time series

$$y_t = \nabla^{d_Y} Y_t$$

is related to an appropriately differenced input series

$$x_t = \nabla^{d_X} X_t$$

by a linear filter whose transfer function is the ratio of two polynomials in the backward shift operator B. (The differencing is used to convert both input and output to stationary time series.) This form of filter enables one to represent the weight function relating the output to the input by means of an acceptably small number of parameters.

The relationship between the output and input will be corrupted by noise or error, which will usually be autocorrelated. This error can be thought of as the result of passing a random series or white noise through another linear filter whose transfer function is the ratio of two polynomials. This leads to the familiar autoregressive-moving average model. Again, the autoregressive-moving average filter enables the weight function relating the error to the white noise series to be represented by an acceptably small number of parameters. The combined transfer function-noise model

$$y_t = c + \frac{\omega(B)}{\delta(B)} x_t + \frac{\theta(B)}{\phi(B)} a_t$$

is capable of representing a very wide range of dynamic behaviour and Dr Bray is right in wanting to represent economic relationships by a model of this kind.

It is important to end up with a model which is as simple as possible, that is, one which contains as few parameters as is necessary to describe the data adequately. This is because an over-parameterized model will lead to difficulties in estimation and also to forecasts which have lower accuracy.

The approach which Professor Box and I have used to avoid these problems is to develop an iterative model-building strategy. We believe that in the past far too much attention has been placed in statistics to model fitting and far too little attention to the more complex, but more important, problem of model building. The first stage in model building is called Identification, in which a rough preliminary data analysis is used to obtain first guesses of the degrees of the four polynomials entering into the transfer function-noise model. Then the parameters in the tentatively entertained model, or models, are estimated by fully efficient non-linear least-squares methods. Finally, diagnostic checks are applied to the fitted models to see whether there is any evidence of model inadequacy. If inadequacies are thrown up, then the nature of these inadequacies can be used to modify the model, which can then be refitted and checked.

In the case of transfer function-noise models, the first step in the identification stage is to fit a model to the input series on its own. The next slide shows that the autocorrelation function of the Gross Domestic Product series X is consistent with non-stationary behaviour. However, the autocorrelations of the first differences are all small and are not inconsistent with the assumption that the series is random. Subsequent least-squares fitting of a range of models showed that the Gross Domestic Product series is well represented by the model

$$\nabla X_t = 0.66 + \alpha_t,$$

where α_t is a random series, that is a random walk with shocks which have a non-zero mean.

The next step is to decide how much differencing is needed to induce stationarity in the input and output. We have just seen that the G.D.P. series needs to be differenced once to induce stationarity. The unemployment series, on the other hand, seems to be stationary over the period observed. It would seem reasonable, therefore, to try and relate either unemployment or the first difference of unemployment to the first difference of G.D.P. There is some evidence that it is better to relate the first difference of unemployment to the first difference of G.D.P.

The third step in the identification process is to obtain rough estimates of the weights in the regression transfer function. In general, one would expect that the cross-correlation function between the appropriately differenced input and output would provide rough estimates of the weighting function in the dynamic regression equation. Unfortunately, what the cross-correlation function is trying to tell us about the weighting function is obscured by the autocorrelation function of the input series. One convenient way of getting over this difficulty is to use the model fitted to the input series to *prewhiten* it, that is to convert it into a random series. If the same prewhitening operation is applied to the output series, the cross-correlation function between the prewhitened input and output is then proportional to the regression weight function. Therefore, the prewhitened cross-correlation function provides a simple visual tool for guessing at the form of model needed to explain the weighting function.

Since the G.D.P. series is converted to a random series by differencing, prewhitening has already been achieved in this example by differencing input and output. It follows that the cross-correlation function between the first difference of unemployment and the first difference of G.D.P. provides a rough estimate of the regression weighting function. The slide shows that this cross-correlation function follows a damped sine wave, suggesting that the denominator $\delta(B)$ in the model should be a second-degree polynomial. The introduction of a first-degree polynomial into the numerator enables the starting values in the damped sine wave to be determined.

A further identification process applied to the noise or error shows that the noise in the first difference of unemployment is nearly random. There is no harm in fitting a model which is slightly more elaborate than is thought to be necessary and so a first-order moving average and a second-order moving average process were tried. The estimation process was then used to determine whether the inclusion of the additional parameters was justified or not.

The next slide summarizes the results of the identification stage. It shows that the unemployment–G.D.P. relationship might be adequately described by a transfer function whose numerator is a polynomial of degree one, and whose denominator is a polynomial of degree two, and by a noise model which is either first-order moving average or second-order moving average, that is,

$$\nabla Y_t = c + \frac{\omega_0 - \omega_1 B}{1 - \delta_1 B - \delta_2 B^2} \nabla X_t + (1 - \theta_1 B - \theta_2 B^2) a_t.$$

These two types of model were then fitted by non-linear least squares to data up to the end of each year from 1965 onwards. The slide shows the model fitted up to the end of 1966 using a first-order moving average noise model

$$\nabla Y_t = c - \frac{\overset{\pm 0.003}{0.0108}(1 - 0.73B)}{\underset{\pm 0.10 \quad \pm 0.08}{1 - 1.73B + 0.82B^2}} \nabla X_t + (1 + \underset{\pm 0.16}{0.33}B) a_t.$$

Examination of the standard errors of the estimated parameters shows that the transfer-function parameters are well estimated but that the moving-average parameter is small compared with its standard error. In fact, it makes little difference to the residual variance if this parameter is left out altogether. This means that the noise in the first difference of unemployment is essentially a random series, that is, that the noise in unemployment itself is a random walk. Thus the model which is finally obtained essentially contains only five parameters and, furthermore, is easy to understand.

Examination of the autocorrelation function of the residuals from this model and the cross-correlation function between the residuals and the prewhitened G.D.P. series shows no evidence of model inadequacy. The model can, therefore, be used with confidence to generate the forecasts.

Dr Bray has rightly emphasized the importance of model building as an essential preliminary to the generation of forecasts. However, once a good model has been produced in the first place, the model will then determine all features of the forecast, including its value at all future times, together with the associated probability limits. It is not necessary to fit regression equations for each forecast lead time as Dr Bray does in some parts of his paper.

The next slide shows the forecasts for eight quarters ahead (made from observation 12 onwards) using a model fitted to data up to the end of 1966. It turns out that this model, containing only five parameters, gives forecasts which are marginally better than the best of Dr Bray's forecasts, which are based on a model containing as many as nine parameters.

It is necessary to point out that there is an unrealistic aspect to these forecasts, since they use the known future values of G.D.P. In practice, these known values would have to be replaced by forecasts of the G.D.P. series, and this would result in an increase in the forecast errors. However, in order to provide an effective comparison, the forecasts shown in the slide have been calculated in the same way as Dr Bray's.

A final interesting point is that the Treasury forecasts, based on the Godley–Shepherd model, make use of a third time series, the quarterly employment figures.

The next slide shows the effect of introducing the employment series into the unemployment–G.D.P. model, namely

$$\nabla Y_t = c - \frac{0\cdot0055(1-0\cdot08B)}{1-1\cdot59B+0\cdot73B^2}\,\nabla X_{1t} - \frac{0\cdot00016(1+0\cdot69B)}{1-1\cdot24B+0\cdot76B^2}\,\nabla X_{2t} + a_t.$$

It can be seen that the transfer function relating employment to unemployment is similar in form to that relating G.D.P. to unemployment. Moreover, the denominators of the two transfer functions have very similar parameter values. Again the noise model in unemployment is a random walk.

The residual variance in this model is appreciably lower than that obtained from the unemployment–G.D.P. model and, although there has not been sufficient time to generate forecasts from this model, it seems to hold out considerable promise as a forecasting tool.

I am sure that we are all grateful to Dr Bray for drawing attention to the need to use better dynamic models for describing economic time series, because better understanding of the dynamic properties of economic relationships must inevitably lead to better control action. I have great pleasure in seconding the vote of thanks to Dr Bray for his paper.

The vote of thanks was put to the meeting and carried by acclamation.

Professor G. E. Box (Universities of Essex and Wisconsin): Dr Bray's model may be written

$$\frac{1-p_1B-p_2B^2-p_3B^3-p_4B^4}{(1-0\cdot5B)(1-0\cdot6B)(1-0\cdot7B)}\,y_t = c + \frac{q_0-q_1B-q_2B^2-q_3B^3}{(1-0\cdot5B)(1-0\cdot6B)(1-0\cdot7B)}\,x_t + a_t$$

or

$$\frac{p(B)}{L(B)} y_t = c + \frac{q(B)}{L(B)} x_t + a_t, \tag{I}$$

the terminal white noise a_t being implied by the least-squares fitting.

It is surprising that this model, at first sight so very different from that described by Professor Jenkins, has given fairly good forecasts. This is all the more mysterious because Dr Bray's approach seems to violate certain important principles.

First, one ought to pay serious attention to noise structure. A statistical model is a recipe for generating white noise. For example, a simple regression model

$$a_t = y_t - \alpha - \beta x_t$$

implies that by subtracting a constant α and a certain multiple β of x_t from y_t we can generate a white-noise sequence a_t. But if, as would be more likely with economic data, the noise sequence has, say, a random-walk structure so that

$$\sum_{j=1}^{t} a_j = y_t - \alpha - \beta x_t \tag{II}$$

or

$$a_t = \nabla y_t - \beta \nabla x_t \tag{III}$$

then fitting y to x by ordinary least squares would yield poor estimates with meaningless standard errors. The equivalence of (II) and (III) illustrates the general point that error structure and model structure are interchangeable. It is at one's peril that ordinary least squares is lightly used to fit model structures involving time series.

Second, over-parametrization of models, always dangerous, is particularly so with rational transfer functions. A transfer function $\omega(B)/\delta(B)$ can equally well be represented by

$$q(B)/p(B) = t(B) \, \omega(B)/t(B) \, \delta(B) \tag{IV}$$

whatever the common factor $t(B)$. So that if an over-parametrizd model $q(B)/p(B)$ is fitted we can expect extreme instability and arbitrariness in the estimates. While Dr Bray's $q(B)$ of third degree and $p(B)$ of fourth degree appear prodigal yet his estimates look fairly stable.

A third peculiarity mentioned by the author is that the arbitrary lagged averages of his equation (1) and Fig. 1 play no part whatever in modelling the transfer between y_t and x_t but appear only in the noise. This is so because the model (I) may be written

$$y_t = c' + \frac{q(B)}{p(B)} x_t + \frac{L(B)}{p(B)} a_t, \tag{V}$$

a form in which the rational function generating the noise structure is forced to have the arbitrary numerator $L(B)$ and a denominator $p(B)$ constrained to be the same as that of the transfer function $q(B)/p(B)$.

The explanation of why, for these particular data, the procedure works as well as it does seems to be as follows. If $q(B)/p(B)$ possesses a common factor $t(B)$ as in equation (IV), then (V) may be written

$$y_t = c' + \frac{t(B) \, \omega(B)}{t(B) \, \delta(B)} x_t + \frac{1}{t(B)} \left\{ \frac{L(B)}{\delta(B)} \right\} a_t.$$

If we fit this expression, or equivalently if (I) is fitted by least squares, then $1/t(B)$ will not be arbitrary but will try its best to take on some form which multiplies the fixed factor $L(B)/\delta(B)$ to give a proper noise structure. If, for example, we take Dr Bray's model from his Table 3 for data to 1968 IV then we find that a near-common factor of this kind occurs and that after this is eliminated we obtain approximately

$$\nabla Y_t \simeq c' - \frac{0 \cdot 012(1 - 0 \cdot 4B)}{1 - 1 \cdot 7B + 0 \cdot 8B^2} \nabla X_t + (1 + 0 \cdot 2B - 0 \cdot 2B^2) a_t$$

which is very similar to the model Professor Jenkins has just described.

One cannot expect that circumstances will always fall out so happily and, as Dr Bray has generously acknowledged, in general it is essential to follow through a model-building procedure whose characteristics are more transparent.

Mr J. R. SHEPHERD (H.M. Treasury): I approach Dr Bray's paper from a somewhat different standpoint from previous speakers as a practising macro-economic forecaster who makes no claim to any deep theoretical knowledge. I did greatly appreciate the emphasis in Dr Bray's paper on showing his method in operation in an applied context; this certainly helped me to get some feeling for what it involves. I think that the comparative evaluation of the predictive performance of Bray and Godley–Shepherd techniques has more fundamental importance. On economic issues different analysts may approach a subject with such different preconceptions and wishing to make (or refrain from) such different *a priori* assumptions that it may often be difficult to devise empirical procedures which help to determine who is right. I believe that comparative forecasting ability is one very relevant approach to such questions which has not been used as much as it might be in economics. However, I think there are substantial difficulties in conducting such tests some of which are illustrated in Dr Bray's paper.

The first problem is that Godley–Shepherd was never designed as an automatic forecasting procedure but rather as a guideline from which to analyse and predict deviations. Future residuals were intended to reflect not only any obvious autocorrelation properties but the forecasters' judgments about the factors in operation which were not correctly incorporated into the model. In order to check on the appropriateness of Dr Bray's treatment of the Godley–Shepherd residuals we thought it would be interesting to try an alternative approach. My colleague, Huw Evans, repeated Dr Bray's test using an automatic rule for extrapolating residuals (devised without reference to the forecasting performance). I should stress that this procedure was an *ad hoc* exercise and bears no relation to the Treasury's actual forecasting methods. The root-mean-square errors were very similar to Dr Bray's but he obtained quite different results in particular instances. The work showed the extreme sensitivity of the results to the exact procedure used (e.g. time periods selected) and underlined the difficulty of reaching conclusions from the small number of extrapolations available. For instance, we obtained much the greatest errors from projections from the end of 1963; from 1964 onwards the Evans version of Godley–Shepherd actually performs better than Dr Bray's preferred version, *B*2. One might argue that if we had actually been forecasting in 1963 we would not have broken the trend at the point selected on the basis of work done in 1968; this meant that a trend was fitted to a mere 3 years' experience.

I am not, however, trying to argue that the Godley–Shepherd procedure really performed relatively well compared with Dr Bray's. I do not even know whether my last comment works in that direction. The point is to emphasize how inconclusive the tests turn out to be and, more generally, the difficulties in making tests of this sort. In a similar vein, I question the validity of Dr Bray's reference (on p. 196) to a 90 per cent level of significance. I do not think that either the projections over different time horizons from a given point or the projections from different starting points are independent in the sense required.

There are other serious problems about retrospective tests of forecasting ability. Even given one's present views about estimating procedures it is hard to reproduce the choice of specification, estimation period, etc. that would actually have been used at the time. I am not clear, for example, whether there would have been sufficient reason at the time for

Dr Bray to choose his *B*2 regressions (which in retrospect performed the best) rather than one of his other versions. Such considerations do, I think, indicate that retrospective comparisons, while potentially a valuable tool, are not quite so simple as might appear at first sight. To make a fair evaluation one must, in effect, devise the rules of quite a complicated game.

My other main point concerns the context in which many forecasters work. This may have some bearing on the choice of estimation technique. One cannot isolate the process of making point predictions and estimating error margins from the wider role of an economic intelligence service. This will consist of interpreting current and projected developments in economic terms and of appraising the likely impact of various decisions or potential decisions upon them. It is not enough to have a means of producing forecasts, however good, if one cannot say why one has made them (in other words the beliefs about economic behaviour underlying them) or how they might be changed by different developments—different economic policies, for example. This means that a set of forecasts will have to be reconcilable with a particular set of hypotheses about economic behaviour—in effect, with a "structural" model of economic behaviour. This does not mean that one cannot be flexible in varying one's relationships or that the logical consequences of one's equations must always be followed through with full rigour: but judgments ultimately have to be made and defended in economic terms. Such an approach will generally lead to more *a priori* restraints on relationships and to more reliance on "economic sense" or on other sources of evidence than would generally be adopted by someone whose first interest is the formal analysis of time series. But while such differences of emphasis undoubtedly exist it is more doubtful whether there are major issues of principle; one should try to combine the strengths of different types of expertise.

The requirements which I have indicated do, however, make it difficult to use methods which do not purport to identify relationships which describe economic behaviour. This applies, in some measure, to the method put forward by Dr Bray. For similar reasons to those applying to the Koyck method of estimating distributed lags, which was widely used by economists until quite recently, Dr Bray's procedure will not generally provide unbiased estimates of structural coefficients when the disturbance terms are autocorrelated. Under realistic conditions the biases may be quite large. Whether or not this matters simply in terms of the quality of the forecast produced—and, if past cyclical patterns are not repeated, it probably does—it clearly does make it more difficult to use such a method to form a view about how the economy works. In the Treasury we are currently using methods which do purport—under certain relatively plausible assumptions—to give consistent estimates. These include both Almon lags and iterative methods which take into account the assumed autocorrelation structure. I understand that Box–Jenkins procedures do make it possible to identify economically meaningful coefficients and I am looking forward to seeing economic applications of these methods.

Professor J. H. WESTCOTT (Imperial College, London): Dr Bray's paper divides into two sections; the first part deals with the view that predictions can be put on a scientific basis and the contributions made by Professors Box and Jenkins have reinforced this. The second theme is that prediction is a means to an end and this end is to have a policy and wish to satisfy it by action. It may interest members to know that transition appears at the average of the number of pages to the paper. I would not claim that these two parts are therefore of equal weight, nor are they independent, but the second theme represents a new viewpoint and one which I am interested in.

As has been said, there is a well-studied field of Control Systems in which much relevant material has been established and, as Professor Sargan said, this has been pointed out around 1950. Why, therefore, has it not been applied before? There are good reasons for this; the first is the extreme brevity of the records available from the statistical point of view, or the perniciousness of the noise, or yet another way of putting it, the paucity of satisfactory measurements. This gives us a very difficult task as the sort of structures we should consider should be no more complicated than is statistically justified. There are extremely large and complicated models which have been constructed. But is this justified from the point of view of action? I think one must very much doubt this. I am convinced that the underlying structure is not fixed but is evolving, consequently to the confusion of the steady-state theory.

The last thing which makes it difficult from a control point of view is the real constraints which exist on the possibilities of action. I am saying that serious intellectual contributions need still to be made if an existing control theory is to be usefully applied to a study of economic systems. I feel that the time is overdue that some serious study should be made.

Dr C. CHATFIELD (Bath University of Technology): I have three brief comments. The first is of a non-statistical nature and concerns the length of the paper: should the Society place some limit on the length of read papers? We have had several long papers recently and in one or two I thought the referees could have been more ruthless with regard to length, and I think this also applies to this paper.

My second comment concerns the relevance of this paper to statisticians. I presume the audience is composed mainly of economists and statisticians. Economists will find the example interesting, and will also find the methods a useful stepping-stone to Box and Jenkins, but as a statistician I cannot see that the techniques will be of much use. As we have heard from Professor Jenkins, his approach gives better estimates with fewer parameters.

My third point concerns the possibility of non-stationarity. If a system is stable, forecasts based on past data will be "good", but if the system changes, then extrapolating from the past to the future may be dangerous. However, in forecasting, extrapolation cannot be avoided, and one looks at the past data and finds the model which fits them the best, but any such forecast must be taken with a pinch of salt, and one should be prepared to modify it in the light of any other information. What I am afraid of is that in a long technical paper of this nature, one may lose sight of this. Perhaps it would be advisable if every paper on forecasting were to carry a compulsory warning on the dangers of extrapolation, just as cigarette packets should carry a compulsory warning on the dangers of smoking.

Mr S. G. B. HENRY (H.M. Treasury): I would like to register my agreement with Dr Bray's emphasis on the importance of control experiments with econometric models. Professor Sargan, in his vote of thanks, argued that such control exercises are not of much value; presumably because he lacks confidence in the ability of econometricians to estimate sufficiently realistic models and to establish appropriate objective functions. Because of these problems he would argue, I think, that control exercises often imply misleading normative decision rules which do not help in the practical problems of regulating the economy. Whilst I agree with a good deal of this scepticism about our ability at present to derive useful decision rules, I would argue that control experiments can be usefully applied to policy-orientated econometric models, particularly macro-models. My argument is simply that estimated models already have implied control behaviour, which depends upon the particular model's general dynamic relationships between objective and control variables, and that these control implications should be explored in a systematic way by assigning an (arbitrary) objective function and going through some maximizing routine. I would regard this merely as part of the investigation of the dynamic properties of the estimated model, the experiments to be done along with such other investigations as, for example, a study of its forecasting behaviour, its dynamic behaviour under policy shocks and the like. Certainly it would not be desirable, I would think, simply to estimate models and leave others to draw dynamic policy implications (and perhaps control-type conclusions about optimal policies) from the model perhaps by using unsystematic methods.

Mr J. P. HUTTON (H.M. Treasury): To a large extent the unease felt by economists about the methods expounded by Dr Bray and by Professors Box and Jenkins arises out of the apparent disregard for economic theory implied by these methods. Economic theory is unfortunately rather untidy and uncertain, so that unique relationships between only two or three clearly defined variables can seldom be postulated. At the same time, as has been pointed out by Dr Bray, economic time-series do not provide enough information satisfactorily to identify the many possible interactions.

It is a reasonable criticism of economists that they do not distinguish between forecasting and structural models: they operate as if they lived in a world where complex structures could be identified with near certainty, so that no conflict need exist between forecasting accuracy and full specification of the economic structure. Nevertheless, if economic theory has any substantive content good structural models must tell us something about cause and effect and hence have forecasting value.

In comparing, therefore, the forecasting accuracy of structural and forecasting models (like Dr Bray's), the criteria must be relevant to the claimed strengths of each method and to the forecasters' own requirements. Over a short period of fairly stable economic activity forecasting one or two years ahead, Bray-type models should have low error variance. But over sufficiently long periods of time to include major shocks or policy changes (war, depressions, exchange rate crises, tariffs wars, economic union, etc.), the structural models should perform more impressively. If, moreover, the forecasters' loss function is such that big errors are very much more costly than small errors, error variance may be an inadequate criterion, and accurate short-term forecasts for 9 years out of 10 may be regarded as a luxury.

The related argument about structural vs reduced-form models is an old one. Present structural estimation methods are at best asymptotically unbiased, while reduced forms are generally impossible to estimate with precision given the shortages of data, collinearity, etc. Dr Bray's solution appears to be smaller models estimated in reduced form, but with more elaborate lag structures than is usual at present.

No one will disagree about the desirability of adequate dynamic specification. What cannot be demonstrated by argument is the value or otherwise of the over-identifying restrictions on the structural equations: that depends on how good the economic theory is, how well represented by the structure, and its demonstration is a matter of adequate comparative tests.

Dr S. J. PRAIS (Graduate Centre for Management Studies, Birmingham): The achievements of economists in establishing useful quantitative relationships for the economy are modest enough, in all truth, for them to welcome assistance from other scientific disciplines. The assistance is doubly welcome when it comes, as in this case, from someone who is not only a scientist but has also been a member of H.M. Government and in that role has taken a close interest in statistics (Dr Bray's masterly handling of the Estimates Committee on Government Statistical Services will be recalled).

Had this paper been rigidly confined to the learned and critical audience here this evening, I would have sat down at this point. But I fear that the *Journal* of our Society falls often into the hands of students not familiar with the background of research in this field, and who may therefore be misled into jumping on an apparently new bandwagon. I should therefore like to warn them against uncritically following the guide-lines for research suggested by our speaker in Section 5 of his paper.

My objection is that in econometric work lags are not at present of the essence of our problem: rather it is to know what are the relevant factors to take into account. If the correct specification of lags had been our problem, we would find that predictions from our equations would be faulty in their timing, but their general level would be correct; in fact we often find that even the trend cannot be correctly predicted because the relevant factors in the period of prediction are not the same as in the sample observations period on which the equations are based. This is brought out by the graphs in Figs. 7 and 12, if we look at the predictions for more than a quarter ahead. From inspection it is not obvious that the predictions are any better than would be given by the classical naïve predictors of "same as last time", or "same as last time plus a trend". The errors in prediction are not randomly distributed, but deviate systematically and increasingly as time proceeds.

What is missing from this paper is a discussion of the *economic factors* that influence the relation between G.D.P. and unemployment. I should like to spend a moment on this in order to illustrate my view that this is the only correct starting point (or, perhaps better, the touchstone) of any econometric investigation.

Movements in unemployment were, until relatively recently, the prime indicator of what was happening to national product, and the two series moved together presumably because general "business-cycle" factors affected both. Today, with full employment policies, the economic situation is entirely changed. If unemployment changes at a given level of G.D.P. it will in large part be due to what are termed "structural" factors, such as regional disequilibrium and lags in adjusting to required changes in the balance of industry as between one branch and another. It is in the nature of economic progress that advances in labour productivity do not take place evenly throughout industry, but tend to be concentrated in particular trades at any time. In those trades, the sequence is that costs fall, prices fall, demand increases, and the total labour required by the industry will fall (though it may rise!) by an amount depending on the price elasticities of demand. The displaced labour has to be absorbed in the less progressive industries, in proportions dependent on income-elasticities of demand. The number of persons unemployed at any time therefore depends on the rate and distribution of technical progress and the ease with which displaced labour is absorbed elsewhere: the latter depends on the incentives for labour to move (presumably inversely related to the levels of redundancy and unemployment benefits) and on whether industry is generally in an expanding or contracting phase as affected by "monetary" factors.

In a few highly simplified sentences I cannot go more deeply into these matters, but I do not believe it is possible to derive a satisfactory understanding of this evening's topic without raising considerations at this level. May I conclude by saying that I can claim no originality for this approach, but that it is the classical position laid down by Tinbergen, Haavelmo and Koopmans in their fundamental papers in the thirties and forties, and it is to these that I would direct the attention of students before any further revolutionary approach in econometrics is accepted as valid.

Mr A. R. THATCHER (Department of Employment): Dr Bray has examined a set of relationships which are of the basic form $U = f(P)$, where U is unemployment, P is the G.D.P. and f is a very complicated function with a very complicated lag structure. However, there is no *a priori* reason to suppose that the G.D.P. is the only factor which affects unemployment. We may expect that unemployment will be affected by changes in employment; and although the number in employment is highly correlated with the G.D.P. it is not a perfect function of it. Other factors like hours of work, holidays and developments in methods and patterns of production can affect the relationship if they change with sufficient abruptness. Moreover, we can expect that unemployment will be affected by changes in the supply of labour, including not only the demographic effects represented by variable D in Fig. 2, but also the effects of changes in the numbers in education.

Another factor which can be expected to affect unemployment is the turnover of labour. Admittedly most of the big changes in unemployment seem to be associated with changes in the number of jobs; but even when the number of jobs is stationary, there is still a continual flow of people changing their jobs. There are about 10 million job-changes each year. In a proportion of these cases the employees concerned will register for a time as unemployed before they start another job, so if more people change their jobs, then unemployment may rise even if there is no change in the number of jobs. We only have direct data on engagements and discharges for the manufacturing industries, but in this sector the turnover of labour in 1966–69 was rather higher than usual. This may help to explain the phenomenon described as "a disturbance passing through the system".

Thus on theoretical grounds one might be tempted to write $U = f(E, L, T)$, where E stands for employment, L for labour supply and T for labour turnover. Of course, this will not be much use as a prediction equation unless we can forecast E, L and T; and if we happen to be in a situation where we can only forecast E as a function of P, and where changes in L and T are expected to be small, then we are back to $U = f(P)$. Nevertheless, the more elaborate equation will still affect our interpretation of the past. Even if we only go so far as to write $U = f(P, H)$, where H stands for "other factors" which reveal their presence as disturbances in Dr Bray's lag structures, then this implies $P = g(U, H)$ and so leaves open the possibility that more than one rate of growth may accompany a given level of unemployment.

Dr Bray also touches on long-term relationships and whether long-term rates of growth are affected by the pressure of demand. On this subject I should like to recommend to those who have not already seen it Phelps Brown's recent book *A Century of Pay*. This contains data on growth rates, prices and wages for five countries over 100 years and throws a great deal of light on the factors which have affected the long-term trends.

Dr P. C. YOUNG (Cambridge University): Dr Bray has presented an interesting paper which has stimulated much discussion. My own comments are restricted to the first part of the paper; namely with the proposed techniques for identifying discrete-time models of dynamic processes. During the past few years in the Control Engineering Group at Cambridge we have been particularly interested in the problem of process identification, and my own work during this time, although principally concerned with the development of discrete methods for identifying processes described by differential equation models (Young, 1965a, b, 1968a, b, 1969a, b, 1970a), shows some similarity, both in concept and detail, with the approach used by Dr Bray. In view of Professor Box's remarks, I should point out that my reason for including exponential weighting (low-pass) filters was to avoid problems associated with differentiation of a noisy signal; the fact that the effect of the filters is "cancelled out" in the manner described by Professor Box is, in fact, essential to the functioning of the differential equation model identification scheme.

I wish to make the following detailed comments on Dr Bray's method of identification; comments that arise directly from our experience at Cambridge and which, I hope, are constructive.

1. The use of the term "regression analysis" tends to imply that the models used are true regression models. It should be stressed, therefore, that they are actually "structural" relationships in which there are measurement errors on those variables (the regressors) associated with the unknown parameters or regression coefficients. As a result, and as Dr Bray points out briefly, the estimates obtained by simple least-squares analysis are generally subject to asymptotic bias. Thus, while the estimated model can be used, as suggested, to obtain a reasonable (although not in general a minimum variance) prediction of the response, any interpretation of the model parameters should be made with great care. If parametric values are required, it is safer to use more sophisticated approaches which recognize that the model is of a structural form; approaches such as that of Box and Jenkins or simpler but less flexible methods such as the Instrumental Variable (e.g. Wong and Polak, 1967) and Generalized Least Squares (Johnson, 1963, p. 193 *et seq.*; Clarke, 1967) procedures. In my own identification studies of this type, a statistically efficient instrumental variable method is used in which the instrumental variables are generated by an adaptive "auxiliary" model of the system under study (Young, 1965b, 1970a).

2. At Cambridge, we have found the use of exponential data weighting for the detection of model variations to be somewhat artificial and inflexible. Our own method of dynamic regression analysis is motivated by the work of R. E. Kalman (1960) on state variable estimation in discrete dynamic systems and is based on the recursive form of the least-squares regression equations. This recursive algorithm is merely a recursive restatement of the normal equations of linear least-squares regression analysis, i.e. using Dr Bray's nomenclature.

$$X'X\,\hat{\mathbf{a}}_t = X'\mathbf{y}$$

or

$$\hat{a}_t = [X'X]^{-1} X'y.$$

The algorithm takes the following form:

$$\hat{a}_t = \hat{a}_{t-1} - P_{t-1}^* \, x_t [x_t' P_{t-1}^* x_t + \sigma^2]^{-1} \{x_t' \hat{a}_{t-1} - y_t\}, \tag{1}$$

$$P_t^* = P_{t-1}^* - P_{t-1}^* \, x_t [x_t' P_{t-1}^* x_t + \sigma^2]^{-1} x_t' P_{t-1}^*, \tag{2}$$

where P_t^* is the estimation error covariance matrix defined as

$$P_t^* \triangleq E\{[a_t - \hat{a}_t] \, [a_t - \hat{a}_t]'\} = \sigma^2 [X'X]^{-1}, \tag{3}$$

while x_t is the vector of regressors $x_i(t)$, $\hat{a}_t$ is the vector of parameter estimates, y_t is the "dependent variable" $y(t)$ and σ^2 is the measurement noise variance.

Another form of (1) is the following:

$$\hat{a}_t = \hat{a}_{t-1} - (P_t^*/\sigma^2) \{x_t \, x_t' \, \hat{a}_{t-1} - x_t \, y_t\} \tag{4}$$

where it will be noted that the term $\{.\}$ is the instantaneous gradient of the least-squares cost function at the tth instant; showing that the recursive least-squares algorithm is, in fact, a multidimensional stochastic gradient (or approximation) algorithm controlled by the weighting matrix P_t^*/σ^2.

The simplest form of dynamic regression analysis requires that we assume the parameter variations are in the form of a random walk, i.e.

$$a_t = a_{t-1} + \eta_t, \tag{5}$$

where a_t is the vector of parameters at the tth instant and η_t is a vector of independent (uncorrelated in time) random variables that supplies a statistical degree of freedom to the parameters, is assumed to be independent of the errors on the data and has a covariance matrix, $E\{\eta_i \, \eta_j'\} = Q \delta_{ij}$, where δ_{ij} is the Kronecker delta function,

$$\delta_{ij} = \begin{cases} 1, & i = j, \\ 0, & i \neq j. \end{cases}$$

By assuming a random walk model for the parameter variations, we have introduced additional prior information into the estimation problem that allows us to make *a priori* updates $\hat{a}_{t/t-1}$ and $P_{t/t-1}^*$ to the estimate $\hat{a}_{t-1}$ and covariance matrix P_{t-1}^* obtained at the $(t-1)$th instant. For instance, since

$$E\{a_t\} = a_{t-1}$$

then

$$\hat{a}_{t/t-1} = \hat{a}_{t-1}. \tag{6}$$

Where the subscript $t/t-1$ indicates the estimate at t based on the estimate at $t-1$ and *a priori* knowledge of the parameter variation law (5). Now, if

$$\tilde{a}_{t/t-1} \triangleq a_t - \hat{a}_{t/t-1}$$

then from (5) and (6)

$$\tilde{a}_{t/t-1} = a_{t-1} + \eta_t - \hat{a}_{t-1};$$

so that, if $a_{t-1} - \hat{a}_{t-1}$ is defined as $\tilde{a}_{t-1}$ and

$$P_{t/t-1}^* \triangleq E\{\tilde{a}_{t/t-1} \, \tilde{a}_{t/t-1}'\},$$

then

$$P_{t/t-1}^* = E\{[\tilde{a}_{t-1} + \eta_t] \, [\tilde{a}_{t-1} + \eta_t]'\};$$

therefore

$$P_{t/t-1}^* = P_{t-1}^* + Q, \tag{7}$$

because

$$P_{t-1}^* \triangleq E\{\tilde{a}_{t-1} \, \tilde{a}_{t-1}'\} \quad \text{and} \quad E\{\tilde{a}_{t-1} \, \eta_t'\} = E\{\eta_t \, \tilde{a}_{t-1}'\} = 0.$$

Equations (6) and (7) can be used to construct the following dynamic least-squares prediction-correction algorithm, i.e. prediction:

$$\hat{\mathbf{a}}_{t/t-1} = \hat{\mathbf{a}}_{t-1}, \tag{8}$$

$$P^*_{t/t-1} = P^*_{t-1} + Q; \tag{9}$$

correction:

$$\hat{\mathbf{a}}_t = \hat{\mathbf{a}}_{t/t-1} - P^*_{t/t-1}\, \mathbf{x}_t[\mathbf{x}'_t\, P^*_{t/t-1}\, \mathbf{x}_t + \sigma^2]^{-1}\{\mathbf{x}'_t\, \hat{\mathbf{a}}_{t/t-1} - y_t\}, \tag{10}$$

$$P^*_t = P^*_{t/t-1} - P^*_{t/t-1}\, \mathbf{x}_t[\mathbf{x}'_t\, P^*_{t/t-1}\, \mathbf{x}_t + \sigma^2]^{-1}\, \mathbf{x}'_t\, P^*_{t/t-1}. \tag{11}$$

Since equation (8) is redundant, these equations differ from the basic least-squares algorithm (equations (1) and (2)) only because of the presence of the covariance prediction equation (9).

In practice, the algorithm (8) $\rightarrow$ (10) can be used in a similar manner to the recursive least-squares algorithm with exponential data weighting. While it is certainly no more complicated to program on a digitial computer, it is inherently more elegant and flexible. For instance, Q can be specified as a diagonal matrix (thus implying uncorrelated parameter variations) with diagonal elements reflecting the expected rates of variation of the parameters composing the parameter vector $\mathbf{a}_t$. In this way, different rates of parameter variation, including a mixture of variable and stationary parameters, can be handled rather easily; thus providing a requirement hinted at by Dr Bray in his section "New Systems and Series". Perhaps more important still, the algorithm is capable of further development should more sophisticated models than the random walk of (5) be available. For example, the algorithm obtained for the general linear model,

$$\mathbf{a}_t = \Phi \mathbf{a}_{t-1} + \Gamma \eta_t,$$

where $\Phi = \Phi(t, t-1)$ and $\Gamma = \Gamma(t, t-1)$ are appropriately defined transition and indical matrices, has been used to estimate the rapidly time variable parameters associated with the dynamic equations of a guided missile (Young, 1969c).

I must apologize for going into so much detail in this simplified derivation of the dynamic regression equations. However, it seems to me that one important difference between Economics and the Natural Sciences is its inherent characteristic of continual structural change. If modelling of economic systems is ever to work satisfactorily, therefore, I feel (as I believe does Dr Bray) that it is necessary that the most sophisticated statistical tools are available to detect significant structural changes and so improve the models predictive ability. The estimation procedure outlined above provides such a tool when models are of the non-mechanistic (black box) type.

In the case of mechanistic (structurally important) state-space models of dynamic systems, the relinearized or extended Kalman filter method of estimating state variables and parameters simultaneously (see Licht, 1970, for continuous-time models; Mehra, 1970, for discrete-time models) appears to be the best currently available general approach to the problem.

This method considers unknown stationary or time variable model parameters as additional state variables and then adjoins them to the state vector. Although the resulting estimation problem is naturally non-linear even for a linear system model, it is possible to apply techniques similar to those of Kalman by using the concept of statistical linearization about the current estimates.

For those not acquainted with Kalman's pioneering work on state variable estimation (Kalman, 1960), I should point out that the discrete Kalman filter-estimator is a general recursive linear estimation procedure that allows directly for non-stationary effects and has wide applicability. I find it somewhat worrying, therefore, that many mathematical statisticians are not acquainted with this work; I would have thought it is of fundamental importance not only in the field of control but also in a more general context.

3. Dr Bray rightly refers to the work of Box and Jenkins. I would merely point out that Åström and Bohlin (1965) and later Bohlin (1970) have carried out conceptually very similar work which is certainly worthy of mention and seems to have attracted more general attention, particularly in the control engineering community. Other work relevant to the present discussion has been carried out by Clarke (1967), Wong and Polak (1967), Hastings-James (1969), Panuska (1969), Peterka and Smuk (1969), Young (1970b), Young and Hastings-James (1970) and others.

4. Dr Bray refers to the possibility of analysing the behaviour of the recursive residuals (the "innovation process", as it would be termed by the control engineer) and utilizing the information to update the exponential weighting parameter, b. The work of Jazwinski (1970) and others on adaptive Kalman filtering uses such an approach to adjust the covariance matrix of the process disturbances. Noting the similarities between the dynamic regression analysis referred to in paragraph 2, above, and Kalman filtering, it is easy to see how, in theory, the covariance matrix Q of parameter variations could be similarly adjusted. Nevertheless, the practical utility of such a scheme would need considerable investigation.

5. During my own work on identifying differential equation models, I used filter sets which are virtually continuous-time analogs of the discrete filters used by Dr Bray. I did detect certain "identifiability" problems, with such filters and have discussed this briefly elsewhere (Young, 1968a). In essence, the high correlation between various similarly filtered functions of the input and output variables did lead to high variance on the parameter estimates, as indicated by high values of certain of the multiple correlation coefficients R_{z_i} associated with the regression of $x_i(t)$ on the remainder of the regressors. Whether such problems can arise with the sort of models and data used by Dr Bray, I do not know, but I would be interested in his comments. I should stress that, for the sort of applications envisaged by Dr Bray, this point is of only academic interest since it has been my experience that, while the parametric estimation variance can be very high, the predictive ability of the model remains very good.

6. Finally, although up to this point I have carefully refrained from any comments on the economic aspects of the paper, I would like to make a layman's comment and hope that it is accepted in the spirit with which it is given. As a complete newcomer to the academic world of economics, I was surprised to hear Dr J. K. Galbraith imply recently that the Keynesian economics are dead! My own feeling is that the Keynesian analysis of the economic situation was intuitively based and still has a lot to offer, provided that the new influential factors that have entered since his time are taken into account. (As Robert Lekachman has said, "Keynes does not cease to be relevant. He becomes relevant in different ways and in different company.") Certainly Keynes's emphasis on fairly simple, albeit pseudo-steady-state models is refreshing to someone like myself who has previously only seen rather complex models of the economy. I am probably very wrong, but it seems to me that combination of simple but inherently time-variable *dynamic* models with sophisticated methods of time-variable parameter estimation offers one approach to economic analysis not yet investigated but certainly worthy of consideration.

The author replied in writing as follows: I am grateful for the many useful points made in the discussion, and regret I cannot refer to them all.

The Jorgenson general rational function-distributed lag model proposed by Professor Sargan would in fact give larger serially correlated residuals, since the implied noise model is more restricted. Professor Sargan ignores the possibility, referred to later by Professor Box and Dr Young, that factors in $P(D)$, $Q(D)$ and $K(D)$ may cancel out, or nearly so. I believe Professor Sargan underestimates the insights and benefits that the application of control theory can now offer to economics. Major advances have been made in control theory itself in the 13 years since the work of Phillips and Theil to which he refers. Also for the United Kingdom, quarterly national income data are only available back to 1955 and, as Professor Westcott said, the data are only now becoming sufficient to identify, estimate and validate the stochastic relationships needed. I would welcome tests (that econometricians would use) which would identify specific incorrect constraints in models. But systematic tests of the error distribution of predictions beyond sample periods and for longer lags, as in my paper, are readily understandable, as well as crucial. Had these tests been applied in much published work they would have shown the inadequacy of many econometric estimations without having to wait for the often disillusioning test of experience. Livesey's control model is a valuable pioneering work; further work could with advantage use Box and Jenkins' estimations of equations, instead of previously accepted forms, leading to fully stochastic control methods. I agree with Mr Henry that it is not desirable to draw dynamic policy implications by unsystematic methods, as at present, particularly with stochastic behaviour as important as it seems to be.

I appreciate Professor Jenkins' application of his methods to the same data, and look forward to seeing his expected and actual forecast errors, and any evidence he can find on longer-term behaviour. I plead guilty on all the counts raised by Professor Box. Since my results are so similar to those found by Professor Jenkins, perhaps Professor Box will accept that my choice of weighting functions is not entirely arbitrary and seems appropriate to many non-seasonal quarterly economic time series. It is the form of the auto-regressive and moving average coefficients (shown in Fig. 10) that matter: the important requirement is that their true values should be well approximated by linear sums of the weighting functions. Nevertheless, I accept that Box and Jenkins' methods, properly used, are preferable to mine.

Mr Shepherd says that in practice adjustments ("residuals") are added to expected values in the Godley–Shepherd method to reflect autocorrelation properties and forecasters' judgments about factors not correctly incorporated in the model. If the adjustments are forecast for different possible out-turns of exogenous variables (in this case for different possible movements of G.D.P.), then it is possible to check forecasts after the event. If adjustments are made for only one possible out-turn of exogenous variables, and often this does not materialize, then the forecast itself is meaningless, with no connection with the real world, and its use in policy making is spurious. If there is no sense in which a forecast can be validated after the event, the forecast is not false, but meaningless. In fact the Godley–Shepherd forecasts have given significant results when checked after the event, and I am glad Mr Shepherd agrees that forecasting ability is a relevant test of economic analysis which has not been used as much as it might be. Any judgment of external factors which could usefully improve the forecasts could equally well be applied with the methods of this paper, or of Box and Jenkins. Since the meeting (Bray, 1971) I have compared Godley–Shepherd and my B2 forecasts on data up to 1971 second quarter, and suggested that the manual "adjustment of residuals" outlined by Shepherd might have been misleading in the management of the economy in 1971.

As Mr Hutton suggests, the links between economic theory, the measurement of economic variables and equations relating these variables are not rigid and fully defined. So I do not accept the suggestion Mr Shepherd seems to make that my method does not purport to describe economic behaviour. I have in mind a wide variety of mechanisms by which I have experienced and observed production in factories, companies and industries affecting employment and the unemployed in towns and regions, and I have observed the different ways in which, over time, these have combined to produce variations in national aggregates. I have felt that the concepts of the Godley–Shepherd equations have oversimplified this behaviour in respect of its stochastics (or type of unpredictability), dynamics (not merely time lags, but the implication that possible growth is independent of past levels of demand), and the relative importance of these and of hours worked and population effects. I have felt that the introduction of the shadow variable "productive potential" in an attempt to describe dynamic behaviour had no industrial or statistical basis and may have seriously prejudiced the making of economic policy. So I sought a form of equation which could accommodate the shifting combinations of behaviour that occur and which could play back the statistics of behaviour that can be expected from different exogenous behaviour in the future, using the evidence of the past. That the equation, or recording device, could also be used for other systems makes it no less "economic". The merit of Box and Jenkins' method is that it is still less constrained, less tied to any one "mechanism" and better able to record economic behaviour. By contrast, Almon lags impose heavy and unnatural constraints on distributed lags, and their combination with postulated auto-correlation structures is likely to produce some curious results.

This problem of the embodiment of economic theory in the form of equations to be estimated can be expressed thus. A form of equation A that accommodated the whole of an economic theory (i.e. allows any behaviour consistent with the theory), and nothing but the theory (i.e. excludes any behaviour inconsistent with the theory), would make beter use of data if the theory is correct, than a form B which accommodated not only the whole of a theory but also alternatives to the theory. If, however, form A is used and the test of forecasting beyond the sample periods and comparing errors with the expected forecast errors fails, then the theory is incorrect, or form A in fact excludes behaviour consistent with the theory. This seems to happen with the Godley–Shepherd equations. If form B passes the test (as the $B2$ equation does) then the estimated equation is not only a theory, but a theory validated by the data. It is probably the case that most equations in the econometric literature impose constraints which exclude behaviour consistent with the economic theory they purport to represent, in that their treatment of dynamics and stochastics is more restrictive than that required by the theory. If a form is more general than any acceptable theory requires, the estimation will narrow down the alternatives to one, and the error test will check its validity. If a form is less general than a theory requires, the estimation process cannot break any offending constraint. There is no justification for saying that form A is more soundly based in economics (as distinct from a particular economic theory) than form B. Indeed, it is less soundly based if form A fails the error test.

Mr Shepherd is right when he says that neither projections over different time horizons from a given point nor projections from different starting points are wholly independent. The latter affects significantly only my 8-step errors, and the effect there, as mentioned in the paper, is equivalent to reducing the degrees of freedom by 1 in the total of 23. Allowance should be made for the former, particularly for 1- and 2-step predictions, reducing the degreees of freedom by about 3. The evidence for this lies in the autoregressive coefficients shown in Fig. 10. The combined effects scarcely affect the conclusion.

Mr Hutton distinguishes between forecasting and structural models. But structural forms can be used for forecasting, and economic theory is as closely linked to reduced forms as it is to structural forms. The distinction between structural and reduced forms was introduced into econometrics to deal, rather unsatisfactorily, with certain estimation problems. The distinction is not made as such in Box and Jenkins' methods or thoery. I do not argue necessarily for smaller models estimated in reduced form, but for that combination of the sophistication (or "parsimony") of dynamics, and the selection of variables, which gives the best predictions (and in due course control), given the available data. And I do suggest that present practice errs on the side of too many variables and too crude dynamics and stochastics, with inadequate testing of results. Also I doubt whether traditional models are as shock-proof over long time periods where uninterrupted series are available as appropriate Box–Jenkins' models with equal access to economic theories valid for the data, but I agree this should be tried. Dr Prais implies that dynamics and stochastics is merely a matter of lags—of saying when an otherwise defined effect will be observed. But there is more to the difference between a whimper and a bang—a little matter of dynamics—than whether it occurs this week or next. The wider range of economic relationships to which Dr Prais refers needs studies similar to that of this paper. Equations 12 to 15 effectively incorporate the "classical naïve" model tests.

I agree with Mr Thatcher that there are plenty of other factors which leave open the possibility that more than one rate of growth can accompany a given level of unemploy-ment. Also, it is not explicitly stated in the paper that the $B2$ equation gives a short-term relation between the rate of growth and the rate of change of unemployment, with no necessary long term correspondence between G.D.P. and the absolute level of unemployment.

Dr Young's filter sets, of which I was not aware, are indeed very similar to the filters I used. I agree with Dr Young on the relevance to economics of the work on system identification to which he refers. The range of techniques available is so wide that only close attention to practical problems in economic management on actual data will make it possible to select, develop and apply appropriate methods of system identification and control. In my view, economists will find it most rewarding first to digest the methods of Box and Jenkins and of Åström and Bohlin on identification and estimation, and then develop the application of adaptive stochastic control methods appropriate to the problem.

REFERENCES IN THE DISCUSSION

ÅSTRÖM, K. J. and BOHLIN, T. (1965). Numerical identification of linear dynamic systems from normal operating records. In *Theory of Self Adaptive Control Systems* (P. H. Hammond, ed.). New York: Plenum Press.

BOHLIN, T. (1970). On the maximum likelihood method of identification. *I.B.M. Jnl. of Res. and Dev.*, **14**, 41–51.

BRAY, J. W. (1971). Will there be a million unemployed? *The Guardian*, 28 June, 14.

CLARKE, D. W. (1967). Generalized least squares estimation of the parameters of a dynamic model. Paper 3.17 at the IFAC Symposium on Identification in Automatic Control Systems, Prague.

HASTINGS-JAMES, R. (1969). Recursive generalized least squares procedure for on-line identification of process parameters. *Proc. I.E.E.*, **116**, No. 12.

JAZWINSKI, A. H. (1970). *Stochastic Processes and Filtering Theory*, pp. 311 *et seq*. New York: Academic Press.

JOHNSON, J. (1963). *Econometric Methods* (Int. Stud. Edition). New York: McGraw-Hill.

KALMAN, R. E. (1960). A new approach to linear filtering and prediction theory. *Trans. A.S.M.E.*, *J. Basic Engng*, **82-D**, 35–45.

LICHT, B. W. (1970). Approximations in optimal non-linear filtering. Report No. SRC 70-1, Systems Research Center, Case Western Reserve University.

MEHRA, R. K. (1970). A comparison of several non-linear filters for re-entry vehicle tracking. *Proc. 9th I.E.E.E. Symposium on Adaptive Processes*. New York: I.E.E.E.

PANUSKA, V. (1969). An adaptive recursive least squares identification algorithm. *Proc. 8th I.E.E.E. Symp. Adapt. Processes*. Pittsburgh: Pennsylvania State University.

PETERKA, V. and SMUK, K. (1969). On-line estimation of dynamic model parameters from input–output data. *Preprints 4th IFAC Congress*, Warsaw.

PHELPS BROWN, E. H. (1968). *A Century of Pay*. London: Macmillan.

WONG, K. Y. and POLAK, E. (1967). Identification of linear discrete-time systems using an instrumental variable method. *Trans. I.E.E.E. on Automatic Control*, **AC-12**, 707–718.

YOUNG, P. C. (1965a). The determination of the parameters of a dynamic process. *Radio and Electron. Engr.* **29**, 345–361.

—— (1965b). Process parameter estimation and self-adaptive control. In *Theory of Self-adaptive Control Systems* (P. H. Hammond, ed.). New York: Plenum Press.

—— (1968a). Identification problems associated with the equation error approach to process parameter estimation. *Proc. 2nd Asilomar Conf. on Circuits and Systems*, pp. 416–422. New York: I.E.E.E.

—— (1968b). The use of linear regression and related procedures for the identification of dynamic processes. *Proc. 7th I.E.E.E. Symp. Adapt. Processes*. New York: I.E.E.E.

—— (1969a). Applying parameter estimation to dynamic systems. *Control Engng*, **16**, Nos. 10 and 11.

—— (1969b). The differential equation error method of real-time process identification. Ph.D. Thesis, Control Engineering Group, Cambridge University.

—— (1969c). On the use of *a priori* parameter variation information to enhance the performance of a recursive least squares estimator. Technical Note TN404-90, Naval Weapons Center, China Lake, California.

YOUNG, P. C. (1970a). An instrumental variable method for real-time identification of a noisy process. *Automatica*, 6, 271–287.

—— (1970b). An extension to the instrumental variable method for the indentification of a noisy dynamic process. Cambridge University, Control Engineering Group Research Note CN/70/1.

—— and HASTINGS-JAMES, R. (1970). Identification and control of discrete-time systems subject to disturbances with rational spectral density. Paper read at the 9th I.E.E.E. Symposium on Adaptive Processes, "Decision and Control", Austin, Texas.

Some Comments on a Paper of Coen, Gomme and Kendall

By George E. P. Box[1] and Paul Newbold[2]

University of Wisconsin

[Received July 1970. Revised February 1971]

Summary

The method of analysis used in a recent paper on economic forecasting is reviewed. Evidence is presented that what were believed to be highly significant relationships making possible the forecasting of the *Financial Times* share index arise because of the inflexibility of the assumed error structure.

1. Introduction

In a recent publication, by Coen, Gomme and Kendall (1969) which for convenience we refer to as the C.G.K. paper, the forecasting of the *Financial Times* ordinary share index using various other lagged series is discussed. It is sufficient for illustration to consider relation (7) of the C.G.K. paper which we write as

$$Y_t = \alpha + \beta_1 X_{1,t-6} + \beta_2 X_{2,t-i} + n_t \tag{1}$$

which is projected to obtain forecasts. In this expression the "output" Y_t is the *Financial Times* ordinary share index. The two "inputs" are $X_{1,t}$, United Kingdom car production, and $X_{2,t}$, the *Financial Times* commodity index, and n_t is an error term. Quarterly data were employed yielding time series containing 51 successive observations. Of course this is only one of a number of such relationships which the authors postulate. However, it is their methods which we are doubtful about and our reservations would apply equally to their other analyses.

The authors built their model (1) by cross-correlating the detrended series which in this instance were the residuals remaining after fitting linear least-squares regressions on time to each series. For example, Fig. 1(a) shows a plot of the sample cross-correlation function† between the *Financial Times* share index (Y_t detrended) and United Kingdom car production ($X_{1,t}$ detrended). The authors display this cross-correlation for positive lags only (Y leading X) and note that a moderately large cross-correlation occurs near lag 5 or 6. The choice of lags for the independent variables in the linear regrassion was made by initially including among the regressors an independent variable at several different lags close to the value where the sample cross-correlation was a maximum in absolute value. A stepwise regression program was used to determine which lags should be included in the final equation. Values of Student's t-statistic of 14·1 and $-9·9$ were computed for the estimates of the parameters β_1 and β_2 in (1) and these appeared to be very highly significant. The authors were thus led to believe, for example, that car production six quarters previously and the *Financial Times* commodity index seven quarters previously could be used to forecast

---

[1] At University of Essex in 1971.

[2] Now at University of Nottingham.

† Our calculated cross-correlations differ somewhat from those given in the C.G.K. paper; however, the general pattern is similar.

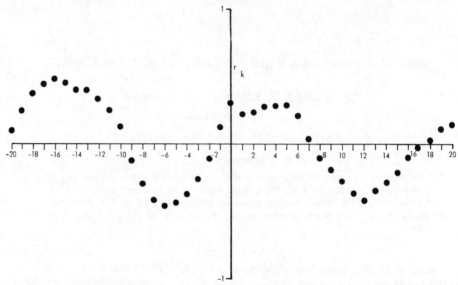

FIG. 1(a). Sample cross-correlations r_k between the *Financial Times* share index (detrended) and lagged values of United Kingdom car production (detrended). Fifty-one pairs of observations.

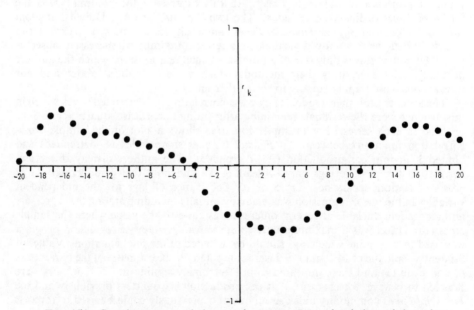

FIG. 1(b). Sample cross-correlations r_k between two unrelated detrended random walks generated from the first two columns of Wold's table of random normal deviates. Fifty pairs of observations.

the *Financial Times* ordinary share index. Because it was felt that the method of detrending itself might give rise to a cross-correlation effect the paper includes an appendix by E. M. L. Beale which shows that *if* individual series were of the form

$$X_t = \alpha + \beta t + a_t, \qquad (2)$$

where a_t are assumed to be independent identically distributed random deviates, then the serial correlations of the residuals obtained when (2) is fitted by ordinary least squares would not differ much from those of a_t unless the sample size was small, thus indicating that sample cross-correlations such as those of Fig. 1 were not created by the detrending procedure. They, furthermore, conducted sampling experiments in which cross-correlations of residuals from detrended *random* series were plotted. They remark that the resulting diagrams are sufficiently unlike the *smooth* curves (see Fig. 1) which characterized the cross-correlations of the economic series as "to indicate that the latter are not artefacts created by the trend removal process, at least so far as concerns random residuals".

We believe that the authors were right to suspect that the apparent lagged relationships which they found might be produced by an artefact. The object of this report is to present evidence that this is so, and to show that this happens because of the inappropriateness of the error structure chosen.

2. EXAMINATION OF THE PROPOSED MODEL

In this paper we suppose throughout that $\dots a_t, a_{t-1}, a_{t-2}, \dots$ are a sequence of *independent* identically distributed random variables having means equal to zero. We shall subsequently call this a *white noise* process.

Let us consider equation (1). Allowing for detrending, the model may be written

$$Y_t = \alpha + \beta_0 t + \beta_1 X_{1,t-6} + \beta_2 X_{2,t-7} + n_t. \qquad (3)$$

A critical assumption on which the C.G.K. analysis hangs is that the n_t's, representing error or "noise", are independent identically distributed random variables. Thus, by employing ordinary least squares, it is tacitly assumed that $n_t = a_t$.

However, it must surely be rare that the noise structure for economic models of this kind can be so represented. One might suspect instead that the n_t's were dependent and possibly best represented by some stable non-stationary noise model such as one in which the first difference of the noise was represented by a stationary process. A particular noise structure which has often proved useful in applications of this kind is the integrated moving average or "noisy random walk".

$$n_t = (1 - \theta) \sum_{j=1}^{\infty} a_{t-j} + a_t, \quad -1 < \theta \leqslant 1, \qquad (4)$$

where the a_t's are independent but for $\theta \neq 1$ the n_t's can be highly dependent.

Characteristics of the integrated moving average model of special interest are:

(i) It may alternatively be written as an infinite autogressive process in which the autogressive weights diminish exponentially

$$n_t = (1 - \theta)(n_{t-1} + \theta n_{t-1} + \theta^2 n_{t-2} + \dots) + a_t$$

with θ between zero and unity. The model thus exponentially discounts past information.

(ii) It follows, as was first shown in Muth (1960), that the model produces the widely used exponentially weighted average as an optimal forecast.

(iii) The model can be written in the convenient alternative form

$$\nabla n_t = a_t - \theta a_{t-1}$$

which implies that the first difference $\nabla n_t = n_t - n_{t-1}$ of the noise is a first-order moving average process and is therefore readily identifiable.

(iv) In the special case $\theta = 1$ we obtain the noise structure assumed in the C.G.K. paper.

(v) In the special case $\theta = 0$ we obtain a noise model which is a pure random walk.

(vi) For intermediate values we have the discounted disturbance structure of (i) which often provides a satisfactory representation of noise in economic series models.

We may now substitute the alternative noise structure (4) in (3) and regard θ as a parameter to be estimated along with the other parameters. If the estimate of θ is close to unity then the simpler error structure assumed in the C.G.K. paper will be vindicated.

After substituting the augmented error structure and differencing we obtain

$$y_t = \beta_0 + \beta_1 x_{1,t-6} + \beta_2 x_{2,t-i} + a_t - \theta a_{t-1},$$

where

$$y_t = Y_t - Y_{t-1}, \quad x_{1,t} = X_{1,t} - X_{1,t-1},$$

$$x_{2,t} = X_{2,t} - X_{2,t-1} \quad \text{and} \quad a_t - \theta a_{t-1} = n_t - n_{t-1}.$$

Now the model may be written in the form

$$a_t = \theta a_{t-1} + y_t - \beta_0 - \beta_1 x_{1,t-6} - \beta_2 x_{2,t-7},$$

whence we may recursively compute the quantities $a_t = (a_t | \theta, \beta_0, \beta_1, \beta_2)$ from $t = 8$ onwards for any given choice of parameters. It will make little practical difference if the starting value of a_7 in this recursion is set equal to its unconditional expected value of zero, or if it too is treated as a parameter to be estimated. In either case the least-squares estimates of the parameters obtained by minimizing $\sum (a_t | \theta, \beta_0, \beta_1, \beta_2)^2$, where summation extends over the whole sample, will closely approximate maximum-likelihood estimates (Barnard *et al.*, 1962).

The least-squares estimates with their approximate standard errors obtained from an iterative nonlinear squares fit are as follows:

$$\hat{\theta} = -0 \cdot 06 \pm 0 \cdot 15, \quad \hat{\beta}_0 = 1 \cdot 78 \pm 2 \cdot 71,$$

$$\hat{\beta}_1 = 0 \cdot 00016 \pm 0 \cdot 00009, \quad \hat{\beta}_2 = -1 \cdot 16 \pm 1 \cdot 18.$$

The analysis is remarkably revealing.

(1) The value of $\hat{\theta}$ is close to zero and not to unity implying that the noise structure is very different from that assumed in the C.G.K. paper and is in fact like a random walk.

(2) While one of the four estimates $(\hat{\beta}_1)$ is $1 \cdot 78$ times its standard error, this can hardly be regarded as unusual. Thus with the less restrictive error structure there is no real evidence of any relation at all between the output on the one

hand and the two lagged inputs on the other hand. Thus among the class of models considered there is in fact little reason to question the unsophisticated model

$$\nabla Y_t = a_t,$$

which implies that Y_t is approximately a random walk and agrees with the frequently confirmed conclusion of Bachelier (1900) concerning the behaviour of stock prices.

(3) It would follow in particular if this model were appropriate that an observation at time $t+l$ could be expressed in terms of that at time t by the equation

$$Y_{t+l} = Y_t + \sum_{j=t+1}^{t+l} a_j.$$

Now (see, for example, Whittle, 1963) the minimum mean-square error (m.m.s.e.) forecast $\hat{Y}_t(l)$ of Y_{t+l} made at origin t for lead time l is given by taking expected values conditional on available knowledge at the time origin t. Hence the m.m.s.e. forecast for l steps ahead would be independent of the inputs $X_{1,t-6}$ and $X_{2,t-7}$ and would be simply the current value of the output

$$\hat{Y}_t(l) = Y_t. \tag{5}$$

The more general error structure proposed above might of course still be unduly restrictive. This could be checked in two ways:

  (i) by considering other error structures;
  (ii) by examining the behaviour of residuals from the fitted models.
A noise structure which presents a plausible alternative to the integrated moving average (4) is a low-order autoregressive process such as the second-order process

$$n_t = \phi_1 n_{t-1} + \phi_2 n_{t-2} + a_t. \tag{6}$$

It is to be noted that with $\phi_1 = 1$ and $\phi_2 = 0$ this coincides with the random walk model $\nabla n_t = a_t$. Thus the two classes of models represented by (4) and (6) intersect at the random walk.

Table 1 summarizes the results from fitting various models and it will be seen that the calculations confirm that the noise model is approximately a random walk. Furthermore, pronounced residual autocorrelations from the C.G.K. model are evident with a highly significant value for the Durbin and Watson (1951) statistic but, no such evidence of inadequacy is found for the other models.

3. Cross-Correlation Patterns of Random Walks

The apparent relationships in the C.G.K. paper between economic series have a number of puzzling aspects. For example, we see from our Fig. 1(a) that when cross-correlations with negative as well as positive lags are plotted one finds even larger cross-correlations existing at negative lags than those found in the C.G.K. paper at positive lags. This might suggest on the reasoning of that paper that the stock prices might be used to forecast car production instead of vice versa. And *a priori* this seems at least equally plausible.

The question thus arises of how cross-correlation patterns of this kind can have arisen. The answer involves the structure of the individual series which are not adequately represented by the classical regression model

$$X_t = \alpha + \beta t + a_t,$$

but rather require a model closer to the random walk form

$$\nabla X_t = \beta + a_t,$$

that is,

$$X_t = X_{t-1} + \beta + a_t$$

or equivalently

$$X_t = \alpha + \beta t + \sum_{j=0}^{\infty} a_{t-j}.$$

TABLE 1

Estimates and standard errors of coefficients in equation (3) for various noise structures

Assumed structure for noise in Y_t	White noise (C.G.K.) $n_t = a_t$	Integrated moving average $n_t = a_t$ $+(1-\theta)\sum_{j=1}^{\infty} a_{t-j}$	Second-order autoregressive $n_t = \phi_1 n_{t-1}$ $+\phi_2 n_{t-2} + a_t$	First-order autoregressive $n_t = \phi_1 n_{t-1} + a_t$	Random walk $n_t = \sum_{j=0}^{\infty} a_{t-j}$
α	653 ± 57		306 ± 108	318 ± 106	
β_0		$1\cdot78 \pm 2\cdot7$	$2\cdot31 \pm 1\cdot0$	$2\cdot04 \pm 1\cdot1$	$1\cdot74 \pm 2\cdot6$
β_1	$0\cdot00047 \pm 0\cdot00004$	$0\cdot00016 \pm 0\cdot00009$	$0\cdot00017 \pm 0\cdot00009$	$0\cdot00018 \pm 0\cdot00009$	$0\cdot00017 \pm 0\cdot00008$
β_2	$-6\cdot13 \pm 0\cdot62$	$-1\cdot16 \pm 1\cdot18$	$-1\cdot76 \pm 1\cdot22$	$-1\cdot87 \pm 1\cdot18$	$-1\cdot27 \pm 1\cdot17$
θ		$-0\cdot06 \pm 0\cdot15$			
ϕ_1			$0\cdot93 \pm 0\cdot16$	$0\cdot82 \pm 0\cdot10$	
ϕ_2			$-0\cdot14 \pm 0\cdot16$		
σ_a^2	497	321	299	298	315
Durbin–Watson statistic	Significant at 1 per cent	Not significant	Not significant	Not significant	Not significant

To gain preliminary insight into the behaviour of cross-correlations between series generated by models of this latter kind, a sampling experiment was performed as follows.

Each column of Wold's table of random normal deviates contains 50 entries. The first five columns on the first page of the table could therefore be used to generate five random walks of 50 observations by computing cumulative sums of column entries. The five independent random walk series so obtained were detrended as in the C.G.K. paper and the sample cross-correlations between each pair computed. Fig. 1(b) shows the cross-correlation function between the series generated from the first two columns of the random deviates. It has a pattern typical of those found for the other pairs.

Now persuasive features of the cross-correlation patterns in the C.G.K. paper, to which the authors have drawn attention are:

  (i) their smoothness;

  (ii) the large absolute magnitude of the biggest cross-correlation.

But it is exactly these features which are displayed by the cross-correlations of the independent random walks. In particular the largest in absolute value of the cross-correlations found and, in brackets, the lag at which this correlation appeared is shown in Table 2.

TABLE 2

Largest cross-correlations (with lag in brackets) found between independent random walks generated from the first five columns of Wold's table of random normal deviates

Column \ Column	2	3	4	5
1	−0·48(5)	−0·42(5)	0·50(−9)	−0·48(8)
2		0·51(1)	0·53(5)	0·54(4)
3			0·49(4)	−0·35(−16)
4				−0·79(18)
5				

Suppose we now treat one detrended random walk series as the detrended "input" X'_t and another as the detrended "output" Y'_t and following the C.G.K. paper fit by ordinary least squares the usual regression model

$$Y'_t = \alpha + \beta X'_{t-j} + a_t,$$

where j is chosen to give the maximum cross-correlation. Then applying the standard t-test it is readily confirmed that *every one* of the ten pairs of series yields a regression "significantly different" from zero *at least* at the 5 per cent point, even though the series are in fact independent.

In the C.G.K. paper the authors mention that much of the early work was done by graphing the series on transparencies to a roughly comparable scale, superposing them and sliding along the time axis to see whether there was any fairly obvious coincident variation. Their Fig. 1 is such a superposition which seemingly shows a remarkably close relationship. Where high cross-correlation is found at the particular lag we would expect to be able to visually demonstrate the relationship by this graphical technique and vice versa. It may be asked then whether a visual impression of a relationship is obtained when two unrelated random walks are treated in this way. Fig. 2 shows the plot for independent random walks 2 and 4 obtained from Wold's random deviates detrended, comparably scaled, and at lag 5 where maximum correlation is produced. The apparent relationship is partly due to the flexibility allowed in what is treated as similar—we can in effect adjust for location, spread, trend and lag before we need find similarity, partly due to the comparative smoothness of what is to be compared—to find a correlation only *a few* detrended rescaled and suitably lagged bumps have to roughly match, and partly due to selection process— among n series there are $\frac{1}{2}n(n-1)$ pairs of series that could show such an apparent relationship.

The reason for the smoothness and large absolute magnitudes of the cross correlations is readily explained from a theoretical viewpoint as follows.

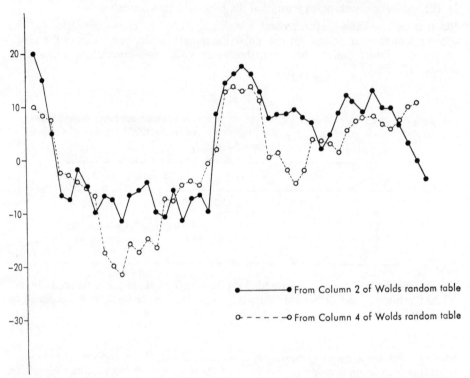

$\bullet$——$\bullet$ From Column 2 of Wolds random table

$\circ$ – – – – $\circ$ From Column 4 of Wolds random table

FIG. 2. A plot of comparably scaled and detrended independent random walks at lag 5.

Smoothness

Suppose we have a series of n values generated by the random walk process

$$(X_t - X_{t-1}) - \beta_1 = U_t$$

or

$$x_t - \beta_1 = U_t$$

and N values of Y generated similarly by

$$(Y_t - Y_{t-1}) - \beta_2 = V_t$$

or

$$y_t - \beta_2 = V_t$$

where U_t and V_t are independent white noise processes and let us define the cross-covariance between the differences x_t and y_t as

$$C_k^* = (N-1)^{-1} \sum_{t=2}^{N-k} (x_t - \bar{x})(y_{t+k} - \bar{y}).$$

Now, suppose we postulate trend relationships of the form

$$X_t = \alpha_1 + \beta_1 t + e_{1,t}$$

and

$$Y_t = \alpha_2 + \beta_2 t + e_{2,t},$$

and let $\hat{\alpha}_1$, $\hat{\alpha}_2$, $\hat{\beta}_1$ and $\hat{\beta}_2$ be *any* estimators of α_1, α_2, β_1 and β_2. The detrended series are then

$$X'_t = X_t - \hat{\alpha}_1 - \hat{\beta}_1 t,$$

$$Y'_t = Y_t - \hat{\alpha}_2 - \hat{\beta}_2 t,$$

and the sample cross-covariances for the detrended series are

$$C_k = N^{-1} \sum_{t=1}^{N-k} (X'_t - \bar{X}')(Y'_{t+k} - \bar{Y}'). \tag{7}$$

It is shown in the appendix that for moderate or large sample sizes to a close approximation

$$\nabla^2 C_{k+1} = -C_k^*. \tag{8}$$

Now (see, for example, Bartlett, 1955) the cross-covariances C_k^* between two independent white noise processes are independently distributed about zero with constant variance. Thus writing $e_k = -C_{k-1}^*$ the e_k's form a white noise process and the C_k's satisfy the difference equation

$$\nabla^2 C_k = e_k$$

the solution of which may be written

$$C_k = \sum_{i=0}^{\infty} \sum_{j=0}^{\infty} e_{k-i-j}.$$

Thus on the assumption made the cross-covariances C_k themselves follow a highly *non-stationary* stochastic process—the cumulative sum of a cumulative sum of random deviates. The appearance of any particular series of cross-covariances and hence of the corresponding cross-correlations is bound therefore to be smooth. Thus with the assumptions made, even though X and Y are generated by independent processes, their cross-covariances and hence their cross-correlations will wander about in a smooth pattern peculiar to each generating set of random numbers, in much the same way as was found for the economic series in the C.G.K. paper. This will be so irrespective of whether, or in which way, the series are detrended.

Size

The above can explain the smooth appearance of the cross-correlations, there remains the question of their large size. The variance of the sample cross-correlations r_k between two independent normal sequences X and Y is given (Bartlett, 1955) approximately by

$$\text{var}(r_k) = (n-k)^{-1} \sum_{\nu=-\infty}^{+\infty} \rho_{xx}(\nu)\, \rho_{yy}(\nu),$$

where $\rho_{xx}(\nu)$ and $\rho_{yy}(\nu)$ are the theoretical autocorrelations. This variance is $(n-k)^{-1}$ for series which are not autocorrelated. However, it can be substantially inflated for correlated sequences. For example, suppose the series under study can be represented by unrelated first-order autoregressive processes each with parameter ϕ.

Then substitution yields

$$\text{var}\,(r_k) = (n-k)^{-1}(1+\phi^2)/(1-\phi^2).$$

The "inflation factor" $(1+\phi^2)/(1-\phi^2)$ becomes large as ϕ approaches unity and as the sequences approximate to the random walks we are considering.

Furthermore, as is noted, for example, by Hannan (1960), the variance of the regression coefficient between two such unrelated autoregressive sequences is inflated approximately by the same factor. The standard errors of the regression coefficients quoted in the C.G.K. paper could thus easily be underestimated by an order of magnitude. This possibly accounts for the high levels of significance obtained.

It is seen then that the observed cross-correlation phenomena are to be expected from unrelated but autocorrelated sequences.

Actual performance of the forecasts

To compare the C.G.K. forecasts with those obtained using equation (5) which totally ignores the inputs X_1 and X_2, forecasts were compared from one step, to six steps, ahead. The forecasting process was begun from the origin 1963/4—that is, the fourth quarter of 1963. All previous data were used to obtain forecasts

(i) from model (1) (C.G.K. forecast),
(ii) from model (5) (present price is forecast price)

The origin was then moved forward to 1964/1 and the whole process was repeated. The origin was moved forward one step at a time to 1967/3, thus producing 16 pairs of forecasts made one step ahead, 15 pairs two steps ahead, and so on. The averages for the squared errors of these forecasts are shown below

	Equation (1)	Equation (5)
One step ahead	969	386
Two steps ahead	1,164	894
Three steps ahead	1,264	1,301
Four steps ahead	1,279	1,270
Five steps ahead	1,274	739
Six steps ahead	1,500	375

Comparison of these results verifies that for these data equation (5) usually provides better forecasts.

Conclusions

Coen, Gomme and Kendall end their paper with the conclusion that their method deserves serious consideration for short-term economic forecasting. We have written this paper because on the contrary we believe this method should not be employed because of an innate and insidious capacity to mislead which we have discussed in some detail. The criticisms we have made are in the spirit of a recently published book (Box and Jenkins, 1970) which is, in turn, based on a number of previous reports and papers there referenced. These latter authors regard the process of model construction as involving first the consideration of an adequately flexible and theoretically sensible family of models followed by the iterative use of the sequence: model identification—model fitting—model diagnostic checking.

In that context we believe we have shown in this paper that:

(i) the *class of* C.G.K. *models* considered—linear multiple regression on lagged input variables with uncorrelated errors—is a demonstrably inadequate family. Adequacy would mean that transformations of the data of the kind

$$n_t = Y_t - \alpha - \beta_0 t - \beta_1 X_{1,t-s_1} - \beta_2 X_{2,t-s_2}$$

for suitable choice of α, β_0, β_1, s_1 and s_2 could produce uncorrelated noise n_t and this has not been found to be so;

(ii) the process of *identification* involving superposition of the highly auto-correlated time series backed by cross-correlation analysis invites the discovery of spurious relationships;

(iii) the process of *fitting* by ordinary least squares with implied uncorrelated errors is inappropriate and could lead to t values inflated by an order of magnitude;

(iv) no diagnostic *checking*, such as analysis of residuals, which would have pointed to these inadequacies, seems to have been attempted.

Acknowledgement

We are grateful to Larry Haugh for carrying out additional calculations and for his help in the revision of this paper. This work was supported by the Air Force Office of Scientific Research and by the U.S. Army Research Office, Durham.

Appendix

Cross-correlation Properties of Detrended Random Walks

We may establish the approximate relation between C_k and C_k^* of equation (8) as follows:

$$(N-1) C_k^* = \sum_{t=2}^{N-k} \left[\left\{ X_t' - (N-1)^{-1} \sum_{t=2}^{N} X_t' \right\} - \left\{ X_{t-1}' - (N-1)^{-1} \sum_{t=1}^{N-1} X_t' \right\} \right]$$

$$\times \left[\left\{ Y_{t+k}' - (N-1)^{-1} \sum_{t=2}^{N} Y_t' \right\} - \left\{ Y_{t+k-1}' - (N-1)^{-1} \sum_{t=1}^{N-1} Y_t' \right\} \right]$$

and approximately

$$(N-1)^{-1} \sum_{t=2}^{N} X_t' = (N-1)^{-1} \sum_{t=1}^{N-1} X_t' = \bar{X}';$$

$$(N-1)^{-1} \sum_{t=2}^{N} Y_t' = (N-1)^{-1} \sum_{t=1}^{N-1} Y_t' = \bar{Y}'.$$

Thus

$$(N-1) C_k^* \simeq \sum_{t=2}^{N-k} [(X_t' - \bar{X}') - (X_{t-1}' - \bar{X}')] [(Y_{t+k}' - \bar{Y}') - (Y_{t+k-1}' - \bar{Y}')],$$

therefore

$$(N-1) C_k^* \simeq \sum_{t=2}^{N-k} (X_t' - \bar{X}')(Y_{t+k}' - \bar{Y}') + \sum_{t=1}^{N-k-1} (X_t' - \bar{X}')(Y_{t+k}' - \bar{Y}')$$

$$- \sum_{t=2}^{N-k} (X_t' - \bar{X}')(Y_{t+k-1}' - \bar{Y}') - \sum_{t=1}^{N-k-1} (X_t' - \bar{X}')(Y_{t+k+1}' - \bar{Y}').$$

For moderate or large samples, on dividing by N the approximate relation (8) is now obtained.

REFERENCES

BACHELIER, L. (1900). Théorie de la spéculation. *Ann. Sci Éc. Norm. Sup.*, *Paris*, Series 3, **17**, 21–86.
BARNARD, G. A., JENKINS, G. M. and WINSTEN, C. B. (1962). Likelihood inference and time series. *J.R. Statist. Soc.* A, **125**, 321–352.
BARTLETT, M. S. (1955). *Stochastic Processes*. Cambridge: Cambridge University Press.
BOX, G. E. P. and JENKINS, G. M. (1970). *Time Series Analysis Forecasting and Control*. San Francisco: Holden-Day.
COEN, P. G., GOMME, E. D. and KENDALL, M. G. (1969). Lagged relationships in economic forecasting. *J.R. Statist. Soc.* A, **132**, 133–152.
DURBIN, T. and WATSON, G. S. (1951). Testing for serial correlation in least squares regression. II. *Biometrika*, **38**, 159–178.
HANNAN, E. J. (1960). *Time Series Analysis*. London: Methuen.
MUTH, G. F. (1960). Optimal properties of exponentially weighted forecasts of time series with permanent and transitory components. *J. Amer. Statist. Ass.*, **55**, 299–306.
WHITTLE, P. (1963) *Prediction and Regulation by Linear Least-squares Methods*. London: English Universities Press.

[13]

J. R. Statist. Soc. A,   131
(1974), **137**, *Part* 2, p. 131

Experience with Forecasting Univariate Time Series and the Combination of Forecasts

By P. Newbold and C. W. J. Granger

University of Nottingham

[Read before the Royal Statistical Society on Wednesday, January 16th, 1974, the President, Professor D. J. Finney, in the Chair]

Summary

A number of procedures for forecasting a time series from its own current and past values are surveyed. Forecasting performances of three methods—Box–Jenkins, Holt–Winters and stepwise autoregression—are compared over a large sample of economic time series. The possibility of combining individual forecasts in the production of an overall forecast is explored, and we present empirical results which indicate that such a procedure can frequently be profitable.

Keywords: FORECASTING; TIME SERIES; BOX–JENKINS; HOLT–WINTERS; EXPONENTIAL SMOOTHING; FORECAST PERFORMANCE; STEPWISE REGRESSION; AUTO-REGRESSIVE MODELS; FORECASTS COMBINED

1. Introduction

In this paper we consider various procedures for forecasting future values of a time series from its own current and past values. That is, given a series of equally spaced observations X_t, $t = 1, 2, ..., n$ on some quantity X, we require to forecast X_{n+h}, $h = 1, 2, 3, ...$

There exist a number of approaches, of varying degrees of complexity, whereby this end can be achieved. The more complex procedures do not produce forecasts as quickly as do the simple ones, but it is to be expected that a pay-off in terms of increased accuracy would obtain through their use, since they allow for a more detailed investigation of the properties of the particular series under consideration. In this context it is useful to distinguish between those approaches for which a single computer program can be written in such a way that, for any given time series, forecasts can be generated without manual intervention and those which preclude such treatment. We refer to the procedures in the former class as 'fully automatic". There is clearly a considerable gain in terms of both speed and cost in using a fully automatic forecasting method, and one of our purposes in this paper is to assess the potential loss in terms of forecast accuracy in so doing.

Of course, one frequently possesses qualitative and quantitative information of potential relevance in addition to current and past values of the series under study and, where practicable, such information ought to be incorporated into the forecasting mechanism. Nevertheless, we feel that univariate time series forecasting methods deserve detailed consideration for a number of reasons. First, such methods are quick and inexpensive to operate, and may well produce forecasts of sufficient accuracy for the purposes at hand. Again, relevant extraneous information may be unavailable or only obtainable at a prohibitively high cost. Univariate forecasting procedures can be useful as a yard-stick against which the success or otherwise of a more elaborate forecasting exercise can be judged. They may also be usefully combined with other forecasting methods in the production of an overall forecast. Such combining can be achieved either on a formal or an informal basis. Finally, one can assess how much of the variation in a quantity can be explained in terms of its own past behaviour, and so form a clearer understanding of what particular behaviour patterns require consideration of extraneous factors for their explanation. Thus, for example, the potential usefulness of other time series in the forecasting of a series of interest can be assessed by examining their ability to predict the univariate forecast errors.

In the bulk of this paper, we review various univariate time series forecasting methods, with particular reference to their application to economic time series, and present the results of a large empirical study designed to assess the relative performances of some of these methods on real data. A particular point of interest is an empirical evaluation of procedures proposed by Bates and Granger (1969) for the combination of forecasts. Section 2 of this paper contains a brief description of the Box–Jenkins approach to univariate time series forecasting, while Sections 3 and 4 discuss various fully automatic forecasting procedures. Exponential smoothing procedures—particularly the Holt–Winters method—are described in Section 3 and Section 4 introduces the possibility of building autoregressive forecasting models by stepwise regression. In Section 5 we describe, and attempt to give some justification for considering, methods for combining individual forecasts. These procedures are of general applicability in forecasting, though for the purposes of this paper we restrict attention to the combination of forecasts derived from univariate time series procedures. Section 6 compares the forecast performances of the Box–Jenkins, Holt–Winters and stepwise autoregressive approaches over a large sample of economic time series, while in Section 7 we present some empirical results on the combination of forecasts generated by these three methods. Finally, in Section 8 we summarize the results of our investigations and outline a number of general points which have arisen from the study.

2. BOX–JENKINS PROCEDURES

In a series of articles and a subsequent book, Box and Jenkins (1970) describe in detail a strategy for the construction of linear stochastic equations describing the behaviour of a time series. These authors assume that the given series X_t is such that it can be reduced to stationarity by differencing a finite number of times. That is, there exists some positive integer d such that

$$W_t = (1 - B)^d X_t \tag{2.1}$$

is stationary, where B is a back-shift operator on the index of the time series so that $BX_t = X_{t-1}$, $B^2 X_t = X_{t-2}$ and so on. It is further assumed that W_t is a mixed autoregressive–moving average process of the form

$$(1 - \phi_1 B - \phi_2 B^2 - \ldots - \phi_p B^p)W_t = \theta_0 + (1 - \theta_1 B - \theta_2 B^2 - \ldots - \theta_q B^q)a_t, \tag{2.2}$$

where the a_t's are a sequence of identically distributed uncorrelated deviates, referred to as "white noise". Combining equations (2.1) and (2.2) yields the basic Box–Jenkins model for non-seasonal time series

$$(1 - \phi_1 B - \phi_2 B^2 - \ldots - \phi_p B^p)(1 - B)^d X_t = \theta_0 + (1 - \theta_1 B - \theta_2 B^2 - \ldots - \theta_q B^q)a_t. \tag{2.3}$$

Equation (2.3) is said to represent an autoregressive integrated moving average process of order (p, d, q) denoted as ARIMA(p, d, q).

Box and Jenkins fit models of the form (2.3) to a given set of data by an iterative three step cycle of identification, estimation and diagnostic checking. At the identification stage, tentative values are chosen for p, d and q. The coefficients $\phi_1, ..., \phi_p, \theta_0, \theta_1, ..., \theta_q$ are then estimated using fully efficient statistical techniques. Finally, diagnostic checks are made to determine whether or not the model fitted adequately describes the given time series. Any inadequacies discovered may suggest an alternative form for the equation, and the whole iterative cycle of identification, estimation and diagnostic checking is repeated until a satisfactory model is obtained.

The details of the steps in the Box–Jenkins model building procedure are summarized in Newbold (1973), and some description, mainly in the context of fitting seasonal models, is given in Chatfield and Prothero (1973).

It is straightforward to show that, standing at time n, the minimum mean squared error forecast of X_{n+h} from (2.3) is its conditional expectation. Forecasts can therefore be obtained from (2.3) by substituting $n+h$ for t in that equation and taking conditional expectations, noting that the conditional expectations for $X_n, X_{n-1}, ...,$ $a_n, a_{n-1}, ...$ are their known values at time n, those for $a_{n+1}, a_{n+2}, ...$ are zero, and those for $X_{n+1}, X_{n+2}, ...$ are the forecasts made at time n. The forecasting prodecure is thus a step by step process, taking in turn $h = 1, 2, 3, ...$

For seasonal time series with period s, Box and Jenkins propose the model

$$(1 - \phi_1 B - \phi_2 B^2 - ... - \phi_p B^p)(1 - \phi_{1s} B^s - \phi_{2s} B^{2s} - ... - \phi_{p_s s} B^{p_s s})$$
$$\times (1 - B)^d (1 - B^s)^{d_s} X_t$$
$$= \theta_0 + (1 - \theta_1 B - \theta_2 B^2 - ... - \theta_q B^q)(1 - \theta_{1s} B^s - \theta_{2s} B^{2s} - ... - \theta_{q_s s} B^{q_s s}) a_t,$$

although the assumption of multiplicativity can be dropped if this is suggested by the identification procedure. The principles of model fitting and forecasting are exactly analogous to those outlined for the non-seasonal model.

The great beauty of the Box–Jenkins approach is in the wide choice of forecast functions available. In any particular case, the data themselves are allowed to suggest the eventual form of the forecast function employed, and one would hope that such freedom would be reflected in the accuracy of the forecasts obtained. It should be stressed that the Box–Jenkins procedure is not fully automatic, in the sense that one cannot simply write a computer program to produce forecasts without manaul intervention. Indeed, a good deal of skill and/or experience is essential if Box–Jenkins models are to be used to best effect—in particular, the identification stage of the model building cycle often demands a high degree of judgment. This being the case it is pertinent to ask whether much the same success could be obtained through a more *ad hoc* procedure.

From the empirical testing point of view, taken up in later sections of this paper, there is a certain amount of difficulty involved in evaluating the merits of the Box–Jenkins predictor. This stems from the fact that it is by no means certain that any two analysts applying the principles of Box and Jenkins to a particular set of data will reach the same conclusions. What we are evaluating in fact, is the Box–Jenkins technique *as applied by ourselves* to a large number of time series. It is difficult to assess the force of this point, but our subjective feeling is that *on the average* the degree of success obtained by any fairly experienced user of the approach would closely approximate our own. We should add that, even at the beginning of this study, one of us already had a good deal of experience with the technique.

3. Exponential Smoothing

In its simplest form, exponential smoothing attempts to estimate locally the level of a time series as a weighted average of the most recent observation and the previous estimate of level. An observed series X_t is thus "smoothed" to produce a series $\bar{X}_t$, given by

$$\bar{X}_t = \alpha X_t + (1-\alpha)\,\bar{X}_{t-1}, \quad 0 < \alpha < 1.$$

The smoothed series $\bar{X}_t$ is thus a weighted average of current and past values of the observed series, with weights decreasing exponentially

$$\bar{X}_t = \alpha \sum_{j=0}^{\infty} (1-\alpha)^j\, X_{t-j}.$$

The latest available smoothed value is then employed to forecast all future values of the series; that is if $\hat{X}_n(h)$ denotes the forecast of X_{n+h} made at time n,

$$\hat{X}_n(h) = \bar{X}_n, \quad h = 1, 2, 3, \ldots.$$

In practice, this simple formulation is rarely employed and several modifications have been developed. These view a time series as being made up locally of trend, level and (possibly) seasonality. One approach due to Holt (1957) and Winters (1960) estimates local trend T as

$$T_t = C(\bar{X}_t - \bar{X}_{t-1}) + (1 - C)\,T_{t-1}, \quad 0 < C < 1.$$

If the series is seasonal with period L, the seasonal estimates S are updated according to

$$S_t = B(X_t/\bar{X}_t) + (1-B)\,S_{t-L}, \quad 0 < B < 1, \tag{3.1}$$

and the smoothed series is given by

$$\bar{X}_t = A(X_t/S_{t-L}) + (1-A)(\bar{X}_{t-1} + T_{t-1}), \quad 0 < A < 1.$$

The forecast of X_{n+h} made at time n is then

$$\hat{X}_n(h) = (\bar{X}_n + hT_n)\,S_{n-L+h}, \quad h = 1, 2, \ldots, L,$$
$$= (\bar{X}_n + hT_n)\,S_{n-2L+h}, \quad h = L+1, L+2, \ldots, 2L, \tag{3.2}$$
$$\vdots$$

The Holt–Winters method thus assumes an additive trend and multiplicative seasonal component, but can be modified in an obvious way to allow either multiplicative trend or additive seasonal. It remains to determine suitable values for the smoothing constants A, B and C. The most objective means of achieving this is to obtain "forecasts", made one time period previously, of the known values $X_n, X_{n-1}, \ldots$ over a grid of possible values of the smoothing constants. That set A, B and C which best "forecasts" the known observations (generally in terms of average squared forecast error) is then employed to forecast the future. In evaluating the performance of the Holt–Winters predictor we have chosen the smoothing constants in this way.

4. Stepwise Autoregression

A great difficulty with exponential smoothing procedures is that they impose a rather severe prior restriction on the form of the eventual forecast function. The data themselves are used only to determine suitable values for the smoothing constants. As an alternative fully automatic procedure, one can build autoregressive models, allowing the given data to prescribe the form of the model fitted through a stepwise regression algorithm.

It has been noted (see, for example, Granger, 1966) that typically economic time series are reduced to stationarity by first-differencing. Accordingly, we analyse changes

$$Z_t = X_t - X_{t-1}$$

of a given series, and consider models of the form

$$Z_t = \alpha + \sum_{j=1}^{M} \beta_j Z_{t-j} + \text{error}. \tag{4.1}$$

At the first step of the model-building process the lagged value Z_{t-j} which contributes most towards explaining variation in Z_t is introduced. At the second step, the particular Z_{t-j} which most improves the fit obtained at step one is added, and so on until addition of further lagged values fails to produce a significant improvement in fit. Lagged values, introduced at an earlier stage, whose contribution to explained variation becomes insignificant, are then dropped.

Forecasts of future values can be obtained by projecting forward equation (4.1). The procedure is fully automatic, and it only remains to choose a suitable value for M. We have found that $M = 13$ for quarterly and shorter monthly series and $M = 25$ for longer monthly series works satisfactorily.

In our empirical study we have used an arbitrary F ratio of 4·0 to determine whether variables should be added to or dropped from the regression equations. (The usual significance tests are, of course, invalid in stepwise regression.) Since our study was completed, Payne (1973) has applied stepwise regression techniques to some of our data, employing a superior cut-off criterion. He achieved one-step-ahead forecasts which, on the whole, were slightly better than ours.

5. THE COMBINATION OF FORECASTS

The idea of combining individual forecasts in the production of an overall forecast was originally proposed by Bates and Granger (1969). In their paper the combination of pairs of forecasts only was discussed, but the methodology can easily be extended to the combination of several forecasts (see Reid, 1969). Suppose one has M forecasts $\mathbf{F}'_T = (F_{1,T}, F_{2,T}, ..., F_{M,T})$ of some quantity X_T, and that these individual forecasts are unbiased. Then the linear combination

$$C_T = \mathbf{k}'_T \mathbf{F}_T, \quad \mathbf{k}'_T \mathbf{1} = 1, \quad 0 \leqslant k_{i,T} \leqslant 1 \quad \text{for all } i, \tag{5.1}$$

where $\mathbf{k}'_T = (k_{1,T}, k_{2,T}, ..., k_{M,T})$ and $\mathbf{1}' = (1, 1, ..., 1)$ will also be unbiased. It is straightforward to show that the variance of the combined forecast error is minimized by taking

$$\mathbf{k}_T = (\Sigma^{-1}\mathbf{1})/(\mathbf{1}'\Sigma^{-1}\mathbf{1}),$$

where

$$\Sigma = E(\mathbf{e}_T \mathbf{e}'_T) \quad \text{and} \quad \mathbf{e}_T = X_T \mathbf{1} - \mathbf{F}_T.$$

It follows that, in general, by appropriate choice of $\mathbf{k}_T$, one can find a combined forecast C_T which has smaller error variance than all the individual forecasts.

Unfortunately, in practice, one does not know the values of the covariance matrix Σ. Bates and Granger propose a number of practical methods of combining. Their suggestions are based on two principles—first that most weight should be given to the forecast which has performed best in the recent past, and second that the weight function should adapt to allow for the possibility of a non-stationary relationship over time between the individual forecasting procedures. Five of their suggested choices of $\mathbf{k}_T$, for one-step-ahead forecasts, extended to the general case are:

(1)
$$k_{i,T} = \left(\sum_{t=T-\nu}^{T-1} e_{i,t}^2 \right)^{-1} \bigg/ \left\{ \sum_{j=1}^{M} \left(\sum_{t=T-\nu}^{T-1} e_{j,t}^2 \right)^{-1} \right\}$$

(2)
$$\mathbf{k}_T = (\hat{\Sigma}^{-1}\mathbf{1})/(\mathbf{1}'\hat{\Sigma}^{-1}\mathbf{1}), \quad \text{s.t. } 0 \leqslant k_{i,T} \leqslant 1 \quad \text{for all } i,$$

where

$$(\hat{\Sigma})_{i,j} = \nu^{-1} \sum_{t=T-\nu}^{T-1} e_{i,t} e_{j,t}.$$

(3)
$$k_{i,T} = \alpha k_{i,T-1} + \left[(1-\alpha) \left(\sum_{t=T-\nu}^{T-1} e_{i,t}^2 \right)^{-1} \bigg/ \left\{ \sum_{j=1}^{M} \left(\sum_{t=T-\nu}^{T-1} e_{j,t}^2 \right)^{-1} \right\} \right], \quad 0 < \alpha < 1.$$

(4)
$$k_{i,T} = \left(\sum_{t=1}^{T-1} W^t e_{i,t}^2 \right)^{-1} \bigg/ \left\{ \sum_{j=1}^{M} \left(\sum_{t=1}^{T-1} W^t e_{j,t}^2 \right)^{-1} \right\}, \quad W \geqslant 1.$$

(5)
$$\mathbf{k}_T = (\hat{\Sigma}^{-1}\mathbf{1})/(\mathbf{1}'\hat{\Sigma}^{-1}\mathbf{1}), \quad \text{s.t. } 0 \leqslant k_{i,T} \leqslant 1 \quad \text{for all } i$$

where

$$(\hat{\Sigma})_{i,j} = \left(\sum_{t=1}^{T-1} W^t e_{i,t} e_{j,t} \right) \bigg/ \left(\sum_{t=1}^{T-1} W^t \right), \quad W \geqslant 1.$$

One might expect that the greatest benefits are to be obtained from combining forecasts of a very dissimilar nature, and indeed Granger and Newbold (1972) have shown that combining statistical and econometric forecasts can be highly rewarding. Nevertheless, we felt that it was well worth while to attempt to combine various univariate time series forecasts, as was done for one particular set of data in Bates and Granger's original paper.

Proponents of the Box–Jenkins approach might find an attempt to combine Box–Jenkins forecasts with those derived from less sophisticated univariate methods intuitively unpromising. After all, the class of models considered in the stepwise autoregression procedure and the non-seasonal (but not the seasonal) variant of the Holt–Winters method are merely subsets of the general ARIMA class of models. Perhaps the problem raised here can best be resolved in terms of the Box–Jenkins framework. It is, of course, true that if one *knew* that a given time series was generated by a particular process of the class (2.3), optimal forecasts could be derived from that model alone. However, much as the Box–Jenkins model-building process tells us about the underlying generating mechanism, we can never be absolutely certain that a particular model is appropriate. Indeed, for small samples the degree of uncertainty can be very high. (This point is noted by Chatfield and Prothero, 1973.) Perhaps a better approach, given M univariate forecasting mechanisms, might be to stipulate a subjective probability k_i as one's degree of belief that the ith mechanism represents the true underlying stochastic process. Suppose now that we wish to predict X_T from $\{X_{T-j}, j>0\}$. If mechanism i denoted the true underlying process, leading to the density function $f_i(X_T)$ with mean $F_{i,T}$ as the conditional density of X_T given past X, then the optimal quadratic loss predictor of X_T would be $F_{i,T}$. However, in subjective terms, our feelings about the conditional density of X_T given past X are represented by the function

$$f(X_T) = \sum_{i=1}^{M} k_i f_i(X_T).$$

The mean of this density function, which provides the optimal predictor in quadratic loss terms, is given by (5.1) and hence one is led naturally to look at forecasts of this form.

In our evaluation studies on the combination of forecasts we have considered in detail only one-step ahead forecasts, although the methods proposed above can be readily extended to deal with forecasting several steps ahead.

6. AN EMPIRICAL COMPARISON OF FORECASTING PROCEDURES

In order to assess the relative performances of univariate time series forecasting methods on real economic data, we assembled a collection of 106 time series, 80 of which were monthly and 26 quarterly. This collection included seasonal and non-seasonal macro-economic series and micro sales data. Our macro series included data on prices, money supply, unemployment, industrial production, vacancies, earnings, exports and imports, retail sales and manufacturing orders in a number of different countries, together with rather more disaggregated series. The micro series were of sales of several products and product lines. (A complete listing of the data used in this study is available from the authors.) Each series was divided into two parts; the first part was employed to fit an appropriate model, and this model was then used to generate forecasts over the second part of the series. We feel that such an operation is essential in evaluating forecasting methods; that is, one should look at actual forecasts rather than fitted values over some period of estimation.

In principle, as noted by Granger (1969), if the forecast error is denoted by e, one can work with any particular cost of error criterion $C(e)$. However, in this and subsequent sections of our paper, we analyse forecasts only in terms of the traditional least squares, or quadratic cost of error function

$$C(e) = ae^2, \quad a > 0,$$

and are thus led to an examination of average squared forecast error. In fact, if one's primary interest is in *comparing* forecast performances, the choice of cost function may not be too crucial (see Granger and Newbold, 1973).

We computed average squared forecast errors arising from the application of the Box–Jenkins, Holt–Winters and stepwise autoregressive procedures to each of the 106 time series in our sample. Table 1 shows the percentage number of times one method outperforms another for forecasts made up to eight steps ahead. We note that the Box–Jenkins approach is clearly superior to the two fully automatic methods for short lead times, but that some of this advantage is lost when forecasting further ahead. This is probably a reflection of the fact that for many non-seasonal time series information available at time t is a highly relevant determinant of the immediate future, but becomes rather less relevant for more distant time periods.

To get some stronger feeling for the possible gains to be obtained from use of the Box–Jenkins approach, we considered the one-step-ahead forecasts in more detail.

TABLE 1

Comparison of Box–Jenkins (B–J), Holt–Winters (H–W) and Stepwise Autoregressive (S–A) forecasts: Percentage of times first named method outperforms second for various lead times

Comparisons	Lead times							
	1	2	3	4	5	6	7	8
B–J : H–W	73	64	60	58	58	57	58	58
B–J : S–A	68	70	67	62	62	61	63	63
H–W : S–A	48	50	58	57	55	56	58	59

Table 2 gives ratios of average squared errors in comparisons of the three predictors. We note that the Box–Jenkins procedure very often markedly outperforms the two fully automatic methods, this feature being particularly pronounced in the case of the Holt–Winters forecasts. It appears that for one-step-ahead forecasts at any rate the performance of stepwise autoregression is much closer to that of Box–Jenkins than is that of the Holt–Winters method.

TABLE 2

Comparison of average squared forecast errors of Box–Jenkins, Holt–Winters and stepwise autoregressive one-step-ahead forecasts in terms of ratios of average squared errors: number of forecasted series in various ranges

	Method A: Method B:	Box–Jenkins Holt-Winters	Box–Jenkins Stepwise	Holt–Winters Stepwise
	0·1–0·2	1	0	0
A.S.E. of Method A	0·2–0·3	3	2	0
A.S.E. of Method B	0·3–0·4	4	4	2
	0·4–0·5	8	4	4
When A is better	0·5–0·6	5	2	4
	0·6–0·7	10	5	6
	0·7–0·8	13	14	13
	0·8–0·9	19	17	10
	0·9–1·0	14	23	12
Two methods identical		0	2	0
	0·9–1·0	11	14	5
	0·8–0·9	8	13	14
A.S.E. of Method B	0·7–0·8	2	3	10
A.S.E. of Method A	0·6–0·7	3	1	12
	0·5–0·6	4	0	5
When B is better	0·4–0·5	0	2	2
	0·3–0·4	1	0	3
	0·2–0·3	0	0	4
	0·1–0·2	0	0	0

A striking feature of Table 2 is the very wide spread of ranges containing an appreciable number of series for the Holt–Winters and stepwise autoregression comparison. This strongly suggests that each method possesses useful features absent in the other, and leads one to ask whether or not a superior fully automatic forecasting mechanism might be obtained by combining Holt–Winters and stepwise autoregressive forecasts.

The geometric means of the various ratios of average squared forecast errors provide useful summary statistics for the information contained in Table 2. The following values were obtained for these geometric means:

$$\frac{\text{Average squared error Box–Jenkins forecasts}}{\text{Average squared error Holt–Winters forecasts}} = 0\cdot80,$$

$$\frac{\text{Average squared error Box–Jenkins forecasts}}{\text{Average squared error stepwise autoregressive forecasts}} = 0\cdot86,$$

$$\frac{\text{Average squared error stepwise autoregressive forecasts}}{\text{Average squared error Holt–Winters forecasts}} = 0\cdot93.$$

7. Some Empirical Results on Combining

For the 80 monthly time series in our sample, we attempted an empirical investigation of the usefulness of combining forecasts, employing the five methods described in Section 5 for one-step-ahead forecasts. Our objective was twofold: first, to determine whether combining could produce a forecast which was, in general, superior to the individual forecasts, and secondly, to investigate differences in performance of the five combining procedures. Now, in retrospect, one can always find an optimal constant weighted combined forecast which will do at least as well as the best individual forecast, and in order to assess the importance of non-stationarity between individual forecasts one can compare the combined forecasts achieved with this optimal forecast.

Forecasts were first combined in pairs, using Methods 1 and 2 with $v = 1, 3, 6, 9, 12$, Method 3 with $v = 1, 3, 6, 9, 12$ and $\alpha = 0\cdot5, 0\cdot7, 0\cdot9$ for each value of v and Methods 4 and 5 with $W = 1\cdot00, 1\cdot50, 2\cdot00$ and $2\cdot50$.

Table 3 shows the percentage number of series for which the combination of a pair of forecasts produced an overall forecast which was superior to *both* individual forecasts. One fact which clearly emerges from this table is that those methods which ignore correlation (Methods 1, 3 and 4) are more successful than those which attempt to take account of correlation (Methods 2 and 5). It can be seen from Table 3 that when Box–Jenkins is combined with one or other of the fully automatic procedures, the combined forecast outperforms both individual forecasts about 40 per cent of the time for the better combining procedures. This naturally leads one to ask how often these combined forecasts outperform the Box–Jenkins forecasts themselves. The answer is given in Table 4, from which it can be seen that for the better combining methods, the combined forecasts do generally outperform the Box–Jenkins forecasts for a slight majority of our series. (One should probably discount Method 1 with $v = 1$, which would only be employed in practice if a very highly non-stationary relationship between the individual forecasts was suspected.)

TABLE 3

Combination of pairs of forecasts. Percentage number of series for which the combined forecast outperforms both individual forecasts for: (A) *Box–Jenkins combined with Holt–Winters,* (B) *Box–Jenkins combined with stepwise autoregressive,* (C) *Holt–Winters combined with stepwise autoregressive*

Method 1				Method 2				Method 3				
(A)	(B)	(C)	ν	(A)	(B)	(C)	ν	α	(A)	(B)	(C)
37·50	27·50	37·50	1	37·50	25·00	37·50	1	0·5	40·00	41·25	46·25
32·50	38·75	46·25	3	26·25	26·25	30·00	1	0·7	41·25	38·75	46·25
37·50	38·75	46·25	6	20·00	25·00	28·75	1	0·9	37·50	40·00	48·75
40·00	40·00	46·25	9	25·00	20·00	33·75	3	0·5	32·50	40·00	45·00
37·50	40·00	45·00	12	21·25	18·75	35·00	3	0·7	38·75	41·25	47·50
							3	0·9	37·50	40·00	50·00

Method 4				Method 5				Method 3 (cont.)				
(A)	(B)	(C)	W	(A)	(B)	(C)	ν	α	(A)	(B)	(C)
35·00	41·25	43·75	1·00	18·75	16·25	30·00	6	0·5	41·25	43·75	48·75
35·00	41·25	48·75	1·50	30·00	26·25	40·00	6	0·7	41·25	40·00	48·75
37·50	41·25	48·75	2·00	35·00	25·00	37·50	6	0·9	37·50	37·50	47·50
37·50	40·00	50·00	2·50	36·25	31·25	38·75	9	0·5	40·00	40·00	45·00
							9	0·7	40·00	36·25	48·75
							9	0·9	36·25	37·50	48·75
							12	0·5	38·75	41·25	50·00
							12	0·7	37·50	38·75	48·75
							12	0·9	33·75	36·25	45·00

TABLE 4

Percentage number of series for which Box–Jenkins is outperformed by (A) *Box–Jenkins combined with Holt–Winters,* (B) *Box–Jenkins combined with stepwise autoregressive*

Method 1			Method 2			Method 3			
(A)	(B)	ν	(A)	(B)	ν	α	(A)	(B)
55·00	48·75	1	53·72	41 25	1	0·5	57·50	58·75
50·00	53·75	3	46·25	42·50	1	0·7	57·50	57·50
55·00	52·50	6	41·25	38·75	1	0·9	55·00	56·25
57·50	53·75	9	47·50	38·75	3	0·5	50·00	53·75
56·25	55·00	12	45·00	37·50	3	0·7	56·25	56·25
					3	0·9	55·00	53·75

Method 4			Method 5			Method 3 (cont.)			
(A)	(B)	W	(A)	(B)	ν	α	(A)	(B)
53·75	55·00	1·00	42·50	37·50	6	0·5	58·75	56·25
52·50	56·25	1·50	46·25	41·25	6	0·7	58·75	55·00
55·00	57·50	2·00	48·75	41·25	6	0·9	55·00	52·50
55·00	56·25	2·50	50·00	46·25	9	0·5	57·50	53·75
					9	0·7	57·50	52·50
					9	0·9	53·75	53·75
					12	0·5	57·50	55·00
					12	0·7	56·25	53·75
					12	0·9	51·25	53·75

We speculated earlier that the combination of the two fully automatic forecasting procedures might well be worth while, and this appears to be borne out by the evidence of Table 5. The better combining procedures do seem to produce an overall forecast which is superior to the individual forecasts on a great majority of occasions.

TABLE 5

Percentage number of series for which the combined Holt–Winters and stepwise autoregressive forecast outperforms: (A) Holt–Winters, (B) stepwise autoregressive

Method 1			Method 2			Method 3			
(A)	(B)	ν	(A)	(B)	ν	α	(A)	(B)
63·75	71·25	1	63·75	65·25	1	0·5	68·75	77·50
67·50	78·75	3	60·00	65·25	1	0·7	71·25	75·00
67·50	78·75	6	57·50	65·25	1	0·9	72·50	76·25
68·75	77·50	9	57·50	71·25	3	0·5	67·50	77·50
68·75	76·25	12	60·00	71·25	3	0·7	70·00	77·50
					3	0·9	71·25	78·75

Method 4			Method 5						
(A)	(B)	W	(A)	(B)	6	0·5	70·00	78·75
					6	0·7	70·00	78·75
68·75	75·00	1·00	57·50	70·00	6	0·9	68·75	78·75
68·75	80·00	1·50	62·50	73·75	9	0·5	68·75	76·25
68·75	80·00	2·00	62·50	72·50	9	0·7	70·00	78·75
68·75	81·25	2·50	63·75	70·00	9	0·9	70·00	78·75
					12	0·5	70·00	80·00
					12	0·7	70·00	78·75
					12	0·9	67·50	77·50

Two further points emerged from our analysis:

(i) The combined forecast was never worse than both individual forecasts in Methods 1, 3 and 4 except for a small number of series for Method 1 with $\nu = 1$ and Method 3 with $\nu = 1$ and $\alpha = 0.5$. For Methods 2 and 5 the combined forecast was generally worse than both individual forecasts for less than 10 per cent of the series.

(ii) The combined forecast was found to perform better than the optimum ex-post constant weights combination for around 5 per cent (for the long memory methods) to around 20 per cent (for the short memory methods) of our series.

As an alternative means of assessing which of the 33 methods employed in selecting the combining weights proved most successful, we ranked each method (giving rank 1 to the best and rank 33 to the worst) for every series and for all three paired combinations. The overall average ranks are shown in Table 6, from which it emerges that the most successful methods are those with long memories—that is, those for which the combining weights adapt relatively slowly. This ties in with the fact noted earlier that the optimum constant weight forecast was rarely outperformed, and suggests that in combining forecasts of the type studied here non-stationarity is rarely of great importance. On the basis of the information given in Table 12, Method 1 with $\nu = 12$ was the most successful, though in fact there is remarkably little to choose on this criterion between the best few methods.

It is of interest to compare the performances of the combined forecasts with the Box–Jenkins forecasts in terms of ratios of average squared forecast errors. We carried out this comparison in terms of the most successful combining method— Method 1, with $v = 12$. The combined Holt–Winters and stepwise autoregressive

TABLE 6

Average overall rankings of various combining procedures

Method 1		Method 2	Method 3		
	v		v	α	
19·47	1	20·94	1	0·5	16·91
16·61	3	20·11	1	0·7	15·95·
15·93	6	19·34	1	0·9	16·74
15·68	9	19·41	3	0·5	16·25
15·09	12	19·51	3	0·7	15·83
			3	0·9	16·23
Method 3		Method 4	6	0·5	15·62
			6	0·7	15·41
	W		6	0·9	16·17
			9	0·5	15·81
15·15	1·00	18·94	9	0·7	15·72
15·11	1·50	18·70	9	0·9	16·32
15·65	2·00	19·62	12	0·5	15·22
16·09	2·50	19·96	12	0·7	15·37
			12	0·9	16·15

forecasts outperformed the Box–Jenkins forecasts on 46·25 per cent of the series in our sample. The geometric means of the ratios of average squared forecast errors were

$$\frac{\text{Average squared error Box–Jenkins and Holt–Winters combined}}{\text{Average squared error Box–Jenkins}} = 0·94,$$

$$\frac{\text{Average squared error Box–Jenkins and stepwise autoregression combined}}{\text{Average squared error Box–Jenkins}} = 0·98,$$

$$\frac{\text{Average squared error Box–Jenkins}}{\text{Average squared error Holt–Winters and stepwise autoregression combined}} = 0·99.$$

It appears that Box–Jenkins forecasts can on the whole be slightly improved by combination with one of the fully automatic procedures, but the most striking aspect of these calculations is the impressive performance of the combined Holt–Winters and stepwise autoregressive forecast—this combination produces a fully automatic forecast of considerable merit.

In order to determine whether further improvement could be achieved, we combined all three forecasts over the 80 monthly series. As can be seen from Table 7, with the exception of the case $v = 1$ in Method 1, this combined forecast outperformed the Box–Jenkins predictor for at least 60 per cent of our series for Methods 1, 3 and 4. The geometric mean for the ratio of the average squared error of the combined forecast to that of the Box–Jenkins forecast for Method 1 with $v = 12$ was 0·92.

TABLE 7

*Percentage number of series for which the combined
Box–Jenkins, Holt–Winters and stepwise autoregressive
forecast outperforms Box–Jenkins*

Method 1		Method 2		Method 3	
	ν		ν	α	
50·00	1	50·00	1	0·5	60·00
65·00	3	52·50	1	0·7	61·25
60·00	6	47·50	1	0·9	60·00
63·75	9	52·50	3	0·5	63·75
62·50	12	51·25	3	0·7	61·25
			3	0·9	61·25
Method 4		Method 5	6	0·5	62·50
			6	0·7	61·25
	W		6	0·9	60·00
			9	0·5	65·00
61·25	1·00	48·75	9	0·7	62·50
65·00	1·50	47·50	9	0·9	62·50
63·75	2·00	47·50	12	0·5	62·50
63·75	2·50	48·70	12	0·7	62·50
			12	0·9	62·50

8. SUMMARY AND CONCLUSIONS

In order to discuss in any meaningful way particular forecasting procedures, we feel that it is imperative to analyse their performances on actual data. To this end, we have examined the behaviour of various univariate time series forecasting methods when applied to a wide collection of economic time series. As we have noted, Box–Jenkins forecasts require a good deal more time and considerably more skill to compute than do their competitors. However, we have found that there is a corresponding pay-off, in the sense that the Box–Jenkins forecasts do seem to be better than those derived from two fully automatic procedures—the Holt–Winters method and stepwise autoregression—for a sizeable majority of the time series in our sample. The tendency of the Box–Jenkins method to produce superior forecasts is particularly marked over the short run (and, indeed, for seasonal series continues in the longer run). Moreover, the gains (in terms of average squared forecast error) from use of the Box–Jenkins approach can be, and often are, quite substantial. These substantial gains do in fact persist when forecasting several steps ahead for many series.

It does appear, however, that Box–Jenkins forecasts can frequently be improved upon by combination with either Holt–Winters or stepwise autoregressive forecasts, and we feel that our results indicate that in any particular forecasting situation combining is well worth trying, as it requires very little extra effort. Further improvement is frequently obtained by considering a combination of all three types of forecast.

It is frequently the case that, for reasons of economy of time or effort, a Box–Jenkins analysis is impracticable, and some fully automatic procedure must be employed. Now, it is a simple matter to construct a computer program which will, for any given series, compute Holt–Winters and stepwise autoregressive forecasts and then produce an overall combined forecast. Judging by our experience on a sample of 80 monthly time series, such a method, while remaining fully automatic, yields a performance which is generally superior to that of the individual procedures, and which furthermore closely approximates that of the individual Box–Jenkins forecast.

We have found that, for two individual forecasts $F_{1,T}$ and $F_{2,T}$ of the type discussed in this paper, a combined forecast

$$C_T = k_T F_{1,T} + (1 - k_T) F_{2,T}$$

generally performs well if the weight

$$k_T = \left(\sum_{t=T-12}^{T-1} e_{2,t}^2 \right) \Big/ \left\{ \sum_{t=T-12}^{T-1} (e_{1,t}^2 + e_{2,t}^2) \right\},$$

where $e_{1,t}$ and $e_{2,t}$ denote the individual forecast errors, is employed.

Having come this far, it is tempting to try to set out well-defined guide-lines for univariate time series forecasting. In our original draft we scrupulously avoided this temptation on the grounds that anything we wrote down would appear overly dogmatic and to carry more force than was justified by the analysis carried out. Furthermore, the choice of forecasting method employed in any particular situation will be in part dictated by the time and resources available, the degree of accuracy required and the forecaster's knowledge of the relative success of various methods on time series of a similar nature. Nevertheless, encouraged by the comments of a referee and the feeling that one ought to say something mildly controversial in a paper read to an Ordinary Meeting of the Society, we have decided to make the attempt.

As a first step, we decided to try to get some feel for the Brown (1959, 1962) and Harrison (1965) procedures by applying them to a small subset of our sample of time series. The forecasts derived from Brown's method were generally rather disappointing, particularly for seasonal time series, and we can think of no circumstances in which this approach would be preferable to that of Holt and Winters. Following Reid (1969), we noted that the Harrison predictor is generally no better (and, on occasion, much worse) than the Holt–Winters approach except on those series which have both a very strong seasonal factor and fairly large random (unpredictable) fluctuations.

We now set out what we hope might be, *in general*, a useful set of guidelines for univariate time series forecasting:

(a) For short time series (less than 30 observations) there is little one can do but employ an exponential smoothing predictor. We suggest that the Holt–Winters approach be used in such circumstances.

(b) For time series of length 30 or more one can calculate stepwise autoregressive forecasts with some degree of confidence, and if the series contains no more than 40–50 observations the most promising approach might be to combine these with Holt–Winters forecasts, using method 1 with $\nu = 12$. For longer series this approach is also to be recommended if resources do not permit the use of the Box–Jenkins method.

(c) For series of length at least 40–50, Box–Jenkins methods can usually be employed with a fair degree of confidence. If these produce forecasts of sufficient accuracy for the purposes at hand, then all well and good. If, however, greater accuracy proves desirable one might try combining Box–Jenkins, Holt–Winters and stepwise autoregressive forecasts, again using Method 1 with $\nu = 12$. It should be borne in mind, however, that the combined forecast could be worse than the individual

Box–Jenkins forecast and accordingly its performance should be monitored. If no improvement is achieved, one can calculate the optimum *ex post* constant weights. If the weight for one forecast is negative or close to zero then that forecast can be dropped, and one should go back and determine whether or not combination of the remaining two forecasts would have proved successful. This would serve as a guide for whether to combine these two forecasts in the future. We feel also that in situations where the Box–Jenkins identification is not clear-cut it would be worth while to fit two or three different ARIMA models, and combine the resulting forecasts using this approach.

(d) Occasionally one meets a time series which proves particularly difficult. For such series it is generally worth while, if at all possible, to work through the Box–Jenkins technique, as it provides considerably more information about the characteristics of the series under study than do any of the fully automatic procedures.

(e) For those series which are strongly seasonal and exhibit large random fluctuations, substitute the Harrison method for that of Holt and Winters in the above.

(f) Never follow blindly the guidelines (a)–(e)! In many practical situations one knows something of value about the series under consideration. This information should, if possible, be employed in any decision as to how the series should be forecast.

Our empirical work was concerned exclusively with economic time series data, and two general points emerged with respect to such series. First, for every time series in our sample, differencing was required in the construction of a Box–Jenkins model. This typical behaviour of economic series has implications not only in univariate model building but also in the building of relationships between series, since for time series of this kind the simple cross-correlation function is a very poor indicator indeed of the strength of any interrelationship. (See, for example, Box and Newbold, 1971). The second point is that in our combining procedures we generally failed to detect evidence of non-stationary behaviour (other than in the random-walk type sense of the ARIMA models) in our time series.

We do not claim to have covered in our work all the various procedures which have been proposed for univariate time series prediction. In particular, there is a great deal of theoretical literature on the topics of non-stationarity and non-linearity. We believe, however, that in order to apply the relevant theory in practice one would need a considerably greater length of data than is generally available for economic time series.

Besides being of interest in itself, this study in univariate time series forecasting also provides, in our opinion, a useful basis for research into multivariate forecasting. We are, at the present time, extending our work in this direction.

ACKNOWLEDGEMENT

This research was supported by a grant from the Social Science Research Council.

REFERENCES

BATES, J. M. and GRANGER, C. W. J. (1969). The combination of forecasts. *Oper. Res. Q.*, **20**, 451–468.

BOX, G. E. P. and JENKINS, G. M. (1970). *Time Series Analysis, Forecasting and Control*. San Francisco: Holden Day.

BOX, G. E. P. and NEWBOLD, P. (1971). Some comments on a paper of Coen, Gomme and Kendall, *J. R. Statist. Soc.* A, **134**, 229–240.

BROWN, R. G. (1959). *Statistical Forecasting for Inventory Control.* New York: McGraw-Hill.
—— (1962). *Smoothing, Forecasting and Prediction.* New York: Prentice Hall.
CHATFIELD, C. and PROTHERO, D. L. (1973). Box–Jenkins seasonal forecasting: problems in a case study, *J. R. Statist. Soc.* A, **136**, 295–336.
GRANGER, C. W. J. (1966). The typical spectral shape of an economic variable. *Econometrica,* **34**, 150–161.
—— (1969). Prediction with a generalized cost of error function. *Oper. Res. Q.,* **20**, 199–207.
GRANGER, C. W. J. and NEWBOLD, P. (1972). Economic forecasting—the atheist's viewpoint. Paper presented to Conference on the *Modelling of the U.K. Economy,* London Graduate School of Business Studies.
—— (1973). Some comments on the evaluation of economic forecasts, *Appl. Econ.,* **5**, 35–47.
HARRISON, P. J. (1965). Short-term sales forecasting. *Appl. Statist.,* **14**, 102–139.
HOLT, C. C. (1957). Forecasting seasonal and trends by exponentially weighted moving averages. Carnegie Institute of Technology.
NEWBOLD, P. (1973). The principles of the Box–Jenkins approach. Paper presented to Conference on *Practical Aspects of Forecasting,* Imperial College, London.
PAYNE, D. J. (1973). The determination of regression relationships using stepwise regression techniques. Ph.D. Thesis, University of Nottingham.
REID, D. J. (1969). A comparative study of time series prediction techniques on economic data. Ph.D. Thesis, University of Nottingham.
WINTERS, P. R. (1960). Forecasting sales by exponentially weighted moving averages. *Man. Sci.,* **6**, 324–342.

DISCUSSION OF THE PAPER BY DR NEWBOLD AND PROF. GRANGER

Dr D. J. REID (Central Statistical Office): I was pleased to be asked to propose the vote of thanks on behalf of the Society to the authors of this evening's paper, partly because the subject is one that has engaged my interest for several years, but also because it comes from my "home stable" so to speak. The paper falls into two parts; an empirical study using three single series prediction techniques to forecast series of a broadly economic nature, and a more extensive comparison of methods of combining forecasts than has hitherto been available: the results of the first part of the paper forming the data for the second.

My comments will likewise be split into two parts. The question motivating the first part seems to be the pragmatic one of which forecasting method is best. One is bound to say that the real choice is unlikely to be limited to one of the three methods described. However, accepting a need for some restriction, and accepting that mean squared error is the most appropriate measure of performance, there seem to be two ways in which one might look at the behaviour of prediction techniques to assess their usefulness. The first is to describe the stochastic process for which each method produces optimal forecasts. A variant of this approach would be to discuss the performance of techniques on certain known processes, either at a theoretical level or by computer simulation. In either form this approach has always struck me as a fairly pointless exercise since if one is typically in the position of knowing the stochastic process generating the data there is no need for portmanteau techniques. One merely builds a predictor using the well-established theory.

The alternative strategy, adopted by the authors and by myself (Reid, 1969), is to look at the performance of the techniques on a large sample of series that are typical of data on which practitioners wish to use the techniques. A major difficulty here is that the population of such series is not defined so one cannot select the data with due regard to sampling theory. In this situation the investigator must choose his series ensuring that they are representative and not merely available but, more than this, it is incumbent on him to describe the characteristics of the series chosen as fully as possible and to discuss the performance of techniques in terms of these characteristics. It was rather disappointing to find that the authors did not do this, so missing an opportunity of using the study to provide an inferential basis for the choice of technique. Frequencies alone are of limited usefulness in this context and it would have been more interesting to have seen various multivariate tools, such as cluster analysis or factor analysis, applied to the results of the study to try to find reasons for differences in performance on different series. As it is the practitioner may be left with a doubt about the relevance of these results to his particular problem.

Turning now to the second part of the paper, on combining forecasts, it is interesting to see a much larger study of the combining procedure than was given by Bates and Granger. As a practical tool for increasing the efficiency of a set of forecasts, combining has the attractions of being purely automatic and conceptually rather simple, and the results displayed are certainly quite impressive. However, there seem to be two major criticisms that can be levelled against it.

In the first place it is very difficult to think of a solid theoretical justification for what is being done. There is, for example, no sense in which the outcome is "dependent" on the forecasts. If the forecasts and outcome co-vary in a consistent way, this is presumably because there are factors influencing both, and hence a more informative approach would seem to be to build a model incorporating these factors. Neither is the Bayesian justification as presented in Section 5 entirely satisfactory. If one feels that there are different mechanisms generating the observations, then the posterior probabilities that each of the various mechanisms generated for X at time t should be reflected in the way in which X_t is used to update the respective forecast models. This is not done since within the individual forecast techniques, all observations are treated as being equally informative. I suspect that a thorough Bayesian treatment would involve building a new model incorporating the features of the individual models being combined.

This brings me to the second shortcoming of the combining approach which is that under alternative, and perhaps more plausible, assumptions it is sub-optimal. Suppose we assume that the reason why one method is better over certain periods but not over others is that both models are inadequate representations of the true generating mechanism. Then the optimum predictor (in a linear least-squares sense), within the scope of the information available, would be obtained from a model incorporating all the explanatory variables in the methods being combined. We might refer to this as the composite model. The sub-optimality of combining is demonstrated geometrically in Fig. 1 for a simple two-forecast situation where each forecast is proportional to a single predictive variable.

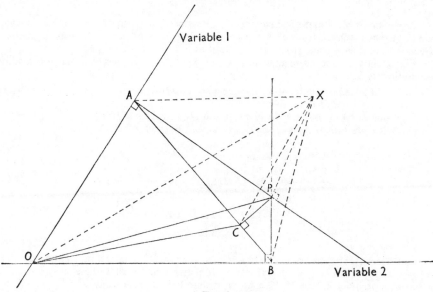

FIG. 1

OX is the quantity to be predicted and the basic forecasts are its projections onto each of the explanatory variables, namely OA and OB. Combined forecasts with non-negative weights, as discussed by the authors, are represented by points on the line segment AB and the combined forecast OC that minimizes the length of XC is obtained by taking XC orthogonal to AB. It is clear that the error XC of the combined forecast can be reduced in the composite model if we take the predictor OP which is the orthogonal projection of OX onto the plane AOB.

In discussing an empirical paper, it is appropriate to include some empirical basis to one's argument, so by way of illustration and without wishing to defend particular choices of techniques, I took the quarterly series for the Standard and Poor index, suitably transformed to stationarity and fitted a Box–Jenkins model to compare with the model given by Coen *et al.* (1969). For a combined forecast it was more convenient for computational reasons to take method 4 with $W = 1.5$ rather than method 1 with $v = 12$, but Table 6 suggests these are good substitutes. The mean squared errors for the individual forecasts, the combined forecast and the forecast from a composite model were:

Box–Jenkins	0·0798
Coen *et al.*	0·0845
Combined forecast	0·1175
Composite forecast	0·0769

supporting the contention that a "composite" model is better than a "combined" one.

In retrospect this turned out to be an unsatisfactory example because the combined forecast did worse than both individual ones, which, whilst not impossible, is untypical. Perhaps it does add emphasis, however, to my earlier point which was that to discuss the merits of techniques merely in terms of frequencies with which they do well without identifying characteristics of the series and techniques which give rise to these relative performances, is less than fully informative.

It is with pleasure that I move the vote of thanks to the authors for their paper which I am sure will generate a lot of interesting discussion.

Professor G. M. Jenkins (University of Lancaster): Dr Newbold and Professor Granger are to be congratulated for their extensive empirical study of various forecasting methods. Nevertheless, I have some major reservations about their conclusions.

Fig. 2 shows three basic questions which need to be answered when forecasting a single time series:

(1) What *weights* should be applied to past observations to generate the forecasts of future values of the series?
(2) What curve or *forecast function* should the forecasts follow?
(3) What *probability limits* should be attached to the forecasts?

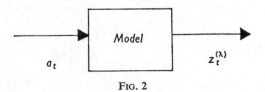

Fig. 2

In the past there has been a tendency to answer these questions in isolation and in an *ad hoc* manner. In our book Professor Box and I argue that these answers are not arbitrary nor independent of each other, but follow automatically once a *parsimonious model* has been obtained which transforms a suitable non-linear function $f(z_t) = z_t^{(\lambda)}$ of the observed time series z_t to a random or white noise series a_t where $z_t^{(\lambda)}$ is some parameter transformation in which λ represents a single parameter or vector of parameters defining the transformation and which may be estimated from the data. In particular, $z_t^{(\lambda)}$ could be a power transformation z_t^λ which becomes $\ln z_t$ when $\lambda = 0$.

If such a model can be found, it follows that the one-step-ahead forecast errors of $z_t^{(\lambda)}$ constitute a random series with a *constant* variance σ_a^2. The three-stage model building procedure consisting of identification, fitting and checking that we have proposed can therefore be thought of as an iterative process which aims to end up with a model which generates residuals or one-step-ahead forecasts which are random.

Dr Newbold and Professor Granger argue that we can never be sure that a particular model may be appropriate and then proceed to combine the forecasts from a Box–Jenkins model with those from two other methods. In particular, they argue in Tables 4 and 7 that the empirical process of selection of the weights that they advocate results in empirical forecast errors which in some cases are slightly smaller than those obtained from Box–Jenkins' forecasts when the latter are combined with one or two other forecasts. Several comments may be made about their procedure for combining forecasts:

1. Since the Holt–Winters and stepwise autoregression methods correspond to special cases of the autoregressive-integrated moving average models proposed by Professor Box and myself, it follows that a linear combination of these forecasts with a Box–Jenkins forecast results in a forecast which corresponds to another more elaborate model in the class of ARIMA processes. If the latter model gives better forecasts than the forecast from the original Box–Jenkins model, the question then arises as to why a close approximation to the more elaborate model, if needed, was not arrived at during the model building stage.

2. As indicated above, the objective should be to end up with residuals or one-step-ahead forecast errors which are random. When checks of the residuals over the length of record to which the model was fitted fail to reveal evidence of non-randomness, it is doubtful whether significant improvements in forecast accuracy can be obtained from a more elaborate model derived by combining forecasts. It is always possible, of course, to achieve reductions in the sum of squares of the residuals by introducing further parameters into the model. However, the addition of more parameters than are necessary to reduce the data to a random series merely results in unnecessarily poor forecasts.

3. The method of combining forecasts advocated by the authors is subject to serious criticism on the grounds that the weights in the combined forecasts are chosen *empirically* from the same set of series that are used to make comparisons between the individual forecasting methods. Any such method must lead to bias in the individual time series and it is difficult to judge whether the error reduction, which is not very large, could not be the result of such bias. The acid test would be if combination weights obtained empirically from, say, the first halves of their series were to lead to reductions in forecast errors when applied to the second halves of their series.

4. The authors have placed considerable emphasis on the need for procedures whereby the data can be fed into the computer and forecasts generated automatically. My first reaction is that their proposal seems unduly laborious since it involves using at least two forecasting methods and then a further stage to combine them. Since the combined forecast corresponds to an ARIMA model, it would seem more expedient to automate the fitting of the ARIMA models in the first place. I understand that at least one American organization has done this. However, it is difficult to understand why there should be such a need to proceed from data to forecasts without going through the intermediate stage of thinking about the data. I doubt, for example, whether many people would want to analyse data from a planned experiment automatically. The fact remains that model building is best done by the

human brain and is inevitably an iterative process. In the case of a univariate time series, there are many decisions which need to be made, such as the choice of the non-linear transformation parameter, the degrees of differencing to induce stationarity, the orders of the seasonal and non-seasonal autoregressive and moving average operators and whether the residual series contains any outlying observations or marked autocorrelation patterns. It is unlikely that such a process can be effectively automated, although with an interactive computer program the computer can be used to do the routine calculations and present them in an appropriate form for the human mind to interpret the intermediate stages of output. Such interactive computer programs for both univariate and transfer function modelling and forecasting have now been developed in collaboration with two time sharing companies.

The authors state that their method can also be used to combine dissimilar forecasts, e.g. a univariate time series forecast with an econometric forecast. Again, I would prefer to use a model rather than an arbitrary method of combining the forecasts. For example, in a production planning problem the question arose as to whether the sales forecasts produced by the sales representatives could be improved by a time series forecast. An empirical comparison over a three-year period showed that the 95 per cent probability limits of the one-step-ahead forecast errors of ± 11 per cent achieved by the salesmen could be reduced to ± 5 per cent using a univariate time series model. However, a transfer function model of the form shown in Fig. 3 succeeded in reducing the probability limits of the one-step-ahead forecast errors to slightly under ± 4 per cent, indicating that the salesmen had some information not contained in the historical data.

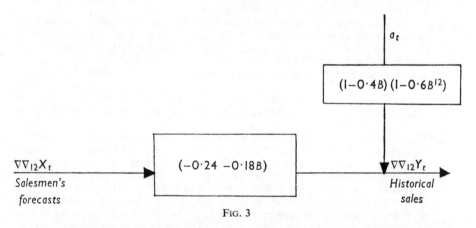

a_t

$(1-0\cdot4B)(1-0\cdot6B^{12})$

$\nabla\nabla_{12}X_t$
Salesmen's
forecasts

$(-0\cdot24\ -0\cdot18B)$

$\nabla\nabla_{12}Y_t$
Historical
sales

Fig. 3

To summarize, I am sceptical about the method of combining forecasts advocated by the authors for the several reasons that I have outlined. Common to all my comments is the belief that it reintroduces a further element of *ad hoc* reasoning into a subject which has too long been plagued by *ad hoc* methods.

Despite my critical comments, I very much support the authors' concern with evaluating forecasting methods using a large number of empirical time series. I have great pleasure in seconding the vote of thanks to Dr Newbold and Professor Granger for their paper.

The vote of thanks was passed by acclamation.

Mr G. J. A. Stern (ICL, Computer House, Euston Centre, London NW1): The excellent work done by the authors could well be supplemented by another survey: which would be to rank forecasting methods not by accuracy but by frequency of use, especially by decision-makers in Government, industry and commerce. If this were done, the classical method of "trend plus seasonals plus residuals" might well head the list. For example, almost the only example of a forecasting technique widely accepted by government ministers is de-seasonalization of unemployment figures and other macro-economic data.

I think that the managers who need a forecast are prepared to understand the idea of a trend and of seasonal effects, because this corresponds to their own way of thinking. Furthermore, in real life one often wants to take some approximate account of other factors without going to the lengths of a full econometric study, for which data are frequently too sparse anyway. Managers can see that after taking out trend and seasonal effect sales were lower than expected and that this might be explained by a price rise, decimalization etc., and they can then apply this experience to modifying the prediction for the year ahead. They will believe this sort of forecast because they understand how it operates, and they are able to modify it to take account of special knowledge they have of the likelihood of being "blown off course", to quote the well-known phrase of our immediate Past President. Also, they do not need tremendous accuracy: quite a common situation is that they have ordered, say, a certain amount of cloth for women's dresses for a season's sales, and all they want is a forecast based on sales of dresses so far this season which merely says: "You've ordered far too much/far too little/about the right amount." The time series used will have neither the length nor the consistency required for elaborate methods like Box–Jenkins, nor would the accuracy gained be required.

I would apply these reflections to the present study by the following remarks. Firstly, Box–Jenkins may have shown up better partly because of the element of manual intervention, which has enabled the authors to input their knowledge of how the time series were likely to go. Even simpler methods than Holt–Winters and stepwise autoregression might have worked better than these did had this possibility of manual intervention existed. Secondly, could it be that many of the series reflected exponential growth or decline, and the underlying models for Holt–Winters and stepwise autoregression did not reflect this as well as Box–Jenkins? Would, for example, a linear trend plus seasonal model on logarithms of the data have done better? It would be useful to publish a list of the series used in the authors' study together with a brief description of their shape, and possibly the Box–Jenkins (p.d.q.) parameters, to help answer these questions. Thirdly, the sort of manual intervention allowed by Box–Jenkins is not really what is needed in the forecasting contexts I have spoken of, because it has to be applied by experts. This means that the decision-maker using the forecast has to have his knowledge filtered both through an expert and through a computer program, instead of being able to see directly what was done. In practice this will often pose an insuperable barrier to the practical use of the technique for decision-making forecasting, even supposing that such experts as the authors are readily available, which is by no means the case.

The combined forecasting methods seem to me to be non-starters. One could adapt St Jerome, that "the whole world groaned to find itself saying 'parsimonious parameterization'." Box–Jenkins could be described as a method of stating in a short but opaque equation much of what is to be said about a time series: other methods could be characterized as less compact in expression and possibly less accurate but gaining in comprehensibility. Is a combined method not in danger of falling between two stools?

I do not wish to give the impression that I am opposed to Box–Jenkins methods under all circumstances: far from it. ICL offer a wide range of forecasting methods, which include several based on Box–Jenkins, and I am clear that this technique has a wide application. What I do favour is fitting the method to the problem, and I suspect that Box–Jenkins is more suited to one-period-ahead forecasts in a technological context (e.g. control of machines), or for studies of long time series of compatible terms. For many other contexts of decision-making forecasting, I suspect that simpler methods are all that can be justified.

In conclusion, I would like to see more research directed to problems of dealing with short, dirty time series with tools that managerial users of the forecast can understand. Studies of error bounds under a wide range of circumstances would be especially useful.

Professor M. B. PRIESTLEY (University of Manchester Institute of Science and Technology): There is now a considerable literature on prediction and forecasting problems, and since the motivation for most of this work was (presumably) to enable people to make more efficient forecasts it is obviously instructive to apply various forecasting approaches to real data and to examine just how well they perform. In this regard, Dr Newbold and Professor Granger's study of a large number of economic series is indeed a most useful one, and they have made some stimulating comments on the results of their analyses. However, interesting and valuable though their results undoubtedly are, we should be careful not to read too much into them—as, of course, we should with any largely empirical study. Let us see, therefore, just what we can reasonably infer from the relative "success" (or "failure") of a particular forecasting approach as applied to a particular group of time series.

The structure of the general univariate forecasting problem may be summarized roughly as follows; we are given past values (up to time t) of a random process, $..., X_{t-2}, X_{t-1}, X_t$, and wish to forecast the value, X_{t+m}, which the process will assume at the future time point, $(t+m)$. In constructing the forecast, $\tilde{X}_{t+m}$, we must first answer the following questions;

(a) What class of random processes are we considering?

(b) What general class of functions of $\{X_s; s \leqslant t\}$ should we consider for $\tilde{X}_{t+m}$?

(c) Having chosen the general class of functions in (b), what criterion of accuracy of $\tilde{X}_{t+m}$ should we use in order to determine the explicit form of $\tilde{X}_{t+m}$ as a function of $X_t, X_{t-1}, ...$?

Of course, if we consider different answers to (b) this will, in general, lead to different forecasts, and if we then agree on a common answer to (c) we can meaningfully compare the relative efficiencies of the different forecasts. For example, if under (c) we choose the "mean square error" criterion, then we could compare the relative efficiency of *linear* forecasts as opposed to, for example, *quadratic* forecasts. However, for all the methods studied in the paper the answers to (a), (b), (c), all turn out to be identical. In fact, all the methods deal only with *stationary process* (or processes which can be rendered stationary by a suitable transformation), all the methods involve only *linear* forecasts, and all are based on the common criterion of "*mean square error*".

What then are the remaining arbitrary features which form the area of dispute? Given (a), (b), (c), the "optimum" forecast is uniquely determined (assuming that the covariance structure is fully known) and no question then arises as to whether one approach is "superior" to another. The Box–Jenkins approach provides a very neat computational algorithm for calculating the linear mean square forecast for series which conform to a particular (albeit, fairly general) class of models, and if this technique works well for a particular series it means that the series under study happens to belong to this class of models. Similarly, if one of the "automatic" methods works well, it means that the series happens to be of the more specialized form for which this *ad hoc* predictor is close to optimal (in the mean square sense). On the other hand, if the Box–Jenkins approach produces unsatisfactory forecasts then either the series does not fit in with the general class of Box–Jenkins models, or if it does, it has not been correctly identified. Thus, the results of the authors' forecasting study tell us rather more about the *models of the series* analysed than about the relative merits of the different types of forecasting methods. Naturally, since the Box–Jenkins approach is the only one of those considered which attempts to match the form of the forecast to the model of the series with any degree of generality, it is hardly surprising that the Box–Jenkins forecasts are generally superior to those produced by the "automatic" methods.

The authors may, perhaps, regard the identification and model-fitting stages as part of the overall Box–Jenkins "procedure", but this interpretation would, I think, be rather misleading. After all, the problems of identification and model fitting are not unique to forecasting but arise in a variety of time series problems—particularly, in the context of stochastic control systems. Here, there is certainly scope for further study, and although the problem of parameter estimation is a fairly straightforward one, the associated problem of determining suitable values for the *orders* of the autoregressive and moving average operators (in a mixed scheme) has not, as yet, been resolved in a thoroughly satisfactory manner. Here, the recent work of Akaike (1972) (aimed at extending his "MFPE" technique to mixed schemes) seems a promising development.

The authors' suggestion about combining different forecasts is an interesting one, but its validity would seem to depend on the assumption that the model used in the Box–Jenkins approach is inadequate—for otherwise, the Box–Jenkins forecast alone would be optimal. However, this general idea raises the question of "robustness"—i.e. how "robust" is an optimal linear forecast with respect to variation in the model parameters? This would be a most worth-while study and one approach would be to generate artificial series of known structure and then investigate the efficiency of "perturbed" predictors.

Dr C. CHATFIELD (Bath University): The authors are to be congratulated for their comprehensive study which has given us a much better idea of the comparative merits of different univariate forecasting procedures.

From Table 2, we see that the median improvement of Box–Jenkins over Holt–Winters is about 15 per cent. If this is judged to be worth the extra cost of the Box–Jenkins procedure, it is worth remembering that the authors have far more experience with the Box–Jenkins method than nearly anyone else in this country. They modestly say that any fairly experienced user would do as well but I suspect that their expertise is way above average. In any case few people are likely to analyse as many series as the authors and first attempts to use the method are likely to have mixed results, as we have found. This is not to say that one should not try the Box–Jenkins method, but one must be prepared to do less well than the authors, at least at first. I would like to ask the authors if they found that the Box–Jenkins method fared progressively better as the study proceeded.

I would now like to report briefly on the work by D. L. Prothero and myself at Bath, during which we made a close study of five time series, comparing the Box–Jenkins and Holt–Winters procedures. One of these series has been discussed elsewhere (Chatfield and Prothero, 1973). In the discussion to that paper it was suggested that the poor forecasts we obtained arose from using the wrong transformation. However, even if one uses the Box–Cox transformation suggested by Dr Wilson, we have subsequently found that the Holt–Winters procedure still gives the smaller mean square forecast error one step ahead. The authors do not mention transformations. I would like to ask if they ever found the need for a Box–Cox transformation when using the Box–Jenkins procedure.

Of the other four series we analysed, Box–Jenkins gave rather better one-step-ahead forecasts for two of the series, but did not do so well for longer lead times. For example, with quarterly sales data supplied by company *Y* (which did not need to be transformed!), the mean absolute forecast errors up to four quarters ahead were calculated as follows:

No. of quarters ahead	Holt–Winters	Box–Jenkins
1	2543	2454
2	2864	2988
3	3174	3416
4	3732	4143

Box–Jenkins is 3 per cent better one step ahead, but 10 per cent worse four steps ahead.

The series where Box–Jenkins gave appreciably better results was that analysed by Tomasek (1972) which is unusually regular. Linear trend and seasonal variation explain 97 per cent of the variation about the mean. Holt–Winters explained 98·9 per cent of the total variation and Box–Jenkins 99·4 per cent. Thus, by the authors' yardstick, Box–Jenkins is 45 per cent better than Holt–Winters. But as the unexplained variation is so small, Holt–Winters may be judged adequate.

We are glad to hear that the authors are extending their work to multivariate forecasting. For the data supplied by company *Y*, a very simple bivariate procedure in which detrended, deseasonalized sales are regressed on stocks two quarters before was found to give a mean absolute forecast error one step ahead of 1,900 which is much better than either of the univariate procedures we tried. If one wants to put in a lot of effort to get a good forecast, it may well be better to try a multivariate procedure than a complicated univariate procedure, although this does not always follow (Naylor *et al.*, 1972).

Mr H. HERNE (Brunel University): I am surprised by three points in this paper.

Firstly, the authors have examined only economic series. None, they say, are stationary. I doubt if many satisfy the further implicit assumption that the stochastic element in each series has a constant variance. None of the many series they have analysed comes from a physical background where simple statistical assumptions are more likely to be valid than for these dubious economic series.

Secondly, their method of combining forecasts seems inconsistent in that it gives a casuistic and seemingly insignificant improvement in the forecast at the expense of discarding the parsimonious parameterization on which the individual forecasts are built.

Thirdly, the authors may discourage other workers with their suggestion that the Box–Jenkins method of time series analysis is time-consuming and expensive. What I understand by the Box–Jenkins method is a traditional analysis in the time domain, and I find a short computer program on some three dozen cards can carry one quickly and cheaply to the stage of identification and preliminary estimation. Admittedly, this particular program does not "deseasonalize" but that is because I suspect economic series with seasonal character are rarely normal time series. I hope other workers with time series will not be intimidated either by the threat that conventional analysis is prohibitively expensive or by the odd results from an analysis of exclusively economic series.

Mr E. J. GODOLPHIN (Royal Holloway College, London): I would like to mention a point which occurred to me on reading tonight's paper.

One property of predictors of non-stationary ARIMA models is that they belong to the class of weighted averages, i.e.

$$\hat{X}_n(h) = \sum_{i=0}^{\infty} w_{hi} X_{n-i},$$

where

$$\sum_{i=0}^{\infty} w_{hi} = 1 \quad (h = 1, 2, \ldots).$$

This is generally true provided that at least one form of differencing ∇, ∇_4 or ∇_{12} is required to induce stationarity in the observations and that $\theta_0 = 0$ which is often the case with non-stationary series. Of course the *w*'s become negligible after a while, as indeed they should with series of finite length, but the upper limit on these summations can be of the order of 20 or even more before there is no appreciable change in performance.

This weighted average property of predictors of non-stationary ARIMA models is of interest here because the authors compare Box–Jenkins predictors with their stepwise autoregression predictors. And these autoregression predictors are themselves weighted averages if $\alpha = 0$, where for example

$$w_{10} = 1 + \beta_1, \quad w_{1i} = \beta_{i+1} - \beta_i \quad (i = 1, 2, ..., M-1),$$

$$w_{1M} = -\beta_M, \quad w_{1i} = 0 \quad (i > M).$$

Furthermore, the parameters M and $\{\beta_i\}$, and therefore the w's also, are *a priori* arbitrary if one takes the suggestion of the authors in Section 4 to consider a "goodness-of-fit" criterion of specification and selection. Presupposing the authors' data series are non-stationary, it follows that autoregression predictors are in principle as general as Box–Jenkins predictors which seems contrary to the authors' assertion in Section 5, and incidentally this degree of generality extends to the case where θ_0, α are not identically zero. In other words, the authors have the means available for constructing a predictor which, on the face of it, should do just as well as Box–Jenkins.

This raises the question why the authors arrive empirically at a different conclusion, since their autoregression predictor is "markedly outperformed" by the Box–Jenkins predictor according to the remarks accompanying Tables 1 and 2. One appreciates the need for caution when drawing conclusions from empirical results; however, I suspect that the selection criteria employed by the authors often avoid autoregression predictors which could do that much better than that selected.

Let me make it clear however that I do not criticize the authors for apparently failing to find the "best" autoregression predictor, because that prospect seems to me to be a daunting one. It is equivalent to estimating simultaneously the individual members of the $\{w_{1i}\}$ sequence which could be converging only slowly to zero. This may involve many unknown parameters and there is the awkward problem of deciding when to stop. It appears to me intuitively to be an unpromising line of approach, and I am reluctant to share the authors' confidence for the autoregression predictor. Would the authors not agree that the advantage of the Box–Jenkins procedure lies not only in the wide choice of forecast functions available but also in the fact that forecast functions can involve many realized observations without necessarily involving the same number of unknown parameters?

Also on the subject of predictor generality, I would mention that the predictors of Brown and Meyer (1961) are special cases of Box–Jenkins predictors, namely the predictors of IMA $(0, d, d)$ processes where the roots of the moving average representation are equal. This result came to light some time ago when P. J. Harrison and myself were engaged jointly on a project at ICI to examine non-seasonal time series.

Dr K. F. WALLIS (London School of Economics): I would like to ask whether the authors can make available further useful information from their valuable study, but first, despite their assumption in the summary that there is nothing even "mildly controversial" in the earlier sections, I wish to take issue with a statement which appears as early as the third paragraph of the paper.

The authors claim that having first carried out a univariate time series analysis one can assess to what extent other explanatory variables are required by correlating such variables with the univariate forecast errors. However, it is known in the context of regression models that this is not a good procedure, and similar results apply in the time series context. As a simple example, consider the regression model

$$y_t = \beta_1 x_{1t} + \beta_2 x_{2t} + u_t.$$

If we first regress y on x_1 and obtain the residuals $e_t = y_t - bx_{1t}$, and then regress these residuals on x_2 to obtain an estimate of β_2, the resulting estimate is biased towards zero if there is any correlation between x_1 and x_2. Thus the extent to which the "other" explanatory variable is required is underestimated. The same result holds asymptotically if x_{1t} is the lagged dependent variable y_{t-1}, and now the condition that x_1 and x_2 are correlated can be replaced by the condition that x_2 is autocorrelated. More generally, in the time series context, consider the transfer function model

$$y_t = \frac{\omega(B)}{\delta(B)} x_t + \frac{\theta_1(B)}{\phi_1(B)} \varepsilon_t, \tag{1}$$

where the polynomials $\phi_1, \theta_1, \delta, \omega$ are of order p_1, q_1, r, s respectively. Suppose that x also has an ARMA (p_2, q_2) representation

$$x_t = \frac{\theta_2(B)}{\phi_2(B)} \xi_t. \tag{2}$$

Then by substituting (2) into (1) we see that y has an ARMA representation

$$y_t = \frac{\theta_3(B)}{\phi_3(B)} \eta_t, \tag{3}$$

where, on the assumption that the polynomials have no common factors,

$$\phi_3(B) = \phi_1(B)\,\phi_2(B)\,\delta(B)$$

is of order $p_1 + p_2 + r$, and $\theta_3(B)$ is of order $\max(p_1 + q_2 + s, p_2 + q_1 + r)$. If a univariate analysis of the y-series is first carried out, then it is the model (3) which one will seek to identify and estimate, and this already incorporates the dynamics of the relation (1). Thus the "potential usefulness" of x_t will be underestimated when it is related to the residuals $\hat{\eta}_t$. (Note that the authors' suggestion differs from the Box–Jenkins suggestion of first fitting the model (2) for the input series, and then "prewhitening" x_t and the transfer function model (1) by applying the operator $\phi_2(B)/\theta_2(B)$, to aid in the identification of δ and ω.)

My request for additional information concerns forecast intervals (or what Box and Jenkins call "probability limits" in a non-standard use of that term). The usual calculation of forecast intervals assumes that the model is correct and that the parameter values are known. A common experience is that models have worse error variances than they "should" when used in forecasting outside the period of fit. In the present context, incorrect forecast intervals may be caused by (a) parameter estimation errors, (b) the wrong choice of model and general data-mining complications, reflecting the uncertainty about the model mentioned by the authors and (c) non-normality of errors. Given the mass of results obtained in the present study, it would be helpful to shed light on this question. Would it be possible for Professor Granger and Dr Newbold to look through their pile of computer output, and tell us what proportion of the time the conventional forecast intervals contained the actual series values—did the forecast errors fall within the estimated ± 1.96 bands approximately 95 per cent of the time, or more, or less—were there any differences between Box–Jenkins and stepwise autoregression—and do they have any conclusions to offer in the light of their very considerable experience?

Mr J. M. CRADDOCK (Meteorological Office): Whatever the views held on the combining of forecasts of time series obtained by different methods, there is no doubt that combined long-range weather forecasts, each based on several predictions founded on different physical principles, are better on average than the predictions given by any single method.

The least-squares criterion is not suitable for the situation in which drawings made from a reservoir in one year must be made up by an income during the next. In this situation the strategy to decide the admissible level of drawings must seek to keep the accumulated error (surplus or deficit) within the bounds fixed by the capacity of the reservoir.

I am surprised that the authors have confined themselves to economic time series, and have not considered, for example, the monthly mean temperatures for Central England for 1698–1952, published by Manley (1953). This series, which has since been extended back to 1680 and forward to the present date, is not subject to inflation, or other short-term, man-made disturbances, and like many other geophysical series the processes which produce it are understood in part. Such series should provide excellent tests for the resolving power of any new statistical method.

Mr M. J. BRAMSON (National Economic Development Office): The Holt–Winters method in order to operate requires two or three starting values, and the forecasts can in some cases be quite sensitive to these; I wonder whether the authors could tell us something about how they chose them.

I would like to support the point Mr Stern made on the question of the exponential growth of economic series. This is a very common feature of many economic series, and it does indicate the need for a type 'of transformation other than straight differencing; economists commonly take the percentage increase or decrease all the way along the series.

I would also like to support those speakers who asked for more work to be done on the characteristics of the series that were studied. Dr Reid was the first speaker to ask for that, and in his own thesis (which the authors list in their references) he gave what I feel is a very useful chart which classifies series on the basis of about five different characteristics and recommends forecasting methods accordingly. I wonder if the authors could comment as to whether their work bears out Dr Reid's views in this respect and add their own views along these lines: this would be a considerable service to those of us who are concerned with practical forecasting.

Lastly I would like to do what appears to be swimming against the tide tonight, and that is to support the idea of automatic forecasting. I think this definitely has a place in certain types of industry. I have had a fair amount of experience in work on stock control and production control. When you are doing stock control and production control you do need short-term forecasts, a matter of a few months or up to a year ahead for each of the products which you are dealing with, and many firms in this country in fact produce a very wide range of different products, amounting in some cases to thousands. I suspect that not even Dr Newbold would be prepared to run thousands of Box–Jenkins analyses, even only once a year.

It is in these circumstances that one badly needs a reliable automatic method of forecasting to put into the computer and churn out the regular forecasts that you need to do a reasonable job of stock control and production control. Certainly one also agrees with the need that other speakers pointed out to be able to incorporate management knowledge with the automatic forecasts, and here is where you need also an automatic monitoring system which will show you how well a forecasting system is doing.

Mr D. H. WARD (Birds Eye Foods Ltd): I should like to endorse what Mr Bramson has said, since not only do you have in industry the problem of one firm trying to look after ten thousand products, but you may also have the problem of it having to look after a couple of hundred products in 30 or 40 depots, and again you cannot intervene into each one individually. A further point is that both in stock control and production control you are not primarily concerned with getting a good forecast of next week's or next month's, or next year's sales, but with getting a cumulative forecast that is correct for the planning period. Since Dr Chatfield's examination showed that even though Box–Jenkins was good for one period ahead, it appeared to be getting worse for four periods ahead, I suspect that in such a situation where errors in estimating a trend become dominant, errors in the cumulative forecasts would make the comparison of Box–Jenkins look even worse against the other methods.

The following contributions were received in writing, after the meeting:

Professor S. M. STIGLER (University of Wisconsin): All too often in the past, competing forecasting methods have been compared on the basis of their performances on a single time series or, worse, on the basis of simulated series. Newbold and Granger are to be commended for the large-scale empirical test they have performed; the work of Section 6 is both timely and important. However, it seems to me possible, indeed likely, that the authors have allowed themselves to be misled as to the advisability of combining other forecasting schemes with Box–Jenkins. Put bluntly, I feel that the methodology the authors have adopted has led to a well-disguised but very real instance of the selection fallacy.

Newbold and Granger state their objective as twofold: "first, to determine whether combining could produce a forecast which was, in general, superior to the individual forecasts, and secondly, to investigate differences in performance of the five combining procedures". I would argue that in their attempt to achieve two goals they have actually opened both of their conclusions ("yes" and "method 1 with $\nu = 12$ is best") to suspicion that their results are at best heavily biased and at worst totally misleading. For no one would (or should) argue with the proposition that it is possible (by combining or otherwise) to produce a forecast which outperforms even an "optimal" scheme *if* one is allowed to select the method of combination on the basis of the same set of series upon which the comparison is based.

Newbold and Granger have performed three studies involving combining Box–Jenkins and other methods, and in each study five methods of combination (in a total of 33 variations) were evaluated. Should the observed results be considered surprising, even under the hypothesis that combining forecasts is mildly detrimental? Any serious attempt to assess a significance probability is likely doomed by the complexity of the situation, but it is perhaps instructive to consider in a simple, admittedly unrealistic situation, how the selection fallacy might distort the truth:

Suppose the series to be forecast are all "white noise"; that is, $\{Z_t\}$ are independent $N(0, \sigma^2)$. Clearly the optimal forecast of Z_{t+1} given $Z_t, Z_{t-1}, \ldots$ is $\hat{Z}_{t+1} \equiv 0$. Indeed, this would be the Box–Jenkins forecast if the model were perfectly identified and fitted. Consider two alternative methods of forecasting, $\hat{X}_{t+1} \equiv \varepsilon$ and $\hat{Y}_{t+1} \equiv -\varepsilon$, ε being a very small positive number. These might be called optimistic and pessimistic respectively. If one then makes 80 forecasts and "selects" one of $\hat{X}$ and $\hat{Y}$ on the basis of the forecast errors, then the *expected* percentage of times the *selected* one outperforms the *optimal* $\hat{Z}$ is about 54·5 per cent! Similar results would hold if $\hat{X}$ and $\hat{Y}$ were replaced by unbiased random predictors—say, different moving averages of past Z's. Of course this example is a gross over-simplification of the situation. But Newbold and Granger consider a great number (of closely related) forecasting schemes, and it is clear that the selection effect could be greatly accentuated both if one combines forecasts as they have done and if the 80 series used are dependent, as would very likely be the case with Newbold and Granger's series. It is also clear, at least in the simplified example, that the effect of selection upon the ratio of expected squared errors would be less dramatic than the effect upon "percentage outperformed"; this too is consistent with the authors' findings.

In fairness to the authors it should be admitted that this argument is not a proof that Method 1 with $\nu = 12$ is not an effective, even "super-optimal", means of forecasting; this question can only be settled by further empirical evaluations, made upon series independent of those Newbold and Granger used. However, when viewed from the perspective of the selection effect, it must be admitted that Table 4 is particularly damaging to their case, and Table 7 is considerably more ambiguous.

Finally, it is perhaps of interest to note that the method of combination of forecasts which Newbold and Granger have studied was earlier used (in the context of point estimation rather than prediction) by Laplace in 1818. Laplace termed the method "impracticable" since the appropriate, optimal weights were unknown (see Stigler, 1973).

Mr D. W. BUNN (The London Graduate School of Business Studies): The suggestion that it might be possible to combine a set of forecasting mechanisms by attaching to each a subjective probability reflecting the user's degree of belief that it represents the true underlying stochastic process would appear to be a promising approach (and, perhaps, a tentative indication of the inevitable Bayesian approach to the combination of forecasts), but one, it seems, not without certain theoretical and operational difficulties.

A forecasting mechanism is an inductive hypothesis on the true underlying stochastic process and as such the question of its being established as logically true or false, unlike that of a realizable event, is generally indeterminable. Subjective probability has achieved success in Bayesian decision theory only as a measure on realizable, future contingent events such as the proposition, "it will rain tomorrow". However, an inductive hypothesis such as the proposition, "all ravens are black", is incapable of confirmation, owing to the necessity of examining each member of a population of unknown size. Thus, if one attempts to measure the subjective probability of an inductive hypothesis in the usual decision theoretic way of offering the decision maker the artificial standard gamble on the truth or falsity of the hypothesis, providing he is rational, he will always bet on its falsity regardless of the pay-offs, since it will not be possible to confirm its truth. For example, a non-black raven might appear (and so refute the hypothesis) but it will never be possible to confirm it by examining all the ravens. Hence the imputed subjective probability of the hypothesis will be zero.

Clearly, a more pragmatic position can be taken by dealing with the approximate rather than the absolute truth of the hypothesis through restricting the domain of its validity. One can obtain a subjective weighting between two or more forecasting mechanisms by offering the standard gamble on which of them will perform better over the next n periods. But such a weighting will not represent one's belief in the underlying "true" stochastic process. Typically, for short lead times an autoregressive mechanism would be given a higher weighting than an econometric one, whereas for a longer lead time the weighting would generally be in favour of the econometric approach.

Professor H. S. KONIJN (Tel Aviv University and London School of Economics): In many instances of prediction of economic time series $\{X_t\}$ one may approximately define two positive numbers m and M such that it is not of great value to achieve a forecast error numerically less than m, but that an error between m and M would have serious consequences, and an error exceeding M would be disastrous. (More generally, m and M may be replaced by relatively short intervals, and m and M need not be the same for positive errors as for negative ones.) Thus, it may be particularly important to predict non-trivial up- or downturns, defined as those which are at least m, and vital to predict up- or downturns larger than M. (This means that, if $\Delta X_t \geqslant m$ and certainly when $\Delta X_t > M$, the prediction P_{t+1} of X_{t+1} at time t should not be $\leqslant X_t$; and if $\Delta X_t \leqslant -m$ and certainly when $\Delta X_t < -M$, P_{t+1} should not be $\geqslant X_t$.)

In practice it is not uncommon that one can find a prediction procedure (I) which as a rule has small or moderate errors but occasionally is way off; and that such a procedure should be considered inferior to any method (II) which has errors considerably bigger than the usual errors of (I) but never or very rarely above M. (Sometimes persons or agencies periodically forecasting some series even find to their consternation that, when for several consecutive periods their forecasts have not been off too seriously, the users come to rely on that!)

By way of illustration, suppose that 9 times out of 10 the errors of (I) have magnitudes $|e_I|$ fluctuating about A with standard deviation $0\cdot2A$ and once out of 10 times $|e_I|$ has the (fixed) value $B > M$; and that for (II) the $|e_{II}|$ fluctuate about $3A$ with standard deviation $0\cdot6A$. Suppose that $6A < M$, so that, by Cantelli's inequality, for an arbitrary random variable Y with variance σ^2 (which states that, for any positive number t, $P\{Y - EY \leqslant t\} \geqslant t^2/\{\sigma^2 + t^2\}$), for no distribution whatever, $|e_{II}|$ exceeds M more than 4 per cent of the time. Then, as long as $B < 9\cdot2A$, $\sum e_I^2 < \sum e_{II}^2$ and the least-squares criterion would rate (I) above (II), contrary to what is desired. (The figures can be made more drastic by taking a particular error distribution.)

I would therefore recommend to the authors to consider, in their future studies, also making comparisons of forecasting methods that have approximate loss functions of the type implied by the above remarks; for use in routine calculations this can be effectuated fairly well by considering as a criterion $\sum e^{2k}$ for some integers k larger than 1.

The authors replied in writing, as follows:

The study we reported constituted an attempt to gain experience of and insight into univariate time series forecasting techniques—particularly Box–Jenkins, Holt–Winters and stepwise autoregression—as applied to a large collection of economic time series, and to pass on our results. We approached the possibility of combining individual forecasts in the same spirit. The results are doubtless open to a range of interpretations, but it was thought that they would prove of value to practitioners of forecasting. When this paper was invited to be presented to an Ordinary Meeting of the Society, our reaction was that it was not sufficiently controversial to provoke stimulating discussion. This forecast proved wildly inaccurate, and we wish to thank the many discussants whose contributions helped clarify our thoughts on forecasting methodology.

The choice of economic time series, questioned by Mr Herne and Mr Craddock, for our study was simply a result of our personal interest in such series. Had other data been employed, then the forecasting methods evaluated would have been different, for whereas the Box–Jenkins method is sufficiently versatile to cope with a wide range of series that of Holt–Winters, for example, is not. Our original paper contained an appendix listing the series, which was removed at the suggestion of a referee. However, as noted by Mr Stern and Mr Bramson, some readers may require more information about our data. This can be obtained by writing to us directly. Dr Reid makes the point (as did Professor Finney informally before the meeting) that it is not feasible to select a random sample of time series for analysis. This implies that it is not possible to make inference about the population of all economic time series using conventional statistical techniques. However, we do feel that at a less specific level it is possible to get an impression of the worth of particular techniques.

Why should we want to compare the performances of forecasting methods? Professor Jenkins and Professor Priestley both make the point that for any given model, optimal forecasts follow immediately. The difficulty is, of course, that we never know the true model, though in this particular situation we have a method (Box–Jenkins) which should often give us a very good chance of getting a close approximation to it. Dr Reid notes that there are several other univariate forecasting methods we might have examined, and Mr Stern suggests in particular the traditional trend + seasonal + residual approach. In fact, as we reported, we did try both the methods of Brown and Harrison on a subset of our series. We also considered Mr Stern's suggestion but rejected it on the grounds that the method is rather arbitrary, requiring judgments about the characteristics of individual series with no well-defined basis for their formulation. In spite of academic distaste for *ad hoc* methods, the importance of fully automatic forecasting procedures in the industrial context is emphasized by Mr Bramson and Mr Ward. Typically, one would not expect such procedures to perform as well as Box–Jenkins, and one of our objectives was to get an impression as to how much might be sacrificed in terms of forecast accuracy by employing them. Professor Jenkins raises the possibility of a fully automatic Box–Jenkins procedure, which has apparently been implemented by an American organization. Although we have no information of the details, this seems to us to be an interesting possibility and one for which there would be considerable demand. We agree with Mr Bramson that an automatic monitoring system (for example, Trigg, 1964) is valuable when fully automatic forecasting methods are used.

With regard to the Box–Jenkins forecasting procedure, our aim was to evaluate its performance by applying the method, as we understood it, to the best of our ability to all our time series. (Unlike Professor Priestley, we regard the identification and model building stages as part of the overall procedure.) Dr Chatfield emphasizes our expertise in Box–Jenkins model building—at least by the time the study was completed, though we did not notice any great improvement in the relative performance of Box–Jenkins as the analysis progressed. The question of expertise, although Professor Jenkins was kind enough not to say so, does of course cut both ways. Dr Chatfield asks if we employed the

Box–Cox transformation. The available material on Box–Jenkins analysis at the time our study was carried out contained only brief mention of the use of the Box–Cox transformation. Further, our understanding of Box and Cox (1964) was that the analysis of transformations was of most use in bringing to light or confirming some natural metric for the analysis of a given set of data. Since we could think of no natural metric, except perhaps the logarithm, for economic time series we did not employ the Box–Cox analysis to any of our data. This is in line with our intention of applying the Box–Jenkins approach as we understood it. Since our analysis was completed, greater emphasis has been laid on instantaneous transformations of the data by Box and Jenkins (1973) and again by Professor Jenkins in his comments on our paper. We would mention two difficulties in this context. First, the autocorrelations of a transformed series are in general different from those of the original series, which raises problems in model identification. Second, care is needed in transforming back optimal forecasts if optimality is to be retained. These points are discussed in detail in a paper by Granger and Newbold (submitted for publication in 1974). Professor Jenkins and Mr Stern emphasize the manual intervention aspect of Box–Jenkins and the probable gains to be obtained therefrom. We agree that this is the great advantage of the approach (and accordingly that the essence of Box–Jenkins is largely lost by the simple use of Mr Herne's programme of three dozen cards). Mr Godolphin urges us to agree that a further advantage of Box–Jenkins is that the forecast function can involve many observations with the use of relatively few parameters. We do so, but would add that the same could be said of Holt–Winters or indeed of any exponential smoothing method.

Professor Jenkins states that Holt–Winters and stepwise autoregression postulate models which are a subset of the class studied by Box and Jenkins. This is not in fact the case for the Holt–Winters seasonal model, where trend is additive and seasonality multiplicative, which we considered, although it is for the variant in which both are taken to be additive. In answer to Mr Bramson, initial values for Holt–Winters were chosen by estimating trend, seasonality and level over the first year's data, these estimates being then updated for subsequent time periods by the Holt–Winters formulae.

In evaluating forecast performance we employed a squared error criterion though it must be accepted, as noted by Professor Konijn, that in some situations other loss functions might be appropriate. Dr Reid and Mr Bramson ask if we can expand our conclusions with regard to the empirical comparisons of individual methods, and in particular assess which method might be a "best bet" for series with particular characteristics. The difficulty here is that if one could specify the characteristics of a given series sufficiently well, the optimal forecast would follow immediately. We have little confidence in such an approach, and would repeat our earlier stated conclusion that if a sufficiently long series is available we can think of no *a priori* grounds for preferring one of the fully automatic methods to Box–Jenkins for any time series if the sole criterion is expected forecast accuracy. We are rather sceptical about the value of the decision tree given by Reid (1969), particularly since the numbers of series studied in most of the 32 classes defined there were so small (see Kendall, 1973, p. 127). In answer to Dr Wallis, we looked at one-step-ahead forecasts for a subsample of 20 of our series, containing a total of 600 forecasts. For Box–Jenkins 93 per cent of these fell within the estimated 95 per cent probability limits, the corresponding figure for stepwise autoregression being 91 per cent.

A number of speakers raised theoretical and philosophical doubts about the combination of forecasts. The temptation to quote Kendall (1973, p. 150)

> "On the other hand, the history of science teaches us that we should not reject empirically observed relationships just because they cannot be explained in our current state of knowledge. The real test, I suppose, is whether the relationships are stable enough to be used in forecasting—whether, in fact, they 'work' "

is irresistible, although the context is a little unfortunate. Professor Jenkins, Mr Stern and Mr Herne dislike combination on the grounds that it is not parsimonious. If by this they are saying, as does Professor Priestley, that combination is not a valid proposition if one of the individual forecasts does not differ significantly from the optimum, we must of course agree. The great difficulty in economic forecasting in general is that the amount of information which could be taken into account in forming the forecast and the number of possible ways of using it are so great that one could rarely have much confidence in a particular set of forecasts being optimum. Faced with sub-optimal forecasts, combination is an attractive possibility. In such a situation, Dr Reid would prefer to build a global model incorporating the individual forecasting models. In theory this is an attractive proposition, but would very often be impractical. How would two large macro-economic models be united in this way? How could one incorporate the element of judgment, so common in economic forecasting, into this global forecasting mechanism? Professor Jenkins notes another attractive possibility—the construction of a transfer function-noise model relating actuals to forecasts. This could easily be generalized to the situation where one requires to combine several sets of forecasts. The chief difficulty here is that one would require a very long run of actual forecasts (not fitted values) for the exercise to be viable. The suggestions of Dr Reid and Professor Jenkins do not take into account the possibility of a non-stationary relationship between the individual forecasts, although perhaps we should expect forecasters to learn from their earlier errors, suggesting the possibility that their relative performances may not remain constant through time. We agree with Dr Bunn's point that in the general context, where the information set is large, the subjective probability approach is not very relevant, since one would have virtually no confidence in any model being "true". We are interested to hear from Professor Stigler that combining (of estimators) dates back to Laplace who rejected it on the grounds that the optimal weights were unknown. In our context, however, it is possible to estimate these unknown quantities from a set of data. As we have hinted, our liking for combination is based primarily on pragmatic grounds—it very often "works". We were therefore particularly interested in the applications mentioned by Mr Craddock and Dr Reid. Mr Craddock tells us of the success obtained from the combining of forecasts in long-range weather forecasting, while Dr Reid produces an example in which the combined forecast is outperformed by both individual forecasts. We do not claim to have solved all the theoretical and methodological problems thrown up by the idea of combining. One difficulty is that we would like to be able to decide fairly quickly when it is appropriate to give weight zero to a particular set of forecasts. Application of conventional significance tests is a possibility, while an alternative might be to reject a set of forecasts of whose generating mechanism we were sceptical. Perhaps on the basis of Box and Newbold (1971) Dr Reid will accept that for his particular example we might well have followed the latter course.

Turning now to the combination of forecasts as employed in this paper, it must be admitted that the circumstances in which we combined (with the exception of the Holt–Winters—stepwise autoregression combination) were about the least favourable imaginable. All these forecasting methods are based on the same information set, and one of them (Box–Jenkins) should give a very good chance of obtaining forecasts close to the optimum. It is not surprising then that, as mentioned by Professor Jenkins and Mr Herne, combination of Box–Jenkins with other methods produced on average only a slight improvement over Box–Jenkins alone. This result would seem to confirm the power of the Box–Jenkins method. Professor Jenkins and Dr Stigler warn that the results presented in Tables 4 and 7 should be treated with caution because of the so-called "selection fallacy". Essentially these results indicate that Box–Jenkins is outperformed by the combined forecasts using Methods 1, 3 and 4 on a slight majority of our series, but this is generally not the case for Methods 2 and 5. If we set out to test the hypothesis that in the population of all economic time series Box–Jenkins is better than combining on at least 50 per cent of occasions then, as Dr Stigler notes, great care would be needed in interpreting these results. Of course, since we have not analysed a random sample of time series we are in no position to perform any such test. Our objective was the more limited one of gaining some insight into the way the various combining procedures operate in situations of this kind. Dr Stigler seems to suggest that one interpretation of our results might be that the two sets of combination methods are intrinsically inferior to Box–Jenkins taken individually, typically differing from it by a small amount. Given a sample of 80 time series one might then expect the more successful combination method to outperform the optimum (Box–Jenkins) for a small majority of series. The case is very well argued, but on the basis of a detailed examination of our results for individual series, we prefer an alternative explanation which is closer in spirit to comments made by Professor Priestley. We feel that it is a mistake to regard the population of economic time series as homogeneous with respect to the Box–Jenkins method. We prefer to think of it as consisting of two groups, the first containing series for which Box–Jenkins analysis will produce forecasts which are near optimum and the other group consisting of series for which it will not. Membership of the first group is comprised of those series whose generating models fall into the ARIMA class with time-invariant parameters and for which the user of the technique is able to build the appropriate models. (We would imagine that the forecasting model derived by Chatfield and Prothero (1973) would fall into the second group.) The relative sizes of the two groups will depend on who is carrying out the Box–Jenkins analysis. For the first group of series, combining is of no value. The Box–Jenkins forecasts should be given a weight of one, or at least very near one. For such series, Methods 1, 3 and 4 will clearly perform badly in comparison to Methods 2 and 5 which themselves will, on the average, be worse than Box–Jenkins forecasts alone. For the second group of series, combination becomes a useful possibility and it may well be that another forecast can be found which optimally should receive non-zero weight in combination with Box–Jenkins. For series where individual methods appear to require significantly non-zero weights, Methods 1, 3 and 4 appear to do a considerably better job of estimating the appropriate weights than do Methods 2 and 5—a conclusion which is supported by comparing our results with the optimum ex-post weights. In summary then, we feel that in this particular situation one would expect to find a large number of series for which combining was of no value, since Box–Jenkins is near optimum. However, for those series for which Box–Jenkins is not near optimum combination using Methods 1, 3 and 4 could well prove profitable—as it did for a large number of series in our collection. It is for this reason that guideline (c) in our summary proposes that, if a sufficiently long series is available, Box–Jenkins be used, but that if this fails to produce forecasts of sufficient quality it might be worth while to *try* combining. Returning to Dr Stigler's theme, we attempted a small experiment. At the beginning of our study, the 80 monthly series were unambiguously numbered 1–80. We looked at the combination of Box–Jenkins, Holt–Winters and stepwise autoregression together for Methods 1 and 2, both with $v = 12$, for series 1–40 and 41–80. The results are summarized in the following table:

Number of series for which first-named forecasting procedure outperforms second

	Series 1–40	Series 41–80
Method 1: Box–Jenkins	24	26
Method 2: Box–Jenkins	18	23
Method 1: Method 2	24	24

As can be seen, Method 1 outperforms the two alternatives for a comfortable majority of series in both sets. We feel that Professor Priestley's question concerning the robustness of forecast performance to model mis-specification warrants further study—the more so since our results on combination do suggest that for some of our series we may well have failed to find the appropriate ARIMA specification (if indeed the true model does lie within that class). Our results on the combination of Holt–Winters and stepwise autoregression are, of course, more clear cut. The resulting fully automatic forecasting mechanism has been seen to perform very well. Professor Jenkins proposes automated ARIMA model building as an alternative. This possibility, of which we have seen no published account, deserves more examination, and it would be most interesting to see an empirical evaluation of its forecast performance compared with that of other methods. We should emphasize here that in choosing the weights for combining we used only data available at the time the forecast was made—the weights were in no way based on future data. We feel that our empirical results are sufficient to indicate that the combination of disparate forecasts is potentially fruitful and surely worthy of further practical consideration.

For many purposes, of course, the study of univariate time series forecasting might be thought of as a stepping stone to the consideration of multivariate methods. Dr Chatfield demonstrates in a particular example the gains which can be obtained from taking into account a related series in forming forecasts. The prize for finding the earliest contentious point in our paper goes to Dr Wallis who regards as dubious the use of univariate forecasting errors in the multivariate context. What we had in mind was the construction of univariate models for every series considered and the examination of the cross-correlations between the residuals from the fitted univariate models. Thus for example, if

$$\phi_1(B)(1-B)^{d_1} X_{1,t} = \theta_1(B) a_{1,t}$$

and

$$\phi_2(B)(1-B)^{d_2} X_{2,t} = \theta_2(B) a_{2,t}$$

then in the bivariate case the series $X_{2,t}$ will be useful in forecasting the series $X_{1,t}$ if and only if corr $(a_{1,t} a_{2,t-j})$ is non-zero for some positive j. We are currently examining the practical possibility of building forecasting models along these lines.

REFERENCES IN THE DISCUSSION

AKAIKE, H. (1972). Use of an information theoretic quantity for statistical model identification. In *Proceedings 5th Hawaii International Conference on System Sciences*, pp. 249–250.

Box, G. E. P. and Cox, D. R. (1964). An analysis of transformations. *J. R. Statist. Soc.* B, **26**, 211–243.

Box, G. E. P. and JENKINS, G. M. (1973). Some comments on a paper by Chatfield and Prothero and on a review by Kendall. *J. R. Statist. Soc.* A, **136**, 337–345.

BROWN, R. G. and MEYER, R. F. (1961). Fundamental theorem of exponential smoothing. *Operns Res.*, **9**, 673–685.

COEN, P. J., GOMME, E. D. and KENDALL, M. G. (1969). Lagged relationships in economic forecasting (with Discussion). *J. R. Statist. Soc.* A, **132**, 133–152.

KENDALL, M. G. (1973). *Time Series*. London: Griffin.

MANLEY, G. (1953). The mean temperature of Central England, 1698–1952. *Quart. J. Met. Soc.*, **79**, 242–261.

NAYLOR, T. H., SEAKS, T. G. and WICHERN, D. W. (1972). Box–Jenkins methods; an alternative to econometric models. *Int. Statist. Rev.*, **40**, 123–137.

STIGLER, S. M. (1973). Laplace, Fisher and the discovery of the concept of sufficiency. *Biometrika*, **60**, 439–446.

TOMASEK, O. (1972). Statistical forecasting of telephone time-series. *ITU Telecomm. J.*, Geneva, December issue, pp. 1–7.

TRIGG, D. W. (1964). Monitoring a forecasting system. *Op. Res. Quart.*, **15**, 271–274.

[14]

© Journal of Business & Economic Statistics, Vol. 2, No. 3, July 1984

A Comparison of Autoregressive Univariate Forecasting Procedures for Macroeconomic Time Series

Richard Meese
School of Business Administration, University of California, Berkeley, CA 94720

John Geweke
Department of Economics, Duke University, Durham, NC 27706

The actual performance of several automated univariate autoregressive forecasting procedures, applied to 150 macroeconomic time series, are compared. The procedures are the random walk model as a basis for comparison; long autoregressions, with three alternative rules for lag length selection; and a long autoregression estimated by minimizing the sum of absolute deviations. The sensitivity of each procedure to preliminary transformations, data, periodicity, forecast horizon, loss function employed in parameter estimation, and seasonal adjustment procedures is examined. The more important conclusions are that Akaike's lag-length selection criterion works well in a wide variety of situations, the modeling of long memory components becomes important for forecast horizons of three or more periods, and linear combinations of forecasts do not improve forecast quality appreciably.

KEY WORDS: Akaike criterion; Autoregression; ARIMA; ARARMA; Forecasting; Macroeconomic time series.

1. INTRODUCTION

In this article we compare the performance of several automated univariate autoregressive forecasting procedures applied to 150 macroeconomic time series. We focus on automated procedures because users of economic data often lack the resources to construct a forecasting model tailored to the idiosyncratic characteristics of each series (such as that suggested by Box and Jenkins 1976), which might well produce superior forecasts in many instances. The application of such automated procedures has grown dramatically in recent years. For example, Statistics Canada and the U.S. Bureau of Labor Statistics now use automated forecasting methods in the seasonal adjustment of thousands of time series. Experimental designs as rich as the one used here further dictate that attention be restricted to automated procedures. Our comparison of univariate forecasting algorithms involves examination of the sensitivity of each technique to the following influences: (a) data transformations (logging, detrending, differencing, etc.), (b) data periodicity, (c) the forecast horizon of interest, (d) the metric used to evaluate forecasts, (e) the loss function employed in parameter estimation, and (f) seasonal adjustment procedures. Section 3 contains a discussion of the experiments that we designed

to account for these potential influences and a description of the five forecasting procedures used in our experiments. The results of our experiments are then summarized in Section 4.

The closest precursor to the present study is the recent forecasting competition conducted by Makridakis et al. (1982). They consider a different set of univariate predictors on a wider range of series. Their study is based on as many as 1,001 series and 24 forecasting procedures. Two of these techniques, autoregressive integrated moving average (ARIMA) modeling and Bayesian forecasting, were not completely mechanical. These techniques were obviously the most time-consuming, and they did not dominate the other, less complicated procedures. Of the 24 models considered by Makridakis et al., we use the same naive model 1 (Makridakis et al. 1982, p. 143) and a technique that is similar to Parzen's ARARMA scheme. Further discussion is provided in Section 3.

This article and the work of Makridakis et al. is further differentiated by our focus on the implications of our results for users of economic time series. A number of recent papers (Meese and Rogoff 1983a,b and Simpson and Porter 1980) have noted the poor forecasting performance of some economic models that appear to fit reasonably well in a sample. In the final

192   Journal of Business & Economic Statistics, July 1984

section of this article, we discuss the discrepancies between in-sample criteria (hypothesis tests, goodness of fit statistics, etc.) and out-of-sample forecasting performance. In particular, we reexamine the recommendations of Nelson and Plosser (1982), who provided in-sample evidence that economic time series are best characterized as borderline nonstationary stochastic processes with no tendency to return to a linear trend. Our out-of-sample forecasting results are inconsistent with this view. Our results highlight the importance of "long memory" or trend estimation, corroborating the recent findings of Parzen (1982), who also relied on out-of-sample performance criteria.

2. A DESCRIPTION OF THE DATA

In our experiments we used 150 domestic and foreign, monthly and quarterly macroeconomic time series. The variables were selected from the Federal Reserve Board's much larger data base and were chosen to be representative of macroeconomic time series in several dimensions. Fifty of the series are sampled monthly and are seasonally unadjusted. The remaining 100 quarterly series are a mix of seasonally adjusted (SA) and seasonally unadjusted (NSA) variables. Of the quarterly (monthly) series, 20 (18) are U.S. variables and 80 (32) are from Germany, Canada, Japan, and the United Kingdom. The series are listed in the Appendix.

Table 1 provides a descriptive cross-classification of all series according to whether they are real or financial, domestic or foreign, and seasonally adjusted or unadjusted. Real series include components of a country's GNP accounts, price indexes, and demographic variables. The financial classification includes monetary statistics, interest rates, and exchange rates. The domestic/foreign breakdown indicates whether a variable comes from a country's domestic or international accounts. The detailed classification for all variables, used in Section 4 to facilitate exposition of our results, is given in the Appendix.

3. EXPERIMENTAL DESIGN

The forecasting procedures considered and the methods of comparison used varied in four dimensions. Five autoregressive forecasting techniques and three comparison criteria were used. The effects of five alternative preliminary transformations were investigated. Finally, all of these procedures were undertaken for both the levels and the logarithm of the data.

The first forecasting procedure employs the naive predictor or random walk model; it requires no estimation. This model is included in our study because the no-change forecast provides one benchmark for the performance of the more sophisticated forecasting procedures. In addition, other researchers (e.g., Kendall 1953 and Meese and Rogoff 1983a, b) have noted that the time series behavior of some economic variables, most notably asset prices, resembles that of a martingale process.

In the second, third, and fourth techniques, forecasts were formed from long autoregressions (AR) estimated by least squares. In the second technique, the length of the lag is $M = M(N) = N/\log(N)$, where N is the sample size. Such deterministic rules have long been used in spectral estimation (e.g., Hannan 1970) and have been applied in distributed lag models (e.g., Sims 1974a). In the third technique, lag length is selected using the Schwarz (1978) criterion, which provides a consistent estimate of lag length when lag length is finite. In the fourth technique, lag length is selected using the Akaike (1974) criterion, which produces asymptotic minimum mean square prediction errors of the dependent variable. For both the Schwarz and Akaike criteria, $M(N)$ was the longest lag length considered. The alternative order-selection criteria proposed by Amemiya (1980), Sawa (1978), Mallows (1973), and Parzen (1974) are similar in their asymptotic and small behavior (Geweke and Meese 1981).

We originally experimented with two additional techniques. The first involved direct application of the Wiener-Kolmogorov prediction formula in the frequency domain, as described in Geweke (1978). Since this procedure gave qualitatively the same results as the long AR, it is not reported here. The second technique involved estimation of the long AR model by weighted least squares. We employed geometrically declining weights so that parameter estimates were more sensitive to recent observations. This procedure did not perform any better than the long AR model, so it is also omitted from the results reported in the next section.

A potential problem with all of these techniques is that they employ criteria based on minimization of squared deviations. These criteria are inappropriate if, for example, some economic time series are drawn from nonnormal stable-Paretian distributions with infinite variances. Our fifth technique constructs forecasts from minimium absolute deviation (MAD) estimates of a long autoregression at order $M(N)$. The MAD estimator was computed by iterative weighted least squares following Mosteller and Tukey (1977); minimization of the sum of absolute deviations is equivalent to minimization of the sum of squared deviations divided by

Table 1. A Classification of the 150 Macroeconomic Time Series

	Total	Domestic			Foreign		
		Total	SA	NSA	Total	SA	NSA
Monthly	50						
Financial	37	28	0	28	9	0	9
Real	13	8	0	8	5	0	5
Quarterly	100						
Financial	22	17	2	15	5	2	3
Real	78	52	36	16	26	8	18

the absolute value of the deviation. We used only five iterations, because initial experiments showed little gain in predictive accuracy from further iterations.

The five techniques were applied to the level of each series. The initial forecasts were generated using half of the available data. An observation was added, the parameter estimates of the various models were updated, and a new set of forecasts was produced. The process continued until all data were exhausted. The forecasts at all horizons were then evaluated on the basis of mean percent error, mean absolute percent error, and root mean square percent error. Specifically, let $k = 1, \ldots,$ 8, 10, 12 denote the 10 forecast steps, N_k denote the total number of forecasts in the projection period for which the actual value $A(t)$ is known, and $F(t)$ denote the forecast value. Then define the percentage mean error (% ME), the percentage mean absolute error (% MAE), and the percentage root mean square error (% RMSE) as follows:

% ME

$$= \left| 100 \cdot \sum_{s=0}^{N_k-1} \frac{[F(t + s + k) - A(t + s + k)]}{[N_k \cdot A(t + s)]} \right|,$$

% MAE

$$= \left| 100 \cdot \sum_{s=0}^{N_k-1} \frac{|F(t + s + k) - A(t + s + k)|}{|N_k \cdot A(t + s)|} \right|,$$

% RMSE

$$= \left| 100 \cdot \sum_{s=0}^{N_k-1} \frac{[F(t + s + k) - A(t + s + k)]^2}{[N_k \cdot A(t + s)^2]} \right|^{1/2}.$$

Five transformations that were preliminary to the forecasting procedures themselves were considered. The first involves removal of a simple linear trend by least squares. The second is to difference the series first, or when the data series is NSA, the difference operator $(1 - L)(1 - L^{12})$ is applied to monthly series and $(1 - L)(1 - L^4)$ to quarterly series. The third transformation removes a deterministic seasonal from NSA time series by dummy variable regression. Experiments were conducted using Sims's (1974b) regression procedure to expand the seasonal parameterization with sample size. Though this procedure for extracting a deterministic seasonal is flexible, on the subset of 50 NSA monthly series it produced results similar to those reported below for dummy variables. The results of these experiments are not reported in Section 4.

The fourth data transformation procedure involves least squares estimation and application of the prefilter $(1 + a_1L + a_2L^{12} + a_3L^{13})$ for monthly NSA series, $(1 + a_1L + a_2L^4 + a_3L^5)$ for quarterly NSA series, or $(1 + b_1L)$ for SA monthly or quarterly series. This procedure was suggested by Geweke (1978), and it is similar in spirit to Parzen (1982). The final adjustment procedure is to analyze the untransformed value of the series.

All procedures were repeated for the logarithm of the data. The logarithmic transformation is frequently used in forecasting because the underlying model is thought to be multiplicative. In empirical econometric work it is attractive because regression coefficients can then often be interpreted as elasticities and because conventional asymptotic distribution theory precludes exponentially growing regressors but permits their logarithms. As a separate exercise we tested for the appropriateness of the logarithmic transformation by comparing the error sum of squares of the long AR model for both the level and the log of each data series divided by its geometric mean. Since the level and log of the series are special cases of the Box-Cox (1962) transformation, this procedure indicates for which transformation the likelihood function is greater. In the next section we compare the results of this in-sample exercise with the results of the out-of-sample prediction experiments.

Two other experiments were conducted for the one-step-ahead forecasts only. First, we formed optimal linear combinations (with weights summing to one) of forecasts taken two at a time as suggested by Granger and Newbold (1977, pp. 268–278). (This procedure is appropriate only when both forecasts being combined are unbiased.) Second, we tested the null hypothesis of equal error variances for each pair of forecasts, following Granger and Newbold (1977, p. 281). This test requires the assumption of joint normality of forecast errors in addition to unbiasedness. The last two experiments were conducted for one-step forecasts only, since even optimally formed k-step ahead $(k \geq 2)$ forecast errors will in general be serially correlated.

Regardless of the model used to construct the forecast, all forecast values are for the original series in levels. Antilogarithms of forecasts are used in logarithmic models, estimated trend and/or seasonals are reinserted, and differences are converted to levels if preliminary differencing was employed. For each NSA series 41 models are considered—(4 estimated models) × (5 preliminary data transformations) × (2 functional forms) + (1 random walk model). For each SA series there are 33 models—4 × 4 × 2 + 1, respectively—since deterministic seasonals are not extracted.

The total computation time for a series of $N = 100$ observations was 90 CPU seconds on an Amdahl 470; computing time increases roughly with the cube of N because of the iterations involved. The MAD estimator is the most expensive to calculate. Coefficient estimates for the deterministic, Schwarz, and Akaike variants of the long AR were computed simultaneously using a Householder recursion.

4. RESULTS

The results are summarized in Table 2. In each of three dimensions—the forecasting model, the prelimi-

194   Journal of Business & Economic Statistics, July 1984

Table 2. Percentage of First- and Second-Place Rankings, Across Three Dimensions

| | Aggregate | | | | | | 1-Step % RMSE | | 6-Step % RMSE | | 12-Step % RMSE | |
| | % RMSE | | % MAE | | % ME | | | | | | | |
	1	2	1	2	1	2	1	2	1	2	1	2
Forecasting Model												
Random Walk	9.0	3.5	9.5	3.4	2.6	2.1	13.9	4.0	9.9	2.0	5.3	3.3
Long AR	15.1	18.5	14.8	16.9	24.4	24.6	15.9	20.5	15.9	15.9	19.9	21.2
Schwarz	16.6	24.9	17.7	24.6	22.8	20.6	9.3	23.8	19.9	21.9	18.5	31.1
Akaike	45.1	37.4	44.9	40.4	23.9	25.7	48.3	32.4	43.0	40.4	39.7	29.1
MAD-AR	14.2	15.7	13.1	14.6	26.3	27.0	12.6	19.2	11.3	19.9	16.6	15.2
Preliminary Transformation												
NSA Series												
None	9.8	7.8	9.8	6.2	13.7	12.7	17.6	16.7	10.8	7.8	3.9	3.9
Linear Detrending	43.1	41.2	42.2	39.6	19.6	20.6	20.6	21.6	45.1	42.2	59.8	52.0
Deterministic Seasonal	10.8	11.8	11.8	12.5	10.8	10.8	15.7	17.6	9.8	11.8	6.9	10.4
Estimated Seasonal Prefilter	30.4	29.4	27.5	31.2	24.5	24.5	36.6	30.4	28.4	31.4	32.4	25.5
First and Seasonal Differencing	5.9	9.8	8.8	10.4	31.4	31.4	9.8	13.7	5.9	6.9	3.9	8.3
SA Series												
None	14.6	12.5	16.7	12.5	16.7	18.8	14.6	10.4	12.5	12.5	16.7	12.5
Linear Detrending	33.3	29.2	31.2	31.2	29.2	27.1	14.6	10.4	43.8	33.3	41.7	39.6
First Differencing	20.8	27.1	25.0	29.2	33.3	33.3	33.3	41.2	16.7	25.0	16.7	20.8
Estimated 1-lag Prefilter	31.2	31.2	27.1	27.1	20.8	20.8	37.5	38.2	27.1	29.2	25.0	27.1
Functional Form												
Level	64.0	50.8	63.2	50.2	60.8	58.3	64.9	42.4	68.2	51.7	59.6	54.3
Log	36.0	49.2	36.8	49.8	39.2	41.7	35.1	57.6	31.8	48.3	46.4	45.7

nary transformation, and the functional form—performance is evaluated on the basis of % RMSE in all cases and on the basis of % MAE and % ME for aggregation over all 10 forecasting horizons. The percentage of time that each model, transformation, or functional form ranks first and second is tabulated. For example, the entry 14.8 in the Aggregate—% MAE column and the Forecasting Model—Long AR row of Table 2 indicates that the long AR model, with order a function of sample size, produced 14.8% of the lowest % MAE forecasts (of which there were (150 series) × (10 forecast horizons) = 1,500). Entries in the 1-, 6-, and 12-step columns are percentages of first- and second-place rankings using the % RMSE evaluation metric over the 150 time series. For each series, the first- and second-place forecasting technique, preliminary data transformation, and functional form are those associated with the minimum % ME, % MAE, or % RMSE model, of which there were 41 (33) possible models for each NSA (SA) series.

It made little difference whether comparisons were based on RMSE or MAE, as a comparison of the first and second columns illustrates. In approximately 45% of the experiments, models fit using the Akaike criterion produced the best out-of-sample forecasts and the random walk was the least successful. Using the level, as opposed to the logarithm, of the series proved to be optimal in a little more than 63% of the experiments. This out-of-sample result is in sharp contrast to the results of the in-sample test for the appropriateness of the level or log transformation. In the latter experiments, the logarithmic transformation maximized the likelihood 48% of the time; there was disagreement between the in- and out-of-sample criteria on whether

the log or level of the series was preferred for approximately 45% of the series.

Linear detrending proved to be the most reliable prefilter, accounting for 43.1% (33.3%) of the best % RMSE forecasts over all prediction horizons for NSA (SA) series. The poor performance of differencing for the NSA series appears to be a consequence of the differencing operator $(1 - L)(1 - L^a)$, $a = 4$ (12) for quarterly (monthly) series. The relative performance of the first differencing operator alone on the 48 SA quarterly series is better, but it is still dominated by linear detrending and the estimated prefilter. Since first and seasonal differences are special cases of least squares estimates, the dominance of least squares is expected asymptotically. It is interesting that for a monthly or quarterly sample of 10–20 years, it is clearly advantageous to estimate rather than impose such differences.

If the evaluation metric is mean error (Column 3), the results change markedly. In this case the long AR model, estimated by minimizing absolute deviations, performed slightly better than the other procedures. The percentage of best forecasts with the random walks model drops to 2.6%, which is not surprising, since all other models include a constant term. The level transformation is still preferred, and differencing produces the best results in terms of the five prefilters.

Comparisons based on RMSE for three selected forecast steps—$k = 1$, 6, and 12—are given in the last three columns of Table 2. The Akaike criterion again produces the largest percentage of best forecasts at each of the selected horizons. For one-step-ahead forecasts, the random walk model accounts for about 14% of the best forecasts; its relative position vis-à-vis the other four procedures deteriorates as the forecast horizon increases. The results of our test for the equality of one-step-ahead forecast error variances indicate, however, that we cannot reject the hypothesis at the 5% significance level and that the best univariate procedure has the same forecast error variance as the random walk model for 50% of the series we analyze. The level of the series is still preferred to the log in all cases, although the number of best forecasts using the level of the series tapers off at the longest forecast horizon. The optimal prefilter varies between linear detrending and the estimated prefilter according to the prediction horizon, possibly because both are capable of approximating the long-memory component of a series. In the experiments reported here, linear detrending produces the highest number of best forecasts for horizons $k = 6$ and 12, and the estimated prefilter works best for shorter horizons. The same comparisons based on % MAE are similar; comparisons using ME provide no information beyond that in Column 3.

At one-step-ahead forecast horizons, we find that optimally formed linear combinations of forecasts taken two at a time (Granger and Newbold 1977, pp. 268–278) rarely improve on the performance of the best model; about 1% of the combined forecasts outperformed the best procedure. This result is generally inconsistent with the forecasting competition of Makridakis et al. (1982), who considered a simple average of all forecasts, which works better than a procedure that optimally weights individual forecasts using the sample covariances of the models' forecast errors. It is also inconsistent with the evidence reported in Newbold and Granger (1974), who found that their most successful combining method outperformed the individual forecasts about 40% of the time. The discrepancy between the present study and those of Newbold and Granger (1974) and Makridakis et al. (1982) is probably attributable to the differences in experimental designs. We studied two data transformations, five prefilters, and five similar autoregressive forecasting techniques to arrive at the best forecast procedure, and this appears to have reduced the gains from combining forecasts. In addition, we did not consider a simple average of individual forecasts as suggested in Makridakis et al. (1982).

To compare the predictability of the monthly and quarterly series, we grouped the % RMSE statistics for both types into three groups: 0%–5%, 5%–10%, and greater than 10%. The statistics for independence of the 2×3 classification are 2.84, 4.56, and 11.3 for $k = 1, 6,$ and 12, respectively. Distributed approximately as $\chi^2(2)$ variates, the test statistics indicate rejection at a 5% significance level of the independence hypothesis only for the longest prediction horizon. Not surprisingly, monthly series are easier to predict 12 months ahead than quarterly series 12 quarters ahead. With respect to the comparison made in Table 2, the only noteworthy differences are that for monthly series (using % RMSE) (a) the Akaike criterion still produces the greatest percentage of optimal forecasts, but that number has dropped to about 33%, and (b) the relative superiority of linear detrending over the estimated prefilter (the closest competitor) is less clear-cut—31% of the optimal forecasts for linear detrending and 24% for the estimated prefilter over all prediction horizons.

The 52 quarterly NSA series and the 48 quarterly SA series indicate that the latter series are more predictable than the former for one-period ($\chi^2(2) = 7.27$) and six-period ($\chi^2(2) = 8.83$) horizons. The result makes intuitive sense, since conventional seasonal adjustment procedures involve smoothing techniques; but it is of little practical consequence because the adjustment filters are two-sided. For the 12-period horizon, there is no significant difference ($\chi^2(2) = 3.35$).

We find no evidence that U.S. macroeconomic time series are any more or less difficult to forecast than series from Japan, Canada, Germany, and the United Kingdom. In addition, we do not find any difference in the relative predictability of those series in our sample labeled real or financial. There is, however, strong evidence that domestic series can be forecast more accurately than foreign series at all prediction horizons: the test statistics are 21.3, 15.8, and 13.3 for the 1-, 6-, and 12-period horizons. The foreign series are those with an international component (e.g., exports, imports, exchange rates, net foreign assets, etc.); they appear to have larger unpredictable components because both domestic and foreign shocks may directly impinge on these variables.

All of the statistics reported thus far are generated from out-of-sample forecasts based on half of the available data for each series. There are many instances in which the forecast period of a particular series covers one or more possible changes in government policy regimes. We made no attempt to control for this deficiency, because there is no general consensus in the economic profession about dating these regime changes or about the practical significance of policy changes on the stochastic structure of a typical economic time series. Recent studies of the out-of-sample predictive accuracy of large macroeconomic models (Fair 1979 and McNees 1979,1982) are also subject to this difficulty.

5. DISCUSSION AND SUMMARY

The empirical regularities of this study can be summarized as follows:

1. The fitting of autoregressive models with order selected by the Akaike criterion on the detrended level of a series, or the Akaike procedure applied to the level of a series passed through an estimated prefilter, produces reasonable forecasts in terms of % RMSE or % MAE for the majority of the monthly and quarterly macroeconomic time series we consider.

2. Economic variables with foreign components are

196   Journal of Business & Economic Statistics, July 1984

harder to predict than domestic variables, and NSA series are generally harder to predict than SA series. The other series classifications we consider—real versus financial, U.S. versus non-U.S., and monthly versus quarterly—do not appear to be related to forecast accuracy.

3. Macroeconomic time series are difficult to predict. Although the naive predictor or random walk model produces the smallest number of best forecasts in our experiments, at one-step-ahead prediction horizons we cannot reject at the 5% significance level the hypothesis that the best procedure in terms of % RMSE has the same forecast error variance as the random walk model for half of the data series in our experiments.

4. The use of root mean square error or mean absolute error when evaluating the forecasts of macroeconomic variables makes little difference. Although our forecast procedure that minimizes the sum of absolute deviations works well on a wide variety of series, it is dominated by least squares autoregression using the Akaike criterion when forecasts are evaluated on the basis of % MAE or % RMSE. The MAD forecast procedure produces the majority of best forecasts when one's evaluation metric is percentage mean error.

5. The optimal forecast procedure, data transformation, or prefilter for a given series is sensitive to the choice of evaluation metric (% ME, % MAE, or % RMSE) and the forecast horizon of interest. For a given series, it is a rare occurrence for the same forecasting procedure to be optimal at all 10 forecast horizons.

6. Our in-sample tests for the appropriateness of the level versus log transformation appear to be unrelated to results of our out-of-sample experiments. There is conflict between these criteria for half of the series considered.

7. Combinations of any two of our autoregressive forecasting techniques based on the correlation structure of the individual forecast errors do not, in general, produce sizable gains in forecast accuracy over the individual methods. Any two methods so combined rarely produce more than a 5% reduction in % RMSE over the best univariate method, and the composition of the combination forecast with lowest % RMSE varies with the time series under analysis.

8. At forecast horizons of roughly three steps or more, producing minimum root mean square error forecasts requires a reasonable estimate of the trend or long–memory component of the series. This empirical regularity is corroborated by Parzen's (1982) recent work. Parzen fits autoregressive (AR) or autoregressive moving average (ARMA) models to the residuals obtained from what he terms *parsimonious "best lag" nonstationary autoregression.* Parzen's parsimonious prefilter is closely related to our estimated prefilter. Our version of this technique produces the second lowest (at long horizons) and lowest (at short horizons) %

RMSE forecasts for the 150 series we analyze.

The most troublesome aspect of our results seems to be Items 5 and 6. Other authors have noted the dismal out-of-sample performance of models that appear to fit well in a sample (Meese and Rogoff 1983a, b and Simpson and Porter 1980). In a recent paper by Nelson and Plosser (1982), the appropriateness of differencing as opposed to linear detrending was explored with the use of "unit root" tests (Fuller 1976, Dickey and Fuller 1979, Hasza and Fuller 1979, and Evans and Savin 1981). Although the unit root tests are known to have little power against borderline stationary alternatives, the in-sample evidence presented by Nelson and Plosser (1982) is still convincing for the hypothesis that macroeconomic time series are best characterized as unit root processes with no tendency to return to a linear trend. The results of our forecasting competition suggest that if minimum % RMSE forecasts are desired, detrending or the application of an estimated prefilter is preferable to first or seasonal differencing, or both. (Comparisons between the current study and that of Nelson and Plosser 1982 are complicated by the fact that the latter study analyzed annual data from 1900 to the present, whereas our study examines monthly (quarterly) data from the past 10 (20) years. The in- and out-of-sample experiments need to be conducted on a common data set.)

If one is to rationalize the conflicting in- and out-of-sample evidence, then the set of models considered by Nelson and Plosser or by us does not adequately characterize the mechanism generating macroeconomic time series. It is difficult, however, to construct an underlying "true" model that, when erroneously estimated by standard linear time series techniques, suggests, for example, that differencing produces minimum % RMSE predictions at one particular horizon and detrending does so at another.

Until a better explanation of the discrepancy between in- and out-of-sample statistics is produced, we remind users of macroeconomic time series that statistical models are rough approximations to the "true" mechanism generating these series. As such, the optimal forecasting technique, prefilter, and data transformation will depend on the investigator's loss function. We hope the results of our experiments will help users of macroeconomic data select techniques best suited to their particular problems.

ACKNOWLEDGMENTS

The authors acknowledge financial support from the Institute for Business and Economic Research at the University of California in Berkeley, the National Science Foundation, and the Sloan Foundation. Robert Hodrick, seminar participants at Berkeley, UCLA, and USC, and several anonymous referees provided comments on an earlier draft of this article.

APPENDIX: DATA

The following abbreviations are used to describe the series. D, domestic, F, financial, For, foreign, M, monthly, NSA, seasonally unadjusted, Q, quarterly, R, real, SA, seasonally adjusted, UK, United Kingdom, US, United States, MR, the source of the variable is described in Meese and Rogoff (1983b), MCM, the source of the variable is the Federal Reserve Board's multicountry model data base, Fed, the source of the variable is the Federal Reserve Board's MDL data base. An asterisk indicates that the untransformed series had negative values; For these series, a positive constant equal to the absolute value of the series' mean and its algebraically smallest value was added before taking logarithms.

1. Deutsche mark-dollar exchange rate: F, For, M, NSA, MR, 1973.1–1981. 6.
2. German consumer price index: D, M, NSA, R, MR, 1973.1–1981.6.
3. UK pound-dollar exchange rate: F, For, M, NSA, MR, 1973.1–1981.6.
4. UK consumer price index: D, M, NSA, R, MR, 1973.1–1981.6.
5. Yen-dollar exchange rate: F, For, M, NSA, MR, 1973.1–1981.6.
6. Japanese consumer price index: D, M, NSA, R, MR, 1973.1–1981.6.
7. German industrial production: D, M, NSA, R, MR, 1973.1–1981.6.
8. German M1: D, F, M, NSA, MR, 1973.1–1981.6.
9. UK industrial production: D, M, NSA, R, MR, 1973.1–1981.6.
10. UK M1: D, F, M, NSA, MR, 1973.1–1981.6.
11. Japanese industrial production: D, M, NSA, R, MR, 1973.1–1981.6.
12. Japanese M1: D, F, M, NSA, MR, 1973.1–1981.6.
13. German three-month interest rate: D, F, M, NSA, MR, 1973.1–1981.6.
14. German taxable bond rate: D, F, M, NSA, MR, 1973.1–1981.6.
15. UK three-month interest rate: D, F, M, NSA, MR, 1973.1–1981.6.
16. UK bond yields: D, F, M, NSA, MR, 1973.1–1981.6.
17. Japanese three-month interest rate: D, F, M, NSA, MR, 1975.1–1981.6.
18. Japanese bond yields: D, F, M, NSA, MR, 1973.1–1981.6.
19. German M2: D, F, M, NSA, MR, 1973.1–1981.6.
20. Deutsche mark-dollar three-month forward rate: F, For, M, NSA, MR, 1973.7–1981.6.
21. UK sterling M3: D, F, M, NSA, MR, 1973.1–1981.6.

22. UK pound-dollar three-month forward rate: F, For, M, NSA, MR, 1973.1–1981.6.
23. Japanese M2: D, F, M, NSA, MR, 1973.1–1981.6.
24. Yen-dollar three-month forward rate: F, For, M, NSA, MR, 1974.1–1981.6.
25. UK monetary base: D, F, M, NSA, MR, 1973.1–1981.6.
26. US consumer price index: D, M, NSA, R, MR, 1973.1–1981.6.
27. German trade balance:* For, M, NSA, R, MR, 1973.1–1981.6.
28. UK trade balance:* For, M, NSA, R, MR, 1973.1–1981.6.
29. Japanese trade balance:* For, M, NSA, R, MR, 1973.1–1981.6.
30. German monetary base: D, F, M, NSA, MR, 1973.1–1981.5.
31. US three-month treasury bill rate: D, F, M, NSA, MR, 1973.1–1981.6.
32. US 10-year+ bond rate: D, F, M, NSA, MR, 1973.1–1981.6.
33. US monetary base: D, F, M, NSA, MR, 1973.1–1981.6.
34. US M3: D, F, M, NSA, MR, 1973.1–1981.6.
35. Trade weighted dollar exchange rate: F, For, M, NSA, MR, 1973.1–1981.6.
36. US trade balance:* For, M, NSA, R, MR, 1973.1–1981.7.
37. US M1: D, F, M, NSA, MR, 1973.1–1981.6.
38. US M2: D, F, M, NSA, MR, 1973.1–1981.6.
39. US industrial production: D, M, NSA, R, MR, 1973.1–1981.6.
40. US government two-year bond rate: D, F, M, NSA, Fed, 1976.6–1981.12.
41. US government 30-year bond rate: D, F, M, NSA, Fed, 1977.3–1981.12.
42. Japanese current account balance:* For, M, NSA, MCM, 1973.1–1979.12.
43. Japanese short-term capital balance:* F, For, M, NSA, MCM, 1973.1–1979.12.
44. Japanese long-term capital balance:* F, For, M, NSA, MCM, 1973.1–1979.12.
45. US one-year government bond rate: D, F, M, NSA, Fed, 1968.9–1981.12.
46. US five-year government bond rate: D, F, M, NSA, Fed, 1968.9–1981.12.
47. US seven-year government bond rate: D, F, M, NSA, Fed, 1969.7–1981.12.
48. US 10-year government bond rate: D, F, M, NSA, Fed, 1968.9–1981.12.
49. US 20-year government bond rate: D, F, M, NSA, Fed, 1968.9–1981.12.
50. US three-year government bond rate: D, F, M, NSA, Fed, 1968.9–1981.12.
51. US average man hours in nonfarm, private busi-

198 Journal of Business & Economic Statistics, July 1984

ness sector: D, Q, SA, R, MCM, 1960.1–1981.4.

52. US total civilian employment: D, Q, SA, R, MCM, 1960.1–1981.4.

53. US total civilian labor force: D, Q, SA, R, MCM, 1960.1–1981.4.

54. US population: D, Q, NSA, R, MCM, 1960.1–1981.4.

55. US discount rate, quarterly average: D, F, Q, NSA, MCM, 1960.1–1981.4.

56. US total time deposits of member banks: D, F, Q, NSA, MCM, 1960.1–1981.4.

57. US aggregate exports in current dollars: For, Q, SA, R, MCM, 1960.1–1981.4.

58. US nonagricultural exports in 1972 dollars: For, Q, SA, R, MCM, 1960.1–1981.4.

59. US nonagricultural exports in current dollars: For, Q, SA, R, MCM, 1960.1–1981.4.

60. US exports of goods and services in 1972 dollars: For, Q, SA, R, MCM, 1960.1–1981.4.

61. US exports of goods and services in current dollars, national income accounts basis: For, Q, SA, R, MCM, 1960.1–1981.4.

62. US service receipts other than investment income: F, For, Q, SA, MCM, 1960.1–1981.4.

63. US total service receipts: F, For, Q, SA, MCM, 1960.1–1981.4.

64. US disposable income: D, Q, SA, R, MCM, 1960.1–1981.4.

65. Canadian exports to the US: For, Q, NSA, R, MCM, 1960.1–1981.1.

66. UK exports to US: For, Q, NSA, R, MCM, 1960.1–1981.1.

67. German exports to the US: For, Q, NSA, R, MCM, 1960.1–1981.1.

68. Japanese exports to the US: For, Q, NSA, R, MCM, 1960.1–1981.1.

69. Exports to US other than Canada, UK, Germany, and Japan: For, Q, NSA, R, MCM, 1960.1–1981.1.

70. US exports to Canada: For, Q, NSA, R, MCM, 1960.1–1981.1.

71. US exports to UK: For, Q, NSA, R, MCM, 1960.1–1981.1.

72. US exports to Germany: For, Q, NSA, R, MCM, 1960.1–1981.1.

73. US exports to Japan: For, Q, NSA, R, MCM, 1960.1–1981.1.

74. US exports to countries other than Canada, UK, Germany, and Japan: For, Q, NSA, R, MCM, 1960.1–1981.1.

75. US total exports: For, Q, NSA, R, MCM, 1960.1–1981.1.

76. Japanese consumption expenditures in constant yen: D, Q, SA, R, MCM, 1965.2–1981.1.

77. Japanese current account balance in dollars: For, Q, NSA, R, MCM, 1961.1–1981.2.

78. Japanese monetary authorities claims on government: D, Q, NSA, R, MCM, 1959.1–1981.2.

79. Japanese index of industrial production: D, Q, NSA, R, MCM, 1959.1–1981.2.

80. Japanese currency component of M1: D, F, NSA, Q, MCM, 1955.1–1981.2.

81. Japanese banks currency holdings: D, F, NSA, Q, MCM, 1960.1–1981.1.

82. Japanese demand deposit component of M1: D, F, NSA, Q, MCM, 1960.1–1981.1.

83. Japanese monetary authorities government deposits: D, F, NSA, Q, MCM, 1957.1–1981.2.

84. Japanese total demand and time deposits: D, F, NSA, Q, MCM, 1963.1–1981.2.

85. Japanese government consumption expenditures in constant yen: D, Q, SA, R, MCM, 1965.2–1981.1.

86. Japanese GNP in constant yen: D, Q, SA, R, MCM, 1965.2–1981.1.

87. Japanese GNP in current yen: D, Q, SA, R, MCM, 1965.2–1981.1.

88. Japanese government consumption expenditure in current yen: D, Q, SA, R, MCM, 1965.2–1981.1.

89. Japanese government fixed investment in current yen: D, Q, SA, R, MCM, 1965.2–1981.1.

90. Japanese private total fixed investment in constant yen: D, Q, SA, R, MCM, 1965.2–1981.1.

91. Japanese private total fixed investment in current yen: D, Q, SA, R, MCM, 1965.2–1981.1.

92. Japanese private residential fixed investment in constant yen: D, Q, SA, R, MCM, 1965.2–1981.1.

93. Japanese private nonresidential fixed investment in constant yen: D, Q, SA, R, MCM, 1965.2–1981.1.

94. Japanese private nonresidential fixed investment in current yen: D, Q, SA, R, MCM, 1965.2–1981.1.

95. Japanese average hours worked per month in all industries: D, Q, SA, R, MCM, 1953.1–1981.2.

96. Japanese fixed investment by government in constant yen: D, Q, SA, R, MCM, 1965.2–1981.1.

97. Japanese employment: D, Q, SA, R, MCM, 1953.1–1981.2.

98. Japanese labor force: D, Q, SA, R, MCM, 1953.1–1981.2.

99. Japanese import unit value: For, Q, SA, R, MCM, 1957.1–1981.2.

100. Japanese population over 14 years of age: D, Q, NSA, R, MCM, 1961. 1–1981.2.

101. Japanese gross domestic capital formation (increase in stocks) in constant yen: D, Q, SA, R, MCM, 1965.2–1981.1.

102. Japanese gross domestic capital formation (increase in stocks) in current yen: D, Q, SA, R, MCM, 1965.2–1981.1.

103. Japanese export unit value: For, Q, SA, R, MCM, 1957.1–1981.2.

104. Japanese monetary authorities' claims on deposit money banks: D, F, Q, NSA, MCM, 1957.1–

1981.2.

105. Japanese average yield on interest bearing bank debentures: D, F, Q, NSA, MCM, 1960.2–1982.1.

106. Japanese short term interest rate: D, F, NSA, Q, MCM, 1957.1–1981.3.

107. Japanese trade balance in dollars: For, Q, R, SA, MCM, 1961.1–1981.2.

108. Japanese time deposit component of M2: D, F, Q, SA, MCM, 1963.1–1981.2.

109. Japanese government transfer payments: D, Q, SA, R, MCM, 1965.1–1981.2.

110. Japanese government revenue: D, Q, SA, R, MCM, 1965.1–1981.2.

111. Japanese unemployed workers: D, Q, SA, R, MCM, 1953.1–1981.2.

112. Japanese wage rate in manufacturing: D, Q, SA, R, MCM, 1965.1–1981.2.

113. Japanese wholesale price index: D, Q, SA, R, MCM, 1953.1–1981.2.

114. Japanese exports of goods: For, Q, NSA, R, MCM, 1960.1–1981.2.

115. German current account balance: For, Q, NSA, R, MCM, 1956.1–1981.2.

116. German current account balance: For, Q, NSA, R, MCM, 1956.1–1981.2.

117. German central bank money: D, F, NSA, Q, MCM, 1960.1–1981.2.

118. German government transfer payments: D, NSA, Q, R, MCM, 1960.1–1981.2.

119. German capital consumption allowance: D, NSA, Q, R, MCM, 1960.1–1981.2.

120. Deutsche mark-dollar three-month forward rate: F, For, NSA, Q, MCM, 1960.1–1981.2.

121. Deutsche mark-dollar exchange rate: F, For, NSA, Q, MCM, 1956.1–1981.2.

122. German government spending: D, NSA, Q, R, MCM, 1960.1–1981.2.

123. German real gross national product: D, NSA, Q, R, MCM, 1960.1–1981.2.

124. German equipment investment: D, NSA, Q, R, MCM, 1960.1–1981.2.

125. German government fixed real investment: D, Q, SA, R, MCM, 1960.1–1981.2.

126. German private gross fixed investment: D, Q, SA, R, MCM, 1960.1–1981.2.

127. German investment in plant: D, Q, NSA, R, MCM, 1960.1–1981.2.

128. German nonresidential private fixed investment: D, Q, SA, R, MCM, 1960.1–1981.2.

129. German private residential fixed investment: D, Q, SA, R, MCM, 1960.1–1981.2.

130. German total fixed investment: D, Q, NSA, R, MCM, 1960.1–1981.2.

131. German government fixed nominal investment: D, Q, NSA, R, MCM, 1960.1–1981.2.

132. German inventory investment:* D, Q, NSA, R,

MCM, 1960.1–1981.2.

133. German labor (including self) employment: D, Q, NSA, R, MCM, 1960.1–1981.2.

134. German labor force: D, Q, SA, R, MCM, 1959.1–1981.2.

135. German unemployed: D, Q, NSA, R, MCM, 1959.1–1981.2.

136. German total real imports: For, Q, NSA, R, MCM, 1956.1–1981.2.

137. German total nominal imports: For, Q, NSA, R, MCM, 1950.1–1981.2.

138. German employment: D, Q, SA, R, MCM, 1960.1–1981.2.

139. German M1: D, F, Q, NSA, MCM, 1948.4–1981.2.

140. German total net foreign assets: F, For, Q, NSA, MCM, 1956.1–1981.2.

141. German absorption deflator: D, Q, SA, R, MCM, 1960.1–1981.2.

142. German gross national product deflator: D, Q, SA, R, MCM, 1960.1–1981.2.

143. German price index for industrial production: D, Q, SA, R, MCM, 1962.1–1981.2.

144. German price index for imports of goods and services: For, Q, SA, R, MCM, 1960.1–1981.2.

145. German short-term interest rate: D, F, Q, NSA, MCM, 1960.1–1982.1.

146. German interest rate on time deposits: D, F, Q, NSA, MCM, 1960.1–1981.3.

147. German tax receipts: D, Q, NSA, R, MCM, 1960.1–1981.2.

148. German real wages: D, Q, SA, R, MCM, 1962.1–1981.2.

149. German real exports of goods: For, Q, NSA, R, MCM, 1956.1–1981.2.

150. German nominal exports of goods: For, Q, NSA, R, MCM, 1950.1–1981.2.

[*Received December 1982. Revised January 1984.*]

REFERENCES

AKAIKE, H. (1974), "A New Look at the Statistical Model Identification," *IEEE Transactions on Automatic Control*, AC-19, 716–723.

AMEMIYA, T. (1980), "Selection of Regressors," *International Economic Review*, 21, 331–354.

BOX, G. E. P., and COX, D. R. (1962), "An Analysis of Transformations," *Journal of the Royal Statistical Society*, Ser. B, 24, 211–243.

BOX, G. E. P., and JENKINS, G. M. (1976), *Time Series Analysis: Forecasting and Control*, San Francisco: Holden-Day.

DICKEY, D. A., and FULLER, W. (1979), "Distribution of the Estimators in Autoregressive Time Series With a Unit Root," *Journal of the American Statistical Association*, 74, 427–431.

EVANS, G. B. A., and SAVIN, N. E. (1981), "Testing for Unit Roots: I," *Econometrica*, 49, 753–780.

FAIR, R. C. (1979), "An Analysis of the Accuracy of Four Macroeconometric Models," *Journal of Political Economy*, 87, 355–378.

FULLER, W. (1976), *Introduction to Statistical Time Series*, New

200   Journal of Business & Economic Statistics, July 1984

York: John Wiley.

GEWEKE, J. F. (1978), "An Efficient Method for Revising Seasonally Adjusted Time Series," Working Paper 7822, University of Wisconsin, Social Systems Research Institute.

GEWEKE, J. F., and MEESE, R. A. (1981), "Estimating Regression Models of Finite but Unknown Order," *International Economic Review*, 22, 55–70.

GRANGER, C. W. J., and NEWBOLD, P. (1977), *Forecasting Economic Time Series*, Academic Press.

HANNAN, E. J. (1970), *Multiple Time Series*, New York: John Wiley.

HASZA, D., and FULLER, W. (1979), "Estimation for Autoregressive Processes With Unit Roots," *Annals of Statistics*, 7, 1106–1120.

KENDALL, M. G. (1953), "The Analysis of Economic Time Series: Part I—Prices," *Journal of the Royal Statistical Society*, Ser. A, 116, 11–34.

MAKRIDAKIS, S., ANDERSON, A., CARBONNE, R., FILDES, R., HIBON, M., LEWANDOWSKI, R., NEWTON, J., PARZEN, E., and WINKLER, R. (1982), "The Accuracy of Extrapolation (Time Series) Methods: Results of a Forecasting Competition," *Journal of Forecasting*, 1, 111–153.

MALLOWS, C. L. (1973), "Some Comments on Cp," *Technometrics*, 15, 661–675.

McNEES, S. K. (1979), "The Forecasting Record for the 1970s," *New England Economic Review*, September/October, 33–53.

——— (1982), "The Role of Macroeconometric Models in Forecasting and Policy Analysis in the United States," *Journal of Forecasting*, 1, 37–48.

MEESE, R. A., and ROGOFF, K. (1983a), "Empirical Exchange Rate Models of the Seventies: Do They Fit Out of Sample?" *Journal of International Economics*, 14, 3–24.

——— (1983b), "The Out-of-Sample Failure of Empirical Exchange Rate Models: Sampling Error or Misspecification?" in *Exchange Rates and International Macroeconomics*, ed. J. Frenkel, Chicago: University of Chicago Press, 67–110.

MOSTELLER, F., and TUKEY, J. W. (1977), *Data Analysis and Regression*, Reading, Mass.: Addison-Wesley.

NELSON, C. R., and PLOSSER, C. I. (1982), "Trends and Random Walks in Macroeconomic Time Series: Some Evidence and Implications," *Journal of Monetary Economics*, 10, 139–162.

NEWBOLD, P., and GRANGER, C. W. J. (1974), "Experience With Forecasting Univariate Time Series and the Combination of Forecasts," *Journal of the Royal Statistical Society*, Ser. A, 137, 131–146.

PARZEN, E. (1974), "Some Recent Advances in Time Series Analysis," *IEEE Transactions on Automatic Control*, AC-19, 723–730.

——— (1982), ARARMA Models in Time Series Analysis and Forecasting," *Journal of Forecasting*, 1, 67–82.

SAWA, T. (1978), "Information Criteria for Discriminating Among Alternative Regression Models," *Econometrica*, 46, 1273–1282.

SCHWARZ, G. (1978), "Estimating the Dimension of a Model," *Annals of Statistics*, 6, 461–464.

SIMPSON, T., and PORTER, R. (1980), "Some Issues Involving the Definition and Interpretation of the Monetary Aggregates," in *Controlling Monetary Aggregates III*, Federal Reserve Bank of Boston Conference Series, 23, 161–234.

SIMS, C. A. (1974a), "Distributed Lags," in *Frontiers of Quantitative Economics*, eds. M. D. Intilligator and D. A. Kendrick, New York: North-Holland.

——— (1974b), "Seasonality in Regression," *Journal of the American Statistical Association*, 69, 618–626.

[15]

©Journal of Business & Economic Statistics, Vol. 1, No. 4, October 1983

Forecasting Economic Time Series With Structural and Box-Jenkins Models: A Case Study

A. C. Harvey
Department of Statistics, London School of Economics, London, WC2A 2AE

P. H. J. Todd
H. M. Treasury, London SW1P 3AG

The basic structural model is a univariate time series model consisting of a slowly changing trend component, a slowly changing seasonal component, and a random irregular component. It is part of a class of models that have a number of advantages over the seasonal ARIMA models adopted by Box and Jenkins (1976). This article reports the results of an exercise in which the basic structural model was estimated for six U.K. macroeconomic time series and the forecasting performance compared with that of ARIMA models previously fitted by Prothero and Wallis (1976).

KEY WORDS: Forecasting; ARIMA models; Structural models; Unobserved components; Kalman filter; Macroeconomic time series.

1. INTRODUCTION

The autoregressive-integrated-moving average (ARIMA) processes introduced by Box and Jenkins (1976) provide a wide class of models for univariate time series forecasting. In the traditional Box-Jenkins framework, the main tools for specifying a suitable model are the correlogram and, to a lesser extent, the sample partial autocorrelation function. However, the correlogram and sample partial autocorrelation function are not always very informative, particularly in small samples. Furthermore, the difficulties in interpretation are compounded when a series has been differenced, and differencing is the rule rather than the exception in economic time series. The result is that inappropriate models are often fitted. Attempts to select ARIMA models by an automatic procedure, based on, say, the Akaike Information Criterion can lead to even worse results; see the examples cited by Jenkins (1982).

Experienced ARIMA model builders usually take into account the type of forecast function that their models imply; see Box, Hillmer, and Tiao (1978) and Jenkins (1982). They also tend to be aware of the type of time series structure that their models imply. Hillmer and Tiao (1982) attempt to make this last point more explicit by defining what constitutes an acceptable decomposition into trend, seasonal, and irregular components. They examine three of the ARIMA models commonly fitted

to economic time series and show that certain restrictions must be placed on the range of parameter values for such a decomposition to exist. However, anyone reading the Hillmer and Tiao article, or the related article by Burman (1980), will realize that the relationship between an ARIMA model and the corresponding decomposition is often complex.

An alternative way of proceeding is to formulate models directly in terms of trend, seasonal, and irregular components. This necessarily limits the choice to those models that have forecast functions satisfying any prior considerations. Such models will be termed *structural* models. The fact that the individual components in a structural model have a direct interpretation opens up the possibility of employing a more formal model selection strategy. The question of developing such a strategy will not, however, be pursued in this article. For many economic time series we believe that one of the simplest structural models, which we call the basic structural model, will be adequate.

In this article we report the results of fitting the basic structural model to a number of economic time series, and then compare the predictions with those obtained using the Box-Jenkins models selected by Prothero and Wallis (1976). The idea of the exercise is not to prove that one method yields better forecasts than the other, but rather to show that for these series at least, the forecasts given by the two methods are comparable.

300   Journal of Business & Economic Statistics, October 1983

Having demonstrated the viability of one of the simplest models within the structural class, we feel that the case for using this class as the basis for univariate time series modeling is a strong one.

From the technical point of view, all aspects of structural models can be handled by putting them into state space form. In particular, the likelihood function can be constructed in terms of the prediction error decomposition by using the Kalman filter; see Harvey (1982). Once estimates of the parameters have been computed, optimal predictions of future observations, together with their conditional mean square errors, can be obtained using the Kalman filter. Finally, optimal estimates of the individual components can be computed using a smoothing algorithm.

2. STRUCTURAL MODELS

Let y_t be the observed variable. The basic structural model has the form

$$y_t = \mu_t + \gamma_t + \epsilon_t, \quad t = 1, \ldots, T, \qquad (2.1)$$

where μ_t, γ_t, and ϵ_t are trend, seasonal, and irregular components, respectively.

The process generating the trend is of the form

$$\mu_t = \mu_{t-1} + \beta_{t-1} + \eta_t, \quad t = 1, \ldots, T \qquad (2.2a)$$

and

$$\beta_t = \beta_{t-1} + \zeta_t, \qquad t = 1, \ldots, T, \qquad (2.2b)$$

where η_t and ζ_t are normally distributed independent white noise processes with zero means and variances σ_η^2 and σ_ζ^2, respectively. The essential feature of this model is that it is a local approximation to a linear trend. The level and slope both change slowly over time according to a random walk mechanism.

The process generating the seasonal component is

$$\gamma_t = -\sum_{j=1}^{s-1} \gamma_{t-j} + \omega_t, \quad t = 1, \ldots, T, \qquad (2.3)$$

where $\omega_t \sim \text{NID}(0, \sigma_\omega^2)$, and s is the number of "seasons" in the year. The seasonal pattern is thus slowly changing but by a mechanism that ensures that the sum of the seasonal components over any s consecutive time periods has an expected value of zero and a variance that remains constant over time. This specification could be modified by replacing the white noise disturbance term by a moving average process.[1] The advantage of doing this is that it allows a smoother change in the seasonal pattern than that permitted by (2.3). However, for the small sample sizes considered in this article we felt it best to

[1] The coefficients of the moving average model can be specified on a priori grounds or treated as additional parameters to be estimated. In the latter case the order of the process must be restricted to $s - 2$ or the model as a whole ceases to be identifiable. In the acceptable decomposition of Hillmer and Tiao (1982) the order of the MA component can be $s - 1$, but only because of the introduction of an additional restriction requiring that the variances of the trend and seasonal disturbance terms be minimized.

restrict our attention to one simple model.

The disturbances η_t, ζ_t, and ω_t are independent of each other and of the irregular component that is a normally distributed white noise process, that is, $\epsilon_t \sim \text{NID}(0, \sigma^2)$. Although the model as a whole is relatively simple, it contains the main ingredients necessary for a time series forecasting procedure in that it projects a local linear trend and a local seasonal pattern into the future.[2] It will be adequate for many economic time series, and it has the attraction that it involves no model selection procedure whatsoever.

The model can be written in the form

$$y_t = \frac{\xi_t}{\Delta^2} + \frac{\omega_t}{S(L)} + \epsilon_t, \quad t = 1, \ldots, T, \qquad (2.4)$$

where L is the lag operator, Δ is the first difference operator, S(L) is the seasonal operator

$$S(L) = \sum_{j=0}^{s-1} L^j, \qquad (2.5)$$

and ξ_t is equivalent to an MA(1) process since it is defined by

$$\xi_t = \eta_t - \eta_{t-1} + \zeta_{t-1}. \qquad (2.6)$$

The first component on the right side of (2.4) is the trend, while the second is the seasonal component. The fact that the operators Δ^2 and S(L) do not have a root in common is important, because it means that the minimum mean square estimates of both components have finite variance; see Pierce (1979). Put in a more informal way this amounts to saying that changes in the seasonal pattern are not confounded with changes in the trend. Note that the same operators are used in the decompositions proposed by Hillmer and Tiao (1982) and Burman (1980).

Expressing the model in the form (2.4) makes it clear that it belongs to the class of unobserved component ARIMA (UCARIMA) models; compare Engle (1978). Models of this kind are discussed at some length in the book by Nerlove, Grether, and Carvalho (1979), but in their work attention is focused on stationary models fitted to the residuals from a polynomial regression. Thus a deterministic trend is adopted as a matter of course. In (2.2), on the other hand, a deterministic (linear) trend only emerges as a limiting case when $\sigma_\eta^2 = \sigma_\zeta^2 = 0$.

2.1 State Space Form

Suppose for simplicity that $s = 4$. The trend and seasonal components can be written in the form

$$\begin{bmatrix} \mu_t \\ \beta_t \\ \gamma_t \\ \gamma_{t-1} \\ \gamma_{t-2} \end{bmatrix} = \begin{bmatrix} 1 & 1 & & & \\ 0 & 1 & & 0 & \\ & & -1 & -1 & -1 \\ & 0 & 1 & 0 & 0 \\ & & 0 & 1 & 0 \end{bmatrix} \begin{bmatrix} \mu_{t-1} \\ \beta_{t-1} \\ \gamma_{t-1} \\ \gamma_{t-2} \\ \gamma_{t-3} \end{bmatrix} + \begin{bmatrix} \eta_t \\ \zeta_t \\ \omega_t \\ 0 \\ 0 \end{bmatrix} \qquad (2.7)$$

[2] A similar model is employed by Kitagawa (1981) except that he has σ_η^2 constrained to be zero.

or, more compactly, as

$$\alpha_t = C\alpha_{t-1} + \tau_t, \qquad (2.8)$$

where $\alpha_t = (\mu_t, \beta_t, \gamma_t, \gamma_{t-1}, \gamma_{t-2})'$, and so on. Defining

$$z_t = (1 \quad 0 \quad 1 \quad 0 \quad 0)', \qquad (2.9)$$

(2.1) can be written as

$$y_t = z_t'\alpha + \epsilon_t, \quad t = 1, \ldots, T. \qquad (2.10)$$

Equations (2.8) and (2.10) can be regarded as the transition and measurement equations of a state space model; see, for example, Harvey (1981a, Ch. 4).

2.2 Estimation

Maximum likelihood estimators of the parameters in structural models can be computed either in the time domain or in the frequency domain. The most attractive time domain procedure is based on the state space representation of the model. As (2.7) makes clear, the state vector in the basic structural model is nonstationary, but starting values for the Kalman filter can be constructed from the first $s + 1$ observations. The likelihood function for $y_{s+2}, \ldots, y_T$ is then given by the prediction error decomposition, that is,

$$\log L = -\frac{(T-s-1)}{2}\log 2\pi - \frac{1}{2}\sum_{t=s+2}^{T}\log f_t^*$$
$$-\frac{1}{2}\sum_{t=s+2}^{T}\frac{\nu_t^2}{f_t^*}, \qquad (2.11)$$

where ν_t is the one-step-ahead prediction error at time t, and f_t^* is its variance; compare Harvey (1981a, pp. 204–207). From the practical point of view an easy way of calculating close approximations to the starting values is to initiate the Kalman filter at $t = 0$ with a diagonal covariance matrix in which the diagonal elements are large but finite numbers.

If the variances of η_t, ζ_t, and ω_t are expressed relative to σ^2, the variance of ϵ_t (i.e., σ_η^2/σ^2, σ_ζ^2/σ^2 and σ_ω^2/σ^2), then the likelihood function can be written in the form

$$\log L$$
$$= -\frac{(T-s-1)}{2}\log 2\pi - \frac{(T-s-1)}{2}\log \sigma^2$$
$$-\frac{1}{2}\sum_{t=s+2}^{T}\log f_t - \frac{1}{2\sigma^2}\sum_{t=s+2}^{T}\frac{\nu_t^2}{f_t}, \qquad (2.12)$$

where the variance of ν_t is $\sigma^2 f_t$. It now becomes possible to concentrate σ^2 out of the likelihood function, leaving

$$\log L = -\frac{(T-s-1)}{2}(\log 2\pi + 1)$$
$$-\frac{(T-s-1)}{2}\log \tilde{\sigma}^2 - \frac{1}{2}\sum_{t=s+2}^{T}\log f_t, \qquad (2.13)$$

where

$$\tilde{\sigma}^2 = (T-s-1)^{-1}\sum_{t=s+2}^{T}\frac{\nu_t^2}{f_t}. \qquad (2.14)$$

The advantage of concentrating σ^2 out of the likelihood function is that numerical optimization can be carried out with respect to three parameters rather than four. The disadvantage is that the ML estimator of σ^2 is sometimes equal to zero. When this is the case, the relative variances in the concentrated likelihood tend to infinity.

Approximate ML estimates[3] can be obtained by expressing the likelihood function in terms of the periodogram of the differenced observations, $\Delta\Delta_s y_t$. These differenced observations are stationary and can be expressed as

$$\Delta\Delta_s y_t = \Delta_s \eta_t + (1 + L + \ldots + L^{s-1})\zeta_{t-1}$$
$$+ \Delta^2\omega_t + \Delta\Delta_s \epsilon_t. \qquad (2.15)$$

The spectral density of the right side of (2.15) is relatively easy to construct using the autocovariance generating function. Frequency domain methods of this kind have been used quite successfully in the estimation of UCARIMA models; see Nerlove, Grether, and Carvalho (1979).

The autocorrelation structure implied by the basic structural model can be derived directly from (2.15). If $\gamma(\tau)$ denotes the autocovariance of $\Delta\Delta_s y_t$ at lag τ, then for quarterly data

$$\gamma(0) = 2\sigma_\eta^2 + 4\sigma_\zeta^2 + 4\sigma_\omega^2 + 4\sigma^2,$$
$$\gamma(1) = \qquad 3\sigma_\zeta^2 - 4\sigma_\omega^2 - 2\sigma^2,$$
$$\gamma(2) = 2\sigma_\zeta^2 + \sigma_\omega^2,$$
$$\gamma(3) = \qquad \sigma_\zeta^2 \qquad + \sigma^2,$$
$$\gamma(4) = -\sigma_\eta^2 \qquad\qquad - 2\sigma^2,$$
$$\gamma(5) = \qquad\qquad\qquad \sigma^2,$$
$$\gamma(\tau) = 0, \quad \tau \geq 6, \qquad (2.16)$$

These equations can be used as the basis for constructing estimators of the unknown parameters from the sample autocovariance function or from the correlogram. However, since there are six nonzero autocovariances and only four unknown parameters, there is no unique way of forming such estimators. Even in special cases where the number of parameters is equal to the number of nonzero autocovariances, efficient estimators cannot be obtained, just as they cannot be obtained for an MA model. Nevertheless, estimates computed from the correlogram may still be useful as preliminary estimates in a maximum likelihood procedure.

2.3 Prediction and Signal Extraction

Once the parameters in the model have been estimated, predictions of future values, together with their conditional mean square errors, can be made from the

---

[3] The likelihood in (2.11) is exact if the first $s + 1$ observations are taken to be fixed, although other assumptions can be made; see Harvey (1982). The frequency domain likelihood would be exact if the differenced observations were generated by a circular process.

302   Journal of Business & Economic Statistics, October 1983

state space form. The forecast function consists of the local trend with the local seasonal pattern superimposed upon it. If y_t is in logarithms, the estimator of β_t at time T can be regarded as the current estimator of the growth rate. This is of considerable importance to policy makers. The fact that it is immediately available in the structural model, together with its conditional MSE, is a great advantage.

Optimal estimates of the trend and seasonal components throughout the series can be obtained by applying a smoothing algorithm. This is sometimes known as signal extraction. In the present context it can be used to provide a method of model-based seasonal adjustment.

2.4 A Class of Structural Models

Although this article is primarily concerned with the basic structural model, it is worth noting how the model can be generalized. In the first place the trend component can be extended so that it yields a local approximation to any polynomial; see Harrison and Stevens (1976). Second, a more elaborate seasonal model can be fitted, as was observed in the discussion after Equation (2.3). In addition, the seasonal pattern in the eventual forecast function can be made to change over time by adding to (2.3) a component, γ_t^*, which satisfies the condition that $S(L)\gamma_t^*$ is white noise. In the third place the irregular component can be modeled by any stationary ARMA process. Finally, a cyclical component can be brought into the model. This can be done by adding it directly to (2.1) or by incorporating it into the trend.[4]

3. CRITERIA FOR MODEL EVALUATION

Models can be evaluated and compared on the basis of goodness of fit both inside and outside the sample period. The criteria employed in our study are set out in this section.

3.1 Prediction Error Variance

The prediction error variance, that is, the variance of the one-step-ahead prediction errors in the models, is a basic measure of goodness of fit within the sample. For an ARIMA model, the prediction error variance is given

---

[4] In a study of annual U.S. economic time series over a period of 100 years, Nelson and Plosser (1982) found that the correlograms had a pattern consistent with the first differences being stationary about a non-zero mean. In all cases the lag one autocorrelation of first differences was positive. A referee has pointed out that series with this property could not have been generated by an annual structural model in which the trend is (2.2) with $\sigma_\zeta^2 = 0$, and the irregular component is white noise. However, for the U.K. series studied later in this paper, we found that the lag one sample autocorrelation for differenced annual data was negative for all series but one, and in that particular case it was less than .05. This behavior is probably accounted for by the relative stability of the U.K. economy over the relatively short sample period covered (the 1950s and 1960s). Were we to consider modeling longer time series of the kind studied by Nelson and Plosser, we would probably do so by setting up a model in which a stochastic cyclical component was built into the trend.

directly by the estimator of the variance of the disturbances. For a structural model, the corresponding estimator is given by

$$\tilde{\sigma}_p^2 = \tilde{\sigma}^2 \bar{f}, \qquad (3.1)$$

where $\tilde{\sigma}^2$ is given by (2.14) and $\bar{f}$ is defined by

$$\bar{f} = \lim_{t \to \infty} f_t. \qquad (3.2)$$

The value of $\bar{f}$ can be found by running the Kalman filter until it reaches a steady state. It can usually be approximated by f_T, although there is an important distinction between $\sigma^2 \bar{f}$ and $\sigma^2 f$, in that the latter is the *finite* sample prediction error variance.

If the variances in the model are not expressed relative to σ^2, as in (2.11), then $\tilde{\sigma}_p^2 = \bar{f}^*$, where $\bar{f}^*$ is defined analogously to $\bar{f}$.

3.2 Post-Sample Predictions

Once the parameters of a model have been estimated within the sample period, predictions can be made in a post-sample period. The sum of squares of the one-step prediction errors then gives a measure of forecasting accuracy. These quantities can then be compared for rival models.

The prediction errors in the post-sample period can also be compared with the prediction errors within the sample. A test statistic can be employed to test whether the prediction errors in the post-sample period are significantly greater than the prediction errors within the sample period. If they are, we can draw three possible conclusions:

1. The variances of the disturbances are increasing over time;
2. The process generating the observations has changed in some way, possibly due to the impact of certain outside interventions; or
3. The fit achieved in the sample period is to some extent a product of data mining.

If the variances of the disturbances are increasing over time, this should normally be detected within the sample period when the residuals are examined. The heteroscedasticity can often be removed by a suitable transformation such as taking logarithms. Predictive failure due to a changing data generation process simply shows up the weakness of univariate time series models, and there is little that can be done about it apart from extending the models to include explanatory variables. The third reason for predictive failure is the most relevant in the present context, since one of the objections to the Box-Jenkins methodology is that the cycle of identification, estimation, and diagnostic checking can lead to models that, while they give a good fit in the sample period, are inappropriate for making predictions in the future. Such models are usually, though not necessarily, over-parameterized.

The mechanics of carrying out a post-sample predictive test are as follows. Consider the basic structural model and suppose that the relative variances of η_t, ζ_t, and ω_t are *known*. In this case $\nu_t \sim \text{NID}(0, \sigma^2 f_t)$ for $t = s + 2, \ldots, T$. If the model is correct, the prediction errors in the post-sample period, ν_t, $t = T + 1, \ldots, T + l$, are distributed in a similar way and so

$$\xi(l) = \frac{(\sum_{t=T+1}^{T+l} \nu_t^2/f_t)/l}{\sum_{t=s+2}^{T} (\nu_t^2/f_t)/(T - s - 1)} \sim F_{l,T-s-1}. \quad (3.3)$$

In the special case when $\sigma_\eta^2 = \sigma_\zeta^2 = \sigma_\omega^2 = 0$, the model is a linear regression with time trend and seasonal dummies, and the test based on (3.3) is then identical to the Chow test.

If T is reasonably large, the Kalman filter will be virtually in a steady state with $f_{T+j} \simeq \bar{f}$ for $j = 1, \ldots, l$. Therefore,

$$\xi(l) \simeq \sum_{t=T+1}^{T+l} \frac{\nu_t^2}{l \bar{\sigma}_p^2}. \quad (3.4)$$

When the relative variances are estimated, the statistic $l \cdot \xi(l)$ has a χ_l^2 distribution under the null hypothesis. However, testing $\xi(l)$ against an F-distribution is still legitimate and may be more satisfactory in small samples.

A post-sample predictive test statistic for an ARIMA model can be derived in a similar way; compare Box and Tiao (1976). The distinction between (3.3) and (3.4) can again be made if a finite sample prediction algorithm is employed; see Harvey (1981b).

3.3 Unconditional Post-Sample Predictions

Another useful measure of forecasting performance is the sum of squares of the prediction errors in the post-sample period for the unconditional predictions. The unconditional predictions are the predictions made for $t = T + 1$ to $T + l$ using the observations up to time $t = T$ only. As pointed out by Box and Tiao (1976), the only formal statistical test of the adequacy of the model is the one based on one-step-ahead predictions. However, looking at predictions several steps ahead is useful as a check that the form of the forecast function is sensible.

4. MODELING MACROECONOMIC TIME SERIES

Prothero and Wallis (1976) fitted Box-Jenkins seasonal ARIMA models to quarterly observations on a number of U.K. economic time series. Their purpose was to compare the performance of these models with that of a small-scale econometric model devised by Hendry. Our purpose is to compare their models with the basic structural model. A subsidiary aim was simply to gain some experience of the problems involved in fitting structural models to relatively short time series.

For each series, Prothero and Wallis presented results for a number of models. In most cases they do not state unequivocally that any one of the models is the preferred specification. However, in light of their comments we have chosen one model in each case. Note that it is the ambiguity surrounding the choice of a suitable ARIMA

model that is one of the weaknesses of the whole Box-Jenkins approach. The cycle of identification, estimation, and diagnostic checking is not only time consuming, but it can also on occasion produce poor results through an excess of data mining. The results for Series 5 (Imports) provide a good example.

We must stress again that only one structural model, the basic structural model, was fitted to each series. Hence no model selection was involved at all. It is quite likely that we could have obtained an even better performance by working with the wider class of models sketched out at the end of Section 2. However, in only one case, Series 4, did we feel that restricting ourselves to the basic model was a significant limitation and even in that case the performance of the model was quite reasonable.

4.1 The Data

The data used in the study by Prothero and Wallis (1976) consisted of various U.K. economic time series published in *Economic Trends*. They fitted models to 42 quarterly observations covering the period 1957/3 to 1967/4. In 1969 the Central Statistical Office changed the data base, and this altered the characteristics of the series. This meant that only the first three observations in 1968 could be used for post-sample predictive testing. It was therefore decided to reestimate the preferred ARIMA specifications over the 37 observations from 1957/3 to 1966/3. The same observations were used to fit the basic structural model, while the eight observations 1966/4 to 1968/3 were used for post-sample predictive testing.

Prothero and Wallis fitted their models without taking logarithms. This was done for comparability with Hendry's econometric model. However, there is evidence of heteroscedasticity in some of the series and, other things being equal, one would almost certainly want to consider taking logarithms in these cases. This should be borne in mind when evaluating the results.

4.2 Estimation

The structural model was estimated via the prediction error decomposition using the concentrated form of the likelihood given in (2.13). The likelihood was maximized using the variable metric Gill-Murray-Pitfield algorithm, E04JBP in the NAG library. Analytic derivatives were not used.

The ARIMA models were reestimated using Prothero's own exact ML program, FMLAMS. The randomness of the residuals was assessed by reference to the values of the Box-Pierce Q-statistic.

4.3 Results

The results of fitting basic structural models and the preferred ARIMA specification of Prothero and Wallis—hereafter denoted as P-W—are summarized in Tables 1 and 2. The following points need to be made

304   Journal of Business & Economic Statistics, October 1983

Table 1. Estimates of Parameters for the Basic Structural Model and for the Preferred Specification of the ARIMA Model

Series	Structural Model					ARIMA Model[a] and Q-Statistic
	$\hat{\sigma}_\eta^2$	$\hat{\sigma}_\zeta^2$	$\hat{\sigma}_\omega^2$	$\hat{\sigma}^2$		
1. Consumer Durables	408.29	.00	181.42	.03	(a)	$\Delta\Delta_4 y_t = (1 - .27L^4)\epsilon_t,\quad Q(15) = 10.02$
2. Other Expenditure	305.51	.00	30.01	181.87	(a)	$\Delta\Delta_4 y_t = (1 - .59L^4)\epsilon_t,\quad Q(15) = 7.48$
3. Investment	1,392.00	.00	.82	111.90	(d)	$(1 - .27L^4 - .05L^n - .12L^{12} - .43L^{16})\Delta y_t = \epsilon_t,$ $Q(12) = 6.90$
4. Inventory Investment	1,204.08	.00	168.89	371.06	(a)	$\Delta\Delta_4 y_t = (1 - .35L^4 + .36L^2)(1 - .60L^4)\epsilon_t,$ $Q(13) = 5.17$
					(e)	$(1 - .25L - .37L^2)(1 - .20L^4 - .06L^n - .14L^{12}$ $- .51L^{16})y_t = \epsilon_t,\quad Q(10) = 4.32$
5. Imports	879.74	.00	.00	268.02	(c)	$(1 + .91L^4 + .94L^n + .89L^{12} + .21L^{16})\Delta_4 y_t$ $= 219.33 + \epsilon_t,\quad Q(11) = 12.13$
6. GDP	3,375.47	.00	599.71	.20	(a)	$\Delta\Delta_4 y_t = (1 - .30L)(1 - .79L^4)\epsilon_t,\quad Q(14) = 9.48$

[a] Letters in parentheses denote the specification in Prothero and Wallis (1976).

for the results on individual series.

1. *Consumers' expenditure on durable goods.* The P-W specification (a) was chosen because P-W considered it to be "an obvious choice." The structural model gave a slightly better fit both within and outside the sample period. Both models clearly fail the post-sample predictive test, but the reason for this is almost certainly the change in vehicle registration policy introduced in 1967; see Prothero and Wallis (1976, p. 484).

2. *Consumers' expenditure on all other goods and services.* Again the preferred ARIMA model is of the simple form adopted in the first series. As before the structural model gives a slightly better fit inside the sample period, but the ARIMA model does better outside the sample period. However, the differences are not great, and as with Series 1, the overall conclusion must be that there is little distinction between the two methods in terms of forecasting performance. The relatively high values of

the post-sample predictive test statistics are almost certainly explained by the heteroscedasticity in the series. This could probably be rectified by modeling the observations in logarithms.

3. *Investment.* P-W considered four models and chose (d) as being the "most reasonable." Unlike the preferred ARIMA models for the previous two series it contains more parameters than the structural model. Perhaps as a result of this it fits slightly better in the sample period. However, it also fits better in the post-sample period, although as with the other two series, the difference in forecasting performance is not great.

Although the preferred ARIMA model appears to be satisfactory for one-step-ahead forecasting (at least for the post-sample period considered), it is less impressive over a longer time horizon. The sum of squares of the unconditional predictions over the sample period was 15,942, which is approximately twice the figure obtained with the structural model. Futhermore, the eventual

Table 2. Forecasting Performance of the Basic Structural Model and the Preferred Specification of the ARIMA Model

Series	Prediction Error Variance		Post-Sample Prediction Sum of Squares		Predictive F-test[a]		Unconditional Post-Sample Prediction Sum of Squares for Structural Model
	Structural	ARIMA	Structural	ARIMA	Structural	ARIMA	
1. Consumer Durables	1,349	1,509	71,705	78,372	6.67	6.49	46,218
2. Other Expenditure	924	1,084	20,211	18,868	2.75	2.17	22,054
3. Investment	1,823	1,745	13,651	12,065	.95	.86	7,551
4. Inventory Investment	3,274	(a) 3,162 (e) 2,157	62,683	(a) 59,596 (e) 43,381	2.40	(a) 2.36 (e) 2.51	76,929
5. Imports	1,532	1,259	57,428	604,080	4.75	59.98	34,223
6. GDP	7,663	7,733	47,794	33,020	.78	.53	56,091

[a] 5% critical value for $F_{8,32}$ is approximately 2.25.

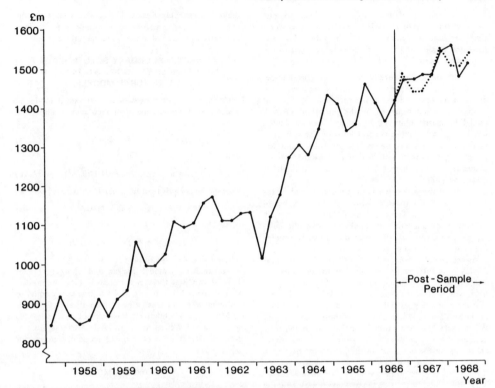

Figure 1. Unconditional Forecasts for Investment Using the Basic Structural Model

forecast function is horizontal, and it seems unlikely that one would want a forecast function of this kind for a series that shows a clear upward movement over time. The forecast function for the structural model over the post-sample period is shown in Figure 1, and one can see that it tracks the series quite well.

4. *Inventory Investment.* P-W observed that an examination of the sample autocorrelation function for various differences of the series suggests the operator $\Delta\Delta_4$. However, the preferred model was one fitted to the undifferenced observations. An examination of the series indicates that this is probably not unreasonable as there are no strong upward or downward movements in the series. Table 1 shows the models P-W fitted to both the differenced ($\Delta\Delta_4$) and undifferenced series. The differenced model has a similar performance to the structural model, but the undifferenced model is clearly superior to both. For this series, therefore, the basic structural model is inadequate and a more general model, in which the irregular component is modeled by an autoregressive process, needs to be employed.

5. *Imports of Goods and Services.* For this series the

preferred specification of P-W was their model (c) "on account of its small residual variance and small value[5] of the Q-statistic." This model has a smaller prediction error variance than the structural model, but its forecasting performance is disastrous. The devaluation of the pound in 1967 meant that any univariate model would have difficulty in forecasting over the post-sample period with any reasonable degree of accuracy, and this is apparent from the post-sample F-statistic value of 4.75 for the structural model. However, the F-statistic of 59.98 achieved with the ARIMA model is of a completely different order of magnitude. The performance of this model is therefore a particularly dramatic example of the dangers inherent in the Box-Jenkins methodology. We should, however, add that P-W's (e) and (f) specifications—which are somewhat more conventional forms—forecasted in much the same way as the basic structural model.

---

[5] P-W had $Q(11) = 4.79$. Our estimates are based on fewer observations and Q is rather larger, although still not significant at the 5% level.

306   Journal of Business & Economic Statistics, October 1983

6. *Gross Domestic Product.* P-W's model (a) is one of the standard forms of an ARIMA model. The prediction error variance is similar to the one obtained in the structural model, and both perform rather well in the post-sample period.

Overall, the performance of the basic structural model is quite good. For Series 1, 2, 3, and 6, its forecasting performance both inside and outside the sample period is similar to that achieved by the preferred ARIMA model. For Series 4, the ARIMA model is clearly better, but in this case a more general form of the structural model is called for. For Series 5, on the other hand, the forecasting performance of the preferred ARIMA model is disastrous while that of the basic structural model is quite reasonable.

For all of the series, the basic structural model produced a sensible forecast function. This is reflected in the last column in Table 2, which shows the sum of squares of the unconditional predictions over the post-sample period. In half the cases it is actually smaller than the sum of squares of the conditional forecast!

As regards the estimated variances in the structural model, it is interesting to note that in all cases the estimate of σ_ζ^2 is consistent with a steady increase over time, which all of the series display. However, the fact that the estimate goes right to zero may be a reflection of the small sample size and the method of estimation. When exact ML estimation is carried out in the time domain, it is not unusual to find some of the estimates ending up on the boundary of the parameter space; see Sargan and Bhargava (1983) and our Appendix for further details. The properties of approximate ML estimates computed in the frequency domain may be quite different, but this is a matter for future investigation.

5. CONCLUSIONS

The forecast function for a structural model can always be reproduced by an ARIMA model. For example, it is clear from (2.15) and (2.16) that the basic structural model is equivalent to an MA($s + 1$) model for $\Delta\Delta_s y_t$ in which the parameters are subject to nonlinear restrictions. The attraction of specifying models in terms of a well-defined structure is that attention is more likely to be confined to models that yield forecast functions of an acceptable form.

The basic model we propose has a similar structure to the Bayesian model of Harrison and Stevens (1976). However, while Harrison and Stevens make assumptions about plausible values for the variances of the disturbances, this article has shown that it is possible to estimate these variances even with a relatively small number of observations. In all the cases examined this led to a sensible forecast function. Furthermore, the forecasting performance of the estimated models compared well with the forecasting performance of ARIMA models selected after the usual process of identification, estimation, and

diagnostic checking. Given these results, we feel that the conceptual advantages of structural models make them attractive as a class of univariate time series models.

APPENDIX: BOUNDARY SOLUTIONS OF MAXIMUM LIKELIHOOD ESTIMATES IN STRUCTURAL MODELS

Consider a simple case of the structural model in which there is no seasonal component and no slope; that is,

$$y_t = \mu_t + \epsilon_t, \quad \epsilon_t \sim \text{NID}(0, \sigma^2) \qquad \text{(A.1a)}$$

and

$$\mu_t = \mu_{t-1} + \eta_t, \quad \eta_t \sim \text{NID}(0, \sigma_\eta^2). \qquad \text{(A.1b)}$$

This model is equivalent to an ARIMA (0, 1, 1) model

$$\Delta y_t = \xi_t + \theta\xi_{t-1}, \quad \xi_t \sim \text{NID}(0, \sigma_\xi^2), \qquad \text{(A.2)}$$

in which

$$\theta = [(q^2 + 4q)^{1/2} - 2 - q]/2,$$

where $q = \sigma_\eta^2/\sigma^2$; see Harvey (1981a, p. 170).

For an MA(1) model, Sargan and Bhargava (1983) have shown that there is a relatively high probability that an exact ML estimate of θ will be *exactly* equal to -1, even when the true value is some distance from -1. In Model (A.1), a relatively low value of σ_η^2 corresponds to a value of θ close to -1 in (A.2). In these circumstances, ML estimates of zero will not be uncommon for σ_η^2.

ACKNOWLEDGMENTS

An earlier version of this article was presented at the Second International Symposium on Forecasting, Istanbul, July 1982. We would like to thank the two referees of this journal for their useful comments on the first draft. The views expressed in this article are not necessarily those of H. M. Treasury.

[*Received August 1982. Revised March 1983.*]

REFERENCES

BOX, G. E. P., HILLMER, S. C. and TIAO, G. C. (1978), "Analysis and Modelling of Seasonal Time Series," in *Seasonal Analysis of Economic Time Series*, ed. A. Zellner, Washington, DC: Bureau of the Census, 309–334.

BOX, G. E. P., and JENKINS, G. M. (1976), *Time Series Analysis: Forecasting and Control* (revised ed.), San Francisco: Holden-Day.

BOX, G. E. P., and TIAO, G. C. (1976), "Comparison of Forecasts With Actuality," *Applied Statistics*, 25, 195–200.

BURMAN, J. P. (1980), "Seasonal Adjustment by Signal Extraction," *Journal of the Royal Statistical Society*, Series A, 143, 321–337.

ENGLE, R. F. (1978), "Estimating Structural Models of Seasonality," in *Seasonal Analysis of Economic Time Series*, A. Zellner (ed.) Washington DC: Bureau of the Census, 281–308.

HARRISON, P. J., and STEVENS, C. F. (1976), "Bayesian Forecasting," *Journal of the Royal Statistical Society*, Series B, 38, 205–247.

HARVEY, A. C. (1981a), *Time Series Models*, Deddington: Philip Allan, and New York: John Wiley.

——— (1981b), "Finite Sample Prediction and Overdifferencing,"

Journal of Time Series Analysis, 2, 221-232.

—— (1982), "Estimation Procedures for a Class of Univariate Time Series Models," LSE Econometrics Program Discussion Paper No. 32.

HILLMER, S. C., and TIAO, G. C. (1982), "An ARIMA-Model-Based Approach to Seasonal Adjustment," *Journal of the American Statistical Association,* 77, 63-70.

JENKINS, G. M. (1982), "Some Practical Aspects of Forecasting in Organizations," *Journal of Forecasting,* 1, 3-21.

KITAGAWA, G. (1981), "A Nonstationary Time Series Model and Its Fitting by a Recursive Filter," *Journal of Time Series Analysis,* 2, 103-116.

NELSON, C. R., and PLOSSER, C. I. (1982), "Trends and Random

Walks in Macroeconomic Time Series: Some Evidence and Implications," *Journal of Monetary Economics,* 10, 139-162.

NERLOVE, M., GRETHER, D. M., and CARVALHO, J. L. (1979), *Analysis of Economic Time Series,* New York: Academic Press.

PIERCE, D. A. (1979), "Signal Extraction Error in Nonstationary Time Series," *Annals of Statistics,* 7, 1303-1320.

PROTHERO, D. L., and WALLIS, K. F. (1976), "Modelling Macroeconomic Time Series," *Journal of the Royal Statistical Society,* Series A, 139, 468-500.

SARGAN, J. D., and BHARGAVA, A. (1983), "Maximum Likelihood Estimation of Regression Models with First-Order Moving Average Errors when the Root Lies on the Unit Circle," *Econometrica,* 40, 617-636.

Comment

Craig F. Ansley
Graduate School of Business, University of Chicago, Chicago, IL 60637

Harvey and Todd (HT) have introduced a simple structural model, a variance components model, which they claim will be adequate for many economic time series. Variants of the same model have been described by Kitagawa (1983), who justifies the models HT(2.2) and (2.3) as smoothness priors, as in Wahba (1978). We will compare the HT model to another that has found wide application for seasonal series, the ARIMA-$(0, 1, 1)(0, 1, 1)_s$ model discussed in Box and Jenkins (1976, Sec. 9.2) and to a related structural model.

HT point out that the variance of ζ_t in their Equation (2.2b) is usually very small, and because of the pile-up effect in maximum likelihood estimation of moving average models, it is more often than not estimated to be zero. The pile-up effect was first described analytically by Cryer and Ledolter (1981); a more complete version appears in their 1980 Technical Report. Monte Carlo evidence of the pile-up effect for other moving average models is given in Ansley and Newbold (1980).

For this reason we consider the simplified version of the model:

$$y_t = \alpha + \beta t + \mu_t + \gamma_t + \epsilon_t, \qquad (1a)$$

$$\mu_t = \mu_{t-1} + \eta_t, \qquad (1b)$$

$$\gamma_t = -\sum_{j=1}^{s-1} \gamma_{t-j} + \omega_t, \qquad (1c)$$

where

$$\epsilon_t \sim N(o, \sigma^2),$$

$$\omega_t \sim N(0, \lambda_1 \sigma^2),$$

$$\eta_t \sim N(0, \lambda_2 \sigma^2).$$

The linear trend term $\alpha + \beta t$ is included because the transformation operations required for stationarity in

this model do not remove the drift β, which must therefore be estimated explicitly. This point is missed by HT.

Applying the difference operators $\Delta \equiv 1 - L$ and $S(L)$ defined in HT(2.5), we have

$$\Delta S(L) y_t = s\beta + \sum_0^{s-1} \eta_{t-j} + \omega_t - \omega_{t-1} + \epsilon_t - \epsilon_{t-s}. \qquad (2)$$

Model (2) is stationary, and has four parameters: λ_1, λ_2, σ^2, and β. HT are effectively advocating the transformation $\Delta S(L)$ to reduce an arbitrary series to stationarity.

Consider now the transformation $\Delta \Delta_s$ used by Box and Jenkins (1976), where $\Delta \Delta_s \equiv 1 - L^s$. Noting that $\Delta S(L) = \Delta_s$, we have from (2)

$$\Delta \Delta_s y_t = \eta_t - \eta_{t-s} + \omega_t - 2\omega_{t-1}$$
$$+ \omega_{t-2} + \epsilon_t - \epsilon_{t-1} - \epsilon_{t-s} + \epsilon_{t-s-1}. \qquad (3)$$

We now suggest an alternative structural model,

$$y_t = \alpha + \beta t + \mu_t + \gamma'_t + \epsilon_t, \qquad (4a)$$

$$\mu_t = \mu_{t-1} + \eta_t, \qquad (4b)$$

$$\gamma'_t = \gamma'_{t-s} + \omega_t. \qquad (4c)$$

In this case we have

$$\Delta \Delta_s y_t = \omega_t - \omega_{t-1} + \eta_t - \eta_{t-s}$$
$$+ \epsilon_t - \epsilon_{t-1} - \epsilon_{t-s} + \epsilon_{t-s-1}. \qquad (5)$$

The difference between models (1) and (4) is essentially the terms $\omega_t - 2\omega_{t-1} + \omega_{t-2}$ and $\omega_t - \omega_{t-1}$ in their stationary derivatives (3) and (5) respectively. This arises from the seasonal components (1c) and (4c). In (1c), $S(L)\gamma_t$ is white noise; in (4c), $S(L)\gamma'_t$ is a random walk. Thus the models differ in the smoothness of the evolution of $S(L)\gamma_t$: HT impose no smoothness prior at all on $S(L)\gamma_t$, while the $\Delta \Delta_s$ transformation implies a model

308   Journal of Business & Economic Statistics, October 1983

with a smoothness prior corresponding to a random walk.

The autocovariances of (5) are

$$c_0 = (4 + 2\lambda_1 + 2\lambda_2)\sigma^2,$$

$$c_1 = -(2 + \lambda_1)\sigma^2,$$

$$c_k = 0 \quad k = 2, \ldots, s - 2,$$

$$c_{s-1} = \sigma^2,$$

$$c_s = -(2 + \lambda_2)\sigma^2,$$

$$c_{s+1} = \sigma^2. \tag{6}$$

We now show how this can approximate the autovariance function of the $\text{ARIMA}(0, 1)(0, 1)_s$ process:

$$y_t = (1 - \theta L)(1 - \Theta L^s)\epsilon_t. \tag{7}$$

The autocovariances for (7) are

$$c'_0 = (1 + \theta^2)(1 + \Theta^2)\sigma^2,$$

$$c'_1 = -\theta(1 + \Theta^2)\sigma^2,$$

$$c'_k = 0 \quad k = 2, \ldots, s - 2,$$

$$c'_{s-1} = \theta\Theta\sigma^2,$$

$$c'_s = -\Theta(1 + \theta^2),$$

$$c'_{s+1} = \theta\Theta\sigma^2.$$

The four distinct nonzero autocovariances satisfy the constraint $c'_1 c'_s = c'_{s-1} c'_0$.

It is easy to see from (6) that if $\lambda_1 \lambda_2$ is small then

$$c_1 c_s / c_{s-1} = \sigma^2(2 + \lambda_1)(2 + \lambda_2)$$

$$\doteq 2\sigma^2(2 + \lambda_1 + \lambda_2) = c_0,$$

so that Model (4) closely approximates an ARIMA-$(0, 1, 1)(0, 1, 1)_s$ process whenever the trend and seasonal terms evolve slowly. Thus the essential difference beween the HT and $\text{ARIMA}(0, 1, 1)(0, 1, 1)_s$ models is simply that the former imposes no smoothness on the evolution of $S(L)\gamma_t$ while the latter does.

We compare these two models further by fitting them to the monthly international airline passenger data 1949–1960 in Box and Jenkins (1976, p. 531) and to the time series of monthly industry sales of printing and writing paper in France 1963–1972 published in Makridakis and Wheelwright (1978, p. 350). (In the latter series an apparent misprint for August 1969 was replaced by 300.000.) Four models were fitted to each series:

I. HT Model (1)
II. Model (4)
III. $\text{ARIMA}(0, 1, 1)(0, 1, 1)_{12}$
IV. A model where $\Delta\Delta_{12} y_t$ had (unconstrained) nonzero autocovariances at lags 1, 11, 12, 13.

Exact maximum likelihood estimation was used in each case.

Summary statistics for the four models are shown in Table 1. $Q(40)$ is the adjusted Box-Pierce statistic for lag

Table 1. Comparison of Model Fit

Model	Airline Data		Paper Sales Data	
	Residual SD	Q(40)	Residual SD	Q(40)
I	.040	78.4*	.055	28.0
II	.038	36.2	.056	27.2
III	.038	29.1	.056	27.1
IV	.037	26.6	.056	27.1

* Significant at 1% level.

40; see Davies, Triggs, and Newbold (1977). The additional residual at $t = 13$ in (2) has been omitted to make the results more comparable.

For the airline data, Models II, III, and IV all fit the data well. Model I, the HT model, shows significant lack of fit in high residual autocorrelations, although the increase in one-step forecast-error was minimal. This finding confirms HT's observation that an ill-fitting model need not necessarily increase the forecast variance. However, the difference between Model I and the other three models lies in the smoothness prior on the evolution of the seasonal component. The lack of fit suggests that $S(L)\gamma_t$ is evolving much more smoothly than (1c) implies, so that Model I will give rise to different, and possibly inappropriate, estimates of the seasonal component. This is a question that deserves further research.

All models fit the paper sales data equally well. Other tests, including likelihood ratio comparisons, confirm the brief impressions conveyed by Table 1.

In fitting Model II to the airline data, estimates $\hat{\lambda}_1 = .85$ and $\hat{\lambda}_2 = .90$ were obtained. The product $\hat{\lambda}_1 \hat{\lambda}_2 = .765$ is about 20% of the variance term $2 + \hat{\lambda}_1 + \hat{\lambda}_2 = 3.75$, so that this model and the $\text{ARIMA}(0, 1, 1)(0, 1, 1)_{12}$ Model III are not very different. This explains the results of Table 1.

For the paper sales data, $\hat{\lambda}_1 = .05$ and $\hat{\lambda}_2 = .04$, so that $\hat{\lambda}_1 \hat{\lambda}_2$ is negligible and Models II and III almost coincide, as confirmed by Table 1. Models I and II fit the paper sales data equally well because filtered estimates of series with very small signal/noise ratios are always very smooth regardless of the underlying model. Some explanation of this point is given by Ansley (1980).

The preceding remarks contrast the HT model with other possible structural models, in particular the $\text{ARIMA}(0, 1, 1)(0, 1, 1)_s$ model, which has a more smoothly evolving seasonal component. While the appeal of a simple structural model cannot be denied, neither can the need to adequately describe the autocorrelation structure of the data, especially if the resulting model is to be used for structural decomposition. Fortunately, simple modifications to (1) can accommodate a variety of different structures, such as the smoother seasonal discussed previously or the positive first-order autocorrelations in first differences noted by Nelson and Plosser (1982).

REFERENCES

ANSLEY, C. F. (1980), "Signal Extraction in Finite Series and the Estimation of Stochastic Regression Coefficients," *Proceedings of the*

American Statistical Association Business and Economic Statistics Section, 251–255.

ANSLEY, C. F., and NEWBOLD, P. (1980), "Finite Sample Properties of Estimators for Autoregressive Moving Average Models," *Journal of Econometrics,* B, 159–183.

BOX, G. E. P., and JENKINS, G. M. (1976), *Time-Series Analysis: Forecasting and Control* (revised ed.), San Francisco: Holden-Day.

CRYER, J. D., and LEDOLTER, J. (1981), "Small-Sample Properties of the Maximum Likelihood Estimator in the First-Order Moving Average Model," *Biometrika,* 68, 691–694. See also Technical Report #74, University of Iowa, Dept of Statistics.

DAVIES, N., TRIGGS, C. M., and NEWBOLD, P. (1977), "Significance Levels of the Box-Pierce Portmanteau Statistic in Finite Samples," *Biometrika,* 64, 517–522.

KITAGAWA, G. (1983), "State Space Modeling of Nonstationary Time Series and Smoothing of Unequally Spaced Data," paper presented at the Office of Naval Research Symposium on Time Series Analysis of Irregularly Spaced Data, Texas A & M University, College Station, Texas, February 10–13, 1983.

MAKRIDAKIS, S., and WHEELWRIGHT, S. C. (1978), *Forecasting Methods and Applications,* New York: John Wiley.

NELSON, C. R., and PLOSSER, C. I. (1982), "Trends and Random Walks in Macroeconomic Time Series: Some Evidence and Implications," *Journal of Monetary Economics,* 10, 139–162.

WAHBA, G. (1978), "Improper Priors, Spline Smoothing and the Problem of Guarding Against Model Errors in Regression," *Journal of the Royal Statistical Society,* Series B, 40, 364–372.

Comment

David F. Findley
Bureau of the Census, Washington, DC 20233

There are very few papers describing the application of powerful time series model fitting procedures to short economic time series. Of course, the definition of *short* is relative. A quarterly series of length 40 with a strong stable seasonal pattern and a moderate, uncomplicated trend could be simpler to forecast or seasonally adjust than a monthly series of length 120 with a slightly more complex trend and seasonal components. The definition also depends on the technology used. For objective model selection, a quarterly series of length 40 seems dauntingly short because of the inapplicability of the asymptotic properties of the statistics usually used for this task. By contrast, a monthly series of length 120 would often be adequately long. Most of the series examined by Harvey and Todd seem complex enough to be short by any definition. Their article is possibly the first to emphasize the application of "structural" trend and seasonal component models, with parameters chosen by a maximum Gaussian likelihood procedure, to the problem of forecasting short series. (Gersch and Kitagawa (1983) discuss the use of a rich class of structural models in forecasting longer series. Findley (1983) applies the closely related models of Akaike (1980a) to seasonally adjust short series.) Given the intense interest in forecasting short series and the seeming appropriateness of structural models for many economic series, the Harvey and Todd article is a welcome addition to the time series literature. Unfortunately, however, it contains a discomforting number of vague or inaccurate statements and implications, some of which are described here along with other discussion points.

1. Harvey and Todd base their choice of model on the implied type of forecasting function and somewhat fuzzy concepts like local linearity. (Akaike (1980b) shows that a Gaussian-shaped trend buried in noise can be estimated well by modeling it to be locally *constant!*) The unavailability of distributional results for the model testing and selecting statistics (see also points 3 and 4) necessarily places increased demands on the modeler's judgment, but it seems cavalier of them to assert that such subjective a priori model selection does not involve model selection.

2. Their *sum of squared unconditional prediction errors in the post-sample forecast period* measure is a natural descriptive statistic to use to compare their forecasts to those of Prothero and Wallis (1976) in order to evaluate the effectiveness of their subjective choice of *increasing horizon* forecast function. However, they do not give the values of this statistic for the ARIMA model forecasts and make this comparison.

3. By virtue of their reference to the paper by Box and Tiao (1976) in the discussion of this prediction-error statistic, the authors use "adequacy of the model" as a synonym for "essential correctness of the model." In situations, presumably including the present one, in which the data are not adequate to determine the essential correctness of an ARIMA model, constrained or otherwise, or when such models are consciously used as *approximate* models, it seems more appropriate to measure model adequacy with reference to the purpose for which the model is being fit. Since forecasting is the purpose in the article, descriptive statistics related to the forecast errors in the (withheld) post-sample period like the measure discussed in point 2 seem likely to be the most useful ones.

4. Even if one believes that the models being fit *could* be essentially correct, special justification is required for using tests based on large-sample distributions for the statistics Q and $\xi(1)$ (or the modified Q statistic of Ljung

310 Journal of Business & Economic Statistics, October 1983

and Box (1978), which Harvey and Todd seem to ignore) with short series. With complex models, especially those of series 3–5, there is no evidence to suggest that the use of the asymptotic distribution of these statistics with short series provides conservative tests (or powerful tests) for the acceptance of such models.

5. If sample size were not an issue, it would still be the case that the authors, in their criticism of the Box-Jenkins methodology, are identifying the methodology with the small part of it used by Prothero and Wallis.

6. It is not clear how the authors are able to choose the Kalman filter's initial seasonal and trend values for a series with seasonal period s using only the first $s + 1$ observations. Perhaps the choice does not matter in their examples because they have twelve periods over which to dissipate its effects. The initialization problem would have been challenging had they had 37 *monthly* seasonal values and therefore only three periods. Gersch and Kitagawa (1983) show that with *good* initial state and state covariance estimates, surprisingly adequate forecasts can sometimes be obtained for a monthly seasonal series of length 24. In Kitagawa (1981), two strategies for initializing the state vector are discussed.

7. Their discussion of the matter does not establish it as important that the seasonal operator s(L) and the trend operator Δ^2 have no root in common: The remark of Pierce about finite variance to which they refer rests upon the widespread misunderstanding that solutions to nonstationary ARMA equations must have infinite variance. As Bell (1983) makes very clear, a solution will have infinite variance only if a starting value is chosen to have infinite variance. To illustrate this simply, given y_0 and a (finite variance) white noise process ϵ_t, the process defined for $t > 0$ by $y_t = y_0 + \sum_1^t \epsilon_{t-j}$ and for $t < 0$ by $y_t = y_0 - \sum_{t+1}^0 \epsilon_t$ satisfies $y_t = y_{t-1} + \epsilon_t$ for all t, and each y_t will have finite variance if y_0 does and not otherwise. Gersch and Brotherton (1981) use s(L) $= I - L^{12}$ and Δ^2, which have the common factor $I - L$, in structural models for seasonal adjustment.

8. It is quite misleading of the authors to associate the examples discussed in their Jenkins (1982) reference with poor performance of Akaike's information criterion (AIC). The models criticized by Jenkins were obtained from a procedure due to D. Reilly that makes no use of AIC (Reilly 1982). In fact, in the contest to which Jenkins refers, which is further discussed in Mehra (1982), the best performance was given by a forecasting method whose model selection is based on the method of Akaike (1976) and uses AIC. Similarly good performance from AIC was obtained in the much larger study reported by Meese and Geweke (1982). This does not mean, of course, that forecasting-model selection should be based on a single statistic, if circumstances permit a more sophisticated approach.

9. I certainly agree with Harvey and Todd that an attractive feature of their models is the provision of an estimate of a statistic that can be interpreted as growth rate, although the validity of this interpretation will need to be demonstrated when the series being modeled cannot be supposed to conform too closely to such a simplistic model.

10. Finally, I appreciated the discussion related to the material in the Appendix. For many structural models the Gaussian likelihood surface seems to be quite flat near the minimum, depending only somewhat on the length or configuration of the series (see Monsell 1983 and Tsang, Glover, and Bach 1981). In the latter reference an alternative estimation criterion is proposed that is intended to be less susceptible to this phenomenon.

These comments should not distract from the important achievement of the Harvey and Todd article, which lies in the authors' demonstration of the basic simplicity, flexibility, and effectiveness of structural models as forecasting tools for short series. I hope this article will encourage forecasters with even shorter series to experiment with this promising class of models and report their results. I congratulate the authors on their contribution.

REFERENCES

AKAIKE, H. (1976), "Canonical Correlation Analysis of Time Series and the Use of an Information Criterion," in *System Identification: Advances and Case Studies*, eds. D. G. Lainiotis and R. K. Mehra, New York: Academic Press.

—— (1980a), "Seasonal Adjustment by a Bayesian Modeling," *Journal of Time Series Analysis*, 1, 1–14.

—— (1980b), "Likelihood and the Bayes Procedure," *Trab. Estad.*, 31, 143–166.

BELL, W. (1983), "Signal Extraction for Nonstationary Time Series," *Annals of Statistics*, forthcoming.

BOX, G. E. P., and TIAO, G. C. (1976), "Comparison of Forecasts With Actuality," *Applied Statistics*, 25, 195–200.

FINDLEY, D. F. (1983), Comments on "Comparative Study of X-11 and BAYSEA Seasonal Adjustment Procedures" by H. Akaike and M. Ishiguro, in *Applied Time Series Analysis of Economic Data*, ed. A. Zellner, Washington: Bureau of the Census, U.S. Department of Commerce.

GERSCH, W., and BROTHERTON, T. (1981), "A Data Analytic Approach to the Smoothing Problem and Some of Its Variations," *Proceedings of the 20th IEEE Conference on Decision and Control*, 1061–1069.

GERSCH, W., and KITAGAWA, G. (1983), "The Prediction of Time Series With Trend and Seasonality," *Journal of Business & Economic Statistics*, 1, 253–264.

JENKINS, G. M. (1982), "Some Practical Aspects of Forecasting in Organizations," *Journal of Forecasting*, 1, 3–21.

KITAGAWA, G. (1981), "A Nonstationary Time Series Model and Its Fitting by a Recursive Filter," *Journal of Time Series Analysis*, 2, 103–166.

LJUNG, G., and BOX, G. E. P. (1978), "On a Measure of Lack of Fit in Time Series Models," *Biometrika*, 65, 243–251.

MEESE, R., and GEWEKE, J. (1982), "A Comparison of Autoregressive Univariate Forecasting Procedures for Macroeconomic Time Series," unpublished manuscript.

MEHRA, R. K. (1982), "Identification in Control and Econometrics," in *Current Developments in the Interface: Economics, Econometrics and Mathematics*, eds. M. Hazwinkel and A. H. G. Rinnooy Kan, Dordrecht, Holland: D. Reidel.

MONSELL, B. (1983), "Using the Kalman Smoother to Adjust for Moving Trading Day," Statistical Research Division Research Report 83/04, U.S. Census Bureau.

PROTHERO, D. L., and WALLIS, K. F. (1976), "Modeling Macro-economic Time Series," *Journal of the Royal Statistical Society,* Series A, 139, 468–500.

REILLY, D. (1982), personal communication.

TSANG, W. L., GLOVER, J. E., and BACH, R. E. (1981), "Identifiability of Unknown Noise Covariance Matrices for Some Special Cases of a Linear, Time-Invariant, Discrete-Time Dynamic System," *IEEE Transactions on Automatic Control,* 26, 970–973.

Comment

Paul Newbold
Department of Economics, University of Illinois, Urbana-Champaign, IL 61820

It is a pleasure to comment on this interesting and provocative paper. Like so much of Harvey's work, it provides a good deal of food for thought. In places the authors' exposition borders on the evangelical, making clear their aim to convert readers to a particular brand of univariate time series model building and forecasting. What is less clear, to this reader at least, is the precise form of the new theology. Are we to embrace structural models in all their generality, or the basic structural model in particular, on the grounds that "it will be quite adequate for many economic time series"? This point is not trivial, for although I am pretty sure I could fit the basic model, it is not clear how I would systematically go about finding, for a specific data set, an appropriate structural model from the general class. Nevertheless, the possibilities are sufficiently intriguing that it is easy to look forward to further work from the authors on this subject. Commentary on the paper is, however, made rather difficult by the fact that while most of the exposition and all of the application is concentrated on the basic model, much criticism is easily diverted by appealing to the possibilities of the more general form.

Right at the outset the authors claim that their approach has "a number of advantages" over the usual ARIMA model building procedure. In the body of the article, however, I detected just two claimed advantages:

1. The structural model, involving a decomposition of a process into components, is somehow logically appealing and is likely to lead to similarly appealing forecast functions.
2. The usual ARIMA model selection process is unsatisfactory, and one would like to avoid its use.

The second point is the more quickly dealt with. Certainly the ARIMA model selection stage can cause difficulties, but these seem to me to be greatly exaggerated. In any case, use of the general structural model form would appear to pose difficulties of the same order of magnitude. Even if we accept the seasonal structure of (2.3) as universally appropriate, there is no particular reason to be satisfied with white noise error terms in Equations (2.1)-(2.3). How do we select appropriate error structures? The other elaborations to the model, suggested at various points in the article, will add further difficulties in model selection. It is only when we stick to just the basic model that we have "the attraction that it involves no model selection procedure whatsoever." But this is surely an old story. For many years, often under the general heading "exponential smoothing," forecasters have developed specific, intuitively appealing, model forms to be imposed on a wide range of time series. In Newbold and Granger (1974), on the basis of a large empirical study, we found that one of these, the Holt-Winters procedure, did not compare favorably, in the prediction of economic time series, with a careful analysis based on fitting ARIMA models. For what it is worth, the basic structural model has no more intuitive appeal to me than the Holt-Winters predictor.

Let us now turn to the apparent logical appeal of structural models. Ignoring for now the question of seasonality, the model for non-seasonal time series is one in which the second differences follow a second order moving average process, which will typically be invertible unless the error term in (2.2b) has zero variance. If differencing involves "throwing out the baby with the bath water"—a remark I have never fully understood—then differencing twice must involve throwing out the tub as well! More seriously, Footnote 4 deserves more prominence. In my experience, it is quite common to find in nonseasonal time series, and not simply annual series, that the first differences are clearly stationary, with large *positive* first sample autocorrelation, and sample autocorrelations of higher orders quite small. I have never found such results intuitively unappealing. On the contrary, such a structure seems plausible. More importantly, it is common! But this does not fit neatly into the structural models of Harvey and Todd. Perhaps, on reflection, this is because their superficial plausibility is really not all that convincing. It is certainly not obvious to me that the logical way to think of nonseasonal economic time series is invariably in terms of local polynomial trend. Why should one expect interest rates or exchange rates, for example, to behave in this way?

312   Journal of Business & Economic Statistics, October 1983

For the analysis of nonseasonal series, I would be reluctant to give up the flexibility of the general ARIMA form. The case of seasonal series is more tricky. It has never seemed to me that the multiplicative seasonal ARIMA models, of the type typically fitted in practice, carried sufficient conviction to exclude all other possibilities. However, I am no more convinced by the form chosen by Harvey and Todd. First, as the authors note, it is not necessary to restrict the error term in (2.3) to white noise for the sum of the seasonal components over a year to have zero mean and fixed variances. Second, it seems likely that one would typically expect (though I realize there are exceptions) that the seasonal factor in August would be more like that in July than like that in January. I cannot see how (2.3) induces any such potential smoothness. The natural appeal of structural models does not strike me with the force that it does Harvey and Todd.

Section 4 of the article devotes quite a bit of space to an empirical comparison of ARIMA analysis and the basic structural model. What we can hope to learn from the analysis of just six series is not very clear, but my interpretation of the results would differ from that of the authors. They claim that for only two of the six series was there much difference in the forecasting performances. In fact, if I am reading Table 2 correctly, the post-sample forecasts for Series 6 also were substantially better for the ARIMA than for the structural model. The authors do acknowledge such an advantage for the ARIMA model in the case of Series 4. This, they say, is because "the basic structural model is inadequate . . . and a more general model . . . needs to be employed." Certainly, but wisdom after the event is not entirely ade-

quate. Returning to an earlier point, we need a procedure for selecting, from the sample data, an appropriate model from the class of structural models, as this particular example clearly demonstrates. The performance on Series 5 of the ARIMA predictor was, as the authors say, "disastrous." Yet it does not persuade me "of the dangers inherent in the Box-Jenkins methodology." There is no reason why it should when that methodology was not designed to predict, or account for, large structural shifts in the forecast period. Neither, incidentally, was the basic structural model, so I am a little worried by its "quite reasonable" forecasts of imports in a period containing a substantial currency devaluation. In fact, the reason for the poor performance of the ARIMA predictor is not difficult to find. By an unhappy coincidence, the model used involves only lags at multiples of four. Naturally, the forecasts from such a model do not adapt quickly to this kind of structural change. I am not as worried as the authors that this particular model is not "conventional"; it just happens to have this property of sluggishness of adaptation to step changes. Perhaps, for this reason, we should not use such models, but the case is far from made on the basis of one special example.

In summary, I have not yet bought the "new religion" of structural models. Considerably more work on the development of a model building cycle, together with more substantial empirical investigation, is still needed. I look forward to seeing both.

REFERENCES

NEWBOLD, P., and GRANGER, C. W. J. (1974), "Experience with Forecasting Univariate Time Series and the Combination of Forecasts," *Journal of Royal Statistical Society*, A, 137, 131–165.

©Journal of Business & Economic Statistics, Vol. 1, No. 4, October 1983

Response

A. C. Harvey and P. H. J. Todd

Before dealing with specific points raised by our discussants, we would like to make a general comment about the model we considered in our article. We defined a structural model as one set up in terms of components, such as trend and seasonal, which have a direct interpretation. The basic structural model is one of the simplest models within this class, and its attraction is that it captures many of the features found in economic time series. As we stated in the Introduction, the idea of our exercise was not to "prove" the superiority of this particular model to models selected from the ARIMA class, but rather to show that in small samples it can give comparable results in terms of forecasting. At the very worst, therefore, the model provides a strong base from which to consider the construction of more elaborate models within a structural framework.

The points raised by the discussants can be grouped conveniently under a number of headings.

Inadequacies of the Basic Structural Model

Both Newbold and Findley question the value of local polynomial trends. But it is precisely this concept that formed the basis of early forecasting procedures, such as those of Brown and Holt, and which lay at the root of the development of ARIMA models; see Box and Jenkins (1976, pp. 146–149), Harrison (1967), and Harvey (1983). The reason the ARIMA model of order $(0, 1, 1) \times (0, 1, 1)_s$ is so common is that it provides a local approximation to a trend and seasonal pattern. One can see this easily by first considering a model with a deterministic linear trend and seasonal pattern, and a white noise disturbance term, that is,

$$y_t = \alpha + \beta t + \sum_j \gamma^{(j)} z_{jt} + \epsilon_t, \qquad (1)$$

where the z_{jt}'s are seasonal dummies. Applying the $\Delta\Delta_s$ operator gives

$$\Delta\Delta_s y_t = (1 + \theta L)(1 + \Theta L^s)\epsilon_t \qquad (2)$$

with $\theta = \Theta = -1$. Trends and seasonal components in economic time series are not normally deterministic, but they are usually fairly pronounced and as a result an invertible model of the form (2) will often give a good fit.

We disagree with Findley when he refers to local linearity as a "somewhat fuzzy concept." This concept has been around for a long time and is fairly fundamen-

tal. Indeed we would argue that a salesman contemplating a graph of his product would find the concept of a local trend a lot less fuzzy than the concept of an ARIMA model! From the statistical point of view, Equations (2.2a) and (2.2b) in our article give a definition of local linearity that is certainly not fuzzy, and statistical models for local approximations to higher order polynomials can also be formulated within this framework; cf. Harrison and Stevens (1976).

Newbold likens the basic structural model to the Holt-Winters forecasting procedure. Since the basic structural model has a similar forecast function to the Holt-Winters predictor, this analogy is a reasonable one (though it must be stressed that the basic structural model is based on a properly formulated statistical model, whereas the Holt-Winters predictor is not). One would therefore expect the two procedures to perform well under similar circumstances. Newbold's remark that Newbold and Granger (1974) found that Holt-Winters "... did not compare favorably, in the prediction of economic time series, with a careful analysis based on the fitting of ARIMA models" is therefore a pertinent one. However, it is also a little misleading, since while it reflects the conclusions of the Newbold-Granger study for samples of size greater than 50, the situation when $T < 50$ is somewhat different. In fact, Granger and Newbold (1977, pp. 183–184) summarize the conclusions of their earlier study for $T < 50$ as follows:

> (a) For very short time series (with less than 30 observations), there is little alternative to use of an exponential smoothing predictor, and generally we would prefer Holt-Winters in such circumstances.
>
> (b) For moderately long series (at least 30 and no more than 40–50 observations), Box-Jenkins is rather difficult to apply (more so for seasonal than nonseasonal series), but stepwise autoregression becomes feasible and its use in combination with Holt-Winters seems the most promising approach.

Other studies, for example, Makridakis et al. (1982), are even more favorable towards Holt-Winters.

Estimation

Findley raises a point (6) about the initialization of the Kalman filter applied to the structural model. In fact, the initialization "problem" for the structural model is no different, in principle, from the initialization problem for an ARIMA model. Suppose, for example, that the ARIMA $(0, 1, 1) \times (0, 1, 1)_s$ model (2) is fitted to a set of T observations on y_t. Because of the differencing, only

313

314 Journal of Business & Economic Statistics, October 1983

$T - (s + 1)$ observations, that is, $\Delta\Delta_s y_t$, $t = s + 2\dots, T$ are available for the estimation of θ and Θ. Furthermore, if the exact likelihood function is defined for these differenced observations, one can show that this is identical to the exact likelihood function defined for the undifferenced observations when $y_1, \dots, y_{s+1}$ are regarded as fixed; cf. Harvey (1981b). Thus the basis upon which a structural model is estimated is exactly the same basis upon which an ARIMA model is normally estimated by full ML.

Other definitions of the likelihood function can be adopted. For example, one can assume that the initial state vector, α_0, is fixed. This is essentially the approach employed by Kitagawa (1981). It would be wrong, however, to infer that his approach in some way solves the initialization problem, while constructing starting values from the first $s + 1$ observations does not; cf. Harvey (1982).

If the series is short, covering only two or three years, then it becomes difficult to obtain sensible estimates of the relative variances σ_η^2/σ^2, σ_ζ^2/σ^2, and σ_ω^2/σ^2. In these circumstances it may be reasonable to fix these parameters on a priori grounds, according to the type of discounting which one wishes to apply to the level, slope, and seasonal components. It may also be reasonable to adopt a Bayesian approach in which a proper prior distribution is put on the state vector at time $t = 0$. This is, in effect, the method used by Harrison and Stevens (1976).

Finally, with regard to "pile-up" effects and flat likelihoods, it is worth stressing that different definitions of the likelihood function will give rise to estimators with different small sample properties; cf. the evidence for ARIMA models in Ansley and Newbold (1980). Furthermore, the use of alternative procedures to ML, as Findley suggested in point (10), may well produce estimators with more desirable properties. All of these issues merit further investigation.

Differencing

Newbold raises the question of differencing in his comment "If differencing involves 'throwing out the baby with the bath water'—a remark I have never fully understood—then differencing twice must involve throwing out the tub as well." The role of differencing has certainly led to a good deal of confusion in time series modeling, and one of the attractions of the structural framework is that it clarifies the issue considerably. Consider a dynamic regression model in which y_t depends on an explanatory variable via a distributed lag, that is,

$$y_t = \mu_t + \sum_{j=0}^{m} \delta_j x_{t-j} + \epsilon_t, \tag{3}$$

where δ_j are the lag coefficients, ϵ_t is a white noise disturbance term, and μ_t is a stochastic trend of the form (2.2). (Additional variables and seasonal effects could be added to the model, but these would simply detract from

the main argument.) Since μ_t is unobservable, the model must be differenced twice in order to yield a stationary disturbance term, that is,

$$\Delta^2 y_t = \sum_{j=0}^{m} \delta_j \Delta^2 x_{t-j} + v_t, \tag{4}$$

where $v_t \sim MA(2)$. When the trend in y_t cannot be completely accounted for by the trend in x_t, it may be appropriate to introduce a stochastic trend, explicitly, as in (3), or implicitly, by differencing as in (4). In certain applications, particularly in macroeconomics, such a situation is ruled out by prior considerations demanding that the model have a steady-state solution; see Davidson et al. (1978). Differencing effectively removes any information on this steady-state solution and so the remark about throwing out the baby with the bath water is a particularly apt one. However, in univariate models, no explanatory variables are available to account for the trend in y_t, and so introducing a trend is almost always necessary. In the extreme case when this trend is deterministic, differencing is inappropriate, though not necessarily incorrect; see Harvey (1981b). In any case the structural model can handle a deterministic trend as a matter of course, simply by having the variances σ_η^2 and σ_ζ^2 equal to zero.

Model Selection

Having a sample size that is not too small opens up the possibility of using the data to help select a suitable structural model. A good deal of empirical work needs to be carried out before a comprehensive model selection strategy can be proposed with any confidence. However, it is worth taking this opportunity to briefly discuss two of the main issues that arise.

The essence of a structural model is that the components should have a direct interpretation. Thus, suppose that we wish to incorporate a trade cycle into the basic structural model. One possibility is to add an AR(2) component to (2.1) or (2.2a); see Section 2.4 and Footnote 4. Various hypotheses about the nature of the cycle can then be formulated in terms of the AR coefficients. In an ARIMA model this is more difficult to do, because the cycle will be mixed up with the trend and seasonal components after differencing.

An alternative way of modeling the cycle is to recognize that the state space formulation does not constrain the individual components to be of the ARIMA form. Thus instead of using an AR(2) process, we might consider modeling a cycle more directly. Let ψ_t denote the cyclical component that is to be added to (2.1) or (2.2a). If the period of the cycle is $2\pi/\lambda$, then ψ_t can be modeled as

$$\begin{bmatrix} \psi_t \\ \psi_t^* \end{bmatrix} = \rho \begin{bmatrix} \cos\lambda & \sin\lambda \\ -\sin\lambda & \cos\lambda \end{bmatrix} \begin{bmatrix} \psi_{t-1} \\ \psi_{t-1}^* \end{bmatrix} + \begin{bmatrix} \xi_t \\ \xi_t^* \end{bmatrix}, \tag{5}$$

where $0 \le \rho \le 1$, and ξ_t and ξ_t^* are white noise disturbance terms; cf. Harrison and Akram (1982). For reasons of identifiability it is necessary to place some restriction on the covariance matrix of the disturbances, and one way of doing this is to let them be independent of each other. It is not difficult to show that $\psi_t \sim \text{ARMA}(2, 1)$, but the advantage of Equation (5) is that the AR part is parameterized in terms of λ and ρ. This last parameter is the modulus of the roots of the associated AR polynomial; if it is unity, the forecast function contains a cycle that does not die away as the forecast horizon goes to infinity.

A second issue concerns the development of test statistics. The Lagrange multiplier principle can be used to develop test statistics in either the time domain or the frequency domain; see Engle and Watson (1981) and Harvey and Hotta (1982). These statistics can then be used to test hypotheses with some structural content, as can Wald and LR statistics, or they can be used simply as diagnostics. We wholeheartedly agree with Findley's point (4) regarding the small sample properties of such test statistics and this is certainly an area for further research. Some progress has already been made in the development of a small sample test for zero variances in the basic structural model; see Franzini and Harvey (1983).

Seasonal Component

As Ansley noted, the seasonal component used in our study has been justified by Kitagawa (1983) on the basis of smoothness priors. Nevertheless, we share the uneasiness that Ansley and Newbold have about this particular form of seasonality. Taking first differences in (2.3) gives

$$\gamma_t = \gamma_{t-s} + \omega_t - \omega_{t-1} \qquad (6)$$

(cf. Ansley's Equation (2)), and this implies that the change from one season to the next may not be very smooth. (This point has also been made to us recently by K. Wallis.) This lack of smoothness can be overcome by replacing ω_t by an MA process, as suggested in the text, or by modeling seasonality by a series of sines and cosines as in (5).

We find models in seasonal differences—as in Ansley's (4c)—rather unappealing. If such models are simulated, the seasonal components go flying off in all directions. This is a practical consequence of Δ and Δ_s having a root in common. If one wants a model that corresponds closely to ARIMA $(0, 1, 1) \times (0, 1, 1)_s$, it seems better to follow Hillmer and Tiao (1982) and to look for a decomposition which, like (2.3), has $S(L)$ as the seasonal operator.

Finally, we believe that the inadequacies of (2.3) are probably more serious for monthly observations than for quarterly ones. The airline data is monthly, but if they are aggregated so as to become quarterly, the prediction error variance, $\tilde{\sigma}_p^2$ in (3.1), is smaller for the basic struc-

tural model than for the ARIMA $(0, 1, 1) \times (0, 1, 1)_s$ model—1.40×10^{-3} as opposed to 1.58×10^{-3}.

Miscellaneous Comments

1. As regards the logical appeal of structural models (see Newbold's remarks), it is surely of some relevance that Hillmer and Tiao (1982) place some importance on the conditions under which an ARIMA model can be converted to what is effectively a structural model.

2. We accept Findley's point (8) regarding the use of AIC in automatic selection procedures for ARIMA models. Nevertheless, we are still wary of approaches of this kind; the ARIMA class of models is broad, and we do not believe that obtaining a good fit in the sample period necessarily results in good forecasts.

3. As regards the forecasting performance of the ARIMA model for imports, we only partly agree with Newbold's analysis of why this was so poor. If one looks at the *unconditional* forecast function, it deviates markedly from any path which the import series could reasonably have taken, with or without a currency devaluation. Thus the inability of the model to adapt to the change that occurred when the pound was devalued is only part of the story.

We would like to thank the discussants for a set of very constructive and stimulating comments. We certainly agree that a good deal of research is needed in this area. If, as Newbold implies, we are religious heretics, we remain unrepentant!

ADDITIONAL REFERENCES

ANSLEY, C., and NEWBOLD, P. (1980), "Finite Sample Properties for Estimators of Autoregressive Moving Average Models," *Journal of Economics*, 13, 159–183.

DAVIDSON, J., HENDRY, D. F., SRBA, F., and YEO, S. (1978), "Econometric Modelling of the Aggregate Time-Series Relationship Between Consumers' Expenditure and Income in the United Kingdom," *Economic Journal*, 88, 661–692.

ENGLE, R. F., and WATSON, M. (1981), "A One Factor Multivariate Time Series Model of Metropolitan Wage Rates," *Journal of the American Statistical Association*, 76, 774–781.

FRANZINI, L., and HARVEY, A. C. (1983), "Testing for Deterministic Trend and Seasonal Components in Time Series Models," *Biometrika* (forthcoming).

GRANGER, C. W. J., and NEWBOLD, P. (1977), *Forecasting Economic Time Series*, New York: Academic Press.

HARRISON, P. J. (1967), "Exponential Smoothing and Short-Term Sales Forecasting," *Management Science*, 13, 821–842.

HARRISON, P. J., and AKRAM, M. (1982), "Generalized Exponentially Weighted Regression and Parsimonious Dynamic Linear Modelling," paper presented at IFS Conference, Valencia, May 1982. To appear in conference proceedings.

HARVEY, A. C. (1983), "A Unified View of Statistical Forecasting Procedures," *Journal of Forecasting* (forthcoming).

HARVEY, A. C., and HOTTA, L. K. (1982), "Specification Tests for Dynamic Models with Unobserved Components," unpublished paper, London School of Economics.

MAKRIDAKIS, S. et al. (1982), "The Accuracy of Extrapolation (Time Series) Methods: Results of a Forecasting Competition," *Journal of Forecasting*, 1, 111–153.

[16]

Forecasting With Bayesian Vector Autoregressions—Five Years of Experience

Robert B. Litterman
Research Department, Federal Reserve Bank of Minneapolis,
Minneapolis, MN 55480

The results obtained in five years of forecasting with Bayesian vector autoregressions (BVAR's) demonstrate that this inexpensive, reproducible statistical technique is as accurate, on average, as those used by the best known commercial forecasting services. This article considers the problem of economic forecasting, the justification for the Bayesian approach, its implementation, and the performance of one small BVAR model over the past five years.

1. INTRODUCTION

Forecasting the economy is a risky, often humbling task. Unfortunately, it is a job that many statisticians, economists, and others are required to engage in. This article describes a technique, economic forecasting with Bayesian vector autoregressions (BVAR), that has proved over the past several years to be an attractive alternative in many situations to the use of traditional econometric models or other time series techniques. The BVAR models are relatively simple and inexpensive to use, and they generate forecasts that have been as accurate, on average, as several of the most expensive forecasts currently available.

Moreover, relative to the widely used macroeconometric models, the BVAR approach has a distinct advantage in two respects. First and most important, it does not require judgmental adjustment. Thus it is a scientific method that can be evaluated on its own, without reference to the forecaster running the model. Second, it generates not only a forecast but a complete, multivariate probability distribution for future outcomes of the economy that appears to be more realistic than those generated by other competing approaches.

I will consider, first, the problem of economic forecasting, second, the justification for the Bayesian approach, third, its implementation, and finally, the performance record of a small BVAR model that has been used during the past five years.

2. THE PROBLEM OF ECONOMIC FORECASTING

The problem of forecasting is to use past and current information to generate a probability distribution for future events. Generally speaking, this is one of the basic problems of statistical analysis, and many well-known statistical procedures have been developed and used successfully to forecast in a variety of contexts.

Some particular difficulties arise, however, in forecasting economic data. First, there is only a limited amount of data, and what is available is often severely contaminated with measurement error. Second, many complicated relationships that are only poorly understood and probably evolving over time interact to generate the data. Finally, it is generally impossible to perform randomized experiments to test hypotheses about those economic structures. In this adverse environment, most of the standard statistical approaches do not work well.

The fact that aggregate economic quantities are usually measured with considerable error is well known. Conceptual problems, seasonal adjustment, changes in the mix of goods and services, and the nonreporting of cash and barter transactions are just a few of the sources of this noise.

The sense in which there is only a limited amount of data is perhaps not so obvious. After all, the total quantity of economic data processed and available on computer data bases today is enormous. The paucity of useful data arises because of the pervasive interdependencies in the economy and therefore in economic data. When we talk of forecasting the economy, we usually are referring to the problem of predicting either values of economic aggregates such as gross national product (GNP) and the price level or values of variables that are closely related to such aggregates. Most forecasts are short to medium term, and much of the variation in these aggregate variables at these horizons seems to be generated by an underlying phenomenon, the business cycle. The sense in which data are scarce is that the entities that we are really trying to measure and forecast are business cycles, and the number of observations of business cycles relevant for use in forecasting today's economy is relatively small. Moreover, the structure of the economy appears to be evolving through time, and government policies are constantly changing, so the relevance of older observations is always called into question. Thus despite the existence of

larger and larger data bases, the small sample size problem
is likely to be with us for the foreseeable future.

Although explanations abound, very little is known with
certainty about what causes and propagates business cycles.
Theories point to a variety of sources of economic shocks
and mechanisms for generating serial correlations in eco-   [25]
nomic data. I believe that a realistic representation of the
current state of economic theory requires a tremendous degree of uncertainty about the structure of the economy. If
this is true, then a Bayesian procedure that can more accurately represent that uncertainty can produce a significant
improvement over conventional techniques in our ability to
generate a realistic probability distribution for future economic events.

The first point in this argument is the assumption that
there is a high degree of uncertainty in our understanding
of the structures that cause and propagate fluctuations in
economic variables. Consider the list one could develop of
the possible mechanisms causing business cycles. It would
have to include a variety of both real and monetary factors.
The real shocks would include, for example, crop failures
and other weather-related events, wars, changes in fiscal
policies, and fluctuations in international trade. The monetary shocks would include fluctuations in the money stock,
changes in the international monetary system, and financial
system shocks such as bank failures, speculative bubbles in
asset prices, and losses of confidence in the payments mechanism. Newer equilibrium business cycle theories focus on
the effects of incomplete information, wage contracts,
and responses to unanticipated changes in nominal quantities.

In recent years there has been a renewed interest in, but
little agreement about, the causes of the Great Depression.
At the time of that event, increased industrial concentration
was a popular explanation, as were a decline in competition
and the failure of the price system. More recent examinations
have stressed both real and monetary causes but come to
less than complete agreement (e.g., see Brunner 1981). On
the one hand, Gordon and Wilcox (1981), for example,
stressed as causes the overproduction of capital due to
"overbuilding of residential housing in the mid-1920s and
the effect on consumer spending of the overshooting of the
stock market during its 1928–29 speculative bubble" (p.
77) followed by declining population growth and its effect
on residential housing. Meltzer (1981), on the other hand,

cited "higher tariffs under Hawley-Smoot . . . and retaliation abroad" (p. 152). He also mentioned attempts to maintain the gold standard as well as anticipations of higher labor costs and lower after-tax returns to capital and changes in budget policy, interest rates, and stock prices.

The point of this discussion is that there are a multitude of economic theories of the business cycle, most of which focus on one part of a complex, multifaceted problem. Most economists would admit that each theory has some validity, though there is wide disagreement over the relative importance of the different approaches. It may be unnecessary to belabor this point; perhaps the profusion of economic theories is obvious. A naive investigation into the workings of the current genre of large macroeconometric models, however, might lead one to a completely opposite conclusion. Each of the behavioral equations in these models is typically based on a specific economic theory, and the theories in different models are often similar. If one were to study only the equations in these models, one might conclude that there is a good deal of consensus on the economic structures involved.

Consider, for example, the investment equations in the Data Resources (DRI) model. These equations are based on "the modern econometric theory of business fixed investment, developed by Dale Jorgenson" (1963), according to the description in Eckstein (1983, p. 129). "Actual investment, in the modern theory, is viewed as a partial adjustment of the capital stock toward the desired level," Eckstein writes (p. 131). The desired level is then expressed as a function of expected output, the production technology, and factor prices. The model includes an equation with investment explained by the lagged stock of capital, the expected utilization rate, and distributed lags on a measure of the rental price of capital, on the ratio of interest payments to cash flow of nonfinancial corporations, and on real output.

Even if one accepts the Jorgenson theory as a reasonable approach to explaining investment, the empirical implementation just described does not adequately represent the true uncertainty about the determinants of investment. In the theory expected output plays a critical role in generating investment. Thus any information that affects the future course of the economy will affect investment. Yet in the DRI equation all such effects are delivered through a proxy term that is simply a fixed distributed lag on output. The empirical implementation of the theory requires many restrictions (here

the exclusion from the expectation formulation of direct influence from variables that affect the course of future output)
that are not particularly motivated by the theory itself.

The prior distribution implicit in the DRI implementation
is not a very realistic representation of the information content of the Jorgenson theory. The flat priors given to coefficients picked out by the theory include no information.
The point priors, at zero, given to coefficients on variables
about which the theory says little are too strong.

A thorough Bayesian would probably not be satisfied to
give probability only to the Jorgenson theory. This type of
analyst might find a dozen theories of investment and give
various weights to them. In a hypothetical calculation of the
implied prior distribution for coefficients, the analyst would
likely find a wide range of variables that one or more of the
theories pick out as likely to affect investment, and the
effects would come through a wide variety of channels. The
analyst would thus find prior distributions for coefficients
on many variables that looked similarly imprecise.

In the non-Bayesian approach to equation specification,
the standard practice (aptly illustrated above), is to include
only a few explanatory variables suggested by a given theory
and to exclude the rest. This practice is based on a practical
recognition by the econometrician that given the relatively
small sample, one can ask only so much from the data. The
problem with this approach is that it has too few choices to
incorporate prior information realistically. From the perspective of the Bayesian who considers several theories plausible, the non-Bayesian begins with similar prior information
for a variety of variables and is forced in each case to make
a decision to include or exclude the variable. For the Bayesian either choice is an extreme: the choice to include rep-   [26]
resents that nothing is known about the coefficient; the choice
to exclude represents that the coefficient is known to be
zero.

3. THE PROBLEM OF DIMENSIONALITY

The standard approach to specifying equations recognizes
that given a limited number of observations, one must be
very parsimonious about adding explanatory variables. Each
additional coefficient must be estimated from the data; and
even though doing this will always improve the fit in sample
(though not always when adjustment is made for degrees of
freedom), in the forecasts generated by the equation there
will be a trade-off between decreased bias and increased

variance. In a Bayesian specification framework, this trade-off disappears in that a mean squared error loss function is minimized by including all relevant variables along with prior information that accurately reflects what is known about the likely values of their coefficients. Of course there are practical limits to the extent to which variables can be included, but the limitations are due to computational feasibility rather than to the lack of degrees of freedom.

One way to think about this problem is to view the forecasting equation as a filter that must pick out from the din of economic noise a weak signal that reveals the likely future course of the variable of interest. The standard approach takes the position that the best one can do is rely on economic theory to suggest at most a few places to look for useful information. The search for information becomes narrowly focused. The alternative BVAR approach is based on a view that useful information about the future is likely to be spread across a wide spectrum of economic data. If this is the case, a forecasting equation that captures and appropriately weights information from a wide range of sources is likely to work better than one with a narrow focus. The appropriate weights are the coefficient estimates, which combine information in the prior with evidence from the data.

We can illustrate the advantage of the Bayesian approach in a simple experiment designed to simulate the problem of modeling in an environment where the structure is uncertain. Suppose the analyst is interested in forecasting the variable Y and believes that Y may be affected by variables x_1 through x_N, which are ordered according to how likely the analyst believes the coefficient on that variable is to be different from zero. In a typical forecasting application, this is likely to be possible. I will represent the analyst's prior as a set of independent distributions, with the coefficients b_j on variable x_j taken to be distributed

$$b_j \sim N(0, j^{-2}). \tag{1}$$

In the usual specification procedure, the analyst either would pick a few of the x's believed to be the most important or he might order them and use a stepwise pretesting procedure to identify those variables to include in the final specification.

I compare the forecast errors made by either of those types of approaches with the results of specifying the Bayesian prior and using the posterior mean estimate as the basis for forecasting. In this simulation I will normalize the x's to be all independent, serially uncorrelated standard Gaussian variates. In each simulation, I generate data on Y by picking random x's and random coefficients from normal distributions specified in the prior. For the purpose of simplifying the calculations, I assume the equation error variance is known. I repeat the experiment 3,000 times, and each time I generate artificial data and reestimate models to determine forecasting performance.

I estimate seven models by ordinary least squares (OLS), models including the most important one, two, three, four, five, and six variables as well as a model in which the number of included variables is chosen by a stepwise procedure that picks the smallest number of variables such that one cannot reject the hypothesis that the excluded variables are all equal to zero at a 5% significance level. I compare the mean squared error (MSE) of coefficient estimates (where coefficients on excluded variables are taken to have estimates of zero) by these methods with the MSE of the Bayesian posterior mean estimates.

$$\text{MSE} \equiv \sum_{s=1}^{3,000} \left[\sum_{j=1}^{6} (b_j - \hat{b}_j)^2 \right] \Big/ 3,000. \qquad (2)$$

The results for various numbers of observations and equation error variances are given in Table 1. Several interesting results are demonstrated in this exercise. First, notice that the usual concern about parsimony is well founded. Excluding variables whose coefficients are likely to be close to zero is better than including them in the standard approach either when the error variance is large, so the R^2 (proportion of variance explained by the regression) is small, or when the number of observations is relatively small. Notice also that the use of a stepwise testing approach does not offer much room for improvement over a shrewd choice of a fixed set of variables to include. Finally, notice that the Bayesian approach offers a very significant advantage over any of the other specifications whenever the number of observations relative to the R^2 is such that exclusionary restrictions might be desirable.

Admittedly, this experiment gives an unrealistic advantage to the Bayesian approach in that the coefficients are drawn from exactly the distribution that is included in the prior used for estimation. Even when the prior variance is off by a factor of four, however, it generally works much better than the standard approach. I include the results from estimation using the prior

$$b_j \sim N[0, (j/2)^{-2}]$$ (3)

as the line "Wrg-Bayes" in the table.

A similar problem arises in choosing a lag length in a time series approach. Many formulas have been suggested for picking the appropriate lag length to satisfy this or that criterion in a variety of contexts. What such formulas ignore is that the reason one wants to choose a lag length in the first place is because one has prior information that more recent values of the variable in question have more information than more distant values. Truncation at a lag length k generates an estimate that reflects inappropriately that there [27] is a clear break in one's prior information about lags k and $k + 1$. An alternative approach that more closely reflects one's actual prior information is to include as long a lag as is computationally feasible, with a prior distribution on the coefficients reflecting the fact that coefficients on longer lags are more likely to be close to zero. Of course this requires one to specify how quickly one's prior tightens around zero, but any such specifications within a wide range should be more appropriate than the prior implicit in either truncation at a given k or truncation based on a function of the evidence in the data.

The BVAR approach does not include any coefficients on moving average terms, as is usual practice in the autoregressive integrated moving average (ARIMA) time series estimation approach. The use of moving average terms is designed to lead to parsimoniously parameterized representations that can generate long, and potentially infinite dimensional, autoregressive representations. The disadvantages of including moving average terms are well known: identification of the order of moving average and autoregressive lag lengths is difficult, and estimation requires a nonlinear procedure. In multivariate contexts, these problems are usually severe; whether they can be overcome in this context is perhaps an open question. To my knowledge there is no evidence available, such as I will present for a BVAR model, to suggest that multivariate ARIMA models can consistently perform at least as well as the standard econometric models in real-time, out-of-sample economic forecasting.

Table 1.   Simulation Comparison of Bayesian With Standard Specification Approaches: Mean Squared Error of Estimated Coefficients

Equation Error Variance	Population R^2	Model	Observations		
			13	19	31
4.0	.27	OLS Variable.1	.902 (46)	.772 (53)	.656 (73)
		OLS Variables (1, 2)	1.092 (78)	.777 (54)	.555 (46)
		OLS Variables (1–3)	1.532 (149)	.954 (90)	.597 (58)
		OLS Variables (1–4)	2.059 (235)	1.221 (142)	.699 (84)
		OLS Variables (1–5)	2.842 (362)	1.567 (211)	.850 (124)
		OLS Variables (1–6)	4.227 (587)	1.934 (284)	1.023 (170)
		OLS Stepwise	1.873 (204)	1.085 (116)	.693 (83)
		Bayesian Variables (1–6)	.615	.503	.379
		Wrg-Bayes Variables (1–6)	.809 (32)	.673 (34)	.518 (37)
1.0	.60	OLS Variable 1	.629 (102)	.585 (152)	.546 (255)
		OLS Variables (1, 2)	.483 (55)	.398 (72)	.330 (109)
		OLS Variables (1–3)	.508 (63)	.357 (54)	.259 (64)
		OLS Variables (1–4)	.584 (88)	.370 (60)	.234 (49)
		OLS Variables (1–5)	.742 (138)	.417 (80)	.238 (51)
		OLS Variables (1–6)	1.059 (240)	.480 (107)	.258 (63)
		OLS Stepwise	.657 (111)	.421 (81)	.267 (69)
		Bayesian Variables (1–6)	.311	.232	.158
		Wrg-Bayes Variables (1–6)	.421 (35)	.320 (38)	.220 (39)
.05	.97	OLS Variable 1	.546 (1,507)	.530 (2,870)	.516 (5,145)
		OLS Variables (1, 2)	.296 (771)	.277 (1,451)	.260 (2,543)
		OLS Variables (1–3)	.184 (442)	.166 (833)	.150 (1,424)
		OLS Variables (1–4)	.117 (244)	.101 (464)	.085 (760)
		OLS Variables (1–5)	.067 (97)	.054 (206)	.041 (319)
		OLS Variables (1–6)	.042 (24)	.019 (7)	.010 (4)
		OLS Stepwise	.055 (62)	.023 (31)	.012 (19)
		Bayesian Variables (1–6)	.034	.018	.010
		Wrg-Bayes Variables (1–6)	.047 (39)	.023 (30)	.012 (19)

NOTE: Percentage increase relative to Bayesian estimate is given within parentheses.

4. THE VECTOR AUTOREGRESSION REPRESENTATION

An mth order autoregressive representation for the n-vector Y is given by

$$\underset{n \times 1}{Y(t)} = \underset{n \times 1}{D(t)} + \sum_{j=1}^{m} \underset{n \times n}{B_j} \underset{n \times 1}{Y(t - j)} + \underset{n \times 1}{\varepsilon(t)}$$

$$t = 1, \ldots, T$$

$$E[\varepsilon(t)\varepsilon(s)'] = \sum \quad \text{if } s = t$$

$$0 \quad \text{otherwise,} \tag{4}$$

where $D(t)$ captures the deterministic component of $Y(t)$. In general $D(t)$ is a linear function of an $n \times d$ matrix of parameters, C. In the examples that follow, $D(t)$ includes a constant term for each component of Y.

The ith equation has the following scalar form:

$$Y_i(t) = d^i(t) + b^i_{11}Y_1(t - 1) + \cdots + b^i_{m1}Y_1(t - m)$$

$$+ b^i_{12}Y_2(t - 1) + \cdots + b^i_{m2}Y_2(t - m)$$

$$+ b^i_{1n}Y_n(t - 1) + \cdots + b^i_{mn}Y_n(t - m)$$

$$+ \cdots + \varepsilon_i(t), \tag{5}$$

where b^i_{jk} is the kth element of the ith row of B_j in matrix notation and $d^i(t)$ is the ith element of the deterministic component. [28]

For ease of exposition we also adopt the somewhat misleading notation (since X includes lagged Y's)

$$\underset{T \times 1}{Y} = \underset{T \times p}{X} \underset{p \times 1}{\beta} + \underset{T \times 1}{\varepsilon} \tag{6}$$

to refer to this equation. Using this notation the estimator suggested here is

$$\beta^k = (X'X + kR'R)^{-1}(X'Y + kR'r). \tag{7}$$

This estimator combines the data generated by the model in (6), assuming $\varepsilon \sim N(0, \sigma^2 I)$, with the prior information contained in specification

$$\underset{q \times p}{R} \underset{p \times 1}{\beta} = \underset{q \times 1}{r} + \underset{q \times 1}{v} \quad v \sim N(0, \lambda^2 I), \tag{8}$$

where $k = \sigma^2/\lambda^2$. Ridge estimators correspond to setting R

$= I$, the identity matrix, and $r = 0$, the p-dimensional zero vector. Stein estimators are generated by taking $R = X$ and $r = 0$. Other estimators of this type, which impose smoothness across coefficients in distributed lag models, have been suggested by Leamer (1972) and Shiller (1973).

Rather than imposing smoothness, the estimator suggested here imposes the information that a reasonable approximation of the behavior of an economic variable is a random walk around an unknown, deterministic component. All equations in the system are given the same form of prior distribution. For the ith equation this distribution is centered around the specification

$$Y_i(t) = Y_i(t - 1) + d^i(t) + \varepsilon_i(t). \tag{9}$$

The parameters are all assumed to have means of zero except the coefficient on the first lag of the dependent variable, which is given a prior mean of one. The parameters are assumed to be uncorrelated with each other and to have standard deviations that decrease the further back they are in the lag distributions. In general, the prior distribution is much looser, that is, has larger standard deviations on lag coefficients of the dependent variable, than it is on other variables in the system. Generally, without observing the data very little is known about the distribution of the parameters of the deterministic component. To represent this ignorance, a noninformative prior is used. The flat prior is not a proper probability distribution but is justified in the usual manner as an approximation to a proper, but suitably diffuse prior.

The prior that has been described here is not derived from a particular economic theory, and in this sense, the restrictions it imposes may be referred to as instrumental. The intuition behind its use is its ability to capture more accurately uncertain a priori information than other standard methods of restricting VAR representations. Probably the most objectionable aspects of this prior are its reflection of complete ignorance about the deterministic components and its prior mean, which reflects a nonstationary process. Both of these specifications are likely candidates for modification in particular applications. On the other hand, these parts of the prior are the areas in which the prior is most uncertain anyway, and thus they are the areas in which the data will dominate most completely. For this reason forecasting performance should be relatively insensitive to specification of other reasonably loose priors with respect to the constant and the first lag of the dependent variable. It certainly may be true, however, that if one is forecasting growth rates of real GNP, for example, a random walk prior is not appropriate; one might do better by specifying a mean of less than one on the first own lag.

The justification for this prior is simply that through its use we are able to express more realistically our true state of knowledge and uncertainty about the structure of the economy. When there are known relationships among variables, whether derived from economic theory or other considerations, that information should be imposed in the estimation process. We are, however, sympathetic to the many economists who feel that the theory that is typically used to identify the equations of econometric models is not valid. Lucas and Sargent (1978), for example, contended that "Modern probabilistic microeconomic theory almost never implies either the exclusion restrictions that were suggested by Keynes or those that are imposed by macroeconometric models" (p. 54). Similarly, Sims (1980) suggested that "claims for identification in these models cannot be taken seriously" (p. 1) and that "a more systematic approach to imposing restrictions could lead to capture of empirical regularities, which remain hidden to standard procedures, and, hence, lead to improved forecasts and policy projections" (p. 14).

5. FORECASTING WITH A VECTOR AUTOREGRESSION

In this section I describe the application of this method in a forecasting experiment with a particular VAR system. The empirical work reported here was performed in 1979. It led to the specification of a model that has been used on a monthly basis for forecasting in subsequent years. The results of that real-time forecasting experiment are reported in the final section of this article. The work reported here is taken from Litterman (1980). More recent surveys of developments in BVAR modeling can be found in Todd (1984), Litterman (1984a), and Doan, Litterman, and Sims (1984). The system includes quarterly observations on the following seven variables: annual growth rates of real GNP (RGNP), annual inflation rates (growth rates of the GNP deflator; INFLA), the unemployment rate (UNEMP), logged levels of the money supply (M1), logged levels of gross private domestic investment (INVEST), the rate on four- to

six-month commercial paper (CPRATE), and the change in
business inventories (CBI). Observations were obtained from
1948:1–1979:3.

Each equation in this seven-variable system includes six
lags of each variable and a constant term, a total of 43 free
parameters. In the context of this system, it is shown first
that the posterior mean estimators can lead to a consistent,
large improvement forecast performance relative to unrestricted OLS estimation.

The prior information I specify treats each equation in the   [29]
same manner. The matrix R is normalized so that λ is the
standard deviation on the first lag of the dependent variable.
Given λ the standard deviations of further coefficients in the
lag distributions are decreased in a harmonic manner. The
coefficient on own lag j, $j = 2, \ldots, 6$, is given an independent normal prior distribution with mean zero and standard deviation λ/j. The standard deviations on lags of variables other than the dependent variable are made tighter
around zero at all lags by a factor $\theta = .2$ to reflect the
assumption that own lags account for most of the variation
of a given variable.

The standard deviations around coefficients on lags of
other than the dependent variable are not scale invariant.
For example, how tight a standard deviation of .1 is on lags
of GNP in an interest rate equation will depend on whether
GNP is measured in dollars or in billions of dollars. Thus
in general, the prior cannot be specified completely without
reference to the data.

This scale problem is usually solved in the ridge regression
context by transforming the data so that $X'X$ is a correlation
matrix. In effect, this scales the implicit prior by the standard
deviations of the independent variables. I am led away from
this approach because I suspect that the scale of the response
of one economic variable to another is more often a function
of the relative sizes of unexpected movements in the two
variables than of the relative sizes of their overall standard
errors. In the results reported here, the measure of the size
of unexpected movements in variable i is taken to be the
estimated standard error $\hat{\sigma}_i$, of the residuals in an unrestricted
univariate autoregression with a constant and six lags.

In summary, letting δ_{ij}^l be the standard deviation of the
prior distribution for the coefficient on lag l of variable j in
equation i, then

$$\delta^l_{ij} = \lambda/l \qquad \text{if } i = j$$
$$= 0\lambda\hat\sigma_i/l\hat\sigma_j \quad \text{if } i \neq j. \qquad (10)$$

Thus to put the prior for the ith equation in the form of (8), make R a diagonal matrix with zeros corresponding to deterministic components and elements $[\lambda/\delta^l_{ij}]$ correspond- [30] ing to the lth lag of variable j. r is a vector of zeros and a 1 corresponding to the first lag of the dependent variable. $R'R$ is singular here, reflecting the improper flat prior on coefficients of the deterministic component. This explains why the prior is expressed as in (5) rather than as a proper probability density for β. As noted before, this procedure is justified as an approximation to a proper, but locally uniform, prior distribution.

A gain in efficiency could be made by estimating all equations together via a seemingly unrelated regression procedure that uses the information contained in the covariances of residuals across equations. I do not attempt such a procedure primarily because of the computational burden; it would require inversion of an $n^2m + nd$ (301 in this case)-order matrix.

If σ^2 and λ^2 were known, the estimator in (7) would have a Bayesian justification as a posterior mean. When σ^2 and λ^2 are not known, one is faced with a problem that is usually encountered in the context of shrinkage estimators—that is, determining how far to shrink. A Bayesian solution that takes λ as given and a diffuse prior distribution for σ leads to a normal-t posterior density for β, which would require an intractable numerical integration to calculate the posterior mean. I chose instead an approximation based on the suggestion by Zellner (1971, sec. 4.2) of using $\hat\sigma$, the estimated standard error of the unrestricted OLS regression in place of σ. I use instead $\hat\sigma_i$, the univariate regression standard error, simply because in large VAR systems with few or no degrees of freedom, $\hat\sigma$ may be an unreliable estimator or may not exist.

The results in Table 2 demonstrate the improvements in forecasting that were produced by imposing the prior on the seven-variable system. Using data beginning in 1948:1, the system in its unrestricted form and combined with the foregoing prior with several degrees of tightness (values of λ) is estimated each quarter from 1971:1 to 1975:3. Each period the resulting estimates are used to make forecasts of one to eight steps ahead, using the chain rule of forecasting. The

Table 2.   Theil Coefficients 1971:1–1975:4

Variable	Forecast Horizon: Quarter Ahead								Average
	1	2	3	4	5	6	7	8	
Real GNP Growth									
No prior	1.89	1.13	1.12	1.23	.98	1.11	1.18	.98	1.20
$\lambda = .5$	.84	.67	.67	.76	.69	.65	.71	.65	.70
$\lambda = .3$	.79	.64	.66	.75	.69	.67	.72	.66	.70
$\lambda = .2$	.77	.64	.67	.75	.70	.68	.73	.67	.70
$\lambda = .1$	.82	.73	.71	.77	.75	.74	.77	.73	.76
Inflation									
No prior	1.90	1.17	1.11	.86	.90	1.05	1.08	1.03	1.14
$\lambda = .5$	1.02	.91	.96	.93	.92	.94	.93	.91	.94
$\lambda = .3$	1.01	.91	.96	.92	.91	.92	.91	.88	.93
$\lambda = .2$	1.00	.92	.95	.91	.91	.92	.91	.89	.92
$\lambda = .1$	.98	.92	.94	.92	.93	.94	.94	.92	.94
Unemployment									
No prior	1.33	1.43	1.60	1.75	1.75	1.66	1.63	1.78	1.62
$\lambda = .5$	.83	.87	.80	.76	.79	.78	.76	.73	.80
$\lambda = .3$	.78	.81	.76	.74	.75	.75	.74	.73	.76
$\lambda = .2$	.77	.79	.74	.74	.75	.76	.76	.76	.76
$\lambda = .1$	.80	.82	.80	.80	.81	.82	.82	.84	.81
Investment									
No prior	1.23	1.33	1.48	1.71	1.61	1.39	1.20	1.20	1.39
$\lambda = .5$	1.07	1.09	1.26	1.32	1.20	1.12	1.08	1.06	1.15
$\lambda = .3$	1.06	1.07	1.23	1.30	1.20	1.14	1.12	1.12	1.15
$\lambda = .2$	1.03	1.03	1.17	1.25	1.17	1.13	1.13	1.14	1.13
$\lambda = .1$	.97	.96	1.04	1.12	1.08	1.07	1.08	1.12	1.06
CBI									
No prior	1.03	.97	.96	10.6	.98	.91	.90	.90	.96
$\lambda = .5$	.93	.85	.91	.95	.86	.80	.80	.82	.87
$\lambda = .3$	.93	.86	.90	.93	.85	.80	.80	.82	.86
$\lambda = .2$	.94	.87	.89	.93	.86	.81	.82	.83	.87
$\lambda = .1$	.96	.91	.91	.95	.89	.85	.86	.87	.90
CPRATE									
No prior	1.09	1.30	1.32	1.43	1.55	1.57	1.45	1.18	1.36
$\lambda = .5$	.87	.95	.88	.77	.69	.66	.60	.52	.74
$\lambda = .3$	.91	.97	.88	.75	.68	.63	.57	.49	.74
$\lambda = .2$	.93	.95	.86	.73	.66	.61	.55	.48	.72
$\lambda = .1$	.93	.92	.84	.74	.68	.63	.57	.52	.73
M1									
No prior	.86	1.03	.94	.85	.83	.87	.93	1.00	.91
$\lambda = .5$	.37	.36	.31	.34	.30	.28	.29	.26	.31
$\lambda = .3$	.37	.32	.26	.28	.25	.24	.24	.22	.27
$\lambda = .2$	.37	.30	.25	.26	.23	.23	.24	.22	.26
$\lambda = .1$	.37	.30	.25	.26	.25	.25	.26	.25	.27

chain rule takes estimated one-step-ahead forecasts as the basis for two-step-ahead forecasts and so on.

MSE and Theil coefficients are calculated for each variable at each forecast horizon. The Theil coefficient scales the root MSE by the root square error of no-change forecasts. This scaling allows comparison to some extent across variables and across horizons. The main result is clear in Table 2. For each of the seven variables, at all horizons, there is an obvious improvement in forecasting as the prior is imposed, relative to the unrestricted model. Values of .5, .3, .2, and .1 were tried for the tightness parameter λ with the prior. Recall that λ is the standard deviation of the first lag of the dependent variable in each equation. All other standard errors are scaled relative to it. The best overall results were [31] generated with $\lambda = .2$. It is clear that forecasting results are not overly sensitive to changes in this parameter.

The improvement in forecasting demonstrated in Table 2 is not particularly surprising. It simply reflects the overparameterization of the unrestricted system. A more interesting question is how well do the posterior mean estimators forecast relative to other alternative methods. One indication is given by a comparison of these results with the forecast performance of univariate autoregressive equations with constant, six lags, and no prior for the same period. Such an equation is, of course, the limiting case of this prior as θ goes to 0 and λ goes to infinity such that $\theta\lambda$ goes to zero. The system with the previously specified prior and appropriate λ's almost uniformly outperforms the univariate equations. There is an obvious qualification to these results, however—the optimal λ could not have been known ahead of time. For this reason an additional experiment was performed to compare this prior and the optimal λ with other forecasting methods over the subsequent period of 1976:1–1979:3. The forecast statistics in the earlier period were compiled as if data for 1976:1 and later were not available, to avoid biasing the second experiment.

This second experiment was designed to allow comparison not only with ARIMA and univariate autoregression models but also with the compiled records of two professional forecasters, Data Resources, Inc. (DRI), and Chase Econometric Associates, Inc. (Chase). The compiled records for these forecasters were taken from the *Statistical Abstract* (published monthly by the Conference Board, New York, NY).

Each of four mechanical forecasts of the quarterly data was updated on a monthly basis using the new or revised information actually available to the professional forecasters at the beginning of the particular month. For example, following the standard convention, the one-step-ahead forecast made in January is a forecast of the fourth-quarter data based on the final data for the third quarter. The February one-step-ahead forecast is of first-quarter data on the basis of preliminary fourth-quarter values. This procedure is followed primarily because it ensures that all of the information used by the models was available to forecasters at the time of their forecast.

The results in Table 3 show that the posterior mean estimator performed favorably in comparison with the other models. It is also clear that during this period no obvious advantage over standard univariate time-series methods was obtained by the professional forecasters' use of structural models, larger information sets, and judgmental adjustment.

6. FORECASTING WITH BVAR's

The preceding empirical work led to my specifying a simple six-variable, six-lag quarterly model with which I

Table 3.   Mean Squared Errors of Forecasts 1976:1–1979:4

	Forecast Horizon: Quarters Ahead						
Variable	2	3	4	5	6	7	8
Real GNP Growth							
DRI	2.726	2.801	2.951	3.388	3.566		
	(42)	(39)	(33)	(19)	(12)		
Chase	3.052	3.391	3.408	3.875	4.224	4.043	3.809
	(42)	(39)	(36)	(33)	(29)	(23)	(14)
ARIMA	2.882	3.071	3.076	3.181	3.209	3.266	3.418
	(42)	(39)	(36)	(33)	(30)	(27)	(24)
Univariate AR	3.192	3.401	3.405	3.656	3.391	3.331	3.374
	(42)	(39)	(36)	(33)	(30)	(27)	(24)
Bayesian VAR	2.841	3.053	2.948	2.959	3.021	2.999	3.281
	(42)	(39)	(36)	(33)	(30)	(27)	(24)
Inflation							
DRI	1.605	1.929	2.277	2.894	2.727		
	(42)	(39)	(33)	(18)	(12)		
Chase	1.565	2.039	2.412	2.780	3.221	3.602	3.151
	(42)	(39)	(36)	(33)	(28)	(23)	(14)
ARIMA	1.674	1.907	1.755	2.211	2.327	2.773	2.773
	(42)	(39)	(36)	(33)	(30)	(27)	(24)
Univariate AR	2.289	2.735	3.111	3.526	3.940	4.235	4.539
	(42)	(39)	(36)	(33)	(30)	(27)	(24)
Bayesian VAR	1.426	1.624	1.441	1.710	1.640	1.793	1.514
	(42)	(39)	(36)	(33)	(30)	(27)	(24)
Unemployment							
DRI	.341	.449	.485	.494	.430		
	(42)	(39)	(33)	(19)	(12)		
Chase	.510	.817	1.040	1.201	1.477	1.817	2.301
	(42)	(39)	(36)	(33)	(29)	(23)	(14)
ARIMA	.466	.712	.915	1.073	1.236	1.384	1.491
	(42)	(39)	(36)	(33)	(30)	(27)	(24)
Univariate AR	.362	.493	.541	.566	.576	.526	.461
	(42)	(39)	(36)	(33)	(30)	(27)	(24)
Bayesian VAR	.383	.497	.559	.627	.738	.845	.961
	(42)	(39)	(36)	(33)	(30)	(27)	(24)

NOTE: Number of observations is given in parentheses.

began to forecast on a regular basis each month, beginning in May 1980. The variables in that model are real GNP, the GNP price deflator, real business fixed investment, the 3-month Treasury bill rate, the unemployment rate, and the money supply. The prior is the same as shown before except that the relative weight parameter, θ, is set at .3. It is now five years later, and I continue to generate forecasts with essentially the same model once a month. In the remainder of this article, I will compare the forecasts generated by that BVAR model with those of three of the best-known commercial forecasting services, DRI, Wharton EFA, and Chase.

Over the past five years, I have sent, at no charge, the BVAR forecasts on a regular basis to a list of interested parties, consisting primarily of academics. A common response has been an impression that there is something different or wrong with the BVAR forecasts because they are too "volatile" or "wild" relative to standard forecasts.

Such a reaction was perhaps to be expected given, for example, that in my first forecast, published May 1, 1980, the unemployment rate was forecast to rise from the then current rate of 6.1% to above 11% by the end of 1982. The DRI, Chase, and Wharton forecasts at that time projected the unemployment rate to peak between 7.5% and 8.2%.

There is at least one obvious explanation for the different behavior of the BVAR forecast from other published forecasts. The BVAR forecast is the unadjusted product of a statistical procedure designed to pick a point as close as

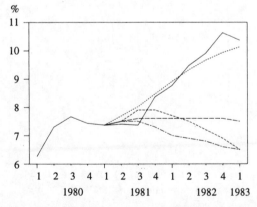

Figure 1. Comparison of Unemployment Rate: Forecasts as of 1981:1. ---, BVAR; – – –, Chase; — —, Wharton; —·—, DRI; ——, Actual. Sources: Actual—U.S. Dept. of Labor and Commerce; Commercial—Conference Board.

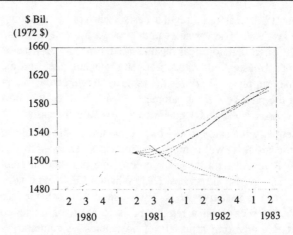

$ Bil.
(1972 $)

Figure 2. Comparison of Real GNP: Forecasts as of Second Quarter 1981. ---, BVAR; – – –, Chase; — —, Wharton; —·—, DRI; ——, Actual. Sources: Actual—U.S. Dept. of Labor and Commerce; Commercial— Conference Board.

possible to the future value of the variable in question. Other forecasts are typically sold to clients and are judgmentally adjusted, presumably in ways that are designed to maximize the demand for the forecast. It is not at all clear that an unbiased forecast is also a profit-maximizing forecast. For [32] example, faced with the outlook for the unemployment rate described above in May 1980, a profit-maximizing forecaster might have published a forecast with the unemployment rate rising only to 9%, even though his own model projected

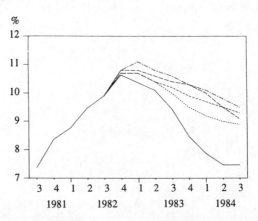

Figure 3. Comparison of Unemployment Rate: Forecasts as of 1982:3. ---, BVAR; – – –, Chase; — —, Wharton; —·—, DRI; ——, Actual. Source: Actual—U.S. Depts. of Labor and Commerce; Commercial—Conference Board.

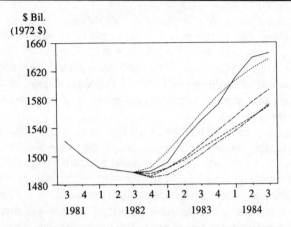

$ Bil.
(1972 $)

Figure 4. Comparison of Real GNP: Forecasts as of Third Quarter
1982. ---, BVAR; − − −, Chase; − −, Wharton; −·−, DRI; ——, Actual.
Sources: Actual—U.S. Depts. of Labor and Commerce; Commercial—Conference Board.

unemployment rising to 11%. The cost in terms of lost credibility of deviating from the range of other forecasters would
have been weighed against the questionable benefit of po-
sitioning one's forecast further above the range of other
forecasters.

For whatever reason, the deviation of the BVAR forecast
from the range of the Chase, DRI, and Wharton forecasts
has been obvious. In Figures 1–6, I illustrate this phenomenon in a few representative forecasts. The deviation of the

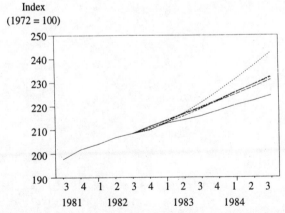

Index
(1972 = 100)

Figure 5. Comparison of the GNP Deflator: Forecasts as of 1982:3.
---, BVAR; − − −, Chase; − −, Wharton; −·−, DRI; ——, Actual.
Sources: Actual—U.S. Depts. of Labor and Commerce; Commer-
cial—Conference Board.

BVAR forecast from the range of DRI, Chase, and Wharton is clear. The reader may also be surprised at how far the actual realized values (the solid line in the figures) are from the range of forecasts. This latter phenomenon illustrates how misleading it can be to follow the common practice of using the range of forecasts as a measure of the range of likely outcomes.

In any case, it should be clear that variance over time in forecasts—or variance with respect to the mean of a distribution of forecasts—is not, in itself, a negative property of a forecasting technique. If the volatility of the forecast represents a correct assessment of the impact of new information, then it is a desirable property. To the extent that a forecasting procedure is too volatile—for example, overly sensitive to new information—that excessive sensitivity will show up as an increased mean squared forecast error. We will use this measure of forecast performance to compare the BVAR forecasts with other published forecasts later in this article.

Another common complaint about BVAR models (and more generally about time series models) is that they never forecast turning points. This criticism is clearly not valid with respect to this BVAR model. Figures 1–4 specifically illustrate how turning points in the real economy over the past four years often have been forecast much more accurately by the BVAR model than by the conventional forecasters.

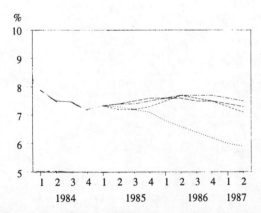

Figure 6. Comparison of Unemployment Rate: Forecasts as of 1985:1. ---, BVAR; – – –, Chase; — —, Wharton; —·—, DRI; ——, Actual. Sources: Actual—U.S. Depts. of Labor and Commerce; Commercial—Conference Board.

This selective sampling of forecasts cannot provide a basis for judging the relative accuracy of the BVAR technique—that is the subject of the rest of this article. Nonetheless, lest I leave the wrong impression from this small selection of forecasts, in Figure 5 the outstanding failure of the BVAR model is shown—that is, its projection of accelerating inflation over the past two years. In Figure 6, I show the most recent forecast of the unemployment rate, which again exhibits a substantial difference between the BVAR forecast and the conventional forecasters.

[33]

7. MEASURING FORECAST PERFORMANCE

Before presenting the comparison, it will be useful to review some of the difficulties in interpreting evidence in forecast performance comparisons. In making this comparison I am, in effect, setting up a form of after-the-fact competition in which the rules and object of the competition were not specified ahead of time to the players. In this situation, there is an obvious potential risk that by selective reporting of results, one could give a misleading picture of the results. This is especially true here, since different models are designed for different purposes, are specified at different levels of aggregation, and are used to forecast over various horizons.

Fortunately, there is widespread agreement that the variables and horizons considered here are indeed those of primary interest. For many years the *Statistical Abstract*, a publication of the Conference Board, has included each month a set of one- through eight-quarter-ahead forecasts of a number of commercial forecasting firms for four variables of primary economic interest: real GNP, nominal GNP, the unemployment rate, and the GNP price deflator. This publication is the source of data and the basis for the forecast comparison I make here.

The timing of release of economic forecasts is another important consideration in any forecasting competition. Forecasts are not generally published on the same date, so they will to some extent be based on slightly different information sets. Forecasts of macroeconomic variables are generally dated according to the National Income and Produce Accounts (NIPA) data available at the time of release, and I follow that convention.

Notice that in the forecast comparison made here, all

participants were operating in real time, making forecasts each month over a period of five years. Thus we need not worry about how to interpret out-of-sample forecasts that are made after the fact. The all too common reporting of results from so-called forecasting experiments in which actual values are used for exogenous variables—those not included in the model—are subject to obvious criticism. Less obvious, but still problematical, are out-of-sample experiments in which a given specification is estimated using data only up to a certain date to make a forecast as of that date. Such simulations are certainly useful in some contexts; results from such an experiment, for example, were the reason I was led to use a Bayesian procedure. But for the most part, such comparisons cannot be used to rank models because it is very difficult to know how important after-the-fact information was in generating the specifications that were used in such an experiment. Today, for example, most conventional econometric models have highly developed energy sectors, which in out-of-sample experiments are quite useful in forecasting the economic data of the seventies. Of course, no one was using those models at the time, and we can only guess today at what structures will be needed to forecast the economy in the future.

In a recent experiment I found that inclusion of two variables, the value of the trade-weighted dollar and a measure of stock prices, dramatically reduced the out-of-sample forecast errors of the model over the last nine years. In particular, for the one variable that has performed most poorly in the model described here, the GNP deflator, this change in specification reduced the one-year-ahead forecast root mean squared error by 32%. I now include these variables in the model, but it would be unfair to compare the performance of this respecified model with the actual real time performance of others.

Another issue that arises is how to define the target that everyone is trying to forecast. The answer is obvious for a series such as an interest rate, which does not get revised, but not so obvious for historical economic data, which are constantly revised. Scheduled revisions take place in NIPA data for at least three years, and benchmark revisions may make the historical data look quite different from the data observed at the time forecasts were made. Since these revisions generally affect levels and short-run growth rates rather than growth over several quarters, one approximate solution to this problem is to use the forecasted growth rates, applied to currently published base levels, to generate multistep level-corrected forecasts that can be compared with currently published levels to measure forecast errors. This is the procedure used here. The exact formula is shown in Equation (12).

Finally, one has to ask what it is that is being judged. Those who have not attempted to use large econometric models are probably unaware of the importance of the judgmental input, sometimes referred to as "tender loving care," that is applied by the forecaster. There is abundant evidence that the standard econometric models cannot be used mechanically to generate forecasts that compare in accuracy with those that are produced with judgmental input. This judgmental input is unfortunate, however, because it makes such forecasts nonreproducible and essentially takes them out of the realm of scientific study. My own guess is that when such input is involved, forecast performance is much more related to the individual producing the forecast than to the model being used. In any case, to judge a model, as opposed to judging the person running the model, one would like to have at least both the unadjusted and the adjusted forecasts for comparison. This information is unavailable, however, since unadjusted forecasts from these models are never published. In these circumstances, it becomes very difficult to know how to interpret the forecast performance of a given commercial model. One might expect the performance to change, for example, when personnel at the firm change.

I think an important distinction can be drawn between forecasts from such models and forecasts from the BVAR model that I have published for the past five years because the latter are purely mechanically produced forecasts without judgmental adjustment. Furthermore, they have been generated by a model whose specification has not changed much over that period of time. They thus represent reproducible data, the statistical properties of which could be expected [34] to remain stable if the model were to be used in the future.

Because the model structure has changed recently, however, one cannot expect the forecast performance statistics to apply exactly to the new structure. What one would like to do is generate procedures that can be expected to give accurate projections of what the performance statistics are likely to be for various model structures. Such a procedure is illustrated below.

8. A FORECAST PERFORMANCE COMPARISON

The forecast performance comparison is based on the monthly forecasts of the BVAR model, the Data Resources model, the Wharton model, and the Chase Econometrics model. The first forecast was made in May 1980 and the last in May 1985. Where observations were not available for one of the forecasters (in a few cases, eight-quarter-ahead forecasts were not published), observations at that horizon and variable for all forecasters were dropped from the sample. Because forecasts of quarterly data are made monthly, there are three forecasts for each observation of a given variable at a given horizon. These are sometimes referred to as "early-," "middle-," and "late-quarter" forecasts, depending on whether they are based on the preliminary or the first or second revised NIPA estimates of the previous quarter. In this comparison, which is presented in Table 4, I aggregate the results for these three months into a single category. Thus, for example, forecasts of data for the first quarter of 1984, made in January, February, and March 1983, are all included as separate observations in the five-quarter-ahead category. (Note that the one-quarter-ahead forecast refers to a forecast of the current quarter.)

The measure of forecast accuracy used is the familiar root mean squared error (RMSE). For the unemployment rate, the RMSE measure of s-quarter-ahead forecast performance is simply

$$\left[\frac{1}{T}\sum_{t=1}^{T}(A_t - {_sF_t})^2\right]^{1/2}, \tag{11}$$

where A_t is the actual value at time t and $_sF_t$ is the forecast made s quarters earlier.

For the variables real GNP, the GNP deflator, and nominal GNP, errors are expressed as percentages of the level of the actual value. Due to the aforementioned correction for historical revisions, the formula for these variables appears somewhat complicated. Letting A_t be the actual value of the level of the variable at time t and $_r\dot{F}_t$ be the forecasted percent growth (not annualized) in quarter t made r periods earlier, the formula for the RMSE at an s-quarter horizon is

$$\left[\frac{1}{T}\sum_{t=1}^{T}\left[A_t - \left\{A_{t-s}\cdot\prod_{r=1}^{s}\left(1 + \frac{_r\dot{F}_{t+1-r}}{100}\right)\right\}\right]^2\bigg/A_t\right]^{1/2}.$$

$$\tag{12}$$

Perhaps the most important point to be made in interpreting the results in Table 4 is that they are based on a small sample. The number of observations listed under each horizon is small to begin with, and the errors in each category, particularly at long horizons, will be highly correlated. It is difficult to judge the results in Table 4 because we know that they are based on a small, correlated sample, and we have no measures of significance.

Despite this high degree of sampling error in Table 4, a few results are clear. It is demonstrated here that a time series forecasting procedure operating in real time, without judgmental adjustment, can produce forecasts that are at least competitive with the best forecasts commercially available. This is not a small achievement. The commercial forecasts [35] are sold for prices in the range of thousands of dollars per year. The BVAR model can be estimated, and forecasts generated, on a personal computer in approximately three minutes.

A second result of interest is that the BVAR model appears to do relatively better at longer horizons. My interpretation of this tendency is that it reflects the significant advantage that the judgmental forecasts had in forecasting the current quarter during the first two years of the forecasting period. In any case, it clearly calls into question a common perception that time series techniques may be useful for very short-term forecasts, but structural models are needed to capture the turning points in business cycles necessary for accurate forecasting at longer horizons. [See, e.g., the opinion of L. R. Klein, as quoted in Lupoletti and Webb (1984, p. 7).]

These conclusions would be stronger if we could approximate the distributions of the performance statistics. Unfortunately, there is not much that can be done to model the statistical properties of a short series of judgmental forecasts. For the BVAR forecasts, however, there is an underlying probability model and a reproducible forecasting procedure that can be used to generate a distribution for the measures of expected forecast error variance. Table 5 shows the actual BVAR performance results (from Table 4) alongside a sampling theoretic measure of the mean and standard error of these statistics. These moments are based on simulations of repeated out-of-sample application of the BVAR forecasting technique to artificial data generated from the original estimated probability model. The exact steps involved in this exercise are given in the Appendix.

Table 4. BVAR Model Forecast Performance Comparison Root Mean Square Forecast Errors, 1980:2–1985:1

Variable	Forecast Horizon in Quarters (number of observations)							
	1 (60)	2 (58)	3 (55)	4 (52)	5 (49)	6 (46)	7 (43)	8 (38)
Real GNP								
BVAR	.833	1.095	1.556	1.829	1.785	1.882	2.170	2.957
Chase	.795	1.367	2.092	2.690	3.124	3.508	3.724	3.576
DRI	.704	1.208	1.901	2.484	2.940	3.405	3.714	3.648
Wharton	.696	1.220	1.869	2.472	2.839	3.234	3.546	3.479
GNP Deflator								
BVAR	.487	1.056	1.874	2.966	4.258	5.571	6.842	8.031
Chase	.345	.569	.929	1.432	2.080	2.761	3.497	4.211
DRI	.340	.560	.838	1.328	1.940	2.633	3.421	4.216
Wharton	.385	.652	1.036	1.555	2.182	2.841	3.595	4.305
Nominal GNP								
BVAR	.998	1.563	2.577	3.567	4.316	5.130	5.615	6.469
Chase	.935	1.645	2.575	3.487	4.347	5.301	6.060	6.343
DRI	.804	1.339	2.198	3.127	4.063	5.137	6.093	6.544
Wharton	.823	1.565	2.501	3.518	4.449	5.395	6.279	6.637
Unemployment Rate								
BVAR	.217	.496	.749	.923	1.061	1.110	1.543	1.696
Chase	.250	.546	.861	1.152	1.441	1.674	1.897	1.938
DRI	.210	.508	.811	1.161	1.500	1.787	1.997	2.019
Wharton	.224	.523	.840	1.105	1.359	1.530	1.645	1.674

The standard errors of the simulation RMSE statistics provide at least a rough guide to the uncertainty of these forecast performance measures. In Table 5 we use the standard error measure to normalize the distance between the BVAR RMSE statistic and that of the best alternative RMSE performance from Table 4 for each variable at each horizon. Using this metric we see that the most significant difference occurs with respect to inflation, in which case for all horizons the BVAR model performance is more than two standard errors worse than the best alternative. On the other hand, for real GNP the BVAR model performs more than one standard error better than the best alternative at the four- through seven-quarter horizons. For nominal GNP these effects are offset, and the BVAR performance is somewhat worse at shorter horizons and a little better at longer horizons. For the unemployment rate the BVAR performs better than the best alternative for the two- through seven-quarter horizons, with the magnitude of the difference reaching one standard error at the six-step horizon.

Although the RMSE is probably the best overall measure of forecast accuracy, it fails to reflect the degree to which the judgmentally adjusted forecasts of the commercial firms tend to bunch together relative to the BVAR model and therefore fails to reflect the relative information content of the BVAR forecast. One measure that does reflect that tendency of other forecasts to bunch together is the proportion of times a given forecaster is closest to the actual. By this measure the results clearly favor the BVAR model. Of the 1,604 forecasts considered, the BVAR model was most accurate 34.8% of the time. The percentage of times each of [36] the other forecasters was most accurate was 16.4, 27.3, and 21.6 for Chase, DRI, and Wharton, respectively.

9. POSTSCRIPT

Over the five years since the model described herein was specified, the state of the art of using BVAR's has advanced considerably. In particular, models with the time-varying parameters and much more sophisticated prior distributions have been developed (e.g., see Sims 1982, Litterman 1984d, and Doan et al. 1984). The Federal Reserve Bank of Minneapolis has developed a larger (46-equation) monthly national forecasting model (Litterman 1984c); several regional BVAR models have been developed (Amirizadeh and Todd 1984); and the BVAR technique has also been used in ap-

Table 5. Monte Carlo Simulation Measures of the Distance Between the BVAR RMSE and the Best Alternative Performance

Variable	Forecast Horizon in Quarters							
	1	2	3	4	5	6	7	8
Real GNP								
BVAR RMSE	.833	1.095	1.556	1.829	1.785	1.882	2.170	2.957
Monte Carlo Simulation Mean	.824	1.271	1.645	1.994	2.360	2.757	3.179	3.593
Monte Carlo Simulation Standard Error	.131	.256	.395	.543	.692	.844	1.023	1.234
Distance (in standard errors) From BVAR to Best Alternative	−1.05	.44	.79	1.21	1.52	1.60	1.35	.42
GNP Deflator								
BVAR RMSE	.487	1.056	1.874	2.966	4.258	5.571	6.842	8.031
Monte Carlo Simulation Mean	.459	.875	1.360	1.897	2.461	3.045	3.652	4.256
Monte Carlo Simulation Standard Error	.060	.159	.293	.465	.680	.926	1.195	1.496
Distance (in standard errors) From BVAR to Best Alternative	−2.45	−3.10	−3.57	−3.56	−3.40	−3.16	−2.85	−2.55
Nominal GNP								
BVAR RMSE	.998	1.563	2.577	3.67	4.316	5.130	5.615	6.469
Monte Carlo Simulation Mean	.980	1.611	2.209	2.760	3.285	3.818	4.391	4.942
Monte Carlo Simulation Standard Error	.149	.276	.434	.640	.887	1.174	1.436	1.716
Distance (in standard errors) From BVAR to Best Alternative	−1.30	−.81	−.87	−.69	−.29	.01	.31	−.07
Unemployment Rate								
BVAR RMSE	.217	.496	.749	.923	1.061	1.110	1.543	1.696
Monte Carlo Simulation Mean	.297	.514	.693	.834	.959	1.088	1.220	1.367
Monte Carlo Simulation Standard Error	.051	.122	.199	.268	.332	.398	.469	.544
Distance (in standard errors) From BVAR to Best Alternative	−.13	.10	.31	.68	.90	1.06	.22	−.04

plications to forecast state revenues (Litterman and Supel 1983), to control the money supply (Litterman 1982), and to measure the costs of intermediate targeting by the Federal Reserve System (Litterman 1984b).

APPENDIX

The bootstrap procedure used to estimate standard errors of the forecast preformance statistics is as follows:

I. The BVAR system is estimated over the base period 1949:3–1980:1.

II. Each quarter from 1980:1 through 1985:1, a one-step-ahead forecast is made for each variable, the forecast errors are saved, and the equation estimates are updated using the Kalman filter. The final coefficient estimates are saved for use in generating artificial data.

III. One hundred simulations are performed. In each simulation the following steps are taken:

A. Artificial data is generated based on the probability structure estimated in steps I and II.

1. One hundred twenty-three (the number of observations in the base period) uniform random integers $I_i, i = 1, \ldots, 123$, are drawn from the interval [1, 123].

2. Artificial data is generated using shocks randomly drawn from the base period residual vectors. Initial conditions are taken to be those as of 1949:2. Then each period, t, from 1949:3 through 1980:1 a new observation is obtained as a sum of the forecast based on the estimated coefficients plus the vector of residuals from period $I_{[t - 1949:3 + 1]}$.

3. A similar procedure is used to generate artificial data for the forecast period. Here 22 random integers $J_i, i = 1, \ldots 22$, are drawn from the interval [1, . . . , 22]. The artificial data through 1980:1 is appended with 22 additional observations obtained as the sum of the forecast at time t plus the vector of forecast errors from the period $J_{[t - 1980:1 + 1]}$.

B. A new BVAR system is estimated on the artificial data using observations 1949:3–1980:1.

C. Each quarter of the forecast period, a one-step-ahead forecast is made of the artificial data, the

forecast errors are saved, and the coefficient estimates are updated using the Kalman filter.
D. The RMSE statistics for each variable at each horizon over the 22-quarter forecast period are calculated.
IV. The mean and standard error across simulations of the RMSE statistics are calculated.

This procedure gives a Monte Carlo measure of the uncertainty of the RMSE statistic obtained when the Bayesian forecasting procedure is applied to a 22-quarter sample of artificial data generated with a probability structure estimated from the actual data.

[*Received March 1985. Revised July 1985.*]

REFERENCES

Amirizedeh, Hossain, and Todd, Richard (1984). "More Growth Ahead for Ninth District States," *Federal Reserve Bank of Minneapolis Quarterly Review*, 4 (Fall), 8–17.

Brunner, Karl (ed.) (1981), *The Great Depression Revisited*, Boston: Nijhoff.

Doan, Thomas, Litterman, Robert, and Sims, Christopher (1984), "Forecasting and Conditional Projection Using Realistic Prior Distributions," *Econometric Reviews*, 3, 1–144.

Eckstein, Otto (1983), *The DRI Model of the U.S. Economy*, New York: McGraw-Hill.

Gordon, Robert J., and Wilcox, James A. (1981), "Monetarist Interpretations of the Great Depression: An Evaluation and Critique," in *The Great Depression Revisited*, ed. Karl Brunner, Boston: Nijhoff, pp. 49–107.

Jorgenson, Dale W. (1963), "Capital Theory and Investment Behavior," *American Economic Review*, 53, 247–259.

Leamer, Edward E. (1972), "A Class of Informative Priors and Distributed Lag Analysis," *Econometrica*, 40, 1059–1081.

Litterman, Robert B. (1980), "A Bayesian Procedure for Forecasting With Vector Autoregression," Working Paper, Massachusetts Institute of Technology, Dept. of Economics.

——— (1982), "Optimal Control of the Money Supply," *Federal Reserve Bank of Minneapolis Quarterly Review*, 6 (Fall), 1–9.

——— (1984a), "Above-Average National Growth in 1985 and 1986," *Federal Reserve Bank of Minneapolis Quarterly Review*, 4 (Fall), 3–7.

——— (1948b), "The Costs of Intermediate Targeting," Working Paper 254, Federal Reserve Bank of Minneapolis, Research Dept.

——— (1984c), "Forecasting and Policy Analysis With Bayesian Vector Autoregression Models," *Federal Reserve Bank of Minneapolis Quarterly Review*, 4 (Fall), 30–41.

——— (1984d), "Specifying Vector Autoregressions for Macroeconomic Forecasting," Staff Report 92, Federal Reserve Bank of Minneapolis, Research Dept. (See also *Bayesian Inference and Decision Techniques With Applications: Essays in Honor of Bruno de Finetti*, eds. P. Goel and A. Zellner, Amsterdam: North-Holland, in press.)

Litterman, Robert B., and Supel, Thomas M. (1983), "Using Vector Autoregressions to Measure the Uncertainty in Minnesota's Revenue Forecasts," *Federal Reserve Bank of Minneapolis Quarterly Review,* 7 (Spring), 10–22.

Lucas, Robert E., Jr., and Sargent, Thomas J. (1978), "After Keynesian Macroeconomics," in *After the Phillips Curve: Persistence of High Inflation and High Unemployment,* Boston: Federal Reserve Bank of Boston, pp. 49–72.

Lupoletti, William M., and Webb, Roy H. (1984), "Defining and Improving the Accuracy of Macroeconomic Forecasts: Contributions From a VAR model," Working Paper 84-6, Federal Reserve Bank of Richmond.

Meltzer, Allan H. (1981), Comments on "Monetarist Interpretations of the Great Depression," in *The Great Depression Revisited,* ed. Karl Brunner, Boston: Nijhoff, pp. 148–164.   [37]

Shiller, Robert J. (1973), "A Distributed Lag Estimator Derived From Smoothness Priors," *Econometrica,* 41, 775–788.

Sims, Christopher A. (1980), "Macroeconomics and Reality," *Econometrica,* 48, 1–48.

——— (1982), "Policy Analysis With Econometric Models," in *Brooking Papers on Economic Activity 1,* ed. William C. Brainard and George L. Perry, Washington, DC: Brookings Institution, pp. 107–152.

Todd, Richard M. (1984), "Improving Economic Forecasting With Bayesian Vector Autoregression," *Federal Reserve Bank of Minneapolis Quarter Review,* 4 (Fall), 18–29.

Zellner, Arnold (1971), *An Introduction to Bayesian Inference in Econometrics,* New York: John Wiley.   [38]

[17]

Journal of Forecasting, Vol. 12, 365–378 (1993)

Forecasting with Generalized Bayesian Vector Autoregressions

K. RAO KADIYALA
Purdue University, West Lafayette, IN 47907, U.S.A

and

SUNE KARLSSON
Stockholm School of Economics, Stockholm, Sweden

ABSTRACT

The effects of using different distributions to parameterize the prior beliefs in a Bayesian analysis of vector autoregressions are studied. The well-known Minnesota prior of Litterman as well as four less restrictive distributions are considered. Two of these prior distributions are new to vector autoregressive models. When the forecasting performance of the different parameterizations of the prior beliefs are compared it is found that the prior distributions that allow for dependencies between the equations of the VAR give rise to better forecasts.

KEY WORDS   Diffuse prior   ENC prior   Normal-Diffuse prior
Normal-Wishart prior   Minnesota prior
Monte Carlo integration   Multivariate time series

The use of Vector Autoregressive (VAR) models in applied economics has increased significantly following the criticism of the Cowles Commission approach to the modelling of systems of simultaneous equations (see, for example, Sims, 1980). There has been a shift from the modelling of economic systems with structural equations towards modelling the joint time-series behaviour of the variables.

The frequent use of VARs for modelling the time-series behaviour can partly be explained by their relative ease of use as compared to the richer class of vector ARMA models. The main advantage of VAR models lies in the identification stage, especially if all variables are taken to enter with identical lags. The estimation problem is also particularly simple in the case of identical lags. In the classical analysis, OLS is efficient under the usual assumptions and the Bayesian case is also considerably more straightforward.

The main disadvantage of the VAR models is the large number of parameters that need to be estimated. With the sample sizes common in economics the classical estimation procedures often run into degrees-of-freedom problems. In a Bayesian framework, on the other hand, sharp posteriors can often be obtained even with relatively uninformative prior distributions. As a consequence, VAR modelling is one of the areas within applied economics where

0277–6693/93/030365–14$12.00
Received September 1991
Revised June 1992

366   Journal of Forecasting   Vol. 12, Iss. Nos. 3 & 4

Bayesian methods have been most extensively used. The Bayesian procedure of Litterman (1980), with the so-called 'Minnesota prior', is the most frequently used method, but the natural conjugate Normal-Wishart prior (Litterman, 1980; Broemeling, 1985) and the diffuse prior (Geweke, 1988) have also seen some use.

The Litterman procedure does not take account of dependencies between the equations and is of a univariate nature. The other two priors, on the other hand, allow for interaction and dependencies between the equations.

In most situations any prior concepts that the researcher may have about the parameter values in the VAR are, at best, expressed in terms of the first and second moments and perhaps the support of the prior distribution. It is, in most cases, very hard to form a prior belief concerning the dependencies between parameters in different equations as well as in the same equation. It is nonetheless important that such dependencies are allowed for and that we 'let the data speak' on this point.

In this paper the effects of various methods of parameterizing the prior beliefs are compared by way of their forecast performance. In order to make the comparisons richer, two additional priors not previously utilized in a VAR setting, the Normal-Diffuse and the ENC priors, are introduced.

In the comparisons of forecasting performance we do not consider the issue of model selection. Two models and data sets available in the literature are simply taken as given for the purpose of the forecasting exercises. The issue of model selection in VAR-based forecasting models is studied by Kling and Bessler (1985) and Edlund and Karlsson (1993).

The rest of the paper is organized as follows. The distributions used to express the prior beliefs are introduced together with the corresponding posterior distributions in the next section. The two forecasting approaches that are considered are discussed in the third section. The numerical methods used to evaluate the posterior distributions are reviewed in the fourth section. The fifth section presents the results of three forecasting experiments and conclusions are presented in the final section.

BAYESIAN ANALYSIS OF VARs

Let y_t be the row vector of q variables of interest observed at time t and x_t a row vector of r exogenous variables that might influence y_t. The VAR can then be written as

$$y_t = \sum_{i=1}^{p} y_{t-i} \mathbf{A}_i + x_t \mathbf{C} + u_t \tag{1}$$

The $\mathbf{A}_i$'s and $\mathbf{C}$ are matrices of unknown parameters, of dimensions $q \times q$ and $r \times q$, respectively. Throughout it will be assumed that the vector of disturbances, u_t, is distributed as multivariate normal with mean vector $\mathbf{0}$ and variance–covariance matrix $\mathbf{\Psi}$ and that u_t, is independent of u_s for all $t \neq s$.

Prior beliefs

The prior beliefs used in the comparison are essentially those embedded in the Minnesota prior of Litterman (1980). A finite distributed lag structure is assumed to describe the time-series behaviour of each of the variables.

These prior beliefs are made operational by specifying the prior moments as follows. The prior means of the regression parameters are set to zero except for the first own lag, which has a prior mean of unity. The prior parameter variances decrease with the lag length, making the prior tighter around zero. The regression parameters on the exogenous variables have a large prior variance, making the prior relatively uninformative on these parameters. The prior covariances are set to zero for simplicity. Finally, the variances are scaled to account for differing variability in the variables. See also Litterman (1986a) for a discussion and motivation of these prior beliefs.

The tightness of the prior distribution, that is, the magnitude of the prior variances, is determined by the three hyperparameters π_1, π_2, and π_3. Where π_1 is the tightness on own lags, π_2 is the tightness on lags of other variables and π_3 is the tightness on lags of exogenous variables. In each case the prior variance of the parameter is proportional to the relevant hyperparameter.

The prior-posterior pairs

For the technical discussion of the prior and posterior distributions the following notation is needed. Write equation (1) as $y_t = z_t \Gamma + u_t$, where $z_t = \{x_t, y_{t-1}, ..., y_{t-p}\}$, $\Gamma = \{C', A_1', ..., A_p'\}'$. Performing the conventional stacking of the row vectors y_t, z_t, and u_t for $t = 1, ..., T$ into Y, Z, and U we have $Y = Z\Gamma + U$. Then, letting the subscript i denote the ith column vector, we can express the equation for each variable as $y_i = Z\gamma_i + u_i$. For y, γ, and u the vectors obtained by stacking the columns of Y, Γ, and U, the system can be written as $y = (I \otimes Z)\gamma + u$. Note that $u \sim N(0, \Psi \otimes I)$. In addition, the tilde denotes parameters of the prior distribution, the bar represents the parameters of the posterior distribution, the OLS estimates of Γ and γ are denoted by $\hat{\Gamma}$ and $\hat{\gamma}$, respectively, and s_i^2, is the residual variance of a p-lag univariate autoregression on variable i.

The Minnesota prior

This is the prior distribution advocated by Litterman (1986a). Each equation is treated separately and the prior beliefs are parameterized as $\gamma_i \sim N(\tilde{\gamma}_i, \tilde{\Sigma}_i)$ with the residual variance, ψ_{ii}, fixed at the value $0.81s_i^2$. The prior variance matrix of the parameters, $\tilde{\Sigma}_i$, is assumed diagonal with diagonal elements

$$0.81\pi_3 s_i^2 \quad \text{for coefficients on exogenous variables}$$

$$\frac{\pi_2 s_i^2}{k s_j^2} \quad \text{for coefficients on lags of variable } j \neq i \tag{2}$$

$$\frac{\pi_1}{k} \quad \text{for coefficients on own lags}$$

where k denotes the lag length.

With normally distributed data this yields the normal posterior distribution $\gamma_i \sim N(\bar{\gamma}_i, \bar{\Sigma}_i)$, with $\bar{\Sigma}_i = (\tilde{\Sigma}_i^{-1} + \psi_{ii}^{-1} Z'Z)^{-1}$ and $\bar{\gamma}_i = \bar{\Sigma}_i(\tilde{\Sigma}_i^{-1}\tilde{\gamma}_i + \psi_{ii}^{-1}Z'y_i)$. Note that this is equivalent to a *multivariate* analysis where the prior distribution of the vectors γ_i is jointly normal with a block-diagonal variance–covariance matrix and *fixed and diagonal* residual variance–covariance matrix.

The researcher using the Minnesota prior is thus claiming knowledge about the residual variance–covariance matrix, while at the same time admitting less than perfect knowledge about the regression parameters in the VAR. We find this to be strange since, in general, it is easier to form an opinion about the regression parameters than about the residual variance–covariance matrix. The assumption that the variance–covariance matrix is known can, to some extent, be justified by the practice of obtaining the diagonal elements from the

368   *Journal of Forecasting*   *Vol. 12, Iss. Nos. 3 & 4*

data. The diagonality assumption is more troublesome, since this rarely is supported by the data. In fact, much of the current controversy over the interpretation of VAR models is centred on the issue of how to achieve a diagonal variance–covariance matrix by transformations of the system of equations (1).

In the remainder of this section we introduce four families of prior distributions which allow for non-diagonal residual variance–covariance matrices. In effect, this takes us from a limited information analysis to a full information analysis of the systems of equations (1) (see Drèze and Richard, 1983, for an overview of these issues in the context of simultaneous-equation systems). In the case of a VAR, the analysis is, however, more straightforward since there are no right-hand side endogenous variables and no *a priori* restrictions on the parameters.

The Normal-Wishart prior[1]

The natural conjugate prior for normal data is the Normal-Wishart where the vector of regression parameters, γ, is normally distributed conditional on the residual variance–covariance matrix Ψ, and Ψ has an inverted Wishart distribution with α degrees of freedom:

$$\gamma \mid \Psi \sim N(\bar{\gamma}, \Psi \otimes (\Omega)), \quad \Psi \sim IW(\bar{\Psi}, \alpha)$$

Integrating out Ψ of the joint prior we have the marginal prior distribution function of the $(pq + r) \times r$ matrix Γ as

$$p(\Gamma) \propto \mid \bar{\Psi} + (\Gamma - \bar{\Gamma})' \bar{\Omega}^{-1} (\Gamma - \bar{\Gamma}) \mid^{-(\alpha + pq + r)/2}$$

A matricvariate t-distribution with α degrees of freedom, $\Gamma \sim MT(\bar{\Omega}^{-1}, \bar{\Psi}, \bar{\Gamma}, \alpha)$, with prior mean and variance $E(\gamma) = \bar{\gamma}$, $\alpha > q$, and $\text{Var}(\gamma) = (\alpha - q - 1)^{-1} \bar{\Psi} \otimes \bar{\Omega}$, $\alpha > q + 1$. The posterior distribution is given by

$$\gamma \mid \Psi, y \sim N(\bar{\gamma}, \Psi \otimes \bar{\Omega}), \quad \Psi \mid y \sim IW(\bar{\Psi}, T + \alpha)$$

where T is the number of observations, $\bar{\Omega} = (\bar{\Omega}^{-1} + Z'Z)^{-1}$, $\bar{\Gamma} = \bar{\Omega}(\bar{\Omega}^{-1}\bar{\Gamma} + Z'Z\hat{\Gamma})$, and $\bar{\Psi} = \hat{\Gamma}'Z'Z\hat{\Gamma} + \bar{\Gamma}'\bar{\Omega}^{-1}\bar{\Gamma} + \bar{\Psi} + (Y - Z\hat{\Gamma})'(Y - Z\hat{\Gamma}) - \bar{\Gamma}'(\bar{\Omega}^{-1} + Z'Z)\bar{\Gamma}$. The marginal posterior distribution of Γ is, of course, matricvariate t, $\Gamma \sim MT(\bar{\Omega}^{-1}, \bar{\Psi}, \bar{\Gamma}, T + \alpha)$. See Zellner (1971) or Drèze and Richard (1983) for a derivation of these results.

The two main shortcomings of the Minnesota prior, the forced independence between equations and the fixed residual variance–covariance matrix, are not present here. On the other hand, the structure of the variance–covariance matrix of γ force us to treat all equations symmetrically.

The prior beliefs are specified as follows. The diagonal elements of $\bar{\Psi}$ are set to

$$\bar{\psi}_{ii} = 0.81(\alpha - q - 1)s_i^2 \tag{3}$$

and the off-diagonal elements are set to zero. The prior marginal expectation of the residual variance–covariance matrix thus coincides with the fixed variance–covariance matrix of the Minnesota prior. The diagonal elements of $\bar{\Omega}$ are then chosen so that the prior variance of γ is $0.81 \pi_3 s_i^2$ for coefficients on exogenous variables and $(\pi_2 s_i^2)/(k s_j^2)$ for the coefficient on lag k of variable j, dependent variable i. Note that the restricted structure of the variance–covariance matrix of γ force us to treat all variables in the same way. As a consequence, the prior variances for own lags differ from the Minnesota prior.

---

[1] Litterman [1980] considered this prior as well as the Minnesota prior but rejected the use of the Normal-Wishart prior on the grounds that it is computationally inconvenient. The calculation of the parameters of the posterior distribution are, however, only marginally more complicated than for the Minnesota prior.

The ith moment of γ exists if $v - q \geq i$ for v the degrees of freedom of the marginal matricvariate t-distribution. For forecasts m periods ahead the mth posterior moment is needed. In addition, the moment of order $2m$ is required for the variance of the forecast. The prior is specified in terms of means and variances of the regression parameters and the prior second moment is needed. That is, $\alpha - q \geq 2$ is needed for specifying the prior and $T + \alpha - q \geq 2m$ is required for forecasting. The prior degrees of freedom are set to

$$\alpha = \max\{q + 2, q + 2m - T\} \tag{4}$$

The diffuse (Jeffreys') prior
The diffuse prior, proposed by Geisser (1965) and Tiao and Zellner (1964), is closely related to the Normal-Wishart in the sense that the posterior distribution is of the same form. Consequently, the posterior variance–covariance matrix of γ suffers from the same restrictions as with the Normal-Wishart prior. Reflecting ignorance about the regression parameters, we have the prior distribution

$$p(\gamma, \Psi) \propto |\Psi|^{-(q+1)/2}$$

The posterior distribution is obtained as

$$\gamma \mid \Psi, y \sim N(\hat{\gamma}, \Psi \otimes (\mathbf{Z'Z})^{-1}), \quad \Psi \mid y \sim IW(\mathbf{Y} - \mathbf{Z}\hat{\Gamma})'(\mathbf{Y} - \mathbf{Z}\hat{\Gamma}), \ T - pq - r)$$

with the marginal posterior distribution of Γ as matricvariate t,

$$\Gamma \sim MT(\mathbf{Z'Z}, (\mathbf{Y} - \mathbf{Z}\hat{\Gamma})'(\mathbf{Y} - \mathbf{Z}\hat{\Gamma}), \hat{\Gamma}, \ T - pq - r).$$

Note that we have $E(\Gamma \mid y) = \hat{\Gamma}$ and $\mathrm{Var}(\gamma \mid y) = (T - pq - r - q - 1)^{-1}(\mathbf{Y} - \mathbf{Z}\hat{\Gamma})'(\mathbf{Y} - \mathbf{Z}\hat{\Gamma}) \otimes (\mathbf{Z'Z})^{-1}$. That is, the posterior moments are similar to what we obtain from Zellner's classical SUR estimator.

The Normal-Diffuse prior
This prior avoids the restrictions on the variance–covariance matrix of γ and still allows for a non-diagonal residual variance–covariance matrix. The multivariate normal prior on the regression parameters of the Minnesota prior is combined with the diffuse prior on the residual variance–covariance matrix. That is, we have prior independence between γ and Ψ with

$$\gamma \sim N(\tilde{\gamma}, \tilde{\Sigma}), \quad p(\Psi) \propto |\Psi|^{-(q+1)/2}$$

This also allows the researcher to specify prior dependence between parameters of different equations. The marginal posterior of the parameters is proportional to the product of the marginal prior distribution and a matricvariate t-distribution. The matricvariate t-factor will give rise to posterior dependence between the equations even if the prior is specified with a diagonal or block-diagonal variance–covariance matrix. The matricvariate t-factor is identical to the posterior associated with the Diffuse prior. The form of the marginal posterior is troublesome in the sense that large differences between the information contained in the prior and in the likelihood function might cause the posterior to be bimodal, and thus the posterior mean to have low posterior probability. In the forecasting exercises the diagonal elements of $\tilde{\Sigma}$ are set as in equation (2) and the off-diagonal elements are set to zero.

The Extended Natural Conjugate prior
The Extended Natural Conjugate (ENC) prior overcomes the restrictions on $\mathrm{Var}(\gamma)$ of the Normal-Wishart prior by reparameterizing the VAR in equation (1). Let Δ be a $q(pq + r) \times q$

370   *Journal of Forecasting*   *Vol. 12, Iss. Nos. 3 & 4*

matrix with the columns γ_i on the diagonal and all other elements zero, that is,

$$\Delta = \begin{pmatrix} \gamma_1 & 0 & \cdots & 0 \\ 0 & \gamma_2 & & \vdots \\ \vdots & & \ddots & 0 \\ 0 & \cdots & 0 & \gamma_q \end{pmatrix}$$

Also let $\Xi = \iota' \otimes Z$, where ι is a $q \times 1$ vector of ones. Equation (1) can then be rewritten as $Y = \Xi\Delta + U$. For the prior distribution

$$p(\Delta) \propto |\tilde{\Psi} + (\Delta - \tilde{\Delta})'\tilde{M}(\Delta - \tilde{\Delta})|^{-\alpha/2}$$
$$\Psi \mid \Delta \sim IW(\tilde{\Psi} + (\Delta - \tilde{\Delta})'\tilde{M}(\Delta - \tilde{\Delta}), \alpha)$$

and normal data, the posterior distribution for this prior is given by Drèze and Morales (1976) as

$$p(\Delta \mid y) \propto |\bar{\Psi} + (\Delta - \bar{\Delta})'\bar{M}(\Delta - \bar{\Delta})|^{-(T+\alpha)/2}$$
$$\Psi \mid \Delta, y \sim IW(\bar{\Psi} + (\Delta - \bar{\Delta})'\bar{M}(\Delta - \bar{\Delta}), T + \alpha)$$

where $\bar{M} = \tilde{M} + \Xi'\Xi$, $\bar{\Psi} = \tilde{\Psi} + \tilde{\Delta}'\tilde{M}\tilde{\Delta} + Y'Y - \bar{\Delta}'\bar{M}\bar{\Delta}$ and $\bar{\Delta}$ is the solution to $\bar{M}\bar{\Delta} = \tilde{M}\tilde{\Delta} + \Xi'Y$. If $\tilde{M}$ is of full rank, $\bar{M}$ will be of full rank and $\bar{\Delta}$ is unique.

The marginal distribution of Δ has the form of a matricvariate t density. However, due to the restricted structure of Δ it is *not* matricvariate t.

When parameterizing the prior beliefs, the following fact (Drèze and Richard, 1983) is used. If $\tilde{\Psi}$ is diagonal, $\tilde{M}$ is block diagonal and $\tilde{\Delta}$ has the same structure as Δ, then the prior distribution of γ factors into independent multivariate t priors with $\alpha - pq - r$ degrees of freedom for the parameters of each equation.

The diagonal elements of $\tilde{\Psi}$ are set as in equation (3) and the off-diagonal elements are set to zero. The prior expectation of Ψ conditional on $\Delta = \tilde{\Delta}$ then coincides with the fixed variance–covariance matrix of the Minnesota prior. From the independent multivariate t's we have

$$\text{Var}(\gamma_i) = \frac{\tilde{\psi}_{ii}}{\alpha - pq - r - 2} \tilde{M}_{ii}^{-1}$$

and the diagonal elements of $\tilde{M}_{ii}$ are chosen such that the prior variances of γ_i are as in equation (2) with the off-diagonal elements zero. A sufficient condition for the existence of the ith moment of γ is given by Drèze and Richard (1983) as $\alpha - q - pq - r \geqslant i$. Consequently, the prior degrees of freedom are set to $\alpha = \max\{2 + q + pq + r, 2m + q + pq + r - T\}$.

The main disadvantage of the Normal-Diffuse and ENC priors is that no closed-form solutions exists for the posterior expectation and variance of γ and they must be evaluated numerically.

FORECASTS

In applications of the Minnesota prior, forecasts are generated using the posterior parameter means and the chain rule of forecasting. The implied loss function behind this approach is the sum of the squared errors for the parameters of the VAR. The chain rule will also be used for the OLS forecasts that are generated for comparative purposes.

For the other posterior distributions presented above, forecasts will be generated using a procedure suggested by Chow (1973). The loss function here is the sum of the squared forecast errors. Consequently the posterior risk is minimized by setting the forecast to the posterior expectation of the forecasted variables. Rewriting equation (1) as a first-order system $\mathbf{y}_t^* = \mathbf{y}_{t-1}^* \mathbf{A} + \mathbf{x}_t \mathbf{D} + \mathbf{u}_t^*$, where $\mathbf{y}_t^* = \{y_t, ..., y_{t-p+1}\}$, $\mathbf{D} = \{\mathbf{C}, \mathbf{0}, ..., \mathbf{0}\}$, $\mathbf{u}_t^* = \{u_t, 0, ..., 0\}$ and

$$
\mathbf{A} = \begin{pmatrix}
\mathbf{A}_1 & \mathbf{I} & \mathbf{0} & \cdots & \mathbf{0} \\
\mathbf{A}_2 & \mathbf{0} & \mathbf{I} & & \vdots \\
\vdots & & & \ddots & \mathbf{I} \\
\mathbf{A}_p & & \vdots & & \mathbf{0}
\end{pmatrix}
$$

The forecasts up to h periods ahead, conditional on γ, is then given by $\mathbf{y}_t^*(h) \mid \gamma = \mathbf{y}_t^* \mathbf{A}^h + \sum_{i=0}^{h-1} \mathbf{x}_{t+h-i} \mathbf{D} \mathbf{A}^i$. The expectation under the posterior distribution is then obtained as the integral

$$
\mathbf{y}_t^*(h) = \int \mathbf{y}_t^* \mathbf{A}^h p(\gamma \mid \mathbf{y}) \, d\gamma + \int \sum_{i=0}^{h-1} \mathbf{x}_{t+h-i} \mathbf{D} \mathbf{A}^i p(\gamma \mid \mathbf{y}) \, d\gamma \tag{5}
$$

Since no closed forms are readily available for the integral in equation (5), it is evaluated numerically.

MONTE CARLO INTEGRATION

Following Kloek and van Dijk (1978), we have chosen to evaluate equation (5) using Monte Carlo integration instead of standard numerical integration techniques.[2] Standard numerical integration is relatively inefficient when the integral has a high dimensionality and we expect to achieve greater precision with a lower computational effort using Monte Carlo integration. An additional benefit is that with Monte Carlo integration probabilistic error bounds are readily available.

For the priors that yield a matricvariate t posterior the procedure is straightforward since draws can be generated directly from the matricvariate t distribution and the integral in equation (5) is estimated as the sample mean of the forecasts. For the other posteriors importance sampling is used, that is, the posterior distribution is approximated by a distribution from which it is known how to generate random numbers. The forecasts calculated from each draw are then weighted by the ratio of the kernel of the posterior and the kernel of the importance function at the draw and the integral is estimated by the weighted mean.

For the ENC posterior the importance function is constructed according to a suggestion of Bauwens (1984). The importance function is the product of independent multivariate t-distribution functions, each approximating the marginal distribution of the parameters of one of the equations. For the Normal-Diffuse posterior, the 2-0 poly t-distribution (Drèze, 1977) is used as the importance function.

Antithetic variates are used in all cases to further reduce the sampling error (see Geweke, 1988, for an example of the effect of antithetic variates in applications like these). Karlsson (1989) gives a full account of the methods used here.

FORECASTING EXPERIMENTS

Three forecasting experiments were conducted in order to assess the performance of the five methods of parameterizing the prior beliefs. The experiments are selected to reflect real-life

---

[2] Other alternatives are the Gibbs sampler and Laplace approximation. For the purpose of this paper we have, however, only considered the use of Monte Carlo integration.

Table I. Hyperparameters of the prior distribution

| | Experiment | | |
| | Canadian data | | US wheat |
Parameter	Small sample	Large sample	export data
π_1	0.07	0.07	0.07
π_2	0.007	0.007	0.007
π_3	$1.4 \cdot 10^5$	$1.4 \cdot 10^5$	$1.4 \cdot 10^5$
α			
(degrees of	9	4	6
freedom)[a]	21	16	19

[a] First row is the Normal-Wishart prior and second is the ENC prior.

situations in which VARs are used. In the experiments part of the data are set aside and the models are fitted to the rest of the data. Forecasts are then generated for the time periods that were set aside. The hyperparameters π_1, π_2, and π_3 were somewhat arbitrarily set to the values in Table I. They are close to the values that Litterman (1986b) and Doan *et al.* (1984) found to work well for the Minnesota prior.

The first two experiments use data on Canadian money and GNP from the first quarter of 1955 to the last quarter of 1977. As is evident from Figure 1, this data set displays very little variation around the trend and should be relatively easy to forecast. The data were obtained from Hsiao (1979) and has also been analysed by Lütkepohl (1982). As indicated in the introduction, we do not consider the issue of model identification. Instead, the model selected by Lütkepohl for the logarithm of nominal *GNP* and the logarithm of *M2* is used with minor modifications. The Normal-Wishart and Diffuse priors require that we have the same right-hand side variables in all equations and the maximum lag length selected by Lütkepohl is used for both variables. In addition, a time trend is included. The right-hand side variables are thus the same in both equations, five lags of log *GNP* and log *M2*, a constant term and a time trend. In both experiments forecasts are made 12 periods (three years) ahead, starting with forecasts made as of the first quarter of 1970.

For the first experiment a subset of the data was used in order to mirror situations where few data are available. Ten sets of forecasts were made and the first set was based on 17 observations and the last set on 26 observations. In this experiment forecasts were not generated from the diffuse posterior since they had no moments for the longer lead times. The

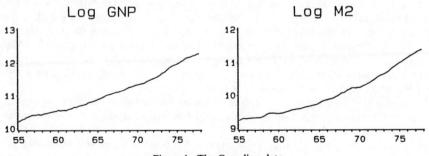

Figure 1. The Canadian data

Table II. Root mean square error, forecasts of Canadian money and GNP, small sample

Variable	Lead time	OLS	Minnesota	Method Normal-Wishart	ENC	Normal-Diffuse
Log *GNP*	1	0.0166[b]	0.0096[a]	0.0099	0.0098	0.0096[a]
	2	0.0270[b]	0.0154	0.0155	0.0153	0.0152[a]
	3	0.0396[b]	0.0272	0.0263[a]	0.0265	0.0266
	4	0.0495[b]	0.0384	0.0371	0.0370[a]	0.0372
	6	0.0736[b]	0.0665[b]	0.0640	0.0635[a]	0.0641[b]
	8	0.1091[b]	0.1050[b]	0.1028	0.1023[a]	0.1028[b]
	10	0.1456	0.1396[b]	0.1408	0.1392	0.1388[a]
	12	0.1831[b]	0.1696[a]	0.1772	0.1734	0.1715
Sum	1–12	1.0870[b]	0.9854[b]	0.9860[b]	0.9749	0.9739[a]
Log *M2*	1	0.0231[b]	0.0104	0.0122[b]	0.0103[a]	0.0103[a]
	2	0.0506[b]	0.0205	0.0241[b]	0.0199[a]	0.0199[a]
	3	0.0719[b]	0.0298	0.0353[b]	0.0289	0.0286[a]
	4	0.0930[b]	0.0390	0.0460[b]	0.0380	0.0371[a]
	6	0.0981[b]	0.0598	0.0669	0.0598	0.0578[a]
	8	0.1244[b]	0.0920[a]	0.0965	0.0930	0.0922
	10	0.1624	0.1213[a]	0.1262	0.1254	0.1249
	12	0.1965[b]	0.1483[a]	0.1564	0.1579	0.1556
Sum	1–12	1.3494[b]	0.8880[a]	0.9537	0.9083	0.8966

[a] The best result for each lead time.
[b] RMSE which differs significantly from the best at the 5% level.

Root Mean Squared Errors of these forecasts are in Table II. We also report those instances when a RMSE differ significantly, at the 5% level, from the lowest RMSE for that lead time.

The significance tests reported in Table II use the procedure of Ashley *et al.* 1980. Note that this procedure tests a sufficient but not necessary condition for the equality of two RMSEs. The test situation is equivalent to testing the joint null of equal variance and squared mean of the forecast errors against the alternative that the differences are both positive. Clearly this differ from testing the necessary condition that the sum of the differences in variance and squared mean is zero. Consequently, the test will fail to reject the null for large differences in the RMSE when, say, the difference in squared mean is significantly negative but partly offset by a large positive difference in variance.

The ENC and Normal-Diffuse priors do best for log *GNP* and the Minnesota and Normal-Diffuse priors do best for log *M2*. The RMSE for OLS is significantly worse than the best RMSE for most of the lead times. It is clear that the introduction of prior information improves the forecasts in this experiment. The Minnesota prior gives the lowest RMSE for several lead times but in no case does this differ significantly from the RMSE of the more general prior distributions. The Minnesota prior is, on the other hand, significantly worse than the ENC or Normal-Diffuse prior in four cases.

In the second experiment the full data set was used and 20 sets of forecasts were made. The first set of forecasts was based on 56 observations and the last set on 75 observations. RMSEs of the forecasts are in Table III.

In this case, the likelihood function dominates the posteriors and the differences between forecasts is small. We do, however, find that the Normal-Diffuse prior does best for log *GNP*

Table III. Root mean square error, forecasts of Canadian money and GNP, large sample

Variable	Lead time	OLS	Minnesota	Normal-Wishart	ENC	Normal-Diffuse	Diffuse
Log *GNP*	1	0.0141	0.0132	0.0131[a]	0.0132	0.0132	0.0141
	2	0.0239	0.0225[a]	0.0228	0.0229	0.0225[a]	0.0239
	3	0.0324	0.0307	0.0314	0.0314	0.0306[a]	0.0324
	4	0.0424[b]	0.0394	0.0403	0.0398	0.0393[a]	0.0425[b]
	6	0.0595[b]	0.0548	0.0561[b]	0.0550	0.0546[a]	0.0600[b]
	8	0.0776[b]	0.0718	0.0747	0.0724	0.0716[a]	0.0783[b]
	10	0.1019[b]	0.0959	0.1004	0.0958	0.0957[a]	0.1034[b]
	12	0.1296[b]	0.1231	0.1293	0.1217[a]	0.1232	0.1328[b]
Sum	1–12	0.8054[b]	0.7540	0.7825	0.7547	0.7527[a]	0.8155[b]
Log *M2*	1	0.0120	0.0105[a]	0.0116	0.0112[b]	0.0105[a]	0.0120[b]
	2	0.0238[b]	0.0218	0.0234	0.0225	0.0217[a]	0.0238[b]
	3	0.0334	0.0325	0.0344	0.0333	0.0324[a]	0.0333
	4	0.0433[b]	0.0439	0.0454	0.0441	0.0436	0.0431[a]
	6	0.0616[b]	0.0652	0.0661	0.0642[b]	0.0644	0.0610[a]
	8	0.0799	0.0855[b]	0.0871[b]	0.0840	0.0842[b]	0.0793[a]
	10	0.0996	0.1062[b]	0.1089[b]	0.1039	0.1042[b]	0.0993[a]
	12	0.1252[a]	0.1322[b]	0.1358[b]	0.1275	0.1295[b]	0.1258
Sum	1–12	0.8033	0.8421[b]	0.8646[b]	0.8280	0.8294[b]	0.8007[a]

[a,b] As Table II.

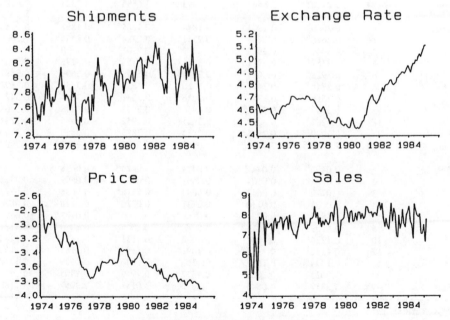

Figure 2. The US wheat export data

Table IV. Root mean square error, forecasts of US wheat export data

Variable	Lead time	OLS	Minnesota	Method Normal-Wishart	ENC	Normal-Diffuse	Diffuse
SALE	1	0.4380	0.4091	0.4288[b]	0.4061	0.4067	0.4380
	2	0.5014	0.4989	0.5143	0.4903[a]	0.4956	0.5015
	3	0.4820[a]	0.4949	0.4933[b]	0.4881	0.4942	0.4829
	4	0.5071[a]	0.5125	0.5339[b]	0.5095	0.5099	0.5081
	6	0.4857	0.4814[b]	0.4925[b]	0.4822[b]	0.4796[a]	0.4839
	8	0.4790[b]	0.4810	0.4953[b]	0.4867	0.4806	0.4769[a]
	10	0.4838	0.4814	0.4708[a]	0.4801	0.4824	0.4828
	12	0.4847[b]	0.4811	0.4768[a]	0.4804	0.4827	0.4887
	18	0.4964	0.4933	0.4922	0.4908[a]	0.4946	0.4991[b]
	24	0.5522[b]	0.5458[b]	0.5564	0.5424[a]	0.5477[b]	0.5594[b]
Sum	1–24	12.029	11.993	12.117	11.955[a]	12.099	12.085
EXCH	1	0.0270	0.0268	0.0269	0.0266[a]	0.0267	0.0270
	2	0.0440	0.0439	0.0440[b]	0.0435[a]	0.0437	0.0439
	3	0.0612[b]	0.0618	0.0615[b]	0.0612	0.0618	0.0610[a]
	4	0.0771[b]	0.0785	0.0774[b]	0.0776	0.0786	0.0768[a]
	6	0.1001	0.1035	0.1009	0.1023	0.1038	0.0996[a]
	8	0.1142	0.1192	0.1145	0.1171	0.1191	0.1128[a]
	10	0.1267	0.1328	0.1253	0.1296	0.1318	0.1234[a]
	12	0.1428	0.1482	0.1377	0.1427	0.1457	0.1370[a]
	18	0.2185	0.2186	0.2026[a]	0.2071	0.2107	0.2052
	24	0.2896	0.2825	0.2561[a]	0.2611	0.2656	0.2639[b]
Sum	1–24	3.8190[b]	3.8487[b]	3.5893[a]	3.6685	3.7328[b]	3.6183
SHIP	1	0.2060[b]	0.1901[b]	0.1844[a]	0.1865[b]	0.1891[b]	0.2060[b]
	2	0.2616[b]	0.2468[b]	0.2331[a]	0.2384[b]	0.2455[b]	0.2609[b]
	3	0.3040[b]	0.2922[b]	0.2739[a]	0.2801[b]	0.2900[b]	0.3035[b]
	4	0.3487[b]	0.3311[b]	0.3143[a]	0.3154[b]	0.3276[b]	0.3468[b]
	6	0.3928[b]	0.3673[b]	0.3544[b]	0.3458[a]	0.3608[b]	0.3897[b]
	8	0.3748[b]	0.3467[b]	0.3320	0.3232[a]	0.3386[b]	0.3692[b]
	10	0.3519[b]	0.3246[b]	0.3036	0.3031[a]	0.3154[b]	0.3429[b]
	12	0.3393[b]	0.3141[b]	0.2916[a]	0.2943	0.3048[b]	0.3308[b]
	18	0.3282[b]	0.3054	0.3011	0.2952[a]	0.2986[b]	0.3234[b]
	24	0.3009[b]	0.2876[b]	0.2851	0.2825[a]	0.2850	0.3006[b]
Sum	1–24	7.8956[b]	7.3723[b]	7.0953	7.0341[a]	7.2313[b]	7.7993[b]
PRICE	1	0.0490[b]	0.0441	0.0434	0.0424[a]	0.0438	0.0490[b]
	2	0.0721[b]	0.0604	0.0592	0.0570[a]	0.0599	0.0722[b]
	3	0.0772	0.0641	0.0644	0.0618[a]	0.0636	0.0773[b]
	4	0.0845	0.0730	0.0731	0.0726[a]	0.0728	0.0850[b]
	6	0.0883[b]	0.0785[b]	0.0769[b]	0.0800[b]	0.0783[b]	0.0892[b]
	8	0.1109[b]	0.1016[b]	0.0988[a]	0.1015	0.1010[b]	0.1121[b]
	10	0.1226[b]	0.1132[b]	0.1082[a]	0.1131	0.1121[b]	0.1240
	12	0.1252[b]	0.1184[b]	0.1091[a]	0.1182	0.1161[b]	0.1262
	18	0.1724[b]	0.1691	0.1568[a]	0.1640	0.1629	0.1712[b]
	24	0.2025[b]	0.2026	0.1817[a]	0.1919	0.1905	0.1959[b]
Sum	1–24	3.2317	3.0845	2.8872[a]	3.0151	2.9957	3.2182[b]

[a,b] As Table II.

and that the Diffuse prior does best for log $M2$. For log GNP, the RMSEs of OLS and the Diffuse prior are significantly worse than the best (Normal-Diffuse) for most lead times. For log $M2$, on the other hand, the Diffuse prior is significantly better than the other methods at several lead times. The evidence on the value of the prior information is thus somewhat mixed in this case. The priors which allow for dependence between the equations tend to do better than OLS and the Minnesota prior—just as for the smaller data set.

The third experiment use a data set and model from Bessler and Babula (1987) (Figure 2). This data set is considerably more noisy than the Canadian data and is thus a tougher test for the forecasting methods. The VAR consists of the following variables: US export shipments of wheat (*SHIP*), an exchange rate index for the US dollar (*EXCH*), the dollar price of wheat (*PRICE*), and US export sales of wheat (*SALE*). Seasonally adjusted logarithms of monthly data for January 1974 to March of 1985 are used. The right-hand variables are three lags of each variable and a constant term. For this experiment 30 sets of forecasts 24 periods (two years) ahead were made, with the first set of forecasts made as of October 1980. The RMSEs for these forecasts are in Table IV.

For the wheat export data, the Normal-Wishart and ENC priors do best overall. For the individual variables, the ENC prior does best for the sales variable, the Diffuse and Normal-Diffuse priors do best for the exchange rate variable, the ENC prior does best for the shipment variable, and the Normal-Wishart prior does best for the price variable. The significance tests does not provide a clear picture for the sales and exchange-rate variables. For the shipments and price variables the Normal-Diffuse and ENC priors clearly dominates the other methods. This forecasting experiment thus lends further support for the use of prior information and prior distributions which allow for dependencies between equations.

In addition to the RMSE, the mean absolute percentage error, mean error, and the log determinant of the forecast error variance–covariance matrix were also calculated. These measures are reported in Karlsson (1989) and the pattern is similar to the one displayed by the RMSE.

CONCLUSIONS

Methods for Bayesian analysis of Vector Autoregressions that allow for dependencies between equations are suggested. When evaluated based on the forecast performance several of the methods suggested here do better than the frequently used Minnesota prior. In no case does the Minnesota prior provide forecasts that are significantly better than the more general prior distributions.

The forecasting experiments indicate that the ability to take account of dependencies between parameters of different equations is an important factor in determining the forecast performance of a statistical model. Since such dependencies most certainly are not a phenomena peculiar to the data sets analysed here, the methods suggested in this paper should be of value in many other applications as well.

In as much as the forecast performance is indicative of the goodness of the fit of a model, the results obtained here should carry over to situations where forecasting is not the main issue. Specifically, the use of prior specifications that allow for dependence between equations should prove profitable also when inference about the parameters of the VAR or functions of the parameters, such as impulse response functions or variance decompositions, is the key concern. The Normal-Wishart and Diffuse priors are especially suitable in this context, since analytic expressions for the first and second posterior moments of the parameters are available.

K. R. Kadiyala and S. Karlsson   *Generalized Bayesian Vector Autoregressions*   377

ACKNOWLEDGEMENTS

Earlier versions of this paper have been presented at the Joint Statistical Meetings in Washington, DC, 1989, at the 13th Nordic Conference in Mathematical Statistics, Odense, 1989, at FIEF and at Uppsala University. We have benefited from comments by participants in these seminars. In particular, we would like to thank Jerry Thursby, Sheng Hu, John Carlson, Erik Ruist, and P.-O. Edlund. The second author wishes to acknowledge the support of the Royal Swedish Academy of Sciences and the Swedish Research Council for Humanities and Social Sciences (HSFR).

REFERENCES

Ashley, R., Granger, C. W. J. and Schmalensee, R., 'Advertising and aggregate consumption: an analysis of causality', *Econometrica*, **48** (1980), 1149–67.

Bauwens, L., *Bayesian Full Information Analysis of Simultaneous Equation Models Using Integration by Monte Carlo*, Berlin: Springer-Verlag, 1984.

Bessler, D. A. and Babula, R. A., 'Forecasting wheat exports: do exchange rates matter?' *Journal of Business & Economic Statistics*, **5** (1987), New York: 397–406.

Broemeling, L. D., *Bayesian Analysis of Linear Models*, New York: Marcel Dekker, 1985.

Chow, G. C., 'Multiperiod predictions from stochastic difference equations by Bayesian methods', *Econometrica*, **41** (1973), 109–18, 796. Reprinted in Feinberg and Zellner (eds), *Studies in Bayesian Econometrics and Statistics in Honor of Leonard J. Savage*, Amsterdam: North-Holland, 1975.

Doan, T., Litterman, R. and Sims, C., 'Forecasting and conditional projection using realistic prior distributions', (with discussion), *Econometric Reviews*, **3** (1984), 1–144.

Drèze, J. H., 'Bayesian regression analysis using poly *t*-densities', *Journal of Econometrics*, **6** (1977), 329–54.

Drèze, J. H. and Morales, J.-A., 'Bayesian full information analysis of simultaneous equations', *Journal of the American Statistical Association*, **71** (1976), 919–23. Reprinted in A. Zellner (ed). *Bayesian Analysis in Econometrics and Statistics*, Amsterdam: North-Holland, 1980.

Drèze, J. H. and Richard, J.-F., 'Bayesian analysis of simultaneous equation systems', in Z. Griliches and M. D. Intrilligator (eds), *Handbook of Econometrics*, Vol. I, Amsterdam: 1983.

Edlund, P.-O. and Karlsson, S., 'Forecasting the Swedish unemployment rate: VAR vs. transfer function modelling', *International Journal of Forecasting*, **9** (1993), forthcoming.

Geisser, S., 'Bayesian estimation in multivariate analysis', *Annals of Mathematical Statistics*, **36** (1965), 150–59.

Geweke, J., 'Antithetic acceleration of Monte Carlo integration in Bayesian inference', *Journal of Econometrics*, **38** (1988), 73–89.

Hsiao, C., 'Autoregressive modelling of Canadian money and income data', *Journal of the American Statistical Association*, **74** (1979), 553–60.

Karlsson, S., *Bayesian Analysis of Vector Autoregressions*, Unpublished doctoral dissertation, Purdue University, 1989.

Kling, J. L. and Bessler, D. A. 'A comparison of multivariate forecasting procedures for economic time series', *International Journal of Forecasting*, **1** (1985), 5–24.

Kloek, T. and van Dijk, H., 'Bayesian estimates of equation system parameters: an application of integration by Monte Carlo', *Econometrica*, **46** (1978), 1–19. Reprinted in A. Zellner (ed.), *Bayesian Analysis in Econometrics and Statistics*, Amsterdam: North-Holland, 1980.

Litterman, R. B., 'A Bayesian procedure for forecasting with vector autoregressions', mimeo, Massachusetts Institute of Technology, 1980.

Litterman, R. B., 'Forecasting with Bayesian vector autoregressions—five years of experience', *Journal of Business & Economic Statistics*, **4**, (1986a), 25–38.

Litterman, R. B., 'Specifying vector autoregressions for macro economic forecasting', in P. Goel and A. Zellner (eds), *Bayesian Inference and Decision Techniques*, Amsterdam: Elsevier Science, pp. 79–94, 1986b.

Lütkepohl, H., 'Differencing multiple time series: another look at Canadian money and income data', *Journal of Time Series Analysis*, **3** (1982), 235–43.

Sims, C. A., 'Macroeconomics and reality', *Econometrica*, **48** (1980), 1–48.

Tiao, G. C. and Zellner, A., 'On the Bayesian estimation of multivariate regression', *Journal of the Royal Statistical Society Ser. B*, **26** (1964), 389–99.

Zellner, A., *An Introduction to Bayesian Inference in Econometrics*, New York: John Wiley, 1971.

Authors' biographies:
K. Rao Kadiyala is Professor of Economics in the Krannert Graduate School of Management, Purdue University. He received his BSc(Hons) from Andhra University, India, MStat from the Indian Statistical Institute, India, and PhD from the University of Minnesota. He was on the faculties of the Indian Statistical Institute, Wayne State University, the University of Western Ontario, and San José State University.

Sune Karlsson is Assistant Professor of Economic Statistics at the Stockholm School of Economics. He holds a BSc in Statistics from the University of Uppsala and a PhD in Economics from Purdue University.

Authors' addresses:
K. Rao Kadiyala, Krannert Graduate School of Management, Purdue University, West Lafayette, IN 47907, USA.

Sune Karlsson, Department of Economic Statistics, Stockholm School of Economics, Box 6501, 11383, Stockholm, Sweden.

[18]

Journal of Forecasting, Vol. 13, 1–9 (1994)

Forecasting from Non-linear Models in Practice

JIN-LUNG LIN AND C. W. J. GRANGER
University of California, San Diego, U.S.A.

ABSTRACT

If a simple non-linear autoregressive time-series model is suggested for a series, it is not straightforward to produce multi-step forecasts from it. Several alternative theoretical approaches are discussed and then compared with a simulation study only for the two-step case. It is suggested that fitting a new model for each forecast horizon may be a satisfactory strategy.

KEY WORDS   Non-linear models   multi-step forecasts   bootstrap estimates

INTRODUCTION

There is growing attention being paid to non-linear time-series models and their use with real data (see, for example, Tong, 1990, for univariate models, Granger and Teräsvirta, 1993, for single-output, multiple-input cases, and Granger, 1991, for a discussion of the use of switching-regime models with stock market prices. A natural question arises as to how these models can be used for forecasting, both single- and multi-step. It will be seen that there are a number of practical problems such as choosing between a parametric model or a non-parametric one and, if the latter, what non-parametric estimate to use. Various techniques can be used to tackle these problems. This paper briefly discusses these approaches and presents the results of a simulation study to compare them. The theoretical properties of the methods have been discussed by Brown and Mariano (1989)—henceforth denoted BM. They obtain expressions in large samples for the bias and variance of forecast errors using parametric models. Here, some of their results are extended to non-parametric models.

ALTERNATIVE TECHNIQUES

For ease of exposition, the following simple data-generating model will be considered:

$$y_t = f(y_{t-1}, \alpha) + \varepsilon_t \tag{1}$$

where ε_t is a zero-mean, independent, and identically distributed sequence, with distribution D. The parameters α of the model have to be estimated. The methods to be discussed can be

0277–6693/94/010001–09$09.50
© 1994 by John Wiley & Sons, Ltd.

Received February 1992
Revised April 1993

extended in straightforward ways to more general, realistic cases, with more lags of the dependent variable, with other explanatory variables and with heteroscedasticity. Some of these generalizations are considered by BM.

The optimum one-step, least-squares forecast is

$$g_{t,1} = E[y_{t+1} \mid y_{t-j}, j \geqslant 0] = f(y_t, \alpha) \tag{2}$$

in the case when the function $f(\ )$ is known and from asymptotic considerations it is reasonable to replace α with $\hat{\alpha}$. Of course, in practice, $f(\ )$ is not known and has to be approximated by some specification search procedure, using a specific function form, a flexible parametric class of models (such as neural nets), or a non-parametric model, as discussed below. The problems arising here are common to the modelling process and are not specific to forecasting. More interesting questions arise when two-step forecasts are considered. Now the optimum two-step forecast, based on the information set I_t: $y_{t-j}, j \geqslant 0$, is

$$\begin{aligned} g_{t,2} &= E[y_{t+2} \mid I_t] = E[f(y_{t+1}, \alpha) \mid I_t] \\ &= E[f[f(y_t, \alpha) + \varepsilon_{t+1}] \mid I_t] \\ &= E[f(g_{t,1} + \varepsilon_{t+1})] \end{aligned} \tag{3}$$

where the last expectation is with respect to D, the distribution of ε. In practice, the specification of f is generally not known, any parameters α have to be estimated and also D is not known. Five alternative approaches are considered, and the first four were also discussed by BM (their names for the techniques are given in parentheses) namely, (1) naive (deterministic), (2) optimal (closed form), (3) Monte Carlo, (4) bootstrap (residual based), and (5) direct modelling. The details and practical properties of the techniques are as follows.

(1) Naive

$$g^n_{t,2} = f(g_{t,1}, \hat{\alpha})$$

so that ε_{t+1} is put only to its mean value of zero at each time. As the expected value of a function is generally not equal to the function of the expected value, the forecast will usually be biased. The direction of the bias will depend on whether the function is convex or concave, as discussed in Granger and Newbold (1976). BM shows that even if $f(\ )$ is known, the bias will be $O(1)$, and so will not go to zero as the sample size, n, becomes large. Although this forecast is widely used and is very easy to implement, it is unlikely to be satisfactory.

(2) Closed form

$$g^c_{t,2} = \int f((g_{t,1} + \varepsilon), \hat{\alpha}) \, dF(\varepsilon)$$

where $F(\ )$ is the distribution function of D. The integral is solved either analytically or numerically. It is clearly important here to know D, which is rarely true in practice. BM assumes D is normal, $N(0,1)$ but this assumption should be tested before use. The forecast is not easily found and may be based on an incorrect assumption. The calculation has to be repeated for each value of $g_{t,1}$.

(3) Monte Carlo

$$g^m_{t,2} = \frac{1}{N} \sum_{j=1}^{N} f(g_{t,1} + e_j)$$

where the sequence e_j is iid and chosen from D. This is a particular form of numerical integration based on simulations. If N is large enough, this forecast has the same disadvantage of the previous one, of needing to know D, but is easier to use. Again, the calculation has to be repeated for each $g_{t,1}$.

(4) Bootstrap

$$g_{t,2}^b = \frac{1}{t} \sum_{k=1}^{t} f(g_{t,1} + \hat{\varepsilon}_k)$$

where $\hat{\varepsilon}_k = y_k - g_{k-1,1}$, $k = 1, \ldots, t$ are the realized one-step forecast errors arising up to time t. The obvious advantage of the bootstrap is that no assumption is needed about D, the forecast is easily formed and should improve as time advances. BM shows that with sample size, n, the bootstrap has a bias $O(n^{-1})$, as do methods 2 and 3 when D is known. They also suggest that the variance of the forecast errors in each case equals the optimum (or true) variance plus a $O(n^{-1})$ term, when f and D are known.

(5) Direct method
In practice, $f(\ )$ is rarely known and has to be approximated by a model from a specification search. The previous methods all involve $f(f(\ ))$ when forming two-step forecasts and so the approximation is used sequentially, which may decrease its quality. An alternative is to directly model the relationship between y_{t+2} and y_t, using the same model search as before, and estimating the new set of coefficients directly. Thus, if

$$\hat{g}_{t,1} = \hat{f}(y_t, \hat{\alpha})$$

a specification of the form

$$\hat{g}_{t,2} = \hat{f}(y_t, \hat{\beta})$$

could be considered. This would be sensible if the model search was over a sufficiently flexible form, such as non-parametric or neural nets. Estimation of parameters may be inefficient as the two-step forecast errors will generally not be white noise. The technique is easy to use and does not have to be estimated for each $g_{t,1}$ unless parameter estimates are updated with each piece of new data.

SIMULATIONS WHEN THE TRUE MODEL IS NOT KNOWN

In the simulations reported below, two approximations to the true function $f(\ )$ were used. The first was a simple neural network model augmented by a linear term, so that

$$y_t = \alpha + \beta y_{t-1} + \pi y_{t-1}(1 + \exp(-\gamma(y_{t-1} - c)))^{-1} + e_t \tag{4}$$

with the coefficients α, β, π, γ, and c being estimated by a hill-climbing maximum likelihood procedure. A full neural network model would use several of the logistic functions shown in equation (4). It has been shown by Hornik *et al.* (1988) that any well-behaved function can be approximated arbitrarily by a neural network model containing enough terms.

The second method of approximating the true function used the non-parametric kernel procedure. Here

$$\hat{f}_n(x) = \frac{\sum y_i k[(x_i - x)/h_n]}{\sum k[(x_i - x)/h_n]} \tag{5}$$

where $k(x)$ is a non-negative function, unimodel and symmetric around $x = 0$, such as a zero-mean Gaussian probability density function. h_n is the bandwidth used with a sample of size n. Essentially, the kernel gives a high weight to points x_i near to the value x at which the function is being estimated and a lower weight for more distant points. It provides a form of weighted moving average, with the bandwidth determining the length of the average. For the simulations, y_i and x_i are set to be y_t and y_{t-1}, $k(x)$ was the normal p.d.f. and $h_n = \sigma(4/3)^{1/5} n^{-1/5}$, where σ is the standard deviation of the independent variable, or its estimate from the data. The obvious advantage of kernel estimators is that they need no estimation.

With any estimator of $f(\ )$, such as those just discussed, it is then used to form forecasts as in the previous section, replacing $f(\ )$ by the estimator. The asymptotic properties of these forecasts may be expected to be similar to those based on the actual function. It is shown in the Appendix that when the kernel estimator is used, the naive forecast still has a bias $0(1)$ but that the bootstrap forecast now has bias $0(n^{-2/5})$ and thus is still asymptotically unbiased. It is called the kernel bootstrap since ε in $E[f(y_t + \varepsilon)]$ is bootstrapped by using the realized one-step forecast error. As before, the mean squared errors of all predictors are $0(1)$.

Data were generated from three univariate models:

(1) Smooth transition autoregressive (STAR), given by

$$y_t = \alpha + \beta y_{t-1} + \pi y_{t-1} [1 + \exp(-\gamma(y_{t-1} + c))]^{-1} + \varepsilon_t$$

where ε_t is iid $N(0, 1)$. The data were simulated with parameter values $\alpha = 0$, $\beta = 0 \cdot 8$, $\gamma = 10$, $c = 0$, $\pi = -0 \cdot 8$.

(2) A simple non-linear AR(1) model

$$y_t = \text{sign}(y_{t-1}) + \varepsilon_t$$

where $\text{sign}(x) = 1$ if x is positive
          $= 0$ if $x = 0$
          $= -1$ if x is negative
and ε_t is as above, and

(3) A linear AR(1) model

$$y_t = \rho y_{t-1} + \varepsilon_t$$

where $\rho = 0.8$ is used to generate the data.

Seven hundred terms were generated for each individual simulation. The first 200 are then discarded, the parameters of the true and neural net models are estimated and the non-parametric kernel model formed from the next 300 terms, and the final 200 terms are used to evaluate the alternative forecasts. Two hundred replications of these simulations were used in the evaluations, which are reported in Table I. In each case, the bias of the forecast, the mean squared forecast error, and the relative MSE of the forecasts using the functions approximations compared to the MSE using the true function are shown in Table I. The one-step forecast results are presented for comparison purposes. The parametric model uses the correct specification for $f(\ )$, but with parameters estimated from the data in the STAR and linear model cases. The two-step direct forecasts used the same model specification as for the true generating mechanism, for the STAR and linear models, and $y_{t+2} = \alpha + \beta \, \text{sign}(y_t) + e_{t+2}$ with α and β estimated by OLS for the sign model. Although the table is compact it involves a considerable amount of programming and computing.

The details of the results lead to the following observations.

J.-L. Lin and C. W. J. Granger   *Forecasting from Non-linear Models in Practice*   5

Star model
As expected, the parametric naive predictor has a much larger bias than that of the parametric kernel, direct, and bootstrap predictors, the last having the smallest bias. The naive predictor has a greater MSE than that of the bootstrap predictor by 3%. It should also be noted that all two-period predictors have a mean squared error larger than the one-period predictor by a factor of 25%. Similar results hold when using kernel-based predictors. The naive predictor generates the largest bias and mean squared error while the optimal and bootstrap predictors have the smallest mean squared error. The direct predictor has the smallest bias but a medium-sized mean square error. The EFF column, computed as the percentage of the non-parametric mean squared error greater than the parametric mean squared error, shows that the kernel predictors are, at most, 2.5% inefficient when compared with the parametric one. This finding is consistent with the results of Moschini *et al.* (1988), who compared the performance of linear and kernel forecast of US hog supply.

The neural network produces somewhat surprising results. The naive predictor is not associated with a large bias although it still gives the largest mean squared error. The EFF is greater than that using the kernel.

Sign model
The results are somewhat different. The parametric naive predictor has a smaller bias than that of the other parametric predictors although its mean squared error is still the largest. The kernel predictors have the same results, with EFF being 5.5% for optimal and bootstrap predictors. The results from the neural network is more consistent with the theory that the naive predictor has the largest bias and mean squared error. However, the EFF for optimal and bootstrap predictors are 46% and 10%, respectively.

Table I. Forecast bias and mean squared error

Period and forecast	Parametric		Kernel			Neural network		
	Bias	MSE	Bias	MSE	EFF[a]	Bias	MSE	EFF[a]
Star model								
1—Forecast	0.0084	1.0043	0.01599	1.0256	2.12	−0.0107	1.0768	7.21
2—Naive	0.1722	1.4450	0.13969	1.4426	−0.17	0.0031	1.4910	4.60
2—Optimal	0.0142	1.4020	0.02375	1.4243	1.59	−0.0180	1.4841	5.86
2—Bootstrap	0.0063	1.4019	0.02555	1.4246	1.62	−0.0141	1.4566	3.90
2—Direct	0.0911	1.4330	0.00948	1.4305	−0.17	−0.0187	1.4578	1.73
Sign model								
1—Forecast	0.0009	0.9963	−0.0017	1.1225	12.67	−0.0431	1.2509	25.55
2—Naive	0.0004	1.6278	−0.0007	1.6387	0.67	0.4720	2.1620	32.82
2—Optimal	0.0017	1.5280	−0.0018	1.6117	5.48	−0.0648	1.7045	46.11
2—Bootstrap	0.0009	1.5302	−0.0014	1.6120	5.35	−0.0442	1.6839	10.04
2—Direct	0.0038	1.9968	0.0031	1.6159	−18.90	−0.0287	1.6853	−15.60
Linear model								
1—Forecast	0.0055	1.0035	−0.0072	1.0523	4.74	−0.0300	1.0140	1.05
2—Naive	0.0093	1.6514	−0.0108	1.7303	4.78	0.0545	1.8903	14.47
2—Optimal	0.0093	1.6514	−0.0107	1.7280	4.64	−0.0496	1.6860	2.10
2—Bootstrap	N/A	N/A	−0.0105	1.7280	N/A	−0.0337	1.6787	N/A
2—Direct	N/A	N/A	−0.0103	1.7022	N/A	−0.0059	1.6848	N/A

[a] EFF is the efficiency of forecast which is computed as the percentage of MSE of a kernel and neural network greater than that of the parametric forecast.

6   *Journal of Forecasting*   *Vol. 13, Iss. No. 1*

Linear model

For the linear model the naive forecast is the optimal two-period forecast. The estimated one- and two-period mean squared error are 1.0035 and 1.6514, which are close to the theoretical values of 1 and 1.64. For the linear model with a functional form assumed known, the two-step naive predictor is optimal and so it does not make much sense to compute the bootstrap and the direct predictor, hence these are not reported here. The bias using the kernel predictor is significantly smaller than using the neural but larger than the parametric model. As within kernel methods, all predictors produce approximately the same bias and mean squared error. For the neural network, the bias mean squared errors for the direct two-period predictor is smaller than the other three.

To summarize, the simulation results show that both the kernel bootstrap predictor and optimal predictors have small bias and mean squared error. However, it should be noted that for the first-order non-linear autoregressive model used in this paper, the forecast performance comparison is not in favour of the neural network predictor, the strength of which lies in its ability to handle high dimensional models. Thus, for the high-order non-linear autoregressive time series the neural network predictor is expected to perform much better than the kernel ones, which suffer from the 'curse of dimensionality.' See White (1989) and the references therein.

CONCLUSION

This paper has discussed the bias and mean square error of various kinds of predictors using parametric and non-parametric methods. The naive two-period predictor is shown to be asymptotically biased in theory and is confirmed by the simulation results. These results lead to a mild recommendation for using the kernel bootstrap predictor since it has a relatively small bias and only, at most, 5% inefficiency in mean squared error when compared with the parametric model using the correct specifications. However, a more affirmative conclusion should come only after more extensive study of broader classes of time-series models.

APPENDIX: ASYMPTOTIC BIAS OF NON-PARAMETRIC PREDICTION

Definition (Rosenblatt, 1970)

A stationary Markov sequence is a G_2 sequence if there exists a positive number, ρ, and integer, n, such that for any bounded Borel function $h(\cdot)$ satisfy $Eh(y_t) = 0$,

$$Ey_1\{E[h(y_n)|y_1]^2\} \leqslant \rho^2 E[h(y_1)^2]$$

To investigate the asymptotic behaviour of the bias of kernel predictors, the following theorem is very useful.

Theorem (Yakowitz, 1985)

Assume that y_t, $t = 1, 2, \ldots$ is a stationary Markov sequence with a continuous stationary density function which satisfies G_2. Also, assume the kernel k is uniformly continuous and

$$k(u) = O(|u^{-1}|) \text{ as } |u| \to \infty$$

and $\int uk(u) \, du = 0$.

Further, if $nh_n \to \infty$, $nh_n^5 \to 0$ then

$$(nh_n)^{1/2}(\hat{f}_n(x) - f(x))$$

is asymptotically normal with variance

$$V = \frac{v(x)}{\pi(x)} \int k^2(u) \, du$$

where $v(x) = \text{var}(y_t/y_{t-1} = x)$ and $\pi(x)$ is the conditional density function of y_t given $y_{t-1} = x$, where

$$\hat{f}_n(x) = \frac{\Sigma \, y_i k[(x_i - x)/h_n]}{\Sigma \, k[(x_i - x)/h_n]}$$

is the kernel estimate of f at x.

As an immediate result, we have

$$\hat{f}_n(x) = O_p(nh_n)^{-1/2}$$
$$(\hat{f}_n(x) - f(x)) = O_p(nh_n)^{-1}$$

The bias of naive predictor, B_t^n, is

$$\begin{aligned}
B_t^n &= E(\hat{y}_{t+2}^n - y_{t+2}) \\
&= E\{\hat{f}[\hat{f}(y_t)] - f[f(y_t) + \varepsilon_{t+1}]\} \\
&= E\{\hat{f}[\hat{f}(y_t)] - f[\hat{f}(y_t)]\} + E\{f[\hat{f}(y_t)] - f[f(y_t) + \varepsilon_{t+1}]\} \\
&= E\eta_t + E\{f[\hat{f}6y_t)] - f[f(y_t)] - f'[f(y_t)](\eta_t + \varepsilon_{t+1}) \\
&\quad - \tfrac{1}{2} f''(\hat{f}(y_t))(\eta_t + \varepsilon_{t+1})^2 + O_p[(\eta_t + \varepsilon_{t+1})^3] \\
&= 2E\eta_t - \tfrac{1}{2} f''[\hat{f}(y_t)](E\eta_t^2 + \sigma^2) + O_p(\eta_t + \varepsilon_{t+1})^3
\end{aligned}$$

where $\eta_t = \hat{f}(\hat{f}(y_t)) - f(\hat{f}(y_t))$.

By applying Yakowitz's theorem with the bandwidth h_n set to be the optimal $O(n^{-2})$, B_t^d can be easily seen to be $O(1)$ due to the middle term σ^2. That is, the naive predictor is asymptotic biased.

Let $\hat{\varepsilon}_t = y_i - \hat{f}(y_{i-1})$, $\varepsilon_i = y_i - f(y_{i-1})$, $\xi_i = \hat{f}(y_i) - f(y_i)$, $\eta_i = \hat{f}(\hat{f}(y_i)) - f(\hat{f}(y_i))$ and $\lambda_{ti} = \hat{f}(f(y_i) + \varepsilon_i + \xi_{i-1}) - f(f(y_i) + \varepsilon_i + \xi_{i-1})$. The bias of the bootstrap predictor, B_t^b after some algebra manipulations becomes

$$\begin{aligned}
B_t^b &= E(y_{t+2}^b + y_{t+2}) \\
&= \left(\frac{1}{t} \sum_{i=1}^t \hat{f}(\hat{f}(y_t) + \varepsilon_i) - Ef(f(y_t) + \varepsilon_{t+1})\right) \\
&= \frac{1}{t} \sum_{i=1}^t (f(f(y_t) + \xi_t + \xi_{i-1} + \varepsilon_i) + \lambda_{ti} - E(f(f(y_t) + \varepsilon_{t+1}))) \\
&= \frac{1}{t} \sum_{i=1}^t \left\{f(f(y_t) + \varepsilon_i) + \frac{1}{t} \sum_{i=1}^t f'(f(y_t) + \varepsilon_i)\right\}(\xi_{i-1} + \xi_t) \\
&= \frac{1}{t} \sum_{i=1}^t \left\{\frac{f''}{2}(\xi_{i-1} + \xi_t)^2 + O_p(\eta_i + \eta_{t+1})^2\right\} - E(f(f(y_t))) + \varepsilon_{t+1}
\end{aligned}$$

8   *Journal of Forecasting*   *Vol. 13, Iss. No. 1*

Assume that

$$\frac{1}{t} \sum_{i=1}^{t} f'(f(y_t) + \varepsilon_i) = F' + O\left(\frac{1}{\sqrt{T}}\right)$$

$$\frac{1}{t} \sum_{i=1}^{t} f''(f(y_t) + \varepsilon_i) = F'' + O\left(\frac{1}{\sqrt{T}}\right)$$

where

$$F' = \plim_{t \to \infty} \frac{1}{t} \sum_{i=1}^{t} f'(f(y_t) + \varepsilon_i)$$

$$F'' = \plim_{t \to \infty} \frac{1}{t} \sum_{i=1}^{t} f''(f(y_t) + \varepsilon_i)$$

Then

$$B_T^b = O(T^{-1/2}) + O(T^{-2/5}) + O(T^{-4/5})$$
$$= O(T^{-2/5})$$

Thus, the bootstrap predictor is asymptotically unbiased.

Since y_{t+2} contains the disturbance term ε_{t+2}, which does not vanish as the sample size grows, the mean squared errors of all predictors are $O(1)$.

ACKNOWLEDGEMENT

This research was partially supported by NSF Grant SES 9023037.

REFERENCES

Brown, B. and Mariano, R., 'Residual-based stochastic predictors and estimation in non-linear models', *Econometrica*, **52**, (1984), 321–43.

Brown, B. and Mariano, R., 'Predictors in dynamic non-linear models: large-sample behaviour', *Econometric Theory*, **5** (1989), 430–52.

Granger, C. W. J., 'Forecasting stock market prices', University of California at San Diego, Economics Department, Discussion Paper 91-23 1991.

Granger, C. W. J. and Newbold, P., 'Forecasting transformed series', *Journal of Royal Statistical Society, Series B*, **38**, (1976) 189–203.

Granger, C. W. J. and Teräsvirta, T., *Modelling Non-linear Economic Relationships*, Oxford University Press, Oxford, 1993.

Hornik, K., Stinchcombe, M. and White, H., 'Multi-layer feedforward networks are universal approximations', University of California at San Diego, Economics Department, Discussion Paper 88-45, 1991.

Moschini, D., Prescott, M. and Stengos, T., 'Nonparametric kernel estimation applied to forecasting: an evaluation based on the bootstrap', in Ullah, A. (ed.), *Semiparametric and Nonparametric Econometrics*, Springer-Verlag, New York, 1988.

Rosenblatt, M., 'Density estimates and Markov sequences', in Puri, M., (ed.), *Nonparametric Techniques in Statistical Inference*, Cambridge University Press, Cambridge, 1970.

Tong, H., *Nonlinear Time Series Models*, Cambridge University Press, Cambridge, 1990.

White, H., 'Some asymptotic results for learning in single hidden layer feedforward networks', *Journal of the American Statistical Association*, **58** (1989), 227–308.

Yakowitz, S. 'Nonparametric density estimation, prediction, and regression for Markov sequences', *Journal of the American Statistical Association*, 1985, 215–21.

Authors' biographies:
Jin-Lung Lin obtained his PhD from the University of California, San Diego, in 1992, for a thesis entitled *Three Essays on Nonlinear Times Series*. He is currently at the Institute of Economics, Academia Sinica, Nankan, Taipei, Taiwan. His research interests include the use of non-parametric techniques with economic time series.
Clive W. J. Granger holds the Chancellor's Associates Chair of Economics at the University of California, San Diego, where he has taught since 1974. Previously he was Professor of Applied Statistics and Econometrics at Nottingham University, UK. He has published a number of books and papers, including works on causality, cointegration, combination of forecasts, and financial markets.

Authors' addresses:
Jin-Lung Lin and **Clive W. J. Granger**, Research Group for Econometric Analysis, Department of Economics, University of California, San Diego, 9500 Gilman Drive, La Jolla, CA 92093-0508, USA.

[19]

The Statistician (1997)
46, *No. 4, pp.* 461–473

Forecasting in the 1990s

By CHRIS CHATFIELD†

University of Bath, UK

[Received August 1996]

SUMMARY
This paper reviews recent developments in time series forecasting with particular emphasis on the use of multivariate and non-linear models, the results of recent forecasting competitions, the computation of prediction intervals and the effects of model uncertainty.

Keywords: Autoregressive conditionally heteroscedastic models; Chaos; Forecasting competitions; Fractional differencing; Generalized autoregressive conditionally heteroscedastic models; Model uncertainty; Neural networks; Non-linear models; Prediction intervals; Structural models; Vector autoregressive moving average models

1. Introduction

This paper reviews recent developments in time series forecasting. Given the voluminous growth in the literature, this survey is necessarily selective. In particular the paper makes no attempt to assess the large field of econometric modelling. The paper updates an earlier review (Chatfield, 1988) which included some general recommendations on the choice of forecasting method based on research evidence up to that time.

One general development has been a substantial expansion in the range of time series texts that are available, especially at an introductory level. Most of these books incorporate some material on forecasting. Some are entirely new (Diggle, 1990; Janacek and Swift, 1993; Mills, 1990; Wei, 1990) while others are new editions (Chatfield (1996a), Harvey (1993), Kendall and Ord (1990) and, for the more advanced reader, Brockwell and Davis (1991) and Fuller (1996)).

There have also been several new books on forecasting (rather than time series analysis). Some expound an approach to forecasting that is based on a particular class of time series models and will be referenced later in this paper. Some more general books on forecasting include the new edition of Montgomery *et al.* (1990), while Granger and Newbold (1986) is still valuable.

One particularly exciting publication is a new third edition of the classic 1970 book by George Box and Gwilym Jenkins with Gregory Reinsel as new co-author (Box *et al.*, 1994). Chapters 12 and 13 of the new edition have been completely rewritten and include material on intervention analysis, outlier detection and process control. The earlier chapters retain the spirit and structure of earlier editions despite some revision and the inclusion of some additional material such as testing for unit roots.

2. Preliminary matters

The basic problem considered here is to forecast future values of an observed time series, denoted by $x_1, x_2, \ldots, x_N$. The forecast made at time N of x_{N+k}, where k denotes the lead time, will be denoted by $\hat{x}(N, k)$.

†*Address for correspondence*: School of Mathematical Sciences, University of Bath, Bath, BA2 7AY, UK.
E-mail: cc@maths.bath.ac.uk

0039-0526/97/46461

The first step in any forecasting exercise is to *clarify the objectives*. Ask questions as necessary to obtain enough background information to formulate the problem properly. The context is crucial. It is a good idea to find out exactly how a forecast will be used.

The second step is to plot the observations against time. The *time plot* is arguably the most important tool in any time series analysis or forecasting study. It enables the analyst to look for trend, seasonality, outliers, turning-points and discontinuities. However, drawing a time plot is not as easy as it sounds, and the graphs produced by many software packages are of a poor standard. The guidelines for producing clear graphs are well known (e.g. Chatfield (1995a)) and include giving the graph a clear self-explanatory title, choosing the scales carefully and labelling axes. A package which allows the user to determine such presentational details when constructing a graph should preferably be used, but sadly many forecasting packages do not have this flexibility.

The time plot is vital, not only for describing the data, but also to help in *model formulation* and in choosing an appropriate forecasting method. Model building is an iterative process which involves formulating a model, estimating the model parameters, carrying out diagnostic checks and then trying alternative models if necessary. Text-books tend to concentrate on the theory of parameter estimation, even though this is usually the easiest stage of model building given current computing software. More generally the literature concentrates on the details of forecasting *techniques*, when most users need more guidance with the *strategy* of forecasting (and of problem solving in general). For example it is easy nowadays to fit an autoregressive integrated moving average (ARIMA) model and to produce the resulting ARIMA forecasts, but it is still difficult to know *when* to use ARIMA modelling and *how* to choose which ARIMA model to fit.

Theory also generally assumes that we know the *true* model and ignores *model uncertainty* and the *model selection biases* which result when a model is formulated and fitted to the *same* data (Chatfield, 1995b). It is strange that we admit model uncertainty by searching for a 'best' model but ignore this uncertainty when making subsequent inferences and forecasts. Computers let us look at tens or even hundreds of models and there is a real danger of overfitting. Recent results (Faraway and Chatfield, 1998) suggest that, when selecting a model, the Bayes information criterion (BIC) should be preferred to Akaike's information criterion (AIC) to penalize the fitting of extra, possibly spurious, parameters satisfactorily although the bias-corrected version of AIC (AIC_c) is also worth considering (Brockwell and Davis (1991), section 9.3). When a model has been formulated from the data, it is easy to demonstrate that the resulting forecast error variances are typically optimistically low and prediction intervals too narrow (Chatfield, 1996b). Partly for this reason, it is always recommended that different forecasting methods and models should be compared, not on within-sample fit, but on genuine *out-of-sample* results (called *ex ante* forecasts by econometricians).

The estimation and/or removal of *trend* and *seasonality* is an age old problem which is still receiving deserved attention. One basic difficulty is that there is no unique decomposition of variation into trend and seasonal terms. Two books which review methods of seasonal adjustment are den Butter and Fase (1991) and Hylleberg (1992), while the discussion of Ball and Wood (1996) demonstrates how difficult it can be to distinguish between different types of trend. It is difficult to define 'trend' and our perception of it may depend on the length of the series. There is a big difference between a *deterministic (global)* linear trend and a *local* linear trend, say $\mu_t = a_t + b_t t$ where μ_t is the local mean level and the coefficients a_t and b_t may change through time. It seems that the deterministic model is generally unrealistic for describing most real time series. For example Franses and Kleibergen (1996) showed that out-of-sample forecasts using first differencing on economic data are better than those obtained by fitting a deterministic trend.

Econometricians distinguish between what they call *difference stationary* series, where stationarity can be induced by taking first differences, and *trend stationary* series, where the deviations from a deterministic trend are stationary. Spurious autocorrelations can readily be induced, either by mistakenly removing a deterministic trend from difference stationary data, or by differencing trend stationary data. This emphasizes the importance of identifying an appropriate model for the trend to assess the appropriate form of differencing. In particular if the original data are non-stationary, but the first differences are stationary, then a *unit root* is said to be present. There is a growing literature on the specialized problem of testing for a unit root and this is written mainly from an econometric viewpoint (e.g. DeJong and Whiteman (1993)). However, it is not always obvious why the existence of a unit root should be taken as the null hypothesis, and in any case the tests usually have poor power. Partly as a result, they are used much less by statisticians and forecasters than by econometricians, and Newbold *et al.* (1993) went so far as to say that 'testing for unit autoregressive roots is misguided'. The topic is too large, complex and unresolved to consider here, except to reiterate that it is generally difficult to distinguish between different types of stationarity and non-stationarity. In forecasting, there is much to be said for using a method which makes few assumptions about the form of the trend and which is *robust* to any changes in it.

Finally we note that the treatment of

(a) outliers,
(b) missing observations and
(c) calendar (or trading day) effects

can be more crucial than the choice of forecasting method. Here again appropriate action is often determined primarily by the context, though there has been continuing general research, especially on the effect of outliers on forecasts under specified model assumptions (e.g. Chen and Liu (1993)).

3. Forecasting methods

This section makes a brief selective review of recent research on the many different forecasting methods that are available.

Forecasting methods can be broadly classified into

(a) *judgmental* methods,
(b) *univariate* methods, where $\hat{x}(N, k)$ depends only on $x_N, x_{N-1}, \ldots$ and/or on the position in time, and
(c) *multivariate* methods.

There is also an important distinction between an *automatic* and a *non-automatic* approach. The former requires no intervention from the analyst and is useful for example in stock control when there are large numbers of items to forecast.

We say nothing about judgmental methods except to note a recent review by Webby and O'Connor (1996) which confirms that such methods sometimes work well and sometimes do not (as is true for all forecasting methods!).

Univariate forecasting methods are still used far more in practice than alternative approaches. There has been rather little recent research on exponential smoothing methods (which include Holt's linear trend for non-seasonal data with trend and the Holt–Winters method for seasonal data with a trend). The flood of research on ARIMA modelling has also abated, though there has been some further work on model identification and estimation (for example see Choi (1992) for an extensive bibliography).

There is also some current research on a variant of ARIMA modelling, namely the use of *fractional differencing*. The usual ARIMA model of order (p, d, q) is written

$$\varphi(B)(1 - B)^d X_t = \theta(B) Z_t$$

where X_t denotes the value of the time series at time t, Z_t denotes the 'error' term, φ and θ are polynomials of order p and q in the backward shift operator B and d is an integer (usually 0 or 1). Fractional ARIMA models extend this class by allowing d to be non-integer. A range of particular interest is $0 < d \leq \frac{1}{2}$ where it can be shown that the process is stationary. A drawback to fractional differencing is that it is difficult to give an intuitive interpretation to a non-integer difference. It is also more difficult to make computations based on such a model.

Stationary fractional ARIMA models are one type of a general class of models called *long memory* models (Beran, 1992, 1994). For most stationary time series models, the auto-correlation function decreases 'fairly fast'. However, for some models the correlations decay to 0 very slowly, implying that observations far apart are still related to some extent. An intuitive way to describe such behaviour is to say that the process has a long memory, or that there is *long-range dependence*. Although it can be difficult to obtain good estimates of some model parameters, notably the mean, it is usually possible to make better forecasts, at least in theory. Intuitively, the larger and more long lasting the autocorrelations, the better should be the forecasts from the model. However, a major problem in practice is distinguishing between a long memory (stationary) process and a non-stationary process, since the empirical autocorrelation function for both models will die out slowly. If it is thought to be worth considering a fractional ARIMA model, the question then is how to estimate d. This is not easy though some progress has been made. One basic question which is often asked is whether d is exactly equal to 1, meaning that a unit root is present—see Section 2. If we manage to fit what appears to be an appropriate fractional ARIMA model to a given set of data, the question then arises whether the resulting forecasts are likely to be better than those from alternative models. Although there are some encouraging results (e.g. Sutcliffe (1994)), the results in Smith and Yadav (1994) suggest that little will be lost by taking first, rather than fractional, differences, while Crato and Ray (1996) say that 'simple ARMA models provide competitive forecasts' to fractional ARIMA models for financial time series.

There has been growing interest in *structural models* since the publication of Harvey (1989), though there has so far been rather little systematic empirical examination of the forecasts which result. The empirical study of Andrews (1994) is one exception and suggests that the models do quite well, especially for long horizons and seasonal data. Structural models are a special case of the class of models called *state space models* by engineers, as are the *unobserved component models* of econometricians and the *dynamic linear models* of West and Harrison (1997)—see below. These classes of model are closely related and are typically updated by the *Kalman filter*, which provides a recursive method of estimating the current state of a system in the presence of noise. (It is also used nowadays for estimating the parameters of an autoregressive moving average (ARMA) model and in other statistical applications).

For the reader who has not seen it before, the *basic structural model* (BSM) assumes additive level, trend, seasonal index and error terms, so that

$$x_t = \text{observation at time } t = L_t + I_t + n_t$$

is the so-called *observation equation*, where

$$L_t = L_{t-1} + T_{t-1} + w_{1,t}$$

$$T_t = T_{t-1} + w_{2,t}$$

$$I_t = -\sum_{j=1}^{p-1} I_{t-j} + w_{3,t}$$

are the three *transition equations* for the three unobservable state variables, namely L_t, the level, T_t, the trend, and I_t, the seasonal index, where p is the number of observations per year. The model is similar in spirit to that implied by the (additive) Holt–Winters method. The latter depends on three smoothing parameters which correspond in some sense to the three error variance ratios, namely σ_1^2/σ_n^2, σ_2^2/σ_n^2 and σ_3^2/σ_n^2 in an obvious notation. The BSM is clearly more complicated to use and explain than the Holt–Winters method but the use of a proper probability model means for example that theoretical prediction intervals can be calculated, and the model can more easily be extended to incorporate explanatory variables.

Bayesian forecasting (West and Harrison, 1997) depends on a class of models called dynamic linear models which, as noted above, are in the even more general class of models called state space models. The model is implemented by updating 'priors' to obtain 'posteriors' using a Bayesian approach, and the procedure which results looks very like a Kalman filter. The approach is particularly useful for short series when there really is some prior information and some examples are given by Pole *et al.* (1994).

Multivariate forecasting methods have given rise to more research than univariate methods have, presumably because there are more unanswered questions and because computational advances have made them more feasible in practice. It seems natural to try to improve forecasts of one variable by including appropriate explanatory variables in the model. Identifying all the relevant variables may not be easy and it is important to study the context, to ask questions and to look for previous empirical regularities. There is always the contrary danger of including unnecessary explanatory variables, which appear to improve the fit but actually lead to poorer out-of-sample forecasts. Although most people expect multivariate forecasts to be better than univariate forecasts, this is not necessarily the case—see Section 4—though they may still improve our understanding of the interrelationships between variables.

There are many types of multivariate model. One basic questions is whether there is a *causal relationship* between the explanatory variables and the response variable, and also whether the system is of *open loop* structure or whether changes in the response variable feed back to affect the explanatory variables in a *closed loop* way. Multiple regression is still the most commonly used method but there can be problems in fitting such models to economic time series data where the variables can be correlated with each other and with time, and where feed-back may be present. Although a good fit can often be obtained, poor forecasts may still result. It is arguable that this is partly because the error structure of regression models is overly simplistic for use with time series data and there has been much work on alternative classes of multivariate time series model notably vector ARMA (VARMA) models—see for example Lütkepohl (1993) and Reinsel (1993). Software has become available but VARMA models are still not easy to fit even with only two or three explanatory variables. Partly because of this, many analysts prefer to restrict attention to vector autoregressive (VAR) models or even further to low order VAR models, and empirical evidence does suggest that restricted VAR models give better out-of-sample forecasts than unrestricted VAR models. *Bayesian vector autoregression* uses appropriate priors to shrink the estimated coefficients of VAR models, which are higher than first order, towards 0—see for example Kadiyala and Karlsson (1993) and the tutorial introduction by Spencer (1993). It is also a good idea, where possible, to use external knowledge to reduce the large number of parameters in VAR models by specifying some coefficients to be 0 to obtain what are called sparse matrices. Another promising approach is to use *co-integration* which uses the fact that, although the individual series may all be non-stationary, it may be possible to find some linear combination of the series which *is* stationary. This may avoid the need to difference the data before trying to fit a model. Some references on co-integration are Engle and Granger (1991) and Banerjee *et al.* (1993), while Murray (1994) gives an amusing introduction. *Transfer function models* (Box *et al.*, 1994) can be regarded as special cases of VARMA models for open loop systems. The *dynamic regression models* of Pankratz (1991) are of a similar type.

There are multivariate versions of both structural modelling and Bayesian forecasting, but they, like econometric models, will not be considered here.

4. Comparison of forecasting methods

A bewildering choice of methods is available. The obvious question which is often asked is 'Which is best?'. The simple answer is 'It depends!'. It depends on the context, the type of data being analysed, the expertise available, the number of series which have to be forecasted and so on. There is a wide variety of problems requiring different treatment, and the sensible forecaster will naturally wish to be selective to try to improve accuracy. Unfortunately it is not easy to give simple advice on choosing a forecasting method, and a good illustration of the difficulty in making general recommendations is provided by Collopy and Armstrong (1992) who listed no fewer than 99 rules to help to make the most appropriate choice from among four univariate methods for annual data.

The answer to the question 'Which is best?' also depends on what is meant by 'best'. A good discussion of ways of measuring forecast accuracy is given by Armstrong and Collopy (1992) and Fildes (1992) and in the discussion which follows.

There have been various *forecasting competitions* over the years to compare the accuracy of various methods on different series. These empirical studies tell us something but not everything. Pre-1988 work was reviewed by Chatfield (1988), section 4.1, who suggested that competitions are mainly useful for assessing automatic methods. For assessing non-automatic univariate methods and multivariate methods, *case-studies* may be more fruitful as competitions between such methods are much more difficult to organize. This is illustrated by the recent M2 competition (Makridakis *et al.*, 1993) which involved 29 time series. Participants also received a variety of additional information. I was one of the participants but found the exercise rather unsatisfactory in some ways, mainly because there was no direct contact with the 'client'. As a result, it was difficult to take full account of the additional information, and so the conditions did not really mimic those that are likely to hold in practice when using such methods. Tashman and Kruk (1996) investigated various protocols for choosing a forecasting method and demonstrated, as would be expected, that substantial gains in accuracy can sometimes be made by choosing a method that is appropriate to the given situation. For example some forecasting competitions applied exponential smoothing to all series in the given study regardless of whether they exhibited trend or not. This hardly seems fair to exponential smoothing as it does not pretend to be able to cope with trend. Various other empirical accuracy studies are reviewed by Fildes and Makridakis (1995), who pointed out that empirical findings have often been ignored by the theoreticians. For example sophisticated methods often fail to outperform simpler methods, while out-of-sample forecasts are typically much worse than would be expected from within-sample fits.

Chatfield (1988) and Chatfield (1996a), section 5.4, gave general advice on the choice of an appropriate forecasting procedure. In brief, a simple *automatic univariate procedure* is useful as a norm, if there are many series to forecast, as a preliminary forecast to be adjusted subjectively or if the analyst's skill is limited. There is little overall difference in accuracy between several methods and so it seems sensible to choose a method which is simple, easily interpreted and for which software is readily available. I recommend using an appropriate form of exponential smoothing (e.g. Holt–Winters for seasonal data) but there are several good alternatives.

If a *non-automatic* approach is indicated, then a general strategy for choosing a *univariate* method is described by Chatfield (1996a), section 5.4.3. Inspection of the time plot remains an invaluable stage of this strategy. For example it may be unwise to try to use any time series method to forecast a series showing a discontinuity (though the use of intervention analysis may sometimes work). The subjective adjustment of a method such as the Holt–Winters method, which is normally regarded as 'automatic', is often fruitful. This would involve a careful choice of the type of seasonality (if any), the starting values and the smoothing parameters, as well as a careful treatment of any outliers. Structural modelling should be added to the list of methods worth considering.

Multivariate methods are worth considering when appropriate expertise is available and when suitable explanatory variables have been identified and measured, especially when one or more of them is a *leading indicator*. Multivariate forecasts are sometimes worth the extra effort that they entail, and multivariate models usually do give a better *fit*. However, it is important to realize that out-of-sample forecasts from multivariate models are not necessarily more accurate than those from univariate models either in theory or practice, because

(a) exogenous variables may have to be forecasted,
(b) economic data are generally *observational* rather than *designed* data, and so may be unsuitable for fitting multivariate models or
(c) 'simple may be best'. It appears that simple univariate methods are often more robust to model misspecification and to changes in the model than more complicated models are.

Multivariate forecasts are more accurate than univariate extrapolations in about half the case-studies that I have seen, but the reverse is true in the remainder. This contest remains unresolved. Despite the research interest in alternatives, such as VAR models, multiple regression is still the most commonly used multivariate model, no doubt because of its simplicity. It is therefore a pity that the dangers mentioned in Section 3 are still not universally recognized.

One general question is whether it is better to difference away trend and seasonal effects (as in the Box–Jenkins approach), to remove trend and seasonality by some other detrending and seasonal adjustment procedure or to use a method which models these effects explicitly. For example, when using the Kalman filter to update the BSM, local estimates of level, trend and seasonality are automatically produced and they can be invaluable for descriptive purposes as well as for forecasting. In contrast, when variation is dominated by trend and seasonal variation, I would not recommend ARIMA (Box–Jenkins) modelling. As always the context and the type of data are the keys to deciding which approach to adopt.

A final comment is that there may be several forecasting methods which appear reasonable for a particular problem. It is now well established (e.g. Clemen (1989)) that more accurate forecasts can often be obtained by taking a weighted average of the individual forecasts rather than by choosing a single best method. Unfortunately this *combination* of methods does not give an interpretable model.

5. Calculating prediction intervals

The literature tends to concentrate on point forecasts even though an interval forecast is often what is required. A *prediction interval* (PI) is an interval forecast associated with a specified probability. A thorough review of methods of computing PIs is given by Chatfield (1993a).

Let

$$e_N(k) = X_{N+k} - \hat{x}(N, k)$$

denote the forecast error. This is a random variable and various methods exist to find its variance. Then, assuming normality and unbiasedness, a 95% PI for the observation at time $N + k$ is given by

$$\hat{x}(N, k) \pm 1.96\sqrt{\operatorname{var}\{e_N(k)\}}.$$

Theoretical formulae for $\operatorname{var}\{e_N(k)\}$ can be found for regression, ARIMA and structural *models* as well as for some exponential smoothing *methods* assuming optimality. Alternatively the prediction error variance may be calculated empirically from the past fitted 'forecast' errors or calculated by some sort of simulation, bootstrapping or Monte Carlo method. Various 'approximate' formulae also exist but some give very inaccurate results, notably the proposal that

$$\operatorname{var}(k\text{-step-ahead error}) \simeq k\operatorname{var}(1\text{-step-ahead error}).$$

Whatever method is used, PIs generally assume that the future is like the past. Partly as a result, PIs are *generally too narrow*. As noted in Section 2, empirical evidence shows that out-of-sample forecasting accuracy is usually (much) worse than within-sample fit. Reasons for this include

(a) the wrong model may have been fitted,
(b) the model may change in future,
(c) the true values of model parameters are unknown and must be estimated or
(d) outliers may be present or the errors may be non-normal.

Generally, it is difficult to capture the effect of *model uncertainty*.

6. Non-linear models

Most theory and practice are concerned with *linear* methods and models, such as ARIMA models and exponential smoothing methods. However, many time series exhibit features which cannot be explained in a linear framework. For example some economic series show different properties when the economy is going into, rather than coming out of, recession. As a result, there has been increasing interest in *non-linear models*.

There are many different classes of non-linear time series model. Tong (1990) gives a detailed authoritative account, while Chatfield (1996a), chapter 11, and Harvey (1993), chapter 8, give introductory accounts. The rewards from using non-linear models can occasionally be substantial. However, on the debit side, they are generally more difficult to fit than linear models are, and it is often difficult to compute forecasts more than one step ahead (Lin and Granger, 1994).

Threshold AR models are one class of non-linear model where the AR coefficients depend on the values of one or more past data values. A simple example of a first-order model, with 0 as the threshold, is

$$X_t = \begin{cases} \alpha^{(1)} X_{t-1} + Z_t & \text{if } X_{t-1} \geq 0, \\ \alpha^{(2)} X_{t-1} + Z_t & \text{if } X_{t-1} < 0. \end{cases}$$

An interesting application of threshold models to economic data is given by Tiao and Tsay (1994). Although little improvement in forecasts resulted from using the model, there was much more insight into the modelling process. A second application by Chappell *et al.* (1996) considered exchange rates within the European Union which are supposed to stay within prescribed bands. This means that thresholds can be expected at the upper and lower ends of the bands. This application *did* lead to improved forecasts.

A simple example of a *bilinear model* is

$$X_t = \alpha X_{t-1} + \beta Z_t + \gamma Z_{t-1} X_{t-1}.$$

The last term is the non-linear term. Applications of this model to forecasting have been rather rare.

The study of multivariate non-linear models (e.g. Granger and Teräsvirta (1993)) is only just beginning and we do not attempt to say anything about them here.

There is particular interest at present in *models for changing variance*, especially for analysing financial time series where understanding *changes in volatility* is important. An introduction to such models is given by Harvey (1993), chapter 8, and by Shephard (1996). The most popular class of models is that called generalized autoregressive conditionally heteroscedastic (GARCH). As a simple example, the GARCH(1, 1) model is the model where the observed time series X_t is given by

$$X_t = \sigma_t \varepsilon_t$$

where ε_t is a series of independent random variables having the same mean (0) and the same variance (1), and the unobservable random variable σ_t is such that its square depends on *one* past value of σ_t^2 and *one* past value of X_t^2 as in

$$\sigma_t^2 = \alpha + \beta \sigma_{t-1}^2 + \gamma X_{t-1}^2.$$

Note that the use of squares in this equation ensures non-negativity. Also, when $\beta = 0$, the model reduces to what is called an ARCH model (Bollerslev *et al.*, 1992).

There are various other models for changing variance, such as *stochastic volatility models* (e.g. Taylor (1994)) where σ_t is assumed to follow a stochastic process.

The ideas involved in modelling the error term in these models can also be applied to more complicated models for X_t. An example is a regression model with ARCH disturbances.

GARCH models have been used in financial statistics to forecast prices of options (derivatives) where an estimation of variance is important in the assessment of risk. However, it is important to realize that GARCH models have little effect on point forecasts of X_t but rather are designed to help to forecast second moments. This makes it hard to compare different models which allow for changing variance, and my assessment of the literature is that the modelling aspect is often more important than forecasting.

Another important class of non-linear models is that of *neural nets*. An introduction to neural nets is given by Ripley (1993). The basic idea is to mimic the structure of the brain by inserting *neurons* (or *nodes*) between the explanatory variables and the response variable. A linear function of the inputs to any neuron may then be transformed by a suitable function, which may be non-linear, to give a numerical value for each neuron. These values are then combined to try to approximate the value of the response variable. In a time series context, the response variable is the value to be forecasted and the explanatory variables are appropriate lagged variables. A large number of parameters are customarily implicit in the model structure and it is sometimes claimed that neural nets can 'learn' the behaviour of a system and produce a good fit and forecasts in a black box way. In our experience (Faraway and Chatfield, 1998) this is a gross simplification. Many questions need to be tackled when fitting a neural net, such as what explanatory variables to include, what structure (architecture) to choose (e.g. how many neurons and how many hidden layers?), how the net should be fitted, and so on.

In the Santa Fe competition (Weigend and Gershenfeld, 1994), six series were analysed. They were very long series (e.g. 34 000 observations) and five were clearly non-linear in the time plots. There was only one economic series. The organizers kept hold-out samples for three of the series. Little contextual information was provided for participants and so I decided not to take part myself. Participants chose their own method of forecasting such as using neural nets, the visual matching of segments or multivariate adaptive regression splines. Neural nets did comparatively quite well, but also produced some of the worst results when used in black box mode without using initial data analysis before applying the algorithm. Some non-linear results were much better than linear results but there are 'unprecedented opportunities for the analysis to go astray'. In particular 'the best, as well as many of the worst, forecasts of Data Set A were obtained with neural networks'. For the exchange rates time series there was a 'crucial difference between training set and test set performance' and 'out-of-sample predictions are on average worse than chance'. So in that case it is better to rely on our old friend the random walk!

Additional empirical evidence (e.g. Chatfield (1993b), Hill *et al.* (1994), de Groot and Wurtz (1991) and Faraway and Chatfield (1998)) suggests that whereas neural nets may give better forecasts for long series with clear non-linear properties (e.g. the sunspots data), the evidence for shorter series is indecisive. Simulations show that linear methods do better than neural nets for data generated by a linear mechanism, as we would intuitively expect. For many economic series, a 'no change' forecast is still found to be better than using a non-linear model or relying on 'experts', while the results of Church and Curram (1996) suggest that neural nets give forecasts which are comparable with (but no better than) those from econometric models, and that 'whichever approach is adopted, it is the skill of choosing the menu of explanatory variables which determines the success of the final results'.

A realistic assessment of the current status of neural nets suggests that more empirical evidence is needed to establish when they are worthwhile to use. Although they are promising for long series with non-linear characteristics, it appears that the analyst needs several thousand observations to be able to fit a neural net with confidence. It is unfortunate that the resulting model is usually difficult to interpret, and that there is plenty of scope for going badly wrong during the modelling process.

Chaos theory (e.g. Isham (1993) and Tong (1995)) has excited much interest. A basic question is whether chaotic series can be forecasted. This is certainly not possible for *long* lead times, but for short lead times it may be possible for low dimensional chaos if we know the model (Berliner, 1991). Unfortunately the analyst generally does not. Granger (1992) gives some cautionary remarks.

My overall impression of the current status of non-linear models is that they constitute a valuable addition to the time series analyst's toolkit, but that gains in forecasting accuracy are often modest. They are much better suited for describing long financial time series data than short sales series. A useful recent collection of papers on applications to financial time series is given in the special April 1996 issue of the *Journal of Forecasting*.

7. Forecasting practice

Most academic research has concentrated on methodological issues such as developing new forecasting methods or improvements to existing methods. The practitioner will also be interested to ask how forecasting *practice* (as opposed to theory) has changed in recent years. Are the newer forecasting methods being used in a commercial setting? How are they used? How are they evaluated? What software is used? Winklhofer *et al.* (1996) reviewed a large number of surveys and case-studies that have been carried out to assess the answers to these and other questions.

It appears that many companies use a forecast as a goal setting device rather than for planning. Sales forecasts are typically prepared up to one year ahead by using judgment or a simple univariate method, whereas longer-term forecasts are more likely to be prepared by using econometric models. Many firms still use internally developed software despite the proliferation of commercial packages, though this is slowly changing. In choosing a forecasting method, commercial users typically rate accuracy as the most important criterion followed by factors such as the ease of use, time horizon and the number of items to forecast. Many companies still prefer judgmental methods though familiarity with quantitative methods is increasing. The Box–Jenkins method appears to be used rather little in practice even though it is taught widely in statistics departments. Although many companies stress the importance of accuracy, it is not clear how this is actually measured in practice, and many companies do not have routine procedures in place to handle large forecast errors and the resulting revisions which may be indicated. It seems that companies still need further help in choosing an appropriate method for a given situation and that further research is needed to establish the importance (or lack of it) of such variables as company size and type of product. Winklhofer *et al.* (1996) went on to suggest various other areas where further research is indicated based on gaps identified in the research literature.

8. Computer software for forecasting

It is difficult to make general remarks on forecasting software as the scene is changing so rapidly. New packages, and new versions of existing packages, continue to come out at ever-decreasing intervals. The reader is advised to read software reviews such as those in the *International Journal of Forecasting* and the *American Statistician*.

Although some packages are specifically written for the non-expert, it remains true that the sensible application of software is vital and that

$$\text{garbage in} \Rightarrow \text{garbage out!}$$

Desirable features of 'good' software include

(a) flexible data entry and editing facilities,
(b) good facilities for exploring data and producing a good clear time plot,
(c) technically sound, computationally efficient routines,
(d) clear output and
(e) easy-to-learn and easy-to-use commands with clear documentation.

Some packages are command driven whereas others are menu driven. Some are written for the personal computer, some for a mainframe and some for both. Some are written for the expert statistician, some for the novice and some for both, though it is difficult to satisfy all types of user at the same time.

Many general statistics packages now include some forecasting capability. For example MINITAB, GENSTAT, SPSS and S-PLUS will all fit ARIMA models. S-PLUS is particularly good for time plots. There are many more specialized forecasting packages, written primarily for personal computers. They include AUTOCAST for implementing the Holt–Winters procedure, AUTOBOX for Box–Jenkins forecasting, STAMP for structural modelling, MTS for VARMA modelling and RATS for time series regression.

One final comment on time series computing is to note that it is one area where different packages may not give exactly the same answer to what is apparently the same question. This is often due to differences in the way that starting values are treated. For example, when fitting an AR(1) model, conditional least squares estimation treats the first observation as fixed, while full maximum likelihood does not. Fortunately the resulting differences are usually small, especially for long series. However, this is not always so as demonstrated by the rather alarming examples in Newbold *et al.* (1994).

9. Closing remarks

By now it should be evident that, in many respects, forecasting in the 1990s is much like forecasting in earlier decades, namely difficult, but exciting and challenging. On the plus side, we now have a wider range of models to choose from with much better software available. However, these developments do not come without a down side. With more models available, it is perhaps even easier to formulate the wrong one, or to choose an inappropriate method or, given the complexities of modern software, to misuse a forecasting package.

It is also salutary to remember that all forecasts are based on assumptions, and so, especially for long-term forecasting, there is much to be said for *not* producing a single point forecast, but rather producing a range of forecasts based on different known assumptions. This is called *scenario analysis* (Schoemaker, 1991).

I close with the following general comments.

(a) It is essential to begin by clarifying exactly how a forecast will be used.
(b) A careful time plot of the data should always be drawn.
(c) The context is crucial in choosing an appropriate forecasting method, though it is not easy to give simple general guidelines on making this choice.
(d) Out-of-sample forecasts are generally not as good as would be expected from within-sample fits, and the comparative accuracy of different forecasting methods should always be assessed on out-of-sample results.
(e) For univariate forecasting, structural modelling and exponential smoothing methods are strong competitors to Box–Jenkins modelling, especially for data showing large trend and seasonal components.

(f) As regards multivariate forecasting, multivariate models are still much more difficult to
     fit than univariate models, while multiple regression remains a treacherous procedure
     when applied to time series data. Bayesian VAR is often preferred to the use of VARMA
     models, while co-integration should always be considered for economic data.
(g) Many observed time series exhibit non-linear characteristics and non-linear modelling is
     of particular current interest, especially for long financial time series. The resulting (out-
     of-sample) forecasts have not always shown as much improvement as might have been
     hoped, and claims for the superiority of neural network models seem particularly
     exaggerated.
(h) Time series model building is generally a tricky process requiring an iterative–interactive
     approach. The BIC and AIC_c model selection critera is is preferred to the (ordinary)
     AIC to try to prevent overfitting.

References

Andrews, R. L. (1994) Forecasting performance of structural time series models. *J. Bus. Econ. Statist.*, **12**, 129–133.
Armstrong, J. S. and Collopy, F. (1992) Error measures for generalizing about forecasting methods: empirical
     comparisons. *Int. J. Forecast.*, **8**, 69–80.
Ball, M. and Wood, A. (1996) Trend growth in post-1850 British economic history: the Kalman filter and historical
     judgment. *Statistician*, **45**, 143–152.
Banerjee, A., Dolado, J., Galbraith, J. W. and Hendry, D. F. (1993) *Co-integration, Error-correction, and the
     Econometric Analysis of Non-stationary Data.* Oxford: Oxford University Press.
Beran, J. (1992) Statistical methods for data with long-range dependence. *Statist. Sci.*, **7**, 404–427.
———(1994) *Statistics for Long-memory Processes.* New York: Chapman and Hall.
Berliner, L. M. (1991) Likelihood and Bayesian prediction of chaotic systems. *J. Am. Statist. Ass.*, **86**, 938–952.
Bollerslev, T., Chou, Y. and Kroner, K. F. (1992) ARCH models in finance. *J. Econometr.*, **52**, 5–59.
Box, G. E. P., Jenkins, G. M. and Reinsel, G. C. (1994) *Time Series Analysis. Forecasting and Control*, 3rd edn.
     Englewood Cliffs: Prentice Hall.
Brockwell, P. J. and Davis, R. A. (1991) *Time Series: Theory and Methods*, 2nd edn. New York: Springer.
den Butter, F. A. G. and Fase, M. M. G. (1991) *Seasonal Adjustment as a Practical Problem.* Amsterdam: Elsevier.
Chappell, D. *et al.* (1996) A threshold model for the French Franc/Deutschmark exchange rate. *J. Forecast.*, **15**, 155–
     164.
Chatfield, C. (1988) What is the 'best' method of forecasting? *J. Appl. Statist.*, **15**, 19–38.
———(1993a) Calculating interval forecasts (with discussion). *J. Bus. Econ. Statist.*, **11**, 121–144.
———(1993b) Neural networks: forecasting breakthrough or passing fad? *Int. J. Forecast.*, **9**, 1–3.
———(1995a) *Problem-solving: a Statistician's Guide*, 2nd edn. London: Chapman and Hall.
———(1995b) Model uncertainty, data mining and statistical inference (with discussion). *J. R. Statist. Soc.* A, **158**,
     419–466.
———(1996a) *The Analysis of Time Series*, 5th edn. London: Chapman and Hall.
———(1996b) Model uncertainty and forecast accuracy. *J. Forecast.*, **15**, 495–508.
Chen, C. and Liu, L.-M. (1993) Forecasting time series with outliers. *J. Forecast.*, **12**, 13–35.
Choi, B. (1992) *ARMA Model Identification.* New York: Springer.
Church, K. B. and Curram, S. P. (1996) Forecasting consumers' expenditure: a comparison between econometric and
     neural network models. *Int. J. Forecast.*, **12**, 255–267.
Clemen, R. T. (1989) Combining forecasts: a review and annotated bibliography. *Int. J. Forecast.*, **5**, 559–583.
Collopy, F. and Armstrong, J. S. (1992) Rule-based forecasting: development and validation of an expert systems
     approach to combining time series extrapolations. *Mangmnt Sci.*, **38**, 1394–1414.
Crato, N. and Ray, B. K. (1996) Model selection and forecasting for long-range dependent processes. *J. Forecast.*, **15**,
     107–125.
DeJong, D. N. and Whiteman, C. H. (1993) Unit roots in US macroeconomic time series: a survey of classical and
     Bayesian perspectives. In *New Directions in Time Series Analysis*, part II (eds D. Brillinger *et al.*). New York:
     Springer.
Diggle, P. J. (1990) *Time Series.* Oxford: Clarendon.
Engle, R. F. and Granger, C. W. J. (1991) *Long-run Economic Relationships: Readings in Cointegration.* Oxford:
     Oxford University Press.
Faraway, J. and Chatfield, C. (1998) Time series forecasting with neural networks: a comparative study using the air
     line data. *Appl. Statist.*, **47**, in the press.
Fildes, R. (1992) The evaluation of extrapolative forecasting methods. *Int. J. Forecast.*, **8**, 81–98.
Fildes, R. and Makridakis, S. (1995) The impact of empirical accuracy studies on time series analysis and forecasting.
     Int. Statist. Rev., **63**, 289–308.

Franses, P. H. and Kleibergen, F. (1996) Unit roots in the Nelson–Plosser data: do they matter for forecasting? *Int. J. Forecast.*, **12**, 283–288.

Fuller, W. A. (1996) *Introduction to Statistical Time Series*, 2nd edn. New York: Wiley.

Granger, C. W. J. (1992) Forecasting stock market prices: lessons for forecasters. *Int. J. Forecast.*, **8**, 3–13.

Granger, C. W. J. and Newbold, P. (1986) *Forecasting Economic Time Series*, 2nd edn. New York: Academic Press.

Granger, C. W. J. and Teräsvirta, T. (1993) *Modelling Nonlinear Economic Relationships*. New York: Oxford University Press.

de Groot, C. and Wurtz, D. (1991) Analysis of univariate time series with connectionist nets: a case study of two classical examples. *Neurocomputing*, **3**, 177–192.

Harvey, A. C. (1989) *Forecasting, Structural Time Series Models and the Kalman Filter*. Cambridge: Cambridge University Press.

———(1993) *Time Series Models*, 2nd edn. Hemel Hempstead: Harvester Wheatsheaf.

Hill, T., Marquez, L., O'Connor, M. and Remus, W. (1994) Artificial neural network models for forecasting and decision making. *Int. J. Forecast.*, **10**, 5–15.

Hylleberg, S. (ed.) (1992) *Modelling Seasonality*. Oxford: Oxford University Press.

Isham, V. (1993) Statistical aspects of chaos. In *Networks and Chaos—Statistical and Probabilistic Aspects* (eds O. E. Barndorff-Nielsen, J. L. Jensen and W. S. Kendall), pp. 124–200. London: Chapman and Hall.

Janacek, G. and Swift, L. (1993) *Time Series: Forecasting, Simulation, Applications*. Chichester: Horwood.

Kadiyala, K. R. and Karlsson, S. (1993) Forecasting with generalized Bayesian vector autoregressions. *J. Forecast.*, **12**, 365–378.

Kendall, M. and Ord, J. K. (1990) *Time Series*, 3rd edn. Sevenoaks: Arnold.

Lin, J.-L. and Granger, C. W. J. (1994) Forecasting from non-linear models in practice. *J. Forecast.*, **13**, 1–9.

Lütkepohl, H. (1993) *Introduction to Multiple Time Series Analysis*, 2nd edn. Berlin: Springer.

Makridakis, S., Chatfield, C., Hibon, M., Lawrence, M., Mills, T., Ord, K. and Simmons, L. F. (1993) The M2-competition: a real-time judgmentally based forecasting study (with commentary). *Int. J. Forecast.*, **9**, 5–29.

Mills, T. C. (1990) *Time Series Techniques for Economists*. Cambridge: Cambridge University Press.

Montgomery, D. C., Johnson, L. A. and Gardiner, J. S. (1990) *Forecasting and Time Series Analysis*, 2nd edn. New York: McGraw-Hill.

Murray, M. P. (1994) A drunk and her dog: an illustration of cointegration and error correction. *Am. Statistn*, **48**, 37–39.

Newbold, P., Agiakloglou, C. and Miller, J. (1993) Long-term inference based on short-term forecasting models. In *Time Series Analysis* (ed. T. Subba Rao), pp. 9–25. London: Chapman and Hall.

———(1994) Adventures with ARIMA software. *Int. J. Forecast.*, **10**, 573–581.

Pankratz, A. (1991) *Forecasting with Dynamic Regression Models*. New York: Wiley.

Pole, A., West, M. and Harrison, J. (1994) *Applied Bayesian Forecasting and Time Series Analysis*. London: Chapman and Hall.

Reinsel, G. C. (1993) *Elements of Multivariate Time Series Analysis*. New York: Springer.

Ripley, B. D. (1993) Statistical aspects of neural networks. In *Networks and Chaos—Statistical and Probabilistic Aspects* (eds O. E. Barndorff-Nielsen, J. L. Jensen and W. S. Kendall), pp. 40–123. London: Chapman and Hall.

Schoemaker, P. J. H. (1991) When and how to use scenario planning: a heuristic approach with illustrations. *J. Forecast.*, **10**, 549–564.

Shephard, N. (1996) Statistical aspects of ARCH and stochastic volatility. In *Time Series Models* (eds D. R. Cox, D. V. Hinkley and O. E. Barndorff-Nielsen), pp. 1–67. London: Chapman and Hall.

Smith, J. and Yadav, S. (1994) Forecasting costs incurred from unit differencing fractionally integrated processes. *Int. J. Forecast.*, **10**, 507–514.

Spencer, D. E. (1993) Developing a Bayesian vector autoregression forecasting model. *Int. J. Forecast.*, **9**, 407–421.

Sutcliffe, A. (1994) Time-series forecasting using fractional differencing. *J. Forecast.*, **13**, 383–393.

Tashman, L. J. and Kruk, J. M. (1996) The use of protocols to select exponential smoothing procedures: a reconsideration of forecasting competitions. *Int. J. Forecast.*, **12**, 235–253.

Taylor, S. J. (1994) Modeling stochastic volatility: a review and comparative study. *Math. Finan.*, **4**, 183–204.

Tiao, G. C. and Tsay, R. S. (1994) Some advances in non-linear and adaptive modelling in time-series. *J. Forecast.*, **13**, 109–131.

Tong, H. (1990) *Non-linear Time Series*. Oxford: Oxford University Press.

———(1995) A personal overview of non-linear time series analysis from a chaos perspective. *Scand. J. Statist.*, **22**, 399–446.

Webby, R. and O'Connor, M. (1996) Judgemental and statistical time series forecasting: a review of the literature. *Int. J. Forecast.*, **12**, 91–118.

Wei, W. W. S. (1990) *Time Series Analysis: Univariate and Multivariate Methods*. Redwood City: Addison-Wesley.

Weigend, A. S. and Gershenfeld, N. A. (eds) (1994) *Time Series Prediction*. Reading: Addison-Wesley.

West, M. and Harrison, J. (1997) *Bayesian Forecasting and Dynamic Models*, 2nd edn. New York: Springer.

Winklhofer, H., Diamantopoulos, A. and Witt, S. F. (1996) Forecasting practice: a review of the empirical literature and an agenda for future research. *Int. J. Forecast.*, **12**, 193–221.

Part IV
The Econometrics of Forecasting

[20]

Journal of Econometrics 52 (1992) 91–113. North-Holland

Prediction in dynamic models with time-dependent conditional variances*

Richard T. Baillie

Michigan State University, East Lansing, MI 48824, USA

Tim Bollerslev

Northwestern University, Evanston, IL 60208, USA

This paper considers forecasting the conditional mean and variance from a single-equation dynamic model with autocorrelated disturbances following an ARMA process, and innovations with time-dependent conditional heteroskedasticity as represented by a linear GARCH process. Expressions for the minimum MSE predictor and the conditional MSE are presented. We also derive the formula for all the theoretical moments of the prediction error distribution from a general dynamic model with GARCH(1, 1) innovations. These results are then used in the construction of *ex ante* prediction confidence intervals by means of the Cornish–Fisher asymptotic expansion. An empirical example relating to the uncertainty of the expected depreciation of foreign exchange rates illustrates the usefulness of the results.

1. Introduction

The ARCH class of models was originally introduced by Engle (1982) as a convenient way of modeling time-dependent conditional heteroskedasticity; see Bollerslev, Chou, and Kroner (1992) for a recent survey. Despite the extensive literature on ARCH and related models, relatively little attention has been given to the issue of forecasting in models where time-dependent conditional heteroskedasticity is present. Bollerslev (1986), Diebold (1988), and Granger, White, and Kamstra (1989) all discuss the construction of one-step-ahead prediction error intervals with time-varying variances. Engle and Kraft (1983) derive expressions for the multi-step prediction error variance in ARMA models with ARCH errors, but do not further discuss the characteristics of the prediction error distribution. The prediction error

*The authors are very grateful to Rob Engle, two anonymous referees, and the participants at the conference on 'Statistical Models of Volatility' at the University of California, San Diego for helpful comments, and thank the NSF for financial support under Grant SES90-22807.

distribution is also analyzed in Geweke (1989) within a Bayesian framework using extensive simulation methods. It turns out that the presence of ARCH effects can make a substantial difference to the conduct of inference, such as constructing *ex ante* forecast confidence intervals and out-of-sample structural stability tests.

This paper considers prediction from a fairly general single-equation model as represented by a nonlinear regression function with ARMA disturbances and innovations with time-dependent heteroskedasticity. After a brief section discussing notation, section 3 describes how the minimum mean square error (MSE) predictor of the future values of the conditional mean can be constructed. In the absence of ARCH in the mean effects, the actual form of the predictor is the same as in the homoskedastic case, but the presence of ARCH changes the MSE of the predictor and can make it larger or smaller than the value obtained under the assumption of conditional homoskedasticity. By expressing the Generalized ARCH (GARCH) model, as in Bollerslev (1986), in a companion form representation, section 4 derives the minimum MSE predictor of future values for the conditional variance. Some theoretical results for the corresponding MSE for the predictions of the conditional variance are given in section 5. Section 6 then derives explicit expressions for all the theoretical moments of the conditional prediction error distribution for the popular GARCH(1, 1) model. This allows the percentiles of the forecast density to be approximated by means of the Cornish–Fisher asymptotic expansion as discussed in section 7. These results are extended in section 8 to the important case in practice where the disturbances from a model have ARMA errors and GARCH(1, 1) innovations. In section 9 the practical relevance of the techniques is illustrated through a simple empirical example relating to the uncertainty of the expected depreciation in the forward foreign exchange rate market. A brief conclusion and suggestions for future work are given in section 10.

2. Notation and assumptions

In many practical contexts it is important to derive multi-step predictions of the conditional mean from dynamic econometric models. To keep the setup as general as possible, let $\{y_t\}$ refer to the univariate discrete time real-valued stochastic process to be predicted and let

$$E_{t-1}(y_t) \equiv \mu_t \tag{1}$$

denote the conditional mean given information through time $t - 1$. The innovation process, $\{\varepsilon_t\}$, for the conditional mean is then given by

$$\varepsilon_t \equiv y_t - \mu_t, \tag{2}$$

with corresponding, possibly infinite, unconditional variance

$$\text{Var}(\varepsilon_t) = \text{E}(\varepsilon_t^2) \equiv \sigma^2. \tag{3}$$

While the unconditional variance is assumed to be time-invariant, the conditional variance of the process is allowed to depend nontrivially on the set of conditioning information, so that

$$\text{Var}_{t-1}(y_t) = \text{E}_{t-1}(\varepsilon_t^2) \equiv \sigma_t^2. \tag{4}$$

It is important to note that both μ_t and σ_t^2 are measurable with respect to the time $t-1$ information set and assumed to be finite with probability one. We also define

$$\nu_t \equiv \varepsilon_t^2 - \sigma_t^2. \tag{5}$$

Similarly to the innovation process for the conditional mean given in (2), $\{\nu_t\}$ is serially uncorrelated through time with mean zero, and is readily interpreted as the time t innovation for the conditional variance.

The above setup allows for a wide variety of dynamic econometric models with time-varying second-order moments. In order to simplify the exposition, in the following analysis we shall concentrate on predictions from the standard ARMA(k,l) class of models, i.e.,

$$\mu_t = \mu + \sum_{i=1}^{k} \phi_i y_{t-i} + \sum_{i=1}^{l} \theta_i \varepsilon_{t-i}. \tag{6}$$

The extension to the case of exogenous explanatory variables allowing for the possibility of co-integration, as in Engle and Granger (1987), is in principle straightforward. It is well-known that if the innovation variance, σ^2, is finite, the ARMA(k,l) model in (6) is covariance-stationary and invertible if and only if all the roots of $1 - \phi_1 z - \cdots - \phi_k z^k = 0$ and $1 - \theta_1 z - \cdots - \theta_l z^l = 0$ lie outside the unit circle.

One important exclusion from this framework concerns the ARCH in mean model, originally due to Engle, Lilien, and Robins (1987). Processes with feedback from the conditional variance to the conditional mean will considerably complicate the form of the predictor and its associated MSE. Analysis of such models is consequently left for future research.

Recently several alternative parameterizations for the time-varying conditional variance, σ_t^2, have been suggested in the econometrics and time series literature. In this study, we shall focus on the popular linear GARCH(p,q)

class of models,

$$\sigma_t^2 = \omega + \sum_{i=1}^{q} \alpha_i \varepsilon_{t-i}^2 + \sum_{i=1}^{p} \beta_i \sigma_{t-i}^2, \tag{7}$$

where $\omega > 0$, and α_i and β_i are restricted so that the coefficients in the infinite distributed lag representation of σ_t^2 in terms of lagged values of ε_t^2 are all positive; see Nelson and Cao (1992). If $\alpha_1 + \cdots + \alpha_q + \beta_1 + \cdots + \beta_p < 1$, $\{\varepsilon_t\}$ is covariance-stationary and

$$\sigma^2 = \omega \left(1 - \alpha_1 - \cdots - \alpha_q - \beta_1 - \cdots - \beta_p \right)^{-1}.$$

Similarly to the ARMA(k, l) model for the conditional mean, the GARCH(p, q) structure could easily be extended to allow for exogenous explanatory variables entering the conditional variance. The particular parameterization in the GARCH(p, q) model in (7) has σ_t^2 expressed as a function of lagged squared innovations. An alternative, although less widely used, representation that could be analyzed in a similar fashion involves σ_t^2 being expressed as a function of serially correlated lagged disturbances $u_t \equiv y_t - f(x_t; b)$, where $f(x_t; b)$ denotes a possible nonlinear regression function; see Bera and Lee (1988) and Bera, Lee, and Higgins (1990).

In part of the subsequent analysis we shall make use of the higher-order conditional moments for the $\{\varepsilon_t\}$ process. For simplicity, we assume that this conditional distribution is symmetric with all the existing even-ordered moments proportional to the corresponding powers of the conditional variance,

$$E_{t-1}\left(\varepsilon_t^{2r+1}\right) = 0, \qquad r = 0, 1, \ldots, K-1, \tag{8}$$

$$E_{t-1}\left(\varepsilon_t^{2r}\right) = \kappa_r \sigma_t^{2r}, \qquad r = 0, 1, \ldots, K. \tag{9}$$

Here κ_r denotes the rth-order cumulant for the conditional density of ε_t, and by definition $\kappa_0 = \kappa_1 = 1$.

For instance, under the assumption of conditional normality often invoked when conducting inference in ARCH-type models, all the moments of the conditional distribution of ε_t are finite and

$$\kappa_r = \prod_{i=1}^{r} (2i - 1), \qquad r = 1, 2, \ldots. \tag{10}$$

With conditional t-distributed errors as in Bollerslev (1987),

$$\kappa_r = (n-2)^r \Gamma(r + 1/2)\Gamma(n/2 - r)\Gamma(1/2)^{-1}\Gamma(n/2)^{-1}, \tag{11}$$

$$r = 1, 2, \ldots, K,$$

where $\Gamma(\cdot)$ denotes the gamma function, $n > 2$ the degrees of freedom in the t-distribution standardized to have a unit variance, and $K = \text{int}(n/2)$. Note, only the first n moments of the t-distribution are finite.

While the vast majority of empirical studies using ARCH models tend to rely on parametric specifications for the conditional density of ε_t given information through time $t - 1$ as in (10) and (11), different nonparametric methods have also been suggested in the literature, including the polynomial expansion in Gallant and Tauchen (1989) and Gallant, Hsieh, and Tauchen (1990) and the nonparametric density estimation in Engle and Gonzalez-Rivera (1991). Although, explicit expressions for the higher-order conditional moments may not be directly available from these methods, the implied κ_r coefficients can easily be evaluated using numerical techniques.[1]

3. Prediction of the mean in ARMA(k, l) models

Many alternative expressions are available for the minimum MSE predictor from the ARMA(k, l) class of models. However, in order to provide an analogy with subsequent material it is convenient to express the ARMA(k, l) model given by (1), (2), (4), and (6) in the companion form representation as

$$
\begin{bmatrix} y_t \\ y_{t-1} \\ \cdot \\ y_{t-k+1} \\ \varepsilon_t \\ \varepsilon_{t-1} \\ \cdot \\ \varepsilon_{t-l+1} \end{bmatrix} = \begin{bmatrix} \mu \\ 0 \\ \cdot \\ 0 \\ 0 \\ 0 \\ \cdot \\ 0 \end{bmatrix} + \begin{bmatrix} \phi_1 & \cdots & \phi_k & \theta_1 & \cdots & & \theta_l \\ 1 & 0 & \cdots & 0 & 0 & \cdots & & 0 \\ 0 & & & & & & & \\ 0 & & \cdots & 1 & 0 & 0 & \cdots & & 0 \\ 0 & & \cdots & & & & \cdots & & 0 \\ 0 & & \cdots & & 0 & 1 & \cdots & 0 & 0 \\ \cdot & & & & & & & \\ 0 & & \cdots & & 0 & 0 & \cdots & 1 & 0 \end{bmatrix} \begin{bmatrix} y_{t-1} \\ y_{t-2} \\ \cdot \\ y_{t-k} \\ \varepsilon_{t-1} \\ \varepsilon_{t-2} \\ \cdot \\ \varepsilon_{t-l} \end{bmatrix} + \begin{bmatrix} \varepsilon_t \\ 0 \\ \cdot \\ 0 \\ \varepsilon_t \\ 0 \\ \cdot \\ 0 \end{bmatrix},
$$

(12)

or more compactly,

$$
Y_t = \mu e_1 + \Phi Y_{t-1} + (e_1 + e_{k+1})\varepsilon_t,
\tag{13}
$$

where e_j refers to the compatible vector of zeros except for unity in the jth element, here a $(k + l)$-dimensional unit vector. Following Baillie (1987), upon repeated substitution in (13) the optimal s-step-ahead predictor is readily seen to be

$$
E_t(y_{t+s}) = \iota_s + \sum_{i=0}^{k-1} \tau_{i,s} y_{t-i} + \sum_{i=0}^{l-1} \lambda_{i,s} \varepsilon_{t-i},
\tag{14}
$$

---

[1] The κ_r coefficients from the density estimation in Engle and Gonzalez-Rivera (1991) are time-invariant by assumption, but the higher-order standardized conditional moments from the seminonparametric method in Gallant and Tauchen (1989) may be time-varying.

where

$$\iota_s = e_1'(I + \Phi + \cdots + \Phi^{s-1})e_1\mu, \tag{15}$$

$$\tau_{i,s} = e_1'\Phi^s e_{i+1}, \qquad i = 0, \ldots, k-1, \tag{16}$$

$$\lambda_{i,s} = e_1'\Phi^s e_{k+i+1}, \qquad i = 0, \ldots, l-1. \tag{17}$$

This is a different and more tractable expression than that given by Baillie (1980) and Yamamoto (1981), where the ARMA process is represented in terms of an infinite-order autoregression.

Furthermore, by direct substitution and iterated expectations the forecast error for the s-step-ahead predictor in (14) is given by

$$e_{t,s} \equiv y_{t+s} - E_t(y_{t+s}) = \sum_{i=1}^{s} \psi_{s-i}\varepsilon_{t+i}, \tag{18}$$

with conditional MSE

$$E_t(e_{t,s}^2) = \text{Var}_t(y_{t+s}) = \sum_{i=1}^{s} \psi_{s-i}^2 E_t(\sigma_{t+i}^2), \tag{19}$$

where

$$\psi_i = e_1'\Phi^i(e_1 + e_{k+1}), \qquad i = 0, \ldots, s-1. \tag{20}$$

Note, the ψ_i's correspond directly to the coefficients in the infinite-order moving average representation of the model.

With conditionally homoskedastic errors the conditional MSE for the optimal s-step-ahead predictor is identical to the unconditional MSE,

$$\text{Var}(y_{t+s}) = \sigma^2 \sum_{i=1}^{s} \psi_{s-i}^2,$$

where σ^2 is assumed to be finite. However, when conditional heteroskedasticity is present, the forecast error uncertainty is generally changing through time, and from (19) the conditional MSE takes the form

$$\text{Var}_t(y_{t+s}) = \sigma^2 \sum_{i=1}^{s} \psi_{s-i}^2 + \sum_{i=1}^{s} \psi_{s-i}^2(E_t(\sigma_{t+i}^2) - \sigma^2).$$

Hence, the conventional first term is appended by a second term reflecting the differences between the average or the unconditional variance of the future innovations and the conditional variance given information through time t. If the process is covariance-stationary and invertible, ψ_i^2 goes to zero and $E_t(\sigma_{t+i}^2)$ to σ^2 for increasing values of i, and the conditional MSE converges to the unconditional variance of the process as the forecast horizon increases. However, with a time-varying variance this convergence is not necessarily monotone. As previously noted by Engle and Kraft (1983), over certain time periods the conditional MSE may exceed the unconditional variance provided $E_t(\sigma^2_{t+i}) > \sigma^2$ for some $1 \le i \le s$.

It is important to note, that the presence of conditional heteroskedasticity does not change the expression for the minimum MSE predictor as given by (14), but the forecast error uncertainty associated with the optimal predictor will be time-varying as reflected in (19). Of course, in order to evaluate the expression for the conditional MSE given by the formula in (19) it is necessary to calculate the conditional expectations for the future conditional variances of the innovation process. This is the subject of the next section.

4. Prediction of the variance in GARCH(p, q) models

Following Bollerslev (1988), the linear GARCH(p, q) model in (4) and (7) can be conveniently rewritten as

$$\varepsilon^2_t = \omega + (\alpha_1 + \beta_1)\varepsilon^2_{t-1} + \cdots + (\alpha_m + \beta_m)\varepsilon^2_{t-m}$$

$$- \beta_1 \nu_{t-1} - \cdots - \beta_p \nu_{t-p} + \nu_t, \tag{21}$$

where $m \equiv \max(p, q)$, $\alpha_i \equiv 0$ for $i > q$, and $\beta_i \equiv 0$ for $i > p$. From the definition in (5), $\{\nu_t\}$ is a serially uncorrelated process, and (21) corresponds to an ARMA(m, p) model for $\{\varepsilon^2_t\}$. Thus, analogous to the ARMA(k, l) representation in (12), the GARCH(p, q) model may be expressed in companion first-order form as

$$
\begin{bmatrix}
\varepsilon^2_t \\
\varepsilon^2_{t-1} \\
\cdot \\
\varepsilon^2_{t-m+1} \\
\nu_t \\
\nu_{t-1} \\
\cdot \\
\nu_{t-p+1}
\end{bmatrix}
=
\begin{bmatrix}
\omega \\
0 \\
\cdot \\
0 \\
0 \\
0 \\
\cdot \\
0
\end{bmatrix}
+
\begin{bmatrix}
\alpha_1 + \beta_1 & \cdots & & \alpha_m + \beta_m & -\beta_1 & \cdots & & -\beta_p \\
1 & & \cdots & 0 & 0 & 0 & \cdots & & 0 \\
& & & & & & & \\
0 & & \cdots & 1 & 0 & 0 & \cdots & & 0 \\
0 & & \cdots & & & & \cdots & & 0 \\
0 & & \cdots & & 0 & 1 & \cdots & 0 & 0 \\
& & & & & & & \\
0 & & \cdots & & 0 & 0 & \cdots & 1 & 0
\end{bmatrix}
$$

$$
\times
\begin{bmatrix}
\varepsilon^2_{t-1} \\
\varepsilon^2_{t-2} \\
\cdot \\
\varepsilon^2_{t-m} \\
\nu_{t-1} \\
\nu_{t-2} \\
\cdot \\
\nu_{t-p}
\end{bmatrix}
+
\begin{bmatrix}
\nu_t \\
0 \\
\cdot \\
0 \\
\nu_t \\
0 \\
\cdot \\
0
\end{bmatrix}, \tag{22}
$$

or more compactly,

$$V_t^2 = \omega e_1 + \Gamma V_{t-1}^2 + (e_1 + e_{m+1}) v_t. \tag{23}$$

Upon repeated substitution,

$$V_{t+s}^2 = \sum_{i=0}^{s-1} \Gamma^i ((e_1 + e_{m+1}) v_{t+s-i} + \omega e_1) + \Gamma^s V_t^2.$$

However, $\varepsilon_{t+s}^2 = e_1' V_{t+s}^2$ and $E_t(v_{t+i}) = 0$ for $i > 0$, and analogously to the derivation of (14) it follows, from pre-multiplication with e_1' and the use of iterated expectations, that the minimum MSE s-step-ahead predictor for the conditional variance from the GARCH(p, q) process is given by[2]

$$E_t\left(\varepsilon_{t+s}^2\right) = E_t\left(\sigma_{t+s}^2\right) = \omega_s + \sum_{i=0}^{p-1} \delta_{i,s}\sigma_{t-i}^2 + \sum_{i=0}^{m-1} \rho_{i,s}\varepsilon_{t-i}^2, \tag{24}$$

where

$$\omega_s = e_1'(I + \Gamma \ldots + \Gamma^{s-1}) e_1 \omega, \tag{25}$$

$$\delta_{i,s} = -e_1' \Gamma^s e_{m+i+1}, \qquad\qquad i = 0, \ldots, p-1, \tag{26}$$

$$\rho_{i,s} = e_1' \Gamma^s (e_{i+1} + e_{m+i+1}), \qquad i = 0, \ldots, p-1; \tag{27}$$

$$\rho_{i,s} = e_1' \Gamma^s e_{i+1}, \qquad\qquad\qquad i = p, \ldots, m-1. \tag{28}$$

As an illustration consider the popular GARCH(1, 1) process, where

$$E_t\left(\sigma_{t+s}^2\right) = \omega \sum_{i=0}^{s-1} (\alpha_1 + \beta_1)^i + (\alpha_1 + \beta_1)^{s-1} \alpha_1 \varepsilon_t^2$$

$$+ (\alpha_1 + \beta_1)^{s-1} \beta_1 \sigma_t^2$$

$$= \omega \sum_{i=1}^{s-1} (\alpha_1 + \beta_1)^i + (\alpha_1 + \beta_1)^{s-1} \sigma_{t+1}^2.$$

If the model is covariance-stationary with $\alpha_1 + \beta_1 < 1$ and $\sigma^2 = \omega(1 - \alpha_1 - \beta_1)^{-1}$, the optimal predictor for σ_{t+s}^2 becomes

$$E_t\left(\sigma_{t+s}^2\right) = \sigma^2 + (\alpha_1 + \beta_1)^{s-1}\left(\sigma_{t+1}^2 - \sigma^2\right),$$

---

[2]An alternative expression for the optimal predictor for the conditional variance is given by the recursions $E_t(\sigma_{t+s}^2) = \omega + \beta_1 E_t(\sigma_{t+s-1}^2) + \cdots + \beta_p E_t(\sigma_{t+s-p}^2) + \alpha_1 E_t(\varepsilon_{t+s-1}^2) + \cdots + \alpha_q E_t(\varepsilon_{t+s-q}^2)$, where by definition $E_t(\varepsilon_{t+i}^2) \equiv E_t(\sigma_{t+i}^2)$ for $i > 0$, while $E_t(\sigma_{t+i}^2) \equiv \sigma_{t+i}^2$ and $E_t(\varepsilon_{t+i}^2) \equiv \varepsilon_{t+i}^2$ for $i \leq 0$.

a result previously derived by Engle and Bollerslev (1986). Once again, as the
forecast horizon increases current information becomes less important, and
the optimal forecast converges monotonically to the unconditional variance.
However, for the Integrated GARCH(1,1), or IGARCH(1,1), model with
$\alpha_1 + \beta_1 = 1$, current information remains important for forecasts of all horizons,

$$E_t(\sigma_{t+s}^2) = \omega(s - 1) + \sigma_{t+1}^2.$$

Shocks to the conditional variance are persistent in the sense of Bollerslev
and Engle (1989), as $E_t(\sigma_{t+s}^2) - E_{t-1}(\sigma_{t+s}^2) = \sigma_{t+1}^2 - \omega - \sigma_t^2 = \alpha_1 \nu_t$ is a non-
trivial function of the information set at time t for all forecast horizons $s > 0$.

The conditional MSE associated with the optimal forecasts for the mean in
the general ARMA(k,l)–GARCH(p,q) class of models is readily obtained
by combining eqs. (19) and (24),

$$\text{Var}_t(y_{t+s}) = \sum_{i=1}^{s} \psi_{s-i}^2 \omega_i + \sum_{i=1}^{s} \psi_{s-i}^2 \left(\sum_{j=0}^{p-1} \delta_{j,i} \sigma_{t-j}^2 + \sum_{j=0}^{m-1} \rho_{j,i} \varepsilon_{t-j}^2 \right).$$

$$(29)$$

For example, for the covariance-stationary AR(1) model with GARCH(1,1)
errors the optimal predictor becomes

$$E_t(y_{t+s}) = \phi_1^s y_t,$$

with associated MSE

$$\text{Var}_t(y_{t+s}) = \sum_{i=1}^{s} \phi_1^{2(s-i)} \left(\sigma^2 + (\alpha_1 + \beta_1)^{i-1} (\sigma_{t+1}^2 - \sigma^2) \right)$$

$$= \sigma^2 (1 - \phi_1^{2s})(1 - \phi_1^2)^{-1} + (\sigma_{t+1}^2 - \sigma^2)$$

$$\times ((\alpha_1 + \beta_1)^s - \phi_1^{2s})(\alpha_1 + \beta_1 - \phi_1^2)^{-1},$$

where the last equality is only valid for $\phi_1^2 \neq \alpha_1 + \beta_1$. The inclusion of the
second term in the above expression for the conditional MSE
may lead to an increase or a decrease in the prediction error variance
compared to the conventional MSE, but as the horizon increases the conditional MSE will converge to the unconditional variance, i.e.,
$\text{var}(y_t) = \omega(1 - \alpha_1 - \beta_1)^{-1}(1 - \phi_1^2)^{-1}$.

5. Uncertainty in predicting future conditional variances

The results in the previous section provide formulae for the calculation of the forecast error variance of the mean in general dynamic econometric models with GARCH(p, q) errors. However, in many applications in financial economics the primary interest centers on the forecast for the future conditional variance itself. Such instances include option pricing as discussed by Day and Lewis (1992) and Lamoureux and Lastrapes (1990), the efficient determination of the market rate of return as in Chou (1989), and the relationship between stock market volatility and the business cycle as analyzed by Schwert (1989). In these situations it is therefore of interest to be able to characterize the uncertainty associated with the forecasts for the future conditional variances also. Some potentially useful results for this purpose are given by Lemma 1.

Lemma 1. For the GARCH(p, q) model given by (4), (5), (7), (8), and (9) the forecast error for the s-step-ahead predictor for the conditional variance σ_{t+s}^2 in (24) equals

$$v_{t,s} \equiv \sigma_{t+s}^2 - \mathrm{E}_t(\sigma_{t+s}^2) = \sum_{i=1}^{s-1} \chi_{s-i} \nu_{t+1}, \qquad (30)$$

and the conditional MSE is

$$\mathrm{E}_t(v_{t,s}^2) = \mathrm{Var}_t(\sigma_{t+s}^2) = (\kappa_2 - 1) \sum_{i=1}^{s-1} \chi_{s-i}^2 \mathrm{E}_t(\sigma_{t+i}^4), \qquad (31)$$

where

$$\chi_i = e_1' \Gamma^i (e_1 + e_{m+1}), \qquad i = 1, \ldots, s-1. \qquad (32)$$

Proof. Since $\sigma_{t+s}^2 - \mathrm{E}_t(\sigma_{t+s}^2) = \varepsilon_{t+s}^2 - \mathrm{E}_t(\sigma_{t+s}^2) - v_{t-s}$, (30) and (32) follow from the companion form in (23) and slight modifications to the derivation of (18) and (19). By (5) and (9) $\mathrm{E}_t(v_{t+i} v_{t+j}) = 0$ for $1 \leq i < j \leq s$, and $\mathrm{E}_t(v_{t+i}^2) = (\kappa_2 - 1) \mathrm{E}_t(\sigma_{t+i}^4)$ for $i > 0$. Hence (31) is a result of iterated expectations. Q.E.D.

To illustrate, consider the GARCH(1, 1) model. From (22) and (32) it follows that $\chi_i = \alpha_1(\alpha_1 + \beta_1)^{i-1}$, $i = 1, \ldots, s-1$. Hence, the forecast error uncertainty associated with predictions of the future conditional variance equals

$$v_{t,s} = \alpha_1 \sum_{i-1}^{s-1} (\alpha_1 + \beta_1)^{i-1} v_{t+s-i},$$

with corresponding conditional MSE

$$\mathrm{E}_t(v_{t,s}^2) = (\kappa_2 - 1)\alpha_1^2 \sum_{i=1}^{s-1} (\alpha_1 + \beta_1)^{2(i-1)} \mathrm{E}_t(\sigma_{t+s-i}^4).$$

The empirical evaluation of this conditional MSE requires an expression for the fourth conditional moment. Such an expression is derived in the next section. However, given the focus in the present paper on optimal predictions for the conditional mean and the distribution of the corresponding prediction errors, we shall not pursue the topic of optimally forecasting the conditional variance any further in this paper.

6. Prediction error distributions in GARCH(1, 1) models

When conducting inference in GARCH(p, q) models, distributional assumptions are generally placed on the conditional distribution of ε_t given σ_t^2. This implies specific values for the cumulants κ_r in (9) that characterize the conditional even-ordered moments. However, in the presence of ARCH the unconditional distribution of ε_t has fatter tails than this conditional one-step-ahead prediction error distribution. In particular, given finite fourth moment $\mathrm{E}_{t-1}(\varepsilon_t^4) - \kappa_2(\mathrm{E}_{t-1}(\varepsilon_t^2))^2 = 0 < \mathrm{E}(\varepsilon_t^4) - \kappa_2(\mathrm{E}(\varepsilon_t^2))^2$. Similarly, the conditional distribution of ε_{t+s} for $s > 1$ given information through time t differs from the conditional distribution for $s = 1$. Even if the distribution of $\varepsilon_{t+s}/\sqrt{\mathrm{E}_t(\sigma_{t+s}^2)}$ is time-invariant for $s = 1$ by assumption, for $s > 1$ and σ_t^2 time-varying the standardized prediction error distribution generally depends nontrivially on the information set at time t. As opposed to the conventional framework with conditionally homoskedastic errors where standardizing with the prediction error variance leads to a time-invariant distribution, the dependence in the higher-order moments for the GARCH(p, q) model substantially complicates conventional multi-step prediction exercises.

For instance, the quantile regression techniques discussed in Granger, White, and Kamstra (1989) as a method for estimating the time-varying one-step-ahead prediction error intervals do not easily extend to multi-step predictors. Similarly, the numerical methods developed by Geweke (1989) for calculating the exact predictive density would require extensive simulations of the prediction error distribution for each particular realization of σ_{t+1}^2.

The presence of heteroskedasticity also alters the structure of the post-sample structural stability tests proposed by Box and Tiao (1976) commonly used as a tool in model evaluation and diagnostic checking; see, e.g., Chong and Hendry (1986), Lahiri (1975), and Lütkepohl (1985, 1988). In particular, under the assumption of conditional normality of the one-step-ahead prediction errors, ε_t/σ_t, it follows that the test statistic

$$Q_{t,s} = \sum_{i=1}^{s} \varepsilon_{t+i}^2 \sigma_{t+i}^{-2}$$

will possess the conventional chi-squared distribution with s degrees of freedom. Ignoring the temporal variation in σ_{t+i}^2 in constructing the test statistic can seriously bias inference.[3]

To overcome this apparent indeterminancy regarding the properties of the prediction error distribution from GARCH models, simple recursive expressions for all the existing conditional moments of the prediction error density for the widely-used GARCH(1, 1) model are provided by Theorem 1.

Theorem 1.   For the GARCH(1, 1) model defined by (4), (8), (9), and

$$\sigma_t^2 = \omega + \alpha_1 \varepsilon_{t-1}^2 + \beta_1 \sigma_{t-1}^2,$$

the 2Kth first conditional moments of ε_{t+s}, $s > 1$, are given by

$$E_t\left(\varepsilon_{t+s}^{2r+1}\right) = 0, \qquad\qquad r = 0, 1, \ldots, K-1, \qquad (33)$$

$$E_t\left(\varepsilon_{t+s}^{2r}\right) = \kappa_r E_t\left(\sigma_{t+s}^{2r}\right), \qquad r = 0, 1, \ldots, K, \qquad (34)$$

where

$$E_t\left(\sigma_{t+s}^{2r}\right) = \omega^r + \sum_{i=1}^{r} \binom{r}{i} \pi_i \omega^{r-i} E_t\left(\sigma_{t+s-1}^{2i}\right) \qquad (35)$$

and

$$\pi_i = \sum_{j=0}^{i} \binom{i}{j} \kappa_{i-j} \alpha_1^{i-j} \beta_1^j. \qquad (36)$$

Proof. Eqs. (33) and (34) follow from (8) and (9) by the law of iterated expectations. On repeated use of the binomial formula and from the law of

[3]For instance, for the GARCH(1, 1) model with $\omega = 0.1$, $\alpha_1 = 0.2$, $\beta_1 = 0.7$, and σ_{t+i}^2 fixed at the unconditional variance of one, the estimated rejection frequencies for $s = 2, 5,$ and 10 based on the 0.05 and 0.01 fractiles in the chi-squared distribution with s degrees of freedom are 0.064, 0.091, 0.114 and 0.027, 0.046, 0.067, respectively.

iterated expectations,

$$E_t(\sigma_{t+s}^{2r}) = E_t\left((\omega + \alpha_1\varepsilon_{t+s-1}^2 + \beta_1\sigma_{t+s-1}^2)^r\right)$$

$$= \sum_{i=0}^{r}\binom{r}{i}\omega^{r-i}E_t\left((\alpha_1\varepsilon_{t+s-1}^2 + \beta_1\sigma_{t+s-1}^2)^i\right)$$

$$= \sum_{i=0}^{r}\binom{r}{i}\omega^{r-i}E_t\left(\sum_{j=0}^{i}\binom{i}{j}\alpha_1^{i-j}\varepsilon_{t+s-1}^{2(i-j)}\beta_1^j\sigma_{t+s-1}^{2j}\right)$$

$$= \sum_{i=0}^{r}\binom{r}{i}\omega^{r-i}\sum_{j=0}^{i}\binom{i}{j}\alpha_1^{i-j}\beta_1^j E_t\left(\varepsilon_{t+s-1}^{2(i-j)}\sigma_{t+s-1}^{2j}\right)$$

$$= \sum_{i=0}^{r}\binom{r}{i}\omega^{r-i}\sum_{j=0}^{i}\binom{i}{j}\alpha_1^{i-j}\beta_1^j E_t\left(\sigma_{t+s-1}^{2j} E_{t+s-2}\left(\varepsilon_{t+s-i}^{2(i-j)}\right)\right)$$

$$= \sum_{i=0}^{r}\binom{r}{i}\omega^{r-i}\sum_{j=0}^{i}\binom{i}{j}\kappa_{i-j}\alpha_1^{i-j}\beta_1^j E_t\left(\sigma_{t+s-1}^{2i}\right),$$

which reduces to (35) and (36).   Q.E.D.

Given the recursive expressions for all the conditional moments in Theorem 1, several alternative asymptotic expansions are available for approximating prediction error distributions.[4] To set out the particular expansion used below in forming prediction error intervals, it is convenient to introduce the standardized cumulants for the s-step-ahead prediction error,[5]

$$\gamma_{r,t,s} \equiv \kappa_{r,t,s}(\kappa_{2,t,s})^{-r}, \qquad r = 2,\ldots,K, \tag{37}$$

where $\kappa_{r,t,s}$ denotes the $2r$th cumulant for $e_{t,s}$ conditional on the time t information set. For the one-step-ahead prediction error $\gamma_{r,t,1}$ will be time-invariant for all r by the assumptions in (8) and (9), but in general $\gamma_{r,t,s}$ will be a nontrivial function of the time t information set for $s > 1$. For instance, from Theorem 1 the conditional excess kurtosis for the two-step-ahead

[4]The conditional moment sequence uniquely determines the conditional distribution if the Carleman condition is satisfied; i.e., $E_t(\varepsilon_{t+s}^2)^{-1/2} + E_t(\varepsilon_{t+s}^4)^{-1/4} + E_t(\varepsilon_{t+s}^6)^{-1/6} + \cdots = \infty$. See Serfling (1980) for sufficient conditions.

[5]The $\gamma_{r,t,s}$'s play an important role in many asymptotic expansions, including the Gramm–Charlier, the Edgeworth, and the Cornish–Fisher approximation used below.

prediction error in the GARCH(1, 1) model is given by

$$\gamma_{2,t,2} = \left(\left(\kappa_2^2 - 3 \right) \alpha_1^2 \sigma_{t+1}^4 + \left(\kappa_2 - 3 \right) \right.$$

$$\times \left(\omega^2 + 2\omega(\alpha_1 + \beta_1)\sigma_{t+1}^2 + \left(\beta_1^2 + 2\alpha_1\beta_1 \right)\sigma_{t+1}^4 \right) \right)$$

$$\times \left(\omega + (\alpha_1 + \beta_1)\sigma_{t+1}^2 \right)^{-2},$$

which under the assumption of conditional normality, i.e., $\kappa_2 = 3$, reduces to

$$\gamma_{2,t,2} = 6\alpha_1^2\sigma_{t+1}^4 \left(\omega + (\alpha_1 + \beta_1)\sigma_{t+1}^2 \right)^{-2}.$$

Obviously, $\gamma_{2,t,2}$ is an increasing function of both σ_{t+1}^2 and α_1. For large values of σ_{t+1}^2 the conditional kurtosis for the two-step-ahead prediction error distribution may exceed the unconditional excess kurtosis for ε_t; i.e., $6\alpha_1^2(1 - \beta_1^2 - 2\alpha_1\beta_1 - 3\alpha_1^2)^{-1}$ where the denominator is assumed to be positive in order to ensure a finite fourth moment. More complicated expressions for the higher-order cumulants and longer forecast horizons from the GARCH(1, 1) model are readily available from Theorem 1.

7. Cornish–Fisher expansion

For the purpose of constructing prediction error intervals that remain valid in the presence of heteroskedasticity, the inverse of the Edgeworth expansion original developed by Cornish and Fisher (1937) is particularly useful; see Barndorff-Nielsen and Cox (1989) for a recent discussion. Thus, let $z_{t,s}(p)$ denote the Cornish–Fisher approximation to the time-varying pth quantile in the conditional distribution for the s-step-ahead prediction error $e_{t,s}$. For symmetric deviations from conditional normality the expression for $z_{t,s}(p)$ then simplifies to

$$z_{t,s}(p) = \rho_{t,s}(p) E_t \left(e_{t,s}^2 \right)^{1/2}, \tag{38}$$

where $\frac{1}{2} \leq p \leq 1$, and

$$\rho_{t,s}(p) = \Phi^{-1}(p) + \rho_2 \left(\Phi^{-1}(p) \right) \gamma_{2,t,s}$$

$$+ \rho_{22} \left(\Phi^{-1}(p) \right) \gamma_{2,t,s}^2 + \rho_4 \left(\Phi^{-1}(p) \right) \gamma_{3,t,s} + \cdots . \tag{39}$$

The first term in (39), $\Phi^{-1}(p)$, refers to the pth quantile in the standard normal distribution, the second term adjusts for conditional excess kurtosis, while the third and fourth terms are due to adjustments for up to the sixth conditional moment, and terms involving eight or higher-order moments have been omitted. Also, three important functions are given by[6]

$$\rho_2(z) \equiv (z^3 - 3z)/24,$$

$$\rho_4(z) \equiv (z^5 - 10z^3 + 15z)/720,$$

$$\rho_{22}(z) \equiv -(3z^5 - 24z^3 + 29z)/384.$$

Of course, the assumption of conditional normality for the s-step-ahead prediction errors corresponds to fixing all these functions in (39) to zero.

In order to check the accuracy of the Cornish–Fisher approximation in obtaining prediction error intervals in the present context a series of simulations were performed for various GARCH(1, 1) parameterizations with conditionally normal one-step-ahead prediction errors. For small values of α_1 and short forecast horizons the convenient assumption of conditional normality of the multi-step predictions appeared to work reasonably well on average, with the estimated coverage probabilities being close to the true size of the intervals. However, consistent with the discussion in the previous section, for longer forecast horizons and/or larger values of α_1 the true conditional prediction error distribution was more peaked at the center and had fatter tails than the normal distribution, and the normal approximation tended to overestimate the 0.50 and 0.20 fractiles while underestimating the 0.01 fractile. Interestingly, the crossing point for the densities for the true prediction error distribution and the normal approximation were generally close to the 5% fractiles. However, the simple Cornish–Fisher expansion in (39) based on the adjustment for up to the fourth conditional moment only, i.e., neglecting $\rho_4(\Phi^{-1}(p))$, $\rho_{22}(\Phi^{-1}(p))$, and higher-order terms, proved a better representation of the extreme fractiles. Also, for large realizations of σ_{t+1}^2 resulting in more marked deviations from conditional normality in the multi-step-prediction error distributions the Cornish–Fisher expansion based on only $\rho_2(\Phi^{-1}(p))$ performed quite well. Full details of these simulation results are available in Baillie and Bollerslev (1990b).

8. Prediction error distributions in ARMA(k, l)–GARCH(1, 1) models

Eqs. (14) and (29) provided explicit expressions for the optimal s-step-ahead predictor and its associated conditional MSE in the ARMA(k, l)–GARCH(p, q) class of models. However, in order to make use of any asymptotic expansions in approximating the prediction error distribution, expressions for the higher-order conditional moments are called for. Theorem 2 provides such a formula for the fourth moment of the prediction errors from a general dynamic econometric model with GARCH(1, 1) innovations.

---

[6]See Abramowitz and Stegum (1972) and Kendall and Stuart (1967) for a definition of the importance functions in terms of Hermite polynomials.

Theorem 2. *The conditional fourth moment for the prediction error for the minimum MSE predictor in the ARMA(k, l)–GARCH($1, 1$) model given by (1), (2), (4), and (6)–(9) equals*

$$E_t(e_{t,s}^4) = \kappa_2 \sum_{i=0}^{s-1} \psi_i^4 E_t(\sigma_{t+s-i}^4)$$

$$+6 \sum_{i=0}^{s-2} \sum_{j=i+1}^{s-1} \psi_i^2 \psi_j^2 \big[(\alpha_1 + \beta_1)^{j-i-1} (\kappa_2 \alpha_1 + \beta_1)$$

$$\times E_t(\sigma_{t+s-j}^4) + \zeta_{i,j} E_t(\sigma_{t+s-j}^2) \big],$$

$$(40)$$

where

$$\zeta_{i,j} = \sum_{h=0}^{j-1-i} \omega(\alpha_1 + \beta_1)^h, \qquad (41)$$

and $E_t(\sigma_{t+i}^2)$ *and* $E_t(\sigma_{t+i}^4)$ *for* $i > 0$ *are given by (35).*

Proof. From (8) the conditional expectation of terms involving ε_{t+i} to odd powers is zero, and therefore

$$E_t(e_{t,s}^4) = E_t \left(\left(\sum_{i=0}^{s-1} \psi_i \varepsilon_{t+s+i} \right)^4 \right)$$

$$= \psi_0^4 E_t(\varepsilon_{t+s}^4) + 6\psi_0^2 E_t \left(\varepsilon_{t+s}^2 \left(\sum_{j=1}^{s-1} \psi_j \varepsilon_{t+s-j} \right)^2 \right)$$

$$+ E_t \left(\left(\sum_{i=1}^{s-1} \psi_i \varepsilon_{t+s-i} \right)^4 \right)$$

$$= \cdots$$

$$= \sum_{i=0}^{s-1} \psi_j^4 E_t(\varepsilon_{t+s-i}^4) + 6 \sum_{i=0}^{s-2} \sum_{j=i+1}^{s-1} \psi_i^2 \psi_j^2 E_t(\varepsilon_{t+s-i}^2 \varepsilon_{t+s-j}^2).$$

For $0 \le i \le s$ it follows directly from (9) that

$$E_t(\varepsilon_{t+s-i}^4) = E_t(E_{t+s-i-1}(\varepsilon_{t+s-i}^4)) = \kappa_2 E_t(\sigma_{t+s-i}^4).$$

Similarly, for $0 \le i < j < s$ it can be shown that

$$E_t\left(\varepsilon_{t+s-i}^2\varepsilon_{t+s-j}^2\right)$$

$$= E_t\left(\varepsilon_{t+s-j}^2\sigma_{t+s-i}^2\right)$$

$$= E_t\left(\varepsilon_{t+s-j}^2\left[\omega + \alpha_1\varepsilon_{t+s-i-1}^2 + \beta_1\sigma_{t+s-i-1}^2\right]\right)$$

$$= E_t\left(\varepsilon_{t+s-j}^2\left[\omega + (\alpha_1 + \beta_1)\sigma_{t+s-i-1}^2\right]\right)$$

$$= \cdots$$

$$= E_t\left(\varepsilon_{t+s-j}^2\left[\omega\left(1 + (\alpha_1 + \beta_1) + \cdots + (\alpha_1 + \beta_1)^{j-2-i}\right)\right.\right.$$

$$\left.\left. + (\alpha_1 + \beta_1)^{j-1-i}\sigma_{t+s-j+1}^2\right]\right)$$

$$= \omega\left(1 + (\alpha_1 + \beta_1) + \cdots + (\alpha_1 + \beta_1)^{j-1-i}\right)E_t\left(\sigma_{t+s-j}^2\right)$$

$$+ (\alpha_1 + \beta_1)^{j-1-i}(\kappa_2\alpha_1 + \beta_1)E_t\left(\sigma_{t+s-j}^4\right),$$

which reduces to (40) and (41) upon substitution. Q.E.D.

Note that if $\alpha_1 + \beta_1 \neq 1$ the expression for $\zeta_{i,j}$ in (41) simplifies to

$$\zeta_{i,j} = \omega\left(1 - (\alpha_1 + \beta_1)^{j-i}\right)(1 - \alpha_1 - \beta_1)^{-1}.$$

As for the formula for the conditional MSE in (19), the results for the conditional fourth moments provided in Theorem 2 apply more generally to all dynamic econometric models with GARCH(1, 1) innovations and prediction errors that can be expressed as in eq. (20). Of course, in the absence of any serial dependence in the conditional mean, i.e., $\psi_1 = \psi_2 = \cdots = \psi_{s-1} = 0$, $e_{t,s} = \varepsilon_{t+s}$, and (40) is just a special case of the more general results for the conditional moments in the GARCH(1, 1) model given in Theorem 1.

To assess the practical importance of the results in Theorem 2 we also carried out several simulations for different AR(1)–GARCH(1, 1) formulations with conditionally normal one-step-ahead prediction error distributions. Not surprisingly, the presence of serial dependence in the disturbances generally led to an increase in the conditional excess kurtosis for the prediction errors, $\gamma_{2,t,s}$, due to the temporal dependence in $E_t(\varepsilon_{t+s-i}^2\varepsilon_{t+s-j}^2)$. For instance, for $\alpha_1 = 0.2$, $\beta_1 = 0.7$, and $s = 2$ the average conditional excess kurtosis increased from 0.228 for $\phi_1 = 0.0$ to 0.516 for $\phi_1 = 0.5$ and 0.642 for

$\phi_1 = 1.0$. This is also borne out by the simulation results obtained for the coverage probabilities for the prediction error intervals. The conditional normal approximations for the AR(1)–GARCH(1, 1) models are too peaked at the center and too thin in the tails, and the serial dependence in the conditional mean tend to enhance these departures from normality even further when compared to the results from the simple GARCH(1, 1) models. Fortunately, the Cornish–Fisher prediction error intervals based on corrections for up to the fourth conditional moment generally provided reasonably close approximations.

9. Empirical example

To illustrate the techniques discussed above we now consider a simple empirical example relating to the uncertainty of four different forward foreign exchange rates as predictors of the corresponding future spot rates. The data are opening bid prices from the New York Foreign Exchange Market from March 1, 1980 to February 2, 1989, and constitutes a total of 462 weekly observations on the UK pound (UK), the West German Deutschemark (WG), the Swiss franc (SW), and the French franc (FR), all vis-a-vis the US dollar. The one-month-forward rates are taken on Tuesdays and the corresponding future spot rates four weeks and two days later on Thursdays;[7] for a more detailed description of the data see Baillie and Bollerslev (1990a). Following Hansen and Hodrick (1980) and Baillie (1989), if the forward rate is an unbiased predictor of the future spot rate, but the sampling time interval of the data is finer than the maturity time of the forward contract, the forecast errors will be serially correlated. To take account of this fourth-order moving average error structure induced by the one-month-forward contracts and overlapping weekly data plus the volatility clustering, an MA(4)–GARCH(1, 1) model was estimated for each of the four currencies,

$$E_{t-1}(y_t) \equiv \mu_t = \mu + \theta_1\varepsilon_{t-1} + \theta_2\varepsilon_{t-2} + \theta_3\varepsilon_{t-3} + \theta_4\varepsilon_{t-4} \tag{42}$$

and

$$\mathrm{Var}_{t-1}(y_t) \equiv \sigma_t^2 = \omega + \alpha_1\varepsilon_{t-1}^2 + \beta_1\sigma_{t-1}^2, \tag{43}$$

where $y_t \equiv \log s_t - \log f_{t-4}$. The estimates reported in table 1 are maximum likelihood estimates obtained under the assumption of conditional normality.[8] In accordance with the results in Baillie and Bollerslev (1990a), the estimates

[7] This generally matches the forward rate with the spot rate in the future that would be used to cover an open position. However, this alignment could be one or two days off around the beginning of a new month; see Hodrick (1987).

[8] For comparison purposes the numbers have been converted to monthly percentage rates by multiplication with 100.

Table 1

Maximum likelihood estimates.[a]

	UK	WG	SW	FR
μ	−0.322 (0.305)	−0.765 (0.317)	−0.915 (0.344)	−0.487 (0.307)
θ_1	0.906 (0.048)	0.925 (0.052)	0.930 (0.048)	0.928 (0.050)
θ_2	0.796 (0.054)	0.819 (0.055)	0.826 (0.053)	0.825 (0.056)
θ_3	0.768 (0.053)	0.754 (0.053)	0.784 (0.053)	0.742 (0.053)
θ_4	0.310 (0.047)	0.298 (0.046)	0.325 (0.047)	0.312 (0.045)
ω	0.158 (0.116)	1.118 (0.523)	0.899 (0.528)	0.960 (0.420)
α_1	0.060 (0.029)	0.199 (0.076)	0.151 (0.062)	0.214 (0.074)
β_1	0.987 (0.050)	0.528 (0.168)	0.662 (0.143)	0.552 (0.137)
κ_2	4.087	4.367	3.643	3.778
$Q(10)$	6.670	9.150	6.293	6.269
$Q^2(10)$	6.371	7.762	9.911	10.909

[a]Maximum likelihood estimates with asymptotic standard errors in parentheses. κ_2 gives the sample kurtosis for the standardized residuals. $Q(10)$ and $Q^2(10)$ refer to the Ljung–Box portmanteau test for up to 10th-order serial correlation in the levels and the squares of the standardized residuals, respectively.

for the four MA coefficients in (42) are all reasonably close to the values implied by the unbiasedness hypothesis and a martingale spot price process, i.e., 0.837, 0.773, 0.686, and 0.258, respectively. In fact for none of the four rates are these implied parameter values rejected by a formal likelihood ratio test constructed under the assumption of conditional normality. Additional diagnostic tests, including the portmanteau tests for remaining serial correlation in the levels and the squares of the standardized residuals reported in table 1, also indicate a reasonably good fit of the models for all the four currencies.

Optimal predictions for the MA(4)–GARCH(1, 1) model are readily available from (14), while the corresponding forecast errors and forecast error uncertainty are given by eqs. (18) and (19), respectively. Note, in this situation $\psi_i = \theta_i$ for $i = 1, \ldots, 4$ and $\psi_i = 0$ for $i > 4$. In order to succinctly summarize the empirical distribution of the forecast errors associated with the expected depreciation from each of the four models, the first three rows in table 2 report the average rejection frequencies across the one- through six-week forecast horizons obtained over the whole sample period using three

Table 2

One percent confidence intervals rejection frequencies.[a]

		UK	WG	SW	FR
1980.3–	Homoskedastic	1.52	1.56	1.30	1.52
1989.2	Heteroskedastic	1.41	1.96	1.70	1.93
	Cornish–Fisher	1.63	1.00	1.04	0.93
1985.2–	Homoskedastic	5.45	3.21	3.53	4.49
1986.2	Heteroskedastic	0.32	4.49	3.21	3.85
	Cornish–Fisher	0.32	2.24	1.92	1.60

[a]Average rejection frequencies with 1% confidence intervals for one- through six-steps-ahead forecast horizons. Homoskedastic denotes the confidence interval constructed under the assumption of conditionally homoskedastic normal errors. Heteroskedastic gives the rejections with a conditional heteroskedastic normal confidence interval, while the Cornish–Fisher intervals adjust for up to the fourth conditional moment.

different 1% confidence intervals.[9] In particular, the entries labelled 'homoskedastic' denote the rejections that occur with a homoskedastic normal confidence interval; i.e., $p = 0.995$, $E_t(\sigma^2_{(t+i)})$ fixed at the unconditional variance, and all the higher-order correction terms in (39) set equal to zero. Similarly, 'heteroskedastic' refers to the average rejection frequencies across the six horizons that obtain by allowing for the GARCH(1, 1) conditional heteroskedastic error structure, but omitting any of the higher-order correction terms for deviations from conditional normality in (39). Finally, the 'Cornish–Fisher' approximation adjusts for up to the fourth conditional moment in the prediction error distribution based on the sample kurtosis for the standardized residuals, i.e., κ_2 in table 1.

For all three methods and four currencies, the actual number of rejections are generally fairly close to the expected values. Interestingly, this is also true for the homoskedastic confidence intervals, since the unconditional sample distribution for the prediction errors are not markedly different from the normal in the present context. It is worth pointing out, that although table 2 only reports the average number of rejections, no systematic pattern across the six forecast horizons is apparent for the four currencies. To illustrate, for the UK the actual number of rejections that occur with the Cornish–Fisher expansion for the six horizons are 7, 5, 5, 8, 10, and 9, respectively, compared to 8, 8, 4, 3, 2, and 2 for West Germany. Also, the results for other sized confidence intervals are very much in line with the findings reported in table 2. For instance, for the UK the average rejection frequencies for the whole

[9]Six observations were excluded in the beginning and the end of the sample to allow for startup problems and predictions up to six steps ahead.

sample with a 5% confidence interval for each of the three different methods equals 4.63, 4.93, and 5.15, respectively.

While the actual rejections for each of the three intervals are quite close over the entire sample period, the results for certain subsamples of the data are very different. To illustrate, consider the one-year period beginning February 26, 1985, corresponding to the peak of the US dollar against the deutschemark at 3.477 mark to the dollar. Over the following year, stimulated by the Plaza agreement on September 22, 1985, the dollar experienced a volatile but fairly systematic depreciation against most major currencies. From table 2 this increase in volatility resulted in far more rejections with the homoskedastic 1% confidence intervals over this one-year period than were to be expected. Whereas the heteroskedastic normal confidence intervals generally do somewhat better, it follows also that correcting for higher-order deviations from conditional normality as in the Cornish–Fisher asymptotic expansion, may be very important under high volatility scenarios. These results for the 1% confidence intervals are also in line with the findings pertaining to other sized tests. For instance for the UK over the 1985.2–1986.2 period the 5% intervals result in average rejection frequencies of 10.90, 3.85, and 4.17, respectively, for each of the three different methods.

10. Conclusion

This paper has considered predictions from a general dynamic time series model with ARMA disturbances and time-dependent conditional heteroskedasticity, as represented by a GARCH process. Tractable formulae for the minimum MSE predictor of both the future values of the conditional mean and conditional variance are presented. Expressions for all the exact moments of the multi-step forecast errors in the presence of GARCH(1, 1) are also derived, and it is shown how the Cornish–Fisher expansion can be used in approximating the forecast densities. As illustrated by the empirical example concerning the depreciation of exchange rates, these adjustment formulae can be especially useful in very volatile periods.

One potentially important issue not addressed relates to the effect of parameter estimation. For the processes considered in this study, the information matrix is block-diagonal between the parameters in the conditional mean and variance equations. This implies that the estimation uncertainty for the conditional variance parameters is irrelevant to the asymptotic MSE for predicting the conditional mean. However, adjustment of higher-order moments for this effect may be important when using asymptotic approximations for the prediction density in small sample sizes. The practical importance of this is hard to ascertain without a detailed Monte Carlo experiment, and is left as an area for future research.

References

Abramowitz, M. and I.A. Stegum, 1972, Handbook of mathematical functions (Dover Publications, New York, NY).

Baillie, R.T., 1980, Predictions from ARMAX models, Journal of Econometrics 12, 365–374.

Baillie, R.T., 1987, Inference in dynamic models containing 'surprise' variables, Journal of Econometrics 35, 101–117.

Baillie, R.T., 1989, Econometric tests of rationality and market efficiency, Econometric Reviews 8, 151–186.

Baillie, R.T. and T. Bollerslev, 1990a, A multivariate generalized ARCH approach to modeling risk premia in forward foreign exchange rate markets, Journal of International Money and Finance 9, 309–324.

Baillie, R.T. and T. Bollerslev, 1990b, Prediction in dynamic models with time dependent conditional heteroskedasticity, Working paper no. 8815 (Department of Economics, Michigan State University, East Lansing, MI).

Barndorff-Nielsen, O.E. and D.R. Cox, 1989, Asymptotic techniques for use in statistics (Chapman and Hall, London).

Bera, A.K. and S. Lee, 1988, On the formulation of a general structure for conditional heteroskedasticity, Unpublished manuscript (Department of Economics, University of Illinois, Urbana-Champaign, IL).

Bera, A.K., S. Lee, and M. Higgins, 1990, Interaction between autocorrelation and conditional heteroskedasticity: A random coefficient approach, Unpublished manuscript (Department of Economics, University of Illinois, Urbana-Champaign, IL).

Bollerslev, T., 1986, Generalized autoregressive conditional heteroskedasticity, Journal of Econometrics 31, 307–327.

Bollerslev, T., 1987, A conditional heteroskedastic time series model for speculative prices and rates of return, Review of Economic and Statistics 69, 542–547.

Bollerslev, T., 1988, On the correlation structure for the generalized autoregressive conditional heteroskedastic process, Journal of Time Series Analysis 9, 121–131.

Bollerslev, T. and R.F. Engle, 1989, Common persistence in conditional variances, Unpublished manuscript (J.L. Kellogg Graduate School of Management, Northwestern University, Evanston, IL).

Bollerslev, T., R.Y. Chou, and K. Kroner, 1992, ARCH modeling in finance: A review of the theory and empirical evidence, Journal of Econometrics, this issue.

Box, G.E.P. and G.C. Tiao, 1976, Comparison of forecast and actuality, Journal of the Royal Statistical Society Series C 25, 195–200.

Chong, Y.Y. and D.F. Hendry, 1986, Econometric evaluation of linear macroeconomic models, Review of Economic Studies 53, 671–690.

Chou, R.Y., 1989, Volatility persistence and stock valuations: Some empirical evidence using GARCH, Journal of Applied Econometrics 3, 279–294.

Cornish, E.A. and R.A. Fisher, 1937, Moments and cumulants in the specification of distributions, Revue de l'Institute International Statistique 5, 307–320.

Day, T.E. and C.M. Lewis, 1992, Stock market volatility and the information content of stock index options, Journal of Econometrics, this issue.

Diebold, F.X., 1988, Empirical modeling of exchange rate dynamics (Springer Verlag, New York, NY).

Engle, R.F., 1982, Autoregressive conditional heteroskedasticity with estimates of the variance of United Kingdom inflation, Econometrica 50, 987–1007.

Engle, R.F. and T. Bollerslev, 1986, Modelling the persistence of conditional variances, Econometric Reviews 5, 1–50.

Engle, R.F. and G. Gonzalez-Rivera, 1991, Semiparametric ARCH models, Journal of Business and Economic Statistics 9, 345–359.

Engle, R.F. and C.W.J. Granger, 1987, Cointegration and error correction: Representation, estimation and testing, Econometrica 55, 251–276.

Engle, R.F. and D.F. Kraft, 1983, Multiperiod forecast error variances of inflation estimated from ARCH models, in: Applied time series analysis of economic data (Bureau of the Census, Washington, DC).

Engle, R.F., D. Lilien, and R.P. Robins, 1987, Estimating time varying risk premia in the term structure: The ARCH-M model, Econometrica 55, 391–407.

Gallant, A.R. and G.E. Tauchen, 1989, Seminonparametric maximum likelihood estimation, Econometrica 55, 1091–1120.

Gallant, A.R., D.A. Hsieh, and G.E. Tauchen, 1990, On fitting a recalcitrant series: The pound/dollar exchange rate 1974–83, in: Nonparametric and semiparametric methods in econometrics and statistics (Cambridge University Press, Cambridge).

Geweke, J., 1989, Exact predictive densities for linear models with ARCH disturbances, Journal of Econometrics 40, 63–86.

Granger, C.W.J., H. White, and M. Kamstra, 1989, Interval forecasting: An analysis based upon ARCH-quantile estimators, Journal of Econometrics 40, 87–96.

Hansen, L.P. and R.J. Hodrick, 1980, Forward exchange rates as optimal predictors of future spot rates, Journal of Political Economy 88, 829–853.

Hodrick, R.J., 1987, The empirical evidence on the efficiency of forward and futures foreign exchange markets (Harwood Academic Publishers, Chur).

Kendall, M.G. and A. Stuart, 1969, The advanced theory of statistics, Vol. 2 (Griffin, London).

Lahiri, K., 1975, Multiperiod prediction in dynamic model, International Economic Review 16, 699–711.

Lamoureux, C.G. and W.D. Lastrapes, 1990, Forecasting stock return variance: Toward an understanding of stochastic implied volatilities, Unpublished manuscript (Department of Economics, University of Georgia, Atlanta, GA).

Lütkepohl, H., 1985, The joint asymptotic distribution of multistep prediction errors of estimated vector autoregressions, Economics Letters 17, 103–106.

Lütkepohl, H., 1988, Prediction tests for structural stability, Journal of Econometrics 39, 267–296.

Nelson, D.B. and C.Q. Cao, 1991, A note on the inequality constraints in the univariate GARCH model, Journal of Business and Economic Statistics, forthcoming.

Schwert, G.W., 1989, Business cycles, financial crises and stock volatility, Carnegie–Rochester Conference Series on Public Policy 31, 83–125.

Serfling, R.J., 1980, Approximation theorems in mathematical statistics (Wiley, New York, NY).

Yamamoto, T., 1981, Predictions of multivariate autoregressive moving average models, Biometrika 68, 485–492.

[21]

Journal of Forecasting, Vol. 12, 617–637 (1993)

On the Limitations of Comparing Mean Square Forecast Errors

MICHAEL P. CLEMENTS

Institute of Economics and Statistics and Nuffield College, Oxford

and

DAVID F. HENDRY

Institute of Economics and Statistics and Nuffield College, Oxford

ABSTRACT

Linear models are invariant under non-singular, scale-preserving linear transformations, whereas mean square forecast errors (MSFEs) are not. Different rankings may result across models or methods from choosing alternative yet isomorphic representations of a process. One approach can dominate others for comparisons in levels, yet lose to another for differences, to a second for cointegrating vectors and to a third for combinations of variables. The potential for switches in ranking is related to criticisms of the inadequacy of MSFE against encompassing criteria, which are invariant under linear transforms and entail MSFE dominance. An invariant evaluation criterion which avoids misleading outcomes is examined in a Monte Carlo study of forecasting methods.

INTRODUCTION

Mean square forecast errors (MSFEs), or their square roots are often used for forecast comparisons across alternative models or methods: for recent examples in macro-economics, see McNees (1990), Wallis (1989), and Wallis and Whitley (1991); for applications to Monte Carlo forecast comparisons, see Engle and Yoo (1987), Brandner and Kunst (1990), and Chambers (1991). Generally, scalar MSFEs are reported, and for scalar variables the concept of MSFE is unambiguous, although its application to multi-step forecasts is not. In systems, however, a number of criteria based on the MSFE matrix (the second moment matrix of forecast errors) are possible, although the trace of the MSFE matrix (TMSFE) is the most commonly applied.

A possible basis for the use of MSFEs in forecast comparisons is that conditional expectations deliver the minimum MSFE when sufficient moments exist, and do so for all non-singular linear transformations of the information set. Nevertheless, MSFEs are shown below to constitute an inadequate and potentially misleading basis for model selection, even in linear models. This arises because of a lack of invariance of MSFEs to non-singular, scale-preserving linear transforms, for a model class that is itself invariant to such transforms. It is obvious

0277–6693/93/080617–21$15.50

© 1993 by John Wiley & Sons, Ltd.

Received November 1991

Revised February 1993

that mean absolute errors (MAEs: see Burns, 1986) are not invariant either across isomorphic model representations, and hereafter are subsumed by the results on MSFEs.

A minimum MSFE (MMSFE) means that the specific model or method has the smallest MSFE in the relevant group of comparisons which ensures MSFE dominance. Then the main result of the paper is that for multi-step forecasts in systems of equations, MMSFE for one linear function of predicted variables does not imply MMSFE on another. This holds even for the matrix MSFE measure. When TMSFEs are used in systems, the result holds for one-step forecasts.

Such non-invariance implies that rankings across models and/or methods based on the commonly used TMSFE can vary by choosing alternative yet isomorphic representations of a given process. For instance, one approach or model can dominate all others for comparisons in the levels of a set of variables, yet lose to one of the others for differences, to a second for cointegrating vectors, and to a third for combinations of variables. This problem is especially apparent in Monte Carlo studies of forecasting methods, where misleading outcomes can result due to the arbitrary choice of which linear transformation of the data to examine. However, it is an equally pertinent issue empirically, and would appear to vitiate the use of TMSFE comparisons in many applications.

The next section illustrates the above claims using simple examples for scalar multi-step forecasts and for forecasts from systems of equations. Two questions are distinguished:

(1)   Does a given measure allow comparisons between different but isomorphic representations of the same system?
(2)   Does the outcome of a comparison depend on which representation is selected?

The forms of admissible transformations are described, and applied to the TMSFE, the MSFE matrix and a determinantal criterion to determine their performance relative to (1) and (2).

In the third section a class of linear dynamic cointegrated systems is formulated for which the results are clear-cut. We believe that our claims hold *a fortiori* in non-linear systems although there are additional problems which make rankings even more susceptible to the choice of variable. The linear model class allows for variables which are integrated of order unity (denoted $I(1)$) and are cointegrated. Thus, one of the transformations we consider is to a stationary representation of the process. We catalogue several estimators in terms of the number of cointegrating restrictions and unit roots they impose. The practical importance of the invariance failure is illustrated within this framework by re-examining the Monte Carlo study of Engle and Yoo (1987): we find that different rankings of the estimators result from the $I(0)$ and $I(1)$ representations of the process.

In the fourth section we demonstrate that the alternative criterion of generalized forecast error second moment (GFESM) is invariant to non-singular, scale-preserving linear transformations for all forecast horizons. The GFESM is the determinant of the forecast error second moment matrix pooled across all horizons. The properties of the GFESM are examined and the reasons for the inadequacy of other MSFE-based measures become apparent. This criterion allows a unique ranking across models or methods and highlights the key role played by one-step forecast accuracy, even when the objective is to forecast for longer horizons.

In the fifth section that result is related to the statistical literature on predictive likelihood (see e.g. Bjørnstad, 1990, for a survey).

The sixth section discusses forecast encompassing, which concerns whether the forecasts of one model can explain the forecast errors made by another (see Chong and Hendry, 1986). Forecast encompassing is formally equivalent to the notion of conditional efficiency in Granger and Newbold (1973) and to the general form of the test for combining econometric and time-series models in Nelson (1972). As established by Lu and Mizon (1991) and Ericsson (1992), MSFE comparisons can fail to reflect non-encompassing: MMSFE is necessary but not sufficient for forecast encompassing, just as variance dominance is necessary but insufficient for parameter encompassing (see Hendry and Richard, 1982). However, forecast encompassing is invariant to non-singular, scale-preserving linear transforms and entails both MSFE and GFESM dominance for one-step forecasts, so it could be used to establish rankings across competing methods or models when parameters are constant. However, forecast encompassing is insufficient to ensure GFESM dominance for longer horizons. The converse is also true in any class of models, but the more demanding forecast-period parameter encompassing in Ericsson (1992) is sufficient for both forecast encompassing and one-step GFESM dominance. Any need to combine one-step forecasts means that the models in question cannot forecast encompass each other, and so entails model mis-specification.

The final section summarizes and concludes the paper.

POTENTIAL PROBLEMS IN MEAN SQUARE FORECAST ERROR COMPARISONS

Since forecasts from large models reflect the judgements, corrections, and inputs of their proprietors as much as the models' properties, historical forecast track records reveal little about model validity. When pure forecast information is available, measures of forecast uncertainty are needed to test model validity, but are rarely provided. Thus, forecast comparisons are often based on mean square forecast errors. Indeed, MSFEs are used in forecast evaluation, forecast comparisons across models, and in simulation studies to assess forecast accuracy as noted above.

In this section, we assume that all the processes under analysis are weakly stationary and have finite unconditional moments of at least second order. The next section examines non-stationary but cointegrated processes. Below, $E[\cdot]$ and $V[\cdot]$ respectively denote expectation and variance.

The mean square forecast error from a model of a univariate process $\{x_t\}$ for a time $t + h$ is:

$$E[(x_{t+h} - \hat{x}_{+h})^2] = E[e_{t+h}^2] = \text{MSFE}_h \tag{1}$$

where $\hat{x}_{t+h}$ is the h-step ahead forecast using information available at time t and $e_{t+h} = x_{t+h} - \hat{x}_{t+h}$ is the forecast error. The MSFE combines the squared bias in forecast errors with the forecast error variance, namely:

$$E[e_{t+h}^2] = \{E[e_{t+h}]\}^2 + E[(e_{t+h} - E[e_{t+h}])^2] = \{E[x_{t+h} - \hat{x}_{t+h}]\}^2 + V[e_{t+h}] \tag{2}$$

In a multivariate setting, the forecast error is denoted by the vector e_{t+h}, and the MSFE matrix is $E[e_{t+h}e_{t+h}'] = V_h$ for all h. A commonly used approach is to measure system forecast accuracy using the trace of this matrix. Thus, the h-step ahead trace MSFE is trace (V_h), denoted TMSFE$_h$. However, other possibilities arise, such as using the determinant of V_h, or, as in e.g. Granger and Newbold (1977, p. 228), choosing the method/model for which $d'V_h d$ is the smallest for every non-zero vector d. We denote this last MSFE matrix criterion by MSFEM.

In sub-section (a) we demonstrate the well-known result that the conditional expectation has the minimum one-step MSFE (which coincides with the MSFEM in the scalar case). Sub-section (b) formalizes the class of isomorphic linear systems. Then (c) and (d) provide examples which address the applicability of the TMSFE and MSFEM to forecast errors (question (1) above). The example in (c) is a first-order, scalar autoregressive process where there is no

620   *Journal of Forecasting*   *Vol. 12, Iss. No. 8*

parameter uncertainty, illustrating the lack of invariance of TMSFEs to isomorphic transformations of processes for multi-step forecasts. In (d) we show that TMSFEs and MSFEMs cannot be applied to one-step forecast errors from systems where outcomes for different combinations of variables are reported. The next two sub-sections show that even when a common comparison basis is agreed (question (2) above), the choice of that basis can determine the rankings of estimators or models. Sub-section (e) illustrates the role of parameter uncertainty by showing that TMSFE rankings can be altered by switching from one isomorphic representation to another. That is, whether forecast accuracy is assessed in terms of levels or differences can affect which estimator, method, or model is selected. Sub-section (f) shows that the MSFEM is not invariant to non-singular, scale-preserving transformations for multi-step forecasts.

(a) MSFEs and conditional expectations

One basis for MSFEs is that the conditional expectation, given all the available information, has the minimum MSFE. Below we demonstrate this proposition for one-step ahead forecasts, while the generalization to h-step ahead forecasts is straightforward. Let $\mathcal{I}_{t-1}$ denote the information set at time t, and decompose x_t as:

$$x_t = E[x_t \mid \mathcal{I}_{t-1}] + u_t = \phi_t + u_t \tag{3}$$

Then $E[u_t \mid \mathcal{I}_{t-1}] = 0$ and $E[u_t\phi_t] = 0$. Let $E[u_t^2 \mid \mathcal{I}_{t-1}] = \sigma_t^2$, and let $G(x_t \mid \mathcal{I}_{t-1}) = \mu_t$ denote any other predictor of x_t. Then setting $\eta_t = \phi_t - \mu_t$ and noting that $E[u_t\eta_t] = E[u_t\phi_t] - E_{\mathcal{I}}(E[u_t\mu_t \mid \mathcal{I}_{t-1}]) = 0$:

$$E[x_t - G(x_t \mid \mathcal{I}_{t-1})]^2 = E[(x_t - \phi_t) + (\phi_t - \mu_t)]^2$$
$$= E[u_t + \eta_t]^2 = \sigma_t^2 + E[\eta_t^2] \geqslant \sigma_t^2 \tag{4}$$

A generalization of equation (4) holds for a vector of variables $\mathbf{x}_t$, whence $E[\mathbf{x}_t \mid \mathcal{I}_{t-1}]$ delivers a MSE matrix which is less than that of $G(\mathbf{x}_t \mid \mathcal{I}_{t-1})$ by a positive semi-definite matrix. At first sight, therefore, minimum MSFE seems a demanding criterion for a model in its class. Unfortunately, outside of the context of scalar one-step forecasts, MMSFE transpires to be an ambiguous notion as shown below. Moreover, the fact that $E[x_t \mid \mathcal{I}_{t-1}]$ is the MMSFE for any given $\mathcal{I}_{t-1}$ does not entail the converse: in a given set of methods or models, the one with the MMSFE need not be the conditional expectation given all the information available to that set since a model not included in the set may have the overall MMSFE. For example, every model may use only a subset of the information. This is analogous to the problem that variance dominance in a group of fitted models is insufficient to ensure model validity (see Hendry and Richard, 1982). That care is required in using some MSFE criteria is shown in sub-sections (c)–(f).

(b) Isomorphic representations of linear systems

Denote a linear forecasting system by the succinct notation:

$$\mathbf{\Phi}\mathbf{s}_t = \mathbf{u}_t \qquad \text{where} \qquad \mathbf{u}_t \sim \mathrm{ID}(\mathbf{0}, \mathbf{\Omega}) \tag{5}$$

when $\mathbf{s}_t' = (\mathbf{x}_t' : \mathbf{z}_t')$, $\mathbf{x}_t$ are the N variables to be forecast and $\mathbf{z}_t$ are k available predetermined variables (perhaps just $\mathbf{x}_{t-1}$) and $\mathbf{\Phi} = (\mathbf{I} : -\mathbf{B})$, say. The parameters are $(\mathbf{B} : \mathbf{\Omega})$, where $\mathbf{\Omega}$ is symmetric, positive semi-definite. Then the likelihood and generalized variance of the system in equation (5) are invariant under scale-preserving, non-singular transformations of the form:

$$\mathbf{M}\mathbf{\Phi}\mathbf{P}^{-1}\mathbf{P}\mathbf{s}_t = \mathbf{M}\mathbf{u}_t \qquad \text{or} \qquad \mathbf{\Phi}^*\mathbf{s}_t^* = \mathbf{u}_t^* \qquad \text{so} \qquad \mathbf{u}_t^* \sim \mathrm{ID}(\mathbf{0}, \mathbf{M}\mathbf{\Omega}\mathbf{M}') \tag{6}$$

In equation (6), $s_t^* = Ps_t$, M, and P are, respectively $N \times N$ and $(k + N) \times (k + N)$ non-singular matrices where $abs(|M|) = 1$ and P is upper block-triangular such that $\Phi^* = (I : -B^*)$. Forecasts and forecast confidence intervals made in the original system and transformed after the event to x_t^* or made initially from the transformed system will be identical. No restrictions are imposed by these transforms, so systems (5) and (6) are isomorphic. Transformations in the class shown in (6) are regularly undertaken in applied work, and include as special cases, differences, cointegrating combinations (see the next section), substitution of identities, and differentials, *inter alia*. The formalization merely makes explicit the fact that a linear model is defined by its invariance under linear transformations (or affine transforms more generally).

(c) Comparisons using MSFEs for scalar multi-step dynamic forecasts
Consider the stationary first-order autoregression (AR(1)):

$$x_t = \rho x_{t-1} + u_t \quad \text{where} \quad u_t \sim IN(0, \sigma^2), |\rho| < 1, x_0 \sim N(0, \sigma^2/[1 - \rho^2]) \tag{7}$$

Here $s_t = (x_t : x_{t-1})'$ and $\Phi = (1 : -\rho)$. When the parameters are known, $E[x_{t+1} | x_t] = \hat{x}_{t+1} = \rho x_t$, so the MSFE for the conditional one-step forecast is:

$$E[(x_{t+1} - \hat{x}_{t+1})^2 | x_t] = E[u_{t+1}^2] = \sigma^2 \tag{8}$$

If, instead, the change $\Delta x_t = x_t - x_{t-1}$ is to be forecast using $\hat{\Delta} x_{t+1} = (\rho - 1)x_t$, then:

$$E[(\Delta x_{t+1} - \hat{\Delta} x_{t+1})^2 | x_t] = E[u_{t+1}^2] = \sigma^2 \tag{9}$$

so the same MSFE results for conditional one-step forecasts of levels and changes. Here, $M = I$, and:

$$P = \begin{bmatrix} 1 & -1 \\ 0 & 1 \end{bmatrix}$$

However, if a two-period (or more distant) forecast is desired, we have:

$$x_{t+2} = \rho x_{t+1} + u_{t+2} = \rho^2 x_t + u_{t+2} + \rho u_{t+1} \tag{10}$$

Using $E[x_{t+2} | x_t] = \hat{x}_{t+2} = \rho^2 x_t$, the MSFE is:

$$E[(x_{t+2} - \hat{x}_{t+2})^2 | x_t] = E[(u_{t+2} + \rho u_{t+1})^2] = (1 + \rho^2)\sigma^2 \tag{11}$$

In terms of changes:

$$\Delta x_{t+2} = (\rho - 1)x_{t+1} + u_{t+2} = (\rho - 1)[\rho x_t + u_{t+1}] + u_{t+2} \tag{12}$$

and hence using the conditional expectation $E[\Delta x_{t+2} | x_t] = \hat{\Delta} x_{t+2} = (\rho - 1)\rho x_t$, the MSFE is:

$$E[(\Delta x_{t+2} - \hat{\Delta} x_{t+2})^2 | x_t] = E[([\rho - 1]u_{t+1} + u_{t+2})^2] = (1 + [\rho - 1]^2)\sigma^2 \tag{13}$$

which is larger (smaller) than equation (11) as $\rho < \frac{1}{2} (> \frac{1}{2})$. Consequently, no valid comparisons of forecast performance can be made between multi-step MSFEs for the level of a variable and its change: a common choice of variable is essential. Note that both $\hat{x}_{t+2}$ and $\hat{\Delta} x_{t+2}$ are the optimal two-step ahead predictors of x_{t+2} and Δx_{t+2}, respectively, since they are the conditional expectations and therefore minimum MSFE predictors (as a generalization of equation (4)). That they cannot be compared follows because the optimal predictors and associated MSFEs differ. Granger and Newbold (1977, p. 285) make this point. In example (e) below, we illustrate the proposition that rankings between forecasts on MSFE-based criteria are not invariant to linear transformation of the variable to be forecast—which is a problem that does not appear to have been fully appreciated hitherto.

(d) Comparisons using one-step MSFE criteria in systems of equations

A simple example will suffice to illustrate that TMSFEs cannot support comparisons across isomorphic representations of systems. Consider the example of a model for exports o_t and imports m_t, with an identity for the balance of trade: $b_t \equiv o_t - m_t$. In the notation of subsection (b), we can define $x_t' = (o_t : m_t)$, so that $N = 2$. Then the model in terms of exports and the balance of trade $x_t^{*\,\prime} = (o_t : b_t)$, is given by the transformations $\mathbf{P} = \mathbf{I}$, and:

$$\mathbf{M} = \begin{bmatrix} 1 & 0 \\ 1 & -1 \end{bmatrix}$$

Let e_{bt+1} denote the one-step ahead error in forecasting b_{t+1}, etc. The conditional expectation for the balance of trade is the conditional expectation for exports minus the conditional expectation for imports. Then, denote by $\mathbf{V}_1(om)$ the MSFE matrix for one-step ahead forecasts for the variables o_t and m_t, and by $\mathbf{V}_1(ob)$ the same for o_t and b_t. Letting $C[\cdot, \cdot]$ denote a covariance:

$$\mathbf{V}_1(om) = \begin{bmatrix} V[e_{ot+1}] & : C[e_{ot+1}, e_{mt+1}] \\ C[e_{mt+1}, e_{ot+1}] & : V[e_{mt+1}] \end{bmatrix} \quad \text{and}$$

$$\mathbf{V}_1(ob) = \begin{bmatrix} V[e_{ot+1}] & : C[e_{ot+1}, e_{bt+1}] \\ C[e_{bt+1}, e_{ot+1}] & : V[e_{bt+1}] \end{bmatrix} \tag{14}$$

For the trace MSFE criterion we have:

$$\text{tr}[\mathbf{V}_1(om)] \gtreqless \text{tr}[\mathbf{V}_1(ob)] \quad \text{depending on whether} \quad V[e_{ot+1}] \gtreqless 2C[e_{ot+1}, e_{mt+1}] \tag{15}$$

In deriving this result we have used $\mathbf{V}_1(ob) = \mathbf{M}\mathbf{V}_1(om)\mathbf{M}'$ so that:

$$V[e_{bt+1}] \equiv V[e_{ot+1} - e_{mt+1}] = V[e_{ot+1}] + V[e_{mt+1}] - 2C[e_{ot+1}, e_{mt+1}] \tag{16}$$

Hence the TMSFE for the estimated model of o_t and m_t may bear any relation to that for o_t and b_t: if one investigator reports the TMSFE for an estimated model of exports, imports, and the balance of trade using $\text{tr}[\mathbf{V}_1(om)]$ (levels) and a second reports $\text{tr}[\mathbf{V}_1(ob)]$ (combinations of levels and differentials), no comparisons of forecast accuracy are possible.

As a precursor to the fourth section, note that the determinant of the MSFE matrix is invariant to the choice of o_t and m_t versus o_t and b_t, since from equation (16) and using:

$$C[e_{ot+1}, e_{bt+1}] = V[e_{ot+1}] - C[e_{ot+1}, e_{mt+1}]$$
$$|\mathbf{V}_1(ob)| = V[e_{ot+1}]V[e_{bt+1}] - (C[e_{ot+1}, e_{bt+1}])^2 \tag{17}$$
$$= V[e_{ot+1}]V[e_{mt+1}] - (C[e_{ot+1}, e_{mt+1}])^2 = |\mathbf{V}_1(om)|$$

We refer to $|\mathbf{V}_1|$ as the one-step generalized forecast error second moment, by analogy with the concept of generalized variance. This measure naturally reveals that the two representations of the system are isomorphic, and forecast accuracy results are comparable irrespective of the transformations $\mathbf{M}$ and $\mathbf{P}$ used in equation (6).

The MSFEM criterion is invariant to any non-singular (not necessarily scale-preserving) $\mathbf{M}$-transformation for one-step forecasts. Let $\mathbf{V}_1$ be the one-step ahead MSFEM for a model of an $N \times 1$ vector x_t, and let $\mathbf{V}_1^*$ be the MSFEM for a rival model of x_t. Consider a non-singular matrix $\mathbf{M}$: then if for x_t, $\mathbf{d}^{*\prime}\mathbf{V}_1\mathbf{d}^* < \mathbf{d}^{*\prime}\mathbf{V}_1^*\mathbf{d}^*$ for all non-zero $\mathbf{d}^*$, it follows that for $\mathbf{M}x_t$, $\mathbf{d}'\mathbf{M}\mathbf{V}_1\mathbf{M}'\mathbf{d} < \mathbf{d}'\mathbf{M}\mathbf{V}_1^*\mathbf{M}'\mathbf{d}$ for all non-zero $\mathbf{d}$ (set $\mathbf{d}^* = \mathbf{M}'\mathbf{d}$). Since $\mathbf{P}$-transforms do not affect one-step forecasts, variable transformations will not induce a switch in the rankings when $(\mathbf{V}_1 - \mathbf{V}_1^*)$ is negative semi-definite.

Nevertheless, unlike equation (17), comparisons across transformations need not be possible using MSFEM in that $(\mathbf{V}_1 - \mathbf{V}_1^*)$ may be indefinite. In terms of the export–import example, setting $\mathbf{d} = (d_1 : d_2)'$, we obtain:

$$\mathbf{d}'\mathbf{V}_1(om)\mathbf{d} \gtreqless \mathbf{d}'\mathbf{V}_1(ob)\mathbf{d}$$

depending upon $\mathbf{d}$, since letting $a = 2\mathbf{C}[e_{ot+1}, e_{mt+1}] - \mathbf{V}[e_{ot+1}]$:

$$\mathbf{d}'\mathbf{V}_1(om)\mathbf{d} - \mathbf{d}'\mathbf{V}_1(ob)\mathbf{d} = (d_2^2 + 2d_1d_2)a$$

The MSFEM does not reveal that the model in terms of $(o_t : m_t)$ is isomorphic to the model in terms of $(o_t : b_t)$, although it does suggest that the two representations cannot be compared. Even so, consider two models denoted by $\tilde{\ }$ and $\hat{\ }$, so that:

$$\mathbf{d}'(\hat{\mathbf{V}}_1(ob) - \tilde{\mathbf{V}}_1(ob))\mathbf{d} = \mathbf{d}'\mathbf{M}(\hat{\mathbf{V}}_1(om) - \tilde{\mathbf{V}}_1(om))\mathbf{M}'\mathbf{d}$$

Then the conditions for positive definiteness of the variance matrices and (semi-)definiteness of their differences entails that:

$$\hat{\mathbf{V}}_1(om) - \tilde{\mathbf{V}}_1(om) > 0 \qquad \text{implies} \qquad \hat{\mathbf{V}}_1(ob) - \tilde{\mathbf{V}}_1(ob) > 0$$

and vice versa, where $>$ denotes that the right-hand side is positive semi-definite. Thus, once a common basis for comparison is established, if one model dominates the other on the $(o_t : m_t)$ metric, it must also do so on the $(o_t : b_t)$. This matches the earlier invariance proof for **M**-transforms. More generally, these results hold for h-step ahead forecasts for **M**-transforms for any single h.

(e) Switching of multi-step scalar MSFE rankings of estimators on isomorphic representations

When parameter uncertainty is introduced, the ranking of two estimators of equation (7) can be reversed by the choice of metric. The one-step forecast error for estimated parameter values based on a sample up to time t, using $\hat{x}_{t+1} = \hat{\rho}x_t$ is:

$$e_{t+1} = x_{t+1} - \hat{x}_{t+1} = u_{t+1} + (\rho - \hat{\rho})x_t \tag{18}$$

with approximate conditional forecast error variance:

$$\mathbf{V}[e_{t+1} \mid x_t] = \sigma^2 + \mathbf{V}[\hat{\rho}]x_t^2$$

Conditional on information available at the beginning of the forecast period, the two-step ahead forecast, $\hat{x}_{t+2}$, is again obtained by backward iteration:

$$\hat{x}_{t+2} = \hat{\rho}\hat{x}_{t+1} = \hat{\rho}^2 x_t \tag{19}$$

whereas:

$$x_{t+2} = \rho x_{t+1} + u_{t+2} = \rho^2 x_t + \rho u_{t+1} + u_{t+2}$$

so that to a first approximation (neglecting the slight dependence of $\hat{\rho}$ on x_t):

$$\mathbf{V}[e_{t+2} \mid x_t] = \mathbf{E}[(\rho^2 - \hat{\rho}^2)^2]x_t^2 + (1 + \rho^2)\sigma^2 \tag{20}$$

In terms of changes, equations (18) and (19) entail:

$$\Delta x_{t+2} - \hat{\Delta} x_{t+2} = (\rho - 1)\rho x_t + u_{t+2} + (\rho - 1)u_{t+1} - (\hat{\rho} - 1)\hat{\rho}x_t$$

and hence the MSFE is:

$$\mathbf{E}[(\Delta x_{t+2} - \hat{\Delta}x_{t+2})^2 \mid x_t] = \mathbf{E}[(\rho^2 - \hat{\rho}^2 - (\rho - \hat{\rho}))^2]x_t^2 + (1 + [\rho - 1]^2)\sigma^2 \tag{21}$$

Since the impact of the estimation error differs between equations (20) and (21), it is possible to find two estimators (denoted ^ and ~ respectively) such that:

$$E[(\rho^2 - \hat{\rho}^2)^2] < E[(\rho^2 - \tilde{\rho}^2)^2] \text{ and } E[(\rho^2 - \hat{\rho}^2 - (\rho - \hat{\rho}))^2] \geqslant E[(\rho^2 - \tilde{\rho}^2 - (\rho - \tilde{\rho}))^2] \quad (22)$$

For example, $\hat{\rho} \equiv 1$ and $\tilde{\rho} \equiv 0$ will satisfy these conditions for ρ near unity, so that an imprecise estimator for the former and a precise estimator for the latter could also. Consequently, the ranking of two estimators by multi-step TMSFE can be altered by switching the basis of comparison from levels to changes: even when a common comparison basis is agreed, invalid conclusions may be drawn using multi-step TMSFE. In terms of the two questions posed in the Introduction; (1) multi-step MSFEs do not allow comparisons between different but isomorphic representations of the same system (sub-section (c)), and furthermore, (2) a common basis for comparison is not sufficient to prevent rank switches.

(f) Non-invariance of the multi-step MSFE matrix in systems of equations

For multi-step forecasts the specification of the MSFEM is ambiguous. If $\mathbf{V}_h$ is defined as the MSFE matrix for the h-step ahead forecasts *alone*, then rank reversals can occur, exactly as the matrix generalization of equation (20) versus equation (21). This is because a switch from $\mathbf{x}_t$ to $\Delta\mathbf{x}_t$ involves a $\mathbf{P}$-transformation which is not covered by the proof of invariance of MSFEMs to $\mathbf{M}$-transforms in (d). If the system is the first-order vector autoregression (VAR) $\mathbf{x}_t = \mathbf{B}\mathbf{x}_{t-1} + \mathbf{v}_t$:

$$\mathbf{s}_t = \begin{bmatrix} \mathbf{x}_t \\ \mathbf{x}_{t-1} \end{bmatrix} \quad \text{and} \quad \mathbf{s}_t^* = \begin{bmatrix} \Delta\mathbf{x}_t \\ \mathbf{x}_{t-1} \end{bmatrix} \quad \text{so that} \quad \mathbf{P} = \begin{bmatrix} \mathbf{I} & -\mathbf{I} \\ \mathbf{0} & \mathbf{I} \end{bmatrix}$$

In terms of levels and changes for known parameters, the MSFEMs are:

$$\mathbf{V}[e_{xt+2} \mid \mathbf{x}_t] = \Omega + \mathbf{B}\Omega\mathbf{B}' \quad \text{and} \quad \mathbf{V}[e_{\Delta xt+2} \mid \mathbf{x}_t] = \Omega + (\mathbf{B} - \mathbf{I})\Omega(\mathbf{B} - \mathbf{I})'$$

Assuming a sufficiently large sample that parameter estimation variances are negligible, it is possible to find two models ~ and ^ as above such that:

$$\hat{\Omega} + \hat{\mathbf{B}}\hat{\Omega}\hat{\mathbf{B}}' - (\tilde{\Omega} + \tilde{\mathbf{B}}\tilde{\Omega}\tilde{\mathbf{B}}') > 0 \quad \text{and} \quad \hat{\Omega} + (\hat{\mathbf{B}} - \mathbf{I})\hat{\Omega}(\hat{\mathbf{B}} - \mathbf{I})' - [\tilde{\Omega} + (\tilde{\mathbf{B}} - \mathbf{I})\tilde{\Omega}(\tilde{\mathbf{B}} - \mathbf{I})'] < 0$$
$$(23)$$

For example, $\hat{\mathbf{B}} \approx \mathbf{I}$ and $\tilde{\mathbf{B}} \approx \mathbf{0}$ when $2\hat{\Omega} - \tilde{\Omega} > 0$ but $\hat{\Omega} - 2\tilde{\Omega} < 0$ creates such an outcome. Thus using a comparison basis of levels, the ~ model appears best on the two-step ahead MSFEM criterion whereas the ^ model wins if first differences are used. Despite using the 'complete' MSFE matrix, it matters for appraising multi-step forecast accuracy which isomorphic representation of the system is selected: investigators could find one system performing better than a second on levels comparisons but worse if the same comparisons were conducted for changes. Potential ranking reversals vitiate the use of a criterion to judge forecasting models or methods.

The results concerning the applicability of MSFEM across isomorphic representations and the (lack of) invariance of MSFEM comparisons to the transformation selected (the two questions raised in the Introduction) can thus be summarized as follows. Even for one-step forecasts, comparisons across transformations may not be possible, but if one model dominates another on a common transformation, it will do so for the class of $\mathbf{M}$- and $\mathbf{P}$-transformations described in sub-section (b). For multi-step forecasts, $\mathbf{P}$-transforms may cause rank reversals, so that the particular basis chosen for comparison may be crucial.

In the fourth section we formalize and extend these results, including a resolution of the difficulty using the GFESM. First, we establish notation for general systems of $I(1)$ variables.

COINTEGRATED LINEAR DYNAMIC SYSTEMS

In this section we outline three isomorphic representations of a system initially formulated in the levels of cointegrated $I(1)$ variables, and discuss a number of commonly used estimators in terms of the number of cointegrating restrictions and unit roots that are imposed or implicitly estimated. We then show that Engle and Yoo's (1987) Monte Carlo finding that the Engle–Granger two-step procedure (see Engle and Granger, 1987) dominates the unrestricted vector autoregression on MSFE calculations is not robust to performing the same calculations on a different representation of the variables.

Let $\mathbf{x}_t$ be the $N \times 1$ vector of time-series variables, $\mathbf{x}_t = (x_{1t}, x_{2t}, ..., x_{Nt})'$. Then a linear dynamic system with p lags can be written as the VAR for $t = 1, 2, ..., T$:

$$\mathbf{A}(L)\mathbf{x}_t = \psi\mathbf{D}_t + \nu_t \quad \text{where} \quad \nu_t \sim \mathsf{IN}(0, \Omega) \quad \text{and} \quad \mathbf{A}(L) = \sum_{j=0}^{p} \mathbf{A}_j L^j \quad \text{with} \quad \mathbf{A}_0 = \mathbf{I}_N \quad (24)$$

In equation (24), $\mathbf{D}_t$ contains deterministic components, and the initial values $\mathbf{x}_{1-p}$, $\mathbf{x}_{2-p}$, ..., $\mathbf{x}_0$ are fixed. Equation (24) can be reparameterized as:

$$\Delta\mathbf{x}_t = \sum_{i=1}^{p-1} \Pi_i \, \Delta\mathbf{x}_{t-i} + \Pi\mathbf{x}_{t-p} + \psi\mathbf{D}_t + \nu_t \tag{25}$$

where:

$$\Pi_i = -\left(\mathbf{I}_N + \sum_{j=1}^{i} \mathbf{A}_j\right) \quad \text{and} \quad \Pi = -\left(\mathbf{I}_N + \sum_{j=1}^{p} \mathbf{A}_j\right) = -\mathbf{A}(1)$$

Ignoring deterministic non-stationarities, the rank of $\Pi (= \text{rank of } \mathbf{A}(1))$ determines how many linearly independent combinations of the variables x_{it} are stationary.

It is assumed throughout that none of the roots of $\det(\mathbf{A}(L)) = 0$ are inside the unit circle, so that explosive variables are excluded. Let n denote the rank of Π where $0 \leqslant n \leqslant N$, then there are $(N - n)$ linear combinations of $\mathbf{x}_t$ which act as common stochastic trends, and n cointegrated linear combinations of $\mathbf{x}_t$ (see Engle and Granger, 1987). We can write Π as $\Pi = \alpha\beta'$ where α and β are $N \times n$, of rank n. The condition that $\alpha'_\perp \Psi \beta_\perp$ is a full-rank matrix is required to rule out $\mathbf{x}_t$ being integrated of order 2, where Ψ is the mean lag matrix of $\mathbf{A}(L)$ evaluated at unity, and $\alpha_\perp$ and $\beta_\perp$ are full-column rank $N \times (N - n)$ matrices such that $\alpha'\alpha_\perp = \beta'\beta_\perp = 0$ (see Johansen, 1992). When $n = 0$, $\Pi = 0$ and the N variables in $\mathbf{x}_t$ are integrated of order unity, denoted $I(1)$, so $\Delta\mathbf{x}_t$ is stationary apart from the possibility of a deterministic trend. For simplicity, we set $p = 1$, noting that the system can be stacked into a first-order form without loss of generality (see Hendry and Mizon, 1993).

Generally, the rank of Π is unknown and investigators might adopt any one of three estimation methods for equation (25). These methods can be categorized in terms of the value imposed on n. Ordinary least squares (OLS) on each equation in the system in turn is the unrestricted VAR estimator (UV), and estimates Π as a full-rank matrix. The polar case is the estimator of the VAR in differences (DV), for which Π is set to the null matrix. The intermediate case imposes some number of cointegrating vectors, and is illustrated by the maximum likelihood (ML) estimator of Johansen (1988), or by the two-step procedure proposed in Engle and Granger (1987) (EG). Estimation and hypothesis testing in closed VARs, where all the variables are jointly endogenous, has been discussed by Johansen (1988) and Johansen and Juselius (1990) for the $I(1)$ case.

System (24) can also be reformulated by partitioning $\mathbf{x}_t$ into $(\mathbf{x}'_{at} : \mathbf{x}'_{bt})'$ where $\beta'\mathbf{x}_t$ and $\Delta\mathbf{x}_{bt}$ are $I(0)$ by construction. Let $\mathbf{w}'_t = (\mathbf{x}'_t\beta : \Delta\mathbf{x}'_{bt})$ and $\alpha' = (\alpha'_a : \alpha'_b)$ which is $(n \times n : n \times (N - n))$.

626   *Journal of Forecasting*   *Vol. 12, Iss. No. 8*

Then, for $p = 1$ the system can be expressed as:

$$\mathbf{w}_t = \mathbf{C}\mathbf{w}_{t-1} + \boldsymbol{\psi}^*\mathbf{D}_t + \boldsymbol{\varepsilon}_t \qquad \text{where} \qquad \boldsymbol{\varepsilon}_t \sim \text{IN}(0, \boldsymbol{\Sigma}) \tag{26}$$

and:

$$\mathbf{C} = \begin{bmatrix} (\mathbf{I} + \boldsymbol{\beta}'\boldsymbol{\alpha}) : \mathbf{0} \\ \boldsymbol{\alpha}_b \quad\;\; : \mathbf{0} \end{bmatrix} \tag{27}$$

In equation (26), $\boldsymbol{\varepsilon}_t' = (\boldsymbol{\varepsilon}_{at}' : \boldsymbol{\varepsilon}_{bt})$, where $\boldsymbol{\varepsilon}_{at} = \boldsymbol{\beta}'\boldsymbol{\nu}_t$ and $\boldsymbol{\varepsilon}_{bt} = (0 : \mathbf{I})\boldsymbol{\nu}_t$.

The forecast accuracy of the alternative estimators can be assessed in terms of $\mathbf{x}_t$ or $\Delta\mathbf{x}_t$ or $\mathbf{w}_t$; the models generated by such linear transformations are isomorphic (that is, have the same likelihood function) for any choice of these variables. One of the main claims of this paper is the inadequacy of measures of forecast accuracy that are sensitive to the choice of $\mathbf{x}_t$, $\Delta\mathbf{x}_t$, $\mathbf{w}_t$, or other linear transformations of the basic variables. The issue is not merely one of academic interest but represents a serious practical difficulty as the following re-examination of the Engle and Yoo (1987) Monte Carlo study illustrates.

Their data generating process (DGP) is a first-order bivariate system where $\mathbf{x}_t = (z_t : y_t)'$:

$$\Delta\mathbf{x}_t = \boldsymbol{\Pi}\mathbf{x}_{t-1} + \boldsymbol{\psi} + \boldsymbol{\nu}_t \qquad \text{where} \qquad \boldsymbol{\nu}_t \sim \text{IN}(0, \boldsymbol{\Omega}) \tag{28}$$

with:

$$\boldsymbol{\Pi} = \begin{bmatrix} a_{11} : -a_{11}\lambda \\ a_{22} : -a_{22}\lambda \end{bmatrix}, \; \boldsymbol{\psi} = \begin{bmatrix} a_{10} \\ 0 \end{bmatrix}, \text{ and } \boldsymbol{\Omega} = \begin{bmatrix} 1 : \rho s \\ \rho s : s^2 \end{bmatrix}$$

Hence $|\boldsymbol{\Pi}| = 0$. For either $a_{11} \neq 0$ or $a_{22} \neq 0$, $n = 1$ and the cointegrating vector is given (up to a scale factor), by the corresponding row of $\boldsymbol{\Pi}$, that is, $(1 : -\lambda)$. Thus, $z_t - \lambda y_t \sim I(0)$.

In terms of $\mathbf{w}_t = (z_t - \lambda y_t : \Delta y_t)'$, the model can be represented as the first-order autoregressive process:

$$\mathbf{w}_t = \mathbf{C}\mathbf{w}_{t-1} + \boldsymbol{\psi}^* + \boldsymbol{\varepsilon}_t \text{ where } \boldsymbol{\varepsilon}_t \sim \text{IN}(0, \boldsymbol{\Sigma}) \tag{29}$$

when:

$$\mathbf{C} = \begin{bmatrix} 1 + a_{11} - \lambda a_{22} : 0 \\ a_{22} \quad\quad : 0 \end{bmatrix}, \boldsymbol{\psi}^* = \boldsymbol{\psi} = \begin{bmatrix} a_{10} \\ 0 \end{bmatrix}, \; \boldsymbol{\varepsilon}_t = \begin{bmatrix} \nu_{1t} - \lambda\nu_{2t} \\ \nu_{2t} \end{bmatrix}$$

so that:

$$\text{E}[\boldsymbol{\varepsilon}_t\boldsymbol{\varepsilon}_t'] = \boldsymbol{\Sigma} = \begin{bmatrix} 1 - 2\lambda\rho s + \lambda^2 s^2 : \rho s - \lambda s^2 \\ \rho s - \lambda s^2 \quad\quad : s^2 \end{bmatrix}.$$

In Engle and Yoo (1987), $\boldsymbol{\psi} = 0$ and constants were not estimated. They compared the multi-period forecast accuracy for $\mathbf{x}_t$ of UV with EG, and we could reproduce all relevant respects in experiment 4 of Clements and Hendry (1992). The two equations of the system are linked by a common cointegrating vector, although the cointegrating parameter and speeds of adjustment differ here, with the 'error-correcting' behaviour being quantitatively more important in Engle and Yoo's DGP. The variances of the independent, standard normal disturbances affect the scaling of the MSFE calculations but are otherwise irrelevant.

Table I of Engle and Yoo (1987) indicates there are gains to using the UV estimator for the shortest forecasts, but that the advantage is increasingly with EG as the horizon lengthens, rising to an increase in forecast accuracy of over 40% after 20 periods. We find little to choose between the estimators at the shortest horizons, but a close correspondence to their findings at the longer horizons, when the basis of comparison is TMSFE on the levels of the variables,

Table I. Measures of relative
forecast accuracy (adapted
from Clements and Hendry,
1992, Table 3). % GAIN/
LOSS($-$) relative to UV

| | | MSFE | |
h	EG	ML	DV
(A)		$\mathbf{x}_t$	
1	1	1	-7
5	5	7	-11
10	15	17	3
20	37	38	29
		$\mathbf{w}_t$	
(B)			
1	0	0	-12
5	-5	1	-31
10	-6	1	-37
20	-6	2	-37
		$\Delta\mathbf{x}_t$	
(C)			
1	1	1	-7
5	0	0	0
10	2	2	2
20	1	1	1
		$|\hat{\phi}|$	
(D)			
1	1	2	-13
5	0	10	-43
10	-3	19	-57
20	5	45	-63

$\mathbf{x}_t$, as in their study. See panel A of Table I, which presents TMSFE calculations for EG, ML, and DV, relative to UV, for ease of comparison, when the basis of comparison is in terms of $\mathbf{x}_t$. Table I is adapted from Table 3 of Clements and Hendry (1992). The small differences in our results compared to those of Engle and Yoo reflect the imprecision of the Monte Carlo given the relatively small number of replications (100 for Engle and Yoo, 1000 in ours) and the particular DGP parameter values selected.

Yet interpreting these results as indicating 'the importance of imposing a long-run constraint rather than the restriction *per se*' (p. 151) is misleading, since the ranking is not robust to performing the calculations on $\mathbf{w}_t = [z_t - \lambda y_t : \Delta y_t]'$ rather than $\mathbf{x}_t$ (see panel B of Table I), illustrating the importance of the particular common basis of comparison chosen for such a measure. In terms of $\mathbf{w}_t$, the UV estimator dominates EG for all forecast horizons, with the gains coming from the improved accuracy of UV in predicting the cointegrating combination. These results are illustrated graphically in Figures 1 and 2 which report the TMSFE calculations for $\mathbf{x}_t$ and $\mathbf{w}_t$; their comparison shows the switch in ranking. All the estimators predict the differences of the variables ($\Delta\mathbf{x}_t$) with approximately the same degree of accuracy (panel C of Table I).

Intuitively, the EG estimator ties the forecasts of z_t and y_t, ($\hat{z}_t : \hat{y}_t$) together, in the sense that the estimated model from which they are generated exhibits an error-correction mechanism, but will tie them together with the wrong cointegrating parameter if the estimate of the cointegrating parameter is poor. What really matters is how close the estimated parameters are to their true values. While the estimates of the parameters on all the $I(0)$ variables (including the cointegrating combination) obtained by the two-step estimator are asymptotically efficient (but not for $\psi \neq 0$), the estimates from the first step may have substantial biases (Banerjee *et al.*, 1986), and may be worse than the estimates of the long run derived from the UV, in which the dynamics are explicitly modelled. Table I also records the results for the ML estimator, corresponding to the non-linear estimator 'which imposes the cross-equation restrictions implicit in the error-correction representation' (p. 151), which Engle and Yoo conjecture would

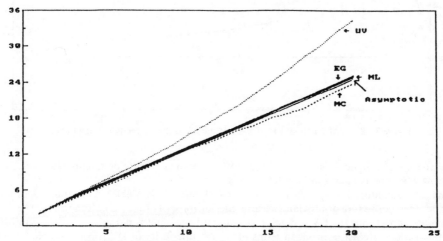

Figure 1. MFSE calculations for the levels of the variables x_t

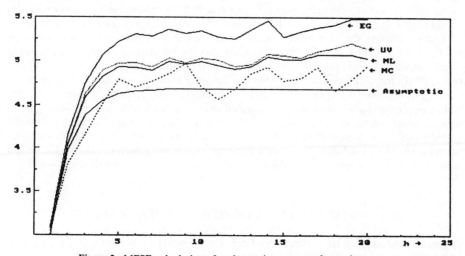

Figure 2. MFSE calculations for the stationary transformation w_t

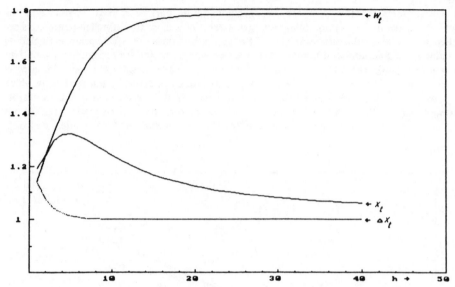

Figure 3. Ratio of trace MSFE of the DV model to the correctly specified case

dominate both estimators. In fact, only the UV estimator is clearly dominated and this only happens when the comparison is in terms of x_t.

The DV estimator, which is clearly mis-specified since the variables cointegrate, does not bear out their conjecture of providing clearly inferior forecasts for comparisons on x_t. The DV estimator outperforms the UV estimator at long horizons, and is not greatly worse than ML for a 20-period forecast horizon. In terms of w_t, the inferiority of DV is considerable (about 40% worse than UV for $h = 20$). Going from x_t to w_t introduces into the MSFE calculations covariance terms between the forecast errors of the elements of x_t which may alter the relative rankings. That the relative losses to using the mis-specified DV model, compared to a correctly specified model, depend on the chosen P-transformation for TMSFEs is evident from Figure 3. This figure compares the asymptotic trace MSFEs for the DV model with those from the correctly specified model. By asymptotic is meant that the estimated parameters are replaced by their true values, as are the covariance matrices of the disturbance terms (see Clements and Hendry, 1992, for a full discussion). The line denoting the ratio of the DV model to the correctly specified model for Δx_t rapidly approaches unity as h increases, indicating that the TMSFEs of the correctly and incorrectly specified models differ only by a term which goes to zero in h. Hence, on the basis of such calculations on Δx_t there is no gain to using a correctly specified model at anything but the shortest forecast horizons. In terms of x_t, the relative losses from using the DV model initially increase then decrease in the forecast horizon, but do not disappear. The relative loss to using the DV model is largest for w_t, and the ratio converges in h.

AN INVARIANT MEASURE OF FORECAST PERFORMANCE

Differencing and cointegration transformations are members of the general class of non-singular scale-preserving linear transformations applicable to a linear dynamic system such as equation (24). If unique forecast accuracy rankings are to result from using any criterion, then that criterion must be invariant across all isomorphic representations of a system. Consider the transformation in equations (5) and (6) from x_t to x_t^* where $|M| = 1$. The h-step ahead forecast errors resulting from x_t and x_t^* are denoted by u_t and e_t respectively. Then, for transformations using M:

(1) The trace MSFE for u_t is not, in general, equivalent to that for e_t: $\text{tr}(MV_hM') \neq \text{tr}(V_h)$;
(2) The determinant of the forecast error second moment matrix is invariant: $|MV_hM'| = |V_h|$ when $|M| = 1$;
(3) The MSFEM is invariant: $d^{*'}V_hd^* < d^{*'}V_h^*d^*$ $\forall d^* \neq 0$ implies that $d'MV_hM'd < d'MV_h^*M'd$ $\forall d \neq 0$. Therefore a change of contemporaneous transformation of the variables will not induce a switch in the rankings providing a common basis is used.

For transformations using P, as happens with the transformation from x_t to w_t or Δx_t, these results continue to hold with the following exceptions:

(1) The trace MSFE is valid for one-step forecasts;
(2) $|V_h|$ is not invariant except for $h = 1$, when the invariance follows from the conditional nature of the expectations operator as with (1).
(3) MSFEM is not invariant for $h > 1$, as shown above.

More generally, for $h > 1$, the covariance terms between the different step ahead forecast errors have to be taken into account, in which case the general forecast error second moment matrix or its determinant (i.e. the GFESM) still provide invariant measures. The general forecast error second moment matrix is formed by stacking the forecast errors from all previous step ahead forecasts as in:

$$|\phi_h| = |E[EE']| \qquad \text{where} \qquad E' = [e_{t+1}', e_{t+2}', ..., e_{t+h-1}', e_{t+h}'] \tag{30}$$

Transforming the data by M where $|M| = 1$ must leave the criterion in equation (30) unaffected; transforming by P leaves the error process unaffected so again equation (30) is invariant.

The MSFEM criterion can be generalized to apply to the pooled or stacked forecast error second moment matrix ϕ_h. In that case, the model denoted by $\tilde{\ }$ dominates $\hat{\ }$ if:

$$\hat{\phi}_h - \tilde{\phi}_h > 0$$

that is, if the difference between the two estimates of the stacked forecast error second moment matrix is positive definite. It follows immediately that MSFEM dominance on the stacked MSFE matrix is sufficient but not necessary for GFESM dominance, that is:

$$\hat{\phi}_h - \tilde{\phi}_h > 0 \Rightarrow |\hat{\phi}| > |\tilde{\phi}_h|$$

since $\hat{\phi}_h$ and $\tilde{\phi}_h$ are positive definite (see, for example, Dhrymes, 1984, proposition 66, p. 77). Thus GFESM dominance is seen to be a weaker condition than MSFEM applied to the stacked MSFE matrix. It can also be related to the statistical literature on the predictive likelihood measure (see the fifth section).

The simulation results for the invariant GFESM measure $|\hat{\phi}_h|$ are recorded in panel D of Table I. There is little to choose between EG and UV on this measure, while the relative superiority and inferiority of ML and DV, respectively, becomes apparent. These findings are independent of whether the calculations are performed in terms of x_t, Δx_t, or w_t: the GFESM criterion has the same value for all of these. In the remainder of this section we demonstrate that the one-step forecast errors determine the complete ranking for the GFESM in a model with white-noise errors when there is no parameter uncertainty, and derive its distribution.

When the parameters are known, ψ drops out of the forecast error calculations so that from equation (24) when $p = 1$:

$$\mathbf{x}_t = \mathbf{B}\mathbf{x}_{t-1} + \mathbf{v}_t \tag{31}$$

where we have simplified notation by setting $\mathbf{B} = \mathbf{A}_1$, consistent with the second section of this paper. Hence:

$$\mathbf{x}_{t+h} = \mathbf{B}^h \mathbf{x}_t + \sum_{j=0}^{h-1} \mathbf{B}^j \mathbf{v}_{t+h-j}. \tag{32}$$

When $\hat{\mathbf{x}}_{t+h} = \mathbf{B}^h \mathbf{x}_t$ and $\mathbf{e}_{t+h} = \mathbf{x}_{t+h} - \hat{\mathbf{x}}_{t+h} = \sum_{j=0}^{h-1} \mathbf{B}^j \mathbf{v}_{t+h-j}$:

$$\mathrm{E}[\mathbf{e}_{t+h}\mathbf{e}'_{t+h}] = \mathbf{V}_h = \sum_{j=0}^{h-1} \mathbf{B}^j \mathbf{\Omega} \mathbf{B}^{j\prime} \tag{33}$$

Thus, for a one-step forecast, the criterion is $|\boldsymbol{\phi}_1| = |\mathbf{V}_1| = |\mathbf{\Omega}| = |\mathbf{\Sigma}|$. For a two-step forecast, the covariance $\mathrm{E}[\mathbf{e}_{t+1}\mathbf{e}'_{t+2}] = \mathbf{\Omega}\mathbf{B}'$, so the complete second moment matrix is:

$$|\boldsymbol{\phi}_2| = \begin{vmatrix} \mathbf{\Omega} & : & \mathbf{\Omega}\mathbf{B}' \\ \mathbf{B}\mathbf{\Omega} & : & \mathbf{\Omega} + \mathbf{B}\mathbf{\Omega}\mathbf{B}' \end{vmatrix} = |\mathbf{\Omega}| \cdot |(\mathbf{\Omega} + \mathbf{B}\mathbf{\Omega}\mathbf{B}') - (\mathbf{B}\mathbf{\Omega})\mathbf{\Omega}^{-1}(\mathbf{\Omega}\mathbf{B}')| = |\mathbf{\Omega}|^2 \tag{34}$$

By partitioned inversion, the determinant in equation (34) is $|\mathbf{\Omega}|^2$. This recursion continues to any order and so the criterion $|\boldsymbol{\phi}_h|$ is just $|\mathbf{\Omega}|^h$ for h-step ahead forecasts. Thus the generalized second moment of the one-step forecast error determines the complete ranking, reinforcing the point that model evaluation should focus on one-step performance (see Chong and Hendry, 1986; Hendry, 1986).

When parameters are unknown and have to be estimated, $\hat{\mathbf{e}}_{t+h} = \mathbf{e}_{t+h} + (\mathbf{B}^h - \hat{\mathbf{B}}^h)\mathbf{x}_t$ so that:

$$\mathrm{E}[\hat{\mathbf{e}}_{t+h}\hat{\mathbf{e}}'_{t+h}] = (\mathbf{I} \otimes \mathbf{x}'_t)\mathbf{Q}(h)' \mathbf{V}[\hat{\mathbf{B}}^v]\mathbf{Q}(h)(\mathbf{I} \otimes \mathbf{x}_t) + \sum_{j=0}^{h-1} \mathbf{B}^j \mathbf{\Omega} \mathbf{B}^{j\prime} \tag{33}^*$$

where ^{v} denotes column vectoring, $\otimes$ is the Kronecker product, and $\mathbf{Q}(h)$ is the derivative of $(\mathbf{B}^h)^v$ with respect to $(\mathbf{B}^v)'$ (see e.g. Schmidt, 1974). The forecast uncertainty is not a monotonically increasing function of the forecast horizon so rankings can alter as h increases even when the complete generalized second moment of forecast errors is used.

Since the asymptotic formulae use the true value of $\mathbf{A}(L)$, an equivalent way of looking at the problem of lack of invariance is in terms of the transformation of $\mathbf{x}_t$, given by $\mathbf{A}(L)$. That is, $\boldsymbol{\xi}_t = \mathbf{A}(L)\mathbf{x}_t = \mathbf{v}_t$. In that case, $\boldsymbol{\xi}_{t+h} = \mathbf{v}_{t+h}$, and $\hat{\boldsymbol{\xi}}_{t+h} = 0$ for all h, so $\boldsymbol{\xi}_{t+h} - \hat{\boldsymbol{\xi}}_{t+h} = \mathbf{v}_{t+h}$. Since:

$$\mathrm{E}[\mathbf{v}_{t+h-i}\mathbf{v}'_{t+h-s}] = \delta_{is}\mathbf{\Omega} \text{ where } \delta_{ii} = 1 \text{ and } \delta_{is} = 0 \text{ for } i \neq s \tag{35}$$

then $\boldsymbol{\phi}_h = \mathbf{I} \otimes \mathbf{\Omega}$ and hence $|\boldsymbol{\phi}_h| = |\mathbf{\Omega}|^h$. We can deduce from the above results that $|\boldsymbol{\phi}_h|$ is invariant to any transformation $\mathbf{M}(L)$ of $\mathbf{x}_t$ for which $|\mathbf{M}(0)| = 1$. This is a property of the transformations from $\mathbf{x}_t$ to $\mathbf{w}_t$, or $\Delta\mathbf{x}_t$, but not of transformations to, say, $[z_t - \lambda y_t : \Delta z_t]'$ for which there is an implicit change in the units of $\mathbf{x}_t$.

$|\boldsymbol{\phi}_h|$ is straightforward to estimate in a Monte Carlo setting where there are independent replications of $\mathbf{E}$. If $\mathbf{E}_j$ denotes the outcome on the jth of M replications, then:

$$\mathbf{E}_j \underset{\mathrm{app}}{\sim} \mathrm{IN}(0, \boldsymbol{\phi}_h) \tag{36}$$

where $\underset{app}{\sim}$ denotes 'is approximately distributed as', and hence:

$$M \cdot S = \sum_{j=1}^{M} E_j E_j' \underset{app}{\sim} W_{Nh}(M, \phi_h) \tag{37}$$

where $W(M, \phi_h)$, is a central Wishart distribution with M degrees of freedom (see Rao, 1965, chapter 8). Then $|S|$ provides a consistent estimator of $|\phi_h|$. Further, the results in Anderson (1984, chapter 7) deliver its distribution:

$$\sqrt{M}\left(\left|\frac{S}{\phi_h}\right| - 1\right) \underset{a}{\sim} N(0, 2Nh) \tag{38}$$

for N equations, an h-step forecast horizon, and M independent replications, using $\underset{a}{\sim}$ to denote 'is asymptotically distributed as'. This formula allows the uncertainty in the Monte Carlo ranking to be estimated. For moderate sample sizes, $(|S|/|\phi_h| - 1)$ will be close to $\log(|S|/|\phi_h|)$.

For evaluating empirical models, Nh is likely to be large and few independent realizations on E will be available, so the GFESM is less likely to be feasible. Other invariant evaluation criteria exist, in particular the log-likelihood, which has many desirable properties. This is considered in the next section. A final criterion discussed in the fifth section is forecast encompassing. Although it is necessary but not sufficient for a valid model, it is invariant to linear transformations of the kind considered here.

PREDICTIVE LIKELIHOOD[1]

In general terms, prediction involves two unknowns: the parameters of the model and the outcomes of the random variables to be predicted. Denote the joint density function of the sample (X) and the variables to be predicted (p) given the parameters of interest, θ say, by $f(p, X | \theta)$. In predicting p, θ become nuisance parameters and must be eliminated from the prediction rule. The approach adopted above corresponded to eliminating θ by replacing it by an estimate $\hat{\theta}$ and when $\hat{\theta}$ is the maximum likelihood estimator (MLE), this leads to a profile predictive likelihood method, noting that 'profile' in statistics denotes the same as 'concentrated' in econometrics. For example from equation (7) using the scalar version of equation (32):

$$x_{t+h} = \rho^h x_t + \sum_{j=0}^{h-1} \rho^j u_{t+h-j} \tag{39}$$

For known parameters $\theta' = (\rho, \sigma^2)$, $p = (x_{t+1}, ..., x_{t+h})'$, $X = (x_1, ..., x_t)'$:

$$p | X, \theta \sim N(rx_t, \phi_h) \text{ where } r' = (\rho, \rho^2, ..., \rho^h) \tag{40}$$

and ϕ_h is defined in equation (30) and e.g. equation (34) for $h = 2$. Thus, the profile predictive log-likelihood is:

$$L_p(p; \hat{\rho}, \hat{\sigma}^2 | X) = K - \tfrac{1}{2}\log|\hat{\phi}_h| - \tfrac{1}{2}(p - \hat{r}x_t)'\hat{\phi}_h^{-1}(p - \hat{r}x_t) \tag{41}$$

Maximizing $L_p(p; \hat{\rho}, \hat{\sigma}^2 | X)$ with respect to p yields $\hat{p} = \hat{r}x_t$ and a further concentrated log-likelihood function which only depends on $\log|\hat{\phi}_h|$. This outcome is invariant to

---

[1] We are grateful to Neil Shephard for suggesting the approach in this section.

transformations with a unit Jacobian, as required of **M** above. However, it is well known from the prediction error decomposition that:

$$f(\mathbf{p} \mid \mathbf{X}, \boldsymbol{\theta}) = \prod_{t+1}^{t+h} f(x_j \mid x_1, \ldots, x_{j-1}; \boldsymbol{\theta}) \tag{42}$$

so the predictive likelihood measure may be applicable in a wider class of model than the generalized second moment. In particular, $|\hat{\phi}|$ assumes the existence of estimator second moments, and the sufficiency of a second moment measure.

FORECAST ENCOMPASSING

Minimum MSFE is neither necessary nor sufficient for a model to have constant parameters, or provide accurate forecasts, both of which one might deem vital concerns for a model to be used in policy. Further, in scalar processes, one-step MMSFE is not sufficient to ensure forecast encompassing although it is necessary, so that encompassing ensures MMSFE: see Ericsson (1992) and Lu and Mizon (1991) who also discuss the relative merits of, and relations between, forecast error encompassing test statistics and parameter constancy tests. Here we are only concerned with showing that forecast encompassing is invariant to non-singular scale-preserving transformations.

Tests for forecast encompassing concern whether the one-step forecasts of one model can explain the forecast errors made by another. Such tests were proposed as a feasible way to evaluate large-scale econometric models by Chong and Hendry (1986), who establish that any need to pool forecasts from disparate sources indicates model mis-specification. Mizon (1984), Mizon and Richard (1986), and Hendry and Richard (1989) provide general discussions of encompassing. See Diebold (1989) for an attempted reconciliation of the pooling and encompassing approaches.

Generally if $\hat{x}_t$ denotes the forecast from model 1 of x_t, and $\tilde{x}_t$ a forecast from model 2 of the same quantity, then the pooled forecast is:

$$\bar{x}_t = (1 - \delta)\hat{x}_t + \delta \tilde{x}_t \tag{43}$$

If δ is neither zero nor unity, then both forecasts are valuable in forecasting x_t but neither is sufficient. However, the linear combination of forecasts in equation (43) generally is not a sensible way to handle information: two models which individually fail to capture the salient features of the data are unlikely to combine on a systematic basis to produce good forecasts. It is much better to sort out the models. A different prescription comes from the early literature on combinations of forecasts, typified by the following quotation from Nelson (1972, p. 914). 'If the bum on the street corner offers free tips to the decision maker on his way to the office, these will be incorporated in composite predictions if they result in any reduction in expected loss.' One can gauge the effect on within-sample predictions of such tips, but their casual nature does not instill confidence in their reliability in the future.

In its implementation, testing for forecast encompassing is formally equivalent to Nelson's (1972) procedure for computing 'conditional efficiency', as introduced by Granger and Newbold (1973), although Nelson only applied the procedure to within-sample predictions, rather than using it explicitly to evaluate forecasts. A forecast is said to be conditionally efficient if the variance of the forecast error from a combination of that forecast and a rival forecast is not significantly less than that of the original forecast alone. We concur with Granger and Newbold (1977) when they state that they regard 'the conditional efficiency criterion as being of great potential value in actual forecast evaluation' (p. 283) but have less sympathy with the combining of sample-period fitted values from different models in an attempt to improve forecasts. Forecast encompassing (and therefore conditional efficiency) was originally intended to evaluate the forecasts from large-scale macroeconometric models for which standard methods may not be operational, and is not, in general, a good way to evaluate models: the drawbacks with forecast encompassing are noted in the Introduction and again at the end of this section. However, as an application of the encompassing principle, the concept of forecast encompassing is more soundly based than the other *ad hoc* evaluation criteria surveyed by Granger and Newbold (1973), which they show are generally inadequate or even misleading.

If the forecast error from model 1 is given by $x_t - \hat{x}_t = \hat{u}_t$, then:

$$x_t - \bar{x}_t = x_t - \hat{x}_t + \delta(\hat{x}_t - \bar{x}_t) = \hat{u}_t + \delta(\hat{u}_t - \bar{u}_t) = \bar{u}_t(\text{say}) \tag{44}$$

so that $V[\bar{u}_t] < V[\hat{u}_t]$ only if $\delta \neq 0$. If $\delta \neq 0$, then the difference between the forecast errors of the two models can help explain the forecast errors of model 1, so that model 1 could be improved by incorporating some of the features of model 2. The forecast encompassing test is implemented by regressing $\hat{u}_t$ on $\hat{x}_t - \bar{x}_t$:

$$x_t - \hat{x}_t = \gamma(\hat{x}_t - \bar{x}_t) + \zeta_t$$

and using a t-test of $H_0 : \gamma = 0$; if there are several competing models and a sufficiently rich parameterization, the F-test of the joint null can be used. If there is a vector of variables, the following multi-equation regression is needed:

$$\mathbf{x}_t - \hat{\mathbf{x}}_t = \Gamma(\hat{\mathbf{x}}_t - \bar{\mathbf{x}}_t) + \zeta_t \tag{45}$$

When $\Gamma = \mathbf{0}$, the first system forecast encompasses the second, but it fails to do so if $\Gamma \neq \mathbf{0}$. Such a forecast encompassing test seems useful only for large systems where more conventional tests are inapplicable.

A switch from $\mathbf{x}_t$ to $\Delta\mathbf{x}_t$ leaves the test unaffected due to the homogeneity of equation (45):

$$\Delta\mathbf{x}_t - \Delta\hat{\mathbf{x}}_t = \Gamma(\Delta\hat{\mathbf{x}}_t - \Delta\bar{\mathbf{x}}_t) + \zeta_t \tag{46}$$

since the $\mathbf{x}_{t-1}$ cancel. Further suppose that forecast encompassing holds for a set of variables in a linear system, so $\Gamma = \mathbf{0}$ in equation (46). Then forecast encompassing must hold for any linear combination of that set of variables with the usual caveat about the possibility of conflicts from finite sample tests at fixed significance levels. Consequently, despite its limitations, if forecast encompassing can be established for all relevant variables, that will ensure population MSFE dominance for all linear combinations such that $|\mathbf{M}| = 1$. Forecast encompassing is sufficient to ensure one-step GFESM dominance as discussed above, but the model which performs best on $|\hat{\phi}|$ need not be able to encompass all the contending models. The forecast parameter encompassing test suggested by Ericsson (1992) is required to avoid conflicts.

SUMMARY AND CONCLUSIONS

Linear models are invariant to non-singular, scale-preserving linear transforms but mean square, and mean absolute, forecast errors need not be. Consequently, different rankings across models or methods can be obtained from various MSFE measures by choosing alternative yet isomorphic representations of a given data generation process. This poses a serious problem because MSFE rankings can be an artefact of the linear transformation selected. A generalized forecast error second moment criterion is proposed which is invariant to non-singular, scale-preserving linear transformations and which highlights the key role of one-step forecast accuracy.

Forecast encompassing is also invariant to non-singular, scale-preserving linear transforms and entails minimum MSFE, whereas MSFE dominance is only necessary for forecast encompassing.

The trace MSFE criterion is sometimes justified in terms of quadratic loss functions. If a model user were certain that one, and only one, non-singular linear transformation of the variables could ever be of interest, then the MSFE for that choice might seem viable. In economics, it seems unlikely that such a condition could be met. An agent interested in the aggregate level of unemployment, for example, is almost certainly interested in its dispersion across regions, occupations, or income groups; and possibly in whether it is increasing or decreasing. The model which delivers the minimum trace MSFE for the first of these need not coincide with that which is best for any one of the decompositions. Such a situation seems intolerable for policy makers: in the UK, we can imagine the response if the Chancellor of the Exchequer were told to use the London Business School model if he or she wanted the minimum MSFE of levels of GNP; the City University Business School model for the MMSFE of changes, etc.! The Chancellor's reaction would be worse still if told to switch to the Treasury model because his or her interest changed from (say) exports and imports to the trade balance.

This first example is precisely the state of affairs suggested by the analysis in Wallis *et al.*, (1987). The RMSEs for four variables—the level and growth of GDP, the inflation rate, and the unemployment rate—are calculated from the forecasts of four leading modelling groups published in autumn 1984 for the following two-year period. The RMSEs are then plotted (see Wallis *et al.*, 1987, Fig. 4.2, p. 78) after scaling by the average for a given variable over the groups, to adjust for varying degrees of difficulty in modelling the variables. However, the scaling is of minor importance since it leaves the rankings of the groups for particular variables unaffected. The RMSE rankings in terms of GDP growth favour the City University Business School model, and place the National Institute model last, while in terms of the level of GDP, the London Business School comes out on top and the Liverpool model fares worst.

As well as illustrating the lack of invariance of MSFE measures, this example reinforces a number of points made throughout the paper. It typifies the common practice of basing comparisons on what are essentially scalar measures even in a multivariate setting. Wallis *et al.* (1987, p. 77) is typical: given a vector of forecast errors for different variables, $\mathbf{e}$, the quadratic form $\mathbf{e}'\mathbf{Ke}$ is constructed, where $\mathbf{K}$ is a symmetric matrix, 'usually...taken to be a diagonal matrix' (p. 77) so no adjustments are made for correlated forecast errors. Second, there is explicit recognition of the fact that no comparisons between modelling teams can be made unless one team dominates another on each of the four variables considered, otherwise rankings will not be invariant to the choice of weights. Compared to our analysis in the second section, the approach here calculates linear combinations of RMSEs of individual variables, rather than (R)MSEs of linear combinations of variables, and therefore ignores covariance terms. Nevertheless, it does appear to suggest that Wallis *et al.* would support our contention that the weights in policymakers' loss functions are not immutable, in which case the non-invariance of MSFE measures becomes a major drawback in policy analysis.

The Chancellor could be spared the confusion of using different models to forecast growth rates versus levels, etc. if it is recognized that maximum likelihood estimates produce maximum likelihood forecasts. Given the limitations of MSFEs as forecast evaluation criteria, more attention should be paid to maximum likelihood forecasts and invariant criteria such as the generalized forecast error second moment or likelihood evaluation.

ACKNOWLEDGEMENTS

Financial support from the UK Economic and Social Research Council under grant R000233447 is gratefully acknowledged. We are indebted to Anindya Banerjee, David Cox, Rob Engle, Neil Ericsson, Grayham Mizon, John Muellbauer, Neil Shephard, and Kenneth Wallis for helpful discussions about the material herein.

REFERENCES

Anderson, T. W., *An Introduction to Multivariate Statistical Analysis*, New York: Wiley, 1984.

Banerjee, A., Dolado, J. J., Hendry, D. F. and Smith, G. W., 'Exploring equilibrium relationships in econometrics through static models: some Monte Carlo evidence', *Oxford Bulletin of Economics and Statistics*, 48 (1986), 253–77.

Bjørnstad, J. F., 'Predictive likelihood: a review', *Statistical Science*, 5 (1990), 242–65.

Brandner, P. and Kunst, R. S., 'Forecasting vector autoregressions—the influence of cointegration. A Monte Carlo study', Research Memorandum, 265, Institute for Advanced Studies, Vienna, 1990.

Burns, T., 'The interpretation and use of economic predictions', *Proceedings of the Royal Society*, A407 (1986), 103–25.

Chambers, M. J., 'A note on forecasting in co-integrated systems', Department of Economics, University of Essex, 1991.

Chong, Y. Y. and Hendry, D. F., 'Econometric evaluation of linear macro-economic models', *Review of Economic Studies*, LIII (1986), 671–90.

Clements, M. P. and Hendry, D. F., 'Forecasting in cointegrated systems', Discussion paper, Oxford Institute of Economics and Statistics, 1992.

Dhrymes, P. J., *Mathematics for Econometrics*, 2nd edition, Springer-Verlag, New York, 1984.

Diebold, F. X., 'Forecast combination and encompassing: Reconciling two divergent literatures', *International Journal of Forecasting*, 5 (1989), 589–92.

Engle, R. F. and Granger, C. W. J., 'Cointegration, and error-correction: Representation, estimation and testing', *Econometrica*, 55 (1987), 251–76.

Engle, R. F., and Yoo, B. S., 'Forecasting and testing in cointegrated systems', *Journal of Econometrics*, 35 (1987), 143–59.

Ericsson, N. R., 'Parameter constancy, mean square forecast errors, and measuring forecast performance: An exposition, extensions, and illustration', *Journal of Policy Modeling*, 14, (1992), 465–95.

Granger, C. W. J. and Newbold, P., 'Some comments on the evaluation of economic forecasts', *Applied Economics*, 5 (1973), 35–47.

Granger, C. W. J. and Newbold, P., *Forecasting Economic Time Series*, New York: Academic Press, 1977.

Hendry, D. F., 'The role of prediction in evaluating econometric models', *Proceedings of the Royal Society*, A407 (1986) 25–33.

Hendry, D. F. and Mizon G. E., 'Evaluating dynamic econometric models by encompassing the VAR', in Phillips, P. C. B., (ed.), *Models, Methods and Applications of Econometrics*: Essays in Honor of A. R. Bergstrom, Oxford: Basil Blackwell, pp. 272–300, 1993.

Hendry, D. F. and Richard, J.-F., 'On the formulation of empirical models in dynamic econometrics', *Journal of Econometrics*, 20 (1982), 3–33.

Hendry, D. F. and Richard, J.-F., 'Recent developments in the theory of encompassing', in Cornet, B. and Tulkens, H. (eds.), *Contributions to Operations Research and Econometrics. The Twentieth Anniversary of CORE*. Cambridge, MA.: MIT Press, pp. 393–440, 1989.

Johansen, S., 'Statistical analysis of cointegration vectors.' *Journal of Economic Dynamics and Control*, 12 (1988), 231–54.

Johansen, S., 'A representation of vector autoregressive processes integrated of order 2', *Econometric Theory*, **8**, (1992), 188–202.

Johansen, S. and Juselius, K., 'Maximum likelihood estimation and inference on cointegration—with applications to the demand for money', *Oxford Bulletin of Economics and Statistics*, **52** (1990), 169–210.

Lu, M. and Mizon, G. E., 'Forecast encompassing and model evaluation', in Hackl, P. and Westlund, A. H. (eds.) *Economic Structural Change, Analysis and Forecasting*, Berlin: Springer-Verlag, pp. 123–38, 1991.

McNees, S. K., 'The accuracy of macroeconomic forecasts', in Klein, P. A. (ed.), *Analyzing Modern Business Cycles*, London: M. E. Sharpe Inc., pp. 143–73, 1990.

Mizon, G. E., 'The encompassing approach in econometrics', in Hendry, D. F. and Wallis, K. F., (eds), *Econometrics and Quantitative Economics*, Oxford: Basil Blackwell, pp. 135–72, 1984.

Mizon, G. E. and Richard, J.-F., 'The encompassing principle and its application to non-nested hypothesis tests'. *Econometrica*, **54**, (1986), 657–78.

Nelson, C. R., 'The prediction performance of the FRB–MIT–PENN model of the U.S. economy', *American Economic Review*, **62** (1972), 902–17.

Rao, C. R., *Linear Statistical Inference and its Applications*, New York: Wiley, 1965.

Schmidt, P., 'The asymptotic distribution of forecasts in the dynamic simulation of an econometric model', *Econometrica*, **42** (1974), 303–9.

Wallis, K. F., Fisher, P. G., Longbottom, J. A., Turner, D. S. and Whitley, J. D., *Models of the UK Economy—A Fourth Review by the ESRC Macroeconomic Modelling Bureau*, Oxford: Oxford University Press, 1987.

Wallis, K. F., 'Macroeconomic forecasting: a survey', *Economic Journal*, **99** (1989), 28–61.

Wallis, K. F. and Whitley, J. D., 'Sources of error in forecasts and expectations: U.K. economic models 1984–8', *Journal of Forecasting*, **10** (1991), 231–53.

[22]

JOURNAL OF APPLIED ECONOMETRICS, VOL. 10, 127–146 (1995)

FORECASTING IN COINTEGRATED SYSTEMS

MICHAEL P. CLEMENTS AND DAVID F. HENDRY

Institute of Economics and Statistics, and Nuffield College, Oxford

SUMMARY

We consider the implications for forecast accuracy of imposing unit roots and cointegrating restrictions in linear systems of $I(1)$ variables in levels, differences, and cointegrated combinations. Asymptotic formulae are obtained for multi-step forecast error variances for each representation. Alternative measures of forecast accuracy are discussed. Finite sample behaviour in a bivariate model is studied by Monte Carlo using control variables. We also analyse the interaction between unit roots and cointegrating restrictions and intercepts in the DGP. Some of the issues are illustrated with an empirical example of forecasting the demand for M1 in the UK.

1. INTRODUCTION

Whether economic time series are integrated of order unity (denoted $I(1)$) or are stationary has important implications for their forecastability. $I(1)$ variables can only be forecast with increasingly wide confidence intervals, although stationary, cointegrating linear combinations of such variables have finite confidence intervals as the horizon grows (see Engle and Yoo, 1987; Clements and Hendry, 1994, for a general exposition of forecasting with $I(0)$ and $I(1)$ variables). In this paper, we undertake analytical and Monte Carlo studies of different models and estimation methods when the number and location of unit roots in the system is unknown to the investigator. The importance of parameter uncertainty is shown by comparing simulation outcomes with control variates and asymptotic formulae. The simulation results also highlight the interaction between parameter uncertainty and the forecast horizon, and the importance of imposing valid reduced-rank restrictions as the estimation sample size gets smaller. Using mean square forecast errors (MSFEs), an empirical model of the demand for M1 in the UK illustrates the impact of the treatment of unit roots on forecast performance.

Clements and Hendry (1993) criticize the MSFE criterion as a measure of forecast accuracy for multi-step forecasts or nonscalar processes. Although they have traditionally been used (for example, Engle and Yoo, 1987; Brandner and Kunst, 1990; Chambers, 1991), MSFEs are not invariant to nonsingular, scale-preserving linear transformations of the model. Hence different rankings may result from alternative yet isomorphic representations of the process. Where the aim is to compare alternative methods of estimation, as in many Monte Carlo studies, this lack of invariance limits the generality of the results to the particular transformation of the data employed in the study. Conversely, when a well-defined loss function exists that exactly specifies the transformation of interest, then these concerns do not apply. Since this paper is concerned with a comparison of methods for which invariance is desirable, we also consider as an invariant measure the determinant of the estimated second moment matrix of stacked forecast errors, denoted by GFESM.

Engle and Yoo report improved relative forecast accuracy from imposing long-run constraints

CCC 0883–7252/95/020127–20

© 1995 by John Wiley & Sons, Ltd.

Received February 1992

Revised July 1994

using the Engle and Granger (1987) two-step procedure, as compared to an unrestricted vector autoregression (VAR). However, this result is not robust to isomorphic transformations of the model, and judged by the GFESM criterion, there is little to choose between the two-step procedure and the VAR for their experimental design. This paper shows that gains in forecast accuracy from imposing long-run constraints become more apparent at small estimation sample sizes. The empirical model also illustrates the alternative rankings that can result from different transformations.

Section 2 exposits alternative representations of cointegrated systems, and categorizes three estimation methods in terms of how they treat unit roots. Section 3 discusses measures of forecast accuracy and Section 4 derives the asymptotic variance formulae. Section 5 presents the Monte Carlo methods, Section 6 the experimental design, and Section 7 presents the simulation results. Section 8 illustrates the issues using an empirical model of the demand for M1 in the UK. Section 9 concludes.

2. SYSTEMS FOR NONSTATIONARY VARIABLES

Cointegration implies restrictions on systems of equations (see, *inter alia*, the Granger representation theorem in Engle and Granger, 1987: Hylleberg and Mizon, 1989, and Engle and Yoo, 1991, provide extensions and simplified proofs using Smith–McMillan–Yoo forms). Here, our interest is in the implications for forecast uncertainty of various transformations of the variables (for example, levels, differences, cointegrating combinations, etc.), and of imposing cointegrating restrictions and unit roots at the estimation stage. We outline the reduced-rank restrictions implied by cointegration in the vector autoregressive (VAR) levels representation and the systems error-correction formulation, and transform to $I(0)$ space in terms of differences and cointegrating combinations of the variables. Three commonly used specifications are discussed within this framework in terms of the number of unit roots and cointegrating restrictions imposed or implicitly estimated in each case.

Let x_t be an $N \times 1$ vector of time-series variables, satisfying the first-order dynamic linear system:

$$x_t = Ax_{t-1} + \Psi D_t + v_t \tag{1}$$

where $v_t \sim \text{IN}(0, \Omega)$ for $t = 1, 2, ..., T$. D_t contains deterministic components, and the initial value x_0 is fixed. A is an $N \times N$ matrix of coefficients. Equation (1) can be reparameterized as:

$$\Delta x_t = \Pi x_{t-1} + \Psi D_t + v_t \tag{2}$$

where $\Pi = A - I_N = \alpha \beta'$ and α and β are $N \times n$ of rank $n < N$ when $x_t \sim I(1)$ and the cointegrating rank is n. Lag systems of an arbitrary order can be stacked into a first-order form after a suitable change of notation. This is well known for equation (1) (namely the companion form), and as shown in e.g. Hendry and Mizon (1993), when $\Psi = 0$ the system in equation (2) becomes:

$$f_t = \begin{pmatrix} \Delta x_t \\ \beta' x_{t-1} \end{pmatrix} = \begin{pmatrix} \Pi & \alpha \\ \beta' & I_n \end{pmatrix} \begin{pmatrix} \Delta x_{t-1} \\ \beta' x_{t-2} \end{pmatrix} + \begin{pmatrix} v_t \\ 0 \end{pmatrix} = \Pi^* f_{t-1} + \varepsilon_t \tag{3}$$

Further terms in Δx_{t-i} merely extend f_t, so there is no loss of generality in analysing equation (3). However, since that notation is inconvenient, we work with the first-order systems (1) and (2).

As well as excluding explosive variables by assuming that none of the roots of $|I - AL| = 0$ lie inside the unit circle, we also rule out x_t being integrated of order 2. Thus, we assume that $\alpha'_\perp \Theta \beta_\perp$ is full rank, where Θ is the mean lag matrix (here A), and $\alpha_\perp$ and $\beta_\perp$ are full column rank $N \times (N - n)$ matrices such that $\alpha' \alpha_\perp = \beta' \beta_\perp = 0$ (see Johansen, 1992).

A convenient reformulation of equation (1) is obtained by partitioning x_t into $(x'_{at} : x'_{bt})'$ where $\beta' x_t$ and $\Delta x_{bt} = \beta_1 \Delta x_t$ are $I(0)$ by construction. β is normalized such that its first n rows are the identity matrix, i.e. $\beta = (I_n : \beta'_2)'$. This ensures that the transformation from x_t to $w'_t = (x'_t \beta : \Delta x'_{bt}) = (w'_{at} : w'_{bt})'$ is scale-preserving. Partitioning conformably, $a' = (a'_a : a'_b)$, which is $(n \times n : n \times (N - n))$, then:

$$w_t = Cw_{t-1} + \Psi_0 D_t + \varepsilon_t \tag{4}$$

where $\varepsilon_t \sim IN(0, \Sigma)$. In equation (4), $\Psi_0 = (\Psi'\beta : \Psi'_b)' = Q\Psi$ where $\Psi_b = J'\Psi$ when $J' = (0 : I)$ and:

$$Q = \begin{bmatrix} \beta' \\ J' \end{bmatrix}, \quad C = \begin{bmatrix} (I + \beta'a) & 0 \\ a_b & 0 \end{bmatrix} = \begin{bmatrix} \mu & 0 \\ a_b & 0 \end{bmatrix} \quad \text{and} \quad \begin{bmatrix} \beta'\Omega\beta & \beta'\Omega J \\ J'\Omega\beta & J'\Omega J \end{bmatrix} \tag{5}$$

The system in equation (4) determines both the conditional and unconditional means and variances of all the $I(0)$ variables. When $a \neq 0$, the long-run solution for the system is defined by:

$$E[w_t] = (I - C)^{-1}Q\Psi = \begin{pmatrix} -(\beta'a)^{-1}\beta'\Psi \\ a_b(\beta'a)^{-1}\beta'\Psi + \Psi_b \end{pmatrix} \tag{6}$$

When $D_t = 1$ (a constant term), Ψ is denoted by the $N \times 1$ vector ψ, so the expectation of Δx_t is:

$$E[\Delta x_t] = E[a\beta' x_{t-1} + \psi + v_t] = aE[w_{at-1}] + \psi$$
$$= [I - a(\beta'a)^{-1}\beta']\psi = K\psi = g_x \tag{7}$$

which defines the growth in the system. The matrix K is nonsymmetric but idempotent with $\beta'K = 0'$ and $Ka = 0$ so $AK = K$. The condition that ψ falls in the cointegrating space is that $\psi = a\psi^*$ where ψ^* is $n \times 1$ (see Johansen and Juselius, 1990). If so:

$$E[\Delta x_t] = E[a(\beta' : \psi^*)(x'_{t-1} : 1)' + v_t] = Ka\psi^* = 0 \tag{8}$$

demonstrating the absence of linear trends in the elements of x_t.

The estimation methods analysed in the Monte Carlo study can be categorized in terms of the number of common trends (Stock and Watson, 1988) or unit roots, $N - n$, and cointegrating restrictions, n, imposed by the estimation method. OLS on each equation in the system in turn is referred to as the unrestricted VAR estimator (UV), and estimates Π as a full-rank matrix, that is, neither unit roots nor cointegrating restrictions are imposed. The polar case is the estimator of the VAR in differences (DV), for which Π is set to the null matrix so that N unit roots are imposed. The intermediate case is illustrated by the maximum likelihood (ML) estimator of Johansen (1988) and Johansen and Juselius (1990). For comparison with other studies the two-step procedure of Engle and Granger (1987) (EG) is also used in some experiments.

A theory of inference in regressions with nonstationary variables has been developed, *inter alia*, by Phillips and his co-authors (see e.g. Phillips, 1991, for references) and Johansen (1988, 1991): Engle and Yoo (1991) provide a good exposition. In general, the asymptotic distributions of coefficient estimators in systems of $I(1)$ variables will be nonstandard, and involve functionals of Wiener processes, but will converge at rate T, faster than the $\sqrt{T}$ rate in regressions involving $I(0)$ variables. West (1988) demonstrates that an even faster of convergence may hold when the differences of the $I(1)$ variables have nonzero means. In that case, the coefficients on stochastic $I(1)$ variables in OLS regressions converge at the rate of $\sqrt{T^3}$ while estimators of the constant term converge at $\sqrt{T}$. Moreover, the distribution of the estimators will be asymptotically normal, so the major contribution to overall forecast uncertainty from estimating parameters will be from the constant term rather than from slope coefficients.

Notwithstanding these rates of convergence, the practical importance of imposing cointegration restrictions for forecast accuracy in small samples is worth study, and is the focus of our Monte Carlo. We do not consider testing for cointegration but contrast the costs of having too few cointegrating vectors versus including spurious combinations of levels terms. Brandner and Kunst (1990), for example, find a tendency to overestimate n when the true value is low, and claim that the costs of incorrectly specifying n are greater for over-estimates (imposing too much 'cointegration'), so they recommend the use of VARs in differences for forecasting. We do not find support for this prescription.

3. MEASURES OF FORECAST ACCURACY

Forecast comparisons are often based on MSFEs, defined for a scalar process as:

$$E[(x_{t+h} - \hat{x}_{t+h})^2] = E[e_{t+h}^2] = \{E[e_{t+h}]\}^2 + V[e_{t+h}] \tag{9}$$

that is, the squared bias in the h-step-ahead forecast error $e_{t+h} = x_{t+h} - \hat{x}_{t+h}$ (when $\hat{x}_{t+h}$ is the forecast) plus the forecast error variance. In a multivariate setting, the MSFE matrix is $E[e_{t+h}e_{t+h}']$, but usually investigators compute the trace MSFE (TMSFE), which is the sum of the individual MSFEs for each variable, $\text{tr}\{E[e_{t+h}e_{t+h}']\}$. As noted in the introduction, such measures are not invariant under nonsingular, scale-preserving linear transformations and can deliver inconsistent rankings across models or methods for alternative, yet isomorphic, representations of a process such as x_t, Δx_t, or w_t. The models generated by such linear transformations are isomorphic as equations (1), (2), and (4) reveal. Using TMSFEs in a simulation study which assesses the multi-step forecast accuracy of estimators in cointegrated systems, Engle and Yoo (1987) find in favour of the Engle–Granger procedure, which imposes cointegration restrictions, over the unrestricted VAR. However, they only report MSFEs for the levels of the variables, x_t, and as shown below, the ranking between the estimators changes when forecast accuracy is assessed in terms of w_t.

A comparison of estimation methods requires measures of forecast accuracy that are invariant to the choice of x_t, Δx_t, w_t, or other scale-preserving linear transformations, since otherwise rankings between estimators or models can be altered by the choice of linear transform. The invariant measure of forecast accuracy proposed by Clements and Hendry (1993) is the generalized forecast error second moment (GFESM):

$$|\Phi_h| = |E[E_h E_h']| \tag{10}$$

where $E_h = [e_{T+1}', e_{T+2}', \ldots, e_{T+h-1}', e_{T+h}']'$, the vector of stacked forecast errors from all previous step-ahead forecasts. $|\Phi_h|$ in equation (10) is invariant under the class of transformations for which the linear model is invariant, irrespective of whether the parameters of the model are known or are estimated. The distinguishing characteristics of equation (10) are that it is a determinantal measure and that it is based on all the forecast errors up to period h and not just on the h-step-ahead forecast error alone.

4. ASYMPTOTIC VARIANCE FORMULAE

We derive asymptotic formulae for the h-step-ahead forecast uncertainty, which provide a first-order approximation for empirical implementation and make Monte Carlo outcomes more interpretable. In turn, the Monte Carlo helps to assess their accuracy in finite samples. In this section, we abstract from many of the sources of forecast error that are likely to arise in practice (such as structural breaks), and in particular, from parameter uncertainty. We first consider the case in which the DGP and econometric model coincide: that is, the econometric model is correctly specified. Results for this case appear in the literature (e.g. Lütkepohl, 1991), but to establish notation, we set out the relations between the forecast second moments for different transformations of the model. Since one of our objectives is to examine the role of imposing unit roots and cointegrating restrictions, we derive the analogous forecast variance formulae when the model is a VAR in differences. The DV model incorrectly imposes unit roots when there is cointegration, but its parameter values can be deduced from the DGP.

Three main types of forecast moments could be derived: $M[e_{T+h}]$, $M[e_{T+h}|x_T]$, and $M[e_{T+h}|X_T^1]$, where $M[\cdot] \equiv E[(\cdot)^2]$ and $X_T^1 = (x_1, ..., x_T)$. The first of these corresponds to the Monte Carlo undertaken below, where X_{T+h}^1 is resampled on each replication; the last involves conditional forecasting after parameter estimation, and corresponds to a Monte Carlo where one set X_T^1 is drawn and sets of independent forecasts are generated from the last data point. The middle is a hybrid, albeit one which is regularly used for computing forecast variance formulae, where taking expectations over x_T will yield the first. Here, we consider the first two types of forecast moment.

4.1 Correctly Specified Econometric Model

We begin with the h-step-ahead covariance matrix for known parameters when $D_t = 1$, so Ψ is the $N \times 1$ vector ψ. Defining the h-step-ahead forecast $\hat{x}_{T+h}$ (for the levels of the series) by the conditional expectation $E[x_{T+h}|x_T]$, and the h-step-ahead forecast error in the level of the series by $e_{x,T+h} = x_{T+h} - \hat{x}_{T+h}$, then the forecast is approximately unbiased with forecast error variance given by:

$$V_{x,h} \equiv V[e_{x,T+h}] = V[e_{x,T+h}|x_T] = \sum_{s=0}^{h-1} A^s \Omega A^{s\prime} \tag{11}$$

An equivalent expression holds in terms of C and Σ for the model defined in equation (4) using w_t:

$$V_{w,h} \equiv V[e_{w,T+h}] = V[e_{w,T+h}|x_T] = \sum_{s=0}^{h-1} C^s \Sigma C^{s\prime} \tag{12}$$

Since $A = (I + \alpha\beta')$ has unit roots, the TMSFE for x_t from equation (11) is $O(h)$, while the TMSFE for w_t from equation (12) is $O(1)$ in h, reflecting the fact that $x_t \sim I(1)$ but $w_t \sim I(0)$ (cf. Engle and Yoo, 1987, Lütkepohl, 1991, sections 2.2 and 11.3).

When the system is expressed in differences, Δx_t, with the predicted value of the h-step-ahead change defined by:

$$\widehat{\Delta x}_{T+h} = E[\Delta x_{T+h}|x_T] = A^{h-1}(\alpha\beta' x_T + \psi)$$

then the forecasts are again approximately unbiased, and the variance formulae are:

$$V_{\Delta x,h} \equiv V[e_{\Delta x,T+h}] = V[e_{\Delta x,T+h}|x_T] = \sum_{s=0}^{h-2} A^s \alpha\beta' \Omega \beta\alpha' A^{s\prime} + \Omega \tag{13}$$

which collapses to Ω when $h = 1$. Since $\mathbf{A}a = a(\mathbf{I} + \beta'a) = a\mu$ where $\mu = (\mathbf{I} + \beta'a)$, then $\mathbf{A}^s a = a\mu^s$. Thus, the MSFE in equation (13) is $O(1)$ despite the terms in $\mathbf{A}^s$. In a bivariate cointegrated system, μ is the eigenvalue of $\mathbf{A}$ strictly less than unity in absolute value so $a\mu^s \rightarrow 0$ as $s \rightarrow \infty$.

4.2 Incorrectly Specified DV Model

Because the DV model is misspecified when $n \neq 0$, the asymptotic variance expressions for the DV model in terms of $\mathbf{x}_t$, $\mathbf{w}_t$, and $\Delta \mathbf{x}_t$ are derived, again ignoring sampling variability. The forecasts from the DV model for $\Delta \mathbf{x}_t$ are calculated by setting $\Delta \mathbf{x}_{T+h}$ equal to the population growth rate $\mathbf{K}\psi$ (defined by equation (7)), so that:

$$\widetilde{\Delta \mathbf{x}}_{T,h} = \mathbf{K}\psi \tag{14}$$

Using equation (14), the expression for the forecast error $\tilde{\mathbf{e}}_{\Delta x, T+h}$ is:

$$\tilde{\mathbf{e}}_{\Delta x, T+h} = \mathbf{A}^{h-1}(a\beta'\mathbf{x}_T + \psi) - \mathbf{K}\psi + \mathbf{v}_{T+h} + \sum_{r=0}^{h-2} \mathbf{A}^r a\beta' \mathbf{v}_{T+h-r-1} \tag{15}$$

so that for $a \neq 0$ and using equation (6):

$$\begin{aligned}
\mathbf{E}[\tilde{\mathbf{e}}_{\Delta x, T+h} \mid \mathbf{x}_T] &= \mathbf{A}^{h-1}(a\beta'\mathbf{x}_T + \psi) - \mathbf{K}\psi \\
&= a\mu^{h-1}\beta'\mathbf{x}_T + \mathbf{A}^{h-1}(\mathbf{I} - \mathbf{K})\psi \\
&= a\mu^{h-1}(\mathbf{w}_{aT} - \mathbf{E}[\mathbf{w}_{aT}])
\end{aligned} \tag{16}$$

whereas equation (13) continues to hold for $\mathbf{V}[\tilde{\mathbf{e}}_{\Delta x, T+h} \mid \mathbf{x}_T]$. Thus, for $\Delta \mathbf{x}_t$ from a DV, the conditional forecasts are biased unless $a = 0$, but tend to zero for large h, and the MSFE is $O(1)$.

To obtain expressions for the unconditional expectations and forecast error variance, take the unconditional expectation in equation (16):

$$\mathbf{E}[\tilde{\mathbf{e}}_{\Delta x, T+h}] = a\mu^{h-1}\mathbf{E}[\mathbf{w}_{aT} - \mathbf{E}[\mathbf{w}_{aT}]] = 0 \tag{17}$$

so the unconditional forecasts from the DV are unbiased when the average growth rate is used as the forecast. However, they would be biased by $-a(\beta'a)^{-1}\beta'\psi$ if $\mathbf{K} = \mathbf{I}$ was used in equation (14), so that the forecast was ψ, as might be incorrectly assumed on setting Π to zero in equation (2).

From equation (4), the unconditional variance matrix of $\mathbf{w}_t$, $\mathbf{V}[\mathbf{w}_t]$, is $\mathbf{G} = \mathbf{C}\mathbf{G}\mathbf{C}' + \Sigma$ so that from equation (5):

$$\begin{bmatrix} \mathbf{G}_{aa} & \mathbf{G}_{ab} \\ \mathbf{G}_{ba} & \mathbf{G}_{bb} \end{bmatrix} = \begin{bmatrix} \mu\mathbf{G}_{aa}\mu' & \mu\mathbf{G}_{aa}a'_b \\ a_b\mathbf{G}_{aa}\mu' & a_b\mathbf{G}_{aa}a'_b \end{bmatrix} + \begin{bmatrix} \Sigma_{aa} & \Sigma_{ab} \\ \Sigma_{ba} & \Sigma_{bb} \end{bmatrix} \tag{18}$$

Consequently, from equation (15) for $a \neq 0$ (the last term on the first line is present only for $h > 1$):

$$\begin{aligned}
\mathbf{V}[\tilde{\mathbf{e}}_{\Delta x, T+h}] &= a\mu^{h-1}\mathbf{V}[\mathbf{w}_{aT}]\mu^{h-1'}a' + \Omega + \sum_{s=0}^{h-2} a\mu^s\beta'\Omega\beta\mu^{s'}a' \\
&= \Omega + a\mathbf{V}[\mathbf{w}_{aT}]a'
\end{aligned} \tag{19}$$

The last expression in equation (19) follows because $G_{aa} = \mu G_{aa} \mu' + \beta' \Omega \beta$ from equation (18), so the first line of equation (19) is:

$$a\mu^{h-2}[\mu G_{aa} \mu' + \beta' \Omega \beta]\mu^{h-2\prime}a' + \Omega + \sum_{s=0}^{h-3} a\mu^s \beta' \Omega \beta \mu^{s\prime} a'$$

$$= a\mu^{h-2} G_{aa} \mu^{h-2\prime}a' + \Omega + \sum_{s=0}^{h-3} a\mu^s \beta' \Omega \beta \mu^{s\prime} a' \tag{20}$$

and so on. Thus, equation (19) is independent of h. In the bivariate case in the Monte Carlo, μ is the scalar $(1 + \beta' a)$ and so $aV[w_{aT}]a' = a\beta' \Omega \beta a'(1 - \mu^2)^{-1}$ using equation (18). From equation (19), therefore:

$$\sum_{s=0}^{h-2} a\mu^s \beta' \Omega \beta \mu^{s\prime} a' = aV[w_{aT}]a' - a\mu^{h-1}V[w_{aT}]\mu^{h-1\prime}a' \tag{21}$$

and substituting this into equation (13):

$$V_{\Delta x,h} \equiv V[e_{\Delta x,T+h}|x_T] = \Omega + aV[w_{aT}]a' - a\mu^{h-1}V[w_{aT}]\mu^{h-1\prime}a' \tag{22}$$

The difference between the correct model and the DV model asymptotic variance formulae for Δx_t in equations (13) and (19) is $a\mu^{h-1}V[w_{aT}]\mu^{h-1\prime}a'$, which goes to zero in h. Hence, when assessing forecast accuracy using the second-moment matrix for Δx_t, there is no measurable gain to using the correctly specified model beyond short forecast horizons.

The analogous expressions for forecasting levels using the DV model are based on forecasts of x_t, derived by integrating the forecasts of Δx_t (given in equation (14)) from the initial value:

$$\tilde{x}_{T+h} = \tilde{x}_{T+h-1} + K\psi = x_T + \sum_{r=0}^{h-1} \Delta\tilde{x}_{T+h-r} \tag{23}$$

After some algebra and using $(A^h - I) = \sum_{r=0}^{h-1} a\mu^r \beta'$:

$$\tilde{e}_{x,T+h} = A^h x_T + \sum_{r=0}^{h-1} A^r \psi + \sum_{r=0}^{h-1} A^r v_{T+h-r} - x_T - hK\psi$$

$$= \sum_{r=0}^{h-1} a\mu^r (w_{aT} - E[w_{aT}]) + \sum_{r=0}^{h-1} A^r v_{T+h-r} \tag{24}$$

Thus, the conditional expectation is:

$$E[\tilde{e}_{x,T+h}|x_T] = (A^h - I)x_T + \sum_{r=0}^{h-1} (A^r - K)\psi = \sum_{r=0}^{h-1} a\mu^r (\beta' x_T - E[\beta' x_T]) \tag{25}$$

whereas the unconditional expectation implies unbiased DV model levels forecasts:

$$E[\tilde{e}_{x,T+h}] = \sum_{r=0}^{h-1} a\mu^r E[w_{aT} - E[w_{aT}]] = 0 \tag{26}$$

The conditional variance $V[\tilde{e}_{x,T+h}|x_T]$ is equivalent to equation (11), but the unconditional variance for the DV forecast of x_t differs and is given by:

$$V[\tilde{e}_{x,T+h}] = \sum_{r=0}^{h-1}\sum_{q=0}^{h-1} a\mu^{r\prime}V[w_{aT}]\mu^{q\prime}a' + \sum_{s=0}^{h-1} A^s\Omega A^{s\prime} \tag{27}$$

Comparing equation (27) to (11), the unconditional variance always exceeds the conditional since the first term is a positive definite matrix. However, it declines asymptotically in h. For example, in the bivariate case, μ is a scalar, so:

$$\sum_{r=0}^{h-1}\sum_{q=0}^{h-1} a\mu^{r\prime}V[w_{aT}]\mu^{q}a' = a V[w_{aT}]a'\left(\sum_{r=0}^{h-1}\sum_{q=0}^{h-1}\mu^{r+q}\right)$$

$$= a V[w_{aT}]a'(1-\mu^h)^2(1-\mu)^{-2} \tag{28}$$

The expressions for the forecast variances of w_t in the DV model can be found by combining the expressions for x_t and Δx_t from equations (24) and (15):

$$\tilde{e}_{w,T+h} = [\tilde{e}'_{x,T+h}\beta : \tilde{e}'_{\Delta x,T+h}J]' \tag{29}$$

so that the formula for the forecast error second-moment matrix of w_t in the DV model is given by:

$$V[\tilde{e}_{w,T+h}] = \begin{bmatrix} \beta'V[\tilde{e}_{x,T+h}]\beta & \beta'E[\tilde{e}_{x,T+h}\tilde{e}'_{\Delta x,T+h}]J \\ J'E[\tilde{e}_{\Delta x,T+h}\tilde{e}'_{x,T+h}]\beta & J'V[\tilde{e}_{\Delta x,T+h}]J \end{bmatrix} \tag{30}$$

We now consider the GFESM criterion defined in equation (10) for the correctly specified model. For a one-step-ahead forecast horizon, $|\Phi_{1,x}| = |\Phi_{1,\Delta x}| = |\Phi_{1,w}|$, where the second equality follows from $|\Omega| = |\Sigma|$, which in turn follows because the nonsingular linear transformation relating w_t to x_t is scale-preserving. Clements and Hendry (1993) establish the equivalences for h-step-ahead forecasts. For a two-step forecast, since the covariance $E[e_{x,T+1}e'_{x,T+2}] = \Omega A'$, then $|\Phi_2| = |\Omega|^2$, a recursion which continues so that $|\Phi_h| = |\Omega|^h$ for h-step-ahead forecasts. Thus, for a correctly specified model with known parameters, the generalized second moment of the one-step forecast error determines the ranking for all h. When the model is misspecified, as in the case of the DV model, or parameters are estimated, there may be additional information from further step-ahead forecasts (see also Ericsson and Marquez, 1993). The GFESM criterion is invariant to the transformations considered above, but the asymptotic formula for the DV model no longer collapses to a simple function of the one-step-ahead value.

When parameters are unknown and have to be estimated, the forecast error variance formulae derived above need to be augmented by a term that reflects parameter estimation uncertainty (see, for example, Schmidt, 1974; Ericsson and Marquez, 1989; Lütkepohl, 1991, sections 3.5 and 11.3). However, since this additional term has a zero probability limit whether or not x_t is a stochastic integrated process, the formulae for estimated parameters and known parameters (as derived above) coincide asymptotically. Various approximations to the parameter uncertainty term are available (see the references quoted above), but as Lütkepohl (1991, p. 378) states, 'little is known about the small sample properties of forecasts based on estimated unstable processes'. Our Monte Carlo seeks to ameliorate this situation.

5. MONTE CARLO TECHNIQUES

In the Monte Carlo, we estimate both TMSFEs and GFESMs. To obtain the former, we simulate the unconditional forecast error second moment matrices (termed $M[e_{T+h}]$ in section 4) by:

$$\hat{M} = R^{-1} \sum_{i=1}^{R} \hat{M}_i = R^{-1} \sum_{i=1}^{R} [\hat{e}_{T+h,i}\hat{e}'_{T+h,i}] \qquad (31)$$

where the summation is over the number of replications ($R = 1000$), and $\hat{e}_{T+h,i}$ is the h-step-ahead forecast error on the ith replication from one of the four estimation methods (UV, ML, EG, DV), and for one of the three transformations of the model (x_i, w_i, Δx_i). The TMSFE is then the trace of equation (31) (the average over replications of $tr\hat{M}_i$). When the forecasts are unbiased, equation (31) delivers the forecast error covariance matrix. Zero mean forecast errors can be shown to result under quite general conditions (see, for example, Hendry and Trivedi, 1972; Dufour, 1984, 1985; Cryer *et al.*, 1990; Magnus and Pesaran, 1991).

As a measure of the precision of the Monte Carlo, we calculate the Monte Carlo standard errors (MCSEs) of the TMSFEs. The sample variance of the Monte Carlo is:

$$\hat{\sigma}^2 = R^{-1} \sum_{i=1}^{R} [tr\,\hat{M}_i - tr\,\hat{M}]^2 = R^{-1} \sum_{i=1}^{R} (tr\,\hat{M}_i)^2 - (tr\,\hat{M})^2 \qquad (32)$$

so that $\hat{\sigma}^2/R$ is an unbiased estimator of the variance of $\hat{M}$ around the population value, and the MCSEs quoted in Table I of section 7 are given by $\hat{\sigma}/\sqrt{R}$.

The GFESM is the determinant of an expectation. The expectation of the stacked matrix of forecast errors is simulated by averaging over replications so $|R^{-1}\sum_{i=1}^{R}E_{h,i}E'_{h,i}|$ estimates $|\Phi_h|$. Since $|E_{h,i}E'_{h,i}| \equiv 0$ for each individual replication, it is impossible to obtain a measure of the sampling variability in the same way as for the TMSFE. However, in a Monte Carlo, with independent replications of E_h denoted by $E_{h,j}$, the outcome on the jth of R replications is:

$$E_{h,j} \underset{app}{\sim} IN(0, \Phi_h) \qquad (33)$$

for $T \to \infty$ where $\underset{app}{\sim}$ denotes 'is approximately distributed as', so that:

$$R \cdot \hat{\Phi}_h = \sum_{j=1}^{R} E_{h,j}E'_{h,j} \underset{app}{\sim} W_{N_h}(R, \Phi_h) \qquad (34)$$

where $W(R, \Phi_h)$ is a central Wishart distribution with R degrees of freedom so that $|\hat{\Phi}_h|$ provides a consistent estimator of $|\Phi_h|$ (see Rao, 1965, Ch. 8). Anderson (1984, Ch. 7) shows that for N equations, an h-step forecast horizon and R independent replications, using $\underset{a}{\sim}$ to denote 'is asymptotically distributed as $R \to \infty$':

$$\sqrt{R}\left(\frac{|\hat{\Phi}_h|}{|\Phi_h|} - 1\right) \underset{a}{\sim} N(0, 2Nh) \qquad (35)$$

For moderate sample sizes, $((|\hat{\Phi}_h|/|\Phi_h|) - 1)$ will be close to $\log(|\hat{\Phi}_h|/|\Phi_h|)$. From equation (35), the uncertainty in the Monte Carlo rankings based on $|\hat{\Phi}_h|$ is $O(4h)$ in the forecast horizon for the bivariate case. In practice, we report estimates of $|\hat{\Phi}_h|^{1/h}$ since the power transform does not affect the qualitative outcome of between-estimator comparisons, but stabilizes estimates of GFESM for large h when $|\Phi_1|$ differs from unity.

Two methods were used to improve the precision of the Monte Carlo. First, a common set of random numbers was used across estimators and across experiments, to highlight between-estimator differences and the differences attributable to different experimental designs. Second, control variates were used for the second moments to control for variation in the Monte Carlo due to the particular random numbers (see e.g. Hendry, 1984; Hendry *et al.*, 1991: a similar approach is adopted by Ericsson and Marquez, 1989, and Chambers, 1991).

The Monte Carlo estimator of the forecast error covariance matrix for known parameter values is denoted by $\mathbf{M}^*$:

$$\mathbf{M}^* = R^{-1} \sum_{i=1}^{R} [\mathbf{e}^*_{T+h,i} \mathbf{e}^{*\prime}_{T+h,i}] \tag{36}$$

where $\mathbf{e}^*_{T+h} = \mathbf{x}_{T+h} - \mathbf{x}^*_{T+h}$ and $\mathbf{x}^*_{T+h} = \mathbf{A}^h \mathbf{x}_T$ (compare equation (31) where $\hat{\mathbf{e}}_{T+h} = \mathbf{x}_{T+h} - \hat{\mathbf{x}}_{T+h}$ and $\hat{\mathbf{x}}_{T+h} = \hat{\mathbf{A}}^h \mathbf{x}_T$ when $\hat{\mathbf{A}}$ is an estimate of $\mathbf{A}$ in equation (1)). Construct the sophisticated Monte Carlo forecast error covariance matrix estimator $\tilde{\mathbf{M}}$ as:

$$\tilde{\mathbf{M}} = \hat{\mathbf{M}} - [\mathbf{M}^* - \mathbf{M}^a] \tag{37}$$

where $\mathbf{M}^a$ is the asymptotic value corresponding to one of equations (11), (12) or (13) (for the correctly specified model). Thus, $E[\tilde{\mathbf{M}}] = E[\hat{\mathbf{M}}]$ since $E[\mathbf{M}^* - \mathbf{M}^a] = 0$, that is, $\mathbf{M}^*$ is an unbiased estimator of the population forecast error covariance matrix $\mathbf{M}^a$. Improved precision of equation (37) over (31) results when (heuristically):

$$V[\tilde{\mathbf{M}}] = V[\hat{\mathbf{M}}] + V\{\mathbf{M}^* - \mathbf{M}^a\} - 2C[\hat{\mathbf{M}}, (\mathbf{M}^* - \mathbf{M}^a)] < V[\hat{\mathbf{M}}] \tag{38}$$

so that the covariance term exceeds the second variance term on the right-hand side of the equality. We could also calculate MCSEs for equation (37) similarly to (32).[1]

6. THE MONTE CARLO EXPERIMENTAL DESIGN

The data generating process (DGP) in the Monte Carlo is a first-order bivariate system as in Engle and Yoo (1987), where $\mathbf{x}_t = (z_t : y_t)'$ so from equation (2) when $\mathbf{v}_t \sim \mathsf{IN}\,(0, \Omega)$:

$$\Delta \mathbf{x}_t = \Pi \mathbf{x}_{t-1} + \psi + \mathbf{v}_t \tag{39}$$

with:

$$\Pi = \begin{bmatrix} a_{11} & -a_{11}\lambda \\ a_{22} & -a_{22}\lambda \end{bmatrix}, \quad \psi = \begin{bmatrix} a_{10} \\ a_{20} \end{bmatrix} \quad \text{and} \quad \Omega = \begin{bmatrix} 1 & \rho s \\ \rho s & s^2 \end{bmatrix}$$

Hence $|\Pi| = 0$, and for either $a_{11} \neq 0$ or $a_{22} \neq 0$, then $n = 1$. Thus, up to a scale factor, the cointegrating vector is given by the corresponding row of Π, that is, $z_t - \lambda y_t \sim I(0)$. Allowing constant terms in general induces nonzero steady-state rates of growth:

$$g_z \equiv E[\Delta z_t] = \frac{\lambda(a_{22} a_{10} - a_{11} a_{20})}{(a_{22}\lambda - a_{11})} \quad \text{and} \quad g_y \equiv E[\Delta y_t] = \lambda^{-1} g_z \tag{40}$$

When both equations are error-correcting, then the condition that the constant terms may be restricted to the cointegrating space ($\psi = \alpha \psi^*$) implies that $a_{22} a_{10} = a_{11} a_{20}$, so from equation (40), $g_y = g_z = 0$. Deriving the steady-state solution for $\{z_t - \lambda y_t\}$ by substituting from equation (40) in (39) shows that the cointegrating combination will have a zero mean when either $a_{10} = a_{20} = 0$, or $a_{10} = a_{20}$ and $\lambda = 1$.

---

[1] Specifically, $\hat{\sigma}^2 = R^{-1} \sum_{i=1}^{R} (\text{tr}(\hat{\mathbf{M}}_i - \mathbf{M}^*_i))^2 - (\text{tr}(\hat{\mathbf{M}} - \mathbf{M}^*))^2$, since $\tilde{\mathbf{M}}_i = \hat{\mathbf{M}}_i - [\mathbf{M}^*_i - \mathbf{M}^a]$.

In generating data from equation (39), x_0 was set equal to zero for each replication. To lessen the influence of this nonrandom initial condition on the simulated data, time series of $\{x_t\}$ were constructed to have 20 more observations than required for estimation and forecasting, and the initial 20 observations were discarded.[2]

In terms of w_t (see equation (4)), the model can be represented as the first-order process with $\varepsilon_t \sim \text{IN}(0, \Sigma)$ where:

$$w_t = Cw_{t-1} + \psi_0 + \varepsilon_t \tag{41}$$

when:

$$C = \begin{bmatrix} 1 + a_{11} - \lambda a_{22} & 0 \\ a_{22} & 0 \end{bmatrix}, \quad \psi_0 = \begin{bmatrix} a_{10} - \lambda a_{20} \\ a_{20} \end{bmatrix}, \quad \varepsilon_t = \begin{bmatrix} v_{1t} - \lambda v_{2t} \\ v_{2t} \end{bmatrix}$$

and:

$$\Sigma = \begin{bmatrix} 1 - 2\lambda\rho s + \lambda^2 s^2 & \rho s - \lambda s^2 \\ \rho s - \lambda s^2 & s^2 \end{bmatrix}$$

The Monte Carlo uses an experimental design similar to that of Engle and Yoo (1987) (see Section 7). A limitation of any Monte Carlo is that the findings are specific to the experiments undertaken and may be a poor guide to performance at other points in the parameter space. A range of experiments exploring the impact of various features of the experimental design was undertaken, and a set of response surfaces summarizing these experiments is available from the authors on request.

7. SIMULATION RESULTS

The presentation of the Monte Carlo results takes the form of TMSFE and GFESM calculations for isomorphic representations of forecasts generated by a DGP similar to that of Engle and Yoo (1987). Table I presents results for an experimental design given by $\{\rho = 0, s = 1, a_{10} = a_{20} = 0, a_{11} = -0.1, a_{22} = 0.25, \lambda = 1\}$ in the notation of Section 6. This essentially reproduces the DGP of Engle and Yoo (1987) where ρ, s, a_{10}, and a_{20} are the same, but $\{a_{11} = -0.4, a_{22} = 0.1, \lambda = 2\}$. The equations for both variables exhibit feedback from the common cointegrating vector in such experiments, although the cointegrating parameter and speeds of adjustment differ, with the 'error-correcting' behaviour being quantitatively more important in Engle and Yoo's DGP. Since $\psi = 0$, we initially follow Engle and Yoo in not estimating constants in the equations. Table I shows the relationships between the Monte Carlo estimates for each estimator, the Monte Carlo control variable estimates (common to all estimators), and the asymptotic values, for both TMSFEs and GFESMs, for a selection of multi-step forecast horizons, and for two estimation sample sizes.

In the notation of Section 5, columns 1 to 4 in panels (a), (b), and (c) of Table I record the estimates, $\tilde{M}_h$, given by equation (37). That condition (38) was generally satisfied was apparent from comparing the results for $\tilde{M}_h$ with those for $\hat{M}_h$ (not shown), and observing that the former were a smoother function of h. The TMSFEs for x_t are $O(h)$ in the forecast horizon, while the TMSFEs for w_t and Δx_t are both $O(1)$, as suggested by equations (11), (12) and (13).

---

[2] Alternatively, we could have generated data from the stationary representation for w_t in equation (41), where w_0 is drawn from a normal distribution with mean and variance given by the unconditional mean and variance of w_t.

Table I. Monte Carlo estimates of forecast accuracy[a] ($R = 1000$ and $T = 50, 100$)

(a) TMSFEs for x_t

h/T	EG 100	EG 50	UV 100	UV 50	ML 100	ML 50	DV 100	DV 50	$\text{tr}M_h^*$ 100	$\text{tr}M_h^*$ 50	$\text{tr}M_h^a$
1	2·04	2·10	2·07	2·13	2·06	2·09	2·32	2·28	1·96	2·07	2·00
	0·07	0·07	0·07	0·07	0·07	0·07	0·07	0·07	0·07	0·07	
5	7·24	7·54	7·60	8·35	7·21	7·43	8·44	8·50	6·90	7·30	7·01
	0·25	0·25	0·26	0·31	0·25	0·25	0·28	0·27	0·25	0·24	
10	13·3	13·7	14·7	17·1	13·2	13·5	15·2	14·5	12·1	13·6	12·9
	0·49	0·55	0·59	0·74	0·49	0·55	0·53	0·53	0·49	0·52	
20	25·1	25·8	31·8	41·6	25·0	25·6	26·9	26·6	22·8	24·5	24·7
	0·9	1·02	1·59	2·10	0·90	1·03	0·92	1·01	0·89	0·99	

(b) TMSFEs for w_t

h/T	EG 100	EG 50	UV 100	UV 50	ML 100	ML 50	DV 100	DV 50	$\text{tr}M_h^*$ 100	$\text{tr}M_h^*$ 50	$\text{tr}M_h^a$
1	3·08	3·22	3·10	3·21	3·11	3·20	3·82	3·71	2·87	3·11	3·00
	0·12	0·13	0·12	0·13	0·12	0·13	0·15	0·15	0·12	0·12	
5	5·00	5·24	4·89	5·03	4·89	5·02	7·08	7·23	4·71	4·54	4·63
	0·18	0·18	0·18	0·18	0·18	0·18	0·26	0·28	0·17	0·16	
	5·32	5·41	5·11	5·13	5·11	5·11	8·63	7·70	4·28	4·77	4·68
	0·19	0·20	0·18	0·18	0·18	0·18	0·33	0·29	0·15	0·17	
20	5·19	5·76	5·08	5·20	5·06	5·30	8·59	8·18	4·64	4·83	4·68
	0·18	0·23	0·17	0·19	0·17	0·21	0·34	0·33	0·16	0·17	

(c) TMSFEs for Δx_t

h/T	EG 100	EG 50	UV 100	UV 50	ML 100	ML 50	DV 100	DV 50	$\text{tr}M_h^*$ 100	$\text{tr}M_h^*$ 50	$\text{tr}M_h^a$
1	2·04	2·10	2·07	2·13	2·06	2·09	2·32	2·28	1·96	2·07	2·00
	0·07	0·07	0·07	0·07	0·07	0·07	0·07	0·07	0·07	0·07	
5	2·24	2·25	2·27	2·31	2·24	2·25	2·25	2·26	2·29	2·19	2·24
	0·07	0·07	0·07	0·07	0·07	0·07	0·07	0·07	0·07	0·07	
10	2·25	2·25	2·27	2·31	2·25	2·25	2·25	2·25	2·21	2·31	2·25
	0·07	0·08	0·07	0·08	0·07	0·07	0·07	0·08	0·07	0·07	
20	2·25	2·25	2·26	2·31	2·25	2·25	2·25	2·25	2·28	2·28	2·25
	0·07	0·07	0·07	0·07	0·07	0·07	0·07	0·07	0·07	0·07	

(d) Determinant of generalized second-moment matrix $|\hat{\Phi}_h|^{1/h}$

h/T	EG 100	EG 50	UV 100	UV 50	ML 100	ML 50	DV 100	DV 50	$|\Phi_h^*|^{1/h}$ 100	$|\Phi_h^*|^{1/h}$ 50
1	1·00	1·17	1·03	1·21	1·01	1·17	1·28	1·36	0·96	1·07
5	1·03	1·03	1·03	1·05	1·02	1·02	1·16	1·14	0·99	0·97
10	1·00	1·04	1·00	1·05	0·99	1·02	1·09	1·11	0·96	0·99
20	0·99	1·00	1·00	1·01	0·98	0·99	1·05	1·05	0·96	0·96

[a] The second row of figures for each horizon are the MCSDs of the TMSFE estimates ($\partial/\sqrt{R}$: see Section 5).

Panel (d) records the simulation results for the GFESM measure $|\hat{\Phi}_h|$ for each estimator, and for $|\Phi_h^*|$ calculated assuming parameters are known ($|\Phi_h|=1$ $\forall h$ so is not reported).

For an estimation sample size of 100 (as used by Engle and Yoo) there appears to be little to choose between EG and UV at the shortest horizons when forecast accuracy comparisons are based on x_t. There is a clear advantage to using EG at longer horizons (observe the size of the MCSDs[3]) matching the findings of Engle and Yoo, an effect which is accentuated for $T = 50$. The small differences in our results compared to those of Engle and Yoo reflect the imprecision of the Monte Carlo given the relatively small number of replications (100 for Engle and Yoo, 1000 in ours) and the particular DGP parameter values selected.

However, the dominance of EG over UV is not robust to switching from x_t to w_t (see panel (b) of Table I), illustrating the importance of the particular common basis of comparison chosen for such a measure. In terms of w_t, again noting the size of the MCSDs, there is little to choose between EG, UV and ML. The UV estimator appears to dominate EG for all but the shortest forecast horizons, with the gains coming from the improved accuracy of UV in predicting the cointegrating combination.

The ML is not appreciably better than EG when the comparison is in terms of x_t. The DV estimator, which is misspecified since the variables cointegrate, does not generate clearly inferior forecasts for comparisons of x_t, and beats UV at long horizons. For an estimation sample size of $T = 50$, the superiority of DV over UV at longer horizons is even more marked. In terms of w_t, though, the inferiority of DV is dramatic (about 40% worse than UV for $h = 20$).

The asymptotic forecast error variance formulae in Section 4 help explain these results. Viewing EG, UV, and ML as correctly specified models, then equations (11), (12) and (13) explain the relationships between the results for these three models and those for the DV model across isomorphic transformations of the variables. For example, DV is only appreciably worse at short horizons for comparisons in terms of x_t (see equation (27)) and Δx_t (see equations (13) and (19)) while numerical evaluation of equation (30) relative to (12) for w_t accurately predicts the poor performance of the DV model on this transformation of the variables.

The simulation results for GFESM, $|\hat{\Phi}_h|^{1/h}$, recorded in panel (d) of Table I, show little to choose between EG and UV. The ML is generally preferred to both EG and UV except at the shortest horizons, while the relative inferiority of DV is apparent.[4]

Table II highlights the information in Table I on the gains and losses from each estimator relative to UV, for the three transformations of the model. From Tables I and II, EG, ML and DV do relatively better than UV at $T = 50$ compared to $T = 100$, showing the importance of valid reduced-rank restrictions in EG and ML when there are fewer degrees of freedom. The significance of the figures for the relative performance of the estimators' TMSFEs in Table II can be deduced by constructing upper and lower bounds, again assuming independence. For example, the 11·6% gain of ML over UV (panel (a) of Table II) for $h = 10$ and $T = 100$ is not statistically significant, whereas the 26·7% gain at the same horizon but for the smaller sample

---

[3] For example, for $h = 20$ and $T = 100$, a 95% confidence interval for EG, assuming normality, is given by $25 \cdot 1 \pm 2 \times 0 \cdot 9 = [23 \cdot 3, 26 \cdot 9]$, compared to $[28 \cdot 6, 35 \cdot 0]$ for UV, so that the difference appears to be statistically significant. These calculations assume that the TMSFEs are independent, whereas they are likely to be positively correlated.

[4] A one percentage point gain or loss at large h is relatively larger than at small h due to raising $|\hat{\Phi}_h|$ to the power of h^{-1}. The adjustment makes sense when parameters are known, but may downplay differences when parameters are estimated.

Table II. Relative forecast accuracy summary: %GAIN/LOSS (−) relative to UV[a] ($R = 1000$ and $T = 50, 100$)

(a) TMSFE x_t

	EG	EG	ML	ML	DV	DV
h/T	100	50	100	50	100	50
1	1·5	1·4	0·5	1·9	−10·8	−6·6
5	5·0	10·7	5·4	12·4	−10·0	−1·8
10	11·0	25·4	11·6	26·7	−2·8	18·0
20	27·0	61·1	27·1	62·4	18·3	56·3

(b) TMSFE w_t

	EG	EG	ML	ML	DV	DV
h/T	100	50	100	50	100	50
1	0·6	−0·3	−0·3	0·3	−18·8	−13·5
5	−2·2	−4·0	0·0	0·2	−30·9	−30·4
10	−3·9	−5·2	0·0	0·4	−40·8	−33·4
20	−2·1	−9·7	0·4	−1·9	−40·9	−36·4

(c) TMSFE Δx_t

	EG	EG	ML	ML	DV	DV
h/T	100	50	100	50	100	50
1	1·5	1·4	0·5	1·9	−10·8	−6·6
5	1·3	2·7	1·3	2·7	0·9	2·2
10	0·9	2·7	0·9	2·7	0·9	2·7
20	0·4	2·7	0·4	2·7	0·4	2·7

(d) $|\hat{\boldsymbol{\Phi}}_h|^{1/h}$

	EG	EG	ML	ML	DV	DV
h/T	100	50	100	50	100	50
1	3·0	3·4	2·0	3·4	−19·5	−11·0
5	0·0	1·9	1·0	2·9	−11·2	−7·9
10	0·0	1·0	1·0	2·9	−8·3	−5·4
20	1·0	1·0	2·0	2·0	−4·8	−3·8

[a] The entries in the table are calculated as $(UV/xx - 1) \times 100$, where xx is either EG, ML, or DV.

size of $T = 50$ is.[5] The differences in the relative performances of the estimators at the longer horizons are insignificant when judged by TMSFEs for Δx_t (panels (c) of Tables I and II), bearing out the asymptotic formulae in section 4.

We also present a set of results exploring the impact of constant terms in the DGP when there is cointegration. In panel (a) of Table III, columns 1, 3, and 5 report $|\hat{\Phi}_h|^{1/h}$ calculations for UV, ML and DV when intercepts are estimated unrestrictedly in the econometric models (but $\psi = 0$). Columns 2, 4, and 6 are the percentage changes relative to Table 1, panel (d) (when constants are not estimated). Panel (b) reports the results of two experiments for which $\psi \neq 0$ and constants are estimated, as percentage changes relative to the results given in columns 1, 3, and 5 in panel (a). In the first experiment (columns 1, 3, and 5 of panel (b)) $\psi = [1 : -1]' \neq \alpha\psi^*$, so that the variables contain linear trends. In the second experiment, $\psi = [1 : -2.5]' = \alpha\psi^*$, so that the constant falls within the cointegration space. In this case, there is the option with ML of imposing the restriction at the estimation stage: the results of doing so are given in column 4(b).

The relative loss of forecast accuracy from estimating constant terms when they do not appear in the DGP increases in h for ML and DV but in comparison is smaller for UV except at very short horizons (see columns 2, 4, and 6 of panel (a)). However, for UV, the increase in $|\hat{\Phi}|^{1/h}$ is large

Table III. The impact of estimating intercepts on forecast accuracy ($R = 1000$ and $T = 100$)

(a) $\psi = 0$

h	1 UV	2 UV	3 ML	4 ML	5 DV	6 DV
1	1·06	2·91	1·04	2·97	1·29	0·78
5	1·05	1·94	1·04	1·96	1·18	1·72
10	1·01	1·00	1·01	2·02	1·11	1·83
20	1·00	0·00	1·01	3·06	1·07	1·90

(b) $\psi \neq 0$

h	1 UV $\psi \neq \alpha\psi^*$	2 UV $\psi = \alpha\psi^*$	3 ML $\psi \neq \alpha\psi^*$	4(a) ML $\psi = \alpha\psi^*$	4(b)	5 DV $\psi \neq \alpha\psi^*$	6 DV $\psi = \alpha\psi^*$
1	1·89	0·0	0·0	0·0	0·0	0·0	0·0
5	2·86	0·0	0.96	0·0	−1·90	0·0	0·0
10	3·96	0·0	0.99	0·0	−0·99	0·0	0·0
20	4·00	0·0	0·0	0·0	−1·98	0·0	0·0

---

[5] Assuming independence, the upper and lower bounds are calculated as the maximum and minimum of

$$\left(\left[\frac{14\cdot7 \pm 2 \times 0\cdot59}{13\cdot2 \pm 2 \times 0\cdot49}\right] - 1\right) \times 100 \quad \text{for } T = 100$$

and of

$$\left(\left[\frac{17\cdot1 \pm 2 \times 0\cdot74}{13\cdot2 \pm 2 \times 0\cdot55}\right] - 1\right) \times 100 \quad \text{for } T = 50$$

Since the former interval contains the origin while the latter is strictly positive, only for $T = 50$ is ML statistically superior to UV.

relative to $\psi = 0$ when $\psi \neq 0$ and $\psi \neq \alpha\psi^*$, while for ML there is no increase for $h = 20$, and for the DV model there is no significant change at any forecast horizon (see columns 1, 3, and 5 of panel (b)). Indeed, as long as constants are estimated, then forecast accuracy using the DV model is invariant to the values of the intercepts in the DGP, at least to the degree of numerical accuracy reported in the table. Furthermore, the UV and ML estimators appear invariant when the constants lie in the cointegrating space, but not otherwise (columns 2 and 4(a)). When this condition holds and is correctly imposed by ML (column 4(b)), there is a 2% gain in forecast accuracy at the longer horizons. Many of these results can be established analytically using antithetic variates.

8. AN EMPIRICAL ILLUSTRATION

In this section, we illustrate the preceding analysis by examining the forecast performance of models of the demand for UK M1, based on a simplified version of the approach in Hendry and Ericsson (1991), Hendry and Mizon (1993), Engle and Hendry (1993) and Hendry and Doornik (1994), *inter alia*. We consider the bivariate system of the (inverse) velocity of circulation v and a learning-adjusted measure of the opportunity cost of holding money R_n (see Hendry and Ericsson, 1991, pp. 844–6, 850–3), where $v = m - p - y$ when m, p, and y are the natural logarithms of nominal UK M1, the total final expenditure deflator and real total final expenditure respectively.

The data are quarterly, seasonally adjusted, and after the creation of lags the estimation period runs from 1964:1 to 1984:2, with the 20 periods from 1984:3 to 1989:2 retained as the forecast period. For this small monetary system, we estimated three second-order models: an unrestricted VAR in the levels of (v, R_n) (termed UV earlier); the DV model imposing two unit roots; and the ML model. The Johansen procedure on the full sample indicated one cointegrating vector, which normalized on v has the form: $w \equiv v + 7 \cdot 7 R_n$, and which we restricted to only enter the velocity equation. Ignoring the possible problems for inference caused by the presence of unit roots,[6] the ML model represents a nonrejectable simplification of the UV (the likelihood ratio test of the three restrictions implicit in the ML relative to the UV yielded a test value of $6 \cdot 6$, which is $\chi^2(3)$ under the null), while the DV was clearly rejected against the UV (test statistic value of $37 \cdot 4$, distributed as $\chi^2(4)$ under the null). These models were then used to generate one-, two-, four-, eight-, and twelve-step-ahead forecasts over the period 1984:3 to 1989:2. Based on the resulting forecast errors, we calculated empirical MSFEs by averaging the 20 squared one-step errors, the 19 squared two-step errors, etc. The root MSFEs (RMSFEs) are given in Table IV.

Both the asymptotic formulae in Section 4 and the results of the Monte Carlo in Section 7 are useful in interpreting the empirical RMSFEs in Table IV. For example, equation (22) in Section 4 suggests that for medium-term horizons there will be little gain from using the correctly specified model (UV or ML) relative to the DV when forecast accuracy is assessed in terms of predicting differences (columns 1 and 2 of Table IV). The column for Δv indicates that the losses from using the DV model are large for short horizons but have all but disappeared for twelve-step-ahead forecasts. The likelihood ratio statistics quoted earlier indicate that the DV model is misspecified for v but not for R_n (the specification of the equations for R_n in the ML and DV models are identical) which explains the similar forecast accuracy of the models for all

---

[6] Sims *et al.* (1990) show that tests of joint significance which include only cointegrated nonstationary regressors have their standard asymptotic distributions, while those that include nonstationary regressors will be nonstandard. Thus the test statistics quoted here have nonstandard distributions. Consistent with this, the tests for the dimension of the cointegrating space in Johansen (1988) have to be compared to nonstandard critical values.

Table IV. Empirical RMSFEs over 1984:3 to 1989:2

(a) UV model

h	Δv	ΔR_n	v	R_n	w
1	0·020	0·017	0·020	0·017	0·12
2	0·026	0·017	0·038	0·028	0·18
4	0·031	0·015	0·083	0·049	0·30
8	0·031	0·0082	0·20	0·067	0·32
12	0·023	0·0085	0·31	0·071	0·25

(b) ML model

h	Δv	ΔR_n	v	R_n	w
1	0·019	0·015	0·019	0·015	0·10
2	0·023	0·014	0·033	0·022	0·14
4	0·026	0·014	0·067	0·037	0·22
8	0·028	0·0083	0·17	0·056	0·27
12	0·023	0·0083	0·28	0·068	0·25

(c) DV model

h	Δv	ΔR_n	v	R_n	w
1	0·034	0·015	0·034	0·015	0·10
2	0·035	0·014	0·066	0·021	0·13
4	0·036	0·013	0·13	0·034	0·20
8	0·033	0·0084	0·26	0·049	0·25
12	0·026	0·0085	0·39	0·060	0·28

steps ahead for ΔR_n. In terms of forecasting the levels of the variables, equation (27) suggests that the DV model will continue to predict worse than the UV and ML as we increase h, and this is evident for v in Table IV. Since the DV model is correctly specified for R_n on a single-equation basis (i.e. ignoring the system characteristics) then it is not surprising that the DV model fares relatively better (and even wins) for predicting the level of R_n.

Finally, we use the results of the Monte Carlo in Section 7. The Monte Carlo indicates that for a bivariate model and for samples as large as $T = 100$ it may be difficult to choose between the ML and UV models. When $T = 50$ the relative differences are more evident, particularly for the levels of the series (see Table II, panel (a)). Our estimation sample size is 82 observations, and differs from the Monte Carlo DGP in that we are estimating second-order models where the 'error-correction' term enters only one equation. However, as in the Monte Carlo the UV fares a little worse than the ML but generally quite a bit better than the DV. An apparent anomaly between the empirical MSFEs and the Monte Carlo results is how well the DV model predicts w. Only at $h = 12$ is it outperformed by the UV and ML models.

9. SUMMARY AND CONCLUSIONS

The paper concerns five main issues. First, we consider the implications for forecast accuracy of imposing unit roots and cointegrating restrictions in linear systems of $I(1)$ variables and show that the rankings alter across representations in levels, differences, and cointegrated combinations. Next, we derive asymptotic variance formulae of multi-step forecasts for each representation, including misspecified models. Third, we examine the finite sample behaviour of forecast variances in a bivariate cointegrated model by Monte Carlo using control variables, and compare these to the asymptotic outcomes. We also analyse the interaction between unit roots and cointegrating restrictions and intercepts in the DGP. Most of these issues are illustrated using an empirical example of forecasting the demand for M1 in the UK.

We show that MSFE evaluations of the ability of models to predict differences of the variables might fail to reject models which incorrectly impose too many unit roots. This is apparent from our asymptotic formulae, is borne out by the Monte Carlo which allows for parameter estimation uncertainty, and is also a feature of our empirical example for medium-term horizons. The asymptotic formulae and Monte Carlo results suggest that comparisons of MSFEs of the ability to predict cointegrating combinations may be more powerful (although this was less evident in the empirical example). This supports the use of an invariant criterion, such as the GFESM, particularly in Monte Carlo studies where the GFESM is feasible to calculate. In empirical practice, though, data availability may be a telling restriction on the length of the maximum step-ahead forecasts for the GFESM; also, rankings may be susceptible to h due to the non-monotonicity of forecast error variances when parameters are estimated. Nevertheless, problems of dependence on the forecast horizon may be compounded by using noninvariant measures such as MSFEs.

The asymptotic formulae for multi-step forecast error variances for each representation reveal a great deal about the behaviour of the various methods and variable selections as forecast horizons increase. In particular, the extent of the dependence of the formulae on the length of the horizon is confirmed by and clarifies some of the Monte Carlo simulation findings, so that the formulae seem relevant for the sample sizes considered in the simulation. Section 8 shows the usefulness of these formulae in interpreting the empirical MSFEs.

The Monte Carlo is for a single experimental design and for a bivariate system, but in such a system, we conclude that there is little benefit from imposing reduced-rank cointegration restrictions (ML versus UV) unless the sample size is small. This conclusion appears to carry over to the empirical example. The maximum likelihood estimator might be expected to dominate the unrestricted vector autoregression more decisively for larger systems of equations when a cointegration relation imposes many more restrictions. Moreover, in practice the number of cointegrating combinations will not be known, and how it is determined from the data may affect the outcome of comparisons across methods.

In terms of empirical practice, it appears that imposing too few cointegration vectors may impose greater costs in forecast accuracy than allowing the presence of 'spurious' levels terms. Intuitively, the former excludes precisely the relationships which keep differentials between the levels of variables stationary, whereas the latter has parameter estimates on $I(1)$ variables which converge at $O_p(T)$ against the growth in forecast error variance at $O(h)$ for h-step-ahead forecasts. We anticipate this result will hold for larger systems: estimating and forecasting with an additional 'spurious' levels term is likely to be no more costly in terms of forecast accuracy than underestimating the cointegrating rank by one. Hence the conjecture above that ML should more convincingly dominate UV in larger systems is expected to hold because the number of restrictions implied by cointegration is positively related to the size of the system, rather than because noncointegrating $I(1)$ levels terms are being excluded.

We find that when the constants fall within the cointegrating space, forecast accuracy is invariant to the value of the constant terms (whatever the estimation method) and that forecast accuracy improvements will result from correctly restricting the intercepts to the cointegration space (ML). Since the local trend is a vital component of forecast accuracy in practice, this finding merits further study.

ACKNOWLEDGEMENTS

Financial support from the UK Economic and Social Research Council under grant R000233447 is gratefully acknowledged. We are indebted to Anindya Banerjee, David Cox, Neil Ericsson, Søren Johansen, Katarina Juselius, Graham Mizon, John Muellbauer, and Neil Shephard for helpful discussions about the material herein. We are pleased to acknowledge helpful comments on earlier drafts from the editor and two anonymous referees. The calculations reported in this paper were carried out using the GAUSS System Version 2.1 and PcFiml Version 8.

REFERENCES

Anderson, T. W. (1984), *An Introduction to Multivariate Statistical Analysis*, John Wiley, New York.

Brandner, P. and R. M. Kunst (1990), 'Forecasting vector autoregressions—The influence of cointegration: A Monte Carlo Study', Research Memorandum No. 265, Institute for Advanced Studies, Vienna.

Chambers, M. J. (1991), 'A note on forecasting in co-integrated systems', Department of Economics, University of Essex.

Clements, M. P. and D. F. Hendry (1993), 'On the limitations of comparing mean square forecast errors', *Journal of Forecasting*, 12, 617–37.

Clements, M. P. and D. F. Hendry (1994), 'Towards a theory of economic forecasting', in C. Hargreaves (ed.), *Non-stationary Time-Series Analyses and Cointegration*, Oxford University Press, Oxford.

Cryer, J. D., J. C. Nankervis and N. E. Savin (1990), 'Forecast error symmetry in ARIMA models', *Journal of the American Statistical Association*, 85, 724–8.

Dufour, J.-M. (1984), 'Unbiasedness of predictions from estimated autoregressions when the true order is unknown', *Econometrica*, 52, 209–15.

Dufour, J.-M. (1985), 'Unbiasedness of predictions from estimated vector autoregressions', *Econometric Theory*, 1, 387–402.

Engle, R. F. and C. W. J. Granger (1987), 'Cointegration and error-correction: representation, estimation and testing', *Econometrica*, 55, 251–76.

Engle, R. F. and D. F. Hendry (1993), 'Testing super exogeneity and invariance in regression models', *Journal of Econometrics*, 56, 119–39.

Engle, R. F. and S. Yoo (1987), 'Forecasting and testing in cointegrated systems', *Journal of Econometrics*, 35, 143–159.

Engle, R. F. and S. Yoo (1991), 'Cointegrated economic time series: an overview with new results' in R. F. Engle and C. W. J. Granger (eds), *Long-Run Economic Relationships*, Oxford University Press, Oxford.

Ericsson, N. R. and J. R. Marquez (1989), 'Exact and approximate multi-period mean-square forecast errors for dynamic econometric models', International Finance Discussion Paper No. 348, Federal Reserve Board, Washington, DC.

Ericsson, N. R. and J. R. Marquez (1993), 'Encompassing the forecasts of U.S. trade balance models', *Review of Economics and Statistics*, 75, 19–31.

Hendry, D. F. (1984), 'Monte Carlo experimentation in econometrics', in Z. Griliches and M. D. Intriligator (eds), *Handbook of Econometrics*, Vol. II, Elsevier Science, Amsterdam.

Hendry, D. F. and J. A. Doornik (1994), 'Modelling linear dynamic econometric systems', *Scottish Journal of Political Economy*, 41, 1–33.

Hendry, D. F. and N. R. Ericsson (1991), 'Modeling the demand for narrow money in the United Kingdom and the United States', *European Economic Review*, 35, 833–86.

Hendry, D. F. and G. E. Mizon (1993), 'Evaluating dynamic econometric models by encompassing the VAR', in P. C. B. Phillips (ed.), *Models, Methods and Applications of Econometrics*, pp. 272–300, Basil Blackwell, Oxford.

Hendry, D. F., A. J. Neale and N. R. Ericsson (1991), *PC-NAIVE: An Interactive Program for Monte Carlo Experimentation in Econometric*, Version 6.1, Oxford Institute of Economics and Statistics.

Hendry, D. F. and P. K. Trivedi (1972), 'Maximum likelihood estimation of difference equations with moving average errors: a simulation study', *Review of Economic Studies*, 39, 117–45.

Hylleberg, S. and G. E. Mizon (1989), 'Cointegration and error correction mechanisms', *Economic Journal* (Conference Supplement), 99, 113–25.

Johansen, S. (1988), 'Statistical analysis of cointegration vectors', *Journal of Economic Dynamics and Control*, **12**, 231–54.

Johansen, S. (1991), 'Estimation and hypothesis testing of cointegration vectors in Gaussian vector autoregressive models', *Econometrica*, **59**, 1551–80.

Johansen, S. (1992), 'A representation of vector autoregressive processes integrated of order 2', *Econometric Theory*, **8**, 188–202.

Johansen, S. and K. Juselius (1990), 'Maximum likelihood estimation and inference on cointegration—with applications to the demand for money', *Oxford Bulletin of Economics and Statistics*, **52**, 169–210.

Lütkepohl, H. (1991), *Introduction to Multiple Time Series Analysis*, Springer-Verlag, New York.

Magnus, J. R. and B. Pesaran (1991), 'The bias of forecasts from a first-order autoregression', *Econometric Theory*, **7**, 222–35.

Phillips, P. C. B. (1991), 'Optimal inference in cointegrated systems', *Econometrica*, **59**, 283–306.

Rao, C. R. (1965), *Linear Statistical Inference and its Applications*, John Wiley, New York.

Schmidt, P. (1974), 'The asymptotic distribution of forecasts in the dynamic simulation of an econometric model', *Econometrica*, **42**, 303–9.

Sims, C. A., J. H. Stock and M. W. Watson (1990), 'Inference in linear time series models with some unit roots', *Econometrica*, **58**, 113–144

West, K. D. (1988), 'Asymptotic normality when regressors have a unit root', *Econometrica*, **56**, 1397–1418.

[23]

The Economic Journal, **107** (*September*), 1330–1357. © Royal Economic Society 1997. Published by Blackwell Publishers, 108 Cowley Road, Oxford OX4 1JF, UK and 350 Main Street, Malden, MA 02148, USA.

THE ECONOMETRICS OF MACROECONOMIC FORECASTING*

David F. Hendry

When an econometric model coincides with the mechanism generating the data in an unchanging world, the theory of economic forecasting is reasonably well developed. However, less is known about forecasting when model and mechanism differ in a non-stationary and changing world. The paper addresses the basic concepts; the invariance of forecast accuracy measures to isomorphic model representations; the roles of causal information, parsimony and collinearity; a reformulated taxonomy of forecast errors; differencing and intercept corrections to robustify forecasts against biases due to shifts in deterministic factors; the removal of structural breaks by co-breaking; and forecasting using leading indicators.

The theory of economic forecasting is reasonably well developed assuming the econometric model coincides with the mechanism generating the data in a (difference) stationary world: see, for example, Klein (1971) and Granger and Newbold (1986). Consider an n-dimensional stochastic process $\mathbf{x}_t$ with density $D_{\mathbf{x}_t}(\mathbf{x}_t | \mathbf{X}_{t-1}, \boldsymbol{\theta})$ for $\boldsymbol{\theta} \in \boldsymbol{\Theta} \subseteq \mathbb{R}^k$, which is a function of past information $\mathbf{X}_{t-1} = (\dots \mathbf{x}_1 \dots \mathbf{x}_{t-1})$. A statistical forecast $\tilde{\mathbf{x}}_{T+h}$ for period $T+h$, conditional on information up to period T is given by $\tilde{\mathbf{x}}_{T+h} = \mathbf{f}_h(\mathbf{X}_T)$, where $\mathbf{f}_h(.)$ reflects that a prior estimate of $\boldsymbol{\theta}$ may be needed. Forecasts calculated as the conditional expectation $\hat{\mathbf{x}}_{T+h} = E(\mathbf{x}_{T+h} | \mathbf{X}_T)$ are unbiased, and no other predictor conditional on only $\mathbf{X}_T$ has a smaller mean-square forecast error (MSFE) matrix:

$$M(\hat{\mathbf{x}}_{T+h} | \mathbf{X}_T) = E[(\mathbf{x}_{T+h} - \hat{\mathbf{x}}_{T+h})(\mathbf{x}_{T+h} - \hat{\mathbf{x}}_{T+h})' | \mathbf{X}_T].$$

However, when the model is mis-specified for the mechanism in an unknown way, and requires estimation from available data, less is known about forecasting, particularly in a non-stationary economy subject to unanticipated structural breaks. In such a setting, not only is it extremely difficult to model the underlying processes correctly, the costs of failing to do so are large. Nevertheless, despite the lack of strong and specific assumptions, many useful insights can be derived, albeit usually articulated in special cases. Consequently, we consider some results that can be established, extending research reported in Clements and Hendry (1993, 1994, 1995 a, b, 1996 b) and Hendry and Clements (1994 a, b).

There are many ways of making economic forecasts, including guessing; 'informal models'; extrapolation; leading indicators; surveys; time-series models; and econometric systems. By focusing on statistical forecasting, we will not be concerned with the first three here, but Section X discusses leading indicators based on Emerson and Hendry (1996). Scalar time-series models include Kalman (1960) and Box and Jenkins (1976), with the latter's

* Royal Economic Society Presidential Address, 1993. Financial support from the ESRC under grants R000233447 and L116250I5 is gratefully acknowledged. This paper is based on recent publications with Michael P. Clements. Thanks are due to Anindya Banerjee, Mike Clements, Jurgen Doornik, Rob Engle, Hans-Martin Krolzig, Grayham Mizon, Bent Nielsen, and Neil Shephard for many helpful discussions about the topics herein.

autoregressive integrated moving-average models (ARIMAs) being a dominant class, based on the Wold decomposition theorem (Wold, 1938: any purely
non-deterministic stationary time series can be expressed as an infinite moving
average; see Cox and Miller, 1965, pp. 286–8, for a lucid discussion). Also see
Harvey and Shephard (1992). The most common multivariate time-series form
is the vector autoregression (VAR): see, e.g., Doan *et al.* (1984). However,
economic forecasting based on econometric models of multivariate time-series
will be our primary focus, since such systems consolidate empirical and
theoretical knowledge of how economies function, provide a framework for a
progressive research strategy, and help explain their own failures as well as
provide forecasts.

The success of econometric model-based forecasts depends upon:

(*a*) there being regularities to be captured;
(*b*) such regularities being informative about the future;
(*c*) the proposed method capturing those regularities; and:
(*d*) excluding non-regularities that swamp the regularities.

The first two are characteristics of the economic system; the last two of the
forecasting method. The history of economic forecasting in the United
Kingdom suggests that there are some regularities informative about future
events, but also major irregularities as well (see, e.g., Burns, 1986, Wallis, 1989,
Pain and Britton, 1992, and Cook, 1995). The dynamic integrated systems with
intermittent structural breaks that are formalised below seem consistent with
such evidence. However, achieving (*c*) without suffering from (*d*) is difficult,
and motivates the conceptual structure proposed below, as well as the emphasis
on issues such as parsimony and collinearity, and the re-examination of the role
of causal information when forecasting models are mis-specified. Several results
transpire to be misleading once model mis-specification interacts with non-
stationary data (denoting thereby the general sense of processes whose first two
moments are not constant over time). Conversely, it becomes feasible to
account for the empirical success of procedures that difference data, or use
intercept corrections (see, e.g., Theil, 1961, Klein, 1971, and Wallis and
Whitley, 1991), although these methods have no rationale when models are
correctly specified. Potential improvements also merit investigation, so co-
breaking is considered, and shown to clarify some problems experienced with
leading indicators.

The structure of the paper is as follows. The first three sections discuss the
background concepts, models, and measures. The next three sections deduce
their implications for causal information, parsimony, and collinearity, in an
attempt to account for recent forecast failures, but only the first seems to be
important. To resolve that problem, a reformulated taxonomy of forecast
errors highlights forecast biases as due to unmodelled shifts in deterministic
factors, providing a rationale for both differencing and intercept corrections to
offset breaks. The alternative of removing regime shifts by co-breaking is
proposed and applied to forecasting using leading indicators.

In more detail, Section I considers the basic concepts needed to develop the analysis of forecasting when the model and mechanism differ. The notions of (un)predictable and forecastable are discussed: despite their close usage, the former is a property whereas forecasting is a procedure. Next, Section II describes the framework for economic forecasting using a vector autoregression in integrated-cointegrated variables. The issue of measuring forecast accuracy is described in Section III, since evaluation may be dependent on the transformations examined for vector processes, or when forecasting more than one-step ahead; that section focuses on the invariance, or otherwise, of putative measures to isomorphic representations of the model.

Then Section IV discusses the role of causal information in economic forecasting, and shows that non-causal variables may outperform in forecasting when the model and mechanism differ in a world subject to structural breaks. An example highlights the potential importance of excluding irrelevant, but changing, effects. The possible role of parsimony in h-step ahead forecasting is discussed in Section V, but only a small effect is found for the constant-parameter cases examined. Section VI shows that collinearity has little effect on forecast accuracy in constant worlds, but a larger effect if the collinearity alters, so parsimony may have a justification in non-constant processes.

Based on the analyses in Hendry and Clements (1994 b) and Clements and Hendry (1996 c), Section VII shows that intercept corrections (non-zero values for a model's error terms over the forecast period) can help robustify forecasts against biases due to structural breaks. The taxonomy of forecast errors in Section VIII allows for structural change in the forecast period, the model and DGP to differ over the sample period, the parameters of the model to be estimated from the data, and the forecasts to commence from incorrect initial conditions. This re-emphasises the possible role of non-causal variables, and warns of the potential dangers of selecting policy models by forecast-accuracy criteria. It also demonstrates the central role of shifts in deterministic factors, confirming the apt naming of intercept corrections, and the potential efficacy of differencing. The differential impact of structural breaks on models with and without cointegration feedbacks highlights that the latter equilibrium correct, but do not error correct between equilibria.

Next, Section IX considers the removal of regime-shift non-stationarity by co-breaking, namely the cancellation of breaks across linear combinations of variables, analogous to cointegration removing unit roots. Such an outcome would allow a subset of variables to be forecast as anticipated. Finally, forecasting using leading indicators is discussed in Section X based on Emerson and Hendry (1996), raising issues of co-integration and co-breaking within the indices, and between their components and macro-economic variables. Since composite leading indicators (CLIs) are unlikely to co-break to mitigate regime shifts, the effects of adding CLIs to macro models may be potentially harmful. Given that most of the conventional results for constant-parameter cointegrated stationary processes do not seem to apply in realistic settings, Section XI concludes that a formal theory of forecasting for mis-specified models under irregular and substantive structural breaks requires development, but is feasible.

I. CONCEPTS

In this section, we define the predictability of a stochastic process relative to the available information, and the resulting forecastability of the series, then draw some implications.

I.1. *Unpredictability*

v_t is an unpredictable process with respect to the information set $\mathcal{I}_{t-1}$ if:[1]

$$D_{v_t}(v_t \mid \mathcal{I}_{t-1}) = D_{v_t}(v_t),\tag{1}$$

so the conditional and unconditional distributions coincide. Unpredictability is invariant under non-singular contemporaneous transforms: e.g. if v_t is unpredictable, so is Bv_t where $|B| \neq 0$. However, unpredictability is obviously not invariant under intertemporal transforms since if $u_t = v_t + Af(\mathcal{I}_{t-1})$:

$$D_{u_t}(u_t \mid \mathcal{I}_{t-1}) \neq D_{u_t}(u_t),$$

when $A \neq 0$. The concept resolves the apparent 'paradox' that (e.g.) although the change in the log of real equity prices may be unpredictable, the level is predictable: since $x_t = \Delta x_t + x_{t-1}$, the 'prediction' of the current level is merely its immediate past value. Below, we assume the time series x_t is of interest, and the information set $\mathcal{I}_{t-1}$ includes at least the history of x_t. When $x_t = v_t$, therefore, x_t must be an innovation, and (weak) white noise when its second moment exists.

Unpredictability is relative to the information set used; e.g., it can happen that for $\mathcal{J}_{t-1} \subset \mathcal{I}_{t-1}$:

$$D_{u_t}(u_t \mid \mathcal{J}_{t-1}) = D_{u_t}(u_t) \quad \text{yet} \quad D_{u_t}(u_t \mid \mathcal{I}_{t-1}) \neq D_{u_t}(u_t).$$

However, $\mathcal{J}_{t-1} \subset \mathcal{I}_{t-1}$ does not preclude predictability. Unpredictability may also be relative to the time period, in that we could have:

$$D_{u_t}(u_t \mid \mathcal{I}_{t-1}) = D_{u_t}(u_t) \quad \text{for} \quad t = 1, \ldots, T,\tag{2}$$

yet:

$$D_{u_t}(u_t \mid \mathcal{I}_{t-1}) \neq D_{u_t}(u_t) \quad \text{for} \quad t = T+1, \ldots, T+H,\tag{3}$$

or *vice versa*. Finally, unpredictability may be relative to the horizon considered in that:

$$D_{u_t}(u_t \mid \mathcal{I}_{t-2}) = D_{u_t}(u_t) \quad \text{yet} \quad D_{u_t}(u_t \mid \mathcal{I}_{t-1}) \neq D_{u_t}(u_t).$$

However, the converse, that:

$$D_{u_t}(u_t \mid \mathcal{I}_{t-1}) = D_{u_t}(u_t) \quad \text{yet} \quad D_{u_t}(u_t \mid \mathcal{I}_{t-2}) \neq D_{u_t}(u_t)$$

is not possible as $\mathcal{I}_{t-2} \subseteq \mathcal{I}_{t-1}$ by definition.

Sequential factorisation of the joint density of X_T^1 yields the prediction representation:

$$D_X(X_T^1 \mid \mathcal{I}_0, \cdot) = \prod_{t=1}^{T} D_{X_t}(x_t \mid \mathcal{I}_{t-1}, \cdot).\tag{4}$$

---

[1] The definition is equivalent to the statistical independence of v_t from $\mathcal{I}_{t-1}$ and does not connote 'wild': indeed, knowing $D_{v_t}(v_t)$ may be highly informative relative to not knowing it.

Consequently, predictability requires combinations with $\mathcal{I}_{t-1}$: the 'causes' must be in train. Such causes need not be direct, and could be very indirect: e.g. a variable's own lags may 'capture' actual past causes. Thus, when the relevant $\mathcal{I}_{t-1}$ is known, structure is not necessary for forecasting, even under changed conditions. Unfortunately, that $\mathcal{I}_{t-1}$ is known is most unlikely in economics, with important implications for understanding why '*ad hoc*' methods can work well, as seen below.

I.2. *Moments*

Forecasting tends to focus on first and second moments assuming these exist. Then, v_t is unpredictable in mean at t if:

$$E(v_t | \mathcal{I}_{t-1}) = E(v_t).$$

Similarly, v_t is unpredictable in variance at t if:

$$V(v_t | \mathcal{I}_{t-1}) = V(v_t).$$

The converse of the latter includes (e.g.) autoregressive conditional hetero-scedastic processes (ARCH or GARCH: see Engle, 1982, Bollerslev *et al.*, 1992, and Bollerslev *et al.*, 1994), or stochastic volatility schemes (see Shephard, 1996). Consequently, unpredictability in mean is not invariant under nonlinear contemporaneous transforms, as in the weak white-noise ARCH process:

$$E(v_t | \mathcal{I}_{t-1}) = E(v_t) = 0 \quad \text{but} \quad E(v_t v_t' | \mathcal{I}_{t-1}) \neq E(v_t v_t').$$

I.3. *Forecastability*

A forecasting rule is any systematic operational procedure for making statements about future events. We will focus on statistical forecasting using formal estimated econometric models. Whereas predictability is a property (of a stochastic process in relation to an information set), forecasting is a process. Moreover, forecasting is undertaken for a purpose, so its evaluation depends on how well it achieves that intent. Consequently, it is extremely difficult to define 'forecastability'. One could perhaps define events as forecastable relative to a loss measure if the relevant procedure produced a lower expected loss than (say) the historical mean. This would be consistent with the change in the log of real equity prices being unforecastable, but the level forecastable using a random walk, on the criteria of bias or MSFE. Unfortunately, as shown in Section III, MSFE rankings for multivariate, multi-step forecasts depend on the transformations used, so can alter in accuracy relative to the historical mean of the transform, rendering most definitions ambiguous.

I.4. *Implications*

These concepts have a number of important implications applicable to most statistical forecasting methods. First, from (1), since the conditional mean of an unpredictable process is its unconditional mean, predictability is necessary for forecastability. However, it is not sufficient, since the relevant information set may be unknown in practice. Further, there is a potential ambiguity in the use of the phrase 'information set' in the contexts of predictability and forecasting: $\mathcal{I}_{t-1}$ denotes the conditioning set generated by the relevant events, whereas forecastability also requires knowledge of how $\mathcal{I}_{t-1}$ enters the conditional density in (1). For example, $\mathbf{v}_{t-1}$ may matter, but in an awkward nonlinear way that eludes empirical modelling.

Secondly, translating 'regularity' as a systematic relation between the entity to be forecast and the available information, then conditions (a)–(d) above are sufficient for forecastability. They may not be necessary in principle (e.g. inspired guessing; precognition etc.), but for statistical forecasting, they seem close to necessary as can be seen by considering the removal of any one of them (e.g. if no regularities exist to be captured).

Thirdly, if the occurrence of large *ex ante* unpredictable shocks (such as earthquakes, or oil crises), induces their inclusion in later information sets (moving from (2) to (3) above), the past will be more explicable than the future is forecastable (cf. stock-market commentators?). Consequently, when the 'true' $\mathcal{I}_{t-1}$ is unknown, to prevent the baseline innovation error variance being an underestimate, forecast-accuracy evaluation may require 'unconditioning' from within-sample rare events that have been modelled *post hoc*.

Fourthly, from (4), intertemporal transforms affect predictability, so no unique measure of predictability, and hence of forecast accuracy, exists. Linear dynamic econometric systems are invariant under linear transforms in that they retain the same error process, and transformed estimates of the original are usually the direct estimates of the transformed system: such transforms are used regularly in empirical research. But by definition, the predictability of the transformed variables is altered by any transforms that are intertemporal (e.g. switching from y_t on y_{t-1} to Δy_t on y_{t-1}).[2] This precludes unique generic rankings of methods, adding to the difficulty of theoretical analysis and practical appraisal.

Next, since new unpredictable components can enter in each period, forecast error variances could increase or decrease over increasing horizons from any given T, as a consequence of (2) versus (3). For integrated processes, $V(x_{T+h}|\mathcal{I}_T)$ is non-decreasing in h when the innovation distribution is homoscedastic. Otherwise, when the initial forecast period T increases with real time, forecast uncertainty will be non-decreasing in h unless the innovation variance is ever-decreasing (since h-steps ahead from T becomes $h-1$ from $T+1$).[3]

Finally, and the focus of Section IV, when the 'true' $\mathcal{I}_{t-1}$ is unknown one cannot prove that genuinely' relevant information must always dominate non-causal variables in forecasting. Rather, one can show in examples that the latter can be the 'best available' forecasting devices on some measures in the absence of omniscience (i.e. when the model is not the DGP). First, however, we need to explain the class of processes and models under analysis, and consider how forecast accuracy will be measured.

---

[2] While one-step MSFEs are invariant to that particular transform, measures such as R^2 are not.

[3] Chong and Hendry (1986) show that forecast confidence intervals may be non-monotonic in h when parameters are estimated: see Section V.

II. THE FRAMEWORK

For an econometric theory of forecasting to deliver relevant conclusions about empirical forecasting, it must be based on assumptions that adequately capture the appropriate aspects of the real world to be forecast. Consequently, we consider a non-stationary (evolutionary) world subject to structural breaks, where the model differs from the mechanism, and requires estimation from available data. The present analysis considers integrated-cointegrated mechanisms which are linear in x_t, but are also subject to shifts in the deterministic factors. Generalisations to longer lags, and nonlinear relations seem feasible but await formal development.

II.1. *The Data Generation Process*

For exposition, the data generation process (DGP) is defined over the period $t = 1, \ldots, T$ by a first-order vector autoregressive process (VAR) in the n variables x_t:

$$x_t = \tau + \Upsilon x_{t-1} + v_t \quad \text{where} \quad v_t \sim \text{IN}_n(0, \Omega), \tag{5}$$

denoting an independent normal error with expectation $E(v_t) = 0$ and variance matrix $V(v_t) = \Omega$. The DGP is integrated of order unity ($I(1)$), and satisfies $r < n$ cointegration relations such that:

$$\Upsilon = I_n + \alpha\beta', \tag{6}$$

where α and β are $n \times r$ matrices of rank r.[4] Then (5) can be reparameterised as the vector equilibrium-correction model (VEqCM):

$$\Delta x_t = \tau + \alpha\beta' x_{t-1} + v_t, \tag{7}$$

where Δx_t and $\beta' x_t$ are $I(0)$. Let:

$$\tau = \gamma - \alpha\mu, \tag{8}$$

where μ is $r \times 1$ and $\beta'\gamma = 0$ so in deviations about means:[5]

$$(\Delta x_t - \gamma) = \alpha(\beta' x_{t-1} - \mu) + v_t, \tag{9}$$

where the system grows at the unconditional rate $E(\Delta x_t) = \gamma$ with long-run solution $E(\beta' x_t) = \mu$.

II.2. *The Model Class*

The form of the model coincides with (5) as a linear representation of x_t, but is potentially mis-specified:

$$x_t = \tau_p + \Upsilon_p x_{t-1} + u_t, \tag{10}$$

where the parameter estimates $(\hat{\tau} : \hat{\Upsilon} : \hat{\Omega})$ are possibly inconsistent, with $\tau_p \neq \tau$

[4] In (5), none of the roots of $|I - \Upsilon L| = 0$ lies inside the unit circle (where L is the lag operator, $L'x_t = x_{t-s}$), and $\alpha'_\perp \Phi\beta_\perp$ is rank $(n-r)$, where Φ is the mean-lag matrix (here Υ), when $\alpha_\perp$ and $\beta_\perp$ are $n \times (n-r)$ matrices of rank $(n-r)$ such that $\alpha'\alpha_\perp = \beta'\beta_\perp = 0$.

[5] $\gamma = \beta_\perp(\alpha'_\perp \beta_\perp)^{-1}\alpha'_\perp \tau$. The decomposition using $\tau = \gamma - \alpha\mu$ is not orthogonal since $\gamma'\alpha\mu \neq 0$, but as a DGP, (9) is isomorphic to (7).

and $\mathbf{Y}_p \neq \mathbf{Y}$. Empirical econometric models like (10) are not numerically calibrated theoretical models, but have error processes which are derived, and so are not autonomous: see Gilbert (1986), Hendry (1995a), and Spanos (1986) *inter alia*. The theory of reduction explains the origin and status of such empirical models in terms of the implied information reductions relative to the process that generated the data. Some reductions, such as invalid marginalisation, affect forecast accuracy directly, whereas others, such as aggregation, may primarily serve to define the object of interest.

Two specific models considered below are defined by ($\tau_p = \tau, \mathbf{Y}_p = \mathbf{Y}$) and ($\tau_p = \gamma, \mathbf{Y}_p = \mathbf{I}_n$). The first model is the DGP in sample. Although empirical econometric models are invariably not facsimiles of the DGP, they could match the data evidence in all measurable respects – i.e. be congruent; but as we allow for forecast-period structural change, the model will not coincide with the DGP in the forecast period. The second model is given by:

$$\Delta\mathbf{x}_t = \gamma + \xi_t$$

which is correctly specified only when $\alpha = 0$ in (9), in which case $\xi_t = \mathbf{v}_t$. It is a VAR in the differences of the variables (DVAR), and is mis-specified in sample by omitting the cointegrating vectors.

III. MEASURING FORECAST ACCURACY

Although econometric analyses could begin by specifying a loss function from which the optimal predictor is derived, a well-defined mapping between forecast errors and their costs is not typical in macroeconomics. Consequently, measures of forecast accuracy are often based on the MSFE matrix:

$$\mathbf{V}_h \equiv \mathrm{E}(\mathbf{e}_{T+h}\mathbf{e}_{T+h}') = \mathrm{V}(\mathbf{e}_{T+h}) + \mathrm{E}(\mathbf{e}_{T+h})\,\mathrm{E}(\mathbf{e}_{T+h}'), \tag{11}$$

where $\mathbf{e}_{T+h}$ is a vector of h-step ahead forecast errors. Such measures may lack invariance to non-singular, scale-preserving, linear transformations for which the associated model class is invariant, so MSFE comparisons may yield inconsistent rankings between forecasting models on multi-step ahead forecasts depending on the particular transformations of variables examined (e.g. level or differences). Clements and Hendry (1993) show analytically that for multi-step forecasts, the trace, determinant, and the whole matrix $\mathbf{V}_h$ lack invariance.

Denote the linear forecasting system by:

$$\mathbf{\Gamma s}_t = \mathbf{u}_t \quad \text{with} \quad \mathbf{u}_t \sim \mathrm{IN}_{n+k}(\mathbf{0}, \mathbf{\Sigma}), \tag{12}$$

where $\mathbf{s}_t' = (\mathbf{x}_t' : \mathbf{z}_t')$, $\mathbf{z}_t$ are the m available predetermined variables and $\mathbf{\Sigma}$ is symmetric, positive semi-definite: for example, in (5), $\mathbf{z}_t' = (1, \mathbf{x}_{t-1}')$ and $\mathbf{\Gamma} = (\mathbf{I}_n : -\tau : -\mathbf{Y})$. Then the likelihood and generalised variance of the system in (12) are invariant under scale-preserving, non-singular transformations of the form:

$$\mathbf{M\Gamma P}^{-1}\mathbf{Ps}_t = \mathbf{Mu}_t$$

so:

$$\mathbf{\Gamma^* s}_t^* = \mathbf{u}_t^* \quad \text{with} \quad \mathbf{u}_t^* \sim \mathrm{IN}_{n+k}(\mathbf{0}, \mathbf{M\Sigma M}'). \tag{13}$$

In (13), $\mathbf{s}_t^* = \mathbf{P}\mathbf{s}_t$, $\mathbf{M}$ and $\mathbf{P}$ are respectively $n \times n$ and $(m+n) \times (m+n)$ known non-singular matrices where $|\mathbf{M}| = 1$, and $\mathbf{P}$ is the upper block-triangular matrix:-

$$\mathbf{P} = \begin{pmatrix} \mathbf{I}_n & \mathbf{P}_{12} \\ \mathbf{0} & \mathbf{P}_{22} \end{pmatrix},$$

with $|\mathbf{P}_{22}| \neq 0$. Then:

$$|\mathbf{M}\Sigma\mathbf{M}'| = |\Sigma|, \tag{14}$$

so the systems (12) and (13) are isomorphic. Forecasts and forecast confidence intervals made in the original system and transformed after the event to $\mathbf{x}_t^*$, or made directly from the transformed system, are identical; and this remains true when parameters are estimated by any method that is invariant (e.g. maximum likelihood). For example, if a system is estimated for $\mathbf{x}_t$ on $\mathbf{x}_{t-1}$ by full-information maximum likelihood with $\widehat{\Delta\mathbf{x}_t}$ obtained by identity, then the forecasts $\widehat{\Delta\mathbf{x}}_{T+h}$ of $\Delta\mathbf{x}_{T+h}$ are identical to those obtained from modelling $\Delta\mathbf{x}_t$ on $\mathbf{x}_{t-1}$ with $\hat{\mathbf{x}}_t$ obtained by identity. A point of potential confusion is that the differences of the forecasts of $\hat{\mathbf{x}}_{T+h}$ may not equal $\widehat{\Delta\mathbf{x}}_{T+h}$ despite using $\Delta\hat{\mathbf{x}}_{T+h} = \hat{\mathbf{x}}_{T+h} - \hat{\mathbf{x}}_{T+h-1}$ if at $h = 1$, the actual initial condition $\mathbf{x}_T$ is subtracted: this adds an intercept correction setting the model back on track, often markedly improving the forecasts as shown below. Nevertheless, the forecasts themselves are invariant to linear transforms; the present issue is the lack of invariance of some measures of their accuracy.

For transformations involving $\mathbf{M}$ only (i.e. $\mathbf{P} = \mathbf{I}_{n+m}$), the matrix measure $\mathbf{V}_h$ and determinant are invariant, but the trace is not: see Granger and Newbold (1986). When $\mathbf{M} = \mathbf{I}_n$, for transformations using $\mathbf{P}$, neither the determinant nor the MSFE matrix is invariant for $h > 1$, even though the distribution of the $\mathbf{u}_t$ is unaffected by (13): see Clements and Hendry (1996a).

Invariance to $\mathbf{P}$ transformations in a measure requires accounting for covariances between different step-ahead errors, leading to a generalised forecast-error second-moment matrix (GFESM, which is close to predictive likelihood: see Bjørnstad, 1990):

$$\Phi_h = \mathrm{E}(\mathbf{E}_h\,\mathbf{E}_h'),$$

where $\mathbf{E}_h$ stacks the forecast errors up to and including h-steps ahead:

$$\mathbf{E}_h' = (\mathbf{e}_{T+1}', \mathbf{e}_{T+2}', \dots, \mathbf{e}_{T+h-1}', \mathbf{e}_{T+h}').$$

Then, $|\Phi_h|$ is also unaffected by $\mathbf{M}$ transforms, since denoting the vector of stacked forecast errors from the transformed model by $\tilde{\mathbf{E}}_h'$:

$$\tilde{\mathbf{E}}_h' = (\mathbf{e}_{T+1}'\mathbf{M}', \mathbf{e}_{T+2}'\mathbf{M}', \dots, \mathbf{e}_{T+h-1}'\mathbf{M}', \mathbf{e}_{T+h}'\mathbf{M}'),$$

we have:

$$|\tilde{\Phi}_h| = |\mathrm{E}(\tilde{\mathbf{E}}_h\,\tilde{\mathbf{E}}_h')| = |\mathrm{E}(\mathbf{E}_h\,\mathbf{E}_h')|,$$

since $|\mathbf{I}_n \otimes \mathbf{M}| = 1$.

Although invariance is useful to determine a unique measure for a fixed model independently of its representation, it is not compelling, and often several forecast-accuracy indices are reported.

IV. CAUSAL INFORMATION IN ECONOMIC FORECASTING

We now consider the role of causal information in economic forecasting first when the model coincides with the mechanism, then when it does not; the mechanism is allowed to be non-constant over time. In the first case, causal information is always useful, and produces better forecasts than non-causal. Adding further variables produces no improvement. Even when the model is mis-specified, causally-relevant information generally improves forecasts providing the mechanism generates stationary data. Such a result cannot be shown for a mis-specified model of a non-constant mechanism, and non-causal additional variables potentially can be more useful than causally-relevant ones so long as the model remains mis-specified.

To demonstrate these claims, we assume all parameters are known: estimation uncertainty would reinforce the main conclusion. While sufficiently poor estimates would weaken any conclusions from the first case, our concern is to establish that causally-relevant variables cannot be relied upon to produce the 'best' forecasts when the model is mis-specified, and parameter uncertainty would strengthen this finding.

IV.1. *Model Coincides with the Mechanism*

Consider the DGP in (5) for the n $I(1)$ variables $\mathbf{x}_t$. Here, (5) is both the model and the DGP, although it could be written in a lower-dimensional parameter space in terms of $I(0)$ transformations of the original variables as in (9) above. The notation is simplest when the mechanism is constant, so we prove the result for 1-step forecasts in that setting first.

The in-sample conditional expectation of $\mathbf{x}_{T+1}$ given $\mathbf{x}_T$ is:

$$E(\mathbf{x}_{T+1} \mid \mathbf{x}_T) = \boldsymbol{\tau} + \mathbf{Y}\mathbf{x}_T$$

and this delivers the (matrix) minimum MSFE. Under the present assumptions, the resulting forecast error is a homoscedastic innovation against all further information:

$$E(\mathbf{v}_{T+1} \mid \mathbf{x}_T) = \mathbf{0} \quad \text{and} \quad V(\mathbf{v}_{T+1} \mid \mathbf{x}_T) = \boldsymbol{\Omega}. \tag{15}$$

Consequently, adding any further variables $\mathbf{z}_{t-1}$ to (5) will not improve the forecast accuracy of mean or variance.

Conversely, replacing any $x_{i,t-1}$ by any or all elements from $\mathbf{z}_{t-1}$ will lead to inefficient forecasts unless there is perfect correlation between $x_{i,t}$ and $\mathbf{z}_t$. Denote the resulting regressor vector by $\mathbf{\bar{x}}_{t-1}$, then, forecasting from:

$$\mathbf{x}_t = \boldsymbol{\delta} + \boldsymbol{\Gamma}\mathbf{\bar{x}}_{t-1} + \mathbf{e}_t,$$

where $E(\mathbf{e}_t \mid \mathbf{\bar{x}}_{t-1}) = \mathbf{0}$ using:

$$\mathbf{\tilde{x}}_{T+1} = \boldsymbol{\delta} + \boldsymbol{\Gamma}\mathbf{\bar{x}}_T,$$

the forecast error is:

$$\mathbf{e}_{T+1} = \mathbf{x}_{T+1} - \mathbf{\tilde{x}}_{T+1} = (\boldsymbol{\tau} - \boldsymbol{\delta}) + \mathbf{Y}\mathbf{x}_T - \boldsymbol{\Gamma}\mathbf{\bar{x}}_T + \mathbf{v}_{T+1}.$$

Let $\mathbf{x}_t = \boldsymbol{\zeta} + \boldsymbol{\Psi}\bar{\mathbf{x}}_t + \mathbf{w}_t$ (say) with $E(\mathbf{w}_t | \bar{\mathbf{x}}_t) = \mathbf{0}$ and $V(\mathbf{w}_t | \bar{\mathbf{x}}_t) = \boldsymbol{\Phi}$, so:

$$\mathbf{e}_{T+1} = (\boldsymbol{\tau} - \boldsymbol{\delta} + \boldsymbol{\Upsilon}\boldsymbol{\zeta}) + (\boldsymbol{\Upsilon}\boldsymbol{\Psi} - \boldsymbol{\Gamma})\bar{\mathbf{x}}_T + \boldsymbol{\Upsilon}\mathbf{w}_T + \mathbf{v}_{T+1}$$

with mean:

$$E(\mathbf{e}_{T+1} | \bar{\mathbf{x}}_T) = (\boldsymbol{\tau} - \boldsymbol{\delta} + \boldsymbol{\Upsilon}\boldsymbol{\zeta}) + (\boldsymbol{\Upsilon}\boldsymbol{\Psi} - \boldsymbol{\Gamma})\bar{\mathbf{x}}_T = \mathbf{0} \qquad (16)$$

so that $\boldsymbol{\delta} = \boldsymbol{\tau} + \boldsymbol{\Upsilon}\boldsymbol{\zeta}$ and $\boldsymbol{\Upsilon}\boldsymbol{\Psi} = \boldsymbol{\Gamma}$; and variance:

$$V(\mathbf{e}_{T+1} | \bar{\mathbf{x}}_T) = \boldsymbol{\Omega} + \boldsymbol{\Upsilon}\boldsymbol{\Phi}\boldsymbol{\Upsilon}'. \qquad (17)$$

Thus, the forecasts are conditionally unbiased (16), but inefficient (17).

Next, in a non-constant DGP, Section IX shows that the main non-constancies of interest concern direct or indirect changes in the deterministic components of (5). Either $\boldsymbol{\tau}$ can change, or if $\boldsymbol{\Upsilon}$ changes, the unconditional means of the I(o) components alter. We only consider the former. Let $\boldsymbol{\tau}$ change to $\boldsymbol{\tau}^*$, so the DGP in the forecast period becomes:

$$\mathbf{x}_{T+1} = \boldsymbol{\tau}^* + \boldsymbol{\Upsilon}\mathbf{x}_T + \mathbf{v}_T. \qquad (18)$$

Since the model also switches to (18) by being the mechanism, the forecast errors have the same properties as in (15), and the previous result is unchanged. Its converse, that (18) will dominate incorrect models, is more tedious to show, but follows from a generalisation of the argument in (16) and (17).

Such powerful results are not surprising; but the assumption that the model coincides with the mechanism is extremely strong and not empirically relevant.

IV.2. *Model Does not Coincide with the Mechanism*

First, we show that if the process is stationary, predictive failure is unconditionally unlikely, irrespective of how badly the model is specified (see Hendry, 1979), but that causal information dominates non-causal. Even so, non-causal might help, if it acts as a proxy for the omitted causal variables. Then we provide an example where causal information need not help once structural breaks are introduced.

Reparameterise the system as in (9):

$$\Delta\mathbf{x}_t = \boldsymbol{\gamma} + \boldsymbol{\alpha}(\boldsymbol{\beta}'\mathbf{x}_{t-1} - \boldsymbol{\mu}) + \mathbf{v}_t. \qquad (19)$$

There are many ways in which a model could be mis-specified for the mechanism in (19), but we only consider omission of the I(o) cointegrating components. Denote the model by:

$$\Delta\mathbf{x}_t = \boldsymbol{\delta} + \boldsymbol{\rho}(\boldsymbol{\beta}_1'\mathbf{x}_{t-1} - \boldsymbol{\mu}_1) + \boldsymbol{\eta}_t, \qquad (20)$$

where $\boldsymbol{\beta}_1'$ is (perhaps a linear transform of) a subset of the r co-integrating vectors in (19), and $\boldsymbol{\mu}_1$ is the unconditional expectation of $\boldsymbol{\beta}_1'\mathbf{x}_t$. Then, as $E(\boldsymbol{\beta}_1'\mathbf{x}_{t-1}) = \boldsymbol{\mu}_1$, $\boldsymbol{\delta} = \boldsymbol{\gamma}$, and hence for known parameters in (20) and forecast $\widehat{\Delta\mathbf{x}}_{T+1} = \boldsymbol{\gamma} + \boldsymbol{\rho}(\boldsymbol{\beta}_1'\mathbf{x}_T - \boldsymbol{\mu}_1)$:

$$E(\widehat{\Delta\mathbf{x}}_{T+1}) = \boldsymbol{\gamma}$$

so forecasts are unconditionally unbiased, though inefficient. Adding any omitted I(o) linear combinations of $\mathbf{x}_{t-1}$ will improve forecasts, as will adding any $\Delta\mathbf{x}_{t-1}$ which proxy for omitted $\boldsymbol{\beta}_2'\mathbf{x}_{t-1}$.

Thus, the notion of basing forecasting on 'causal models' still has substance, perhaps qualified by the need to estimate parameters from small samples of badly-measured data. However, once the model is not the mechanism and the mechanism is non-constant, the dominance of causal information over non-causal cannot be shown. We consider a counter example where non-causal information dominates causal on at least one forecast criterion, unless omniscience is assumed. The result may help explain some of the apparent success of the approach in Box and Jenkins (1976).

Consider a world in which GNP (Y) is 'caused' by the exchange rate (E):

$$Y_t = \alpha E_{t-1} + \epsilon_t \quad \text{with} \quad \epsilon_t \sim \text{IN}(0, \sigma_\epsilon^2) \quad \text{for} \quad t \in \mathcal{T}_1, \tag{21}$$

where $\mathcal{T}_1 = (1, T_1)$. Then at $T_1 + 1$, the DGP changes to:

$$Y_t = \beta R_{t-1} + v_t \quad \text{with} \quad v_t \sim \text{IN}(0, \sigma_v^2) \quad \text{for} \quad t \in \mathcal{T}_2, \tag{22}$$

where $\mathcal{T}_2 = (T_1 + 1, T)$. The collapse of Bretton Woods, leaving the ERM, or entering EMU are potential examples, albeit that the model is overly simplistic. We assume that E_t and R_t are driftless random walks, but are always positive (otherwise, shifts in intercepts would be needed), given by $\Delta E_t = e_t$ and $\Delta R_t = r_t$ with mean-zero, white-noise innovations e_t and r_t, and variances σ_e^2 and σ_r^2.

Throughout, Y_t is predictable in mean from the universal information set, since (setting $D_t = 1$ when $t \in \mathcal{T}_1$, zero otherwise):

$$E(Y_t | \mathscr{I}_{t-1}) = \alpha D_t E_{t-1} + \beta (1 - D_t) R_{t-1}.$$

However, using the criterion of unbiasedness of forecasts, Y_t is forecastable from (E_{t-1}, R_{t-1}) after T_1 only if the switch point is known. For example, the model based on regressing Y_t on E_{t-1} and R_{t-1}, namely:

$$Y_t = \psi_1 E_{t-1} + \psi_2 R_{t-1} + u_t \tag{23}$$

will not suffice as:[6]

$$E\left[\begin{pmatrix} \hat{\psi}_1 \\ \hat{\psi}_2 \end{pmatrix}\right] = \begin{pmatrix} \psi_1 \\ \psi_2 \end{pmatrix} \simeq \begin{bmatrix} K\alpha \\ (1-K)\beta \end{bmatrix},$$

where $K = T_1(T_1 - 1)/[T(T-1)]$. Forecasting using $\hat{Y}_t = \psi_1 E_{t-1} + \psi_2 R_{t-1}$ for $t \in \mathcal{T}_2$ yields:

$$E(\hat{Y}_t | \mathscr{I}_{t-1}) \simeq K\alpha E_{t-1} + (1-K)\beta R_{t-1} = \beta R_{t-1} + K(\alpha E_{t-1} - \beta R_{t-1}),$$

so that:

$$E(Y_t - \hat{Y}_t | \mathscr{I}_{t-1}, D_t = 0] = -K(\alpha E_{t-1} - \beta R_{t-1}).$$

As E is the relative price of two currencies, it could move wildly due to the other country's behaviour, swamping any predictability from R to produce badly biased forecasts.

Consider an alternative forecasting procedure that ignores the information

[6] The analytical calculations depend on what is assumed about the time-series properties of E_t and R_t. If these are not independent driftless random walks, but are correlated, for example, or have heteroscedastic errors after the regime shift, than a somewhat different, but related, analysis is needed. Appendix A provides the derivation.

on E_{t-1}, R_{t-1} and simply uses the time series on Y_t. For example, differencing once yields:

$$\Delta Y_t = \alpha e_{t-1} + \Delta \epsilon_t, \; t \in \mathcal{T}_1,$$

$$\Delta Y_{T_1+1} = \beta R_{T_1} - \alpha E_{T_1-1} + v_{T_1+1} - \epsilon_{T_1},$$ (24)

$$\Delta Y_t = \beta r_{t-1} + \Delta v_t, \; t > T_1 + 1,$$

so for $t \in \mathcal{T}_2$:

$$E(\Delta Y_t) = E(\beta r_{t-1} + \Delta v_t) = 0$$

and hence the forecast $\tilde{Y}_t = Y_{t-1}$ is unconditionally unbiased (albeit 'inefficient'). Thus, even though Y_{t-1} does not directly enter the DGP, $\tilde{Y}_t = Y_{t-1}$ is better in terms of bias than $\hat{Y}_t$, which included the correct causal variable R_{t-1}. However, Y_t is slightly biased conditionally on Y_{t-1}, since after the break:[7]

$$E(Y_t - \tilde{Y}_t \mid Y_{t-1}) = E(\Delta Y_t \mid Y_{t-1}) = E(\beta r_{t-1} + \Delta v_t \mid Y_{t-1}) = E(v_{t-1} \mid Y_{t-1}) \neq 0.$$

The inability to prove that causally-relevant variables will dominate for mis-specified models has important implications. First, there exist methods of robustifying forecasts against structural breaks that have occurred: the differencing in (24) is one example, and others are noted below. Alternatively, other forms of non-causal information may prove relevant, such as intercept corrections. Secondly, the differenced process in (24) is close to an ARIMA with a large negative moving-average root and an outlier at the break point, although that is not the DGP (see the analysis of multi-step estimators in Clements and Hendry, 1996d). Thirdly, for large enough unmodelled breaks, 'causal' models will lose on MSFE (and related criteria) to models that are robustified against breaks; this is examined further in Section VIII below. Finally, while the example is specifically constructed to demonstrate the possibility of dominating causal information, Section VIII provides a general class that also does so, and highlights the distinction between error-correction and equilibrium-correction mechanisms.

V. PARSIMONY

It is not easy to find formal reasons for the advantages of parsimony in forecasting, despite a general folklore that it matters. Estimated parameter variances decline with sample size, whereas inconsistencies do not, so any trade-off rapidly moves against parsimony: we show below that in correct model specifications, large parameter variances due to 'collinearity' cannot be a justification. The origins of the arguments for parsimony in the methods of Box and Jenkins (1976) are because of lack of identification in ARIMA models when there are redundant common factors, so do not generalise to other model classes. There is some evidence that empirically, parsimony may help (see, e.g., the basis for 'Bayesian DVARS' in Doan *et al.*, 1984). In practice, model mis-specification and structural change seem likely to be more important than

---

[7] At the switch point, since $K \simeq 1$, the relative biases conditional on $\mathcal{I}_{T_1}$ could go either way as $E(Y_{T_1+1} - \hat{Y}_{T_1+1} \mid \mathcal{I}_{T_1}) \simeq \beta R_{T_1} - \alpha E_{T_1}$, whereas $E(Y_{T_1+1} - \tilde{Y}_{T_1+1} \mid \mathcal{I}_{T_1}) = \beta R_{T_1} - \alpha E_{T_1-1} - E(\epsilon_{T_1} \mid \mathcal{I}_{T_1})$, and hence could be constructed to be smaller for Y_{T_1+1}.

parameter uncertainty, leading to an alternative justification noted below, but we first consider a case where parsimony can be shown to matter. We focus on h-step ahead scalar forecasts under correct specification, drawing on Hendry and Clements (1993).

Consider a stationary first-order autoregression defined by:

$$y_t = \rho y_{t-1} + \epsilon_t \quad \text{where} \quad \epsilon_t \sim \text{IN}(0, \sigma_\epsilon^2),$$

with $|\rho| < 1$. Then $E(y_t) = 0$ and $E(y_t^2) = \sigma_y^2 = \sigma_\epsilon^2/(1-\rho^2)$.

We examine the effect on forecasting h-steps ahead of estimating ρ relative to imposing it at zero. Since:

$$y_{T+h} = \rho^h y_T + \sum_{j=0}^{h-1} \rho^j \epsilon_{T+h-j}, \tag{25}$$

the h-step conditional forecast error from the estimated model using $\hat{y}_{T+h} = \hat{\rho}^h y_T$ in (25) is:

$$\hat{\epsilon}_{T+h} = y_{T+h} - \hat{y}_{T+h} = (\rho^h - \hat{\rho}^h) y_T + \sum_{j=0}^{h-1} \rho^j \epsilon_{T+h-j}, \tag{26}$$

so that for forecasting the level y_{T+h} on a MSFE basis (see Schmidt, 1974; Baillie, 1979; Chong and Hendry, 1986; Campos, 1992, noting the caveats in Clements and Hendry, 1993):

$$M(\hat{\epsilon}_{T+h} | y_T) = \frac{(1-\rho^{2h}) \sigma_\epsilon^2}{(1-\rho^2)} + T^{-1} h^2 \rho^{2(h-1)} (1-\rho^2) y_T^2,$$

$$= \sigma_y^2 [(1-\rho^{2h}) + T^{-1} h^2 \rho^{2(h-1)} (1-\rho^2) y_T^{\dagger 2}], \tag{27}$$

where $y_T^\dagger = y_T/\sigma_y$. When a forecast of zero (the unconditional mean) is used instead, so $\tilde{y}_{T+h} = 0 \,\forall h$, then (again for levels):

$$M(\tilde{\epsilon}_{T+h} | y_T) = \frac{(1-\rho^{2h}) \sigma_\epsilon^2}{(1-\rho^2)} + \rho^{2h} y_T^2$$

$$= \sigma_y^2 [(1-\rho^{2h}) + \rho^{2h} y_T^{\dagger 2}]. \tag{28}$$

Hence, the relative MSFE, denoted $R(\cdot)$, is:

$$R(\tilde{\epsilon}, \hat{\epsilon}, h) = \frac{M(\tilde{\epsilon}_{T+h} | y_T) - M(\hat{\epsilon}_{T+h} | y_T)}{\sigma_y^2}$$

$$= T^{-1} \rho^{2(h-1)} (1-\rho^2) (\phi_{\rho=0}^2 - h^2) y_T^{\dagger 2}, \tag{29}$$

where $\phi_{\rho=0}^2 = T\rho^2/(1-\rho^2)$ is the non-centrality parameter of the F-test of H_0: $\rho = 0$ in (25). Thus, the condition for retaining the estimated coefficient rather than imposing it arbitrarily at zero becomes increasingly stringent as h increases, crudely expressed as needing $t_\rho > h$. Although the term as a whole is tending to zero, this provides some basis for parsimony in estimation for forecasting. A cross-over of sign in $R(\cdot)$ must occur at some h: there always exists an h at which negative $R(\cdot)$ values occur. The formula in (29) also explains why forecast confidence bands are non-monotonic in h, and can exceed the unconditional forecast uncertainty (see Chong and Hendry, 1986; Ericsson and Marquez, 1989). Further, when $\phi^2_{\rho=0} > 1$, a weighted average of the estimated and imposed models will outperform either, matching the optimal weight for pooling the models obtained in Hendry and Clements (1994b). This leads in turn to a scientific basis for intercept corrections using zero as the long-run outcome (e.g. for second-differenced data). At first sight, therefore, a formula such as (29) seems promising.

Unfortunately, Hendry and Clements (1993) show that the result does not generalise easily, nor is the effect large in Monte Carlo studies. Single parameters in vector systems cannot be selected by such a criterion, since powering a matrix has very indirect effects on its elements. More generally, parameter uncertainty is of order $O(T^{-1})$ in stationary processes, and even smaller for unit-root processes, as against other errors of $O(1)$. Consequently, sampling uncertainty does not seem to be the most serious problem, particularly as we now show that collinearity cannot justify parsimony for forecasting unless structural breaks occur.

However, as noted earlier, one argument for parsimony is excluding non-constant aspects. If an 'irrelevant' variable with a non-zero mean is nevertheless estimated as significant in a model, perhaps because it proxies another omitted effect (or acts like E_{t-1} in (23)), biased forecasts will result when that variable undergoes a change in its time-series behaviour. After a break, re-estimation on a least-squares criterion will reveal its irrelevance, so the model will revert to a relatively constant fit despite the forecast failure. However, a 'more parsimonious' model that excluded that effect would have produced better forecasts. One route that such effects may act along is collinearity, so we next look at that.

VI. COLLINEARITY IN FORECASTING

One might anticipate that parsimony would have a more important role when there was substantial 'collinearity' in the explanatory variables. Despite the non-uniqueness of collinearity (see Hendry, 1995a), we investigate such a possibility in this section using the static regression model:

$$y_t = \boldsymbol{\beta}'\mathbf{x}_t + \nu_t \quad \text{when} \quad \nu_t \sim \text{IN}(0, \sigma^2_v), \tag{30}$$

with $\mathbf{x}_t \sim \text{IN}_k(\mathbf{0}, \boldsymbol{\Omega})$ independently of $\{\nu_t\}$. For large T:

$$\sqrt{T}(\hat{\boldsymbol{\beta}} - \boldsymbol{\beta}) \underset{a}{\sim} \text{N}_k(\mathbf{0}, \sigma^2_v \boldsymbol{\Omega}^{-1}).$$

Then for k regressors with estimated coefficients and known future values of $\mathbf{x}$:

$$\hat{y}_{T+1} = \hat{\boldsymbol{\beta}}'\mathbf{x}_{T+1},$$

so that the forecast error:

$$\hat{\nu}_{T+1} = y_{T+1} - \hat{y}_{T+1} = \nu_{T+1} - \mathbf{x}'_{T+1}(\hat{\boldsymbol{\beta}} - \boldsymbol{\beta}),$$

and hence:

$$\text{M}(\hat{\nu}_{T+1} | \mathbf{x}_{T+1}) \simeq \sigma^2_v(1 + T^{-1}\mathbf{x}'_{T+1}\boldsymbol{\Omega}^{-1}\mathbf{x}_{T+1}). \tag{31}$$

Factorise $\boldsymbol{\Omega}$ as $\mathbf{H}'\boldsymbol{\Lambda}\mathbf{H}$ where $\boldsymbol{\Lambda}$ is diagonal, $\mathbf{H}'\mathbf{H} = \mathbf{I}_k$ and $\mathbf{H}\mathbf{x}_t = \mathbf{z}_t$, so that $\mathbf{z}_t \sim \mathrm{IN}_k(\mathbf{0}, \boldsymbol{\Lambda})$, and:

$$y_t = \boldsymbol{\gamma}'\mathbf{z}_t + \nu_t \quad \text{where} \quad \boldsymbol{\gamma} = \mathbf{H}\boldsymbol{\beta}. \tag{32}$$

Then $\mathbf{x}'_{T+1}\boldsymbol{\Omega}^{-1}\mathbf{x}_{T+1}$ equals:

$$\mathbf{x}'_{T+1}(\mathbf{H}'\boldsymbol{\Lambda}\mathbf{H})^{-1}\mathbf{x}_{T+1} = \mathbf{x}'_{T+1}\mathbf{H}'\boldsymbol{\Lambda}^{-1}\mathbf{H}\mathbf{x}_{T+1} = \mathbf{z}'_{T+1}\boldsymbol{\Lambda}^{-1}\mathbf{z}_{T+1} = \sum_{i-1}^{k} \frac{z_{i,T+1}^2}{\lambda_i}. \tag{33}$$

On average, $\mathrm{E}(z_{i,T+1}^2) = \lambda_i$, and therefore, $\mathrm{E}(\mathbf{x}'_{T+1}\boldsymbol{\Omega}^{-1}\mathbf{x}_{T+1}) = k$. Hence:

$$\mathrm{M}(\hat{\nu}_{T+1}) \simeq \sigma_v^2(1 + T^{-1}k). \tag{34}$$

This shows that any 'collinearity' in $\mathbf{x}_t$ is irrelevant to forecasting so long as the marginal process remains constant. Alternatively, the model is invariant under linear, and therefore orthogonal, transforms as shown in (32), so one-step forecasts are unaffected.

However, when $\boldsymbol{\beta}$ stays constant, but $\boldsymbol{\Omega}$ changes to $\boldsymbol{\Omega}^*$, with $\boldsymbol{\Lambda}$ changing to $\boldsymbol{\Lambda}^*$ then:

$$\mathrm{E}\left(\sum_{i-1}^{k} \frac{z_{i,T+1}^2}{\lambda_i}\right) = \sum_{i-1}^{k} \frac{\lambda_i^*}{\lambda_i}, \tag{35}$$

so:

$$\mathrm{M}(\hat{\nu}_{T+1}) \simeq \sigma_v^2\left(1 + T^{-1}\sum_{i-1}^{k} \frac{\lambda_i^*}{\lambda_i}\right).$$

Thus, changes in the eigenvalues of the least-well determined β_i corresponding to the smallest λ_i will induce the biggest relative change in $\mathrm{M}(\hat{\nu}_{T+1})$. For example, when $\lambda_1 = 0.001$ but $\lambda_1^* = 0.1$ then even for $T = 100$, the error variance is doubled. Thus, simplification could pay dividends for *ex ante* forecasting in such a state of nature.

Generalisations to dynamic systems are less clear cut, since the collinearity can alter only if the system specification changes, which anyway induces a structural break in some equations. However, (30) might be the only equation of interest in a system, in which case the analysis applies. Again we see a potential case for tighter parameterisation once breaks are allowed.

VII. INTERCEPT CORRECTIONS

Intercept corrections (ICs) are non-zero values for a model's error terms added over a forecast period to adjust a model-generated forecast to prior beliefs, allow for anticipated future events that are not explicitly incorporated in a model, or 'fix-up' a model for perceived mis-specification over the past: see, for example, Wallis and Whitley (1991). A general theory of the role of intercept corrections in macro-econometric forecasting is provided in Hendry and Clements (1994b): here we establish the effects of one commonly-used IC following Clements and Hendry (1996c).

A typical IC for a one-step ahead forecast is to add in the residual from the final sample observation to the first period forecast value. To see the consequences, consider the simple example of a stationary first-order autoregressive process:

$$y_t = \rho y_{t-1} + \epsilon_t \quad \text{where} \quad \epsilon_t \sim \text{IN}(0, \sigma_v^2) \tag{36}$$

and $|\rho| < 1$. Let $\hat{\rho}$ denote the estimate of ρ, then the conventional forecast of period $T+1$ given T is:

$$\hat{y}_{T+1} = \hat{\rho} y_T,$$

with forecast error:

$$\hat{\epsilon}_{T+1} = y_{T+1} - \hat{y}_{T+1} = (\rho - \hat{\rho}) y_T + \epsilon_{T+1}.$$

The intercept-correcting forecast is:

$$\hat{y}_{i,T+1} = \hat{y}_{T+1} + \hat{\epsilon}_T = \hat{\rho} y_T + \hat{\epsilon}_T,$$

with a forecast error $\hat{\epsilon}_{i,T+1}$ given by

$$\hat{\epsilon}_{i,T+1} = y_{T+1} - \hat{y}_{i,T+1} = (\rho - \hat{\rho}) y_T + \epsilon_{T+1} - \hat{\epsilon}_T = \Delta \hat{\epsilon}_{T+1},$$

so that the IC differences the original forecast error. We use this result in the next section to help correct for forecast biases arising from unanticipated structural breaks.

VIII. A TAXONOMY OF FORECAST ERRORS

To clarify the impact of structural breaks on forecasting, we reconsider the taxonomy of forecast errors in Clements and Hendry (1994). Despite allowing general structural change in the forecast period, the model and DGP to differ over the sample period in any way, the parameters of the model to be estimated (perhaps inconsistently) from the data, and the forecasts to commence from initial conditions (denoted by $\hat{\mathbf{x}}_T$) which may differ from the 'true' values $\mathbf{x}_T$, nevertheless some useful results can be established. The present analysis will highlight the role of changes in deterministic terms.

Write the closed system (5) in $\mathrm{I}(0)$ space using the n variables $\mathbf{y}_t$ (r of which are $\boldsymbol{\beta}'\mathbf{x}_{t-1}$ and $n-r$ are $\Delta\mathbf{x}_t$) as:[8]

$$\mathbf{y}_t = \boldsymbol{\phi} + \boldsymbol{\Pi}\mathbf{y}_{t-1} + \boldsymbol{\varepsilon}_t \quad \text{with} \quad \boldsymbol{\varepsilon}_t \sim \text{IN}_n(\mathbf{0}, \boldsymbol{\Omega}_\epsilon), \tag{37}$$

where by construction, the unconditional mean of $\mathbf{y}_t$ is:

$$E(\mathbf{y}_t) = (\mathbf{I}_n - \boldsymbol{\Pi})^{-1}\boldsymbol{\phi} = \boldsymbol{\varphi} \tag{38}$$

so:

$$\mathbf{y}_t - \boldsymbol{\varphi} = \boldsymbol{\Pi}(\mathbf{y}_{t-1} - \boldsymbol{\varphi}) + \boldsymbol{\varepsilon}_t.$$

This formulation is convenient for distinguishing between changes that induce biased forecasts, and those that do not.

The h-step ahead forecasts at time T for $h = 1, \ldots, H$ are (using $\hat{\boldsymbol{\varphi}} = (\mathbf{I}_n - \hat{\boldsymbol{\Pi}})^{-1}\hat{\boldsymbol{\phi}}$):

$$\hat{\mathbf{y}}_{T+h} - \hat{\boldsymbol{\varphi}} = \hat{\boldsymbol{\Pi}}(\hat{\mathbf{y}}_{T+h-1} - \hat{\boldsymbol{\varphi}}) = \hat{\boldsymbol{\Pi}}^h(\hat{\mathbf{y}}_T - \hat{\boldsymbol{\varphi}}), \tag{39}$$

where ' ^ 's on parameters denote estimates, and on random variables, forecasts.

[8] The identities determining the future values of the cointegrating vectors are omitted for simplicity: see Hendry and Doornik (1994). The analysis is conditional on assuming such vectors remain unchanged, so the transformed system remains $\mathrm{I}(0)$ after the structural change.

Table 1
Forecast Error Taxonomy

$$
\begin{aligned}
\hat{\varepsilon}_{T+h} \simeq\ & [(\mathbf{\Pi}^*)^h - \mathbf{\Pi}^h]\,(\mathbf{y}_T - \boldsymbol{\varphi}) && (ia) && \text{slope change} \\
& + [\mathbf{I}_n - (\mathbf{\Pi}^*)^h]\,(\boldsymbol{\varphi}^* - \boldsymbol{\varphi}) && (ib) && \text{equilibrium-mean change} \\
& + (\hat{\mathbf{\Pi}}^h - \mathbf{\Pi}_p^h)\,(\mathbf{y}_T - \boldsymbol{\varphi}) && (iia) && \text{slope mis-specification} \\
& + (\mathbf{I}_n - \mathbf{\Pi}_p^h)\,(\boldsymbol{\varphi} - \boldsymbol{\varphi}_p) && (iib) && \text{equilibrium-mean mis-specification} \\
& - \mathbf{F}_h\,\delta_{\mathbf{\Pi}}' && (iiia) && \text{slope estimation} \\
& - (\mathbf{I}_n - \mathbf{\Pi}_p^h)\,\delta_{\boldsymbol{\varphi}} && (iiib) && \text{equilibrium-mean estimation} \\
& - (\mathbf{\Pi}_p^h + \mathbf{C}_h)\,\delta_{\mathbf{y}} && (iv) && \text{initial condition uncertainty} \\
& + \sum_{i=0}^{h-1} (\mathbf{\Pi}^*)^i \varepsilon_{T+h-i} && (v) && \text{error accumulation.}
\end{aligned}
$$

Although the initial condition is uncertain, we assume $E(\hat{\mathbf{y}}_T) = \boldsymbol{\varphi}$ so on average it is unbiased.

Prior to forecasting, $(\boldsymbol{\phi}:\mathbf{\Pi})$ changes to $(\boldsymbol{\phi}^*:\mathbf{\Pi}^*)$ where $\mathbf{\Pi}^*$ still has all its eigenvalues less than unity in absolute value, so from $T+1$ the data are generated by:

$$
\mathbf{y}_{T+1} = \boldsymbol{\phi}^* + \mathbf{\Pi}^* \mathbf{y}_T + \boldsymbol{\varepsilon}_{T+1}.
$$

Letting $\boldsymbol{\phi}^* = (\mathbf{I}_n - \mathbf{\Pi}^*)\,\boldsymbol{\varphi}^*$:

$$
\mathbf{y}_{T+h} - \boldsymbol{\varphi}^* = \mathbf{\Pi}^*(\mathbf{y}_{T+h-1} - \boldsymbol{\varphi}^*) + \boldsymbol{\varepsilon}_{T+h} = (\mathbf{\Pi}^*)^h\,(\mathbf{y}_T - \boldsymbol{\varphi}^*) + \sum_{i=0}^{h-1} (\mathbf{\Pi}^*)^i \boldsymbol{\varepsilon}_{T+h-i}.
\tag{40}
$$

Many other factors could induce serious forecast errors such as large blips (e.g. 1968 (1) and (2) for consumers' expenditure in the United Kingdom, but we construe the first blip to be the above change in the mean, followed by a second shift superimposed thereon. From (39) and (40), the h-step ahead forecast error $\hat{\boldsymbol{\varepsilon}}_{T+h} = \mathbf{y}_{T+h} - \hat{\mathbf{y}}_{T+h}$ is:

$$
\hat{\boldsymbol{\varepsilon}}_{T+h} = \boldsymbol{\varphi}^* - \hat{\boldsymbol{\varphi}} + (\mathbf{\Pi}^*)^h\,(\mathbf{y}_T - \boldsymbol{\varphi}^*) - \hat{\mathbf{\Pi}}^h(\hat{\mathbf{y}}_T - \hat{\boldsymbol{\varphi}}) + \sum_{i=0}^{h-1} (\mathbf{\Pi}^*)^i \boldsymbol{\varepsilon}_{T+h-i}.
\tag{41}
$$

Deviations between sample estimates and population parameters are denoted by $\delta_{\boldsymbol{\varphi}} = \hat{\boldsymbol{\varphi}} - \boldsymbol{\varphi}_p$, where $\boldsymbol{\varphi}_p = (\mathbf{I}_n - \mathbf{\Pi}_p)^{-1}\boldsymbol{\phi}_p$, and $\delta_{\mathbf{\Pi}} = \hat{\mathbf{\Pi}} - \mathbf{\Pi}_p$, with $(\hat{\mathbf{y}}_T - \mathbf{y}_T) = \delta_{\mathbf{y}}$. To obtain a clearer interpretation of the various sources of forecast errors, we ignore powers and cross-products in the δs for parameters, but not those involving parameters interacting with initial conditions. Appendix B details the derivation, and defines $\mathbf{C}_h$ and $\mathbf{F}_h$.

Table 1 combines the possible sources of forecast errors that arise from the above decompositions.

In the present formulation, the second and fourth rows alone induce biases, whereas the remainder only affect forecast-error variances. The role of econometrics in reducing each of the forecast errors is discussed in Clements and Hendry (1994) and Hendry and Clements (1994a): here we concentrate on the consequences and properties of breaks.

First, we establish the approximate unbiasedness of forecasts based on estimates of Π in equation (37) when the model is correctly specified and $\phi = o$, even though $E(\delta_\Pi^v) \neq o$. Since $\varepsilon_t \sim IN_n(o, \Omega_\varepsilon)$, an antithetic-variate argument based on normality (or more generally, any symmetric error distribution: see, e.g., Hendry and Trivedi, 1972) can exploit $P(\varepsilon_t) = P(-\varepsilon_t)$. Since $y_t(\varepsilon_t) = -y_t(-\varepsilon_t)$ in VARs, whereas $\hat{\Pi}$ is an even function of ε_t, so $\hat{\Pi}(\{\varepsilon_t\}) = \hat{\Pi}(\{-\varepsilon_t\})$, denoting forecast errors by $\hat{}$ and $\tilde{}$ respectively when the generating process is $\{\varepsilon_t\}$ ($\{-\varepsilon_t\}$), for one-step ahead:

$$\hat{\varepsilon}_{T+1} = (\Pi - \hat{\Pi})\, y_T + \varepsilon_{T+1} \quad \text{and} \quad \tilde{\varepsilon}_{T+1} = -(\Pi - \hat{\Pi})\, y_T - \varepsilon_{T+1} \qquad (42)$$

and these average to zero for every possible error process drawing. Although the system is a dynamic process, the parameter estimate bias does not necessarily bias the forecasts. When $E(\delta_\phi) \neq o$, or for more complicated processes, the result is not exact, but suggests that finite-sample forecast error biases are unlikely to be the most serious problem.

Next, taking expectations in Table 1, assuming such finite-sample biases are negligible:

$$E(\hat{\varepsilon}_{T+h}) = [I_n - (\Pi^*)^h]\,(\varphi^* - \varphi) + (I_n - \Pi_p^h)\,(\varphi - \varphi_p). \qquad (43)$$

However, almost all estimation methods ensure that residuals have zero means in-sample, in which case the second term is zero by construction. Then, forecasts will be biased only to the extent that the long-run mean shifts from the in-sample population value. The forecast-error bias is zero for mean-zero processes ($\varphi_p = \varphi^* = o$), or when shifts in ϕ^* offset those in Π^* to leave φ unaffected ($\varphi^* = \varphi$). Only direct or induced shifts in the deterministic factors lead to serious forecast biases. Moreover, such effects do not die out as the horizon increases, but converge to the full impact of the shift. There are variance effects as well, which are detrimental on a MSFE basis; and the *ex ante* forecast-error variance estimates will mis-estimate those ruling *ex post*, but these problems seem likely to be dominated by mean-shift structural breaks. Although nonlinearities, asymmetric errors, or roots moving onto the unit circle could generate more complicated outcomes, the basic finding points up the requirement for eliminating systematic forecast-error biases.

By way of contrast, changes in the dynamics, and dynamic parameter mis-specifications, are both multiplied by mean-zero terms, so vanish on average: indeed, they would have no effect whatever on the forecast errors if the initial condition equalled the equilibrium mean. Conversely, the larger the dis-equilibrium at the time of a shift in slope, the larger the resulting impact; but as Π^*, Π and Π_p (by assumption) have all their roots inside the unit circle, these effects die out as the horizon expands.

At the time when the parameter change occurs, forecasts will be incorrect from almost any statistical procedure. However, consider the period following the break. Forecasting $T+2$ from $T+1$ using (39) will generate the same bias as $T+1$ (given by (43) for $h = 1$). However, some robustness to regime shifts which would otherwise bias forecasts can be obtained either by intercept corrections (ICs) that carry forward the shift from time $T+1$; or by suitable differencing to eliminate the changed intercept in later periods. For the former, at time $T+1$ to forecast time $T+2$, subtracting the previous forecast error will on average produce unbiased forecasts (at a cost in forecast-error variance):

$$E(\hat{\boldsymbol{\epsilon}}_{T+2} \mid \mathcal{I}_{T+1}) - E(\hat{\boldsymbol{\epsilon}}_{T+1} \mid \mathcal{I}_T) = 0. \tag{44}$$

This IC again differences the forecast errors that would otherwise have been made, but possibly at a large cost in terms of increased forecast error variance for larger values of h: see Clements and Hendry (1996c).

Alternatively, first differencing the I(o) data produces the naive forecast $\Delta \tilde{\mathbf{y}}_{T+2} = \mathbf{0}$, or $\tilde{\mathbf{y}}_{T+2} = \mathbf{y}_{T+1}$, and as $E(\mathbf{y}_{T+h}) = \boldsymbol{\varphi}^* + (\boldsymbol{\Pi}^*)^h (\boldsymbol{\varphi} - \boldsymbol{\varphi}^*)$, the mean forecast error is:

$$\begin{aligned}
E(\tilde{\boldsymbol{\epsilon}}_{T+2}) &= E(\mathbf{y}_{T+2} - \tilde{\mathbf{y}}_{T+2}) \\
&= (\boldsymbol{\Pi}^*)^2 (\boldsymbol{\varphi} - \boldsymbol{\varphi}^*) - \boldsymbol{\Pi}^*(\boldsymbol{\varphi} - \boldsymbol{\varphi}^*) \\
&= \boldsymbol{\Pi}^*(\mathbf{I}_n - \boldsymbol{\Pi}^*) (\boldsymbol{\varphi}^* - \boldsymbol{\varphi}).
\end{aligned}$$

The bias vanishes at $\boldsymbol{\Pi}^* = \mathbf{0}$ and is smaller than (43) in general. Thus, once again, a non-causal variable $(\mathbf{y}_{t-1})$ can dominate on some forecast-accuracy measure; and overdifferencing need not be disadvantageous (noting that some of the $\Delta \mathbf{y}_t$ are second-differenced $\mathbf{x}_t$).

Clements and Hendry (1996c) show that a VEqCM and DVAR for (5) have identical forecast-error biases when a forecast is made before a break occurs for a horizon that includes the break. This is so despite the former including, and the latter excluding, all the cointegration information; however, their forecast-error variances will differ. The biases for the VEqCM do not depend on whether the forecast starts pre or post the break: thus, there is no error correction after the break. However, the DVAR has different biases pre and post for breaks in $\boldsymbol{\alpha}$ and $\boldsymbol{\mu}$, and these are usually smaller than the corresponding biases from the VEqCM. A forecasting model like $\Delta^2 \tilde{\mathbf{x}}_{T+1} = \Delta^2 \mathbf{x}_T$ seems robust to many of the shifts, but may 'over-insure' by not predicting any developments of interest, merely 'tracking' by never being badly wrong.

Although such devices can improve forecast accuracy, especially on bias measures, they entail nothing about the usefulness for other purposes of the forecasting model. Even if the resulting (intercept corrected or differenced) forecast is more accurate than that from (39), this does not imply choosing the 'robustified' model for policy, or later modelling exercises. If any policy changes were implemented on the basis of mechanistic forecasts, the latter would have the odd property of continuing to predict the same outcome however large the policy response. Thus, there may be benefits to pooling robust predictors with forecasts from econometric systems in the policy context, and this is a hypothesis to consider if encompassing fails: see Hendry and Mizon (1996).

IX. CO-BREAKING

At this point in the analysis, econometric systems do not seem to be doing well relative to rather naive methods when the objective is forecasting. We cannot establish the relevance of causal information, yet can show cases where such systems perform poorly. Parsimony has not been demonstrated as uniformly beneficial, and *ad hoc* adjustments such as intercept corrections appear to be of value. We now introduce an alternative approach to handling structural breaks that seems well suited to econometric systems, and transpires to link back closely to cointegration.

Co-breaking is defined as the cancellation of breaks across linear combinations of variables. The breaks could be changes in any of α, β, γ, or μ as before, but again we focus on one-off shifts in the last two (so Υ stays constant). Thus, the relevant regime shifts are $\mu^* = \mu + \nabla\mu$ and $\gamma^* = \gamma + \nabla\gamma$ where:

Then from (45):
$$\Delta\mathbf{x}_{T+1} = \gamma^* + \alpha(\beta'\mathbf{x}_T - \mu^*) + \mathbf{v}_{T+1}. \tag{45}$$

$$\begin{aligned} \Delta\mathbf{x}_{T+1} &= [\gamma + \alpha(\beta'\mathbf{x}_T - \mu) + \mathbf{v}_{T+1}] + (\nabla\gamma - \alpha\nabla\mu) \\ &= \overline{\Delta\mathbf{x}_{T+1}} + (\nabla\gamma - \alpha\nabla\mu). \end{aligned} \tag{46}$$

The first term is the constant-parameter value of $\Delta\mathbf{x}_{T+1}$ and the second term is the composite intercept shift. Form the m linear combinations $\phi'\Delta\mathbf{x}_{T+1}$:

$$\phi'\Delta\mathbf{x}_{T+1} = \phi'\overline{\Delta\mathbf{x}_{T+1}} + \phi'(\nabla\gamma - \alpha\nabla\mu). \tag{47}$$

Then m-dimensional equilibrium-mean co-breaking requires that $\phi'\alpha\nabla\mu = \mathbf{o}$; whereas q-dimensional drift co-breaking requires $\phi'\nabla\gamma = \mathbf{o}$. We now establish that each is almost certain to occur, so a sub-system will be independent of the breaks (see Hendry, 1995 c, for a general formulation and analysis of co-breaking).

First, 'common trends' are equilibrium-mean co-breaking. Since $\alpha'_\perp \alpha = \mathbf{o}$, when $\nabla\gamma = \mathbf{o}$:
$$\alpha'_\perp \Delta\mathbf{x}_{T+1} = \alpha'_\perp \gamma + \alpha'_\perp \mathbf{v}_{T+1}. \tag{48}$$

Thus, the $n-r$ dimensional subset $\alpha'_\perp \Delta\mathbf{x}_{T+1}$ is unaffected by the shift in the equilibrium mean. This result comes close to explaining the effectiveness of differencing as a 'solution' to intercept shifts, noted above. Alternatively, it could be used to characterise 'common trends' as those combinations not affected by shifts in underlying equilibria.

Secondly, cointegrating vectors are drift co-breaking when they are trend free (i.e. $\beta'\gamma = \beta'\gamma^* = \mathbf{o}$). Thus premultiply (45) by β' when $\nabla\mu = \mathbf{o}$:

$$\beta'\Delta\mathbf{x}_{T+1} = \beta'\alpha(\beta'\mathbf{x}_T - \mu) + \beta'\mathbf{v}_{T+1}, \tag{49}$$

thereby eliminating the shift in the drift parameter. Providing $\beta'\alpha \neq \mathbf{o}$, the resulting subsystem is unaffected by changes in the trend rates of growth in the economy. Conversely, a vector that eliminated such breaks would look like a cointegration vector, so discrimination between cointegration and co-breaking may not be easy (and may be perhaps unnecessary). Thus, a subset of equations remains constant despite the break. If these were really 'structural' (see e.g. Hendry, 1995 b) they would continue to be constant across further breaks. The remaining variables to be forecast would need extra differencing or intercept corrections pending further developments.

Consequently, there are concepts that suggest that econometric systems may yet prove a superior vehicle even in the forecasting context. We now apply this notion to help account for the potential benefits of econometric systems over leading indicators, precisely because the former involves causal information and the latter does not.

X. FORECASTING USING LEADING INDICATORS

Indices of leading indicators are often used in both forecasting and in macroeconomic modelling: see, *inter alia.* Artis *et al.* (1993), Diebold and Rudebusch (1989, 1991 *a, b*), Lahiri and Moore (1991), Neftci (1979), Stock and Watson (1989, 1992), and Zarnowitz and Braun (1992). However, the procedures used to select the components of composite leading indicators (CLIs), and construct the resulting indices, are altered frequently. It is proposed in Emerson and Hendry (1996) that this phenomenon may be due to ignoring issues of cointegration within the indices, and between their components and macroeconomic variables, and to the possibility that non-causal indicator systems are unlikely to co-break to mitigate regime shifts.

First, an indicator is any variable believed informative about another variable of interest; an index is a weighted average of a set of component indicators. A leading indicator is any variable whose known outcome occurs in advance of a variable that it is desired to forecast; a CLI is a combination of such variables. The Harvard A–B–C curves were the earliest construction meant to serve as a prediction system (see Persons, 1924).

Co-breaking provides conditions under which regime shifts vanish for linear combinations of variables. Such an outcome either entails a coincidentally equal effect, or a genuine relationship: across many breaks, the former seems unlikely, leading to poor forecasts. This highlights the key distinction between an indicator – which is non-causal of, and non-caused by, the target – and a causally-related variable. The former is unlikely to systematically experience the same shifts as the target. Thus, although CLIs and econometric models face similar problems for *ex ante* forecasting in a world of regime shifts, CLIs should suffer relatively when the mappings of the indicators to the outcomes are not causal relations.

Non-constant processes pose problems for all forecasting approaches. In leading-indicator methods, breaks can occur for reasons that would not affect an econometric model which embodied co-breaking relations. For example, the demand for money alters for portfolio reasons as well as transactions changes, so the demand function could be stable for a regime shift in interest rate policy, yet the correlation with GNP be unstable. Conversely, CLIs with a causal basis, that are both cointegrated with, and co-break with, the target, will maintain constant relationships with that target and hence provide a useful forecasting procedure, but one that is tantamount to an econometric model.

X.1. CLIs added to Econometric Systems

Next, consider adding a CLI to a DVAR for the DGP in (5):

$$\Delta \mathbf{x}_t = \mathbf{\theta} + \mathbf{\Theta} \Delta \mathbf{x}_{t-1} + \mathbf{v}_t. \tag{50}$$

As shown above, such approximations can be robust to regime shifts, particularly in $\mathbf{\mu}$ (see Clements and Hendry, 1995b). Denote the CLI by $c_{t-1} = \mathbf{\varphi}' \mathbf{x}_{t-1}$ and add it to (50), taking the special case $\mathbf{\Theta} = \mathbf{0}$ for simplicity, so that the augmented DVAR becomes:

$$\Delta \mathbf{x}_t = \mathbf{\delta} + \mathbf{\rho} c_{t-1} + \mathbf{u}_t. \tag{51}$$

When $\mathbf{\varphi}' = \mathbf{h}'\mathbf{\beta}'$ (where $\mathbf{h}$ is $r \times 1$), the CLI is a cointegrating combination, so $\{\mathbf{u}_t\}$ will be stationary. Generally $\mathbf{\rho} \neq \mathbf{0}$, with $\mathbf{\rho}\mathbf{\varphi}'$ of rank 1 and $E(c_t) = \mathbf{h}'\mathbf{\mu}$ (if $\mathbf{\varphi}'$ does not cointegrate $\mathbf{x}_t$, $\{\mathbf{u}_t\}$ will be stationary only if $\mathbf{\rho} = \mathbf{0}$). When $\mathbf{\Theta} \neq \mathbf{0}$, both $\Delta \mathbf{x}_{t-1}$ and c_{t-1} will proxy the omitted cointegrating vectors, probably reducing the significance of the latter. However, if c_{t-1} does enter empirically, the intercept in (51) will depend on $\mathbf{\mu}$. Similar reasoning applies to a CLI based on differenced data.

There are interesting implications of this analysis under regime shifts in $\mathbf{\gamma}$ and $\mathbf{\mu}$. The CLI will improve forecasting performance relative to the DVAR only if co-breaking occurs using the CLI's weights. Since $\mathbf{\beta}$ is co-breaking for shifts in the growth rate $\mathbf{\gamma}$ when the cointegrating vectors do not trend (so $\mathbf{\beta}'\mathbf{\gamma} = \mathbf{0}$), whereas $\{\mathbf{u}_t\}$ depends on $\mathbf{\gamma}$, a CLI will be a poor proxy in such a state of nature relative to the correct cointegrating vectors. Further, although the DVAR is little affected by changes in $\mathbf{\mu}$, the CLI-based model in (51) depends on $\mathbf{\mu}$ and will experience similar predictive failure to the VEqCM, so the robustness of (50) to shifts in the equilibrium mean is lost as well. Emerson and Hendry (1996) offer some empirical evidence supporting this argument.

XI. CONCLUSION

Despite the relatively weak assumptions that the economy under analysis is non-stationary and subject to unanticipated structural breaks, that the model may differ from the mechanism in unknown ways, and that it requires estimation from available data, many useful insights can be derived. The resulting implications often differ considerably from those derived when the model is assumed to coincide with a constant mechanism. The fundamental concepts of predictability and forecastability point towards many of the general problems confronting successful forecasting. Causal information cannot be shown to dominate non-causal uniformly in such a setting, and there are no unique measures of forecast accuracy although some measures are not even invariant across isomorphic model representations. Also, intercept corrections have a theoretical justification in a world subject to structural breaks of unknown form, size, and timing by 'robustifying' forecasts against deterministic shifts. Such ICs reveal that the best forecasting model is not necessarily the best policy model.

There is a case for increased parsimony when making multi-step forecasts in constant-parameter worlds, but it is weak, particularly given the absence of any role for collinearity. However, even if the forecasting model remains constant, a break in the correlation structure of the regressors can induce poor forecasts due to variance effects from the least significant variables retained, consistent with the need to eliminate non-systematic effects.

The taxonomy of sources of forecast error clarifies the roles of model mis-specification, sampling variability, error accumulation, initial condition mis-measurement, intercept shifts, and slope-parameter changes. While structural breaks reduce forecastability, the consequences of many forms of break can be derived analytically. Further, models may be differentially susceptible to structural breaks, as shown analytically for VEqCMs and DVARs.

Co-breaking suggests the possibility of eliminating structural breaks by taking linear combinations of variables, which may help produce more robust subsystems. Finally, while leading indicators based on *ex post* correlations should forecast well in constant-parameter processes, they seem unlikely to provide a reliable forecasting approach under structural breaks as their intercepts are not likely to co-break when variables are genuine indicators that are not linked causally to the target. Thus, causal information retains a central role.

In many ways, this research aims to discover why methods such as Box–Jenkins or DVARs 'work' when econometric systems fail. Some potential answers have been proposed, namely, that they impose (so do not estimate) unit roots; that their formulation therefore retains the full values of the previous levels of the transformed variables which ensures a form of error correction; they restrict the information used by appealing to parsimony claims, and thereby happen to exclude non-systematic effects that might otherwise swamp forecastability; and overdifferencing removes permanent breaks in deter-ministic factors (perhaps at the cost of inducing negative moving-average residuals) demonstrated above to be central to avoiding systematic forecast error biases. Their very advantages as forecasting devices that are robust against deterministic shifts mitigate against their use in a policy setting.

The case for continuing to use econometric systems seems to depend in practice on their competing successfully in the forecasting arena. Cointegration, co-breaking, model selection procedures and rigorous testing help, but none of these ensures immunity to predictive failure from new forms of break. Thus, there is a powerful case for adopting more robust forecasting approaches than intercept corrections: a key development must be error-correction methods that do not eliminate other sources of information such as cointegration. An approach that incorporates causal information in the econometric system for co-breaking and policy, but operates with robustified forecasts merits development.

Many of the conclusions entail positive prescriptions for action; many are at first sight counterintuitive (but then intuition is just the legacy of previously unquestioned beliefs); and many of the difficulties have possible remedies. In particular, we have only just begun to explore the implications of forecasting across structural breaks with mis-specified models, and many surprises undoubtedly await future researchers.

Nuffield College

Date of receipt of final typescript: October 1996

REFERENCES

Artis, M. J., Bladen-Hovell, R. C., Osborn, D. R., Smith, J. P. and Zhang, W. (1993). 'Turning point prediction in the UK: Preliminary results using CSO leading indicators.' Presented to the Royal Economic Society Conference, York.

Baillie, R. T. (1979). 'The asymptotic mean squared error of multistep prediction from the regression model with autoregressive errors.' *Journal of the American Statistical Association*, vol. 74, pp. 175–84.

Bjørnstad, J. F. (1990). 'Predictive likelihood: a review.' *Statistical Science*, vol. 5, pp. 242–65.

Bollerslev, T., Chou, R. S. and Kroner, K. F. (1992). 'ARCH modelling in finance – A review of the theory and empirical evidence.' *Journal of Econometrics*, vol. 52, pp. 5–59.

Bollerslev, T., Engle, R. F. and Nelson, D. B. (1994). 'ARCH models.' In (R. F. Engle and D. McFadden, eds.), *The Handbook of Econometrics*, Volume 4, pp. 2959–3038. Amsterdam: North-Holland.

Box, G. E. P. and Jenkins, G. M. (1976). *Time Series Analysis, Forecasting and Control*. San Francisco: Holden-Day.

Burns, T. (1986). 'The interpretation and use of economic predictions.' In *Proceedings of the Royal Society*, Series A, vol. 407, pp. 103–25.

Campos, J. (1992). 'Confidence intervals for linear combinations of forecasts from dynamic econometric models.' *Journal of Policy Modeling*, vol. 14, pp. 535–60.

Chong, Y. Y. and Hendry, D. F. (1986). 'Econometric evaluation of linear macro-economic models.' *Review of Economic Studies*, vol. 53, pp. 671–90. Reprinted in (C. W. J. Granger, ed.) (1990), *Modelling Economic Series*. Oxford: Clarendon Press.

Clements, M. P. and Hendry, D. F. (1993). 'On the limitations of comparing mean squared forecast errors.' *Journal of Forecasting*, vol. 12, pp. 617–37. With discussion.

Clements, M. P. and Hendry, D. F. (1994). 'Towards a theory of economic forecasting.' In (C. Hargreaves, ed.), *Non-stationary Time-series Analyses and Cointegration*, pp. 9–52. Oxford: Oxford University Press.

Clements, M. P. and Hendry, D. F. (1995a). 'Forecasting in cointegrated systems.' *Journal of Applied Econometrics*, vol. 10, pp. 127–46.

Clements, M. P. and Hendry, D. F. (1995b). 'Macro-economic forecasting and modelling.' ECONOMIC JOURNAL, vol. 105, pp. 1001–13.

Clements, M. P. and Hendry, D. F. (1996a). 'An empirical study of seasonal unit roots in forecasting.' *International Journal of Forecasting*. Forthcoming.

Clements, M. P. and Hendry, D. F. (1996b). 'Forecasting in macro-economics.' In Cox *et al.* (1996), pp. 101–41.

Clements, M. P. and Hendry, D. F. (1996c). 'Intercept corrections and structural breaks.' *Journal of Applied Econometrics*. Forthcoming.

Clements, M. P. and Hendry, D. F. (1996d). 'Multi-step estimation for forecasting.' *Oxford Bulletin of Economics and Statistics*. Forthcoming.

Cook, S. (1995). 'Treasury economic forecasting.' mimeo, Institute of Economics and Statistics, University of Oxford.

Cox, D. R., Hinkley, D. V. and Barndorff-Nielsen, O. E. (eds.) (1996). *Time Series Models In Econometrics, Finance and Other Fields*. London: Chapman and Hall.

Cox, D. R. and Miller, H. D. (1965). *The Theory of Stochastic Processes*. London: Chapman and Hall.

Diebold, F. X. and Rudebusch, G. D. (1989). 'Scoring the leading indicators.' *Journal of Business*, vol. 62, pp. 369–91.

Diebold, F. X and Rudebusch, G. D. (1991a). 'Forecasting output with the composite leading index: an ex ante analysis.' *Journal of the American Statistical Association*, vol. 86, pp. 603–10.

Diebold, F. X. and Rudebusch, G. D. (1991b). 'Turning point prediction with the composite leading index: an ex ante analysis.' in Lahiri and Moore (1991), pp. 231–56.

Doan, T., Litterman, R. and Sims, C. A. (1984). 'Forecasting and conditional projection using realistic prior distributions.' *Econometric Reviews*, vol. 3, pp. 1–100.

Emerson, R. A. and Hendry, D. F. (1996). 'An evaluation of forecasting using leading indicators.' *Journal of Forecasting*, vol. 15, pp. 271–91.

Engle, R. F. (1982). 'Autoregressive conditional heteroscedasticity, with estimates of the variance of United Kingdom inflations.' *Econometrica*, vol. 50, pp. 987–1007.

Ericsson, N. R. and Marquez, J. R. (1989). 'Exact and approximate multi-period mean-square forecast errors for dynamic econometric models.' International finance discussion paper 348, Federal Reserve Board.

Gilbert, C. L. (1986). 'Professor Hendry's methodology.' *Oxford Bulletin of Economics and Statistics*, vol. 48, pp. 283–307. Reprinted in (C. W. J. Granger, ed.) (1990), *Modelling Economic Series*. Oxford: Clarendon Press.

Granger, C. W. J. and Newbold, P. (1986). *Forecasting Economic Time Series* 2nd edn. New York: Academic Press.

Harvey, A. C. and Shephard, N. (1992). 'Structural time series models.' In (G. S. Maddala, C. R. Rao and H. D. Vinod, eds.), *Handbook of Statistics*, Vol. 11. Amsterdam: North-Holland.

Hendry, D. F. (1979). 'Predictive failure and econometric modelling in macro-economics: the transactions demand for money.' In (P. Ormerod, ed.), *Economic Modelling*, pp. 217–42. London: Heinemann. Reprinted in D. F. Hendry (1993), *Econometrics: Alchemy or Science?* Oxford: Blackwell Publishers.

Hendry, D. F. (1995*a*). *Dynamic Econometrics*. Oxford: Oxford University Press.

Hendry, D. F. (1995*b*). 'Econometrics and business cycle empirics.' ECONOMIC JOURNAL, vol. 105, pp. 1622–36.

Hendry, D. F. (1995*c*). 'A theory of co-breaking.' Mimeo, Nuffield College, University of Oxford.

Hendry, D. F. and Clements, M. P. (1993). 'On model selection when forecasting.' Mimeo, Economics Department, University of Oxford.

Hendry, D. F. and Clements, M. P. (1994*a*). 'Can econometrics improve economic forecasting?' *Swiss Journal of Economics and Statistics*, vol. 130, pp. 267–98.

Hendry, D. F. and Clements, M. P. (1994*b*). 'On a theory of intercept corrections in macro-economic forecasting.' In (S. Holly, ed.), *Money, Inflation and Employment: Essays in Honour of James Ball*, pp. 160–82. Aldershot: Edward Elgar.

Hendry, D. F. and Doornik, J. A. (1994). 'Modelling linear dynamic econometric systems.' *Scottish Journal of Political Economy*, vol. 41, pp. 1–33.

Hendry, D. F. and Mizon, G. E. (1996). 'Selecting econometric models for policy analysis by forecast accuracy.' Mimeo, Nuffield College, University of Oxford.

Hendry, D. F. and Trivedi, P. K. (1972). 'Maximum likelihood estimation of difference equations with moving-average errors: a simulation study.' *Review of Economic Studies*, vol. 32, pp. 117–45.

Kalman, R. E. (1960). 'A new approach to linear filtering and prediction problems.' *Journal of Basic Engineering*, vol. 82, pp. 35–45.

Klein, L. R. (1971). *An Essay on the Theory of Economic Prediction*. Chicago: Markham Publishing Company.

Lahiri, K. and Moore, G. H. (eds.) (1991). *Leading Economic Indicators: New Approaches and Forecasting Records*. Cambridge: Cambridge University Press.

Neftci, S. N. (1979). 'Lead-lag relations, exogeneity and prediction of economic time series.' *Econometrica*, vol. 47, pp. 101–13.

Pain, N. and Britton, A. (1992). 'The recent experience of economic forecasting in Britain: some lessons from national institute forecasts.' Discussion paper (new series) 20, National Institute.

Persons, W. M. (1924). *The Problem of Business Forecasting*. No. 6 in Pollak Foundation for Economic Research Publications. London: Pitman.

Schmidt, P. (1974). 'The asymptotic distribution of forecasts in the dynamic simulation of an econometric model.' *Econometrica*, vol. 42, pp. 303–9.

Shephard, N. G. (1996). 'Statistical aspects of ARCH and stochastic volatility.' In Cox et al. (1996), pp. 1–67.

Spanos, A. (1986). *Statistical Foundations of Econometric Modelling*. Cambridge: Cambridge University Press.

Stock, J. H. and Watson, M. W. (1989). 'New indexes of coincident and leading economic indicators.' *NBER Macro-Economic Annual*, pp. 351–409.

Stock, J. H. and Watson, M. W. (1992). 'A procedure for predicting recessions with leading indicators: econometric issues and recent experience.' Working paper 4014, NBER.

Theil, H. (1961). *Economic Forecasts and Policy*, 2nd edn. Amsterdam: North-Holland.

Wallis, K. F. (1989). 'Macroeconomic forecasting: a survey.' ECONOMIC JOURNAL, vol. 99, pp. 28–61.

Wallis, K. F. and Whitley, J. D. (1991). 'Sources of error in forecasts and expectations: U.K. economic models 1984–8.' *Journal of Forecasting*, vol. 10, pp. 231–53.

Wold, H. O. A. (1938). *A Study in The Analysis of Stationary Time Series*. Stockholm: Almqvist and Wicksell.

Zarnowitz, V. and Braun, P. (1992). 'Major macroeconomic variables and leading indicators: Some estimates of their interrelations, 1886–1982.' Working paper 2812, National Bureau of Economic Research, New York.

APPENDICES

A. *Parameter Estimates*

From the properties of the $I(1)$ variables in the example, the expectations of the estimates of λ_1 and λ_2 in (23) are:

$$E\left[\binom{\hat{\lambda}_1}{\hat{\lambda}_2}\right]$$

$$= E\left[\begin{pmatrix} T^{-2}\sum\limits_{t-1}^{T} E_{t-1}^2 & T^{-2}\sum\limits_{t-1}^{T} E_{t-1}R_{t-1} \\ T^{-2}\sum\limits_{t-1}^{T} E_{t-1}R_{t-1} & T^{-2}\sum\limits_{t-1}^{T} R_{t-1}^2 \end{pmatrix}^{-1} \begin{pmatrix} T^{-2}\sum\limits_{t-1}^{T} E_{t-1}Y_t \\ T^{-2}\sum\limits_{t-1}^{T} R_{t-1}Y_t \end{pmatrix}\right]$$

$$\simeq \left[\begin{pmatrix} T^{-2}\sum\limits_{t-1}^{T} E(E_{t-1}^2) & 0 \\ 0 & T^{-2}\sum\limits_{t-1}^{T} E(R_{t-1}^2) \end{pmatrix}^{-1} \begin{pmatrix} \alpha T^{-2}\sum\limits_{t-1}^{T_1} E(E_{t-1}^2) \\ \beta T^{-2}\sum\limits_{t-T_1+1}^{T} E(R_{t-1}^2) \end{pmatrix}\right]$$

$$= \left[\begin{pmatrix} T^{-2}\sum\limits_{t-1}^{T}(t-1) & 0 \\ 0 & T^{-2}\sum\limits_{t-1}^{T}(t-1) \end{pmatrix}^{-1} \begin{pmatrix} \alpha T^{-2}\sum\limits_{t-1}^{T_1}(t-1) \\ \beta T^{-2}\sum\limits_{t-T_1+1}^{T}(t-1) \end{pmatrix}\right]$$

$$= \left[\begin{pmatrix} 2T(T-1)^{-1} & 0 \\ 0 & 2T(T-1)^{-1} \end{pmatrix}\begin{pmatrix} \tfrac{1}{2}\alpha T^{-2}T_1(T_1-1) \\ \tfrac{1}{2}\beta T^{-2}[T(T-1)-T_1(T_1-1)] \end{pmatrix}\right]$$

$$= \binom{K\alpha}{(1-K)\beta},$$

where:

$$K = \frac{T_1(T_1-1)}{T(T-1)}.$$

B. *Taxonomy Derivations*

First, we make the approximation:

$$\hat{\Pi}^h = (\Pi_p + \delta_\Pi)^h \simeq \Pi_p^h + \sum_{t-0}^{h-1} \Pi_p^t \delta_\Pi \Pi_p^{h-t-1} = \Pi_p^h + C_h. \tag{52}$$

Also, using (52), letting $(\cdot)^v$ denote forming a vector and $\otimes$ a Kronecker product:

$$C_h(\mathbf{y}_T - \boldsymbol{\varphi}_p) = [C_h(\mathbf{y}_T - \boldsymbol{\varphi}_p)]^v = \left[\sum_{t-0}^{h-1} \Pi_p^t \otimes (\mathbf{y}_T - \boldsymbol{\varphi}_p)' \Pi_p^{h-t-1'}\right]\delta_\Pi^v = F_h \delta_\Pi^v.$$

To highlight components due to different effects (parameter change, estimation inconsistency, and estimation uncertainty), we decompose the terms $(\Pi^*)^h (\mathbf{y}_T - \boldsymbol{\varphi}^*)$ and $\hat{\Pi}^h(\hat{\mathbf{y}}_T - \boldsymbol{\varphi})$ in (41) into:

$$(\Pi^*)^h (\mathbf{y}_T - \boldsymbol{\varphi}^*) = (\Pi^*)^h (\mathbf{y}_T - \boldsymbol{\varphi}) + (\Pi^*)^h (\boldsymbol{\varphi} - \boldsymbol{\varphi}^*)$$

and:

$$\hat{\mathbf{\Pi}}^h(\hat{\mathbf{y}}_T - \hat{\mathbf{\phi}}) = (\mathbf{\Pi}_p^h + \mathbf{C}_h)\,[\mathbf{\delta}_y - (\hat{\mathbf{\phi}} - \mathbf{\phi}_p) + (\mathbf{y}_T - \mathbf{\phi}) - (\mathbf{\phi}_p - \mathbf{\phi})]$$
$$= (\mathbf{\Pi}_p^h + \mathbf{C}_h)\,\mathbf{\delta}_y - (\mathbf{\Pi}_p^h + \mathbf{C}_h)\,\mathbf{\delta}_\phi + (\mathbf{\Pi}_p^h + \mathbf{C}_h)\,(\mathbf{y}_T - \mathbf{\phi}_p)$$
$$= (\mathbf{\Pi}_p^h + \mathbf{C}_h)\,\mathbf{\delta}_y - (\mathbf{\Pi}_p^h + \mathbf{C}_h)\,\mathbf{\delta}_\phi + \mathbf{F}_h\,\mathbf{\delta}_\Pi^v + \mathbf{\Pi}_p^h(\mathbf{y}_T - \mathbf{\phi}) - \mathbf{\Pi}_p^h(\mathbf{\phi}_p - \mathbf{\phi})$$

so $(\mathbf{\Pi}^*)^h\,(\mathbf{y}_T - \mathbf{\phi}^*) - \hat{\mathbf{\Pi}}^h(\hat{\mathbf{y}}_T - \mathbf{\phi})$ yields:

$$[(\mathbf{\Pi}^*)^h - \mathbf{\Pi}_p^h]\,(\mathbf{y}_T - \mathbf{\phi}) - \mathbf{F}_h\,\mathbf{\delta}_\Pi^v - (\mathbf{\Pi}_p^h + \mathbf{C}_h)\,\mathbf{\delta}_y$$
$$- (\mathbf{\Pi}^*)^h\,(\mathbf{\phi}^* - \mathbf{\phi}) + \mathbf{\Pi}_p^h(\mathbf{\phi}_p - \mathbf{\phi}) + (\mathbf{\Pi}_p^h + \mathbf{C}_h)\,\mathbf{\delta}_\phi. \quad (53)$$

The interaction $\mathbf{C}_h\,\mathbf{\delta}_\phi$ is like a 'covariance', but is omitted from the table. Hence (53) becomes:

$$[(\mathbf{\Pi}^*)^h - \mathbf{\Pi}^h]\,(\mathbf{y}_T - \mathbf{\phi}) + (\mathbf{\Pi}^h - \mathbf{\Pi}_p^h)\,(\mathbf{y}_T - \mathbf{\phi})$$
$$- (\mathbf{\Pi}^*)^h\,(\mathbf{\phi}^* - \mathbf{\phi}) + \mathbf{\Pi}_p^h(\mathbf{\phi}_p - \mathbf{\phi})$$
$$- (\mathbf{\Pi}_p^h + \mathbf{C}_h)\,\mathbf{\delta}_y - \mathbf{F}_h\,\mathbf{\delta}_\Pi^v + \mathbf{\Pi}_p^h\,\mathbf{\delta}_\phi.$$

The first and third rows have expectations of zero, so the second row collects the 'non-central' terms.

Finally, for the term $\mathbf{\phi}^* - \hat{\mathbf{\phi}}$ in (41), we have (on the same principle):

$$(\mathbf{\phi}^* - \mathbf{\phi}) + (\mathbf{\phi} - \mathbf{\phi}_p) - \mathbf{\delta}_\phi.$$

Name Index

The International Library of Critical Writings in Economics

Privatization in Developing and Transitional Economies
Colin Kirkpatrick and Paul Cook

The Economics of Intellectual Property
Ruth Towse

The Economics of Tourism
Clem Tisdell

The Economics of Organization and Bureaucracy
Peter Jackson

Realism and Economics: Studies in Ontology
Tony Lawson

The International Economic Institutions of the Twentieth Century
David Greenaway

The Economics of Structural Change
Harald Hagemann, Michael Landesmann and Roberto Scazzieri

The Economics of the Welfare State
Nicholas Barr

Path Dependence
Paul David

Alternative Theories of the Firm
Richard Langlois, Paul Robertson and Tony F. Yu

The Economics of the Mass Media
Glenn Withers

The Economics of Budget Deficits
Charles Rowley

The Economic Theory of Auctions
Paul Klemperer

The Economics of Regional Policy
Harvey W. Armstrong and Jim Taylor

Forms of Capitalism: Comparative Institutional Analyses
Ugo Pagano and Ernesto Screpanti

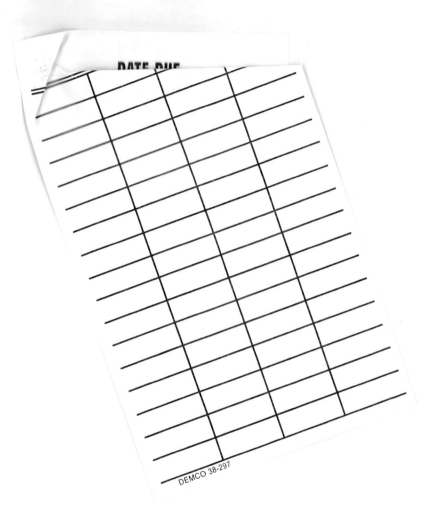

DATE DUE

DEMCO 38-297